T0304327

Informal Economy and Sustainable Development Goals

Informal Economy and Sustainable Development Goals: Ideas, Interventions and Challenges

EDITED BY

A. VINODAN
Central University of Tamil Nadu, India

S. MAHALAKSHMI
Central University of Tamil Nadu, India

AND

S. RAMESHKUMAR
Central University of Punjab, India

United Kingdom – North America – Japan – India – Malaysia – China

Emerald Publishing Limited
Emerald Publishing, Floor 5, Northspring, 21-23 Wellington Street, Leeds LS1 4DL.

First edition 2024

British Library Cataloguing in Publication Data
A catalogue record for this book is available from the British Library

ISBN: 978-1-83753-981-9 (Print)
ISBN: 978-1-83753-980-2 (Online)
ISBN: 978-1-83753-982-6 (Epub)

Printed and bound by CPI Goup (UK) Ltd, Croydon, CR0 4Y

INVESTOR IN PEOPLE

Contents

List of Acronyms

ABA	Alexandria Business Association
AI	Artificial Intelligence
ALMPs	Active Labour Market Policies
ARD	American Research and Development
CAGR	Compound Annual Growth Rate
CAPMAS	Central Agency for Public Mobilization and Statistics
CBFM	Community-Based Facilities Management
CDI	Cluster Development Initiative
CKCL	Clean Kerala Company Limited
CWS	Current Weekly Status
DAY-NRLM	Deendayal Antyodaya Yojana-National Rural Livelihoods Mission
DCYT	Decentralized Cotton Yarn Trust
DGT	Directorate General of Training
DMEs	Directory Manufacturing Establishment
DSD	Department of Social Development
EGDI	E-Government Development Index
EPA	Environmental Protection Agency
EPR	Extended Producer Responsibility
ERF	Economic Research Forum
FCS	Food Consumption Score
FII	Financial Inclusion Index
FTP	First Telecommunications Project
GARID	Greater Accra Resilient and Integrated Development
GATC	German Agency for Technical Cooperation
GB	Grameen Bank
GCSCA	Ghana Cooperative "Susu" Collectors Association
GDP	Gross Domestic Product
GEAR	Ghana Environmental Assessment Regulations

GIFEC	Ghana Investment Fund for Electronic Communications
GIS	Geographic Information Systems
GIZ	Deutsche Gesellschaft Fuer Internationale Zusammenarbeit
GVA	Gross Value Added
HDI	Human Development Index
ICDS	Integrated Child Development Services
ICLS	International Conference of Labor Statisticians
ICT	Information, Communication and Technology
ICT4AD	ICT For Accelerated Development
IFMEC	International Facility Management Expert Centre
IHDS	India Human Development Survey
IIA	Independence of Irrelevant Alternatives
IIPA	Indian Institute of Public Administration
ILO	International Labour Organization
IMF	International Monetary Fund
IS	Information System
ITC	Industrial Training Centres
ITI	Industrial Training Institutes
IWA	Informal Waste Actors
JLG	Joint Liability Group
JSS	Jan Shikshan Sansthan
LFPR	Labour Force Participation Rate
LFS	Labour Force Surveys
LGS	Local Government Service
LMPS	Labour Market Panel Surveys
M&E	Monitoring and Evaluating
MCF	Material Collection Facilities
MDAs	Ministries, Departments, and Agencies
MDG	Millennium Development Goals
MDM	Mid-Day Meal Scheme
MENA	Middle East and North African
MEUs	Micro Enterprise Units
MFIs	Microfinance Institutions
MGNCRE	Mahatma Gandhi National Council of Rural Education

MLGDRD	Ministry of Local Government, Decentralization, and Rural Development
MLR	Multiple Linear Regression
MMDAs	Metropolitan, Municipal, and District Assemblies
MoC	Ministry of Communications
MOSPI	Ministry of Statistics and Programme Implementation
MoT	Ministry of Textile
MSDE	Ministry of Skill Development and Entrepreneurship
MSEs	Micro and Small Businesses
NABARD	National Bank for Agriculture and Rural Development
NAPS	National Apprenticeship Promotion Scheme
NCAER	National Council of Applied Economic Research
NCEUS	National Commission for Enterprises in The Unorganised Sector
NCF	National Curriculum Framework
NCO	National Classification Occupation
NDC	National Development Commission
NDMEs	Non-Directory Manufacturing Establishments
NEP	National Education Policy
NIC	National Industry Classification
NIESBUD	National Institute of Entrepreneurship and Small Business Development
NIFT	National Institute of Fashion Technology
NIRDPR	National Institute of Rural Development and Panchayati Raj
NPA	Non-Performing Assets
NRFIP	National Rural Financial Inclusion Plan
NRLM	National Rural Livelihoods Mission
NRO	National Resource Organization
NSFI	National Strategy for Financial Inclusion
NSSO	National Sample Survey Office
OBC	Other Backward Caste
OCYF	Operation Clean Your Frontage
OECD	Organization for Economic Cooperation and Development
OJT	On Job Training
OMEs	Own Account Manufacturing Enterprises

P&T	Posts and Telecommunications
PDS	Public Distribution System
PLFS	Periodic Labour Force Survey
PMGKAY	Pradhan Mantrigaribkalyan Anna Yojana
PMJDY	Pradhan Mantri Jan Dhan Yojana
PMKY	Pradhan Mantri Kaushal Vikas Yojana
PMO	Prime Minister's Office
PNSDP	Per Capita Net State Domestic Product
PPE	Personal Protective Equipment
PSI	Private Sector Initiative
PSIRU	Public Services International Research Unit
RC	Rural Cooperatives
RCC	Regional Coordinating Council
RDESE	Regional Directorates of Skill Development and Entrepreneurship
RIDF	Rural Infrastructure Development Fund
RSETIs	Rural Self Employment Training Institutes
SC	Scheduled Caste
SCBFM	Sustainable Community-Based Facilities Management
SDGs	Sustainable Development Goals
SEDGs	Socially and Economically Disadvantaged Groups
SEM	Structural Equation Modelling
SHG	Self-Help Groups
SPSS	Statistical Package for Social Sciences
SRLMs	State Rural Livelihoods Missions
SSA	Sub-Saharan Africa
SSI	Social and Sustainable Institutions
STP	Second Telecommunications Project
SVEP	Start-Up Village Entrepreneurship Programme
SWM	Solid Waste Management
SWTS	School-to-Work Transition Survey
TDGW	Tethered On-Demand Gig Workers
UN	United Nations
UNDP	United Nations Development Programme
UNEP	United Nations Environment Programme
UNSD	United Nations Statistics Division
UNTFHS	United Nations Trust Fund for Human Security

UR	Unemployment Rate
USSD	Unstructured Supplementary Service Data
VVGNLI	V.V. Giri National Labour Institute
WAAPP	West African Agriculture Productivity Programme
WBES	World Bank Enterprise Surveys
WCED	World Commission on Environment and Development
WEDP	Women's Entrepreneurship Development Programmes
WHO	World Health Organization
WMD	Waste Management Department
WFPR	Workforce Participation Rate

List of Contributors

Anthony Acquah	*Bluecrest University College, Ghana*
Philippe Adair	*University Paris-Est Créteil, France*
Yewande Adewunmi	*University of the Witwatersrand, South Africa*
Bita Afsharinia	*Indian Institute of Science, India*
Anthony Nkrumah Agyabeng	*University of Professional Studies, Ghana*
Razdan Alam	*Rabindra Bharati University, India*
Shireen AlAzzawi	*Santa Clara University, USA*
T. P. Arjun	*Central University of Tamil Nadu, India*
Ashique Ali K. A.	*Central University of Tamil Nadu, India*
Shantanu Baidya	*Jadavpur University, India*
Shashi Bala	*VV Giri National Labour Institute, India*
Manas Ranjan Bhowmik	*Ramakrishna Mission Vidyamandira, India*
Avishek Bose	*University of Calcutta, India*
Ganesh R.	*St. Mary's College, India*
Anjula Gurtoo	*Indian Institute of Science, India*
Sumit Haluwalia	*CHRIST (Deemed to be University), India*
Vladimir Hlasny	*Ewha Womans University, Korea*
K. Jafar	*MIDS Chennai, India*
Rohan Kanti Khan	*Maulana Abul Kalam Azad University of Technology, India*
Nomita P. Kumar	*Giri Institute of Development Studies, India*
Sushobhan Mahata	*University of Calcutta, India*
Soumyajit Mandal	*St. Xavier's College (Autonomous), India*
Umanath Malaiarasan	*MIDS Chennai, India*
James Kwame Mensah	*University of Ghana Business School, Ghana*
Naresh G.	*Indian Institute of Management Tiruchirappalli, India*
Sigamani Panneer	*Jawaharlal Nehru University, India*
Shiba Shankar Pattayat	*CHRIST (Deemed to be University), India*

Kalpana Rajsinghot	*Ministry of Communication, India*
Renjith Ramachandran	*Indian Institute of Management Ranchi, India*
Rahana Salahudeen Raseena	*Central University of Tamil Nadu, India*
V. P. Nirmal Roy	*Gulati Institute of Finance and Taxation, India*
Debolina Saha	*Rabindra Bharati University, India*
Priyabrata Sahoo	*Banaras Hindu University, India*
Prisca Simbanegavi	*University of the Witwatersrand Johannesburg, South Africa*
Puja Singhal	*NCSL-National Institute of Educational Planning and Administration, India*
Rameshkumar Subramanian	*Central University of Punjab, India*
B. S. Sumalatha	*Gulati Institute of Finance and Taxation, India*
Achala Srivastava	*Giri Institute of Development Studies, India*
Fathima Sherin Ottakkam Thodukayil	*Central University of Tamil Nadu, India*
P. Udhayakumar	*Central University of Tamil Nadu, India*
U. G. Unnimaya	*MIDS Chennai, India*
Malcolm Weaich	*University of the Witwatersrand, South Africa*
Nandani Yadav	*Banaras Hindu University, India*

Preface

In the vast landscape of global economic systems, the informal economy is a vibrant yet often overlooked realm, teeming with resilience, innovation, and dynamism. Within this intricate tapestry of informal transactions, unregistered enterprises, and marginalised labour forces, we find both profound challenges and immense opportunities for sustainable development. As editors of *Informal Economy and Sustainable Development Goals: Ideas, Interventions and Challenges*, it is our privilege to present a collection of scholarly contributions that delve deep into the heart of this complex domain, shedding light on its multifaceted dimensions and its critical role in the pursuit of sustainable development goals (SDGs).

The chapters within this volume represent diverse perspectives, methodologies, and empirical insights, offering a comprehensive exploration of the informal economy's intersections with key themes such as food security, financial inclusion, digital transformation, waste management, gender disparities, and rural entrepreneurship. Through empirical studies, theoretical frameworks, and policy analyses, our contributors navigate the labyrinthine complexities of informal economies, presenting innovative ideas, effective interventions, and pressing challenges that demand our attention and action.

The journey begins with exploring the invisible pathways of informal lending, a bibliometric study that unveils the intricate networks and dynamics underpinning informal financial transactions. From there, we embark on a journey across continents, examining the digital transformation of economies and its implications for the informal sector, from the bustling streets of Ghana to the vibrant textile sectors of India. Along the way, we encounter the resilience and vulnerabilities of migrant women workers, the persistent challenges of industrial concentration, and the impacts of foreign capital inflows on informal economies, offering nuanced analyses that deepen our understanding of these complex phenomena.

As we delve deeper into the book, we encounter chapters that present interventions aimed at addressing the myriad challenges faced by informal economies. From initiatives to enhance food security and financial inclusion to collaborations for climate action and waste management, our contributors offer practical strategies and innovative approaches to empower informal workers and enhance their socio-economic well-being. Through case studies, policy analyses, and stakeholder collaborations, these interventions provide a roadmap for policymakers, practitioners, and researchers striving to foster inclusive and sustainable growth in diverse socio-economic contexts.

However, amidst the wealth of ideas and interventions, we must recognise the stark realities and pressing challenges confronting informal economies and the communities they support. From the gig economy's impact on labour rights to the gender disparities that pervade informal employment, our contributors highlight the persistent inequalities and structural barriers that hinder the realisation of SDGs. They challenge us to confront these injustices and advocate for meaningful change through rigorous research and critical analysis, offering insights and perspectives that inspire action and transformation.

As editors, we are deeply grateful to our esteemed contributors for their scholarly rigour, intellectual curiosity, and unwavering commitment to advancing knowledge and promoting social change. Their collective efforts have enriched this volume with invaluable insights, innovative ideas, and practical solutions that have the power to shape policy, inform practice, and inspire future research in the fields of informal economy and sustainable development.

In conclusion, *Informal Economy and Sustainable Development Goals: Ideas, Interventions and Challenges* is more than just a book; it is a testament to the resilience, ingenuity, and potential of informal economies to contribute to a more just, equitable, and sustainable world. We hope readers find inspiration, knowledge, and motivation within these pages to join us on this journey towards a future where informal workers are empowered, and communities thrive. Sustainable development has become a reality for all.

Thank you for embarking on this journey with us.

Sincerely,
A. Vinodan
S. Mahalakshmi
S. Rameshkumar

Ideas

Chapter 1

A Conceptual Framework for Managing Public Services Delivered by Environmental Enterprises in Informal Settlements

Yewande Adewunmi, Prisca Simbanegavi and Malcolm Weaich

School of Construction Economics and Management, University of the Witwatersrand, Johannesburg, South Africa

Abstract

Informal settlements are frequently located in hazardous areas with a high risk of natural disasters. Upgrading informal settlements can be difficult due to the time and expense needed to complete the process. This chapter advocates using a management framework of public services in informal settlements. In doing so, it addresses 17 of the 17 UN sustainable development goals (SDGs). The study reviewed the literature to investigate current ways of managing environmental enterprises in informal settlements in South Africa. Thereafter, the challenges of managing public services were explored, and a conceptual framework for managing public services by social enterprises in such communities was developed. The chapter found that environmental enterprises are classified as 'green spaces' and infrastructure, water and sanitation services, energy systems, and recycling initiatives. Essential aspects of sustainable community-based facilities management (SCbFM) for managing public services are maintenance, governance, community project management, environment service delivery, service performance, governance, community project management, environment service delivery, service performance, well-being and health and safety, disaster management, and finance. Some of the problems of managing public services in informal settlements include the limited skills of managers, the focus of government on new projects rather than managing existing projects, not choosing the right indicators to measure service performance, and limited guidelines for the health and safety of managers

Informal Economy and Sustainable Development Goals:
Ideas, Interventions and Challenges, 3–27
Copyright © 2024 by Yewande Adewunmi, Prisca Simbanegavi and Malcolm Weaich
Published under exclusive licence by Emerald Publishing Limited
doi:10.1108/978-1-83753-980-220241001

and disaster management. Thus, a new conceptual framework was needed and developed based on the principles of social capital and capability for managing services in informal settlements in South Africa.

Keywords: Community-based facilities management; environmental enterprises; informal settlements; public services; sustainable development goals; South Africa

1. Introduction

Community-based facilities management (CbFM) can be applied regionally to achieve socio-economic objectives. Facilities management can considerably contribute to community infrastructure and service provision, regeneration, the creation of skilled job opportunities, and trade skill development. Additionally, it could allow communities to correctly participate in planning and administrating services and the urban environment (Alexander & Brown, 2006). Facilities management in informal settlements will promote access to infrastructure, sustainable real estate, and people's safety by working with communities to design and administer services and the urban environment (Bertotti et al., 2011; Bolinger & Brown, 2015; Napier, 2007).

In the global South, informal settlements are home to almost one billion people, which have grown over the past several decades. The creation and survival of informal settlements are influenced by the many social, economic, and even political forces/dynamics of the cities that serve as homes in these communities (UN-Habitat, 2013). Informal settlements have several traits in common (Gancarczyk & Ujwary-Gil, 2021). Informal settlements often house vulnerable people in unstable housing conditions that lack tenure security with limited access to essential basic services. Informal settlements also have a beneficial impact on urban life by being a shelter for the disadvantaged. These informal settlements possess sizeable storage of newly constructed homes, excess human resources, and 'dead capital' – legally unrecognised and undervalued land holdings (De Soto, 2001). According to Chigbu and Onyebueke (2021, p. 116), informal settlements: 'provide unique city life experiences such as slum tourism to many rural–urban migrants that have rights to the city'. Also, low-income citizens do not tolerate the decreasing environmental conditions in their areas. Instead, they start to initiate and support initiatives to produce and upgrade public services, generate new livelihood opportunities and are encouraged to improve their living conditions (Thieme, 2015).

Good urban governance must have 'processes and procedures for managing a city and its activities which have at their core the participation and involvement of all citizens of informal settlements for transparency and accountability' (McAuslan, 2011, p. 5). When local community members collaborate to create and exchange commodities and services using the current social framework for running such activities, the community behaves as a social enterprise (Carvalho et al., 2012).

According to Van Belle et al. (2020), environmental and social enterprises should be equal and need knowledge of urban governance systems for adequate measures and accountability of informal settlements. Persistence, leadership, the appropriate culture, careful planning, familiarity with formal processes, and primarily financial resources are required to organise an environmental community enterprise (Weppen & Cochrane, 2012). The difficulties occur when funding for management services stops and puts environmental enterprises' services at risk (Chen et al., 2020; Denoon-Stevens & Ramaila, 2018).

Hence, this chapter recommends a conceptual framework for managing public services by environmental enterprises in informal settlements. The use of the framework will help communities have services that are effective and efficient and aligned to the UN SDGs. This chapter examined the types of environmental enterprises in informal settlements and the management framework used by public services/social enterprises in South Africa. In doing so, we examined the challenges of managing public services and developed a framework for managing public services by social enterprises in such under-resourced communities. This section introduces the chapter, whilst the next section looks at the role and forms of environmental entrepreneurship in informal settlements. The third section covers aspects of SCbFM. The fourth section covers informal settlements in South Africa, whilst the fifth section proposes a framework for the management of informal settlements, and the sixth section discusses the conceptual and application challenges of the proposed framework. The last section focuses on the recommendations.

2. Role and Forms of Environmental Entrepreneurship in Informal Settlements

Sustainability concerns are mainly focused on the environment in less developed markets. Some broad environmental elements include energy efficiency, environmental concerns, purchasing, reusing and recycling, and the ecosystem. Energy efficiency, as defined by the United Nations Environment Programme (UNEP) (UNEP, 2007 quoted in Adewunmi et al., 2012), is the capacity to provide the same (or greater) level of energy services, such as thermal comfort and high-quality lighting, at a lower cost and with less energy usage. Some of the main challenges affecting informal settlements are desertification, environmental pollution, biodiversity loss, urban environmental degradation and slum expansion, gully erosion and floods and deforestation. One particularly serious challenge is the problem of properly managing waste. Whilst there are several types of solid waste, waste recycling is an interesting strategy for attaining an integrated, effective method of managing municipal solid waste (Adewunmi et al., 2012; Temeljotov Salaj & Lindkvist, 2021). Environmental entrepreneurs provide waste services in informal settlements (Gutberlet et al., 2016). Environmental entrepreneurship seeks to generate income by addressing environmental problems, including the lack of dependable waste collection services in informal settlements. In many large cities, urban planners do not see the need to prioritise economic liberalisation processes and public management changes as these are commonly linked to the lack of essential public services in informal settlements (Otsuki, 2016). As a result, many private efforts are available to fill the gap left by a deficiency in governmental infrastructure management, such as the activities of environmental enterprises providing sanitation, water, and waste services. Through such innovative entrepreneurial activities, these environmental enterprises market these services/ resources for profit.

In this section, 'green space' infrastructure, landscaping, hygienic practices, waste disposal, and energy management were the primary topics of this study on environmental entrepreneurial efforts in informal settlements.

2.1. Green Spaces and Infrastructure

This includes governance of urban green infrastructure in institutional frameworks, agents and alliances, resources, processes, and social enterprises, including collective gathering places, crafts, leisure, and tourism. There is a need for 'green spaces' that can be provided by low-cost techniques (Cheshmehzangi et al., 2021).

2.2. Waste and Sanitation Services

These enterprises offer waste removal and cleaning services. Examples of this type of environmental enterprise in informal settlements that incorporate social and environmental challenges include social, environmental, institutional, mixed-economic, and waste entrepreneurship (Uzairiah Mohd Tobi et al., 2013). Opportunities for waste and sanitation include community cleaning, the construction of facilities that treat waste, and informal pit-emptiers (Gutberlet, 2010; O'Keefe et al., 2015; Thieme, 2015). Pit-emptiers exceeded the institutional and practical parameters/mandate required to offer sanitation services (Mallory et al., 2021). Another entrepreneurial opportunity is providing a transfer station that a private company maintains to transport waste from informal settlements. Some incentives, institutions, and power relationships can contribute to or hinder the effectiveness of sanitation services (Mallory et al., 2022).

2.3. Energy Systems Enterprises

Energy enterprises use solar energy and other efficient energy systems. The study discovered that home-based small- and medium-sized businesses benefit from energy availability in terms of employment and expansion potential. Electricity costs can exceed those of charcoal and kerosene, frequently bought in modest amounts each day by informal settlers. Rising daily expenditures might impact the capacity of households to pay for other vital services (Christley et al., 2021). Opportunities can come from solar energy systems that contribute to the development of local jobs, reduce operational costs, increase end-user affordability, and provide economic advantages (Conway et al., 2019). There are also opportunities to use IoT to improve energy infrastructure and promote the growth of businesses (Chambers & Evans, 2020). Planning and regulations can be used to coordinate access to energy to help families access affordable energy through financial incentives. Incentives and subsidies support informal settlements' access to energy. Through government-coordinated loans and subsidies, connection costs for power can be reduced. A lifeline tariff that pays less than the normal tariff can cover monthly payments, which can be established using prepayment techniques (Christley et al., 2021).

2.4. Recycling

These are social enterprises that relate to different recycling efforts. Research has also shown that opportunities for recycling enterprises also exist for e-waste (Gutberlet, 2012). There are variables driving the creation and expansion of informal e-waste operations (Asibey et al., 2021). Employees can be encouraged to participate in such activities (Ssekamatte et al., 2019). Recycling scavengers are at the bottom of the e-waste ladder, and re-use and open disposal of e-waste are regular practices. Poverty is the key motivator for getting involved in the processing of e-waste.

Another opportunity for job creation is to encourage the youth to recycle manufactured goods. For example, research conducted in Namibia by Winschiers-Theophilus et al. (2017) that employed the Havanna Entrepreneur technique of social enterprises to examine youth entrepreneurship in informal settlements and found that recycling of manufactured goods (e-waste) may be a feasible entrepreneurship opportunity amongst young people to earn an income whilst preserving green infrastructure.

Previous studies on environmental papers on the management of environmental enterprises such as Campos and Zapata (2014) focused on waste management. Thieme (2015) also studied environmental enterprises. Studies on sanitation enterprises were mainly from Kenya, including those of Tsinda et al. (2015), Otsuki (2016), Mallory et al. (2021), and Mallory et al. (2022). Gutberlet et al. (2016) studied socio-environmental enterprises. Green infrastructure was the focus of Adegun (2016), Gashu et al. (2019), and Wijesinghe and Thorn (2021). Christley et al.'s (2021) study was on electricity and liquefied petroleum gas, whilst Conway et al.'s (2019) study was on solar energy systems. Chambers and Evans (2020) focused on the Internet of Things (IoT). Cheshmehzangi et al.'s (2021) paper on environmental enterprises was conceptual. Other contexts besides those where the investigations above were conducted have particular environmental difficulties. Future studies can also examine environmental enterprises from the viewpoint of climate change and take more inclusive and participatory positions.

3. Management of Services in Informal Settlements

3.1. Sustainable Community-based Facilities Management

Essential aspects of SCbFM for managing public services enhance all mentioned SDGs through maintenance, governance, community project management, environment service delivery, service performance, well-being and health and safety, disaster management, and finance. As explained in Alexander and Brown (2006, p. 263), CbFM enables the management of facilities and the delivery of services to reflect the community and environment in which they reside and operate. It is the process by which all the stakeholders in a community work together to plan, deliver, and maintain an enabling environment within which the local economy can prosper, quality services can be delivered, and natural resources can be protected so that citizens can enjoy a quality of life.

The aspects of sustainable development are environmental, social, and economic sustainability (Nielsen et al., 2016). Including socio-technical systems at the building level, buildings and their operation, usage, maintenance, and management procedures is critical to sustainable facilities management.

A look at the previous studies on sustainable community facilities management shows that none focused directly on SDGs and the capabilities of the manager/management skills. Some of these papers were from the United Kingdom, such as Alexander and Brown (2006), Tammo and Nelson (2014), and Hutchings et al. (2015), which were focused on service, economics, and water. Boyle and Michell (2018) in South Africa considered the process-based approach, but it was not implemented. In Serbia, Vukmirovic and Gavrilovi (2020) used place-making and public participation geographic information systems but were not comprehensive and focused on using Geographic Information Systems. Also, Grum and Kobal Grum (2020) focused mainly on social sustainability. Temeljotov Salaj et al. (2020) in Norway explored sustainable community FM through action research and the design of a Facebook interactive tool.

3.2. Aspects of Sustainable Community-based Facilities Management

Sustainable facilities management contributes to the realisation of 17 SDGs, (Lok et al., 2013). A study by the International Facility Management Expert Centre (IFMEC, 2018, cited in Opoku & Lee, 2022) in the Netherlands showed that strategic Sustainable Facilities Management (SFM) can achieve the 17 SDGs because the facilities manager can integrate SDGs at all levels of the community, from strategic to the operational levels and can influence behavioural changes of individuals in the community. The facilities manager can contribute to the realisation of SDG 12 (responsible consumption and production) by promoting policies and practices that source resources through sustainable and circular procurement strategies to ensure that only healthy are used in communities; they also prevent the loss of biodiversity (Goal 15: life on land, biodiversity). Such policies and actions will reduce the sector's CO_2 emission and carbon footprint (Goal 13: climate action), which could be absorbed into oceans and seas (Goal 14: life below water). The facilities manager partners with people, organisations, and authorities (Goal 17: partnership for the goals) to maintain safety and security (Goal 16: peace, justice, and strong institutions) in communities.

Also, the facilities manager provides economic and social improvement for individuals in communities through job creation (SDG 8: decent work and economic growth). It can also help address SDG 1: no poverty. The FM profession, through support services, health and safety, and supply chain, helps institutions and communities through the food supply chain in addressing SDG 2: zero hunger and SDG 3: good health and well-being, responsible for the sustainable maintenance of buildings in cities and communities (SDG 11: sustainable cities and communities), which includes managing building energy usage (SDG 7: affordable and clean energy) and by water conservation practices (SDG 6: clean water and sanitation) in communities. The FM manager manages educational facilities to meet the communities' goals, thereby improving quality education for all, SDG 4: quality education. The FM sector has a record of diverse employees (Goal 9: reduced inequalities, equal rights in wages, and career opportunities for women, demonstrating gender equality, SDG5). The FM uses relevant technologies such as artificial intelligence and the IoT to produce smart communities to achieve SDG 9: industry, innovation, and infrastructure.

3.2.1. Governance
Institutions and other parties involved in decision-making for communities include informal settlements. The operational department managing and maintaining the community appears to be split between the strategic goals established within municipal goals and political agendas. According to Lindkvist et al. (2021), several players and networks are active in governance. There is a view in FM that because of the political borders it is created within, service delivery and especially maintenance can be challenging. Residents in the informal community suffer from the consequences of inadequate service delivery. Through involvement from various sectors, including education, consultation, involvement, collaboration, and empowerment, CbFM seeks to increase connectivity in smart cities to establish a connection with communities (Lindkvist et al., 2021; Simbanegavi & Ijasan, 2022). Over time, it becomes challenging to maintain infrastructure due to poor local and national governance capability, minimal community engagement, and lack of government assistance. Service delivery is impacted by agents' lack of trust and collaboration, hindering local participation in management (Silvestri et al., 2018).

3.2.2. Maintenance
Politicians may not have the maintenance of the current structure as a top priority because they think more obvious changes will significantly impact their term in office. However, politicians can neglect to maintain old infrastructure, which diminishes their long-term sustainability. Also, it can make these places less desirable as places to live and diminish the energy efficiency in a poorly kept structure. To promote long-term societal engagement in sustainable renewal efforts and to produce sufficient incentives to stimulate and encourage creativity, the facilities manager is more proactive, as seen in the community (Lindkvist et al., 2021).

3.2.3. Community Project Management
The built environment design, individual quality of life, a community's social arrangement, and success are all related. FM's value and serviceability show the ability to contribute actively to the design of new projects. In addition to new

facilities (such as public services like schools, elderly homes, and medical centres) and coordinating new services, extending FM to the broader community helps assume more social responsibility in these communities (Temeljotov Salaj et al., 2020).

3.2.4. Environment Service Delivery

Nazali Mohd Noor and Pitt (2009) contend that by concentrating on the unique operating procedures of the organisation, FM may be strategically used to manage support services and operations in organisations and communities. Atkin and Brooks (2000) assert that for FM to be effective, both 'hard skills', like finance, and 'soft skills', like people management, must be considered. Hence, FM includes all aspects of an organisation's operations by coordinating all skills and activities that deal with planning, developing, and managing its physical resources.

3.2.5. Service Delivery Performance

The goal is to identify those facilities that are doing poorly in the community and ensure that facilities are managed and acquired strategically rather than for political purposes. An evaluation of facilities is centred on service delivery as a 'return on investment', as a going concern by paying close attention to the government's primary outcomes. Thus, stakeholder participation is essential to the project's success (Brackertz & Kenley, 2002).

3.2.6. Well-being and Community Safety

This aspect involves complete compliance with health and safety policies, personnel, procedures, and training that will improve the well-being and safety of the community (Eaton & Nocerino, 2000).

3.2.7. Disaster Management

It is not enough to merely prepare for disasters. Facilities managers working with the underprivileged in informal settlements need business continuity and disaster recovery procedures. Such disaster planning is needed to handle the immediate reaction to a disaster and promptly restore routine community services following any catastrophe. The plan must be widely shared with the community, and emergency situations must be regularly exercised (Warren, 2010).

3.2.8. Finance

Facilities rely on financing to pay for the costs of providing community services and supplies. Lack of finance limits the underprivileged's access to public services. Thus, the 'the user pays' principle may not be possible. Since informal settlement users might be unable to pay for essential community services. This lack of income stream can shut down the supply of essential services to these communities that need them. Promoting community responsibility for spending money on essential services also involves monitoring the expenditure/use of such revenues obtained at the facility. Another source of funding is direct funding from the government from tax revenue (Waweru et al., 2013).

4. Informal Settlements in South Africa

Unplanned urbanisation has contributed to the ongoing rise in informal settlements. Lack of essential utilities, pollution, congestion, and inadequate waste management are features of informal communities. The availability of essential fundamental services, including water, sanitation, roads, trash management, and community amenities, varies greatly amongst informal settlements. The levels of supply range from delivering the complete range of essential services to limited or none at all (Department of Human Settlements, 2021). Informal communities are typically found in unfavourable locations at high risk of floods, sinkholes, high winds/mine sand pollution, and inaccessible and unsafe mountainous terrain.

In 2002, there were 300 such informal villages in South Africa. According to a StatsSA 2018 estimate, 14% of the population resides in unofficial, informal settlements, increasing rapidly. There are now 2,453 informal settlements in South Africa (2018). The Parliamentary Monitoring Group (PMG) estimate that this number will increase to 2,700 informal settlements by 2022.

The number of informal settlements is increasing due to migration to cities from rural areas. However, data from the 2010 national census show that informal settlements increased significantly in the Western Cape, North West, and Northern Cape provinces.

The Millennium Development Goals (MDGs) and other international pronouncements that focused directly on eradicating poverty impacted the creation of an informal settlement improvement initiative in South Africa (Huchzermeyer, 2006). Breaking New Ground is such an initiative that emphasises: 'poverty eradication, reduction of vulnerability, and promotion of social inclusion' together with its companion 'Informal Settlements Upgrading Programme' (Marais & Ntema, 2013, p. 87).

The rehabilitation of land for upgrading instead of developments regarding greenfield, tenure security, ensuring adequate access to social and economic amenities as well as temporary services (water and sanitation), and social inclusion from participatory layout planning were all purposed to achieve these three MDG (Huchzermeyer, 2006).

It is still a difficult task for the government to upgrade informal settlements. It can take up to seven or eight years to improve living conditions through service delivery, and it is a costly exercise. Given the difficulties and the fact that informal settlements appear to be expanding daily, the government has raised concerns about its capacity to reach performance objectives (PMG, 2022).

Informal settlements face obstacles like poor transportation, accessibility, crowded living quarters, inadequate services, poor living conditions and health (some are used as dumps/landfills for waste), poor urban appearance, unemployment and poverty, and high crime rates (UN-Habitat, 2013). Limitations to the administration of public services might result from insufficient supplies, a lack of investment in health and safety, community conduct, workplace risks for personnel, working hours, and management support (Ssekamatte et al., 2019). The sustainability of public services provided by social enterprises might be significantly impacted by a lack of community involvement in administering such services. Due to crime and instability, access to services might be difficult in some countries (O'Keefe et al., 2015). A community's attitude towards public services may be influenced by social variables, including gender and culture, and behaviour change can be promoted through marketing, communication, and community involvement (Okurut et al., 2015).

According to the University of Buffalo Global Health Equity (2019), to improve the quality of life in informal settlements, the following steps need to be taken: involve community planning; provide better government support; create tenure through land pooling; regularise urban types; control urban sprawl; implement information management systems; improve exterior spaces; provide a variety of housing; and invest in education, healthcare, and social services. Understanding the issues affecting informal settlement communities is crucial for efficiently managing public services.

5. Conceptual Framework for the Management of Services in Informal Settlements

Theories assist in building knowledge (Nielsen et al., 2016), and these theories applied in this context include those of social capital and capability regimes (refer to Fig. 1.1). It reveals FM's principles and added value in a community (Tammo & Nelson, 2014). Putnam's social capital community engagement drives improved services and efficient public institutions that are cooperative, equitable, trustworthy, and comply with the community's norms (Adhikari & Goldey, 2010; Putnam, 1993).

Regarding social capital theory, having access to social capital motivates taking action (Coleman, 1988), and it makes it possible to have some services that would otherwise be impossible. Networks, norms, and trust are the three primary elements of social capital theory.

On the other hand, the theory that deals with capabilities is that of capabilities. Lavie (2006) introduced three capability reconfiguration instruments for change: capability substitution, evolution, and transformation. These procedures result in newly acquired, transformed, or changed skills based on various learning sources and mechanisms instruments. 'Capability substitution' takes place by replacing old skills with more recent ones. The second instrument to improve capability is the 'capability evolution' process. The 'capability evolution' process involves changing current procedures or adapting capabilities to new demands. Dynamic capabilities are important to this technique since capabilities are path-dependent. The organisation itself serves as the learning resource. This instrument involves investigation at the level of particular specific

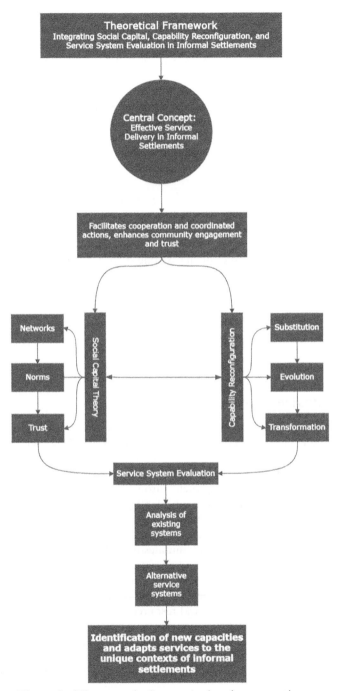

Fig. 1.1.   Theoretical Framework. *Source*: Authors' own creation.

practices continuously (Lavie, 2006, p. 154). A combination of internal and external factors contributes to learning. It is a midway response that applies at a specific capability level (Lavie, 2006, p. 154). Applying this theory would help those managing sustainable enterprises know which capabilities to discard and which to acquire.

According to van Welie et al. (2019), evaluating the service systems already developed in informal settlements is essential to determine what kind of new capacities a service would require to function there. Various service providers have developed skills that align with the different service structures that make up informal settlements. Therefore, service providers should carefully examine the capabilities of the other service providers and work collaboratively to enhance their integration.

A comparative framework for identifying other skills a service would need for effective operation in informal settlements is provided.

This systemic framework suggests the following kinds of processes:

1. Analyse the characteristics of the existing service system in which the manager operates.
2. Obtain the corresponding capabilities for this service system.
3. Analyse the characteristics of other service systems established in the new enterprise context.
4. Find the capabilities to enable the manager to succeed in another service system.
5. Find the change in the way capability is planned.

6. Conceptual and Application Challenges

The administration of services at the community level is conceptually and practically difficult for each CbFM aspect (see Table 1.1 for an overview). Each activity in Table 1.1 of the SCbFM framework contributes to the 17 SDGs (Lok et al., 2023). The framework was crafted to help managers apply sustainable community facilities management through platforms of networks, trust, and capabilities. These platforms help identify problems that need solutions that SCbFM enterprises can provide to improve services in informal settlements in South Africa. Some of the conceptual issues are managing facilities and providing services in a way that imitates the goal of the area and the environment in which they are located and operate. It is a process through which all the community's stakeholders work together to design, implement, and maintain a climate that enables the local economy to thrive, provides high-quality services, and conserves scarce natural resources so that citizens live in dignity. The following recommendations focus on solving the application's problems and how the framework can be applied in practice. Using the framework, facilities managers who work in or establish sustainable enterprises can also determine how well they can contribute to SDG goals and differentiate themselves in service delivery.

Table 1.1. Conceptual and Application Challenges.

Sustainable Community Services Management	Relevant SDGs	Conceptual Challenge	Application Challenge
Maintenance	2, 9, 11, 12, 13	Limitations to using people and processes that keep the community facilities running smoothly, from the infrastructure to the assets and equipment It ranges from using maintenance to procurement and technology for sustainable services	• Managers do not have the necessary skills to maintain services at the community level • Lack of engagement and trust with the community regarding the maintenance of services • There is limited provision in terms of policy for managing services at the community level
Governance	1, 9, 12, 17	Limitations to contributions from the manager towards the optimal use of community services over short-medium-, and long-term It includes coming up with policies that promote sustainable practices	• The management team is unable to address climate change issues • Insufficient priority is given to maintenance challenges by the government • Lack of cooperation and support from the government on ongoing projects • Managers are not part of the community decision-making process for service provision
Community project management	5, 8	Challenges towards the manager's input in community projects, especially at the design stage. When designed correctly, these projects will create jobs in the community, encourage inclusion, and ensure that services are provided sustainably	• Managers are not involved in the design stage of community service provision • There are limited policies for CbFM input in developing countries • The community has limited trust at the design stage in the competence of managers

(Continued)

Table 1.1. (*Continued*)

Sustainable Community Services Management	Relevant SDGs	Conceptual Challenge	Application Challenge
Environment service delivery	2, 3, 7, 12, 15, 13, 14	Problems with the management of community services that relate to the environment Environmental practices can include water conservation, clean energy and biodiversity, responsible consumption, promoting climate change, and sourcing for sustainability	• New knowledge regarding the logistics/practicalities of management facilities at the community level is lacking • Limited community participation and collaboration in service delivery management of projects • Lack of equitable access to land can negatively impact service delivery and management • Inequitable access to properly managed services due to the community's social status • Inadequate remuneration for managers and staff • Lack of communication about the role of CbFM to community members • Restrictive, bureaucratic procedures that lead to delays in approvals • Service providers do not always implement sustainable practices • Limited supplies regarding the procurement of supplies for services managed • The marginalisation of particular groups and the misconception that they cannot participate in service delivery

Service delivery performance	All SDGs	Problem with measurement of performance of services provided at the community level to meet SDG goals	• There is little understanding of how to apply the right tools to measure the performance of services at the community level • There are no indicators to assist with the sustainability of environmental services
Well-being and safety of the community	3, 16	Problems with the safe use and management of community services	• Some of the services are not safe to use • Exposure of staff to occupational hazards • Limited access to services due to crime and insecurity • Limited investment in occupational health • Poor health and safety practices of the community
Disaster management	16	Ensuring that services and the community are safe before, during, and after an emergency is challenging	• Many of the informal settlements are prone to natural disasters • Community attitude and participation in response to disasters • Lack of detailed disaster planning and risk assessment • Managers do not have emergency preparedness skills to assist people experiencing poverty • Lack of comprehensive guidelines for managers to follow in response to emergencies

(Continued)

Table 1.1. (*Continued*)

Sustainable Community Services Management	Relevant SDGs	Conceptual Challenge	Application Challenge
Finance	1	Problems with access to funds for managing services provided at the community level	• Managers do not have access to resources to manage community services • High cost of managing services • The unwillingness of users to pay for services results in break-even problems • Injudicious disbursement of funds for public services leads to trust problems • Preference by the government to spend on new facilities rather than to maintain existing ones • Initial cost engaging FM

Source: Authors own creation.

7. Recommendations for the Management of Informal Settlements

Based on the literature review, the following recommendations were made and are also reflected in Fig. 1.2.

7.1. Having the Right Policies in Place

This study should encourage facilities managers to get involved in community initiatives through government policy to contribute from the beginning. This is based on the facilities manager's competency relating to strategic roles and facilities planning where they are involved in projects at the design stage.

Additionally, legislation should be passed to support public service administration to ensure sustainability. Such policies should include clear instructions/ guidance/directives on managing such services according to best practices.

Fig. 1.2.   Conceptual Framework for Managing Public Services in Informal Settlements. *Source*: Authors own creation.

Policies should be utilised to encourage public engagement, collaborative partnerships, and the quick introduction of initiatives (Boyle, 2016).

7.2. Having an Integrated Management Platform

CbFM can solve many problems in South African informal settlements. Firstly, a centralised, comprehensive management platform can help save scarce resources and cut unnecessary expenses (Boyle & Michell, 2018).

7.3. Improving Public Sector Relevance

FM is a fairly new profession and is unknown and acknowledged in many institutions (Roper & Payant, 2014). The strategic relevance of FM still needs to be promoted for institutions and communities to realise the benefits and the impact that this profession can make, especially in meeting SDGs, amongst other benefits. We have a situation in South Africa where more facilities managers work for corporations and the private sector than in the public sector. Hence, the contributions of public sector FMs need to be made more well-known to strengthen the public sector.

7.4. Having a Vision for the Community

Managers should be able to cope with the various degrees of engagement and community actors whilst working within the framework of their communities. At the community level, managers should be able to create plans to address issues with management and sustainability of services offered whilst ensuring that such communities' objectives are realised.

It can be challenging to coordinate a range of stakeholders' abilities into a cohesive and workable plan. A strong community vision that embraces sustainability can be facilitated through practical cooperation that can direct leadership at different levels.

Additionally, managers of community projects can assist in integrating the expertise and perspectives of many stakeholders into a workable strategy. An example of such a middleman is the CIDs, as stated in the study by Boyle and Michell (2018) in Cape Town, where an area-based approach was used to increase neighbourhood property values by improving the management of an urban district. They also helped to expedite government on various levels (Boyle & Michell, 2018).

7.5. Identification of Training Capabilities

Identifying training capabilities in the community is needed to ensure that everyone involved in the management of services can play their roles and responsibilities within the governance structures and at the community level. For community initiatives to be implemented correctly, it is crucial to understand the different training requirements of the agents involved in administering public services.

Additionally, it is critical to comprehend how social interactions, geographic locations, and organisational structures are related to any new and current initiatives (van Welie et al., 2019).

Training is also required to promote community members' involvement in project management. Thwala (2008) stated that a lack of follow-up post-maintenance of infrastructure projects was the cause behind the failure of many of these economic development programmes in other regions of Africa. For instance, managers require training in areas such as emergency response in underdeveloped communities.

Furthermore, few tertiary institutions in South Africa and the rest of Africa provide degrees specifically designed for people who work in municipalities with skills and knowledge to administer community facilities. When FM training is available at educational institutions, it is often designed to meet the demands of the private sector instead of the public sector.

7.6. Minimising Bureaucratic Procedures

Municipalities should prioritise processing applications that can contribute to the sustainable administration of public services. Creating policies that support NGOs or organisations planning to handle these services can help to support such businesses (Boyle, 2016). Government bodies' institutional ability may be unable to accommodate CbFM concepts due to South Africa's lack of experience with urban development. Thus, such capacity should be sourced from outside government institutions (Boyle & Michell, 2018).

7.7. Formalisation of Informal Settlements Through Title Deeds

To change the boundaries of human settlement and create sustainable communities, it is vital to remember that the government is actively involved in formalising informal settlements. Formalising informal settlements can be done through the provision of serviced sites and the issuance of title deeds. Individual property titles should not be disregarded as such when provided, and they need to be viewed as a long-term goal. The goal is to enhance the availability of legal urban land in many places and at many price points, and with various tenure choices (public or private rental, leasehold, freehold) to meet the demands of various socio-economic groups (Lekonyane & Disoloane, 2013).

7.8. Inclusive Community Participation

Government policies should continue to encourage participation in the local administration of public services. Examples may also be found in South African models like the Expanded Public Works scheme, a labour-intensive scheme that offers employment possibilities or funding for infrastructure project management (Nzimakwe, 2008). The challenge with such schemes has been in their execution since individuals continue to think that their primary responsibility is to complete projects rather than to create jobs and oversee such enterprises.

Other difficulties include a preference by the government for short-term work over long-term employment or options for business development. Therefore, it is necessary to rethink how these programmes operate and teach government employees how to run such projects (Nzimakwe, 2008).

7.9. Building Trust

Building trust with people who oversee community services is essential. Managers of community projects ought to be well-liked and reliable/have a track record of managing successful projects in the neighbourhood.

7.10. Disaster Management Guidelines Should Be Outlined

Guidelines need to show how communities may be managed to avert disasters, such as disaster planning by individuals in charge of managing communities. Those in charge of community initiatives should follow this critical safety directive.

7.11. Addressing Contextual Issues in Communities

According to Boyle and Michell (2018), the Department of Social Development in South Africa is less equipped to pinpoint the contextual requirements of a community and provide a coordinated response. Facility managers should address the contextual issues in those communities. Social enterprises typically operate as micro-businesses within a niche market where they have a deep awareness of the problems that face their communities. The fact that these enterprises in South Africa recognise the need to have meaningful discussions with communities to advance a development agenda relevant to that community is another crucial characteristic of these enterprises.

7.12. Health and Safety in Community Services Management

Managers and senior government officials/managers should encourage the safety of services whenever necessary. In certain countries, like South Africa, crime may be an issue. A closer partnership between governmental agencies such as the police and the community in the delivery of services may be seen in the interaction between a community's security services and the neighbourhood (Moghayedi et al., 2022).

Project managers and operators should receive professional/accredited training on health and safety.

7.13. Finance

Open and responsible management systems should be created to build confidence, allowing for communication amongst project stakeholders about how money is allocated to various initiatives. Additionally, by mitigating unaffordable start-up expenses with tax-free incentives, the government and other essential stakeholders could encourage social entrepreneurship efforts. In addition, public–private partnerships can help with this challenge as long as finances are well-regulated. At the same time, those who oversee community initiatives should be fairly compensated to promote openness and efficiency at work.

7.14. Choosing Indicators Carefully

Monitoring and evaluating indicators are essential to ensure they represent the community's objectives concerning the performance of community services. This suggests that acquiring technical and operational abilities will help improve management skills at the local community level. Better administration of public services also needs interpersonal and communication capabilities (Nxumalo et al., 2018).

8. Conclusion

The study reviewed the literature to examine the types of environmental enterprises in informal settlements and the management of public services in South Africa. From this review, this study developed a conceptual framework for managing public services by social enterprises in such communities and strategies by first identifying the conceptual and application challenges of implementing each aspect of SCbFM. The framework was aligned with the 17 SDG goals. It provided recommendations for using the developed framework for managing public services.

The chapter identified various forms of environmentally aware enterprises and characteristics of SCbFM to manage public services. A few of the issues with managing public services in informal settlements are the lack of managerial expertise, the government's preference for new projects over the management of ongoing ones, the failure to select the appropriate performance indicators, the lack of safety and health guidelines for managers, and disaster management planning.

The administration of public services produced by social enterprises requires the implementation of appropriate policies, an increase in the relevance of facility management for the public sector, identification of stakeholder training capacities, inclusive community engagement, and trust. The limitation of the study is that the research question and the findings should be tested empirically in future studies.

References

Adegun, O. B. (2016). *Informal settlement intervention and green infrastructure: Exploring just sustainability in Kya Sands, Ruimsig and Cosmo City in Johannesburg* (Doctoral Dissertation, University of the Witwatersrand, Faculty of Engineering and the Built Environment, School of Architecture and Planning, Johannesburg, South Africa).

Adewunmi, Y., Omirin, M., & Koleoso, H. (2012). Developing a sustainable approach to corporate FM in Nigeria. *Facilities, 30*, 350–373.

Adhikari, K. P., & Goldey, P. (2010). Social capital and its "downside": The impact on the sustainability of induced community-based organizations in Nepal. *World Development, 38*(2), 184–194.

Alexander, K., & Brown, M. (2006). Community-based facilities management. *Facilities, 24*(7/8), 250–268.

Asibey, M. O., Michael, P.-B., & Isaac Osei, A. (2021). Residential segregation of ethnic minorities and sustainable city development: Case of Kumasi, Ghana. *Cities, 116*, 103297.

Atkin, B., & Brooks, A. (2000). *Total facility management*. Wiley.

Bertotti, M., Sheridan, K., Tobi, P., Renton, A., & Leahy, G. (2011). Measuring the impact of social enterprises. *British Journal of Healthcare Management, 17*(4), 152–156.

Bolinger, A. R., & Brown, K. D. (2015). Entrepreneurial failure as a threshold concept: The effects of student experiences. *Journal of Management Education, 39*(4), 452–475.

Boyle, L. (2016). *Urban facilities management as a systemic process to achieve urban sustainability in South Africa* [Master's thesis, University of Cape Town].

Boyle, L., & Michell, K. (2018, June). A management concept for driving sustainability in marginalised communities in South Africa. *Urban Forum, 29*(2), 185–204.

Brackertz, N., & Kenley, R. (2002). A service delivery approach to measuring facility performance in local government. *Facilities, 20*(3/4), 127–135.

Bröchner, J., Haugen, T., & Lindkvist, C. (2019). Shaping tomorrow's facilities management. *Facilities, 37*(7/8), 366–380.

Campos, M. J. Z., & Zapata, P. (2014). The travel of global ideas of waste management. The case of Managua and its informal settlements. *Habitat International, 41*, 41–49.

Carvalho, M. D. S., Rosa, L. P., Bufoni, A. L., & Oliveira, L. B. (2012). Putting solid household waste to sustainable use: A case study in the city of Rio de Janeiro, Brazil. *Waste Management & Research, 30*(12), 1312–1319.

Chambers, J., & Evans, J. (2020). Informal urbanism and the Internet of Things: Reliability, trust and infrastructure reconfiguration. *Urban Studies, 57*(14), 2918–2935.

Chen, J. C. P., Tsaih, L. S. J., & Li, Y. F. (2020). Exploring views on communal amenities and well-being in housing for seniors in Taiwan. *Building Research & Information, 48*(3), 239–253.

Cheshmehzangi, A., Butters, C., Xie, L., & Dawodu, A. (2021). Green infrastructures for urban sustainability: Issues, implications, and solutions for underdeveloped areas. *Urban Forestry & Urban Greening, 59*, 127028.

Chigbu, U. E., & Onyebueke, V. U. (2021). The COVID-19 pandemic in informal settlements: (Re)considering urban planning interventions. *The Town Planning Review, 92*, 115–121.

Christley, E., Ljungberg, H., Ackom, E., & Nerini, F. F. (2021). Sustainable energy for slums? Using the Sustainable Development Goals to guide energy access efforts in a Kenyan informal settlement. *Energy Research & Social Science, 79*, 102176.

Coleman, J. S. (1988). Social capital in the creation of human capital. *American Journal of Sociology*, 94, S95–S120.

Conway, D., Robinson, B., Mudimu, P., Chitekwe, T., Koranteng, K., & Swilling, M. (2019). Exploring hybrid models for universal access to basic solar energy services in informal settlements: Case studies from South Africa and Zimbabwe. *Energy Research & Social Science, 56*, 101202.

Denoon-Stevens, S. P., & Ramaila, E. (2018). Community facilities in previously disadvantaged areas of South Africa. *Development Southern Africa, 35*(4), 432–449.

Department of Human Settlements. (2021). *Baseline evaluation of informal settlements targeted for upgrading in the 2019-2024 MTSF*. Department of Human Settlements.

De Soto, H. (2000). *The mystery of capital: Why capitalism triumphs in the West and fails everywhere else*. Basic Books.

Eaton, A. E., & Nocerino, T. (2000). The effectiveness of health and safety committees: Results of a survey of public-sector workplaces the effectiveness of health and safety committees. *Industrial Relations: A Journal of Economy and Society, 39*(2), 265–290.

Gancarczyk, M., & Ujwary-Gil, A. (2021). Entrepreneurial cognition or judgment: The management and economics approaches to the entrepreneur's choices. *Journal of Entrepreneurship, Management and Innovation, 17*(1), 7–23.

Gashu, K., Gebre-Egziabher, T., & Maru, M. (2019). Drivers for urban green infrastructure development and planning in two Ethiopian cities: Bahir Dar and Hawassa. *Arboricultural Journal, 41*(1), 48–63.

Grum, B., & Kobal Grum, D. (2020). Concepts of social sustainability based on social infrastructure and quality of life. *Facilities, 38*(11/12), 783–800.

Gutberlet, J. (2010). Waste, poverty and recycling. *Waste Management, 30*(2), 171–173.

Gutberlet, J. (2012). Informal and cooperative recycling as a poverty eradication strategy. *Geography Compass, 6*(1), 19–34.

Gutberlet, J., Kain, J. H., Nyakinya, B., Ochieng, D. H., Odhiambo, N., Oloko, M., Omolo, J., Omondi, E., Otieno, S., Zapata, P., & Zapata Campos, M. J. (2016). Socio-environmental entrepreneurship and the provision of critical services in informal settlements. *Environment and Urbanization, 28*(1), 205–222.

Huchzermeyer, M. (2006). The new instrument for upgrading informal settlements in South Africa: Contributions and constraints. In M. Huchzermeyer & A. Karam (Eds.), *Informal settlements: A perpetual challenge?* (pp. 41–61). UCT Press.

Hutchings, P., Chan, M. Y., Cuadrado, L., Ezbakhe, F., Mesa, B., Tamekawa, C., & Franceys, R. (2015). A systematic review of success factors in the community management of rural water supplies over the past 30 years. *Water Policy*, 17(5), 963–983.

Lavie, D. (2006). Capability reconfiguration: An analysis of incumbent responses to technological change. *Academy of Management Review, 31*(1), 153–174.

Lekonyane, B. C., & Disoloane, V. P. P. (2013). Determining strategies to manage informal settlements. *Administratio Publica, 21*(2), 57–72.

Lindkvist, C., Temeljotov Salaj, A., Collins, D., Bjørberg, S., & Haugen, T. B. (2021). Exploring urban facilities management approaches to increase connectivity in smart cities. *Facilities, 39*(1/2), 96–112.

Lok, K. L., Opoku, A., Smith, A., Vanderpool, I., & Cheung, K. L. (2023, May). Sustainable facility management in UN development goals. *IOP Conference Series: Earth and Environmental Science, 1176*(1), 012022.

Mallory, A., Mdee, A., Agol, D., Hyde-Smith, L., Kiogora, D., Riungu, J., & Parker, A. (2022). The potential for scaling up container-based sanitation in informal settlements in Kenya. *Journal of International Development, 34*(7), 1347–1361.

Mallory, A., Omoga, L., Kiogora, D., Riungu, J., Kagendi, D., & Parker, A. (2021). Understanding the role of informal pit emptiers in sanitation in Nairobi through case studies in Mukuru and Kibera settlements. *Journal of Water, Sanitation and Hygiene for Development, 11*(1), 51–59.

Marais, L., & Ntema, J. (2013). The upgrading of an informal settlement in South Africa: Two decades onwards. *Habitat International, 39*, 85–95.

McAuslan, P. (2011, September). Urban planning law in Liberia: The case for a transformational approach. *Urban Forum, 22*(3), 283–297.

Moghayedi, A., Le Jeune, K., Massyn, M., & Michell, K. (2022, November). Investigating the safety and security of the open campus using community-based facilities management and technological innovation principles: University of Cape Town. *IOP Conference Series: Earth and Environmental Science, 1101*(6), 062023.

Napier, M. (2007). *Informal settlement integration, the environment and sustainable livelihoods in sub-Saharan Africa.* Council for Scientific & Industrial Research in South Africa.

Nazali Mohd Noor, M., & Pitt, M. (2009). A critical review on innovation in facilities management service delivery. *Facilities, 27*(5/6), 211–228.

Nielsen, S. B., Sarasoja, A. L., & Galamba, K. R. (2016). Sustainability in facilities management: An overview of current research. *Facilities, 34*(9/10), 535–563.

Nxumalo, N., Goudge, J., Gilson, L., & Eyles, J. (2018). Performance management in times of change: Experiences of implementing a performance assessment system in a district in South Africa. *International Journal for Equity in Health, 17*, 1–14.

O'Keefe, M., Lüthi, C., Tumwebaze, I. K., & Tobias, R. (2015). Opportunities and limits to market-driven sanitation services: Evidence from urban informal settlements in East Africa. *Environment and Urbanization, 27*(2), 421–440.

Okurut, K., Kulabako, R. N., Chenoweth, J., Charles, K. (2015). Assessing demand for improved sustainable sanitation in low-income informal settlements of urban areas: A critical review. *International Journal of Environmental Health Research, 25*(1), 81–95.

Opoku, A., & Lee, J. Y. (2022). The future of facilities management: Managing facilities for sustainable development. *Sustainability, 14*(3), 1705.

Otsuki, K. (2016). Infrastructure in informal settlements: Co-production of public services for inclusive governance. *Local Environment, 21*(12), 1557–1572.

Parliamentary Monitoring Group (PMG). (2018). *Upgrading of informal settlements programme; human settlements policies & processes working session.* https://pmg.org.za/committee-meeting/27038/

Putnam, R. D. (1993). The prosperous community. *The American Prospect, 4*(13), 35–42.

Roper, K., & Payant, R. (2014). *The facility management handbook.* Amacom.

Silvestri, G., Wittmayer, J. M., Schipper, K., Kulabako, R., Oduro-Kwarteng, S., Nyenje, P., Komakech, H., & Van Raak, R. (2018). Transition management for improving the sustainability of WASH services in informal settlements in Sub-Saharan Africa – An exploration. *Sustainability, 10*(11), 4052.

Simbanegavi, P., & Ijasan, K. (2022). *Inclusive, affordable, and smart housing in Africa in understanding African real estate markets* (p. 13). Routledge.

Ssekamatte, T., Isunju, J. B., Balugaba, B. E., Nakirya, D., Osuret, J., Mguni, P., Mugambe, R., & van Vliet, B. (2019). Opportunities and barriers to effective operation and maintenance of public toilets in informal settlements: Perspectives from toilet operators in Kampala. *International Journal of Environmental Health Research, 29*(4), 359–370.

Tammo, M., & Nelson, M. (2014). Emergent theories for facilities management in community-based settings. *Journal for Facility Management, 8*, 22–33.

Temeljotov Salaj, A., Gohari, S., Senior, C., Xue, Y., & Lindkvist, C. (2020). An interactive tool for citizens' involvement in the sustainable regeneration. *Facilities, 38*(11/12), 859–870.

Temeljotov Salaj, A., Roumboutsos, A., Verlič, P., & Grum, B. (2018). Land value capture strategies in PPP–What can FM learn from it? *Facilities, 36*(1/2), 24–36.

Temeljotov Salaj, A., & Lindkvist, C. M. (2021). Urban facility management. *Facilities, 39*(7/8), 525–537.

Thieme, T. A. (2015). Turning hustlers into entrepreneurs, and social needs into market demands: Corporate–community encounters in Nairobi, Kenya. *Geoforum, 59*, 228–239.

Thwala, W. D. (2008). Employment creation through public works programmes and projects in South Africa: Experiences and potentials. *Acta Commercii, 8*(1), 103–112.

Tsinda, A., Abbott, P., & Chenoweth, J. (2015). Sanitation markets in urban informal settlements of East Africa. *Habitat International, 49*, 21–29.

UN-Habitat. (2013). *State of the world's cities 2012/2013: Prosperity of cities.* Routledge.

University of Buffalo Global Health Equity. (2019). *Strategies for improving informal settlements.* http://www.buffalo.edu/content/www/globalhealthequity/Resources/policy-briefs/issue-2-strategies-for-improving-informal settlements/_jcr_content/par/download/file.res/02_Final_Policy%20Brief_Smith_NCL.pdf

Uzairiah Mohd Tobi, S., Amaratunga, D., & Mohd Noor, N. (2013). Social enterprise applications in an urban facilities management setting. *Facilities, 31*(5/6), 238–254.

Van Belle, S., Affun-Adegbulu, C., Soors, W., Srinivas, P. N., Hegel, G., Van Damme, W., Saluja, D., Abejirinde, I., Wouters, E., Masquillier, C., Tabana, H., Chenge, F., Polman, K., & Marchal, B. (2020). COVID-19 and informal settlements: An urgent call to rethink urban governance. *International Journal for Equity in Health, 19*(1), 1–2.

van Welie, M. J., Truffer, B., & Gebauer, H. (2019). Innovation challenges of utilities in informal settlements: Combining a capabilities and regime perspective. *Environmental Innovation and Societal Transitions, 33*, 84–101.

von der Weppen, J., & Cochrane, J. (2012). Social enterprises in tourism: An exploratory study of operational models and success factors. *Journal of Sustainable Tourism, 20*(3), 497–511.

Vukmirovic, M., & Gavrilović, S. (2020). Placemaking as an approach of sustainable urban facilities management. *Facilities, 38*(11/12), 801–818.

Warren, C. M. (2010). The role of public sector asset managers in responding to climate change: Disaster and business continuity planning. *Property Management, 28*(4), 245–256.

Waweru, E., Opwora, A., Toda, M., Fegan, G., Edwards, T., Goodman, C., & Molyneux, S. (2013). Are health facility management committees in Kenya ready to implement financial management tasks: Findings from a nationally representative survey. *BMC Health Services Research, 13*(1), 1–14.

Wijesinghe, A., & Thorn, J. P. (2021). Governance of urban green infrastructure in informal settlements of Windhoek, Namibia. *Sustainability, 13*(16), 8937.

Winschiers-Theophilus, H., Cabrero, D. G., Chivuno-Kuria, S., Mendonca, H., Angula, S. S., & Onwordi, L. (2017). Promoting entrepreneurship amid youth in Windhoek's informal settlements: A Namibian case. *Science, Technology and Society, 22*(2), 350–366.

Chapter 2

Digital Transformation and Implications for the Informal Sector of Ghana

Anthony Acquah[a], Anthony Nkrumah Agyabeng[b] and James Kwame Mensah[c]

[a]*Department of Business Administration, Bluecrest University College, Accra, Ghana*
[b]*Department of Business Administration, University of Professional Studies, Accra, Ghana*
[c]*Department of Public Administration, University of Ghana Business School, Accra, Ghana*

Abstract

The chapter explores the implications of digitalization on the informal economy of Ghana, focusing on the agricultural, microcredit, transportation, and retail sectors. The study was designed as a qualitative study with data collected from books, articles, government reports, business reports, and newspapers. The data collected were analyzed using qualitative content analysis. The study argues that in the agricultural sector, e-agriculture initiatives and digital tools have improved farming practices, providing timely scientific knowledge to farmers and increasing yields. The microcredit sector has been transformed through digital financial services, which have expanded financial inclusion, lowered costs, and simplified regulatory compliance. In the transportation sector, digital platforms like Uber and local startups have streamlined operations, improved safety, and created economic opportunities for drivers. Additionally, e-commerce platforms have facilitated stock ordering and delivery for retailers, reducing downtime and formalizing their transactions. These digital innovations are crucial in enhancing the formalization of the informal economy in Ghana, providing numerous benefits for businesses and individuals in these sectors.

Keywords: Informal sector; digitization; digital transformation; digitization policy; microcredit Services

Informal Economy and Sustainable Development Goals:
Ideas, Interventions and Challenges, 29–51
Copyright © 2024 by Anthony Acquah, Anthony Nkrumah Agyabeng and
James Kwame Mensah
Published under exclusive licence by Emerald Publishing Limited
doi:10.1108/978-1-83753-980-220241002

Introduction

The sustainable development goals (SDGs) were established during the 2012 United Nations Conference on Sustainable Development which was held in Rio de Janeiro, Brazil (Sarabhai, 2015). The objective was to develop a list of global goals connected to the environmental, political, and economic issues that humanity faces. The United Nations adopted 17 universal goals to transform the world to be implemented over the period 2015–2030. The 17 global sustainable goals came to replace the 8 millennium development goals (Fukuda-Parr, 2016).

The SDGs represent a commitment to addressing the world's most pressing issues and are interconnected (Fukuda-Parr, 2016). The SDGs are a worldwide call to action to respond responsibly to the challenge of climate change by improving how we manage our fragile natural resources, fostering peace and inclusive communities, reducing inequities, and contributing to economic growth (Mpofu, 2022). Since its inception, the SDGs have aspired to achieve the so-called 2030 Agenda, which seeks to promote shared prosperity in a sustainable future in which all people may lead productive lives while living in peace and on a healthy planet (Villalba-Eguiluz et al., 2020).

SDG goal 10 is to reduce inequalities among and within countries. Goal 10 calls for reducing inequalities in income as well as those based on age, sex, disability, race, ethnicity, origin, religion, or economic or other status within a country. Target 10.1 seeks to progressively achieve and sustain income growth of the bottom 40% of the population at a rate higher than the national average by 2030. Digitalization has been hailed as a crucial strategy for reducing inequality in the informal economy. Digitization can play a significant role in transforming the informal economy into a formal economy by bringing transparency, efficiency, and accountability to economic activities that were previously unregulated and often conducted off the books (Lindgren et al., 2019). Digitization can connect informal businesses to larger, formal markets. Online marketplaces and e-commerce platforms enable informal businesses to reach a broader customer base, expand their product offerings, and compete more effectively (Lindgren et al., 2019). Ivanović-Đukić et al. (2019) argue that digitization contributes incrementally to economic growth. There is ample evidence to suggest that countries that have embraced digitalization gain about 20% more economic benefits in terms of boosting productivity, creating new jobs, improving the ease of doing business, and promoting improvements in societal quality of life than those with less digitalization experience (Sabbagh et al., 2012). Countries with extensive digitalization are able to reduce unemployment, increase citizens' access to public services, improve their quality of life, and expose the government to greater transparency and efficiency (Casalino & Bednar, 2015). By providing access to technology and information to disadvantaged persons in society, digitalization seeks to eliminate inequality within and across countries and communities (Heeks, 2001). One way to reduce inequality is the creation of digital tools to produce, utilize, transmit, or obtain data for economic activities in the informal sector (Agwu, 2021). Against this background, the government has been putting measures in place to develop and execute a solid foundation for a digital economy.

Vice President Dr. Bawumia stated during the 2022 Civil Service Week Awards Ceremony in Accra that the government's digitization plan was the sure route to improve the economy and generate jobs. Dr. Bawumia declared that Ghana cannot continue to grow its economy with "brick and mortar" but must instead use technology to achieve economic transformation. Several digital solutions have been introduced to make business and life easier and more efficient. Some of these digital solutions include Mobile Money Interoperability Payment System, National Identification System (Ghana Card), Ghana.gov, Paperless Port Systems, National Property Address System, GhanaPay, etc.

Through digitalization, the government has been able to reform and enhance Ghana's institutional and regulatory procedures (Addo, 2022). For example, the Ghana card has enabled the government to expand the number of Ghanaians having Tax Identification Numbers guaranteeing that the government is able to cast its tax net wide (Towah, 2019). The Ghana card is now used as a travel document, and diasporans are able to use it as visa to Ghana. The country has been able to reduce bureaucracy in the delivery of public services, enhance efficiency, reduce the cost of doing business, and make life easier for Ghanaians through the adoption of digital platforms (Towah, 2019). Although it is an established fact that digitalization has transformed the formal economy of Ghana (Addo, 2021), the implication of digitalization in the informal sector is missing in the extant literature. The informal sector must position itself to capitalize on the burgeoning digital economy, which offers unprecedented prospects for rapid development. This chapter explores the digital transformation and its implications for the informal economy of Ghana. The informal economy plays a significant role in Ghana's economic landscape, contributing to employment, income generation, and poverty reduction. Understanding how digital transformation affects the informal sector is significant for inclusive economic growth and development and the formalization of the study. The study is structured into the following themes: an overview of the informal sector of Ghana, the history of Ghana's digitalization journey, digitalization policy for the informal sector, the implication of digitalization for the agricultural sector, microcredit sector, transportation sector, retail sector, and conclusion.

Informal Sector

An informal economy (also known as the informal sector or shadow economy) is any sector of the economy that is not officially taxed or regulated (Feige, 1990). Vosko (2002) defined the informal economy as all economic activities performed by workers that are not covered or inadequately covered by official arrangements. Hussmanns (2001) defines the informal sector in terms of the features of the firms (production units) in which the activities take place, rather than the characteristics of the people participating or their occupations. As a result, those engaged in the informal sector were classified as everyone who worked in at least one informal sector production unit during a particular reference period, regardless of their employment status or whether it was their primary or secondary job.

In paragraph 5 (1) of the 15th International Conference of Labor Statisticians resolution, the informal sector is defined as units engaged in the production of goods or services with the primary goal of generating employment and income for the persons concerned. These units often work at a low organizational level, with little or no division of labor and capital as production elements, and on a small scale. Where labor ties exist, they are generally based on family, personal, or social relationships, rather than contractual partnerships with formal assurances.

International Labour Organization Office (2002) defined informal sector production units as a subset of unincorporated enterprises owned by households, that is, production units that are not constituted as separate legal entities independent of the households or household members who own them, and for which no complete sets of accounts (including balance sheets of assets and liabilities) are available to allow a clear distinction. For this study, the definition of informal economy by Feige (1990) is adopted, that is, the sector of the economy that is not officially taxed or regulated.

Overview of the Informal Sector of Ghana

The informal sector in Ghana has expanded over the years due to various economic, social, and structural factors. Ghana's population has been steadily increasing over the years, leading to a larger labor force (Adeniran et al., 2020). Many individuals in the workforce turn to the informal sector for income-generating opportunities when formal sector jobs are scarce. Furthermore, the formal sector in Ghana has not been able to absorb the growing workforce. This has led to a lack of formal employment opportunities, pushing more people to seek work in the informal sector (Adeniran et al., 2020). Moreover, the informal sector often requires fewer qualifications, permits, or startup capital compared to formal businesses. This makes it more accessible for people with limited resources and skills to start their businesses or engage in various informal activities. Also, rural–urban migration has led to the growth of informal activities in urban areas as people move to cities in search of better opportunities. Many of these migrants engage in informal trading, services, and small-scale manufacturing (Zakaria, 2017). In addition, agriculture is a significant part of the informal sector in Ghana. Many smallholder farmers engage in subsistence and cash-crop farming outside the formal sector, contributing to the expansion of the informal economy (Zakaria, 2017). In addition, street vending, market trading, and other forms of informal trade have grown due to consumer demand and the flexibility these activities offer. These types of businesses are often easier to establish without formal registration. Likewise, in some cases, the government's limited capacity to enforce regulations has allowed the informal sector to thrive. Some informal businesses may operate without adhering to all formal rules and regulations.

In terms of its varied nature, the informal sector in Ghana is divided into two main categories:

(i) Rural informal economy.
(ii) Urban informal economy.

Rural Informal Economy

The following activities are undertaken by the rural informal economy:

(i)   *Agriculture*: These are mostly farming groups that rely on family labor and include a considerable number of small farmers in rural and semi-urban areas. Farmers are typically illiterate or semi-illiterate, with little formal education. Apprenticeship is used to learn farming skills. Family labor and low-technology pooled labor are frequently accessible, and land is typically purchased on a usufruct base from family units and communal resources (Osei-Boateng & Ampratwum, 2011). Agriculture is a major source of employment in Ghana, with a significant portion of the population engaged in farming, fishing, and related activities. This sector provides livelihoods for a large portion of the population, especially in rural areas (Zakaria, 2017). Agriculture is essential for ensuring food security in Ghana. It provides the majority of the country's food supply, including staples like maize, cassava, yam, and cocoa (Zakaria, 2017). A robust agricultural sector helps reduce the country's reliance on food imports and stabilizes food prices. Agriculture provides raw materials for various agro-based industries in Ghana, including the food and beverage industry, textile industry, and pharmaceutical industry. This helps to diversify the economy and create value-added products. A thriving agriculture sector can help reduce poverty by increasing the income of smallholder farmers and rural communities. It provides opportunities for income diversification and entrepreneurship in rural areas (Zakaria, 2017).

(ii) *Activities involving fishing and fish processing*: These are usually located along Ghana's coastline and are generally made up of males aged 18–40. These primarily illiterate employees learned to swim via experience during their childhood age. The value-added and processing tasks, such as smoking and marketing the fish, are mostly carried out by women who are either the fishermen's wives or close relatives. The fishing industry provides employment opportunities to a large number of Ghanaians. It is estimated that millions of people are directly or indirectly employed in fishing and related activities, including fish processing and marketing. Many coastal and inland communities rely on fishing as a primary source of income (Asiedu et al., 2018).

(iii) *Agro-processing business in rural areas*: Palm wine tapping, local gin distillery, cassava bread, processing, groundnut, palm kernel, copra oils, local pito brewery, soap-making, etc. These activities are dominated by females, the majority of whom are uneducated. Their skills are passed onto them through their family. Their experience with seasonal underemployment is severe. They are mostly married and have children, yet they are not covered by social security (Osei-Boateng & Ampratwum, 2011). There are also forest product workers, most of whom are males, such as woodworking machine operators, carpenters, wood carvers, and bamboo artisans. The agro-processing sector is a major employer in Ghana, providing jobs for a significant portion of the population. This includes jobs in food processing, packaging, distribution, and related services, both in rural and in urban areas. These jobs help reduce unemployment and alleviate poverty, particularly in rural communities (Gyil, 2020). Other sectors other than agriculture, fishing and fish processing, agro-processing are not common because of the economic structure of rural Ghana. The historical and cultural significance of agriculture in Ghana has led to an economy heavily reliant on farming. The majority of the population in rural areas is engaged in agricultural activities, and it has become deeply ingrained in the way of life. In addition, rural areas often lack the necessary infrastructure, such as roads and electricity for diversifying into other sectors. This limits opportunities for investment and growth in nonagricultural industries. Also, a large portion of the rural population has limited access to education and training, which is a barrier to participating in nonagricultural sectors that often require more specialized skills and knowledge.

Urban Informal Economy

The urban informal sector in Ghana is notable for its diversity and variability. Studies on the urban informal sector in Ghana indicate a diverse variety of operations that may be classified as (i) services, (ii) construction, and (iii) manufacturing.

(i) *Services*:

- *Urban food dealers*: market vendors, itinerant wholesalers and retailers, bakers, caterers, and cooked-food vendors are examples of urban food dealers and processors. These employees are usually women who are illiterate or semi-illiterate. They get much of their information and skills from their families.
- *Health and sanitation workers*: night soil carriers, traditional/herbal healers, drugstore operators, funeral undertakers, chemical sellers, refuse collectors, and traditional birth attendants and attendants in private maternity homes.
- Domestic workers, who are primarily women and have limited social protection and job security.
- Mechanical or electronic equipment repairers, radio and refrigeration repairers, who are mostly young male workers and have either received some basic education or are drop-outs, but among whom are to be found skilled workers whose skills are largely acquired through years of apprenticeship.
- *Garages*: auto mechanics, sprayers, welders, vulcanizers, and auto electricians, many of whom obtained some minimal formal education alongside numerous dropouts and learned their trade through years of apprenticeship.
- Graphic designers, primarily men, two to six individuals per unit who learned their trade through minimal vocational training and apprenticeship.
- *Audio–visual sector professionals*: cinema, photographers, artist, film makers. These are talented professionals who have had basic formal education but lack formal vocational training. These people are often male, but the number of females in the industry keeps on growing.
- Barbers/salon operators, private security workers who are in their youth with low educational qualifications and don't have job security.

The service sector makes a substantial contribution to Ghana's Gross Domestic Product. It accounts for a significant portion of the country's economic output. The service sector provides employment opportunities, improves the quality of life, supports economic diversification, and plays a critical role in attracting foreign investment and tourists to the country (Deladem et al., 2021). As Ghana continues to develop and modernize its economy, the service sector plays an important role.

(ii) *Construction workers*:
The construction sector provides employment opportunities for a significant portion of the country's workforce (Boadu et al., 2020). This includes both skilled and unskilled labor, such as architects, engineers, masons, carpenters, and laborers. The sector's labor-intensive nature helps reduce unemployment and underemployment. The construction sector is responsible for building and maintaining critical infrastructure such as roads, bridges, ports, airports, schools, hospitals, and housing. Improved infrastructure contributes to economic growth by facilitating trade, reducing transportation costs, and enhancing the quality of life. The construction sector also generates revenue for the government through various means, including taxes and permits. Government revenues are used to fund public services, infrastructure projects, and social development programs.

(iii) *Manufacturing*:
The common activities in this sub-sector of the informal sector include food processing, textile and garment production, wood processing, and metal work. Women dominate in food processing, whereas males dominate in metalworking and woodworking. Apprenticeship is the most prevalent method of acquiring skills and finding work in urban informal manufacturing units. The manufacturing sector plays a significant role in contributing to the economy of Ghana, as it drives economic growth. The manufacturing sector is a major source of employment in Ghana. It provides jobs for a significant portion of the population, including skilled and unskilled labor, which helps reduce unemployment and poverty levels (Baffour et al., 2020). Manufacturing diversifies the economy by adding value to raw materials and promoting the development of various industries. This diversity helps reduce the country's vulnerability to fluctuations in commodity prices, which often affect primary sectors like agriculture and mining. Furthermore, the manufacturing sector produces goods for export, contributing to foreign exchange earnings and improving the balance of trade (Baffour et al., 2020). Ghana exports manufactured products to regional and international markets, generating revenue and boosting the country's economic stability (Baffour et al., 2020).

History of Ghana's Digitalization Journey

The government of Ghana has recognized the crucial role that the telecommunications industry plays in transforming the economy. In this regard, various policies and actions have been implemented over time to maximize the sector's potential (Kpessa & Atuguba, 2013). The push for digitization has become a central agenda for Ghana's development, with its origins tracing back to the economic liberalization in the early 1980s. This marked the end of the monopolistic practices of the Ghana Postal and Telecommunication Services, which had been the sole supplier of telecommunication services in the country (Alhassan, 2004).

In 1976, the Ghana Posts and Telecommunications Corporation initiated the First Telecommunications Project to enhance service quality and restore the country's telecommunications network. Subsequently, the Second Telecommunications Project was launched in 1987, aimed at expanding infrastructure, installing earth-receiving satellites, and improving the switch network in urban and rural areas, among other objectives (Osei-Owusu, 2017). The second phase faced delays, stretching its completion to 1994 due to project execution and funding disbursement issues. Despite these efforts, telecommunications services were far from being universally accessible, primarily limited to urban areas. In 1987, the government, as part of the World Bank and International Monetary Fund structural adjustment program, allowed private businesses to enter the industry. This move attracted approximately 40 telecommunication firms, mostly subsidiaries of established international companies from the United States and Europe, which began providing and maintaining telecommunication infrastructure (Osei-Owusu, 2017).

With the advent of the internet, the government formulated the Information, Communication, and Technology (ICT) for Accelerated Development (ICT4AD) Policy in 2003, aligning with socioeconomic development frameworks such as Vision 2020, the Ghana Poverty Reduction Strategy, and the Coordinated Programme for Economic and Social Development (Kubuga et al., 2021). The ICT4AD Policy aimed to leverage ICT to address developmental challenges and transform Ghana into an information-rich, knowledge-based society and economy. The policy emphasized the deployment of ICT in various sectors, including agriculture, public service delivery, education, health, human resource management, research and development, justice, infrastructure, governance, community mobilization, and private sector development (Kwami, 2010). The ultimate goal was to mainstream technology in service provision, governance, and economic management.

To facilitate the implementation of the ICT4AD Policy, various legislations and policies were enacted, and a National Broadband Policy and Implementation Strategy were put in place to promote digital technologies in both commercial and public organizations. The policy aimed to enhance broadband network capacity, promote socioeconomic change, encourage private sector participation, and create an environment conducive to efficient broadband service adoption (Kubuga et al., 2021). The national broadband strategy was seen as essential for achieving inclusivity and cost-effectiveness while creating employment opportunities and infrastructure for sustainable development. As part of this digitalization drive, the government invested in interoperable broadband infrastructure networks to promote e-government and enhance public service delivery.

Ghana's digital technology ecosystem has rapidly evolved under successive administrations, with digitalization becoming a central focus. This has opened doors for citizens to access government services electronically, fostering transparency, reducing corruption, and minimizing bureaucracy (Hossan & Bartram, 2010). In 2018, Ghana made significant progress, transitioning from middle to a high level in the E-Government Development Index, earning recognition for its ICT efforts (World Bank, 2019). The country's digital transformation has attracted global attention, with companies like Google and Twitter establishing regional offices in Ghana. Notably, Accra boasts a state-of-the-art data center, contributing to Ghana's digital prowess. Various digital solutions have been introduced, such as the digital national identification card, e-smart driver's license, e-justice, e-property addressing, mobile money interoperability, and more (Demuyakor, 2021).

One of the significant developments is the Ghana.Gov platform, enabling citizens to access government services conveniently. Additionally, a unique digital addressing system known as Ghana Post GPS was introduced, simplifying navigation and property identification. While these advancements have been substantial, challenges remain in deploying such technologies effectively in a dynamic and unpredictable environment. Efforts have been made to provide Wi-Fi connectivity to enhance access to digital services for all segments of society. These initiatives collectively contribute to Ghana's digitalization journey and its potential for economic growth and social development.

Digitalization Policy for the Informal Sector of Ghana

Section 3.8 of the ICT4AD report outlines Ghana's policy guidelines for the informal sector's integration of ICT. The government acknowledges the vital importance of expanding access to ICTs throughout society as Ghana enters the digital age. To ensure that the benefits of this technological transformation reach all segments of the population, the government is committed to implementing policy measures aimed at extending the reach of ICT applications, services, and access to the vast informal sector, which includes many of the most disadvantaged individuals. In pursuit of this goal, concerted efforts have been made to encourage the adoption of technology in rural, urban, and underserved populations as part of a broader strategy to promote the adoption and utilization of ICT within the informal sector. It is widely recognized that the growth of Ghana's information society is closely linked to the extent and equitable distribution of ICT access within the informal sector.

The overarching objective of this program is to transform the informal sector through ICT by:

(i) Fostering a high-income informal economy driven by the trading of ICT products and services, (ii) nurturing an informal economy characterized by a substantial commercial services sector and a thriving ICT services sub-sector and industry, (iii) creating an informal economy where a majority of the working population is engaged in information and communications-related activities, either directly or indirectly, (iv) establishing an informal economy where a significant portion of the population has access to information and communications technology products and services, (v) cultivating an informal economy within a literate society with a high proportion of computer literates, (vi) empowering an informal economy through the use of ICT to facilitate trade. To achieve these policy objectives, several initiatives have been launched. For example, the Ghana Investment

Fund for Electronic Communications (GIFEC) has taken steps to reduce the rural connectivity gap by undertaking various projects. Notably, GIFEC partnered with Mobile Telephone Network (MTN) and Ericsson in a $12 million Rural Telephony Project aimed at extending mobile telephone service coverage to around 40 rural communities in the country (Arthur, 2016). Similar projects have also been introduced by GIFEC, the Ministry of Communications, and the World Bank. Moreover, more than 200 community and regional innovation centers have been established to offer a range of communication and innovation services to rural and underserved populations (Arthur, 2016).

The ICT4AD policy aims to leverage information and communication technology to drive socioeconomic development, including efforts to formalize the informal sector. One of the key strategies was to increase financial inclusion through digital means. By promoting the use of mobile money and digital payment systems, the informal sector workers, such as small-scale traders and artisans, could gain access to formal financial services. This will help them in keeping records of their transactions and financial activities, which is an essential step in formalization. Furthermore, the government aims to provide various services online, making it easier for informal sector workers to interact with government agencies. This includes business registration, tax payment, and access to permits and licenses. Offering these services digitally reduces the need for face-to-face interactions, which is an important step toward formalization (Prokop & Tepe, 2022). In addition, the ICT4AD policy aims to provide training and capacity-building programs to empower informal sector workers with digital skills. This will enable Small, Medium Scale Enterprises (SMEs) to better manage their businesses and interact with formal institutions, such as banks and government agencies, more effectively. Moreover, ensuring that informal sector workers have access to relevant information and market data through ICT tools can help them make informed decisions and improve their businesses. This access can enhance their ability to operate more efficiently and formally. Also streamlining regulations and simplifying administrative processes for informal sector businesses were part of the policy's approach. Reducing bureaucratic barriers and making it easier for informal businesses to comply with regulations can encourage formalization. Again, the implementation of digital identification systems can help formalize the informal sector by creating a way to track and identify individuals and businesses. This can be used for taxation, access to credit, and other formalization processes.

Ghana's ICT4AD policy has the potential to drive economic development and improve the lives of its citizens by harnessing the benefits of information and communication technology. However, the digital divide is a key challenge that is hindering the attainment of the goals of the policy (Yalley, 2022). Lack of digital literacy or the ability to effectively use digital devices and navigate the internet exacerbates the digital divide. People who lack digital skills are less likely to benefit from online educational resources, job opportunities, and government services. Despite efforts to promote digital literacy, disparities in access to and proficiency in ICT skills persist, particularly in rural areas (Yalley, 2022). These disparities hinder the policy's effectiveness (Yalley, 2022). Urban areas in Ghana generally have better access to digital infrastructure, including broadband internet and mobile networks, compared to rural areas. However, many remote and under-served communities still lack reliable internet connectivity, making it difficult for residents in these regions to access digital services. Furthermore, low-income individuals and families often face barriers to affording digital devices (e.g., smartphones and computers) and internet subscriptions. The cost of data, devices, and electricity prohibits many Ghanaians, particularly in rural and marginalized communities from using ICT (Yalley, 2022). Again, people with higher levels of education tend to have better digital literacy and are more likely to make use of digital technologies. The digital divide is exacerbated by disparities in the quality of education between urban and rural areas (Yalley, 2022). Moreover, while Ghana has made significant strides in expanding its internet infrastructure and mobile network coverage, challenges remain. Infrastructure limitations, including unreliable electricity supply, hinder internet access in some areas (Yalley, 2022).

Methodology

The study was designed as a qualitative study. The key reason for choosing a qualitative design is to explore the research issue in-depth. Qualitative research is more concerned with gaining a deep understanding of the subject matter (Mwita, 2022). The researchers were able to delve into the complexities, nuances, and underlying reasons for the phenomena under investigation. A desk review was conducted by collecting data from secondary data sources such as articles, books, government reports, business reports, and newspapers. In analyzing the data, qualitative content analysis was used. Qualitative content analysis is a data analysis approach that allows for the subjective analysis of text through a methodical categorization procedure of coding and finding themes (Driesen, 2019). Exploring the meaning of text is greatly aided by qualitative content analysis (Driesen, 2019).

Contemporary Observations of the Digitalization Initiatives

Ghana has been making efforts to digitize various aspects of its economy, including initiatives in the informal sector. Some contemporary observations regarding Ghana's digitalization initiatives in the informal sector include digital payments and mobile money, digital financial inclusion, digital identification, digital marketplaces, and e-commerce and fintech startups (Asamoah & Owusu-Agyei, 2020). Ghana has been promoting the use of mobile money and digital payment solutions in the informal sector. Mobile money services such as MTN Mobile Money and Vodafone Cash have gained significant popularity. This has made it easier for individuals and small businesses in the informal sector to send and receive money, pay bills, and even access credit. The government and various financial institutions have been working to improve financial inclusion in the informal sector. Initiatives like "Ghana Digital Financial Services" have aimed to provide financial services to informal sector participants, helping them access credit, insurance, and savings products (Asamoah & Owusu-Agyei, 2020). The Ghana Card, a biometric national identification card, has been introduced to enhance the identity verification of individuals. This facilitates access to various government services and financial products, especially for those in the informal sector (Asamoah & Owusu-Agyei, 2020). The growth of digital marketplaces and e-commerce platforms has provided a channel for informal sector businesses to expand their reach (Asamoah & Owusu-Agyei, 2020). Sellers and artisans can now list their products online, reach a wider customer base, and receive payments digitally. Fintech startups in Ghana have been developing solutions to address the needs of the informal sector. These include microloans, savings platforms, and payment solutions tailored to the unique challenges faced by informal businesses and individuals.

Implication of Digitalization in the Agricultural Sector of Ghana

Digitalization is being used to promote contemporary agriculture practices in the country. Policymakers launched an e-agriculture initiative under the West African Agriculture Productivity Programme, which was a World Bank-sponsored project that is aimed at leveraging the utility value of ICT to provide farmers with well-timed scientific knowledge and to improve the yield of farmers. E-farm information is a project that provides information on toll-free lines; e-field extension – a project that collects and provides feedback to farmers; and e-learning and resource centers – provide information for youth in agriculture, and regular web publications and dissemination of news and information on innovations, new methods, and practices across the agriculture value chain.

The e-agriculture initiative, which is viewed as a method of bridging gaps between farmers and technology, employs electronic means to provide extension services as well as to generate, store, and retrieve information. The program registers farmers and uses Unstructured Supplementary Service Data (USSD) numbers to electronically provide crucial codes for farmers to obtain fertilizers and other farm inputs. Thus, under this initiative, registered farmers may use their USSD number to identify and claim their fertilizer allotment in their communities, preventing corruption and smuggling to neighboring states. According to Nyarko and Kozári (2020), the fundamental goal of the e-agriculture initiative is to offer inexpensive, timely, and effective agricultural service delivery via the use of ICTs.

To save farmers' time and effort, the e-agriculture allows farmers to access information using technological means at home, as opposed to previous arrangements that required them to visit district officers to be educated on issues such as increasing yields, handling products in the post-harvest phase, and marketing their products. Farmers using smartphones as part of this initiative engage in live conversations with extension officers and receive immediate replies on problems via technology applications.

Digital farming has removed obstacles to farming, making it more inventive and fascinating for the youth to explore, as well as comforting farmers, particularly those who are hesitant to use inorganic fertilizers for fear of poisoning their lands. The evolution of digital farming began 30 years ago when tiny agricultural hand tools such as hoes, cutlasses, and rakes were replaced with low-tech mechanical engineering instruments such as tractors, plows, planters, etc.

A higher and more advanced technology was introduced that uses sensors and contains a significant amount of software-based artificial intelligence that is a combination of mechanics and electronics, commonly referred to as mechatronics or robotics such as livestock farming tech. Ghana has been identified as one of the digitalization trailblazers in the agriculture sector (Odusola, 2021).

Corporations have advanced agriculture digitization in Ghana by creating payment systems, credit platforms, and digital insurance. Many digital platforms, such as Esoko, Farmerline, Cowtribe, and AgroCenta, have evolved in recent years to provide diverse services. These systems provide agribusinesses with digital data collection, farmer profiling, management, and analytics for field monitoring, farm mapping, and food procurement. Agribusiness uses digital applications to teach farmers, audit farmers for compliance and certification, such as Rainforest Alliance and Fairtrade, and perform voice polls with farmers in many languages (Loukos & Javed, 2018).

The application provides farmers with digital identities and financial records, trains farmers on improved farming practices and business tips through digital channels such as voice calls and talking books, provides farmers with weather updates in local languages, supplies farm inputs on credit to farmers, and distributes these inputs (Farmerline, 2020). These activities are carried out with the help of Mergdata, a web and mobile application that is used to power many farmers in Ghana, including modules for farmer profiles, certification, traceability, mapping, and messaging (Farmerline, 2020).

Aerial photos from satellites or drones, weather forecasts, and soil sensors are allowing crop development to be managed in real-time. If there are variations from typical growth or other causes, automated systems offer early warnings. Precision farming organizations collect and analyze soil data such as temperature, nutrients, and vegetative health to assist farmers in applying the appropriate fertilizer and irrigating their crops effectively. By facilitating data-driven agricultural techniques for small-scale farmers, the approach increases farm output and lowers input waste. Big data and analytic skills are used by technology corporations to turn farmers into a knowledge-based community to enhance production through precision insights. This aids in the adjustment of irrigation and determining the demands of specific plants.

Aside from precision farming, financial options for farmers are flourishing. Digitalization exposes unbanked and underserved smallholder farmers to access credit while also assisting financial institutions in cost-effectively expanding their agricultural loan portfolios. Pricing data is provided by technology corporations to reduce price asymmetry between farmers and buyers, allowing farmers to earn more. Farmerline and AgroCenta, both established in Ghana, use mobile and online technology to deliver farming advise, weather predictions, market information, and financial guidance to farmers who have previously been out of reach owing to connectivity, literacy, or language obstacles. Sokopepe provides farmers with market information and agricultural record management services via short message service (SMS) and web technologies.

Corporations have enhanced agricultural digitization in Ghana by developing payment systems, credit platforms, and digital insurance. Another breakthrough in this field is the use of the mobile phone as a trading platform. These platforms connect buyers and sellers in geographically dispersed markets, and they often specialize in a primary cash crop of the chosen region. These structured platforms, in contrast to traditional marketplaces, enable farmers, merchants, processors, and financial institutions to engage in legally defined trading and financial arrangements. They operate by digitizing and automating price discovery methods such as identifying and announcing auction winners, communicating price information, and enabling farmers to access other electronic marketplaces. The digital platforms inform farmers about current market prices, boost market competitiveness, and improve price search transparency. They lower information costs at various stages of the agricultural chain by instantly linking distant market actors. Farmers take advantage of previously untapped trade prospects and learn about previously undiscovered innovative methods. As a result, cost savings result in increased welfare and income (Nakasone et al., 2014). Examples of apps developed for the agricultural sector include Agrimall, Esoko, Farmerline, etc. Farmers who use these platforms enter their requests to purchase or sell items into a centralized national database; the app then processes discovering successful trades, and both parties are notified. Rather than enabling buyers and sellers to browse a list of possible trading partners, the matching algorithm matches offers focused on increasing the platform's trade profits. Various characteristics make these apps appealing to farmers.

First, customers not only enter the desired price and amount of their bid but also restrict the possibilities of their intended transaction, for example, wet versus cleaned maize and shelled versus unshelled grains. Second, the platforms allow users to trade with every trader in the country and the app's algorithm considers trip expenses when suggesting pairings. The Farmerline platform enables customers with in-village assistance and a contact center, which increases its dependability. Users trade on these platforms in these ways: by SMS, USSD application, website, or by calling a contact center representative. All of these solutions offer the same functionality to their customers: purchase, sell, and quote/request pricing information.

Implication of Digitalization in Microcredit Services

Digitalization in microcredit services has significantly contributed to the formalization of the sector by making operations more efficient, transparent, and inclusive. This benefits both microcredit providers and borrowers, while helping regulatory authorities ensure that the sector operates within established guidelines. The microcredit industry benefits from digital innovation in a variety of ways, including improved service delivery, product selection, convenience, competitive timeliness, and pricing in "Susu" (local name for microcredit) business processes (Dzogbenuku, 2017).

Digital financial services provide opportunities to enhance financial inclusion while also lowering the cost of mobilizing savings. Products such as mobile money have made it possible to reach a large section of the unbanked across various demographics and genders. Bringing the financially excluded into the financial sector has a large potential to drive low-cost savings mobilization and dramatically decrease funding costs, as well as a high potential for supporting microcredit establishments through inexpensive lending.

In July 2011, the Bank of Ghana released guidelines and standards for microcredit firms whether previously registered with the Ghana Cooperative "Susu" Collectors Association or not, under TIER 4 encompassing Business Form; Capital; Permissible Activities; Branch Expansion; and Prudential Reporting (Sarpong, 2018). The Bank of Ghana issued a directive on Crowd Funding that prioritized the unbanked by facilitating Crowd Funding Policy Directive, technology platforms, and other non-bank financial institutions such as Credit Unions and the Ghana Cooperative "Susu" Collectors Association to allow the unbanked access to financial services in the context of overall payment system reforms (Quartey & Afful-Mensah, 2014).

Through its Crowd Funding Policy, the Bank of Ghana aims to digitize the "Susu" scheme (Sarpong, 2018). Since 2011, the foregoing legislation, as well as the Bank of Ghana's instructions and directives, has established an enabling financial sector environment for the financial inclusion of the unbanked in the informal economy (Sarpong, 2018). Two essential components of these standards required microfinance firms to deposit their funds with commercial banks and to report their activities to the Bank of Ghana on a regular basis, which meant that these small groups had to immediately prepare themselves for submitting standardized financial reports (Sarpong, 2018).

The new laws provide microfinance enterprises with an opportunity to expand their operations. Microfinance companies developed a "Susu" system that includes a point of sale "POS" device that Susu collectors bring with them (Quartey & Afful-Mensah, 2014). When customers make their deposits, the POS prints a receipt for the customer and transmits the information back to the "Susu" company's home office information system (IS), also provided by "Susu" firms, for real-time reconciliation (Quartey & Afful-Mensah, 2014). Connectivity is provided by a dual Subscriber Identity Module (SIM) system in the POS so that if one mobile network happens to be down at that moment, the other SIM kicks in to provide coverage. Many "Susu" collectors were spending more than an hour in the office each evening, trying to reconcile their paper tracking logs against the old IS system and preparing a report of the day's transactions; now, the transactions are already reconciled when they get back to the office and they just need to print out their reports (Adusei & Appiah, 2012).

The automated system also helps the "Susu" companies manage fraud risk, which can always be a problem with manual cash collection systems (Adu, 2019). Customers are also happy to see the new POS devices in action. It gives them confidence in the system when they see immediate balance reports that jibe with their expectations (Adu, 2019). The solution enables "Susu" enterprises to provide their clients with a full "one-stop shop" experience, including depository, credit, and asset finance services, as well as the IS and collection tools (Adu, 2019). And the more deposits "Susu" enterprises have on hand for their banking activities, which is the lifeblood of every bank, the better their "Susu" clients do (Adu, 2019). Deposits at "Susu" companies have increased as a result of the digitalization drive by the government (Adu, 2019). "Susu" enterprises are able to provide these services at a profit and offer even more value-added services to customers (Dzogbenuku, 2017).

We are witnessing widespread acceptance of the use of these new technologies in the provision of financial services for the unbanked. Microfinance organizations have used digital technologies to create new methods to communicate with clients. Microfinance organizations, for example, have begun to use WhatsApp and Chat banking to provide financial services to consumers remotely. By using these technologies, microfinance institutions enabled clients to make inquiries while continuing to provide fundamental financial services.

On the part of individuals and businesses in the informal sector, digitalization ensures financial inclusion. Many individuals and businesses in the informal sector lack access to traditional banking services due to geographical limitations, inadequate infrastructure, or a lack of formal documentation (Dzogbenuku, 2017). Digitization, especially through mobile banking and digital wallets, provides an alternative means of accessing basic banking services. This allows them to make transactions, save money, and even apply for credit without visiting a physical bank. Furthermore, digital financial services often have lower transaction costs compared to traditional banking, and thus individuals and businesses in the informal sector find it more affordable to use digital platforms for financial transactions, making it economically viable for them to participate in the formal financial ecosystem.

Also, digitalization helps to overcome geographic barriers associated with banking in the informal sector. In many regions, physical banks and branches are few and far between, making it challenging for individuals in remote areas to access financial services (Dzogbenuku, 2017). Digitization breaks down these geographical barriers by allowing anyone with a mobile phone and an internet connection to access banking services. This extends the reach of financial institutions to the informal sector (Dzogbenuku, 2017).

Moreover, digital financial data are used to assess creditworthiness, enabling individuals and businesses in the informal sector to access credit. For example, the implementation of the Ghana card has resulted in increased adoption of digital financial services by making it easier for the unbanked to open a bank account while also simplifying documentation requirements and enabling more cost-effective customer onboarding that can be conducted remotely. Digital identity systems improve security credentials and make it a more secure procedure for individuals and businesses in the informal sector to gain financial inclusion (Dzogbenuku, 2017).

Digital financial services provide informal sector workers and businesses with access to the formal financial system. This inclusion allows them to save, borrow, and invest more easily. Financial institutions are able to assess the creditworthiness of individuals and businesses in the informal sector based on their digital transaction history (Dzogbenuku, 2017). Digitalization has allowed individuals and businesses in the informal sector to access financial services (Dzogbenuku, 2017).

This access to formal financial services has helped individuals and businesses in the informal sector build a financial track record, which is a crucial step toward formalization.

Implication of Digitalization in the Transportation Sector of Ghana

In general, the digital platform business model, which often depends on small, self-employed service providers, fits well with a significant number of such firms. Digital platforms connecting self-employed drivers to customers have quickly acquired traction in Ghana's informal transportation sector. Uber, Bolt, and Yango are the common digital transportation services in the country.

Similar start-ups catering to local markets include the motorbike taxi app (Okada) app. Digital platform drivers fare better than taxi drivers. Because the platform driver has more prospective clients, he or she spends less time waiting or searching for customers, saving fuel. Prices are determined and adhered to, reducing contractual risks. Furthermore, customer and driver rating systems limit the possibility of route and fee disagreements.

It is apparent that the emergence of Uber and others has put severe competitive pressure on existing taxi businesses and drivers (as well as operators of other modes of transportation).

In Ghana, the emergence of platform driving is altering the commercial passenger industry in a variety of ways. In contrast to the previous system, which is based on the negotiating abilities of drivers and passengers, the metered pricing system imposes some amount of certainty. For example, price increases and traffic jams might raise the expense of the journey. Nonetheless, ride-hailing excursions are often seen as less expensive than renting traditional taxicabs. The traceability of ride-hailing journeys is thought to lower the risk of injury when traveling and enhance the likelihood of retrieving lost belongings or tracing harms/crimes and offenders. Also, the vans that provide services to riders' homes are quite modern and well-maintained, typically with air conditioning. In addition to raising the quality of road transportation, ride-hailing has created economic opportunities in the informal sector. It has made it possible for people to commercialize their driving abilities.

The digitalization of transportation extends beyond the urban informal sector as it has reached rural Ghana. Ghana's rural people are mostly engaged in agriculture, and digital solutions have been created to help farmers with their jobs. Farming equipment transportation has become less stressful as a result of agricultural transportation applications. A Trotro Tractor Limited (TTL), for example, is an agricultural technology business that provides mechanization.

TTL has created an "Uber-like" technology-enabled equipment hire platform that connects farmers with tractor operators and other agricultural machinery service providers (Satyasai & Balanarayana, 2018). Farmers may request and schedule tractor and agricultural machinery services using TTL's USSD short code. Tractor owners utilize TTL's digital apps and online sites to remotely monitor the efficiency and profitability of their tractors. Aggregators gain access to farmers and produce using TTL's data management system, as well as other upstream agricultural services.

Digitalization has played a significant role in helping to formalize the informal transport sector in Ghana in several ways: First, digital platforms and apps provide a transparent system for both passengers and drivers. Passengers can see information about the driver, the vehicle, and the price before booking a ride. This transparency reduces the risk of overcharging and ensures that drivers adhere to established rates. Second, many digital platforms have safety features such as driver background checks, GPS tracking, and the ability to share ride details with others. This enhances passenger safety and creates accountability within the sector, making it less likely for drivers to engage in unethical or illegal behavior. Third, digital platforms have quality and service standards that drivers must adhere to. These standards include vehicle conditions, driver conduct, and customer service. This standardization helps formalize the sector by providing a consistent level of service to passengers. Also, some digital platforms offer training and support to drivers, helping them develop professional skills and customer service abilities. This training contributes to the formalization of the sector by raising the standards of service. Fourth, digital platforms have helped to transform informal transportation work into more formal employment. Some platforms offer benefits like insurance and retirement plans to drivers, making their work more secure and formal. Fifth, digital platforms make it easier for passengers to find rides quickly, reducing wait times and the inefficiencies often associated with informal transportation. This convenience encourages more people to use formalized services and lastly, and digitalization has lowered barriers to entry for new players in the transportation sector. This increased competition has led to better services and fairer pricing, contributing to the formalization of the industry.

Implication of Digitalization in the Retail Sector of Ghana

Store operators understand that sales are only as good as the items they have in stock. The majority of micro and small businesses in Ghana's retail sector confront two obstacles: small working capital and difficulties restocking inventory on a regular basis. The majority of such merchants are informal, with the majority of their money invested in inventory. When items do not sell, they must find a means to restock the items that are selling in order to continue receiving revenue. In these instances, restocking in-demand items frequently can help. However, merchants in Ghana often go to the main market to restock, requiring them to close down for several hours. Needless to say, every minute the store is closed, or an item remains out of stock represents a potential lost sale, and every cedi matters for these businesses' bottom lines.

E-commerce platforms have emerged to assist in the resolution of these issues. E-commerce provides retailers with easy stock ordering and delivery. Rather than traveling to the market to buy supplies, businesses register on e-commerce platforms and then order things using mobile phones (or by dialing in for poor literacy and non-smartphone clients). Boost Ghana, for example, provides regular, low-cost delivery straight to retailers, allowing them to resupply their mobiles without leaving their stores. Boost Ghana is able to give retailers a variety of reasonably priced goods that are delivered to their door via the platform. This implies that merchants have things in stock when consumers need them and can simply and conveniently refill them.

Store owners just SMS their orders or use the mobile app to place them, and they are delivered the same day. E-commerce platforms contribute to a bigger development priority: the digitization of the informal economy, by assisting merchants in growing and documenting their transactions and purchases. Despite the introduction of mobile money, business-2-business supply chains in Ghana continue to largely deal with cash (Naab & Bans-Akutey, 2021). E-commerce is propelling merchants' digital transformation by making it simple to purchase items online and make digital payments via bank deposits or mobile money, all while maintaining a digital record of their transaction history. E-commerce order and payment records legitimize procurement by providing businesses with a documented ledger of their purchase and payment history, which serve as formal accounts from a financial standpoint.

The growth of e-commerce in Ghana has enabled many retailers to establish an online presence. These online platforms provide a formalized way for retailers to showcase their products and services, reach a wider customer base, and conduct transactions securely. E-commerce platforms offer a structured and organized way for retailers to present their products. These platforms typically provide templates and tools for creating product listings, allowing retailers to display items in a standardized manner. This formality improves the customer's shopping experience. The growth of e-commerce in Ghana has transformed the retail landscape, offering a formalized way for retailers to connect with customers and conduct business in an efficient, secure, and cost-effective manner. Digitalization is playing a significant role in formalizing the informal retail sector by bringing small, unregistered businesses, street vendors, and local markets into the formal economy. Digitalization brings these businesses into the formal economy by providing tools and technologies that make it easier for them to operate, track transactions, and make informed decisions based on customer demand and trends.

Conclusion

In conclusion, the implications of digitalization in various sectors of Ghana's informal economy are profound and far-reaching. Digitalization has played a significant role in transforming and formalizing the informal sector, contributing to economic growth and enhancing the overall quality of life in the country. Digitalization has facilitated the adoption of modern agricultural practices, connecting farmers with valuable information and resources. It has improved efficiency, increased yields, and reduced risks, making farming more attractive and productive for both traditional and tech-savvy farmers. Digital financial services have expanded access to credit for individuals and businesses in the informal sector. It has reduced costs and barriers, enabling a broader segment of the population to participate in the formal financial system. This, in turn, has helped formalize the sector and build financial track records for previously underserved individuals. In the area of transportation, digital platforms like Uber and Bolt have introduced transparency, accountability, and safety in the informal transportation sector. Digitalization has provided economic opportunities for self-employed drivers and created a more reliable and efficient system for both passengers and drivers. For informal retail operators, digital platforms have improved inventory management and supply chain logistics for retailers, allowing them to restock quickly and efficiently. Moreover, these platforms enable businesses to establish an online presence, formalizing their operations and expanding their customer reach.

Overall, digitalization has bridged the gap between the informal and formal sectors in Ghana, offering tools and technologies that empower businesses and individuals to participate in the formal economy. This transformation has contributed to reducing inequalities, improving efficiency, and fostering economic growth in the country. The continued integration of digitalization into various sectors of the informal economy holds great promise for the future of Ghana's sustainable development and shared prosperity.

References

Addo, A. (2022). Information technology and public administration modernization in a developing country: Pursuing paperless clearance at Ghana customs. *Information Systems Journal, 32*(4), 819–855.

Addo, A. (2021). Controlling petty corruption in public administrations of developing countries through digitalization: An opportunity theory informed study of Ghana customs. *The Information Society, 37*(2), 99–114.

Adeniran, A., Ishaku, J., & Yusuf, A. (2020). Youth employment and labor market vulnerability in Ghana: Aggregate trends and determinants. In M. L. McLean (Ed.), *West African youth challenges and opportunity pathways* (pp. 187–211). Palgrave Macmillan.

Adu, J. S. N. (2019). *The effects of internet banking on the performance of rural banks: A case study of Kaaseman Rural Bank* [Doctoral dissertation, University of Cape Coast].

Adusei, M., & Appiah, S. (2012). Evidence on the impact of the 'susu' scheme in Ghana. *Global Journal of Business Research, 6*(2), 1–10.

Agwu, M. E. (2021). Can technology bridge the gap between rural development and financial inclusions?. *Technology Analysis & Strategic Management, 33*(2), 123–133.

Alhassan, A. (2004). *Development communication policy and economic fundamentalism in Ghana*. Tampere University Press.

Arthur, E. (2016). *Market orientation and firm performance in Ghana's telecommunications industry* [Doctoral dissertation, London Metropolitan University].

Asamoah, J. Y., & Owusu-Agyei, L. (2020). The impact of ICT on financial sector policy reforms in post-financial crisis era in Ghana: An institutional theory perspective. *International Journal of Finance & Banking Studies, 9*(2), 82–100.

Asiedu, B., Failler, P., & Beygens, Y. (2018). Ensuring food security: An analysis of the industrial smoking fishery sector of Ghana. *Agriculture & Food Security, 7*(1), 1–11.

Baffour, P. T., Ebo Turkson, F., Gyeke-Dako, A., Oduro, A. D., & Abbey, E. N. (2020). Innovation and employment in manufacturing and service firms in Ghana. *Small Business Economics, 54*, 1153–1164.

Boadu, E. F., Wang, C. C., & Sunindijo, R. Y. (2020). Characteristics of the construction industry in developing countries and its implications for health and safety: An exploratory study in Ghana. *International Journal of Environmental Research and Public Health, 17*(11), 4110.

Casalino, N., & Bednar, P. (2015). Managerial governance and transparency in public sector to improve services for citizens and companies. *Open Review of Management, Banking and Finance, Regent's University, London, UK, 1*(1), 45–51.

Deladem, T., Xiao, Z., Siueia, T. T., Doku, S., & Tettey, I. (2021). Developing sustainable tourism through public-private partnership to alleviate poverty in Ghana. *Tourist Studies, 21*(2), 317–343.

Demuyakor, J. (2021). COVID-19 pandemic and higher education: Leveraging on digital technologies and mobile applications for online learning in Ghana. *Shanlax International Journal of Education, 9*(3), 26–38.

Driesen, C. (2019). Category positioning – A qualitative content analysis approach to explore the subjective importance of a research topic using the example of the transition from school to university. *Forum Qualitative Sozialforschung/Forum: Qualitative Social Research, 20,* 3.

Dzogbenuku, R. K. (2017). *Identifying antecedents of marketing orientation of microfinance institutions in Ghana: The case study of microfinance companies* [Doctoral dissertation, London Metropolitan University].

Farmerline. (2020). *Solutions for farmers, for business and government's (webpage).* Retrieved May 10, 2023, from https://farmerline.co/2019/11/21/farmerlines-mergdata-named-to-times-list-of-100-best-inventions-of-2019/

Feige, E. L. (1990). Defining and estimating underground and informal economies: The new institutional economics approach. *World Development, 18*(7), 989–1002.

Fukuda-Parr, S. (2016). From the millennium development goals to the sustainable development goals: Shifts in purpose, concept, and politics of global goal setting for development. *Gender & Development, 24*(1), 43–52.

Gyil, M. B. (2020). *Participation in agro-processing and its effects on household welfare in the Sissala East Municipality of Ghana* [Doctoral dissertation, University of Cape Coast].

Heeks, R. (Ed.). (2001). *Reinventing government in the information age: International practice in IT-enabled public sector reform* (Vol. 1). Psychology Press.

Hossan, C., & Bartram, T. (2010). The battle against corruption and inefficiency with the help of eGovernment in Bangladesh. *Electronic Government, an International Journal, 7*(1), 89–100.

Hussmanns, R. (2001). *Informal sector and informal employment: Elements of a conceptual framework* [Paper presentation]. Fifth meeting of the Expert Group on Informal Sector Statistics. Delhi Group.

International Labour Office. (2002). *ILO compendium of official statistics on employment in the informal sector* [STAT Working papers, No. 2002-1]. International Labour Office, Bureau of Statistics.

Ivanović-Đukić, M., Stevanović, T., & Rađenović, T. (2019, January). Does digitalization affect the contribution of entrepreneurship to economic growth. *Proceedings of Rijeka Faculty of Economics: Journal of Economics and Business, 36*(2), 653–679.

Kpessa, M., & Atuguba, R. (2013). Grounding with the people: Participatory policy making in the context of constitution review in Ghana. *Journal of Politics and Law, 6*(1), 99–110.

Kubuga, K. K., Ayoung, D. A., & Bekoe, S. (2021). Ghana's ICT4AD policy: Between policy and reality. *Digital Policy, Regulation and Governance, 23*(2), 132–153.

Kwami, J. D. (2010). *Information and communication technologies for development and gendered realities in the South: Case studies of policy and practice in Ghana* [Doctoral dissertation, University of Oregon].

Lindgren, I., Madsen, C. Ø., Hofmann, S., & Melin, U. (2019). Close encounters of the digital kind: A research agenda for the digitalization of public services. *Government Information Quarterly, 36*(3), 427–436.

Loukos, P., & Javed, A. (2018). Opportunities in agricultural value chain digitisation: Learnings from Ghana. *Journal of Agriculture Value Chain, 3*(2), 30–45.

Mpofu, F. Y. (2022). Green taxes in Africa: Opportunities and challenges for environmental protection, sustainability, and the attainment of sustainable development goals. *Sustainability, 14*(16), 10239.

Mwita, K. (2022). Factors influencing data saturation in qualitative studies. *International Journal of Research in Business and Social Science, 11*(4), 414–420.

Naab, R., & Bans-Akutey, A. (2021). Assessing the use of e-business strategies by SMEs in Ghana during the Covid-19 pandemic. *Annals of Management and Organization Research, 2*(3), 145–160.

Nakasone, E., Torero, M., & Minten, B. (2014). The power of information: The ICT revolution in agricultural development. *Annual Review of Resource Economics, 6*(1), 533–550.

Nyarko, D. A., & Kozári, J. (2020). Influence of socio-economic characteristics of cocoa farmers on the use of E-agriculture in Ghana. *Asian Journal of Agricultural Extension, Economics & Sociology, 38*(6), 82–91.

Odusola, A. (2021). Case studies from Africa. In A. Odusola (Ed.), *Africa's agricultural renaissance: From paradox to powerhouse* (pp. 237–303). Springer International Publishing.

Osei-Boateng, C., & Ampratwum, E. (2011). *The informal sector in Ghana.* Friedrich-Ebert-Stiftung.

Osei-Owusu, A. (2017). Policy foundation of the Ghana telecom industry. *Nordic and Baltic Journal of Information and Communications Technologies, 2017*(1), 45–64. https://doi.org/10.13052/nbjict1902-097X.2017.004

Prokop, C., & Tepe, M. (2022). Talk or type? The effect of digital interfaces on citizens' satisfaction with standardized public services. *Public Administration, 100*(2), 427–443.

Quartey, P., & Afful-Mensah, G. (2014). Financial and monetary policies in Ghana: A review of recent trends. *Review of Development Finance, 4*(2), 115–125.

Sabbagh, K., Friedrich, R., El-Darwiche, B., Singh, M., Ganediwalla, S., & Katz, R. (2012). Maximizing the impact of digitization. In S. Dutta & B. Bilbao-Osorio (Eds.), *The global information technology report 2012: Living in a hyper-connected world* (pp. 121–133). INSEAD & World Economic Forum.

Sarabhai, K. V. (2015). ESD for sustainable development goals (SDGs). *Journal of Education for Sustainable Development, 9*(2), 121–123.

Sarpong, S. (2018). Ensuring sanity in Ghana's financial sector: A focus on Ghana's microfinance institutions. In B. Díaz Díaz, S. O. Idowu, & P. Molyneux (Eds.), *Corporate governance in banking and investor protection: From theory to practice* (pp. 287–301). Springer.

Satyasai, K. J. S., & Balanarayana, M. (2018). Can mechanization in agriculture help achieving sustainable development goals?. *Agricultural Economics Research Review, 31*(347-2018-5155), 147–156.

Towah, W. (2019). *The impact of good governance and stability on sustainable development in Ghana* [Doctoral dissertation, Walden University].

Villalba-Eguiluz, U., Egia-Olaizola, A., & Pérez de Mendiguren, J. C. (2020). Convergences between the social and solidarity economy and sustainable development goals: Case study in the Basque country. *Sustainability, 12*(13), 5435.

Vosko, L. F. (2002). Decent work' the shifting role of the ILO and the struggle for global social justice. *Global Social Policy, 2*(1), 19–46.

World Bank. (2019). Global financial development report 2019/2020: Bank regulation and supervision a decade after the global financial crisis. *The World Bank.*

Yalley, C. E. (2022). A tracer study on challenges affecting the use of ICT in pre-tertiary school administration in Ghana: Administrators' perspective. *Cogent Education, 9*(1), 2062893.

Zakaria, H. (2017). The drivers of women farmers' participation in cash crop production: The case of women smallholder farmers in Northern Ghana. *The Journal of Agricultural Education and Extension, 23*(2), 141–158.

Chapter 3

How Do the Socio-economic Characteristics of Migrant Workers Shape Their Financial Behaviour?

Rameshkumar Subramanian[a], T. P. Arjun[b] and Ashique Ali K. A.[b,c]

[a]*Department of Financial Administration, Central University of Punjab, India*
[b]*Department of Commerce, Central University of Tamil Nadu, India*
[c]*School of Law, SVKM'S NMIMS Deemed-to-be University, Hyderabad Campus, India*

Abstract

Personal financial management is gaining momentum in modern society, as it plays a vital role in shaping the financial behaviour of people looking forward to adequate financial well-being. Hence, people in general and the weaker sections of society in particular are expected to show desirable financial behaviour for achieving individual as well as societal well-being. The present study investigates the impact of socio-economic characteristics on the financial behaviour of migrant workers who have migrated to the state of Tamil Nadu. The primary data were collected using the interview schedule from 200 migrant workers selected using the snowball sampling technique. The results show that migrant workers have mediocre financial behaviour. Furthermore, it is also found that migrant workers' financial behaviour is not influenced by their socio-economic characteristics, such as gender, age, marital status, family type, and family income. However, the level of education has a significant positive role in shaping the financial behaviour of the migrant workers. The study outlines the need for specially engineered financial education for migrant workers.

Keywords: Financial literacy; financial education; financial behaviour; migration; migrant workers

Informal Economy and Sustainable Development Goals:
Ideas, Interventions and Challenges, 53–66
Copyright © 2024 by Rameshkumar Subramanian, T. P. Arjun and Ashique Ali K. A.
Published under exclusive licence by Emerald Publishing Limited
doi:10.1108/978-1-83753-980-220241003

1. Introduction

Today, there is a national as well as global focus on sustainable development. Growth with equity has emerged as the primary objective of the planning process of various economies in the world. Policymakers have been taking numerous initiatives to make the growth process more inclusive and sustainable. Achieving sustainable development goals (SDGs) becomes a question mark if economic development benefits are not reaching the weaker sections of society. It is crucial to bring the marginalised individuals into the formal financial system to achieve not only the SDGs but also inclusive growth. However, it is worth noting that unless they exhibit desirable financial behaviour, including them in the mainstream financial system and improving their financial literacy may not yield the desired results of achieving financial well-being (Sabri et al., 2023; Shim et al., 2009). Financial behaviour pertains to an individual's choices regarding their finances, encompassing day-to-day decisions to achieve a sense of satisfaction with their actions (Kamakia et al., 2017). Understanding how individuals handle, oversee, and utilise their financial resources is crucial to attaining financial well-being.

The changing trends in the economy, various complexities involved in the financial market environment, and the availability of innovative products and services make it necessary for people, particularly those in the informal economy, to exhibit desirable financial behaviour. One of the important groups mainly and actively engaged in the country's informal sector is the migrant workers. Economic development is invariably accompanied by the migration of people from rural to urban locations in search of jobs. People who move, the migrants, are relatively more adventurous compared to other people who stay behind in their native place, the settlers. As development accelerates, the ever-growing migrant population contributes significantly to a country's economic and social dynamics. Migrant workers' remittances help decrease regional spending differences among their families. The migrants add to diversity in customs and social practices as they integrate with the society at their workplace. Thus, they are a key segment of a rapidly urbanising society resulting from the economic and social transformation brought about by economic development.

Migrant workers are noted as one of the marginalised sections of society and are mostly engaged in 3-D jobs – dirty, dangerous, and demanding (sometimes degrading or demeaning) (Moyce & Schenker, 2018). They are often exposed to higher risk for mental health and social well-being issues, workplace accidents, exposure to hazards, etc., due to the nature of the jobs they perform (Aktas et al., 2022). While having low wages by working for longer hours in worse conditions, migrant workers are constantly subjected to human rights violations (Moyce & Schenker, 2018) and financial exploitations, making them vulnerable to financial emergencies and economic instability (Chen & Lemieux, 2016).

The challenges of uneven income flows, settlement issues, unsecured remittances, and limited access to savings instruments lead to cash flow volatility at source, which makes migrant households highly vulnerable. Migrant workers need adequate knowledge and skills not only to manage their day-to-day expenses but also to meet their needs throughout their lives. They need knowledge and skills to widely use financial services – saving, borrowing, and insurance – that can help them reduce vulnerability and build assets. In order to make informed financial decisions and achieve desirable financial well-being, migrant workers must have adequate financial skills and abilities. This eventually makes them capable of facing financial emergencies and economic instability, leading them to have stable lives while effectively utilising available financial resources.

Challenging financial circumstances, such as lower individual and family income, wage disparities, and increased responsibilities for household expenses, may compel the Indian migrant groups to engage in undesirable financial practices. Furthermore, limited financial capabilities, such as a lack of knowledge and awareness about financial products and services, lower financial skills and ability to conduct various financial transactions, along with a negative financial attitude, contribute to the propensity for migrant workers to exhibit irresponsible financial behaviours. The recent National Financial Literacy and Inclusion Survey 2019 (NCFE-FLIS) (NCFE, 2019) also highlights a heightened likelihood of undesirable financial behaviour among the marginalised sections of Indian society as merely 27% of the Indians are financially literate, and only 53% exhibit desirable financial behaviours. However, little is known about the financial behaviour of Indian migrant workers. This necessitates an empirical investigation of the Indian migrant workers in order to understand their current level of financial behaviour and facilitate necessary policy implications for their empowerment. Therefore, this study intends to fill this gap by empirically investigating the financial behaviour of migrant workers who have migrated to Tamil Nadu, one of the fastest-growing states in India, for jobs in the informal sectors. Furthermore, this study also analyses how various socio-economic characteristics of migrant workers shape their financial behaviour.

The remainder of the chapter is as follows: Section 2 consolidates the extant literature on the topic, followed by the methodology in Section 3. The results of the study are discussed in Section 4. Finally, Section 5 concludes the study.

2. Literature Review

2.1. Financial Behaviour

Financial behaviour is the actions and conducts of individuals that shape both short- and long-term financial well-being (NCFE, 2019). According to Altfest (2004, p. 54), financial behaviour is 'a process which assimilates all components of individual financial interest. These include cash flow management, investments, risk management, retirement planning, tax planning and real estate planning'. Xiao (2008) defined it as any human behaviour relevant to managing money-related transactions such as cash, credit, and savings. It is the capability of an individual to understand the impact of his/her financial choice on his/her circumstance and make appropriate decisions on cash management, precautionary measures, and opportunities for budget planning (Zeynep, 2015). Financial behaviour generally encompasses any behaviour related to managing, borrowing, saving/investing, insuring, or any money-related behaviour aimed at enhancing individual well-being (Xiao & Kumar, 2023).

Earlier studies measured financial behaviour using proxies (Meneau & Moorthy, 2022), such as actual consumer debt (Bapat, 2020). These proxies failed to cover a broader financial behaviour framework as these only covered one or two dimensions (Meneau & Moorthy, 2022). Previous studies on antecedents and outcomes of financial behaviour often defined financial behaviour as a set of behavioural components encompassing budgeting, cash flow management, consumption, savings, investment, borrowing, and insurance (Goyal et al., 2021). Therefore, the choice of financial behaviour measure in these studies varies considerably depending on researchers' preferences for specific behavioural components. For example, Kim et al. (2003) used a financial behaviour scale that covers five content areas such as planning, saving, budgeting, cutting down spending, and credit management, whereas Perry and Morris's (2005) scale only covered three content areas, such as budgeting, saving, and controlling spending. Dew and Xiao's (2011) scale, covering four content areas, such as spending, borrowing, saving, and planning for the future, was found to be a popular financial behaviour scale among the researchers as it is psychometrically validated (Bapat, 2020; Goyal et al., 2021).

2.2. Socio-economic Characteristics and Financial Behaviour

Human behaviour is shaped by socio-economic characteristics. Similarly, various literatures have noted that the financial behaviour of individuals is correlated with their socio-economic characteristics (Fachrudin et al., 2022; Goyal et al., 2021). Among these characteristics, age, gender, marital status, education, family type, and income were common (Goyal et al., 2021; Xiao & Kumar, 2023).

2.3. Gender

Individual behavioural patterns can differ based on gender (Caterall & Maclaran, 2001). Various studies have noted that financial decisions and habits have varied based on gender (Goyal et al., 2021). Male investors have higher confidence in their investment perception than female investors and hold a bigger portfolio (Chandra et al., 2017). Households with male heads have shown a higher propensity to plan and a longer planning horizon (Xiao & O'Neill, 2018b). Previous studies found that women's financial retirement planning has become ineffective as they lack better financial skills and cause financial difficulties during their post-retirement days (Kumar et al., 2019).

2.4. Age

Age is one of the common demographic characteristics expected to impact financial behaviour significantly as it represents different stages of life (Xiao & Kumar, 2023). Responsible financial behaviour is reflected by Indian young adults with the increase in their age (Bapat, 2020). Similarly, older individuals are shown to make better financial decisions in terms of performance measures of sunk cost and credit card repayment decisions and self-report measures of money management and financial decision outcomes (Eberhardt et al., 2019). However, Loke (2017) found that Malaysians in the higher age group had worse financial management practices than their lower age groups.

2.5. Education

Like ageing, education level is also an important factor affecting individuals' cognitive development and changing their behaviour according to various contexts. It was observed that education is one of the major factors identified by various studies that had a favourable impact on financial literacy (Goyal & Kumar, 2021). Based on the review by Goyal et al. (2021), financial behaviour has been found to be desirable among the different target groups with higher levels of education. For instance, consumer cash-flow management and budgeting behaviour were desirable among different target groups with higher education based on the review conducted by Subramanian and Arjun (2023).

2.6. Marital Status

Marital status is also one factor that can influence an individual's financial behaviour. After the marriage, the individuals' various financial decisions and actions can be highly influenced by their partner. Married individuals are shown desirable financial behaviour (Pepin, 2019; Sachitra et al., 2019; Xiao & O'Neill, 2018a).

2.7. Family Type

Similar to personal characteristics, an individual's financial behaviour can also be influenced by their family-oriented attributes. When a person resides within a joint family with multiple financial decision-makers, responsibility for various financial choices may be diminished, as many family members will be involved in the decision-making process. Conversely, in a nuclear family setting, an individual's financial obligations tend to be more significant, as fewer family members share the financial responsibilities. Consequently, individuals from nuclear families are more likely to exhibit favourable financial behaviour than those from joint families. However, living in a joint family setting can also offer opportunities to positively shape financial behaviour by observing other family members' desirable financial practices. In such cases, a joint family can contribute to the development of desirable financial behaviour in an individual (Borda & Rólczyńska, 2016; Mudzingiri et al., 2018).

2.8. Family Income

Another prominent family-oriented factor is family income (Gunay et al., 2015). Goyal et al. (2021) found that various studies reported that both individual and family income had a significant positive impact on financial behaviour. For instance, high-income Malaysians had more desirable financial behaviour than their lower-income counterparts (Loke, 2017). Similarly, undergraduates from high-income families have shown favourable financial habits compared to their peers from low-income families (Sachitra et al., 2019).

Based on the extensive literature review, we formulated the following hypothesis:

H1. Socio-economic characteristics such as age, gender, marital status, education, family type, and family income of the migrant workers have a significant impact on their financial behaviour.

3. Methodology

3.1. Empirical Analysis

We performed multiple linear regression (MLR) analysis using Jamovi 2.2.5, an open-source software built on R statistical language. The MLR analysis was performed by including six socio-economic characteristics such as age (x_1), gender (x_2), level of education (x_3), marital status (x_4), family type (x_5), and monthly family income (x_6) as independent variables, and financial behaviour (y) as the dependent variable. The MLR equation is as follows:

$$y = \alpha + \beta_1 x_1 + \beta_2 x_2 + \beta_3 x_3 + \beta_4 x_4 + \beta_5 x_5 + \beta_6 x_6 + e$$

whereas y is the dependent variable (financial behaviour), x_1–x_6 are the independent variables, e denotes the error term in the regression equation, α refers to the constant, and $\beta_1 - \beta_6$ are the regression coefficients.

3.2. Measure

Financial behaviour, the dependent variable, was measured using a scale devised by Dew and Xiao (2011). However, we adopted a modified version of Dew and Xiao's (2011) scale used in the study conducted by Bapat (2020), which modified the scale according to the Indian context. A 5-point Likert scale, ranging from strongly agree to strongly disagree, was used to present 10 items in the financial behaviour scale. The independent variables were measured through multiple-choice items, except for age, which is considered a metric variable measured in years. All other independent variables, including gender, level of education, marital status, family type, and monthly family income, were converted into dummy variables. Table 3.1 presents a description of the variables included in the analysis.

3.3. Population, Sampling, and Data Collection

The present study focused on the target population, comprising individuals who have migrated to Tamil Nadu in search of jobs and are engaged in informal sector occupations, such as construction work, carpentry, painting, and others.

Table 3.1.   Description of the Variables.

Variable	Description
Financial behaviour	*Metric*: financial behaviour score was calculated by summating the item scores. The financial behaviour scale includes 10 items covering spending, borrowing, saving, and planning for the future areas. One point is given if the respondent agrees to the item (strongly agree or agree); otherwise, zero point is given
Gender	*Binary*: if the respondent is male = 1, otherwise = 0
Level of education	
Less than matriculation	*Binary*: if the level of education of the respondent is less than matriculation = 1, otherwise = 0
Matriculation and above	*Binary*: if the level of education of the respondent is more than matriculation = 1, otherwise = 0
Monthly family income	*Binary*: if the monthly family income of the respondent is more than Rs. 35,000 = 1, otherwise = 0
Marital status	*Binary*: if the respondent is married = 1, otherwise = 0
Family type	*Binary*: if the respondent is living in a joint family = 1, otherwise = 0
Age	*Metric*: age in years

Source: Authors' own creation.

Since the exact population is unknown, we used a snowball sampling method to collect data. The snowball sampling method is most appropriate to secure a list of the unknown population from a few known potential respondents (Wang et al., 2023). Firstly, we collected the details of potential respondents from known migrants working nearby places, builders, friends, and relatives. During the interaction with the initially identified migrant workers, we made a further list of migrant workers based on their contact and recommendations. We approached the migrant workers with an interview schedule and collected data. However, we had a language barrier during the data collection since the migrant workers came from different states of India and spoke different languages. We included a translator and minimised the language barrier. We also faced a non-response barrier since many potential respondents were not interested in replying to the survey, as it extracts personal finance-related information. Some of them explicitly mentioned that details, particularly personal finance-related information collected from them, might be used to get hold of various Government benefits they receive or tend to receive. Even though we cleared the misunderstanding, they were not convinced to respond to the survey. Some potential respondents declined to participate in the survey, mentioning that it might jeopardise their job opportunities.

Nevertheless, we received 200 valid responses. Hair et al. (2017) suggested a rule of thumb for determining the required sample size for MLR analysis, which typically recommends having 15–20 observations for each independent variable. Following this guideline, our study required a total of 120 valid observations, as we employed 6 independent variables in the MLR analysis. Hence, we could meet the sample size criteria in order to avoid sampling error and get a robust result from the present study.

4. Results and Discussion

4.1. Descriptive Statistics

The various socio-economic characteristics and the descriptive analysis of the financial behaviour of the migrant workers are shown in Table 3.2.

Table 3.2. Socio-economic Characteristics and Financial Behaviour of the Migrant Workers.

Socio-economic Characteristics		Frequency	Percentage
Gender	Male	171	85.5
	Female	29	14.5
	Total	200	200
Level of education	No formal education	30	15
	Less than matriculation	148	74
	Matriculation and above	22	11
	Total	200	100
Marital status	Married	152	76
	Unmarried/widowed/divorced	48	24
	Total	200	100
Family type	Joint family	19	9.5
	Nuclear family	181	90.5
	Total	200	100
Monthly family income	Below Rs. 35,000	164	82
	Above Rs. 35,000	36	18
	Total	200	100
	Minimum	*Maximum*	*Average score*
Financial behaviour 1		10	4.98

Source: Authors' own creation.

The sample consists of a majority of males (85.5%), married individuals (76%), and people who live in nuclear families (90.5%). Only 11% of the respondents have an educational level of matriculation or above, and 15% have no formal education. This indicates the low literacy level among the migrant workers. More than three-fourths of the respondents have a lesser monthly family income. The average age of the respondents was 35 years (authors' calculation). The average financial behaviour score obtained was 4.98, and the standard deviation was 1.47.

4.2. Classification of Financial Behaviour

The respondents were classified into three categories based on their level of financial behaviour: desirable, mediocre, and undesirable, using the following method. The migrant workers whose financial behaviour score was above mean plus standard deviation (4.98 + 1.47 = 6.45) are considered to have desirable financial behaviour, whereas those with a score below mean minus standard deviation (4.98 – 1.47 = 3.51) are considered to have undesirable financial behaviour. The other respondents who score lying between these two values (3.51–6.45) show mediocre financial behaviour.

Eighty per cent of the migrant workers have mediocre financial behaviour, and only 9.5% were able to exhibit desirable financial behaviour (Fig. 3.1).

4.3. Regression Results

A multiple regression model was carried out. The model includes financial behaviour as the dependent variable and gender, educational qualification, marital status, family type, age, and monthly family income as the independent variables. The measures of each variable are described in Table 3.1. Table 3.3 displays the results of multiple regression.

The regression model has an explanatory power of 13.8% ($R^2 = 0.138$, $p < 0.001$), to explain the variance in financial behaviour by socio-economic

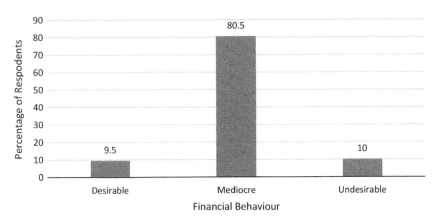

Fig. 3.1.   Classification of Financial Behaviour. *Source*: Authors' own creation.

Table 3.3.   Regression Results.

Predictor	Categories (Reference Category)	Estimate	SE	t	p
Intercept		3.3222	0.6137	5.414	<0 .001
Gender	Female (male)	0.0860	0.2871	0.299	0.765
Education qualification	Below matriculation (no formal education)	0.7589	0.2955	2.568	0.011
	Above matriculation (no formal education)	2.1236	0.3951	5.374	<0 .001
Marital status	Unmarried/widowed/divorced (married)	−0.1028	0.2398	−0.428	0.669
Family type	Nuclear family (joint family)	0.4440	0.3700	1.200	0.232
Age		0.0133	0.0132	1.005	0.316
Monthly family income	Higher income (lower income)	0.0734	0.2839	0.258	0.796
R^2	Adjusted R^2	F	df1	df2	p
0.138	0.106	4.39	7	192	<0 .001

Source: Authors' own creation.

characteristics of the migrant workers. Among the independent variables, level of education is the sole significant predictor of financial behaviour ($p < 0.05$). The beta coefficients indicate that better financial behaviour is achieved when they have a higher level of education ($\beta = 0.76$ for below matriculation, $\beta = 2.12$ for matriculation and above). Compared to migrant workers with no formal education, others with school education (below matriculation and above matriculation) have better financial behaviour. The result is in line with the findings of Goyal et al. (2021) and Subramanian and Arjun (2023) that higher education brings desirable financial behaviour among individuals. Strong cognitive abilities coupled with knowledge gained through experience enable individuals to exhibit desirable financial behaviour, as they are adept at making rational financial decisions, considering various possibilities, and adhering to desirable financial habits (Eberhardt et al., 2019).

Other personal characteristics such as gender, age, and marital status were insignificant in predicting migrant workers' financial behaviour and failed to support various previous literature findings. For instance, as per the findings of D. Bapat (2020) and Eberhardt et al. (2019), it was expected that migrant workers would possess more desirable financial behaviour in accordance with their ageing. However, we failed to support their results and concluded that age does not significantly predict migrant workers' financial behaviour. While contradicting (Chandra et al., 2017; Kumar et al., 2019; Xiao & O'Neill, 2018b) and supporting (Kumar et al., 2023) extant literature, the present study found gender differences do not hold any significant influence on the financial behaviour of migrant workers. Contrary to the findings of Pepin (2019), Sachitra et al. (2019), and Xiao and O'Neill (2018a), our observations indicate that there is no discernible variation in financial behaviour among migrant workers based on their marital status. Hence, it can be concluded that migrant workers show similar kinds of financial behaviour irrespective of their personal characteristics. This arises from their shared economic and living conditions, coupled with the nature of their similar employment. In this context, distinctions such as gender-based income disparities or age-related job opportunities become inconsequential for migrant workers when engaging in various financial activities and adopting financial habits, as their circumstances are characterised by common living conditions and expenses.

A similar kind of finding was found on family-oriented attributes. Neither family type nor family income does not influence migrant workers' financial behaviour. They are engaged in similar financial behavioural practices despite their family type and family income. However, earlier studies observed that family-oriented factors such as family type (Borda & Rólczyńska, 2016; Mudzingiri et al., 2018) and family income (Goyal et al., 2021; Khalisharani et al., 2022; Loke, 2017; Sachitra et al., 2019) are significant predictors of financial behaviour. The migrant workers are forced to stay away from their native household, and during the stage of earning a livelihood and taking care of their family, they often make individual decisions rather than consulting with other family members. Hence, the migrant workers' current family setting has a minimal role in shaping their financial behaviour. Most migrant workers have limited family income, which serves as both their primary source of sustenance and the means for sending financial support to their families back in their hometowns. Consequently, they may allocate these resources towards meeting immediate expenses rather than saving and investing for the future. Hence, most migrant workers cannot explore sophisticated financial services, and the influence of experiencing such financial services is meagre in shaping their financial behaviours.

5. Implications and Scope for Future Research

Migrant workers migrate from their homeland to other parts of the country in search of livelihood, and hence, they are more likely to possess similar demographic features. However, the present study's findings reiterate the importance of education in developing better financial behaviour. The educational level is the only personal attribute that significantly changes migrant workers' financial behaviour despite their common living conditions and job environment. Having a higher level of education helps the migrant workers to practice much more desirable financial behaviour. Governments can proactively offer equivalency courses, such as matriculation equivalency, to required migrant workers to provide a chance to access formal education opportunities. This will enable them to manage their hard-earned money in a better way.

Furthermore, the findings necessitate specially engineered financial education initiatives by host states as the states receive migrant workers from various states of the country. Hence, the Government, NGOs, and other interested agencies might design financial education modules exclusively for the migrant workers. It also mandates a financial awareness campaign to make them aware of various financial scams and malpractices that are happening around them, as there is a higher chance of approaching private money transfer intermediaries for the immediate transfer of money to their families.

The present study only considered the selective socio-economic characteristics of migrant workers to understand their impact on financial behaviours. Further studies have to be conducted by considering various antecedents that might play a major role in shaping the financial behaviour of migrant workers, such as psychological characteristics (including materialism, impulsiveness, self-efficacy, etc.), financial education, financial socialisation, and financial accessibility. Future researchers might explore how financial behaviour influences the financial well-being, quality of life, net worth, etc., of migrant workers. Additionally, the relationship between financial literacy, financial behaviour, and financial well-being of the migrant workers may also be investigated to formulate better policies to uplift this marginalised section of society.

6. Conclusion

The present study investigated the influence of socio-economic characteristics on the financial behaviour of migrant workers in Tamil Nadu. The study employed a survey method to gather primary data from migrant workers and analysed the data using multiple regression. Most migrant workers displayed mediocre financial behaviour, which is not up to the mark. The level of education significantly influences migrant workers' financial behaviour, which outlines the need for offering financial literacy promotion programmes to improve their financial behaviour. The major reasons for migration include meeting household expenses, repaying debts, and accumulating savings, all of which could be done in a better manner when they exhibit desirable financial behaviour. Otherwise, the money they earn may not serve all their purposes.

References

Aktas, E., Bergbom, B., Godderis, L., Kreshpaj, B., Marinov, M., Mates, D., McElvenny, D. M., Mehlum, I. S., Milenkova, V., Nena, E., & Glass, D. C. (2022). Migrant workers occupational health research: An OMEGA-NET working group position paper. *International Archives of Occupational and Environmental Health*, *95*(4), 765–777. https://doi.org/10.1007/s00420-021-01803-x

Altfest, L. (2004). Personal financial planning: Origins, developments and a plan for future direction. *American Economist*, *48*(2), 53–60. https://doi.org/10.1177/056943450404800204

Bapat, D. (2020). Antecedents to responsible financial management behavior among young adults: Moderating role of financial risk tolerance. *International Journal of Bank Marketing*, *38*(5), 1177–1194. https://doi.org/10.1108/IJBM-10-2019-0356

Bapat, D. M. (2020). Segmenting young adults based on financial management behavior in India. *International Journal of Bank Marketing*, *38*(2), 548–560. https://doi.org/10.1108/IJBM-01-2019-0016

Borda, M., & Rólczyńska, P. K. (2016). Impact of demographic factors on household financial decisions – Evidence from Poland. *International Journal of Risk Assessment and Management, 19*(1/2), 106. https://doi.org/10.1504/IJRAM.2016.074438

Caterall, M. A., & Maclaran, P. B. (2001). Gender perspectives in consumer behaviour: An overview and future directions. *The Marketing Review, 2*(4), 405–425. https://doi.org/10.1362/1469347012863853

Chandra, A., Sanningammanavara, K., & Nandini, A. S. (2017). Does individual heterogeneity shape retail investor behaviour? *International Journal of Social Economics, 44*(5), 578–593. https://doi.org/10.1108/IJSE-04-2015-0097

Chen, Z., & Lemieux, C. M. (2016). Financial knowledge and behaviors of Chinese migrant workers: An international perspective on a financially vulnerable population. *Journal of Community Practice, 24*(4), 462–486. https://doi.org/10.1080/10705422.2016.1233475

Dew, J., & Xiao, J. J. (2011). The financial management behavior scale: Development and validation. *Journal of Financial Counseling and Planning, 22*(1), 43–59.

Eberhardt, W., Bruine de Bruin, W., & Strough, J. N. (2019). Age differences in financial decision making: The benefits of more experience and less negative emotions. *Journal of Behavioral Decision Making, 32*(1), 79–93. https://doi.org/10.1002/bdm.2097

Fachrudin, K. A., Pirzada, K., & Iman, M. F. (2022). The role of financial behavior in mediating the influence of socioeconomic characteristics and neurotic personality traits on financial satisfaction. *Cogent Business and Management, 9*(1), 1–16. https://doi.org/10.1080/23311975.2022.2080152

Goyal, K., & Kumar, S. (2021). Financial literacy: A systematic review and bibliometric analysis. *International Journal of Consumer Studies, 45*(1), 80–105. https://doi.org/10.1111/ijcs.12605

Goyal, K., Kumar, S., & Xiao, J. J. (2021). Antecedents and consequences of personal financial management behavior: A systematic literature review and future research agenda. *International Journal of Bank Marketing, 39*(7), 1166–1207. https://doi.org/10.1108/IJBM-12-2020-0612

Gunay, G., Boylu, A. A., & Oğuz, A. (2015). Determinants of financial management behaviors of families. In Z. Copur (Ed.), *Handbook of research on behavioral finance and investment strategies: Decision making in the financial industry* (pp. 236–254). Business Science Reference/IGI Global. https://doi.org/10.4018/978-1-4666-7484-4.ch014

Hair, J. F., Black, W. C., Babin, B. J., & Anderson, R. E. (2017). *Multivariate data analysis.* Pearson Education Limited. https://doi.org/10.1002/9781118895238.ch8

Kamakia, M. G., Mwangi, C. I., & Mwangi, M. (2017). Financial literacy and financial well-being of public sector employees: A critical literature review. *European Scientific Journal, 13*(16), 233. https://doi.org/10.19044/esj.2017.v13n16p233

Khalisharani, H., Johan, I. R., & Sabri, M. F. (2022). The influence of financial literacy and attitude towards financial behaviour amongst undergraduate students: A cross-country evidence. *Pertanika Journal of Social Sciences and Humanities, 30*(2), 449–474. https://doi.org/10.47836/pjssh.30.2.03

Kim, J., Garman, E. T., & Sorhaindo, B. (2003). Relationships among credit counseling clients' financial well-being, financial behaviors, financial stressor events, and health. *Journal of Financial Counseling and Planning, 14*, 1–4.

Kumar, P., Islam, M. A., Pillai, R., & Sharif, T. (2023). Analysing the behavioural, psychological, and demographic determinants of financial decision making of household investors. *Heliyon, 9*(2), e13085. https://doi.org/10.1016/j.heliyon.2023.e13085

Kumar, S., Tomar, S., & Verma, D. (2019). Women's financial planning for retirement: Systematic literature review and future research agenda. *International Journal of Bank Marketing, 37*(1), 120–141. https://doi.org/10.1108/IJBM-08-2017-0165

Loke, Y. J. (2017). The influence of socio-demographic and financial knowledge factors on financial management practices of Malaysians. *International Journal of Business and Society, 18*(1), 33–50. https://doi.org/10.33736/ijbs.488.2017

Meneau, L. K., & Moorthy, J. (2022). Struggling to make ends meet: Can consumer financial behaviors improve? *International Journal of Bank Marketing, 40*(2), 263–296. https://doi.org/10.1108/IJBM-12-2020-0595

Moyce, S. C., & Schenker, M. (2018). Migrant workers and their occupational health and safety. *Annual Review of Public Health, 39*, 351–365. https://doi.org/10.1146/annurev-publhealth-040617-013714

Mudzingiri, C., Muteba Mwamba, J. W., & Keyser, J. N. (2018). Financial behavior, confidence, risk preferences and financial literacy of university students. *Cogent Economics and Finance, 6*(1), 1–25. https://doi.org/10.1080/23322039.2018.1512366

NCFE. (2019). *Financial literacy and inclusion in India.* https://www.ncfe.org.in/images/pdfs/reports/NFLIS_2019.pdf

Pepin, J. R. (2019). Beliefs about money in families: Balancing unity, autonomy, and gender equality. *Journal of Marriage and Family, 81*(2), 361–379. https://doi.org/10.1111/jomf.12554

Perry, V. G., & Morris, M. D. (2005). Who is in control? The role of self-perception, knowledge, and income in explaining consumer financial behavior. *Journal of Consumer Affairs, 39*(2), 299–313. https://doi.org/10.1111/j.1745-6606.2005.00016.x

Sabri, M. F., Anthony, M., Law, S. H., Rahim, H. A., Burhan, N. A. S., & Ithnin, M. (2023). Impact of financial behaviour on financial well-being: Evidence among young adults in Malaysia. *Journal of Financial Services Marketing*, 1–20. https://doi.org/10.1057/s41264-023-00234-8

Sachitra, V., Wijesinghe, D., & Gunasena, W. (2019). Exploring undergraduates' money-management life: Insight from an emerging economy. *Young Consumers, 20*(3), 167–189. https://doi.org/10.1108/YC-07-2018-00828

Shim, S., Xiao, J. J., Barber, B. L., & Lyons, A. C. (2009). Pathways to life success: A conceptual model of financial well-being for young adults. *Journal of Applied Developmental Psychology, 30*(6), 708–723. https://doi.org/10.1016/j.appdev.2009.02.003

Subramanian, R., & Arjun, T. P. (2023). Consumer cash-flow management and budgeting behavior. In J. J. Xiao & S. Kumar (Eds.), *A research agenda for consumer financial behavior* (1st ed., Issue 2011, pp. 59–72). Edward Elgar Publishing. https://doi.org/10.4337/9781803922652.00013

Wang, D., Chen, Y., Tuguinay, J., & Yuan, J. J. (2023). The influence of perceived risks and behavioral intention: The case of Chinese international students. *SAGE Open, 13*(2), 1–17. https://doi.org/10.1177/21582440231183435

Xiao, J. J. (2008). Applying behavior theories to financial behavior. In J. J. Xiao (Ed.), *Handbook of consumer finance research* (pp. 1–424). Springer. https://doi.org/10.1007/978-0-387-75734-6

Xiao, J. J., & Kumar, S. (2023). Introduction to a research agenda for consumer financial behavior. In J. Jian Xiao & S. Kumar (Eds.), *A research agenda for consumer financial behavior* (pp. 1–15). Edward Elgar. https://doi.org/10.4337/9781803922652.00008

Xiao, J. J., & O'Neill, B. (2018a). Mental accounting and behavioural hierarchy: Understanding consumer budgeting behaviour. *International Journal of Consumer Studies, 42*(4), 448–459. https://doi.org/10.1111/ijcs.12445

Xiao, J. J., & O'Neill, B. (2018b). Propensity to plan, financial capability, and financial satisfaction. *International Journal of Consumer Studies, 42*(5), 501–512. https://doi.org/10.1111/ijcs.12461

Zeynep, T. (2015). Financial education for children and youth. In Z. Copur (Ed.), *Handbook of research on behavioral finance and investment strategies: Decision making in the financial industry* (pp. 69–92). IGI Global. https://doi.org/10.4018/978-1-4666-7484-4.ch005

Chapter 4

Mapping the Invisible Pathways: A Bibliometric Study on Informal Lending in the Informal Economy

R. Ganesh[a] and G. Naresh[b]

[a]*PG and Research Department of Commerce and Management Studies, St. Mary's College, Kerala, India*
[b]*Finance & Accounting, Indian Institute of Management Tiruchirappalli, Tamil Nadu, India*

Abstract

This chapter explores an analytical method to understand the decades-long literature on informal lending in the informal sector. Assessing the predominance and interrelationships of numerous issues in informal loans in the informal economy helps in identifying emerging research trends. The analysis employs a method of investigation by thematically analyzing research publications indexed by Scopus from the first publication to 2023 using bibliometrix and PRISMA model in R Studio. Research ideas may be visualized using thematic slices and other visual representations that show their evolution and interconnectedness. Key concepts like "rural credit" and "informal sector" become apparent, shedding light on the evolution of these concepts through time with the help of thematic analysis. Findings on trending themes and tree maps improve thematic comprehension. The study majority restricted to thematic analysis in depth confined to available information. The results may be used as a road map for further study and policy choices in the field of informal lending. Informal lending research promotes financial inclusion and sustainable informal sector economic growth. This bibliometric analysis illuminates informal lending

Informal Economy and Sustainable Development Goals:
Ideas, Interventions and Challenges, 67–80
Copyright © 2024 by R. Ganesh and G. Naresh
Published under exclusive licence by Emerald Publishing Limited
doi:10.1108/978-1-83753-980-220241004

research themes and their consequences for informal economy issues. The results enhance informal lending research and policy development.

Keywords: Informal lending; informal economy; financial inclusion; informal sector; thematic analysis; bibliometric study

1. Introduction

In the vast and complicated world of global economies, there are informal financial instruments that play a significant role in people's financial lives (Banerjee & Duflo, 2007). These instruments operate quietly outside the traditional financial system and have a big impact on individuals and communities (Macias & Cazzavillan, 2010; Neves & Du Toit, 2012). Imagine a bustling market where people buy and sell things with a secret financial system that operates outside regular banks and rules, called the informal economy. A crucial part of it is informal lending where trust and interpersonal relationships serve as the foundation for financial transactions (Kear, 2016; Liu et al., 2016; Weiping, 2023). When formal banks cannot help, informal lending offers hope and support for more than 1,700 million people across the globe who have not had any experience with structured banking systems (World Bank, 2018). Whereas, the 2021 edition of the world bank survey shows their global findex database with 1,28,000 people from 123 countries updated on the use of organized and unorganized financial instruments during the period of the COVID-19 pandemic (World Bank, 2021). However, these databases acknowledge their limitations in the survey by quoting there is a paucity in their survey because the survey excludes women and poor adults in using any organized banking systems. Informal lending becomes vital for these people, as it provides them with much-needed money and support (Aryeetey & Nissanke, 1998; Germidis et al., 1991). Understanding their influence is like a journey to discover the intricate world of finance. So, to comprehend the hidden world of informal lending in the informal economy, the study uncovers important information that can help us make a difference in the lives of many people who are part of this mysterious financial network. Poirine (1997) presents the notion of an implicit and informal loan agreement among close relatives for migrant money transfer, offering empirically testable propositions and policy prescriptions for maximizing emigrant remittance flows, which will improve the current argumentation on informal lending within ancestral and migratory contexts. Dabla-Norris et al. (2008) add to the conversation on informal economies by investigating the factors that determine the size of informal sector and highlighting the interconnected influence of variables like tax burden, development of financial markets, caliber of the legal system, etc. Asongu (2013) examined the relationship between mobile phone penetration and financial development in Africa and found that while traditional financial intermediaries revealed a negative correlation, the informal sector revealed a positive correlation underlining the expanding role of informal finance. Mallick (2012) examined the impact of microfinance programs intervention on moneylender interest rates in Northern Bangladesh, and the results of the study indicate that higher program coverage is associated with higher moneylender interest rates, especially in villages where loans are primarily used for productive economic activities rather than our consumption.

In this paper, the study goes on a journey to learn about informal lending in the informal economy with bibliometric analysis which will help to find out who has contributed to it and see what is currently being explored. By looking at the academic literature, we hope to find out what we know and what we still need to learn about informal lending. The goal is to raise awareness about informal lending's significance in the informal economy and how it can affect society and economic development. Therefore, understanding this topic might help to create better policies and support for those who are often overlooked in the financial system.

The balance of the manuscript has been arranged as: Section 2 will detail the study's methodology, while the findings are given and discussed in Section 3. Finally, Section 4 is about the conclusion of the study by summarizing key findings, discussing their implications and limitations of the study, while also suggesting potential avenues for further exploration in this area for research aspirants who are interested in this area.

2. Research Methodology

The present study employs a bibliometric research design to comprehensively explore the thematic analysis of informal lending in the informal economy. Through qualitative analysis, the study delves into the themes present in the corpus of research papers, aiming to identify the relationships within the textual data. The dataset consists of research papers focusing on informal lending in the informal economy. To ensure robustness, a rigorous search on the previous studies from Scopus-indexed database has been done. Details of the research papers indexed in Scopus were extracted up to July 2023, encompassing publications from the earliest to the latest dates. Careful measures were taken to remove any duplications in the dataset. The keywords such as informal loan, informal finance, informal lending, informal economy, informal credit, unorganized sector, informal sector, unofficial sector, gray economy, grey economy, black economy, hidden economy, shadow economy, and non-formal economy were used to generate the database from the Scopus-indexed journals for the analysis. For the robustness of the analysis, transparency, and trustworthiness, PRISMA model (the preferred reporting item for systematic reviews and meta-analysis) has to be applied (Panic et al., 2013).

The software used for the study is R Studio. The importance and how much each has developed are assessed by using the methodology of Callon Centrality and density in the thematic analysis (Aria et al., 2020, 2021; Cobo et al., 2011). Through a four-quadrant graph output, thematic evolution is analyzed by keeping X-axis as centrality and in Y-axis density (Cahlik, 2000). Centrality analyzes external strength, and density in Y-axis shows internal strength. Both external and internal strength are assessed by the value. The higher the value, higher the strength is. The high value of centrality indicates a strong linkage of clusters and priority of the subject. The high value of density points about the strength of internal links and a common subject.

The research also extends the analysis on trend analysis to explain the evolution of key sub topics in each cluster across time underlying the understanding of the road map of research over the time.

Tree map analysis has also been applied here to highlight the significance of thematic concerns on informal lending through a graphical presentation. This helps the researcher to identify topic and patterns for understanding and improving the knowledge in a better and easy way.

Sankey diagram is used for understanding the topic developments during the period 1985–2008 and 2009–2023 (Aria & Cuccurullo, 2017; Aria et al., 2020). The goal of splitting the study on informal finance into two phases is to study before and after the global financial crisis. The study also attempts to look into the shift in interest of the researchers in the area and to understand the innovation in each phase during each phase. Incorporating these methodological approaches, the study aims to provide valuable insights into the thematic analysis of informal lending in the informal economy.

3. Results and Discussion

The study initially retrieved several research materials published in Scopus indexed database from the period of first publication in that area to 2023. However, the retrieved number of articles from the Scopus database may have to be eliminated from the analysis. To ensure transparency and trustworthiness, **PRISMA** model is applied and presented here in Fig. 4.1.

From Fig. 4.1, there were 158 research materials identified from the Scopus database in 2023. The study first inspected whether any duplicate entries were

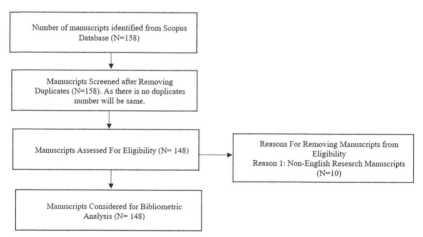

Fig. 4.1.   Visualizing Insight: Exploring the Unseen with **PRISMA** Flowchart.
Source: Author's creation.

there in the database. However, as there was no trace of duplicate entries, all were considered in the initial screening process. Then, the manuscripts written in a language other than English were counted, and 10 research papers were identified and removed. Eventually, 148 manuscripts were considered for the study. The first article published in the area was written by Hansen in 1985. Informal lending and arrangements for borrowing from unofficial agencies are crucial in the lives of the public in meeting uncertainty (Hansen, 1985).

4. Thematic Analysis

Thematic evolution of research papers on informal lending in the informal economy, covering the period from 1985 to 2023 published in Scopus-indexed journals, revealed two distinct slices: Slice 1 (1985–2008) and Slice 2 (2009–2023). In Slice 1, the prominent themes addressed were rural credit, the informal sector, developing countries, and developing regions. On the other hand, Slice 2 focused on themes such as the informal sector, financial system, economics, financial policy, and accessibility.

5. Thematic Slice 1 (1985–2008) Analysis

In this slice, the most significant themes identified were related to rural credit. The top keywords in this thematic slice were "rural credit," "credit market," "informal credit," and "savings." This suggests that during this period, researchers emphasized understanding the dynamics of rural credit, credit markets, and informal credit systems in the context of developing countries and regions.

Betweenness centrality: The X-axis often denotes the measure of "Betweenness Centrality." The concept of betweenness centrality refers to a metric within network analysis that aims to quantify the degree to which a certain cluster, or node, serves as a connector or mediator between other clusters in a given network. To put it another way, it gauges how commonly a cluster appears on the shortest path between other clusters. A higher betweenness centrality value indicates that the cluster plays a more critical role in connecting different clusters and facilitating information flow between them.

The Y-axis shows the "Closeness Centrality." Another measure of centrality in a network is called "closeness centrality," and it measures how closely one cluster is connected to every other cluster in the network. The cluster is more easily available compared with other clusters in the network if its proximity centrality score is high.

Researchers may find clusters that are pivotal in connecting others (high betweenness centrality) and groups that are central and easy to reach (high proximity centrality) by analyzing the visual output using these centrality metrics.

Researchers may learn a lot about the framework of the theme network, where information and power are flowing, as well as where critical clusters are located, by interpreting centrality values. This helps the researchers to explore new trends and understand future directions of research.

Table 4.1.   Key Themes: Clusters and Centrality Measures.

Cluster	Cluster Label	Betweenness Centrality	Closeness Centrality	PageRank Centrality
1	Rural credit	337.50837	0.00171	0.00509
2	Informal sector	669.09462	0.00172	0.00923
3	Developing country	518.15379	0.00177	0.00731
4	Zambia	463.73140	0.00172	0.00316
5	Developing region	467.41127	0.00170	0.00430
6	Eastern hemisphere	47.36407	0.00158	0.00475

Source: Bibliometrix R Studio.

For a more comprehensive understanding of the outcomes from thematic slice 1, the study presents the results in Table 4.1 as follows:

Table 4.1 showcases the salient findings obtained through the thematic evolution analysis. The table presents six pivotal clusters, each offering distinctive thematic features and mean score of betweenness centrality, closeness centrality, and pagerank centrality.

Cluster 1, centered around "rural credit," exhibits a moderate betweenness centrality of a mean score of 337.51 and a relatively low closeness centrality of a mean score of 0.00171, indicating its significant position as a mediator between other clusters in the network. Moreover, the PageRank centrality of a mean score of 0.00509 indicates its notable influence within the research domain. The second cluster named internal sector has a mean score of 669.09 on the betweenness centrality value in connecting various other clusters. On the other hand, the mean score stood at 0.00172 for the closeness centrality while PageRank centrality's mean score is 0.00923. The theme of Cluster 3 is on "developing country." Centrality mean score of cluster 3 stood at 518.15 indicating an intermediary role in the thematic network. The mean score of 0.00177 of closeness centrality and PageRank centrality stood at 0.00731 highlighting the significance of the research area.

Cluster 4 lies on the theme Zambia. This theme shows 463.73 for the centrality mean score and 0.00172 as the mean score of closeness centrality. PageRank centrality of cluster 4 lies relatively a lower value which stood at 0.00316 indicating less influence when compared to previous clusters. Cluster 5 is titled as developing region which has a centrality of mean score of 467.41, closeness centrality mean score stood at 0.00170, PageRank centrality at 0.00430. The statistics of cluster 5 explain the significance of the theme in the research field. Cluster 6 is named as Eastern Hemisphere. The centrality mean score of cluster 6 lies at 47.36, the mean score of centrality stood at 0.00158, and PageRank centrality at 0.00475. The statistics of cluster 6 point out that though the cluster 6 significantly contributes to the research area its influence among other clusters stood at very low.

Clusters like informal sector and rural credit suggest their prominence in shaping the research landscape as they have high centrality value. While cluster titled

Zambia and developing region plays a role of meeting point for new opinions in the research field. Thus, these findings provide an understanding of clusters during both phases. The phase during 2009–2023 is analyzed in the second thematic slice.

6. Thematic Slice 2 (2009–2023) Analysis

In thematic slice 2, the keywords mainly explored are credit provision, financial services, interest rate, lending behavior microfinance, and financial system. In addition to this region like China, Africa and India also came into the field. Thematic 2 slice indicates a shift in the exploration of research in the informal sector by highlighting the unique features of informal lending in regions like China, India, and Africa. The regions like India and China play a major role in influencing the economy of those countries. African regions also played a similar role in attracting researchers because of the dynamic environment.

The results of thematic slice present the results in Table 4.2 with corresponding mean score of centrality measures. Each cluster highlights the themes that emerged in the research domain during the period 2009–2023. The mean score of betweenness centrality of cluster 1 signifies the role of an intermediary in connecting the themes of research in the area of informal lending. With a closeness centrality of mean score 0.00269 and a PageRank centrality of mean score 0.00749, this cluster holds considerable influence and centrality in the research network. The average value of betweenness centrality lies at 578.04, which also showcases a fostering connectivity among the different areas. Cluster 3's centrality of mean score lies in the value of 265.58 indicating its role as a meeting point among various themes.

The fourth cluster titled economics centrality value highlighted 387.99 as a mean score of 387.99. The statistical value points out as a crucial role in linking other themes of research in informal lending. The theme financial policy is considered here as cluster 5 which stood at a value of 3.33 as mean score of centralities. Though cluster five has a commanding position in influencing the researches in the research theme of informal lending, the influence on other clusters is meager.

Table 4.2.   Emerging Thematic Patterns and Centrality Analysis.

Cluster	Cluster Label	Betweenness Centrality	Closeness Centrality	PageRank Centrality
1	Tanzania	262.94686	0.00269	0.00749
2	Informal sector	578.04130	0.00246	0.01413
3	Financial system	262.58347	0.00251	0.00980
4	Economics	387.99230	0.00269	0.00641
5	Financial policy	33.32754	0.00241	0.00443
6	Accessibility	239.44806	0.00264	0.01015

Source: Bibliometrix R Studio.

The above evidence showcases the period 2009–2023 and represents the above-mentioned themes that have gained prominence in the research of informal lending. The themes informal sector and Tanzania have achieved a crucial part in the research world, while clusters, namely financial policy and accessibility, have the role of mediator in extending the linking of the research on different themes. These results help the future research aspirants in contributing new ideas to the field of research. By assimilating the insights obtained from both theme segments, researchers may get a holistic comprehension of the dynamic patterns within the study field, enabling them to make well-informed choices for future inquiries.

7. Thematic Map Interpretation

The thematic map provides an overview of how themes were categorized based on Callon centrality and density measures. The four quadrants in the thematic map are emerging/disappearing themes, niche themes, motor themes, and basic themes.

(1) *Emerging/disappearing themes*:
The themes categorized in this quadrant include "Developing region," "Economics education," and "Developing countries." These themes might have emerged as relatively important topics during the study period, but they could be experiencing a decline in research interest or relevance.

(2) *Niche themes:*
The themes falling into this quadrant are "Eastern Hemisphere," "World," "Female," "Male," "Human," "Financial dualism," and "Urban economy." These themes might have a specific focus and appeal to a niche audience, exploring distinct aspects of informal lending in the informal economy.

(3) *Motor themes*:
The dominant themes categorized in this quadrant are "Developing country," "Informal finance," "Rural credit," and "Credit market." These themes have shown high centrality and density, indicating their significance in shaping research on informal lending in the informal economy. They are the driving forces and key areas of interest in the field.

(4) *Basic themes*:
The themes in this quadrant are "Informal banking system," "Money lending," "Developing world," "Microenterprise," "Accessibility," and a small portion of "Informal credit" and "Credit market." These themes serve as foundational elements in the study of informal lending and complement the motor themes in shaping the overall research landscape.

Although the thematic map clearly illustrates the overarching themes prevalent in research on informal lending, it lacks the ability to unveil the nuanced temporal patterns and evolving emphases that characterize the development of these subjects. To effectively mitigate the constraints and include the dynamic character of research interests, this study integrates a thorough examination of developing patterns and developments. The objective of this strategy is to improve comprehension of the chronological development of important study subjects, hence augmenting the collective knowledge of previous popular themes. Fig. 4.2 shows the outcomes of trend themes.

Fig. 4.2 depicts a graphical illustration of the evolving research emphasis in the domain of unregulated borrowing within the informal economy throughout the course of time. The horizontal axis in this graph shows time, while the vertical axis reflects the frequency of appearances of certain thematic words. This concise but informative visualization effectively illustrates significant research trajectories across time.

A deeper examination of the data reveals some intriguing details on the changing landscape of research objectives. The interest in a few theme words such as "informal sector," "lending behaviour," and "credit provision" has remained consistent throughout time underlining the persistence of these problems.

In addition to recurring ideas, the graph shows other temporal patterns. The terms "microfinance" and "developing country" both had meteoric rises and falls

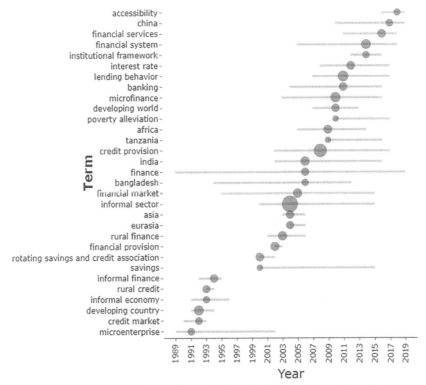

Fig. 4.2.   Mapping Research Shifts: Trends in Informal Lending Studies.
Source: Bibliometrix R Studio.

in the early 2000s, for example. But the "financial market" enjoyed a resurgence in the latter part of the 2010s, which means that researchers are becoming more interested in this area. Emerging themes are further emphasized in the visual display. A shift toward studying more compact financial operations and accessibility issues has been shown by the rising academic interest in the terms "microenterprise," "savings," and "accessibility" during the last few years.

The "trend topics map" goes further by illuminating complex temporal dynamics and revealing new avenues of inquiry in contrast to the "theme map" which provides a high-level summary of key themes.

Overall, by using trend themes analysis, we can better understand how interest in studying informal lending has changed over time. The ability to easily track trends, spot fresh questions, and propose possible new lines of inquiry makes this visual depiction potentially very useful for academics, politicians, and practitioners. We may have a better grasp of the complexities of informal lending and all its many features by embracing this integrated approach. Fig. 4.2 shows a topic trend analysis and the development of research themes. To make it easier to determine the dominant theme, Table 4.3 summarizes the results and highlights the top 10 main topics.

Table 4.3 provides a summary of the primary topics, the year in which they were first published, the median year, which is the year that falls in the middle of earlier and later studies, and the final column, which accounts for 75% of all occurrences, which demonstrates the time period in which research was conducted with the greatest intensity. All of these information can be found in the table.

The study uses a tree map to visually portray the research environment, which allows for a more thorough assessment of major results. This infographic shows how common and dispersed certain themes are in the collection of informal

Table 4.3.   Trend Topics: Key Research Themes over Time.

Topic	Total Occurrences	Emergence Year	Median Year	Advanced Focus Year
Informal sector	93	2000	2004	2015
Credit provision	51	2002	2008	2017
Lending behavior	25	2007	2011	2017
Microfinance	19	2003	2010	2016
Developing country	18	1991	1992	1994
Financial system	16	2005	2014	2018
Financial market	14	1995	2005	2016
India	14	2002	2006	2016
Financial provision	13	2002	2002	2003
Rural finance	13	2001	2003	2006

Source: Bibliometrix R Studio.

lending documents. One flexible and dynamic tool for representing the relative importance of several research topics is the tree map, which provides a clear picture of the dominance and interconnections of each.

The study of tree map analysis enhances the results of earlier investigations. Researchers in the field of informal lending might benefit from a deeper comprehension of the complex network of ideas by adopting this novel strategy. Providing useful insights into the key subjects of academic inquiry is the inclusion of the average number of repetitions for each phrase as well as the degree of repetition for each phrase expressed as a percentage. A mean frequency of 93 indicates that the term "informal sector" is one of the most frequently used terms, accounting for around 17.99% of all occurrences of the term. One might deduce from this that there is a substantial emphasis placed on exploring this concept against the background of informal lending.

Results for "credit provision" (51 occurrences) and "lending behavior" (25 occurrences), representing 9.86% and 4.84% of the total, respectively, have been discovered. The intricacy of credit and lending operations is shown by these observations. Among the many noteworthy phrases found in the analysis was "microfinance," which came up 19 times (or 3.68% of the total volume). The phrase "developing country" was also used 18 times, making up 3.48% of the total. The term "financial system" was also used 16 times, making up 3.09% of the total. Money and developmental factors both had a major impact on the text under investigation, as shown by the results. Keep in mind that out of all the phrases found, "Asia," "banking," and "financial services" account for 1.93% of the overall frequency, which is quite a little. The results pointed out financial systems and services are captured as common interest in the research of informal lending. The tree map analysis, thus, brings the key issues in the research on informal lending and also gives an insight to academicians where to concentrate their future research.

8. Conclusion

By performing a thematic analysis of research articles that focused on informal lending within the informal economy, the objective of this study was to provide major insights into the shifting landscape of this issue. This was accomplished by doing the study. Inside the confines of this investigation, the identification and analysis of relevant topic clusters were completed by using a qualitative research methodology and the use of analytical tools inside R Studio. This was done in order to fulfill the objectives of this study. The study also looked at the degree of centrality and density of these clusters within the framework of informal lending in the informal sector. This was done in addition to the previous point. The research was conducted during a period of time ranging from 1985 to 2008 and 2009 to 2023, and it shed light on the ever-changing research trends that have happened over the course of time. The study covered two distinct topic slices.

Within the context of the research landscape, the identification of significant subjects such as "rural credit," "informal sector," and "financial system" highlights the key areas of attention that are being examined. Through the acquisition of knowledge of these fundamental themes, it is possible that future research efforts will be focused toward addressing important challenges in the informal lending business. Furthermore, these themes may serve as a template for future study. Graphical representations of theme evolution, such as the four-quadrant graph and the Sankey diagram, provide visualizations that assist in recognizing the development of a variety of study topics and the interrelationships between them. These visualizations are offered by the Sankey diagram and the four-quadrant graph. All of these different kinds of visualizations have the potential to make communication within the scientific community more effective and to make the dissemination of established knowledge more straightforward.

A further advantage of using thematic slices is that they make it feasible to get a comprehensive understanding of theme patterns that have emerged throughout certain time periods. This realization exposes shifts in the focus of research as well as emerging areas of interest in the educational system. It is possible for researchers to make use of these insights in order to analyze the route of study advancement in this discipline and to discover potential research gaps that need to be examined.

The study results are presented with important new information on broad subjects relevant to the domain of unlawful lending in the shadow economy sector. This research was designed to investigate the shadow economy. The findings emphasize the significance of the issues of "rural credit," "informal sector," and "financial system" and "financial inclusion," and they provide supporting images to make the information more easily digestible.

9. Limitations and Prospects for Future Research

Although this study provides vital insights, it is crucial to acknowledge that it has constraints. As a means of getting things started, the research relied on material that was extracted from Scopus, which may not have included all of the articles that ended up being published on the theme informal lending. Even though we searched extensively and removed duplicates, we may have missed some important publications from journals that aren't indexed or from other sources, which might have affected how thorough our analysis was. This study primarily emphasizes theme analysis as its main focus, potentially overlooking other crucial aspects of investigation, such as qualitative evaluations of content or factors influencing research themes. However, it does provide significant and valuable insights into patterns related to themes.

Though the study acknowledges the limitations of the study, it serves as a valuable groundwork for subsequent research. This study looks into the exploration of time-based subthemes, utilizes a combination of qualitative and quantitative methodologies, and expands the scope of data sources. By incorporating these elements, the study lays a solid foundation for further investigations in this field. The findings of this study provide a fundamental basis for prospective inquiries into the unregulated lending practices within the shadow economy. Investigating the temporal evolution of specific subtopics among the identified clusters may shed light on the dynamic nature of research trends. Moreover, an in-depth awareness of geographic differences in research focus can be achieved through global comparisons, thereby facilitating the development of more precise policies and initiatives. The present study represents a pioneering effort to enhance our understanding of the informal lending sector, thereby laying the groundwork for future legislative measures and innovative interventions in this domain.

References

Aria, M., Alterisio, A., & Scandurra, A. (2021). The scholar's best friend: Research trends in dog cognitive and behavioral studies. *Animal Cognition, 24*(3), 541–553.

Aria, M., & Cuccurullo, C. (2017). Bibliometrix: An R-tool for comprehensive science mapping analysis. *Journal of Informetrics, 11*(4), 959–975.

Aria, M., Misuraca, M., & Spano, M. (2020). Mapping the evolution of social research and data science on 30 years of social indicators research. *Social Indicators Research, 149*(3), 803–831.

Aryeetey, E., & Nissanke, M. K. (1998). *Financial integration and development. Liberalization and reform in sub-Saharan Africa.* Routledge.

Asongu, S. A. (2013). How has mobile phone penetration stimulated financial development in Africa?. *Journal of African Business, 14*(1), 7–18.

Banerjee, A. V., & Duflo, E. (2007). The economic lives of the poor. *Journal of Economic Perspectives, 21*(1), 141–167.

Cahlik, T. (2000). Search for fundamental articles in economics. *Scientometrics, 49*(3), 389–402.

Cobo, M. J., López-Herrera, A. G., Herrera-Viedma, E., & Herrera, F. (2011). Science mapping software tools: Review, analysis, and cooperative study among tools. *Journal of the American Society for Information Science and Technology, 62*(7), 1382–1402.

Dabla-Norris, E., Gradstein, M., & Inchauste, G. (2008). What causes firms to hide output? The determinants of informality. *Journal of Development Economics, 85*(1–2), 1–27.

Germidis, D. A., Kessler, D., & Meghir, R. (1991). *Financial systems and development: What role for the formal and informal financial sectors?.* Development Centre of the Organisation for Economic Co-operation and Development.

Hansen, K. T. (1985). Budgeting against uncertainty: Cross-class and transethnic redistribution mechanisms in urban Zambia. *African Urban Studies, 21*(1), 65–73.

Kear, M. (2016). Peer lending and the subsumption of the informal. *Journal of Cultural Economy, 9*(3), 261–276.

Liu, Q., Luo, J., & Tian, G. G. (2016). Managerial professional connections versus political connections: Evidence from firms' access to informal financing resources. *Journal of Corporate Finance, 41*(1), 179–200.

Macias, J. B., & Cazzavillan, G. (2010). Modeling the informal economy in Mexico. A structural equation approach. *The Journal of Developing Areas, 44*(1), 345–365.

Mallick, D. (2012). Microfinance and moneylender interest rate: Evidence from Bangladesh. *World Development, 40*(6), 1181–1189.

Neves, D., & Du Toit, A. (2012). Money and sociality in South Africa's informal economy. *Africa, 82*(1), 131–149.

Panic, N., Leoncini, E., de Belvis, G., Ricciardi, W., & Boccia, S. (2013). Evaluation of the endorsement of the preferred reporting items for systematic reviews and meta-analysis (PRISMA) statement on the quality of published systematic review and meta-analyses. *PloS One, 8*(12), 1–7.

Poirine, B. (1997). A theory of remittances as an implicit family loan arrangement. *World Development, 25*(4), 589–611.

Weiping, L. (2023). The reconstruction of trust system and the modernization transformation of regional finance. *Social Trust: Informal Finance and Economic Transformations, 1*(1), 179–197.

World Bank. (2018). *Financial inclusion on the rise, but gaps remain, global Findex database shows.* Findex. Retrieved July 24, 2023, from https://www.worldbank.org/en/news/press-release/2018/04/19/financial-inclusion-on-the-rise-but-gaps-remain-global-findex-database-shows

World Bank. (2021). *The global Findex database 2021: Financial inclusion, digital payments, and resilience in the age of Covid-19.* Findex. Retrieved July 24, 2023, from https://www.worldbank.org/en/publication/globalfindex#:~:text=The%202021%20edition%2C%20based%20on,behaviors%20that%20enable%20financial%20resilience

Chapter 5

Industry 4.0, AI and Textile Sector in India*

Manas Ranjan Bhowmik[a] and Shantanu Baidya[b]

[a] *Ramakrishna Mission Vidyamandira, West Bengal, India*
[b] *Jadavpur University, Kolkata, India*

Abstract

Industry 4.0 broadly implies the digital transformation of industrial works. In India's industrial arena, the textile industry is extremely important in the non-farm sector, both regarding value addition and employment generation. This chapter attempts to think about new avenues of research while integrating different streams of literature. For example – literature on innovation, literature on the industrial ecosystem, literature on industry 4.0, and consequences for the Indian economy – all such streams of literature have been considered synoptically to think of a new research program. The focus of this research program is to explore pathways of synergizing these different literatures and thinking about how to integrate and apply innovations for the betterment of the unorganized manufacturing sector in India. The unorganized manufacturing sector is a vast area in India, so here, we focus on some specific sections of the textile sector which is the handloom weaving industry. How have changes in techniques happened within the handloom weaving sector so far? What are the possible ways of applying these new technologies in altering the products and processes within the textile sector? What can the government do in this regard? These are the research questions that need attention in today's context, and we

*This chapter is a part of the research work under a Major Research Project sponsored by Indian Council of Social Science Research (ICSSR). The authors gratefully acknowledge the financial support of ICSSR, New Delhi, for this research work.

Informal Economy and Sustainable Development Goals:
Ideas, Interventions and Challenges, 81–98
Copyright © 2024 by Manas Ranjan Bhowmik and Shantanu Baidya
Published under exclusive licence by Emerald Publishing Limited
doi:10.1108/978-1-83753-980-220241005

have not found serious works in this direction in the context of the Indian economy; hence, we are investigating these issues in this chapter.

Keywords: Innovation; ecosystem; unorganized manufacturing; textile; handloom

1. Introduction

In the textile sector of India, technology adoption in today's context has become a critical issue. Why should we focus on the textile sector in India? Why technology adoption is such a crucial issue? To understand such questions, we should, at the outset, focus on the current post-COVID-19 juncture. Presently in the post-COVID-19 era amidst fragile recovery industries of the unorganized sector in developing countries are facing serious challenges. Uncertainties of the market have been further exacerbated due to the Russia–Ukraine ongoing war and supply chain disruptions. Apart from such issues, the advent of new technologies is also threatening the employment situation in the industrial sector. Gains that have been achieved for the last few decades regarding poverty alleviation, and nutritional attainment, such gains may be hampered due to the advent of new technologies and the consequent potential of mass unemployment. In this globalized era, it has become increasingly difficult to create decent jobs for the masses in developing countries. Growing inequality is a matter of concern in this regard. Hence to promote equality, create or maintain employment, and alleviate poverty using new technological innovations in the unorganized manufacturing sector in countries like India is of paramount importance. The technology question cannot be avoided any more in social science research. We have to deal with this issue head-on and squarely and contemplate how millions of unorganized sector worker–owners of micro-small enterprises can reap the benefits of such technological innovation and can safeguard themselves from possible loss of jobs and income.

In this regard, questioning existing institutions–organizations and rethinking about new institutional set-ups are extremely important. Many existing institutional set-ups may become unworthy in this new regime of innovation and for Industry 4.0. Hence in this regard, the ecosystem theory of developing industrial clusters may come as a handy theoretical apparatus. In the ecosystem research paradigm, organizations like universities, research labs, etc., may come as a handy tool, and it has been pointed out repeatedly that in India the collaboration practices between industry and educational organizations have not been explored adequately. Here in this chapter, following the ecosystem research, we will try to point out some of the concrete ways of collaboration between industry and academia so that the industrial sector can learn well about the latest advances in the technological domain. Apart from this, another requirement especially in India is to know enough about the actual situation of the unorganized industrial sector from time to time. National-level sample surveys cannot capture the full picture;

hence, data deficiency is a real issue here in India for policymakers. In this regard, once again universities or research institutes may come up for help by collecting data from local industrial clusters on a regular basis. The benefits of such collaborations may be significant for all, especially for the firms in the unorganized manufacturing sector. While discussing artificial intelligence (AI) and such new technological innovations, the issue of possible job loss often comes up as a topic of research, yet almost none of the researchers have talked about the theme that how such new innovations can be guided or used for the benefit of Micro Small Medium Enterprise (MSMEs) in the unorganized sector in India.

India's recent gross domestic product (GDP) estimates have shown a 7.2% growth rate provisionally, yet as per many scholars' performance in the manufacturing sector is not so promising as it has grown only 1.3%, which is the second lowest after the year 2019–2020 when output declined. India's manufacturing share of GDP is 17.7% as per the recent data and 2011–2021 period 3 million jobs were added in the Indian manufacturing sector (Himanshu, 2023). One can argue that a major chunk of this employment has happened in the unorganized manufacturing sector and not in the organized manufacturing sector. Hence, the question arises isn't it pertinent to think about how to boost this unorganized manufacturing sector amidst advents of various disruptive technologies?

Here, we consider some of the following frontier technologies such as AI, and related developments. We would like to evaluate economic benefits and country-wide capabilities while using these innovations. In the last two decades especially, these technologies have seen exponential uptake. All the waves of automation are coupled with threats to jobs. This issue has remained serious, and it is more serious at this time given some of the grim predictions. Nevertheless, we have to remember that all jobs cannot be automated; moreover, automation also leads to new jobs, new markets, new products, and new tasks; hence on balance job destruction and job creation need to be evaluated. If we look at the international innovation landscape in this regard, we can observe that countries like the United States and China are dominating the scene by jointly holding more than 60% of patents. Other competing countries are Germany, France, Japan, India, the United Kingdom, and the Republic of Korea (Mazzucatto, 2014). In this realm of frontier technologies, some are more mature and some are still developing; for example, AI has become significantly mature, but IoT, that is, Internet-of-Things technology seemingly still needs some time to attain a stage of maturity. As we are focusing on developing countries, especially on India's economy, here, millions of firms in the MSME sector need to develop capabilities to harness the benefits of such technologies. And, to develop such capabilities, scientific skill is not enough rather developing an ecosystem that takes care of infrastructure, policy implementation, and implementing regulations. The government or a reimagined "entrepreneurial state" must play a pivotal role not only in developing policies and regulations but also in promoting such ecosystems within the country (Mazzucatto, 2014). To grasp the issue from a comparative perspective, it is pertinent to report the findings of the Readiness Index 2023 which studies indicators for skills, R&D, ICT, finance, and industrial capacity; among 166 countries – top performers are the United States, Sweden, etc., and

India's rank is 46, China is at 35, and Brazil is at 40. Countries in Latin America, sub-Saharan Africa, and the Caribbean have performed poorly in this Readiness Index (UNCTAD, 2023).

One should not ignore the importance of the textile[1] industry which has been the backbone of many industrialized nations. Regarding innovation, it has become imperative to study the textile industry of India due to the fact that the textile industry remains one of the highest employment-generating sectors right after agriculture. The Indian textile sector is the second highest (after China) in the world in terms of manufacturing and export; employment in the textile and apparel sector in India stands at 45 million with an additional employment of 60 million in allied sectors, hence total employment figure stands at 105 million (Ministry of Textiles (MoT), 2019). The handloom weaving industry is an important part of the textile sector in India; the handloom weaving sector has contributed in terms of total production of 7,000 square meters and $288.36 million worth of exports in the year 2017–2018 (MoT, 2019).

Moreover, with respect to SDGs (sustainable development goals), the handloom weaving sector and the issue of technology adoption may be crucial as it can influence multiple SDGs. If technology adoption happens adequately, then SDGs regarding poverty alleviation, promotion of decent work (skilled work within handloom weaving), and environmentally sustainable job creation all such issues can be addressed to some extent (Bhowmik, 2021). On the contrary, if the handloom weaving sector fails to catch the "technology train" this time, then like many other countries, the handloom sector may face an existential crisis. And, in turn, if a labor-intensive activity like handloom weaving suffers, then many of the SDGs may also become distant dreams for India.

Section 2 talks about the unorganized sector in India; Section 3 highlights a brief history of industrial revolutions and the handloom weaving sector. Section 4 chalks out innovations within the handloom weaving industry. Section 5 is about ecosystem theory; Section 6 analyzes the issues in the handloom weaving sector, and Section 7 offers discussion and conclusion.

2. On Unorganized Sector in India

Developing countries with a history of colonization often portray a dualistic pattern of economic development, and India is no exception in this regard.

---

[1]Indian textile sector is comprised of three parts – first organized textile mills, second power-looms and third handlooms. Major big textile mills are part of the organized sector, in which mainly the spinning operation takes place. There are independent spinning mills and then there are composite mills with separate spinning section. In the informal or unorganized sector production under – decentralized handlooms and power looms take place. An important feature of the unorganized sector is that here enterprises are not registered and hence reliable data on employment and output is difficult to obtain.

The divide between the formal sector and informal[2] sector (i.e., organized and unorganized sector) within the economy is evident; the formal sector consists of large-scale factories, with domestic, state, and foreign capitalist investment toward, big corporate wholesale and retail chains, etc., and informal sector consists of peasants, petty commodity producers, artisans, domestic workers, retailers, etc. The organized sector is usually large-scale, capital-intensive, and technology-dependent; the unorganized sector is generally marked by small-scale, labor-intensive, traditional technique-based production activities. Adding to this, it is important to mention a working definition of the unorganized sector firms. Firms in the unorganized sector employ less than 10 workers, are not registered under the Factory Act, do not pay taxes, and do not abide by labor laws or other such regulations applicable to registered firms under the organized sector. Moreover, workers working within the firms in the unorganized sector do not enjoy social security, retirement benefits, or any type of health benefits.

In terms of composition, around 90% of the workforce is involved in the unorganized sector in India. As per the NSSO report (2017) number 582 titled "Economic Characteristics of Unincorporated Non-Agricultural Enterprises (excluding construction) in India," the share of workers in the unorganized manufacturing sector is 32.4%, among the total number of enterprises 31% is in the manufacturing sector (Government of India, 2017). Within the manufacturing sector as per this report, 85.5% are OAEs or Own Account Enterprises, that is, enterprises that do not employ any hired labor. Some of the major segments within the unorganized manufacturing[3] sector are food processing, textile, garments, etc.

It is important to note that industrialization based on large-scale factories has not taken off in India, and the share of large-scale factory employment within the total manufacturing employment is around 25% (Basole & Basu, 2011). Capital-intensive nature of production, ongoing casualization and subcontracting, increasing speculation and lower priority toward accumulation and re-investment, and penetration of informalization within the formal sector are some of the well-known reasons (Basole & Basu, 2011). Hence mainly, the Indian

---

[2]Informal sector as a terminology has been used in academia and in general discussions; on the other hand, within the reports of Government of India, informal sector has been termed as unorganized sector. Hence, in government reports, formal–informal divide is termed as organized–unorganized sectors' divide. Sengupta commission (NCEUS, 2007, p. 2) has proposed the following definition of the informal sector. "The unorganized sector consists of all unincorporated private enterprises owned by individuals or households engaged in the sale and production of goods and services operated on a proprietary or partnership basis and with less than ten total workers." Here, in this chapter, formal–informal and organized–unorganized are terms we have used interchangeably.

[3]Extensive scope of the informal manufacturing sector is noteworthy – production of food products, beverages, tobacco products, cotton, wool, silk textiles, wool, paper, leather, chemical, metal, plastic, electrical, machine tools, capital equipment, repair, and installation of machinery and equipment.

manufacturing sector has remained overwhelmingly informalized, and flexibility of labor employment has also remained a common phenomenon.

Reasons behind the existence and proliferation of unorganized manufacturing enterprises may be summarized as follows – in order to avoid labor and other regulations, in order to avoid tax payments, horizontal expansion rather than vertical expansion has become the norm. Two recent characteristics of the unorganized manufacturing sector are – one, firms within this sector have now become a part of global value chains, and two, the recent trend in India is the rising importance of smaller workshop-based production at the cost of large-scale factory-based production NCEUS (2009). One lingering issue is that large-scale firms are unable to create jobs to any significant extent, as it is argued in NCEUS's (2009) report that formal sector manufacturing employment has been stagnant since the 1980s; hence, small-scale unorganized employment still remains important. As per the latest available NSSO data (73rd round survey on unincorporated enterprises 2015–2016), the data on the unorganized sector point out the following characteristics of this sector. As per this data, it has been estimated that there are over 60 million such enterprises in India. In this sector, the dominating enterprise is the Own Account Enterprises,[4] covering 84.2% (Government of India, 2017).

Studies on the unorganized sector have been carried out broadly following these three strands – poverty-centered, developmental-centered, and exploitation-centered. It is evident that an innovation-centered approach is missing while studying the unorganized sector (Basole & Basu, 2011; Breman, 1996; Wilkinson-Weber, 1997). This study is an attempt to develop an innovation-centered approach toward the unorganized manufacturing sector.

As we are discussing innovation with respect to the unorganized sector firms, it is intriguing to use an innovation ecosystem framework. This is because this framework has not been used for Indian industries; despite this framework is so useful to study industries. And since we are discussing the innovation ecosystem in the unorganized manufacturing sector, it is important to briefly talk about the organizational morphology of this sector. Varieties of putting out arrangements can be observed within the unorganized sector. One, in which the fixed capital is owned by the working owner, and the working capital is supplied by the intermediary. Two, in which the fixed as well as the working capital are owned by others and not by the worker–owner; in this arrangement, the product is taken by the others, that is, the intermediary, yet the process is controlled by the worker–owner. These arrangements are about home-based cottage industries in the unorganized sector in India, in which the owner himself/herself is the main worker and he/she produces within the home premises using the labor of the family members, that is, the women and the children (usually) (Basole & Basu, 2011).

---

[4]Own Account Enterprises refer to those enterprises that do not employ any hired worker on a fairly regular basis.

Also, regarding sub-contracting and connecting to the global network of big firms or big brands, production is subcontracted out to small producers in developing countries. These actual producers face stiff competition; on the other hand, retailers and multinationals with brand value possess market power using which they can pay low prices to these actual producers (Heintz, 2006). In this way, those big brands work with a decentralized network of production, and surplus value extraction happens in such a way in this system that very little value remains for the actual producer and most of the value-added usually is appropriated by the intermediaries and the big firm. Now to co-create value and retain this value, it is important to pursue and move up using the innovation ladder. If the small producers fail to do this, then their situation may be worsened in the near future. Hence, this innovation bus should not be missed this time.

3. A Brief History of Industrial Revolutions and Handloom

The history of industrial revolutions shows a close relationship with the textile sector. The first industrial revolution happened during the 18th century after the invention of steam engine and power loom. Hence, industry of transportation and textile industry in this way were impacted due to such inventions of that time. It truly revolutionized cloth production and the ramifications of such innovations were felt globally even in India. During the colonial rule, cheap imports of such power loom cloths flooded Indian markets and Indian handloom weavers suffered as a result. Hence, innovations and developments of coal, iron, shipbuilding, railways, and textile industry remained as important achievements of the first industrial revolution of the 18th century. Next, the second industrial revolution began toward the end decades of the 19th century with the developments of communication technology, airplanes, further development of mass production technologies, etc. More and more use of newer technologies such as petroleum and natural gas also happened during this period. After this, the third industrial revolution happened after the 1960s with the invention of computers and the large-scale use of automation, industrial computing. Next, the fourth industrial revolution started with further usage of automation and ICT, in the recent past. During this fourth industrial revolution, more and more use of information technology, smart factories, the Internet of Things, AI, and Big Data such things have become the norm. This fourth industrial revolution which is happening at present all over the world also often has been referred to as Industry 4.0 – in which networked integration of all domains of the value creation process has been attempted (Omrane et al., 2023).

3.1. A Profile of the Textile Sector and Handloom

Textile sector can be considered the most important sector regarding employment generation after agriculture. The textile sector has largely three components – big mills and factories, power loom, and handloom units. Here, we would like to mainly focus on the unorganized segment of the textile sector which comprises micro, small, and medium factories using handlooms; how these micro-small firms can obtain the benefits of new technologies is the key issue in this chapter.

The latest All India Handloom Census report (MoT, 2019) has shown a rise in the number of handloom weavers' households in the present decade (2010–2019) from 27.83 lakhs (2.7 million) to 31.45 lakhs (3.1 million). The handloom weaving sector is very important because it is creating a substantial number of employment opportunities in rural areas of India. Handloom weaving is a labor-intensive activity that needs very little capital investment; unlike power loom, handloom weaving does not require industrial power consumption; hence, it is more environment friendly. However, individual handloom weavers are facing manifold problems in the competitive market environment of today; some of the issues are obtaining good quality input, that is, hank yarn at affordable prices, getting good marketing opportunities, credit supply at cheaper interest rates, technological upgradation and training, innovation of new designs, and availability of insurance (Bhattacharya & Sen, 2018; Dev et al., 2008).

Currently, it is estimated that about 84% of the total handlooms in the world are installed in India (Mitra et al., 2009) and 88.7% of Indian handlooms are situated in rural areas according to the latest handloom census report (MoT, 2019). The majority of the weaver households reside in the following four states: Assam (10.9 lakhs or 1 million), West Bengal (3.4 lakhs or 0.3 million), Manipur (2.1 lakhs or 0.2 million), and Tamil Nadu (1.7 lakhs or 0.1 million). Handloom weaving is still predominantly a rural activity since 88.7% of weaver households are located in rural areas (Bhowmik, 2019; MoT, 2019).

The exotic designs, innovative usage of color, India's cultural heritage – all such things provide handloom weaving a unique status. It has been declared by UNESCO that the Jamdani is an "intangible cultural heritage of humanity" (Sinha, 2013). On the one hand, the deep-rooted cultural ethos of India, its spiritual heritage, quick adaptations of new designs through the technology installed in the *jacquard*[5] looms, small-scale nature of inventories also offer handloom a crucial cutting edge in the global textile market. Nevertheless, it is the highly skilled weavers of India for generations who are producing handloom products should be considered the real asset for our country; they are capable of producing designs that cannot be easily replicated and matched by the power loom or any other competitor.

Despite these potential advantages, a large section of handloom weavers has been struggling to earn the subsistence level of living. The viability and survival of handloom weavers have remained a perennial issue. Since independence, many policies have been designed to uplift this sector, yet implementation of these policies has remained poor. After liberalization productivity, efficiency, and export potential – all such parameters have obtained greater importance; hence, policy orientation toward the handloom sector has changed (Bhattacharya & Sen, 2018).

---

[5]Jacquard looms are a relatively new variety of looms for handloom weavers. In the Jacquard looms, it is relatively easier to change designs, and as a result, adaptability increases substantially for handloom weavers.

4. History of Innovation in Handloom

Going beyond the overwhelming narrative of lack of change and almost no innovation in the industries in the unorganized sector, it is first of all important to ponder over the history of changes that happened within the handloom sector using cotton.

First of all, in the nature of cotton itself changes happened. India captured one of the top positions in cotton production in the world. But over time, the nature of cotton has changed. Earlier cotton was produced mainly of short staple variety which was appropriate for hand spinning, slowly a change happened in cotton variety, and there has been a shift toward long staple variety of cotton which is appropriate for machine spinning without breakage (Menon & Uzramma, 2017).

The next task is to transform cotton into yarn through spinning, earlier through hand spinning it used to happen. Inventions that led to the advent of machine spinning are the spinning jenny of the 1760s, then the water frame of 1768, and the mule of 1780 to which steam power was used. Eventually, spinning activities shifted from home to factories. Broadly, there are two types of yarn – hank yarn and cone yarn; hank yarn goes for handloom production, and cone yarn goes for the production of cloths in mills and factories (Menon & Uzramma, 2017).

The next stage after producing the yarn is dyeing (Table 5.1), that is, adding color. Two kinds of dyeing could be pointed out – one is natural dye by extracting color from indigo or other vegetables, and another type of dyeing was developed later, that is, chemical dye using vat dyes or naphthol dyes. In the past, natural dyeing practices dominated in India, but eventually, they were replaced by chemical dyes, and nowadays, it is very difficult to find practices of natural dyeing (Menon & Uzramma, 2017).

The next stage in handloom production is preparing bobbins; in this process, hank yarn can be transformed into a linear form. Winding and then preparing

Table 5.1.   Technology and Developmental Possibilities.

Technology	Social Group	New Possibilities
Yarn preparing	Yarn supplier	NA
Dyeing	Dyer	Natural dye
Warping drum	Warper	–
Sizing shed	Sizer	–
Loom	Weaver	Improved punch cards, use of AI in creating punch cards
Marketing – digital platforms	Weaver, coops, Mahajans	Digital marketing
Designing	Designer	Use of AI
Retailing	Retailer	Digital retailing

Source: Authors' conceptualization.

warp and weft happens after preparing bobbins. This process is for preparing yarns before starting weaving. Then, using a warping drum warp has to be prepared (Das, 2001).

The next step is called street sizing in which yarns are in the morning in the handloom weaving villages – here, warps are stretched out, and natural adhesives are usually applied there; for this purpose, rice starched with coconut or ground nut oil, such things are used. This process is mainly important to ensure the strength of the yarn so that it can be woven without breakage too many times (Das, 2001).

The next step is to attach the warp to the loom; after this, weaving can be done. Hence, before weaving, these many processes are there. We are noting here all these processes because we are curious about the possibilities of innovation of products, designs, and processes (Das, 2001).

5. Ecosystem Theory

Before delving into details of the industrial ecosystem framework, it would be pertinent to clarify why we are using it here. From our understanding of the current globalized context, we have observed that standalone industrial initiatives may fail miserably due to global forces. Hence, it is important to focus on the holistic development of an industrial sector, focusing on various complementarities and competitive aspects. To cater to this holistic approach, we would like to use here this industrial ecosystem framework.

There are two main components of an industrial ecosystem – capability domains and sectoral value chains, and by linking these two components, the production space of the industrial ecosystem can be curved out. The industrial ecosystem usually follows a multi-tiered complex structure in which firms, several institutions, and demand side actors are embedded in a web of structural interdependencies. Due to existing structural interdependencies among supply and demand side actors within an industrial ecosystem, co-value creation happens in the ecosystem. An industrial ecosystem refers to multi-tiered production systems with heterogeneous agents operating in sectoral value chains and contributing to the capability domains of the ecosystem with closely complementary but dissimilar sets of resources and capabilities (Andreoni, 2018).

Hence, within an industrial ecosystem firms, other supporting organizations, different institutions, and demand side actors all remain embedded and interconnected and take part in the co-creation of value. After defining the ecosystem, it is pertinent to define the concept of the capability domain. The capability domain refers to the different clusters, organizations, and institutions of resources and capabilities – including firms, intermediaries, etc. Here, in our analysis, the unit of analysis is firm, that is, micro–small–medium enterprises; mainly micro and small enterprises operating in the unorganized portion within the textile sector. Each type of productive activity is referred to as a production base or technological base. A firm may have many such bases and such bases act as pools of resources from which a firm can extract services or capabilities. Also, a move toward a new base implies a firm must achieve expertise in a significantly new area of production or toward a new technological area. So, in capability domains, various clusters of dissimilar capabilities with close complementarity exist. Some of the important ecosystems are the Greater Boston ecosystem, the German industrial ecosystem, and Massachusetts ecosystem (Andreoni, 2018).

5.1. Dynamic Capabilities and Role of Universities

A novel area of research is to link the concept of dynamic capabilities with the notion of innovation ecosystems, in which mediating roles between firms and ecosystem may be played by actors like universities (Linde et al., 2021). Innovation ecosystem may emerge organically, and it is also possible to nurture and manage the creation and sustenance of innovation ecosystem through judicious interventions from different social actors – such as research institutes and universities. When elements of our ecosystem exist but do not coordinate among themselves, then this coordination role should be played by some actor/s. In concrete, the "triple helix" case of coordination between academia–industry–government can be pointed out here which may lead to effective coordination toward an innovation ecosystem. Here specifically, we are focusing on what universities, colleges, and research institutes can contribute in this regard as theoretical framework concepts like dynamic capabilities have been utilized here. Dynamic capabilities refer to "… ability to integrate, build and reconfigure internal and external competencies to address rapidly changing environments" (Teece et al., 1997). Sensing opportunities, seizing opportunities, and then maintaining competitiveness by adjusting assets – these three remain important aspects of dynamic capabilities (Teece, 2007). In the presence of uncertainties which is a mark of our time, strong dynamic capabilities matter significantly. To a great extent, dynamic capabilities depend on organizations' routines and managerial decision-making processes; moreover, all these are embedded in the prevailing tacit organizational culture. Cultures, routines such things are path-dependent and slow to change. Yet at times transformation happens in the performances of different organizations through new dynamic leadership (Hsu & Kenney, 2005). Here, we are trying to theorize the role of universities in the Indian context in promoting innovation ecosystems – through sensing, seizing, and transforming opportunities and processes. Within the framework of dynamic capabilities, asset orchestration is a crucial task. It refers to the process of persuasion and consensus building toward a strategy, pursuing people to direct investments toward a particular direction for growth, holding workshops and conferences in pursuing this issue more sincerely, business incubator program launching and finally changing laws, etc. For example, in the United States, such examples are plenty – the first venture capital firm American Research and Development (ARD) in the United States was founded in 1946 by the former dean of Harvard Business Schools and former president of Massachusetts Institute of Technology (MIT). ARD helped launch MIT-based start-ups and worked closely with several firms in New England (Hsu & Kenney, 2005).

Since in the Indian context, we are not going to discuss any advanced stages of the ecosystem; hence, we would like to focus only on the first stage of building an innovation ecosystem. The first portion, that is, the case of sensing, is the highlight of this chapter. Moving toward sensing opportunities and building effective coordination of several organizations around it remains an initial challenge in India. Typical characteristics are few enterprises, almost no channel of interaction among them, and lack of activities on behalf of any supporting agency – such is the situation in the Indian unorganized manufacturing sector's target ecosystem.

In the theory of innovation ecosystem, initial stage, development stage, and renewal stage – these three stages have been pointed out, yet for developing countries such as India we would like to focus now on the initial stage since developed innovation ecosystems are very rare in India and in most of the developing countries. The question we raise here is – what can a university do in this initial stage? Scholars have suggested the following functions for a university – supporting faculty entrepreneurship, supporting start-up incubators, hosting networking events, performing outreach with emerging technologies, building linkages with local firms, etc. With all such activities, a university, a college, or a research institute can attempt to sense opportunities in a given regional area. Sensing would be a key dynamic capability in this regard.

> During the initial stage, an innovation ecosystem exhibits low density, a limited identity, and few linkages. Firms and other actors begin to cooperate on key activities. To be successful, the ecosystem must build a critical mass of companies, entrepreneurs, talent, and investment – a process that can take years and is not a guarantee of success. During this stage, a university can help create preconditions by ensuring a research and outreach presence in promising technology fields with regional potential (Heaton et al., 2019, p. 6).

For instance, in the United States, apart from well-known examples of MIT and Stanford University's role in promoting the innovation ecosystem, universities such as Carnegie Melon, UC Barkley, and the University of Pennsylvania also did significantly well. For example, in Carnegie Melon since the 1970s, the process of industry collaboration started and slowly it paid off and played a significant role in transforming the surrounding industrial area of Pittsburgh. Pittsburgh was transformed in the process which was erstwhile a steel-producing area; nowadays, it has become a hub of technology firms, thanks to the university–industry collaboration with Carnegie Mellon (Heaton et al., 2019).

In the Indian context with respect to the textile sector, establishing this linkage between dynamic capabilities of firms' and innovation ecosystem may be orchestrated by universities, research and educational institutes, and research labs. Small businesses often face problems of R&D, knowledge about recent innovations, and institutional mechanisms. That goes from textile sector also. For example, from our field works, we know that handloom weavers of West Bengal do not have much idea about new and novel design innovations due to their lack of education and institutional access. Left to their own, they may never be able to harness the benefits of already existing technologies and designs. In this regard, universities and research labs may come forward in integrating the knowledge creation and industrial application by conducting workshops for these small producers.

6. Issues in the Handloom-Weaving Industry

Today as per many scholars, a significant threat to handloom products is imitations by power looms; as per the Reservation Act (1985), such imitations cannot be done. This practice has seriously affected markets for products like *Gadwal*, *Pochampally, Mangalagiri, Santipuri sarees*, etc. Even in government-sponsored handloom exhibitions, it is regularly witnessed that a mix of power-loom and handloom sarees is on display. Many committees were formed in order to address this problem – Mira Seth committee (1996), Satyam committee (2000), etc., and almost all these committees directly or indirectly called for mechanization (Srinivasulu, 1997). But from various accounts, it is evident that pure handloom products enjoy adequate market demand at the national and international levels. And no other country can satisfy this demand except India, as no other country in the world possesses so many working handlooms except India.

6.1. Policy Interventions by the Government

How to think about improving the economic conditions of millions of handloom weavers? What kinds of interventions can make life better for them? These are some of the critical questions for the policymakers of the handloom weaving industry. Some of the state interventions in terms of inventions and innovations we will discuss here.

In Fig. 5.1, it is shown that innovation can happen in input provisioning, output production, marketing aspects, and different organization–institutional setups. In the input market, it is required that weavers are able to obtain quality yarns at affordable prices. Innovation should happen in dyeing processes and chemical use, in experimentation with different colors. In the case of production organization, the issue is to ensure that the real producers get adequate remuneration and are not exploited by the intermediaries; in this regard, institutional innovation may happen.

We can differentiate between two concepts invention and innovation – invention means creating something new and innovation means putting something new in use. Especially, in the last decade, innovation became so important for business that it seems innovation is the engine of growth. Innovation can happen through R&D, from practice, etc. Innovation can happen in product, process, machinery, marketing, business model, and organization, that is, in the realm of organizations and institutional norms. The competitiveness of any sector in this globalized world depends heavily on innovation; hence in a way, continuous innovation is imperative in today's context.

As per the report on innovation by the Ministry of Textile (MoT, 2014, p. 12), the objectives regarding innovation in the textile sector are focusing on the innovations in the textile sector, mapping opportunities for innovations; helping to create innovation eco-systems; encouraging young talents and local colleges,

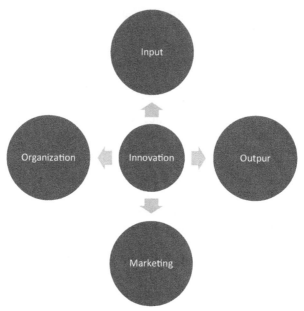

Fig. 5.1.   Role of Innovation in Different Aspects of Handloom Weaving.
Source: Authors.

universities, research institutes, and industries to join hands; identifying talents in this area and talk about success stories; organizing seminars, workshops; encouraging innovations in the delivery of public services, etc. This chapter can be considered a first step in the research regarding the development of the innovation ecosystem in handloom in India and the role of colleges and universities. Since we are laying the foundations of a new research area here, since it is beyond our scope to provide a full analysis of innovation ecosystems, this chapter is an attempt to chalk out the contours of this new paradigm.

In this regard, we will mention here some of the recent developments under the guidance of the Ministry of Textiles. First, it has been attempted to train artisans with new designs by providing them with financial assistance for attending the training. Also, design and training workshops have been arranged. Second, to provide infrastructural and skill development support, common facility centers have been set up and at present there are 100 common facility centers in different handloom clusters all over India. Third, it has been attempted to develop and supply modern toolkits to artisans every year so that artisans can use the latest technologies. Fourth, institutional mechanisms have been developed to reach out and provide support to artisans by using public organizations like National Institute of Fashion Technology (NIFT) and related research institutes (MoT, 2014).

Under the government schema, NIFT has been given ample importance for innovation and dissemination of new designs as well as new know-how. To sensitize students about grassroots level innovation, "The Cluster Development Initiative (CDI)" was started by NIFT. By providing students with research projects in the areas of handloom and handicraft, NIFT has been trying to build inroads into rural artisanal clusters. Systematic information collected in this way can pave the way for better suitable interventions in the future. As per the CDI process, each student of the design and management departments must visit a cluster at least once during their course at NIFT; they can undertake surveys or conduct workshops whichever is suitable for the project and cluster's development.

6.2. Why to Innovate

In the handloom weaving, craft sector innovation is needed for the following issues – improving the working conditions of the weavers, developing and designing products with improved functional properties, improving the productivity of the weavers, and increasing the overall efficiency of the micro-small enterprises, to develop less time-consuming and cost-effective processes, to replace older and conventional machines by faster technologically advanced machines, and to improve visibility in the national and international market (MoT, 2014).

Apart from all these factors, the linkages between market dynamics, availability of raw materials, and concerns regarding sustainability are important regarding innovation. It implies that innovation is required in products and processes so that sustainability issues can be addressed. It can be pointed out that more innovations for the usage of cotton fabrics rather than polyester mixed raw materials are better for the environment and human health (Palacios-Mateo et al., 2021). Yet the problem is that good quality cotton-based raw material is hard to find and costlier. Hence to cut costs often, the quality of raw materials gets sacrificed in the Indian textile sector. Hence regarding the issue of sustainability, it is pertinent to think of innovations keeping in mind the issue of cost and making available good quality cotton-based hank yarn, that is, the raw material for the handloom weavers of India. This is not an easy task.

6.3. Some of the Inventions and Innovation

Many new inventions are happening in this sector. And, innovations have been attempted in products, process, machinery, marketing, business model, and organization.

While producing hank yarn for handloom fabric production rather than traditional charkha, high-speed charkha has been invented. Charkha provides employment and livelihoods for many people in India, and now to improve productivity and overall efficiency, high-speed charkha has been invented. The pedal system has been changed to reduce efforts and a gear has been added to increase productivity. Due to such new features, the high-speed charkha has been adopted by many people in many handloom clusters in India.

In the dyeing process especially while dyeing of cotton textiles, it has been attempted to develop a no salt, low alkali dyeing, and a process has been tried for enzymatic preparation of cotton textiles. Also, some organizations like Dastkar and decentralized cotton yarn trust tried to develop natural dyeing processes using vegetables for dyeing and avoiding chemical dyeing altogether.

New types of looms have been developed which are ergonomically better for weavers so that they can work for longer hours. Moreover, new software has been developed for design purpose; yet as per our field work in handloom weaving areas, usage of software for design purpose is still very limited. AI-based developments also have happened especially in the area of design, yet in the handloom weaving sector uptake of such inventions is low and slow. In this area, universities and research institutes may come forward and help. It may be possible to come up with new designs using AI tools, and there will not be any copyright issues with such designs. With speedier utilization of such a technology, handloom weaving may proliferate and contribute toward the SDGs.

7. Discussion and Conclusion

Here, different streams of literature have been considered to make a case for the unorganized manufacturing small firms in India in today's context of the ongoing technological revolution. This chapter has been attempted to develop an outline of a research program that can illuminate ways and means of advancing the interest of these small firms. Literature on innovation ecosystem, dynamic capabilities have been considered to explore the case of the Indian textile sector, in general, and the handloom weaving sector, in particular. Also, it has been attempted to connect all these with respect to SDGs.

> The Government should ... put more emphasis on supporting start-ups with the potential to bring about economic development rather than the potential for growth, whose social benefit is unknown. In order to benefit every population stratum, there is a need to build a more inclusive and accessible start-up ecosystem. The intervention of government agencies at various scales can correct the tendencies of private capital to concentrate. Possible policies include the creation of specific funds for entrepreneurs in tier-2, tier-3 cities, and rural areas, accompanied by active marketing of the schemes amongst underprivileged populations; the implementation of reservations in the start-up funds created by the government based on household incomes; and the development of support structures (incubators, accelerators, Fab Labs) in tier-2 and tier-3 cities and secondary education institutes ... there is a large potential for innovation at the grassroots level. So far, this potential has been surprisingly untapped in India (Rault & Mathew, 2019, pp. 49–50).

From the above analysis, we can point out that in India to promote an innovation ecosystem more decentralized approach may become further beneficiary. The role of NIFT has been well-studied, yet when NIFT may act as a nodal agency, the regional or district-level universities, colleges, and research institutes may be better suited to intervene in the clusters. So, more and more district-level institutions should be promoted to do this work. Institutional mechanisms need to be developed in these institutes/organizations so that they can effectively intervene in the various rural clusters prevailing in the district. Developing innovation ecosystems should be seen as a long-term project, gestation periods in such investments used to be longer, and target-based, quick-fix approaches may not work well in this regard.

References

Andreoni, A. (2018). The architecture and dynamics of industrial ecosystems: Diversification and innovative industrial renewal in Emilia Romagna. *Cambridge Journal of Economics, 42*(6), 1613–1642.

Basole, A., & Basu, D. (2011). Relations of production and modes of surplus extraction in India. *Economic and Political Weekly, 46*(14), 63–79.

Bhattacharya, R., & Sen, S. (2018). *Pride and prejudice: The condition of handloom weavers in West Bengal* [Centre for Sustainable Employment, Azim Premji University, Working Paper 2018–16]. http://publications.azimpremjifoundation.org/245/1/Pride%20and%20Prejudice_The%20Condition%20of%20Handloom%20Weavers%20in%20West%20Bengal.pdf

Bhowmik, M. R. (2019). Fourth handloom census: Government's claims belie ground reality. *Economic and Political Weekly, 54*(49).

Bhowmik, M. R. (2021). SDGs, social responsibilities, institutions and cooperatives: Evidence from the handloom weaving sector in India. *International Journal of Rural Management, 97*(IS), 97s–114s.

Breman, J. (1996). *Footloose labor: Working in India's informal economy.* Cambridge University Press.

Das, S. K. (2001). *The warp and woof: An inquiry into the handloom industry in West Bengal.* K.P. Bagchi & Company.

Dev, S. M., Galab, S., Reddy, P. P., & Vinayan, S. (2008). Economics of handloom weaving: A field study in Andhra Pradesh. *Economic and Political Weekly, 43*(21), 43–51.

Government of India. (2017). *Key indicators of unincorporated non-agricultural enterprises (excluding construction) in India.* https://microdata.gov.in/nada43/index.php/catalog/139/related_materials

Heaton, S., Siegel, D. S., & Teece, D. J. (2019). Universities and innovation ecosystems: A dynamic capabilities perspective. *Industrial and Corporate Change, 28*(4), 921–939.

Heintz, J. (2006). *Globalization, economic policy and employment: Poverty and gender implications* [ILO Employment Strategy Papers]. https://cse.azimpremjiuniversity.edu.in/wpcontent/uploads/2017/10/NCEUS2009_ChallengeofEmploymentinIndia.pdf

Himanshu. (2023). *India's slow but sure de-industrialization is worrying.* mint. https://www.livemint.com/opinion/columns/indias-manufacturing-sector-faces-worsening-decline-implications-for-growth-employment-and-income-11686851477882.html

Hsu, D. H., & Kenney, M. (2005). Organizing venture capital: The rise and demise of American Research & Development Corporation, 1946–1973. *Industrial and Corporate Change, 14*(4), 579–616.

Linde, L., Sjodin, D., Parida, V., & Wincent, J. (2021). Dynamic capabilities for ecosystems orchestration: A capability based framework for smart city innovation initiatives. *Technological Forecasting and Social Change, 166.*

Mazzucatto, M. (2014). *The entrepreneurial state: Debunking public vs. private sector myths.* Anthem Press.

Menon, M., & Uzramma (2017). *A frayed history: The journey of cotton in India.* Oxford University Press.

Ministry of Textiles (MoT). (2014). *Innovations in the textile and apparel industry.*

Ministry of Textiles (MoT). (2019). *Fourth all Inda handloom census 2019–20.*

Mitra, A., Choudhuri, P. K., & Mukherjee, A. (2009). A diagnostic report on cluster development programme of Shantipur handloom cluster, Nadia, West Bengal, Part I_ Evolution of the cluster and cluster analysis. *Indian Journal of Traditional Knowledge, 8*(4), 502–509.

NCEUS. (2009). *The challenge of employment in India: Informal economy perspective* [Volume-I Main report]. https://cse.azimpremjiuniversity.edu.in/wpcontent/uploads/2017/10/NCEUS2009_ChallengeofEmploymentinIndia.pdf

Omrane, A., Akbari, M., & Patra, G. (2023). How to digitize human resource management in the age of Industry 4.0? In A. Omrane, G. Patra, & S. Datta (Eds.), *Digital technologies for smart business, economics and education: Towards a promising future* (pp. 1–18). Springer.

Palacios-Mateo, C., Meer, Y. V., & Seide, G. (2021). Analysis of the polyester clothing value chain to identify key intervention points for sustainability. *Environmental Sciences Europe, 33*(1), 1–25.

Rault, Y.-M. & Mathew, S. (2019). An imbalanced ecosystem: Start-ups in India. *Economic and Political Weekly, LIV*(45), 45–50.

Sinha, K. (2013). Unesco declares Jamdani saris intangible cultural heritage. *The Times of India.*

Srinivasulu, K. (1997). High-powered committee, low voltage report: Mira Seth report on handloom. *Economic and Political Weekly, 32*(24), 1381–1384.

Teece, D. J., Pisano, G., & Shuen, A. (1997). Dynamic capabilities and strategic management. *Strategic Management Journal, 18*(7), 509–533.

Teece, D. J. (2007). Explicating dynamic capabilities: The nature and microfoundations of (sustainable) enterprise performance. *Strategic Management Journal, 28*(13), 1319–1350.

UNCTAD. (2023). *Technology and innovation report 2023: Opening green windows technological opportunities for a low-carbon world.* https://unctad.org/tir2023

Wilkinson-Weber, C. M. (1997). Skill, dependency, and differentiation: Artisans and agents in the Lucknow embroidery industry. *Ethnology, 36*(1), 49–65. https://doi.org/10.2307/3773935

Chapter 6

Persisting Industrial Concentration and Signs of Industrial Dispersion: Evidence from Formal and Informal Manufacturing Sector

Renjith Ramachandran

Indian Institute of Management Ranchi, India

Abstract

The spatial concentration of the manufacturing employment and production is the general feature in all the economy. Indian economy is not an exception from this scenario. The spatial pattern of Indian manufacturing sector reports a significant regional disparity. Since manufacturing is becoming more vital in the Indian economy, it is essential to understand the spatial distribution of the manufacturing sector. This chapter provides a detailed picture of India's spatial distribution pattern in formal and informal manufacturing sectors. Using the well-known Ellison–Glaeser index, we measure the industrial agglomeration for all National Industry Classification (NIC) three-digit industries and further incorporate statewise manufacturing activity distribution. From the analysis, it is evident that there is a substantial regional concentration of manufacturing activity; however, the recent regional distribution pattern also depicts some signs of industrial dispersion.

Keywords: Industrial agglomeration; formal manufacturing; informal manufacturing; India; regional disparity

Informal Economy and Sustainable Development Goals:
Ideas, Interventions and Challenges, 99–126
Copyright © 2024 by Renjith Ramachandran
Published under exclusive licence by Emerald Publishing Limited
doi:10.1108/978-1-83753-980-220241006

1 Introduction

Regional concentration of economic activity, explicitly manufacturing production, is considered the general feature of developing economies (Fan & Scott, 2003; Lu & Tao, 2009; Ramachandran et al., 2020). Due to this concentration of economic activity, some regions flourish, and many lag behind. Literature on Economic Geography incorporated this as one of the core areas in its discussion. The initial strand of literature analyses the plausible determinants behind this spatial concentration (Ellison & Glaeser, 1999; Rosenthal & Strange, 2001), while the second strand of literature emphasises the cost–benefit analysis of this concentration, specifically the impact on productivity and pollution (Cainelli et al., 2015; Dong et al., 2020; Li et al., 2021; Tveteras & Battese, 2006). Furthermore, recently, the measures of industrial agglomeration and Geographic Information System mapping enhanced the popularity of this subject matter and assisted policymakers with regional and urban development.

The existing literature highlights the strategy behind the location choice of industrial activity and associated benefits; along with these discussions, measuring and understanding the geographic map of an economy's industrial activity are essential. Even though all the economies marked a high concentration of economic activity, more recent studies started to observe an industrial dispersion rather than further agglomeration. India is not an exception from this scenario. Mukim (2015) measures the co-location of the formal and informal manufacturing sector in India and observes a reduction in the co-location pattern. Furthermore, Ramachandran et al. (2020) reported a spatial dispersion in the location of cross-border greenfield investment and local manufacturing production in India. Given this exciting fact, this chapter analyses the spatial and sectoral distribution of formal and informal manufacturing activity during 2005–2015. Specifically, we are trying to address two issues: (i) identify the changing pattern of industrial agglomeration in India and (ii) analyse the industrial location in India to identify concentration/dispersion status of industrial activity.

Interestingly, studies pertaining to industrial agglomeration and industrial location in the context of India are limited. Therefore, given this backdrop, we make the following contributions to the literature. Firstly, we analyse India's changing industrial concentration/industrial location pattern at a more disaggregated level (NIC 3 digit). Understanding these statewise and sectoralwise distributions of manufacturing activity can provide valuable insights for policy recommendations. Secondly, we are incorporating spatial distribution of informal sector in India. According to the Labour Force Participation Survey 2017–2018, more than 80% of manufacturing workers in India engaged in the informal sector. However, barring Ghani and Kanbur (2013) and Mukim (2015), studies about the spatial distribution of the informal sector are relatively scant in the literature. Therefore, this study intends to provide an elaborative picture of the spatial distribution of the informal sector in India.

The remaining part of the chapter is organised as follows: Section 2 discusses stylised facts about the formal sector and provides a detailed picture of the industrial agglomeration. In contrast, Section 3 incorporates the same for the informal sector in India. Section 4 concludes the chapter.

2. Formal Manufacturing Sector in India: Stylised Facts

According to the Factories Act of 1948 and the Beedi and Cigar workers Act 1966, formal manufacturing includes those units or plants registered as factories under sections 2(m)(i) and 2(m)(ii). Accordingly, a plant that employs more than 10 workers with power and more than 20 workers without power is considered the formal manufacturing sector. More than 80% of Indian manufacturing output is produced in formal sector. The evidence from different Annual Survey of Industries reports observes that there has been growth in all the main characteristics of formal sector during this period. The number of factories records a substantial increase with an annual growth of 5.2% during 2005–2015. On the other hand, in terms of formal employment, the annual growth rate was 4.55% during the same period. Furthermore, the growth rate of the value of output and inputs during the same period was 13.65% and 13.73%, respectively. Hence, during the period under the study, we observed a positive change in the number of factories, employees and output providing evidence of formal manufacturing sector growth in India.

Given the objective of this study, we set forth to identify how formal manufacturing activities are spatially distributed in India. To analyse this, we have compiled different annual survey of industries (ASI) reports and observed different factors, especially the number of factories, number of workers and value of output distributed among Indian states during 2005–2015. During the period 2006–2015, there was a considerable increase in formal manufacturing activity in terms of number of factories, number of workers and value of output. The number of factories in the formal sector recorded positive growth in all the states, while the union territories of Andaman & Nicobar Islands and Chandigarh recorded negative growth. The state of Himachal Pradesh reports the highest growth rate in the number of factories (15.6%), followed by Uttarakhand (14.7%) and Manipur (11.26%). In the growth rates of formal sector, Andhra Pradesh, Bihar and Delhi recorded a negative growth rate. In terms of number of formal workers, Uttarakhand recorded the highest growth (23.64%), followed by Meghalaya (17.3%) and Himachal Pradesh (15.91%).

Traditionally, the formal manufacturing activities were located in states like Tamil Nadu, Maharashtra, Andhra Pradesh, Gujarat and Uttar Pradesh. However, when we analyse the recent data, we observe a tendency of industrial dispersion. For example, the growth rate of formal sector is predominant in the states of Himachal Pradesh, Uttarakhand, Manipur, Meghalaya, Odisha and Rajasthan. However, the annual growth of the formal sector in the industrially developed states reports lower values than the emerging regions. We may attribute this trend to the agglomeration diseconomies forces like congestion, increased competition and land cost. Therefore, our initial descriptive analysis points to spatial dispersion of formal manufacturing sector.

Furthermore, we analyse this trend by different industry groups. We measure industrial agglomeration using the Ellison–Glaeser index (EG index by Ellison & Glaeser, 1997) at the three-digit industry classification.[1] EG index has certain advantages, for example, it allows for comparability across industries. Furthermore, the scale of the index allows for comparison with a "no agglomeration" benchmark (EG index = 0). In addition, the construction of the EG index only requires one variable (employment). Hence, it is not hampered by the little information which is available regarding plant level distribution. Equation 1 gives a formal representation of the EG index.

$$\gamma_j = \frac{\sum_{r=1}^{M}(S_r - x_r)^2 - (1 - \sum_r x_r^2)\sum_i z_i^2}{(1 - \sum_r x_r^2)(1 - \sum_i z_i^2)} \tag{1}$$

where s_r is state r's share in the industry j's employment; x_r stands for state r's share in total manufacturing employment and z_i is the share of plant i in the industry's employment. $P_i z_i^2$ shows the Herfindahl index of the plant size distribution. For measuring EG index, we need detailed information concerning the establishment of each plant. As mentioned, we use the employment data from ASI plant-level panel data to construct this index.

Table 6.1 reports the agglomeration pattern by industry classification. Following the standard practice, based on standard EG classification, we classify the industries into (i) highly concentrated industries (EG > 0.05), (ii) concentrated (0.02 < EG < 0.05), and (iii) least concentrated industries (EG < 0.02). For the year 2006, we observe that 33 industries belong to the highly concentrated category. Among the various industries, the manufacture of fur is the most highly concentrated industry with an EG value of 0.47, followed by the manufacture of knitted and crocheted apparel (0.46) and manufacture of coke oven products (0.31). During 2015, the number of industries under the highly concentrated category declined marginally. Manufacture of knitted and crocheted apparel reproduction of recorded media and manufacture of fur articles are found to be highly concentrated. In terms of the least concentrated industry, manufacture of dairy products remained the least concentrated during the study period. Furthermore, the number of the least concentrated industries increased from 6 to 10 during 2006–2015. Similarly, during the study period, 35 three-digit industries showed a reduction in the EG index value. This trend points to the dispersion of industries rather than further agglomeration.

Furthermore, Table 6.2 reports the top five states, based on the share of workers in each industry (22 two-digit industries). It shows the change in the top five positions of states in each industry category during 2006–2015. In the formal sector, we do not observe any substantial changes among the top five states in terms of the employment share. When we attempt to map the share of the top five states across two-digit industry category, we observe little change in their positions during 2006–2010.

---

[1]The 3-digit NIC classification includes a total of 63 industry categories.

Table 6.1.   Industrial Agglomeration Pattern of Formal Sector (2006–2015).

	2006			2015	
NIC 3 Digit	Description	EG Index	NIC 3 Digit	Description	EG Index
Highly concentrated (EG > 0.05)					
142	Manufacture of articles of fur	0.472	143	Manufacture of knitted and crocheted apparel	0.479
143	Manufacture of knitted and crocheted apparel	0.468	182	Reproduction of recorded media	0.471
191	Manufacture of coke oven products	0.311	142	Manufacture of articles of fur	0.375
302	Manufacture of railway locomotives and rolling stock	0.31	191	Processing and preserving of meat	0.319
268	Manufacture of magnetic and optical media	0.23	268	Manufacture of magnetic and optical media	0.301
264	Manufacture of consumer electronics	0.198	120	Manufacture of tobacco products	0.224
120	Manufacture of tobacco products	0.19	302	Manufacture of railway locomotives and rolling stock	0.203
203	Manufacture of man-made fibres	0.189	264	Manufacture of consumer electronics	0.203
152	Manufacture of footwear	0.186	303	Manufacture of air and spacecraft and related machinery	0.183
182	Reproduction of recorded media	0.174	191	Manufacture of coke oven products	0.18
301	Building of ships and boats	0.17	252	Manufacture of weapons and ammunition	0.167

(Continued)

Table 6.1.   (Continued)

	2006			2015	
NIC 3 Digit	Description	EG Index	NIC 3 Digit	Description	EG Index
151	Tanning and dressing of leather	0.165	151	Tanning and dressing of leather	0.151
101	Processing and preserving of meat	0.157	304	Manufacture of military fighting vehicles	0.15
252	Manufacture of weapons and ammunition	0.156	301	Building of ships and boats	0.148
141	Manufacture of wearing apparel, except fur apparel	0.154	152	Manufacture of footwear	0.147
272	Manufacture of batteries and accumulators	0.15	102	Processing and preserving of fish, crustaceans, and molluscs	0.144
304	Manufacture of military fighting vehicles	0.148	141	Manufacture of wearing apparel, except fur apparel	0.107
310	Manufacture of furniture	0.136	201	Manufacture of basic chemicals	0.095
309	Manufacture of transport equipment	0.118	267	Manufacture of optical instruments	0.094
201	Manufacture of basic chemicals	0.112	309	Manufacture of transport equipment	0.091
303	Manufacture of air and spacecraft and related machinery	0.107	266	Manufacture of irradiation equipment	0.087
231	Manufacture of glass and glass products	0.101	242	Manufacture of basic precious and other non-ferrous metals	0.087
102	Processing and preserving of fish, crustaceans and molluscs	0.097	241	Manufacture of basic iron and steel	0.083

139	Manufacture of other textiles	0.091
161	Sawmilling and planning of wood	0.087
242	Manufacture of basic precious and other non-ferrous metals	0.077
266	Manufacture of irradiation equipment	0.076
262	Manufacture of computers and peripheral equipment	0.075
192	Manufacture of refined petroleum products	0.074
103	Processing and preserving of fruit and vegetables	0.071
291	Manufacture of motor vehicles	0.07
107	Manufacture of other food products	0.069
267	Manufacture of optical instruments	0.069
274	Manufacture of electric lighting equipment	0.06
293	Manufacture of parts and accessories for motor vehicles	0.06
106	Manufacture of grain mill products, starches, and starch products	0.051
203	Manufacture of man-made fibres	0.076
161	Sawmilling and planning of wood	0.074
262	Manufacture of computers and peripheral equipment	0.073
231	Manufacture of glass and glass products	0.065
292	Manufacture of bodies for motor vehicles	0.065
293	Manufacture of parts and accessories for motor vehicles	0.063
273	Manufacture of wiring and wiring devices	0.06
274	Manufacture of electric lighting equipment	0.057
291	Manufacture of motor vehicles	0.052
272	Manufacture of batteries and accumulators	0.052
192	Manufacture of refined petroleum products	0.051

(Continued)

Table 6.1. (Continued)

	2006			2015	
NIC 3 Digit	**Description**	**EG Index**	**NIC 3 Digit**	**Description**	**EG Index**
		Concentrated (0.02 < EG < 0.05)			
263	Manufacture of communication equipment	0.047	310	Manufacture of furniture	0.043
241	Manufacture of basic iron and steel	0.043	107	Manufacture of other food products	0.042
273	Manufacture of wiring and wiring devices	0.043	263	Manufacture of communication equipment	0.042
259	Manufacture of other fabricated metal products	0.042	210	Manufacture of pharmaceuticals	0.039
131	Spinning, weaving, and finishing of textiles	0.041	261	Manufacture of electronic components	0.037
251	Manufacture of structural metal products	0.04	103	Processing and preserving of fruit and vegetables	0.037
292	Manufacture of bodies for motor vehicles	0.039	162	Manufacture of products of wood, cork, straw, and plaiting materials	0.036
210	Manufacture of pharmaceuticals	0.037	131	Spinning, weaving, and finishing of textiles	0.036
104	Manufacture of vegetable and animal oils and fats	0.036	259	Manufacture of other fabricated metal products	0.032
202	Manufacture of other chemical products	0.034	239	Manufacture of non-metallic mineral products	0.031

Code	Industry	Value	Code	Industry	Value
261	Manufacture of electronic components	0.034	275	Manufacture of domestic appliances	0.028
239	Manufacture of non-metallic mineral products	0.029	281	Manufacture of general purpose machinery	0.027
271	Manufacture of electric motors	0.027	243	Casting of metals	0.026
275	Manufacture of domestic appliances	0.026	106	Manufacture of grain mill products, starches, and starch products	0.026
222	Manufacture of plastics products	0.026	265	Manufacture of measuring equipment	0.025
221	Manufacture of rubber products	0.025	222	Manufacture of plastics products	0.023
110	Manufacture of beverages	0.025	108	Manufacture of prepared animal feeds	0.022
181	Printing and service activities related to printing	0.022	110	Manufacture of beverages	0.02
282	Manufacture of special-purpose machinery	0.022	104	Manufacture of vegetable and animal oils and fats	0.02
265	Manufacture of measuring equipment	0.02			
243	Casting of metals	0.02			

(Continued)

Table 6.1. *(Continued)*

	2006			2015	
NIC 3 Digit	**Description**	**EG Index**	**NIC 3 Digit**	**Description**	**EG Index**
		Least concentrated (EG < 0.02)			
105	Manufacture of dairy products	0.004	105	Manufacture of dairy products	0.005
170	Manufacture of paper and paper products	0.013	170	Manufacture of paper and paper products	0.006
279	Manufacture of other electrical equipment	0.014	279	Manufacture of other electrical equipment	0.01
108	Manufacture of prepared animal feeds	0.015	139	Manufacture of other textiles	0.011
162	Manufacture of products of wood, cork, straw, and plaiting materials	0.017	202	Manufacture of other chemical products	0.014
281	Manufacture of general purpose machinery	0.019	181	Printing and service activities related to printing	0.015
			221	Manufacture of rubber products	0.016
			251	Manufacture of structural metal products	0.018
			282	Manufacture of special-purpose machinery	0.018
			271	Manufacture of electric motors	0.019

Note: Own calculations using Annual Survey of Industries data.

Table 6.2.   Top Five States in Terms of Employment Share (Formal Sector).

	2006			2015	
NIC	State	Share	NIC	State	Share
10	Kerala	17.625	10	Maharashtra	14.476
	Uttar Pradesh	13.252		Kerala	13.257
	Maharashtra	11.869		Uttar Pradesh	10.673
	Andhra Pradesh	9.659		Tamil Nadu	9.3308
	Assam	7.2258		Andhra Pradesh	8.9719
11	Uttar Pradesh	15.17	11	Andhra Pradesh	12.802
	Andhra Pradesh	12.558		Maharashtra	12.091
	Maharashtra	11.591		Uttar Pradesh	9.8157
	Punjab	9.1111		Karnataka	9.0946
	Karnataka	7.3115		Tamil Nadu	8.3338
12	Andhra Pradesh	72.725	12	Andhra Pradesh	74.016
	Maharashtra	11.752		Maharashtra	9.8556
	West Bengal	2.7256		Uttar Pradesh	3.5525
	Uttar Pradesh	1.9932		Odisha	2.6134
	Madhya Pradesh	1.8948		Karnataka	1.8885
13	Tamil Nadu	23.377	13	Tamil Nadu	18.946
	West Bengal	18.918		Gujarat	18.338
	Gujarat	11.378		West Bengal	14.107
	Maharashtra	9.7422		Maharashtra	9.7121
	Punjab	6.8736		Punjab	6.9251
14	Karnataka	36.788	14	Karnataka	35.512
	Tamil Nadu	25.723		Tamil Nadu	27.473
	Haryana	15.904		Haryana	10.21
	Delhi	5.8439		Uttar Pradesh	8.2282
	Uttar Pradesh	5.6495		Punjab	3.9422
15	Tamil Nadu	41.485	15	Tamil Nadu	41.847
	Uttar Pradesh	31.416		Uttar Pradesh	20.221
	West Bengal	5.0669		Haryana	9.7543
	Haryana	4.7296		West Bengal	9.1044
	Delhi	2.6346		Andhra Pradesh	3.4748

(*Continued*)

Table 6.2.   (*Continued*)

2006			2015		
NIC	**State**	**Share**	**NIC**	**State**	**Share**
16	Kerala	11.105	16	Andhra Pradesh	17.757
	West Bengal	9.3849		West Bengal	9.7947
	Uttar Pradesh	8.591		Tamil Nadu	9.2352
	Tamil Nadu	8.5371		Gujarat	8.4386
	Gujarat	7.9784		Maharashtra	7.6975
17	Andhra Pradesh	12.767	17	Tamil Nadu	12.463
	Tamil Nadu	9.8814		Maharashtra	11.119
	Gujarat	9.5836		Gujarat	10.184
	Karnataka	9.0979		Andhra Pradesh	8.7419
	Maharashtra	9.0189		Karnataka	8.4899
18	Tamil Nadu	21.154	18	Maharashtra	17.099
	Maharashtra	15.643		Tamil Nadu	14.767
	Uttar Pradesh	11.856		Uttar Pradesh	12.211
	Karnataka	9.3997		Andhra Pradesh	9.6863
	Delhi	7.6756		Karnataka	8.9878
19	Gujarat	27.681	19	Gujarat	20.263
	Jharkhand	17.628		Maharashtra	11.045
	Maharashtra	12.216		Kerala	10.919
	Assam	10.59		Uttar Pradesh	8.9441
	West Bengal	7.2324		West Bengal	8.8935
20	Gujarat	25.095	20	Gujarat	25.153
	Tamil Nadu	20.898		Tamil Nadu	14.27
	Maharashtra	15.285		Maharashtra	12.711
	Uttar Pradesh	6.2163		Uttar Pradesh	6.0521
	Andhra Pradesh	4.5548		Uttaranchal	5.6199
21	Andhra Pradesh	17.999	21	Andhra Pradesh	18.919
	Gujarat	17.857		Maharashtra	15.602
	Maharashtra	17.45		Gujarat	14.975
	Karnataka	6.1674		Uttaranchal	9.0939
	Madhya Pradesh	5.4395		Karnataka	6.4267

Table 6.2. (*Continued*)

	2006			2015	
NIC	**State**	**Share**	**NIC**	**State**	**Share**
22	Maharashtra	17.009	22	Tamil Nadu	13.779
	Tamil Nadu	11.862		Maharashtra	13.44
	Gujarat	8.7129		Gujarat	9.3478
	Punjab	8.3203		Karnataka	8.1033
	Andhra Pradesh	8.0568		Uttaranchal	7.7991
23	Gujarat	13.03	23	Gujarat	13.191
	Andhra Pradesh	9.8166		Andhra Pradesh	10.338
	Rajasthan	7.7276		Rajasthan	7.4583
	Tamil Nadu	7.6075		Tamil Nadu	7.2595
	Punjab	7.5387		Haryana	6.729
24	Jharkhand	14.877	24	Odisha	21.173
	West Bengal	13.109		Maharashtra	11.44
	Maharashtra	11.277		Chhattisgarh	10.842
	Odisha	11.175		West Bengal	10.715
	Chhattisgarh	10.236		Jharkhand	8.7476
25	Maharashtra	17.043	25	Maharashtra	17.062
	Uttar Pradesh	16.49		Tamil Nadu	14.009
	Tamil Nadu	14.547		Uttar Pradesh	13.957
	Gujarat	10.119		Gujarat	9.2679
	Punjab	8.1556		Haryana	6.6685
26	Uttar Pradesh	17.432	26	Maharashtra	18.546
	Maharashtra	15.108		Uttar Pradesh	12.843
	Karnataka	9.6643		Tamil Nadu	11.185
	Andhra Pradesh	8.0309		Karnataka	10.046
	Gujarat	7.9466		Kerala	7.5718
27	Maharashtra	17.166	27	Maharashtra	13.498
	Andhra Pradesh	11.55		Tamil Nadu	10.174
	Madhya Pradesh	8.2986		Uttaranchal	9.6419
	Karnataka	7.6449		Andhra Pradesh	8.941
	Gujarat	7.6062		Gujarat	7.9767

(*Continued*)

Table 6.2.   (*Continued*)

2006			2015		
NIC	**State**	**Share**	**NIC**	**State**	**Share**
28	Maharashtra	20.637	28	Maharashtra	20.889
	Tamil Nadu	13.933		Tamil Nadu	19.212
	Gujarat	12.592		Gujarat	17.522
	Haryana	8.3191		Karnataka	7.2708
	Karnataka	8.1772		Haryana	6.4002
29	Tamil Nadu	25.52	29	Tamil Nadu	27.65
	Maharashtra	24.317		Maharashtra	18.973
	Haryana	15.082		Haryana	18.064
	Karnataka	6.5474		Karnataka	8.6312
	Uttar Pradesh	5.856		Uttaranchal	5.3536
30	Punjab	19.89	30	Haryana	21.69
	Haryana	19.467		Maharashtra	14.241
	Maharashtra	17.188		Punjab	12.43
	West Bengal	7.69		Uttaranchal	10.686
	Tamil Nadu	7.6181		Tamil Nadu	7.1179
31	Maharashtra	43.944	31	Maharashtra	24.127
	Karnataka	8.0115		Tamil Nadu	17.51
	Tamil Nadu	7.4186		Karnataka	10.052
	Uttar Pradesh	5.1829		Rajasthan	9.7221
	Andhra Pradesh	4.7679		Uttar Pradesh	9.0654

Note: Authors calculation based on ASI, 2006 and 2015, NIC denotes National Industrial Classification.

Given that the bulk of the existing literature on the regional distribution of the manufacturing sector in India primarily focuses on formal manufacturing, we extend this to include the informal sector to overcome the limitation of the previous studies. Since 90% of the manufacturing workers in India belong to the informal sector, it is imperative to analyse the spatial distribution of informal sector manufacturing (Ramachandran & Sasidharan, 2021). In the next section, we analyse the trends and patterns of the spatial distribution of informal manufacturing.

3. Informal Manufacturing Sector in India

Informal activities in developing economies contribute to gross domestic product in the form of employment generation and industrial output (ILO, 2011–2012).

However, the contribution of informal sector in non-agriculture gross value added varies from 14% in eastern European and central Asian countries to as high as 50% in sub-Saharan Africa. Furthermore, regarding employment, 24% of employment in transition economies are involved in informal sector. Similarly, 50% of Latin American and 70% of sub-Saharan African workers are part of informal sector (Jutting & de Laiglesia, 2009; Marjit & Kar, 2009).

According to the Labour Force Participation Survey 2017–2018, more than 80% of manufacturing workers in India engaged in the informal sector. This figure includes all the workers in the informal sector and the informal sector workers in the formal sector on contract. Informal manufacturing sector in India consists of all other manufacturing enterprises not part of sections 2 m(i) and 2m(ii) of the factories act, 1948; manufacturing enterprises covered under section 85 of factories act, 1948; and beedi and cigar enterprises which are not registered under Beedi and Cigar Workers Act, 1966. Furthermore, those enterprises included in the informal manufacturing sector are categorised as: (i) own account manufacturing enterprises (OAMEs) and establishments – includes enterprises without any hired workers regularly. On the other hand, establishments employ a minimum one hired worker regularly. Establishments can be further classified as (i) non-directory manufacturing establishments (NDMEs) – which employ one to five workers and (ii) directory manufacturing establishment (DMEs) – which employ six or more than six workers.

According to the NSSO 62nd and 73rd survey, OAMEs account for dominant share of the enterprises. At the all India level, 85.6% enterprises belong to the OAME category, while the remaining 14.4% belong to establishments (DMEs and NDMEs) during 2005–2006, and this composition remains virtually unchanged even after a decade. Similarly, there is no significant change in the share of OAMEs and establishments in rural areas during the same period (with a share of 91.6 and 8.4, respectively). In the case of urban areas, the share of OAMEs increased from 70.8% in 2005–2006 to 76.5% by 2015–2016. On the other hand, establishments recorded a decline from 29.10% to 23.4% during the same period.

Another important feature of the informal manufacturing sector is the migration of informal sector into the urban areas. During 1989–2005, there is a substantial movement of formal sector from urban areas to rural areas, which recorded a decline of employment share from 69% to 57%. During the same period, on the other hand, the share of informal manufacturing employment in urban region increased from 25% to 37% (Ghani et al., 2011a, 2011b). Therefore, it is argued that the urbanisation in developing economies is occurring through informal sector. Hence, given the dynamics of informal sector, it becomes imperative for urban and regional policy makers to recognise the regional distribution of informal activity.

In Table 6.3, we analyse the migration pattern of informal manufacturing sector statewise during the 2005–2015 period. Like the overall pattern, statewise figures also show the migration of informal manufacturing sector from the rural areas to urban areas. Comparison between NSSO 62nd and NSSO 73rd rounds reveals a substantial informal sector movement within the states. Among the Indian states (without considering union territories), Sikkim shows

Table 6.3.   Statewise Rural–Urban Distribution of Enterprises (in %).

State	62nd (2005–2006)		73rd (2015–2016)		CAGR (2005–2015)
	Rural	Urban	Rural	Urban	
Andhra Pradesh	70.78	29.21	55.78	44.21	4.2
Arunachal Pradesh	62.98	37.01	38.68	61.31	5.1
Assam	89.81	10.18	80.63	19.36	6.6
Bihar	85.88	14.11	71.26	28.73	7.3
Chhattisgarh	83.19	16.8	67.9	32.09	6.6
Delhi	3.727	96.27	0.755	99.24	0.3
Goa	44.1	55.89	24.45	75.54	3
Gujarat	45.96	54.03	23.57	76.42	3.5
Haryana	52.01	47.98	47.13	52.86	0.9
Himachal Pradesh	93.48	6.519	88.75	11.24	5.5
Jammu & Kashmir	81	18.99	64.73	35.26	6.3
Jharkhand	92.2	7.798	88.22	11.77	4.2
Karnataka	68.95	31.04	56.75	43.24	3.3
Kerala	74.81	25.18	47.97	52.02	7.5
Madhya Pradesh	66.05	33.94	61.87	38.12	1.1
Maharashtra	49.37	50.62	47.76	52.23	0.3
Manipur	68.16	31.83	66.06	33.93	0.6
Meghalaya	93.31	6.688	79.11	20.88	12
Mizoram	64.53	35.48	45.69	54.3	4.3
Nagaland	72.35	27.64	70.8	29.19	0.5
Odisha	90.97	9.021	83.97	16.02	5.9
Punjab	51.22	48.77	46.38	53.61	0.9
Rajasthan	62.98	37.01	45.64	54.35	3.9
Sikkim	89.78	10.23	60.25	39.74	14.5
Tamil Nadu	57.38	42.61	36.69	63.3	4
Telangana	–	–	60.99	39	0
Tripura	85.73	14.26	69.09	30.9	8
Uttar Pradesh	72.24	27.75	60.06	39.93	3.7
Uttaranchal	78.07	21.92	62.86	37.13	5.4
West Bengal	80.78	19.21	74.48	25.51	2.8
Andaman & Nicobar Islands	80.82	19.17	48.73	51.26	10.3

Table 6.3. (*Continued*)

State	62nd (2005–2006)		73rd (2015–2016)		CAGR (2005–2015)
	Rural	**Urban**	**Rural**	**Urban**	
Chandigarh	54.84	45.22	3.564	96.43	7.8
Dadra & Nagar Haveli	82.24	17.85	58.43	41.56	8.8
Daman & Diu	55.47	44.52	27.66	72.33	4.9
Lakshadweep	64.23	35.76	5.698	94.3	10.1
Pondicherry	29.89	70.09	19.95	80.04	1.3

Note: (i) Compiled from different NSSO reports; (ii) CAGR (2005–2015) shows the compound annual growth rate of informal manufacturing in urban areas.

the highest annual growth rate of migration from rural areas to urban areas (14.5%). Among the industrially developed states, Andhra Pradesh reports the highest amount of informal sector migration (with an annual rate of 4.2%), followed by Tamil Nadu (4%) and Uttar Pradesh (3.7%). At the same time, Maharashtra recorded only a 0.3% growth rate in the movement of informal sector from rural to urban areas.

To identify the concentration of different industry groups within the informal sector, we measure the industrial agglomeration of 59 NIC three digit informal sector enterprises. Table 6.4 provides the agglomeration pattern of all the industries. In 2006, 36 industries were listed as highly concentrated industries. Manufacture of weapons and ammunition is the highest concentrated industry, followed by the manufacture of irradiation equipment and non-metallic mineral products. By 2015–2006, the list of highly concentrated industries expanded and 42 industries were listed as highly concentrated. Compared to the year 2006, the number of least concentrated industries increased from 6 to 10 by 2015. However, during the same period, 40 industries recorded an increase in the EG index value. Therefore, compared to the formal sector, informal sector shows agglomeration. This trend may be because of the migration of informal sector workers from rural to urban areas (Ghani & Kanpur, 2011).

Table 6.4 presents agglomerated industries at the three-digit level. Finally, Table 6.5 reports the distribution of informal industry categories across various Indian states. Table 6.5 reports the top five states in each of the two digit industries based on the share of employment. Compared to the formal sector (which shows a consistency in the top five states during 2005–2015), the informal sector shows a changing trend in the employment share of top five states by each industry. To cite an example, for the year 2005, informal employment in the manufacture of beverages was concentrated in states like West Bengal, Uttar Pradesh, Bihar, Odisha, and Madhya Pradesh. However, by 2015, except for the state of Odisha, other states were no longer in the top five lists. Similarly, only Tamil Nadu retained its position among the top five states in the case of wood products.

Table 6.4. Industrial Agglomeration Pattern of Informal Sector (2006–2015).

	2006			2015	
NIC 3 Digit	Description	EG Index	NIC 3 Digit	Description	EG Index
	Highly concentrated (EG > 0.05)				
252	Manufacture of weapons and ammunition	0.956	266	Manufacture of irradiation equipment	0.92
266	Manufacture of irradiation equipment	0.902	203	Manufacture of man-made fibres	0.763
239	Manufacture of non-metallic mineral products	0.421	252	Manufacture of weapons and ammunition	0.538
302	Manufacture of railway locomotives and rolling stock	0.323	102	Processing and preserving of fish, crustaceans, and molluscs	0.45
139	Manufacture of other textiles	0.302	231	Manufacture of glass and glass products	0.424
291	Manufacture of motor vehicles	0.286	108	Manufacture of prepared animal feeds	0.372
279	Manufacture of other electrical equipment	0.278	267	Manufacture of optical instruments	0.354
107	Manufacture of other food products	0.267	210	Manufacture of pharmaceuticals	0.35
282	Manufacture of special-purpose machinery	0.202	264	Manufacture of consumer electronics	0.35
162	Manufacture of products of wood, cork, straw, and plaiting materials	0.191	302	Manufacture of railway locomotives and rolling stock	0.343
259	Manufacture of other fabricated metal products	0.177	291	Manufacture of motor vehicles	0.341

Code	Industry	Value
272	Manufacture of batteries and accumulators	0.302
279	Manufacture of other electrical equipment	0.252
192	Manufacture of refined petroleum products	0.24
201	Manufacture of basic chemicals	0.235
265	Manufacture of measuring equipment	0.235
274	Manufacture of electric lighting equipment	0.231
182	Reproduction of recorded media	0.225
191	Manufacture of coke oven products	0.186
202	Manufacture of other chemical products	0.182
309	Manufacture of transport equipment	0.177
293	Manufacture of parts and accessories for motor vehicles	0.149
143	Manufacture of knitted and crocheted apparel	0.139
267	Manufacture of optical instruments	0.169
203	Manufacture of man-made fibres	0.163
309	Manufacture of transport equipment	0.156
281	Manufacture of general purpose machinery	0.14
143	Manufacture of knitted and crocheted apparel	0.119
202	Manufacture of other chemical products	0.119
301	Building of ships and boats	0.116
170	Manufacture of paper and paper products	0.111
110	Manufacture of beverages	0.109
102	Processing and preserving of fish, crustaceans, and molluscs	0.106
131	Spinning, weaving, and finishing of textiles	0.099
251	Manufacture of structural metal products	0.099

(Continued)

Table 6.4. *(Continued)*

	2006			2015	
NIC 3 Digit	Description	EG Index	NIC 3 Digit	Description	EG Index
273	Manufacture of wiring and wiring devices	0.094	275	Manufacture of domestic appliances	0.128
263	Manufacture of communication equipment	0.093	273	Manufacture of wiring and wiring devices	0.125
261	Manufacture of electronic components	0.084	271	Manufacture of electric motors	0.121
108	Manufacture of prepared animal feeds	0.082	281	Manufacture of general purpose machinery	0.118
192	Manufacture of refined petroleum products	0.082	301	Building of ships and boats	0.104
264	Manufacture of consumer electronics	0.08	152	Manufacture of footwear	0.1
182	Reproduction of recorded media	0.077	142	Manufacture of articles of fur	0.096
243	Casting of metals	0.077	261	Manufacture of electronic components	0.094
151	Tanning and dressing of leather	0.07	263	Manufacture of communication equipment	0.089
201	Manufacture of basic chemicals	0.069	103	Processing and preserving of fruit and vegetables	0.08
191	Manufacture of coke oven products	0.067	242	Manufacture of basic precious and other non-ferrous metals	0.079
231	Manufacture of glass and glass products	0.06	151	Tanning and dressing of leather	0.078

139	Manufacture of other textiles	0.069
110	Manufacture of beverages	0.067
104	Manufacture of vegetable and animal oils and fats	0.064
292	Manufacture of bodies for motor vehicles	0.062
181	Printing and service activities related to printing	0.057
241	Manufacture of basic iron and steel	0.056
243	Casting of metals	0.054
120	Manufacture of tobacco products	0.051
Concentrated (0.05 > EG > 0.02)		
274	Manufacture of electric lighting equipment	0.049
222	Manufacture of plastics products	0.048
265	Manufacture of measuring equipment	0.047
221	Manufacture of rubber products	0.047
106	Manufacture of grain mill products, starches, and starch products	0.046
131	Spinning, weaving, and finishing of textiles	0.046
170	Manufacture of paper and paper products	0.046
221	Manufacture of rubber products	0.044
210	Manufacture of pharmaceuticals	0.042
142	Manufacture of articles of fur	0.039
105	Manufacture of dairy products	0.036
282	Manufacture of special-purpose machinery	0.034

(Continued)

Table 6.4. (*Continued*)

	2006			2015	
NIC 3 Digit	Description	EG Index	NIC 3 Digit	Description	EG Index
293	Manufacture of parts and accessories for motor vehicles	0.039	101	Processing and preserving of meat	0.025
275	Manufacture of domestic appliances	0.036			
105	Manufacture of dairy products	0.034			
222	Manufacture of plastics products	0.033			
271	Manufacture of electric motors	0.03			
103	Processing and preserving of fruit and vegetables	0.029			
292	Manufacture of bodies for motor vehicles	0.028			
152	Manufacture of footwear	0.027			
120	Manufacture of tobacco products	0.026			
241	Manufacture of basic iron and steel	0.026			
242	Manufacture of basic precious and other non-ferrous metals	0.023			

Least concentrated (0 < EG < 0.02)

Code	Industry	EG	Code	Industry	EG
141	Manufacture of wearing apparel, except fur apparel	0.004	141	Manufacture of wearing apparel, except fur apparel	0.002
310	Manufacture of furniture	0.004	310	Manufacture of furniture	0.005
161	Sawmilling and planning of wood	0.008	107	Manufacture of other food products	0.006
104	Manufacture of vegetable and animal oils and fats	0.013	181	Printing and service activities related to printing	0.006
101	Processing and preserving of meat	0.014	251	Manufacture of structural metal products	0.008
272	Manufacture of batteries and accumulators	0.015	106	Manufacture of grain mill products, starches, and starch products	0.009
			259	Manufacture of other fabricated metal products	0.011
			162	Manufacture of products of wood, cork, straw, and plaiting materials	0.012
			161	Sawmilling and planning of wood	0.016
			239	Manufacture of non-metallic mineral products	0.019

Note: Authors own calculation using NSSO 67th and 73rd round survey.

Table 6.5.   Informal Sector Employment Share of Top Five States.

2006			2015		
NIC	**State**	**Share (%)**	**NIC**	**State**	**Share (%)**
10	Uttar Pradesh	13.68	10	Uttar Pradesh	10.96
	Tamil Nadu	8.06		Tamil Nadu	10.33
	West Bengal	7.925		Andhra Pradesh	9.767
	Andhra Pradesh	7.293		West Bengal	9.069
	Gujarat	7.01		Maharashtra	6.386
11	West Bengal	24.1	11	Andhra Pradesh	13.42
	Uttar Pradesh	13.49		Tamil Nadu	11.01
	Bihar	9.731		Odisha	8.981
	Odisha	9.242		Jharkhand	8.472
	Madhya Pradesh	5.623		Kerala	7.962
12	Tamil Nadu	23.81	12	Andhra Pradesh	24.18
	Bihar	8.163		Madhya Pradesh	15.32
	Uttar Pradesh	8.016		West Bengal	13.67
	Andhra Pradesh	7.649		Tamil Nadu	10.47
	Kerala	7.503		Karnataka	8.697
13	Maharashtra	13.26	13	Tamil Nadu	19.59
	Andhra Pradesh	10.41		Uttar Pradesh	16.99
	Tamil Nadu	9.71		West Bengal	15.92
	Uttar Pradesh	9.34		Maharashtra	5.019
	Madhya Pradesh	7.561		Gujarat	4.702
14	Tamil Nadu	13.58	14	Tamil Nadu	10.38
	Andhra Pradesh	8.859		Uttar Pradesh	9.428
	Gujarat	8.337		Andhra Pradesh	8.79
	Maharashtra	8.116		West Bengal	8.723
	Rajasthan	7.833		Maharashtra	6.991
15	Andhra Pradesh	14.82	15	Uttar Pradesh	24.69
	Tamil Nadu	14.82		West Bengal	18.48
	Maharashtra	14.77		Tamil Nadu	12.4
	Madhya Pradesh	8.768		Delhi	7.02
	Gujarat	6.784		Andhra Pradesh	5.346

Table 6.5. (*Continued*)

2006			2015		
NIC	**State**	**Share (%)**	**NIC**	**State**	**Share (%)**
16	Uttar Pradesh	17.25	16	Tamil Nadu	11.67
	West Bengal	11.35		Uttar Pradesh	8.806
	Bihar	7.614		West Bengal	7.869
	Odisha	6.347		Karnataka	6.295
	Andhra Pradesh	5.183		Jammu & Kashmir	6.117
17	Maharashtra	14.39	17	Delhi	20.75
	Jharkhand	11.95		Tamil Nadu	13.69
	Tamil Nadu	10.15		Uttar Pradesh	11.92
	Rajasthan	8.997		West Bengal	9.211
	Andhra Pradesh	7.84		Karnataka	5.488
18	Tamil Nadu	21.55	18	Kerala	11.6
	Maharashtra	12.77		Tamil Nadu	10.95
	Karnataka	10.74		West Bengal	8.023
	Gujarat	8.986		Uttar Pradesh	7.566
	Rajasthan	7.195		Maharashtra	7.566
19	West Bengal	21.5	19	West Bengal	22.79
	Uttar Pradesh	18.27		Uttar Pradesh	12.5
	Odisha	11.82		Andhra Pradesh	12.5
	Dadra & Nagar Haveli	7.526		Tamil Nadu	12.5
	Meghalaya	4.301		Tripura	7.352
20	Tamil Nadu	21.44	20	Tamil Nadu	55.38
	Rajasthan	8.576		West Bengal	6.102
	Uttar Pradesh	8.026		Karnataka	5.995
	Andhra Pradesh	7.586		Delhi	4.532
	Maharashtra	6.816		Andhra Pradesh	3.604
21	Uttar Pradesh	14.46	21	Uttar Pradesh	26.39
	Jammu & Kashmir	8.805		West Bengal	14.21
	Gujarat	8.805		Kerala	9.644
	Madhya Pradesh	7.547		Karnataka	7.106
	Kerala	7.547		Andhra Pradesh	6.598

(*Continued*)

Table 6.5.   (*Continued*)

2006			2015		
NIC	State	Share (%)	NIC	State	Share (%)
22	Tamil Nadu	22.67	22	Delhi	20.62
	Maharashtra	10.24		Tamil Nadu	14.68
	Rajasthan	9.431		West Bengal	13.07
	Andhra Pradesh	8.494		Gujarat	6.093
	Gujarat	8.432		Kerala	5.625
23	Uttar Pradesh	12.51	23	West Bengal	21.51
	West Bengal	10.91		Uttar Pradesh	14.61
	Bihar	9.426		Tamil Nadu	11.31
	Punjab	7.606		Madhya Pradesh	8.977
	Andhra Pradesh	5.459		Andhra Pradesh	6.647
24	Uttar Pradesh	13.94	24	Delhi	19.64
	Gujarat	11.45		Uttar Pradesh	16.46
	Tamil Nadu	10.65		West Bengal	13.09
	Maharashtra	8.366		Gujarat	8.035
	Andhra Pradesh	8.167		Tamil Nadu	6.349
25	Tamil Nadu	10.53	25	Uttar Pradesh	12.13
	Maharashtra	9.213		Maharashtra	7.96
	Uttar Pradesh	9.001		Tamil Nadu	7.875
	Andhra Pradesh	8.007		West Bengal	7.242
	West Bengal	7.034		Kerala	5.682
26	Rajasthan	19.55	26	Haryana	19.64
	Maharashtra	15.08		Uttar Pradesh	11.73
	Andhra Pradesh	14.52		Delhi	11.43
	Tamil Nadu	12.84		West Bengal	11.14
	Gujarat	9.217		Pondicherry	10.55
27	Tamil Nadu	21.13	27	Delhi	22.56
	Rajasthan	9.453		West Bengal	16.31
	Andhra Pradesh	9.346		Maharashtra	7.886
	Maharashtra	9.134		Uttar Pradesh	5.366
	Gujarat	8.072		Punjab	5.257

Table 6.5. (*Continued*)

2006			2015		
NIC	State	Share (%)	NIC	State	Share (%)
28	Tamil Nadu	13.71	28	Punjab	13.74
	Maharashtra	10.4		Uttar Pradesh	11.21
	Madhya Pradesh	9.205		Tamil Nadu	10.5
	Uttar Pradesh	8.664		Gujarat	8.925
	Rajasthan	8.002		Maharashtra	8.767
29	Andhra Pradesh	16	29	Maharashtra	17.41
	Gujarat	15.57		Tamil Nadu	12.43
	Tamil Nadu	13.05		Uttar Pradesh	8.955
	Maharashtra	9.684		Haryana	7.794
	Madhya Pradesh	9.263		West Bengal	7.296
30	Madhya Pradesh	32.62	30	Punjab	15.64
	Chhattisgarh	14.11		West Bengal	14.96
	Tamil Nadu	10.77		Kerala	14.28
	Andhra Pradesh	10.16		Jharkhand	8.163
	Maharashtra	8.497		Tamil Nadu	8.163
31	Uttar Pradesh	13.46	31	West Bengal	13.59
	Gujarat	10.58		Uttar Pradesh	10.73
	Tamil Nadu	8.944		Assam	5.745
	Andhra Pradesh	8.047		Andhra Pradesh	5.545
	Rajasthan	6.675		Madhya Pradesh	5.448

Note: Authors' calculation based on NSSO, 2005–2006 and 2015–2016.

4. Concluding Remarks

Understanding the location of economic activity can assist rural and urban poli-cymakers in policy framing. This chapter endeavours to depict a detailed picture of the spatial distribution pattern of the manufacturing sector in India. It is evident that India is also characterised by regional concentration of economic activity in some specific states, same as other economies. However, despite this higher regional concentration of industrial activity, the more recent distribution pattern of formal manufacturing activity shows a sign of dispersion than further agglomeration. On the other hand, the informal manufacturing sector reports a decline in the informal activities in the rural areas in terms of the number of enterprises and the number of workers, which indicates the migration of the informal manufacturing activity from rural areas to urban areas.

References

Cainelli, G., Fracasso, A., & Vittucci Marzetti, G. (2015). Spatial agglomeration and productivity in Italy: A panel smooth transition regression approach. *Papers in Regional Science, 94*, S39–S67.

Dong, F., Wang, Y., Zheng, L., Li, J., & Xie, S. (2020). Can industrial agglomeration promote pollution agglomeration? Evidence from China. *Journal of Cleaner Production, 246*, 118960.

Ellison, G., & Glaeser, E. L. (1997). Geographic concentration in US manufacturing industries: A dartboard approach. *Journal of Political Economy, 105*(5), 889–927.

Ellison, G., & Glaeser, E. L. (1999). The geographic concentration of industry: Does natural advantage explain agglomeration?. *American Economic Review, 89*(2), 311–316.

Fan, C. C., & Scott, A. J. (2003). Industrial agglomeration and development: A survey of spatial economic issues in East Asia and a statistical analysis of Chinese regions. *Economic Geography, 79*(3), 295–319.

Ghani, E., Goswami, A. G., & Kerr, W. R. (2012). *Is India's manufacturing sector moving away from cities?* (No. w17992). National Bureau of Economic Research.

Ghani, S. E., & Kanbur, R. (2013). *Urbanization and (in) formalization* [World Bank Policy Research Working Paper No. 6374].

Jutting, J., & Laiglesia, J. R. D. (2009). Is informal normal?: Towards more and better jobs in developing countries. Development Centre of the Organisation for Economic Co-operation and Development.

Li, X., Xu, Y., & Yao, X. (2021). Effects of industrial agglomeration on haze pollution: A Chinese city-level study. *Energy Policy, 148*, 111928.

Lu, J., & Tao, Z. (2009). Trends and determinants of China's industrial agglomeration. *Journal of Urban Economics, 65*(2), 167–180.

Marjit, S., & Kar, S. (2009). A contemporary perspective on the informal labour market: Theory, policy and the Indian experience. *Economic and Political weekly*, 60–71.

Mukim, M. (2015). Coagglomeration of formal and informal industry: Evidence from India. *Journal of Economic Geography, 15*(2), 329–351.

Ramachandran, R., Sasidharan, S., & Doytch, N. (2020). Foreign direct investment and industrial agglomeration: Evidence from India. Economic Systems, 44(4), 100777.

Ramachandran, R., & Sasidharan, S. (2021). Co-location of formal and informal manufacturing and firm's performance: Evidence from India. *The Indian Economic Journal, 69*(4), 600–613.

Rosenthal, S. S., & Strange, W. C. (2001). The determinants of agglomeration. *Journal of Urban Economics, 50*(2), 191–229.

Tveteras, R., & Battese, G. E. (2006). Agglomeration externalities, productivity, and technical inefficiency. *Journal of Regional Science, 46*(4), 605–625.

Chapter 7

Foreign Capital Inflow, Product Market Imperfection, and the Informal Sector: A General Equilibrium Analysis

Sushobhan Mahata[a], Rohan Kanti Khan[b], Soumyajit Mandal[c] and Avishek Bose[a,d]

[a]*Department of Economics, University of Calcutta, Kolkata, West Bengal, India*
[b]*Department of Applied Economics, Maulana Abul Kalam Azad University of Technology, Kolkata, West Bengal, India*
[c]*Department of Economics, St. Xavier's College (Autonomous), Kolkata, West Bengal, India*
[d]*University of Calcutta, Kolkata, West Bengal, India*

Abstract

With the onset of globalization in developing economies, policymakers express serious concerns about the role of the informal economy, a concern also mirrored in the United Nations (UN) sustainable development goals (SDGs). Numerous attempts have been made to analyse the general equilibrium consequences of globalization in terms of foreign capital inflow on the informal sector in a developing economy. These studies examined the impact of foreign capital inflow through the channels of resource reallocation across sectors and adjustment in the factor and commodity prices. Nevertheless, the efficacy of these channels is contingent upon the assumption of perfectly competitive product markets that is pertinent in the majority of the studies. This chapter attempts to incorporate imperfect competition in the informal economy in a Heckscher–Ohlin-type multi-factor, multi-sector general equilibrium setup. We assume the existence of imperfection in both a homogeneous good-producing industry and a product-differentiating industry and examine how foreign capital inflow in the presence of imperfect competition affects the informal workers, industrial and firm output, product diversity, national income, and welfare. We also

Informal Economy and Sustainable Development Goals:
Ideas, Interventions and Challenges, 127–154
Published under exclusive licence by Emerald Publishing Limited
doi:10.1108/978-1-83753-980-220241007

analyse how the consequences of foreign capital inflow on the informal economy can vary with the degree of product market imperfection. It is obtained that varying degrees of product market imperfection in the informal economy have only quantitative (magnitude) effects; however, qualitative (directional) effects remain unchanged.

Keywords: Imperfect product market; general equilibrium; foreign capital inflow; differentiated product; informal sector; sustainable development

1. Introduction, Literature, and Motivation

The role of the informal sector is paramount all over the world, especially in developing economies. According to the International Labour Organization (ILO), the informal economy encompasses more than 6 out of 10 workers and 4 out of 5 enterprises.[1] Based on the findings of ILO (2018), it is evident that the informal sector employs 60% of the world's employed population, with approximately 2 billion men and women living in the informal economy without decent working conditions. The concern of informatization has also been reflected (directly or indirectly) in the UNSDGs. In 2015, the United Nations adopted the SDGs to achieve the 2030 agenda to foster economic well-being, tackle disparities, and safeguard the environment.[2] The objective of *SDG 8* is to 'promote sustained, inclusive and sustainable economic growth, full and productive employment and decent work for all'. Within this framework, *target 8.3* aims to advocate for 'development-oriented policies' that bolster 'productive activities', facilitate the creation of 'decent jobs', promote 'entrepreneurship, creativity and innovation', and it also endorses the 'formalization and growth of micro-, small- and medium-sized enterprises, including access to financial services' that is directly concerned about the formalization of the economy.[3] However, there are other SDGs like SDG 1 (no poverty), SDG 5 (gender equality), SDG 10 (reduced inequalities), SDG 16 (peace, justice, and strong institutions), and SDG 17 (partnerships for the goals), indirectly pertinent to the concept of informality. Initiatives geared towards progressively formalizing the informal economy will contribute to the advancement of these interconnected goals.[4]

The onset of globalization and liberalization has stimulated an intensified discourse among researchers concerning the informal economy. Additionally,

---

[1]For more details, see https://www.ilo.org/global/topics/employment-promotion/informal-economy/lang-en/index.htm.

[2]The details regarding the SDGs are retrieved from https://www.undp.org/sustainable-development-goals.

[3]The precise targets outlined within different SDGs are obtained from https://sdgs.un.org/.

[4]For more discussion related to informal economy and SDGs, visit https://www.ilo.org/global/topics/dw4sd/themes/informal-economy/lang-en/index.htm#1.

UNCTAD (2004) contends that globalization and liberalization policies are interconnected with sustainable development in specific cases. Therefore, a critical examination is necessary to explore the impact of foreign capital inflow, a key element of globalization, on the informal economy within a developing nation. This chapter attempts to address this question.

In the realm of trade theory, Jones's general equilibrium analysis gained importance in the understanding of the informal economy and its dimensions, especially in developing economies. Ronald Jones's seminal contribution in providing a formal and simple structured general equilibrium (GE, henceforth) model has widely impacted various sub-domains of economics, for example public economics, development economics, labour economics, and international trade policies, including the intersection of these sub-disciplines. The basic models in the early works such as Jones (1965, 1971) and Jones and Neary (1984) have not only been extended to many sub-domains of economics but several micro-foundations have been provided in later works by scholars across the globe analysing a variety of policy issues using such applied general equilibrium models. The common feature includes the assumption of a perfectly competitive factor and commodity market, the production functions are characterized by constant returns to scale technology, factors are mobile across sectors, and in the absence of any distortion, all factors are fully employed. Commodity prices are usually taken as a datum owing to the assumption of a small open economy. The results are qualitative rather than quantitative given the simple assumptions with a limited set of parameters that fail to capture the complexity of several interconnected parameters. These basic assumptions have turned out to be the major limitations of such GE models. However, over time numerous attempts have been made to make the GE models more rigorous. These include incorporating factor–market distortions, rural–urban migration, endogenized labour supply, neo-classical growth dynamics, etc. (for some relevant works, see Chaudhuri & Yabuuchi, 2007; Gupta, 2020; Marjit & Mandal, 2016, among others). In the past few years, these GE models have attracted heavy criticism for such simplistic assumptions. Among all the criticisms, the most highlighted is the assumption of a perfectly competitive final product market.

In the realm of general equilibrium literature, a substantial amount of scholarly works has been focused on the relationship between globalization and the informal economy. The work of Chaudhuri and Mukhopadhyay (2013), Maiti and Marjit (2008), Marjit et al. (2007), Chaudhuri and Banerjee (2007), and Chaudhuri and Yabuuchi (2007) is among many others that give emphasis on the debate surrounding economic reforms in the light of globalization and liberalization and the informal economy. Furthermore, the general equilibrium framework has been employed to analyse other dimensions, such as the informal credit market (Chaudhuri & Gupta, 2014), migration and informal economy (Chaudhuri, 2000; Marjit & Mandal, 2016), economic recession and informal economy (Chaudhuri, 2009; Mahata et al., 2020; Marjit et al., 2011), corruption and informal economy (Khan et al., 2022; Mahata et al., 2023; Marjit et al., 2014), pandemic and informal economy (Khan et al., 2023; Mahata et al., 2022), among many others. However, this literature exhibits limitations in relation to the features of the general equilibrium models, as previously discussed.

Against this backdrop, the purpose of this chapter is twofold. Initially, we attempt to integrate product market imperfections into the Jonesian simple general equilibrium structure in the presence of the informal sector. This involves incorporating a homogeneous good-producing oligopolistic industry, a differentiated good-producing monopolistic industry, in addition to the perfectly competitive industry. Hence, it introduces a combination of imperfectly competitive and perfectly competitive industries, deviating from the universal assumption of competitive product markets. This departure alleviates the constraints associated with conventional general equilibrium models. Secondly, our objective is to investigate the influence of product market imperfections on determining the magnitude and direction of equilibrium values for variables such as informal wage, informal sector production, the number of product varieties, real national income, and welfare. This examination is conducted in the context of an exogenous shock, specifically in terms of foreign capital inflow. The majority of the scholarships have used a competitive general equilibrium set up to analyse the effect of foreign capital inflow, a few of these include Gupta (1997, 1998), Beladi and Marjit (2000), Gupta and Basu (2004), Chaudhuri (2014), Chaudhuri and Biswas (2016), Chaudhuri et al. (2016), Chaudhuri and Chaudhuri (2019), among others.[5] This analysis delves into how the attributes of the informal economy influence the effects of foreign capital inflow, shedding light on implications for SDGs. We show that the variation in the degree of product market imperfection has only quantitative (magnitude) effects; however, qualitative (directional) results remain unchanged owing to an inflow of foreign capital. Interestingly, we also obtained that as the degree of product market imperfection plummets, it becomes difficult for the product differentiating industry to survive and it vanishes in the extreme case of complete absence of market power.

The itinerary of the chapter is as follows. In Section 2, we describe the basic structure of the model that incorporates a homogeneous good producing an imperfectly competitive informal industry and analyse the effect of foreign capital inflow. In Section 3, the basic model is extended by incorporating a product-differentiating informal industry characterized by increasing returns to scale. In Section 4, the limiting cases of the variation in the degree of product market imperfection are analysed. Finally, Section 5 concludes the chapter.

2. The Model

We consider a small open developing economy with two broad final commodity production industries: a homogeneous good-producing competitive industry (sector 1) and another homogeneous good-producing oligopolistic industry

---

[5]There are exceptions with regard to incorporation of commodity market imperfection in GE set-up. Some of the pioneering works include Helpman (1981), Chao and Yu (1997), Konishi et al. (1990), Neary (2003a, 2003b), Gupta and Dutta (2012), among many others; however, most of these existing papers are either based on Ricardian type one factor economy or these have not considered explicitly the role of the degree of product market imperfection in influencing the results of various trade policies.

(sector 3). Both sector 1 and sector 3 comprise the informal economy. Sector 1 is an export sector, while sector 3 is a non-traded industry. Commodity 2 is assumed to be entirely imported and consumed by the domestic residents. The economy is endowed with two main factors of production –informal labour ($\bar{L}$) and capital ($\bar{K}$). The aggregate capital stock in the economy is composed of domestic capital stock ($\bar{K}_D$) and foreign capital stock ($\bar{K}_F$).

Firstly, let us elucidate the demand side of the economy. The economy is populated with a continuum of identical consumers with unit mass, the preference of which is represented by the following utility function:

$$U = D_1^\alpha D_2^\beta D_3^{1-\alpha-\beta} \; ; \; \alpha + \beta < 1 \tag{1}$$

where D_ρ is the consumption demand for good $\rho = \{1,2,3\}$. Commodity 2 is entirely imported at a given world price, P_2^*. The economy is constrained by the following budget equation:

$$Y = D_1 + P_2^* D_2 + P_3 D_3 \tag{2}$$

where P_3 is the domestic price of commodity 3 and the price for commodity 1 is normalized to unity. Y represents the real national income.

Maximization of equation (1) subject to equation (2) yields the following demand functions:

$$D_1(Y) = \alpha Y \tag{3.1}$$

$$D_2(P_2^*,Y) = \frac{\beta Y}{P_2^*} \tag{3.2}$$

$$D_3(P_3,Y) = \frac{(1-\alpha-\beta)Y}{P_3} \tag{3.3}$$

The aggregate volume of imports is given by equation (3.2) since imports are not produced domestically.

The production side of the economy is described as follows. Sector 1 produces a homogeneous commodity (X_1) using informal labour and capital characterized by constant returns to scale technology in a perfectly competitive environment, where w and r are the informal wage and interest rate, respectively. Thus, profit maximization in this sector is implied by the following price-average cost parity condition:

$$w a_{L1} + r a_{K1} = 1 \tag{4}$$

where a_{L1} and a_{K1} are the unit labour and capital requirements in sector 1, respectively.

Industry 3 is an oligopolistic industry that produces a homogeneous product with 'n' number of firms competing simultaneously in a Cournot–Nash fashion, where n is exogenously determined. Each firm in this industry 3 faces an identical marginal cost. The profit equation for the k th firm ($k = 1, 2, \dots n$) is given by the following equation:

$$\pi_{3k} = P_3(X_3)x_{3k} - C(w,r)x_{3k} \tag{5}$$

where x_{3k} is the output produced by the k th firm in the industry. Profit maximization under symmetric equilibria owing to identical marginal cost leads to the following first-order condition:

$$\frac{\partial \pi_{3k}}{\partial x_{3k}} = P_3(.) + x_{3k}P_3{}'(.)\frac{\partial X_3}{\partial x_{3k}} - C'(.) = 0 \tag{6}$$

Given that firms with identical marginal costs in industry 3 compete simultaneously in a Cournot-Nash fashion, thus, equation (6) boils down to the following expression:

$$wa_{L3} + ra_{K3} = P_3\left(1 - \frac{1}{n\varepsilon}\right) \tag{6.1}$$

The right-hand side (RHS) of equation (6.1) is the marginal revenue of each firm, where 'ε' is the absolute value of elasticity of demand and the left-hand side (LHS) is the usual marginal cost function which is identical for all n firms in the industry, where $n\varepsilon > 1$. a_{L3} and a_{K3} are the labour and capital coefficients in this sector, respectively. Symmetric equilibrium owing to identical marginal cost implies $nx_3 = X_3$, using (3.2) this boils down to

$$nx_3 = \frac{(1 - \alpha - \beta)Y}{P_3} \tag{7}$$

Using Shephard's lemma and market clearing conditions, the full-employment conditions are obtained as follows:

$$a_{L1}X_1 + a_{L3}nx_3 = \overline{L} \tag{8}$$

$$a_{K1}X_1 + a_{K3}nx_3 = \overline{K} = \overline{K}_D + \overline{K}_F \tag{9}$$

The trade-balance condition in this economy is given by

$$X_1 - D_1 = P_2^*D_2^* \tag{10}$$

Assuming income accruing to foreign capital owners is completely repatriated, the national income could be expressed in terms of value-added as

$$Y = X_1 + nP_3x_3 - r\overline{K}_F \tag{11}$$

Using equations (4), (6.1), (8), and (9), the national income expression in equation (11) can be expressed in terms of aggregate factor income and profits of n identical firms in sector 3 as[6]

---

[6]The last term in the expression of national income in equation (11.1) represents the total profit earned by all the n firms in the oligopolistic industry (sector 3). Given

$$Y = w\bar{L} + r\bar{K}_D + \frac{P_3 x_3}{\varepsilon} \tag{11.1}$$

The welfare function is proxied by the indirect utility function, V, which is obtained by substituting equations (3.1)–(3.3) in equation (1) which boils down to the following expression:

$$V = U(P_2, P_3, Y) = \alpha^\alpha \beta^\beta (1 - \alpha - \beta)^{1-\alpha-\beta} (P_2^*)^{-\beta} P_3^{\alpha+\beta-1} Y \tag{12}$$

This completes the description of the economy. The main endogenous variables in the model are $w, r, P_3, X_1, x_3, Y, V$ and the four-factor coefficients which are itself a function of factor price ratio owing to cost minimization in each sector with the same number of equations [equations (4), (6.1), (7), (8), (9), (11.1), and (12)]. Equations (4) and (6.1) solve for w and r as a function of P_3. Solving simultaneous equations (8) and (9), we get X_1 and x_3 as a function of P_3. Equation (11.1) solves for Y as a function of P_3. Substituting all these in equation (7), we have one equation in one unknown P_3. Thus, we obtain the final equilibrium value of P_3 as a function of $\bar{K}_F$. Once P_3 is obtained, the final equilibrium values of all the above unknowns can be obtained as a function of $\bar{K}_F$ only. Finally, once the equilibrium values of factor prices are obtained, the values of all variable factor coefficients can be determined. This completes the description of the determination of the equilibrium values of the variables in the general equilibrium system.

2.1. Foreign Capital Inflow and Variation in Commodity Market Imperfection

An increase in foreign capital inflow accentuates the aggregate capital endowment of the economy. Both the informal production sectors (sectors 1 and 3) form a sub-system with two common mobile factors, labour and capital; thus, the factor-intensity condition between the industry would determine the direction of variation in sectoral output and output of each firm as in a standard competitive environment. However, the factor shares in the imperfectly competitive industry (sector 3) depend on the number of firms in this industry. Let us assume that sector 3 is relatively more capital-intensive compared to sector 1 which is implied by the following condition:

$$|\lambda|_{13} = \lambda_{L1}\lambda_{K3} - \lambda_{L3}\lambda_{K1} > 0$$

where $\lambda_{L1} = (a_{L1}X_1/\bar{L})$, $\lambda_{K1} = (a_{K1}X_1/\bar{K})$, $\lambda_{L3} = (na_{L3}x_3/\bar{L})$, and $\lambda_{K3} = (na_{K3}x_3/\bar{K})$ are the factor shares in industry 1 and industry 3, respectively. Alternatively, the

---

that foreign capital income is completely repatriated, thus, national income takes the following form $Y = w\bar{L} + r\bar{K}_D + n\pi_{3k}$. Provided symmetric equilibrium outcome, thus, using equation (7) in the above expression (equation 11), it boils down to equation (11.1).

factor-intensity ranking can be expressed in terms of cost share in each sector as follows:

$$|\theta|_{13} = \theta_{L1}\theta_{K3} - \theta_{L3}\theta_{K1} > 0$$

where θ_{ji} represents the cost share of the j th factor in the i th sector.

Given the above assumption, we explain the primary effects on output, factor prices, national income, and welfare. To obtain the primary effect on output level for given commodity prices, we partially differentiate equations (8) and (9) simultaneously with respect to $\bar{K}_F$ that leads to the following:

$$\frac{\partial x_3}{\partial \bar{K}_F} = \frac{\lambda_{L1}\eta_{KF}x_3}{|\lambda|_{13}\,\bar{K}_F} > 0 \qquad (13)$$

$$\frac{\partial X_1}{\partial \bar{K}_F} = -\frac{\lambda_{L3}\eta_{KF}X_1}{|\lambda|_{13}\,\bar{K}_F} < 0 \qquad (14)$$

where η_{KF} is the physical share of foreign capital in total capital endowment (see Appendix 2.2). The above result is just a consequence of the standard output-magnification effect (Rybczynski effect) where the relatively capital-intensive industry 3 expands, while the labour-intensive industry 1 contracts. Owing to identical marginal costs in the oligopolistic industry (industry 3), the output of each firm in industry 3 increases. Given that profit of each firm in industry 3 increases, thus, Y increases for given commodity prices.

Given the negatively sloped average revenue and marginal revenue curves, an expansion of output of each firm in sector 3 causes its industry-wide price (P_3) to fall, while an increase in Y accentuates the demand for commodity 3 (average revenue) which escalates the value of P_3. We derive that under the sufficient condition $\lambda_{L1} < \lambda_{K_D1}$, the former effect dominates the latter effect, thus P_3 falls.[7] Given the factor-intensity ranking in the value sense, a fall in P_3 causes a fall in the value of r and an increase in the value of w (equations 4 and 6.1); this is the standard Stolper–Samuelson effect. The effect on welfare can be derived by totally differentiating equation (12).

$$\frac{\hat{V}}{\hat{\bar{K}}_F} = \frac{\hat{Y}}{\hat{\bar{K}}_F} - (1-\alpha-\beta)\frac{\hat{P}_3}{\hat{\bar{K}}_F} \qquad (15)$$

where the symbol '∧' is used to represent the relative change in the variable. The effect on welfare includes both positive real income effect and negative price effect. We obtained that under few sufficient conditions $\dfrac{\hat{P}_3}{\hat{\bar{K}}_F} < 0$ and $\dfrac{\hat{Y}}{\hat{\bar{K}}_F} > 0$; thus, welfare improves owing to foreign capital inflow. The following proposition is immediate.

---

[7]See Appendices 1 and 2 for detailed mathematical derivation.

P1. In the presence of oligopolistic competition, an inflow of foreign capital results in an expansion of output of each informal firm in the oligopolistic industry, contraction of output in the competitive informal industry, informal wage improves while returns to capital plummets. Both real national income and welfare improve.

We construct a numerical example to analyse how the variation in the degree of commodity market imperfection captured in terms of variation in the value of 'ε' alters the effect on the equilibrium values of the variables due to foreign capital inflow. We assume the following hypothetical numerical values for the parameters in the model which is consistent with the assumptions in the model: $\lambda_{L1} = 0.8$, $\lambda_{K1} = 0.3$, $\lambda_{L3} = 0.2$, $\lambda_{K3} = 0.7$, $\theta_{L1} = 0.8$, $\theta_{K1} = 0.2$, $\theta_{L3} = 0.3$, $\theta_{K3} = 0.7$, $\eta_{KF} = 0.1$, $\lambda_{3Y} = 0.2$, $\lambda_{KY} = 0.1$, $\lambda_{LY} = 0.7$, $n = 2$, and the cross-price elasticity of substitution between the factors in each sector is assumed to be 0.5. The above data are used to simulate the relationship between the equilibrium values of $\hat{w}$, $\hat{r}$, $\hat{P}_3$, $\hat{Y}$, and $\hat{V}$ against $\bar{K}_F$ for alternative values of ε.

The above figures (Figs. 7.1–7.5) plot the relationship between proportionate change in factor prices, commodity price, real national income, and welfare (measure along the vertical axis) against proportionate change in $\bar{K}_F$ (measured along the horizontal axis) corresponding to the following values of ε: 1.5, 3, 6, 12, and 24. An increase in the value of ε implies a reduction in commodity market imperfection. The solid line, long-dashed line, short-dashed line, dashed-dot line, and dot line correspond to the value of ε: 1.5, 3, 6, 12, and 24, respectively. All the straight lines in Figs. 7.1–7.5 lie in the respective quadrants which confirm the direction of change of the variables due to foreign capital inflow. Notice that in the above figures an increase in the value of ε leaves the quadrant unchanged; however, the slope of the line changes. For example, in Fig. 7.1, the straight line becomes steeper which implies the magnitude of proportionate change in w accentuates as the value of ε is increased. This implies that as the degree of product market imperfection falls in the oligopolistic industry, the magnitude of the effect of foreign capital inflow on accentuating the informal wage becomes larger; however, the quadrant remains unchanged. In other words, a fall in the degree of product market imperfection accelerates the increase in informal wage rate due to an inflow of foreign capital. This clearly shows that variation in commodity market imperfection has only a quantitative effect (magnitude effect), while there is an absence of any qualitative effect (directional effect) on the equilibrium values of the variables. The following propositions are immediate.

P2. An inflow of foreign capital and a lower degree of product market imperfection in the informal economy

> (2a) accelerates the increase in informal wage rate and real national income,
> (2b) accelerate the fall in real returns to capital,
> (2c) dampens the magnitude of increase in social welfare, and
> (2d) decelerates the fall in the price of the imperfectly competitive non-traded industry.

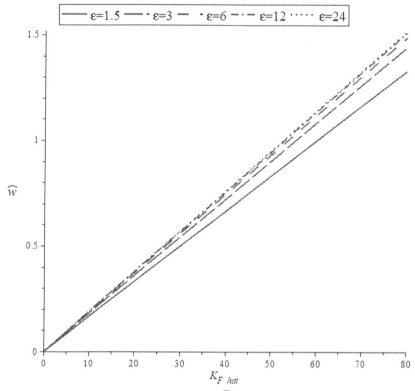

Fig. 7.1.   Effect of Foreign Capital Inflow ($\bar{K}_F$) on w for Different Values of ε.
Source: This figure has been generated based on authors' own construct of numerical values using **MAPLE 2015**.

P3. Variation in the degree of commodity market imperfection has only a quantitative effect, while no qualitative change occurs in the equilibrium values of the endogenous variables owing to an increase in the inflow of foreign capital.

3. An Extension with Product Differentiating Industry

We now relax the assumption that imports are entirely imported by introducing an import-competing industry (sector 2). Commodity 2 is a horizontally differentiated product with 'm' number of domestic brands which are closed substitutes for each other and 'm^*' number of imported (foreign) brands; thus, we define the aggregate output and price index for this commodity in Dixit and Stiglitz (1977) fashion.

$$X_2 = [\sum_{i=1}^{m} x_{2i}^{\sigma-1/\sigma} + \sum_{j=1}^{m^*} x_{2j}^{*\sigma-1/\sigma}]^{\sigma/\sigma-1} \tag{16}$$

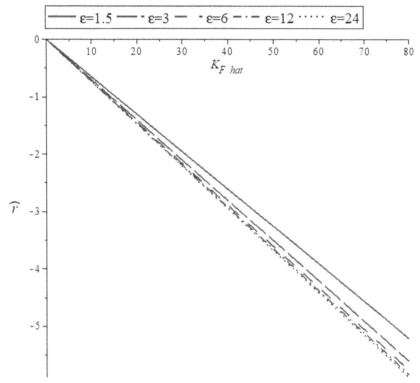

Fig. 7.2.   Effect of $\bar{K}_F$ on r for Different Values of ε. *Source*: This figure has been generated based on authors' own construct of numerical values using MAPLE 2015.

$$P_2 = [\sum_{i=1}^{m} p_{2i}^{1-\sigma} + \sum_{j=1}^{m^*} p_{2i}^{*1-\sigma}]^{1/1-\sigma} \tag{17}$$

where x_{2i} and x_{2j}^{*} are the output of each i th domestic brand and j th foreign brand, respectively, and 'σ' is the price elasticity of demand for the ith variety.[8] Using two-stage budgeting, we obtain the following demand functions.[9]

$$x_{2i} = p_{2i}^{-\sigma} P_2^{\sigma-1} \beta Y \tag{18}$$

$$x_{2i}^{*} = p_{2i}^{-\sigma^*} P_2^{\sigma-1} \beta Y \tag{19}$$

The aggregate output in industry 2 using equation (3.2) boils down to

---

[8]'σ' also implies elasticity of substitution between different domestically produced varieties (see Sen et al., 1997).
[9]See Appendix 2.1 (equations A.17–A.23) for detailed derivation.

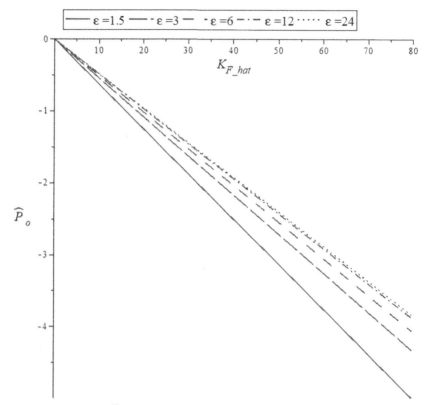

Fig. 7.3.   Effect of $\bar{K}_F$ on P_3 for Different Values of ε. *Source*: This figure has been generated based on authors' own construct of numerical values using MAPLE 2015.

$$X_2 = \frac{\beta Y}{P_2} \qquad (20)$$

In the monopolistically competitive industry (sector 2), there are 'm' number of firms, each firm enjoys market power over its brand that implies equality between marginal revenue and marginal cost at the equilibrium which is given by the following equation:

$$wa_{L2} + ra_{K2} = \frac{p_2(\sigma - 1)}{\sigma} \qquad (21)$$

p_2 is the price for each variety and a_{L2}, a_{K2} are the respective factor-coefficient in each firm within the industry.[10] Finally, Chamberlin's group equilibrium implies

---

[10]Identical technology in the industry implies symmetric equilibria across firms within sector 2, thus the subscripts 'i' are subsequently dropped for the relevant variables.

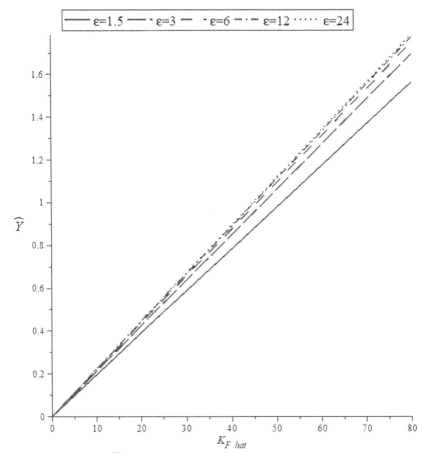

Fig. 7.4. Effect of $\bar{K}_F$ on Y for Different Values of ε. *Source*: This figure has been generated based on authors' own construct of numerical values using MAPLE 2015.

the equality between the price of each variety and the corresponding average cost for each firm, represented by the following equation:

$$wa_{LF} + ra_{KF} = \frac{p_2 x_2}{\sigma} \tag{22}$$

where a_{LF} and a_{KF} are the total amount of labour and capital used in each firm as overhead, and the LHS of equation (22) represents the total overhead expenses for each firm, respectively.

Thus, the full-employment of labour and capital in the economy is given by the following equations, respectively:

$$a_{L1}X_1 + (a_{L2}x_2 + a_{LF})m + a_{L3}nx_3 = \bar{L} \tag{23}$$

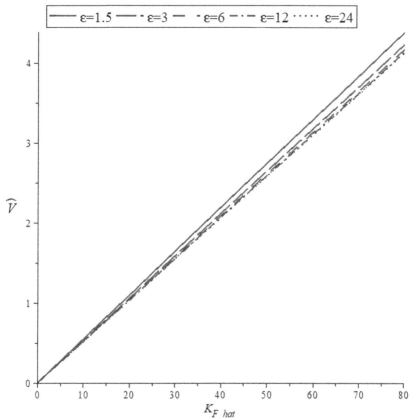

Fig. 7.5.   Effect of $\bar{K}_F$ on V for Different Values of ε. *Source*: This figure has been generated based on authors' own construct of numerical values using MAPLE 2015.

$$a_{K1}X_1 + (a_{K2}x_2 + a_{KF})m + a_{K3}nx_3 = \bar{K} \tag{24}$$

The balanced-trade condition in this economy remains the same as in equation (11); however, the real national income is expressed as follows:

$$Y = X_1 + mp_2x_2 + nP_3x_3 - r\bar{K}_F \tag{25}$$

This completes the description of the economy. The endogenous variables in the model are $w, r, X_1, x_2, p_2, x_2^*, x_3, P_3, Y, m$. Equations (4) and (21) solve for w and r as a function of p_2. Substituting these values in equation (22), we get x_2 as a function of p_2. From equation (6.1), we obtain P_3 as a function of p_2. Solving simultaneous equations (23) and (24), we get X_1 and x_3 as a function of p_2 and m. Equation (11.1) solves for Y as a function of p_2 and m. Substituting all these in equations (7) and (18), we have two equations (say, equations 7.1 and 18.1) in two unknowns p_2 and m. Thus, we obtain the final equilibrium values of P_2 and m as a function for parameters only. Once these are obtained, the equilibrium values of P_2, x_2^*, and X_2 can be solved using equations (17), (19), and (20), respectively. Finally, once the equilibrium values of factor prices are obtained, the values of all variable factor-coefficients can be determined. This completes the determination of the equilibrium values of the variables in this general equilibrium system.

An increase in foreign capital inflow accentuates the aggregate capital endowment of the economy. We consider the direct (primary) effects of foreign capital inflow for given values of other variables.[11] Partially differentiating the equilibrium values of X_1 and x_3, we obtain the following:

$$\frac{\partial X_1}{\partial \bar{K}_F} = -\frac{X_1 \lambda_{L3} \eta_{KF}}{\bar{K}_F |\lambda|_{13}} \tag{26}$$

$$\frac{\partial x_3}{\partial \bar{K}_F} = \frac{x_3 \lambda_{L1} \eta_{KF}}{\bar{K}_F |\lambda|_{13}} \tag{27}$$

where λ_{L1} and λ_{L3} are the allocative share of labour in sector 1 and sector 3, respectively; $|\lambda|_{13}$ is the factor-intensity ranking in physical sense between sector 1 and sector 3; and η_{KF} is the physical share of foreign capital in total capital endowment (see Appendix 2.2). We assume sector 1 to be more labour-intensive relative to capital than sector 3 which implies $|\lambda|_{13} > 0$. It follows from the Rybczynski theorem that $\dfrac{\partial X_1}{\partial \bar{K}_F} < 0$ and $\dfrac{\partial x_3}{\partial \bar{K}_F} > 0$ (equations 23 and 24). Thus, sector 3 expands at a cost to sector 1.

Partially differentiating the equilibrium value of Y, we obtain

$$\frac{\partial Y}{\partial \bar{K}_F} = \frac{(1 - \lambda_L - \lambda_K)\lambda_{L1}\eta_{KF}Y}{|\lambda|_{13} \bar{K}_F} > 0 \tag{28}$$

The logic behind this is simple. The profit earned by the firms in the oligopolistic industry (sector 3) is part of the national income (equation 11.1). An expansion of output in sector 3 accentuates the profit level in this industry which augments the national income for a given level of commodity and factor prices.

On the demand side, an increase in the real national income, Y, escalates the domestic demand for commodities 2 and 3 and the demand for the imported commodity (equations 3, 18, and 19) owing to the pure income effect. This causes an upward shift of the average revenue and marginal revenue curves for each firm in sector 2 that leads to an increase in p_2 and x_2. Owing to positive profit caused by an expansion in this sector, new firms enter the market; thus, m rises. This also implies that product variety in this differentiated industry increases. Due to a rise in p_2, it then follows from the price-magnification effect that w falls and r rises provided sector 1 is relatively more labour-intensive in value sense relative to capital than sector 2, that is $|\theta|_{12} > 0$ (see equations A.28 and A.29 in Appendix 2.2).

---

[11]There are certain secondary effects as well which affect the equilibrium values of the variables; however, in this class of general equilibrium models, the primary effects are found to dominate the secondary effects under certain sufficient conditions.

It follows from the zero-profit condition in sector 2 (Chamberlain large group case) that the magnitude of decrease in w is smaller than an increase in r (equation 21). Owing to this effect on the equilibrium values of factor prices, the marginal cost in sector 3 rises that causes P_3 to rise (equation 6.1).

As already defined, welfare of the economy is measured by the indirect utility function in equation (15) which is a negative function of commodity prices and a positive function of real national income. The effect on welfare remains ambiguous which hinges on the relative strength of the negative price effect owing to an increase in p_2 and P_3 and the positive income effect owing to an increase in the value of Y. The following proposition summarizes the result.

> *P4.* In the presence of both oligopolistic and product differentiating monopolistic informal industry, an inflow of foreign capital results in

> (4a) an expansion of output of each informal firm in the oligopolistic industry and product-differentiated industry,
> (4b) contraction of output in the competitive informal industry,
> (4c) an increased product varieties in the product-differentiating informal industry,
> (4d) a decrease in informal wage rate while returns to capital improve. However, the effect on welfare remains ambiguous.

4. The Limiting Cases and the Role of Imperfection in the Commodity Market

In this section, we analyse how and how far the variation in the commodity market imperfection alters the equilibrium values of the variables in the model and whether it has only directional (qualitative) effect or magnitude (quantitative) effect or both.

As already mentioned, there are two imperfectly competitive sectors: sector 2 (monopolistically competitive) and sector 3 (oligopolistic structure). The terms 'σ' and 'ε' capture the degree of imperfection in both the commodity markets, respectively. From the comparative static results for $\hat{K}_F > 0$, for a higher value of σ, the magnitude of the equilibrium changes will increase while there will be no qualitative changes. For example, from equations (A.28) and (A.29), we obtain

$$\hat{w} = -\frac{\theta_{K1}}{|\theta|_{12}}(\frac{\sigma-1}{\sigma})\hat{p}_2 \text{ and } \hat{r} = \frac{\theta_{L1}}{|\theta|_{12}}(\frac{\sigma-1}{\sigma})\hat{p}_2, \text{ and we can observe that an increase}$$

in the value of σ would leave the sign of $\hat{w}$ and $\hat{r}$ unaltered which hinges only on the factor-intensity ranking, that is $|\theta|_{12}$, while the magnitude of this change will increase in absolute value. Similar logic holds for a higher value of ε.

We can discuss intuitively the effect of an increase in the value of σ which implies a reduction in the degree of commodity market imperfection. From equation (21), the RHS increases which leads to a Stolper–Samuelson type effect; thus, it has a similar implication on factor prices. Given that sector 2 is relatively more capital-intensive than sector 1, thus w falls and r rises. From equation (22), we observe that LHS falls; it implies that fall in w dominates rise in r. In equation (6.1), it causes a fall in P_3. Given that fall in w dominates rise in r and P_3 falls for a given level of output, thus, it causes real national income (Y) to plummet (equation 11.1). A fall in Y depresses the domestic demand for both the non-traded commodities (2 and 3) which causes contraction of output in these sectors.

Let us now consider the following two extreme cases:

Case 1: $\sigma \to \infty$. The limiting value of $\sigma \to \infty$ implies that the firms in the monopolistically competitive sector (sector 2) lose control over the market price owing to the perfectly elastic demand curve. The RHS of equation (22) collapses to zero; however, owing to positive overhead costs ($wa_{LF} + ra_{KF} > 0$), the operation of the firm in the industry becomes unsustainable. Thus, sector 2 would cease to exist. Vanishing of sector 2 would reduce six equations (equations 16, 17, 19, 20, 21, and 22) and six unknowns ($p_2, x_2, P_2, X_2, x_2^*,$ and m) such that the system remains consistent for the determination of the remaining other endogenous variables.

Case 2: $\varepsilon \to \infty$. The magnitude of the market power varies inversely with the value of ε. Even though firms in the oligopolistic industry (sector 3) lose their market power owing to $\varepsilon \to \infty$, sector 3 could exist provided it turns to a perfectly competitive non-traded sector. The positive level of profit earned in this sector will reduce to economic profit only. This reduction in surplus profit would cause the level of real national income to fall given that $\dfrac{P_3 x_3}{\varepsilon} = 0$ as $\varepsilon \to \infty$ (equation 11.1).

P5. In the limiting case of our argument, if the demand for good 2 becomes infinitely elastic, sector 2 vanishes (shuts down), while in sector 3, the oligopolistic sector faces a perfectly elastic demand, it survives and starts to act like a perfectly competitive sector, and therefore, the standard results on qualitative changes that we stress on remain unchanged.

5. Concluding Remarks

In seeking to understand how foreign capital inflow influences the informal economy in a developing nation, this chapter endeavours to highlight the market imperfection impact. This nuanced perspective aims to assist policymakers in enhancing the labour formalization process in alignment with SDGs. In the domain of theoretical studies, the structure of the simple general equilibrium model presented in the seminal works of Jones (1965, 1971) had found its wide application in various sub-disciplines. Despite several criticisms about its assumption of the perfectly competitive market, it had been the simple way to analyse public policies, trade policies, etc. The simple structure is also easy to modify to incorporate various sectors or factors according to the objective of analysis. However, in recent times, the GE structure is facing tremendous challenges due to one of its main assumptions of the perfectly competitive commodity market. Hence, this chapter attempted to examine the divergence between the outcomes derived from a perfectly competitive general equilibrium model and the effects of imperfect competition in the product market, specifically concerning an exogenous change in foreign capital inflow in the presence of the informal economy. We built a simple *mixed* general equilibrium model that is characterized by the presence of imperfect competition in both homogeneous goods and a horizontally differentiated good-producing informal industry. The propositions presented offer a nuanced understanding of the intertwined interlinkages between foreign capital inflow, market competition, and other key economic variables. Firstly, it sheds light on the impact of foreign capital inflow, highlighting improvements in informal wages, real national income, and welfare, but also noting a decline in returns to capital. *P3* emphasized the quantitative effects of commodity market imperfection on equilibrium values. *P4* delves into the intricate consequences of both oligopolistic and product-differentiating monopolistic industries, revealing shifts in output, informal wages, and the number of product varieties. Moreover, the limiting case underscores the resilience of certain sectors and the persistence of qualitative changes. Together, these propositions contribute to a comprehensive understanding of the intricate interplay between foreign capital inflow and the informal economy, providing valuable insights for policy considerations and SDGs. It further implies that the influence on the informal economy is not uniform. Consequently, the policy implications will vary depending on the nature of production within the informal economy. Moreover, we obtained that variation in the degree of commodity market imperfection has only a quantitative effect while no qualitative changes occur. Hence, the assumption of the perfect competition in the commodity market which makes the algebra simple but allows to analyse a wide variety of economic issues should not be a hindrance towards achieving rigorous qualitative results; however, if the objective is to estimate the exact magnitude of change in the equilibrium values of the variables, then advanced market structures may be suitable compared to the basic GE framework.

Acknowledgement

The authors are grateful to (Late) Professor Sarbajit Chaudhuri for his suggestions and motivations for this chapter. The authors remember him with great fondness and respect.

References

Beladi, H., & Marjit, S. (2000). A general equilibrium analysis of foreign investment an intersectoral linkage. *The Journal of International Trade and Economic Development*, 9(2), 213–218.

Chao, C. C., & Yu, E. (1997). Trade liberalization in oligopolistic competition with unemployment: A general equilibrium analysis. *The Canadian Journal of Economics*, 30(2), 479–496.

Chaudhuri, S. (2000). Rural–urban migration, the informal sector, urban unemployment, and development policies: A theoretical analysis. *Review of Development Economics*, 4(3), 353–364.

Chaudhuri, S. (2009). *Economic recession and informal sector.* https://papers.ssrn.com/sol3/papers.cfm?abstract_id=1492321

Chaudhuri, S. (2014). Foreign capital, non-traded goods and welfare in a developing economy in the presence of externalities. *International Review of Economics and Finance, 31,* 249–262.

Chaudhuri, S., & Banerjee, D. (2007). Economic liberalization, capital mobility and informal wage in a small open economy: A theoretical analysis. *Economic Modelling, 24*(6), 924940.

Chaudhuri, S., & Biswas, S. (2016). Endogenous labour market imperfection, foreign direct investment and external terms-of-trade shocks in a developing economy. *Economic Modelling, 59,* 416–424.

Chaudhuri, S., & Chaudhuri, S. (2019). Foreign direct investment and credit market reform in a developing economy: Could these be alternative policies?. *International Review of Economics and Finance, 62,* 321–331.

Chaudhuri, S., Ghosh, A., & Deb, S. (2016). Foreign direct investment and rural firm and non-firm sectors in a developing economy. *Journal of Quantitative Economics, 16*(3), 787–810.

Chaudhuri, S., & Gupta, M. R. (2014). International factor mobility, informal interest rate and capital market imperfection: A general equilibrium analysis. *Economic Modelling, 37,* 184–192.

Chaudhuri, S., & Mukhopadhyay, U. (2013). Foreign direct investment, environmentally sound technology and informal sector. *Economic Modelling, 31,* 206–213. https://doi.org/10.1016/j.econmod.2012.11.023

Chaudhuri, S., & Yabuuchi, S. (2007). Economic liberalization and wage inequality in the presence of labour market imperfection.

Dixit, A. K., & Stiglitz, J. E. (1977). Monopolistic competition and optimum product diversity. *The American Economic Review, 67*(3), 297–308.

Gupta, K., & Basu, T. (2004). Foreign capital inflow, skilled-unskilled wage gap and welfare in the presence of the informal sector. *The Pakistan Development Review, 43*(2), 125147.

Gupta, M. R. (1997). Foreign capital and the informal sector: Comments on Chandra and Khan. *Economica, 64,* 353–363.

Gupta, M. R. (1998). Foreign capital and technology transfer in a dynamic model. *Economica, Journal of Economics, 67*(1), 75–92.

Gupta, M. R. (2020). Globalization, crime and wage inequality: A theoretical analysis. *Indian Growth and Development Review, 14*(1), 97–121.

Gupta, M. R., & Dutta, P. B. (2012). Skilled-unskilled wage inequality, product variety, public input and increasing returns: A static general equilibrium analysis. *Economic Modelling, 29*(2), 502–513.

Helpman, E. (1981). International trade in the presence of product differentiation, economies of scale and monopolistic competition: A Chamberlin–Heckscher–Ohlin approach. *Journal of International Economics, 11*(3), 305–340.

ILO. (2018). *Women and men in the informal economy: A statistical picture.* https://www.ilo.org/global/publications/books/WCMS_626831/lang-en/index.htm

Jones, R. (1971). A three-factor model in theory, trade and history. In J. Bhagwati, R. Jones, R. Mundell, & J. Vanek (Eds.), *Trade, balance of payments and growth* (pp. 3–21). North-Holland.

Jones, R. W. (1965). The structure of simple general equilibrium models. *Journal of Political Economy, 73*(6), 557–572.

Jones, R. W., & Neary, P. J. (1984). The positive theory of international trade. In R. W. Jones & P. B. Kenen, *Handbook of international economics* (pp. 1–62). Elsevier.

Khan, R. K., Mahata, S., & Nag, R. N. (2022). Capital and crime–corruption nexus in the shadow of the law: A theoretical analysis of public policy. *Public Finance Review*. https://doi.org/10.1177/10911421221127098

Khan, R. K., Mahata, S., & Nag, R. N. (2023). Pandemic crisis, contact intensity and gender disparity in a developing economy*. *Economic Papers: A Journal of Applied Economics and Policy, 42*(1), 30–53. https://doi.org/10.1111/1759-3441.12379

Konishi, H., Fujiwara, M. O., & Suzumura, K. (1990). Oligopolistic competition and economic welfare: A general equilibrium analysis of entry regulation and tax-subsidy schemes. *Journal of Public Economics, 42*(1), 67–88.

Mahata, S., Khan, R. K., Chaudhuri, S., & Nag, R. N. (2022). COVID-19 lockdown, family migration and unemployment in a gendered society. *Research in Economics, 76*(3), 218236. https://doi.org/10.1016/j.rie.2022.07.010

Mahata, S., Khan, R. K., & Nag, R. N. (2020). Economic recession, informal sector and skilled–unskilled wage disparity in a developing economy: A trade-theoretical analysis. *Foreign Trade Review, 55*(2). https://doi.org/10.1177/0015732519894132

Mahata, S., Khan, R. K., Nag, R. N., Mandal, S., & Chaudhuri, S. (2023). Crime, corruption and capital: A general equilibrium analysis in the presence of political cronyism. In K. Gupta & J. K. Dwibedi (Eds.), *International trade, economic development and national welfare* (pp. 80–104). Routledge India.

Maiti, D., & Marjit, S. (2008). Trade liberalization, production organization and informal sector of the developing countries. *Journal of International Trade and Economic Development, 17*(3), 453–461.

Marjit, S., Kar, S., & Beladi, H. (2007). Trade reform and informal wages. *Review of Development Economics, 11*(2), 313–320. https://doi.org/10.1111/j.1467-9361.2007.00409.x

Marjit, S., Kar, S., & Chaudhuri, S. (2011). Recession in the skilled sector and implications for informal wage. *Research in Economics, 65*(3), 158–163.

Marjit, S., & Mandal, B. (2016). International trade, migration and unemployment – The role of informal sector. *Economics & Politics, 28*(1), 8–22.

Marjit, S., Mandal, B., & Roy, S. (2014). Trade openness, corruption and factor abundance: Evidence from a dynamic panel. *Review of Development Economics, 18*(1), 45–58. https://doi.org/10.1111/rode.12068

Neary, J. P. (2003a). Competitive versus comparative advantage. *The World Economy, 26*(4), 457–470.

Neary, J. P. (2003b). Globalization and market structure. *Journal of the European Economic Association, 1*(2–3), 245–271.

Sen, P., Ghosh, A., & Barman, A. (1997). The possibility of welfare gains with capital inflows in a small tariff-ridden economy. *Economica, 64*(254), 345–352.

UNCTAD. (2004). *Making FDI work for sustainable development*. United Nations Conference on Trade and Development and Sustainable Business Institute at the European Business School. https://digitallibrary.un.org/record/520391?ln=en

Appendix 1. The Model of Imperfect Competition Under Product Homogeneity

A1.1. Equations of Change

Totally differentiating equations (4) and (6.1), we obtain

$$\theta_{L1}\hat{w} + \theta_{K1}\hat{r} = 0 \tag{A.1}$$

$$\theta_{L3}\hat{w} + \theta_{K3}\hat{r} = (1 - \frac{1}{n\varepsilon})\hat{P}_3 \tag{A.2}$$

Solving equations (A.1) and (A.2) using Cramer's rule, we can express $\hat{w}$ and $\hat{r}$ in terms of $\hat{P}_3$ as follows:

$$\hat{w}(\hat{P}_3) = -\frac{\theta_{K1}}{|\theta|_{13}}(1 - \frac{1}{n\varepsilon})\hat{P}_3 \tag{A.3}$$

$$\hat{r}(\hat{P}_3) = \frac{\theta_{L1}}{|\theta|_{13}}(1 - \frac{1}{n\varepsilon})\hat{P}_3 \tag{A.4}$$

where $|\theta|_{13} = \theta_{L1}\theta_{K3} - \theta_{K1}\theta_{L3} > 0$.

Taking the total derivative of equations (8) and (9), we obtain the following:

$$\lambda_{L1}\hat{X}_1 + \lambda_{L3}\hat{x}_3 = -\frac{(\lambda_{L1}S_{LK}^1 + \lambda_{L3}S_{LK}^3)(1 - \frac{1}{n\varepsilon})\hat{P}_3}{|\theta|_{13}} \tag{A.5}$$

$$\lambda_{K1}\hat{X}_1 + \lambda_{K3}\hat{x}_3 = \eta_{KF}\hat{\bar{K}}_F + \frac{(\lambda_{K1}S_{KL}^1 + \lambda_{K3}S_{KL}^3)(1 - \frac{1}{n\varepsilon})\hat{P}_3}{|\theta|_{13}} \tag{A.6}$$

Solving equations (A.5) and (A.6) simultaneously using Cramer's rule, we obtain $\hat{X}_1$ and $\hat{x}_3$ in terms of $\hat{P}_3$ as follows:

$$\hat{X}_1(\hat{P}_3, \hat{\bar{K}}_F) = -\frac{\lambda_{L3}\eta_{KF}\hat{\bar{K}}_F}{|\lambda|_{13}} - (1 - \frac{1}{n\varepsilon})B\hat{P}_3 \tag{A.7}$$

$$\hat{x}_3(\hat{P}_3, \hat{\bar{K}}_F) = \frac{\lambda_{L1}\eta_{KF}\hat{\bar{K}}_F}{|\lambda|_{13}} + (1 - \frac{1}{n\varepsilon})C\hat{P}_3 \tag{A.8}$$

where

$$|\lambda|_{13} = \lambda_{L1}\lambda_{K3} - \lambda_{K1}\lambda_{L3} > 0$$

$$B = \frac{(1 - \frac{1}{n\varepsilon})\{\lambda_{K3}(\lambda_{L1}S_{LK}^1 + \lambda_{L3}S_{LK}^3) + \lambda_{L3}(\lambda_{K1}S_{KL}^1 + \lambda_{K3}S_{KL}^3)\}}{|\lambda|_{13}|\theta|_{13}} > 0$$

$$C = \frac{(1-\frac{1}{n\varepsilon})\{\lambda_{K1}(\lambda_{L1}S_{LK}^1 + \lambda_{L3}S_{LK}^3) + \lambda_{L1}(\lambda_{K1}S_{KL}^1 + \lambda_{K3}S_{KL}^3)\}}{|\lambda|_{13}|\theta|_{13}} > 0$$

Totally differentiating equation (11.1), we get

$$\hat{Y}(\hat{P}_3, \hat{\bar{K}}_F) = \hat{P}_3\left\{(1-\frac{1}{n\varepsilon})(\frac{\lambda_{KY}\theta_{L1} - \lambda_{LY}\theta_{K1}}{|\theta|_{13}} + \lambda_{3Y}(C+1)\right\} + \frac{\lambda_{3Y}\lambda_{L1}\eta_{KF}\hat{\bar{K}}_F}{|\lambda|_{13}} \qquad (A.9)$$

where λ_{3Y} is the share of aggregate profit of firms in industry 3 in the real national income.

Taking the total derivative of equation (7) and using equation (11.1), we obtain the final expression of $\hat{P}_3$ in terms of $\hat{\bar{K}}_F$

$$\hat{P}_3(\hat{\bar{K}}_F) = \frac{\dfrac{\lambda_{L1}\eta_{KF}(1-\lambda_{3Y})\hat{\bar{K}}_F}{|\lambda|_{13}}}{(1-\dfrac{1}{n\varepsilon})\dfrac{(\lambda_{KY}\theta_{L1} - \lambda_{LY}\theta_{K1})}{|\theta|_{13}} - (1-\lambda_{3Y})\{1+C(1-\dfrac{1}{n\varepsilon})\}} \qquad (A.10)$$

Substituting equation (A.10) in equations (A.3), (A.4), (A.7), (A.8), and (A.9), we obtain the following equilibrium values, respectively:

$$\hat{w}(\hat{\bar{K}}_F) = -\frac{\theta_{K1}}{|\theta|_{13}} \frac{(1-\dfrac{1}{n\varepsilon})\dfrac{\lambda_{L1}\eta_{KF}(1-\lambda_{3Y})\hat{\bar{K}}_F}{|\lambda|_{13}}}{(1-\dfrac{1}{n\varepsilon})\dfrac{(\lambda_{KY}\theta_{L1} - \lambda_{LY}\theta_{K1})}{|\theta|_{13}} - (1-\lambda_{3Y})\{1+C(1-\dfrac{1}{n\varepsilon})\}} \qquad (A.11)$$

$$\hat{r}(\hat{\bar{K}}_F) = \frac{\theta_{L1}}{|\theta|_{13}} \frac{(1-\dfrac{1}{n\varepsilon})\dfrac{\lambda_{L1}\eta_{KF}(1-\lambda_{3Y})\hat{\bar{K}}_F}{|\lambda|_{13}}}{(1-\dfrac{1}{n\varepsilon})\dfrac{(\lambda_{KY}\theta_{L1} - \lambda_{LY}\theta_{K1})}{|\theta|_{13}} - (1-\lambda_{3Y})\{1+C(1-\dfrac{1}{n\varepsilon})\}} \qquad (A.12)$$

$$\hat{X}_1(\hat{\bar{K}}_F) = -\frac{\eta_{KF}\hat{\bar{K}}_F}{|\lambda|_{13}}\left[\lambda_{L3} + \frac{(1-\dfrac{1}{n\varepsilon})B\lambda_{L1}(1-\lambda_{3Y})}{(1-\dfrac{1}{n\varepsilon})(\dfrac{\lambda_{KY}\theta_{L1} - \lambda_{LY}\theta_{K1}}{|\theta|_{13}}) - (1-\lambda_{3Y})\{1+C(1-\dfrac{1}{n\varepsilon})\}}\right]$$

$$(A.13)$$

$$\hat{x}_3(\hat{\bar{K}}_F) = \frac{\lambda_{L1}\eta_{KF}\hat{\bar{K}}_F}{|\lambda|_{13}}\left[\frac{(1-\frac{1}{n\varepsilon})(\frac{\lambda_{KY}\theta_{L1}-\lambda_{LY}\theta_{K1}}{|\theta|_{13}})-(1-\lambda_{3Y})}{(1-\frac{1}{n\varepsilon})(\frac{\lambda_{KY}\theta_{L1}-\lambda_{LY}\theta_{K1}}{|\theta|_{13}})-(1-\lambda_{3Y})\{1+C(1-\frac{1}{n\varepsilon})\}}\right] \quad (A.14)$$

$$\hat{Y}(\hat{\bar{K}}_F) = \frac{\lambda_{L1}\eta_{KF}\hat{\bar{K}}_F}{|\lambda|_{13}}\frac{\left[(1-\frac{1}{n\varepsilon})(\frac{\lambda_{KY}\theta_{L1}-\lambda_{LY}\theta_{K1}}{|\theta|_{13}})-\lambda_{3Y}\{1+C(1-\frac{1}{n\varepsilon})\}(2\lambda_{3Y}-1)\right]}{(1-\frac{1}{n\varepsilon})(\frac{\lambda_{KY}\theta_{L1}-\lambda_{LY}\theta_{K1}}{|\theta|_{13}})-\lambda_{3Y}\{1+C(1-\frac{1}{n\varepsilon})\}}$$

$$(A.15)$$

The effect on welfare could be decomposed into income and price effect by differentiating equation (12) with respect to $\bar{K}_F$ which is as follows:

$$\frac{\hat{V}}{\hat{\bar{K}}_F} = \frac{\hat{Y}}{\hat{\bar{K}}_F} - (1-\alpha-\beta)\frac{\hat{P}_3}{\hat{\bar{K}}_F} \quad (A.16)$$

A1.2. Proof of the Results

An inflow of foreign capital implies $\hat{\bar{K}}_F > 0$. Using equations (A.10)–(A.16), we obtain the following results:

$$\frac{\hat{P}_3}{\hat{\bar{K}}_F} < 0 \text{ under the sufficient condition } \lambda_{L1} < \lambda_{K_D1}$$

$$\frac{\hat{Y}}{\hat{\bar{K}}_F} > 0 \text{ provided } \lambda_{3Y} > 1/2$$

Given that $\lambda_{L1} < \lambda_{K_D1}$ and $\lambda_{3Y} > 1/2$, we have the following outcomes on the output and factor prices:

$$\frac{\hat{X}_1}{\hat{\bar{K}}_F} < 0; \frac{\hat{x}_3}{\hat{\bar{K}}_F} > 0; \frac{\hat{w}}{\hat{\bar{K}}_F} > 0; \text{ and } \frac{\hat{r}}{\hat{\bar{K}}_F} < 0$$

Given that under the above sufficient conditions, both price and income effect move in the opposite direction; thus, the effect on welfare is obtained as follows:

$$\frac{\hat{V}}{\hat{\bar{K}}_F} > 0$$

Appendix 2. The Model of Imperfect Competition with Product-differentiating Industry

A2.1. Derivation of Demand Functions

In the first stage, maximization of the utility function in equation (1) subject to the income constraint in equation (2) yields the Marshallian demand functions given by equations (3.1)–(3.3).

In the second stage of the optimization problem, we maximize equations (3.1–3.3) subject to the following constraint:

$$P_2 X_2 = \sum_{i=1}^{m} p_{2i} x_{2i} + \sum_{j=1}^{m^*} p_{2j}^* x_{2j}^* \tag{A.17}$$

Using equation (3.2), the maximization problem could be stated as

$$\text{Max,} \quad X_2 = [\sum_{i=1}^{m} x_{2i}^{\sigma-1/\sigma} + \sum_{j=1}^{m^*} x_{2j}^{*\sigma-1/\sigma}]^{\sigma/\sigma-1}$$

$$\{x_{2i}\},\{x_{2j}^*\}$$

$$\text{subject to} \quad \beta Y = \sum_{i=1}^{m} p_{2i} x_{2i} + \sum_{j=1}^{m^*} p_{2j}^* x_{2j}^*$$

The Lagrangian function can be expressed as follows:

$$\phi = [\sum_{i=1}^{m} x_{2i}^{\sigma-1/\sigma} + \sum_{j=1}^{m^*} x_{2j}^{*\sigma-1/\sigma}]^{\sigma/\sigma-1} + \delta[\beta Y - \sum_{i=1}^{m} p_{2i} x_{2i} + \sum_{j=1}^{m^*} p_{2j}^* x_{2j}^*] \tag{A.18}$$

Assuming interior solution, we obtain the following first-order conditions:

$$\frac{\partial \phi}{\partial x_{2i}} = [\sum_{i=1}^{m} x_{2i}^{\sigma-1/\sigma} + \sum_{j=1}^{m^*} x_{2j}^{*\sigma-1/\sigma}]^{(\sigma/\sigma-1)-1} x_{2i}^{-1/\sigma} - \delta p_{2i} = 0 \tag{A.19}$$

$$\frac{\partial \phi}{\partial x_{2\omega}} = [\sum_{i=1}^{m} x_{2i}^{\sigma-1/\sigma} + \sum_{j=1}^{m^*} x_{2j}^{*\sigma-1/\sigma}]^{(\sigma/\sigma-1)-1} x_{2\omega}^{-1/\sigma} - \delta p_{2\omega} = 0 \quad \forall \omega \neq i \tag{A.20}$$

$$\frac{\partial \phi}{\partial x_{2j}^*} = [\sum_{i=1}^{m} x_{2i}^{\sigma-1/\sigma} + \sum_{j=1}^{m^*} x_{2j}^{*\sigma-1/\sigma}]^{(\sigma/\sigma-1)-1} x_{2j}^{*(-1/\sigma)} - \delta p_{2j}^* = 0 \tag{A.21}$$

$$\frac{\partial \phi}{\partial x_{2\psi}^*} = [\sum_{i=1}^{m} x_{2i}^{\sigma-1/\sigma} + \sum_{j=1}^{m^*} x_{2j}^{*\sigma-1/\sigma}]^{(\sigma/\sigma-1)-1} x_{2\psi}^{*(-1/\sigma)} - \delta p_{2\psi}^* = 0 \quad \forall \psi \neq j \tag{A.22}$$

Using equations (A.19)–(A.22) in the constraint, we obtain the following:

$$\beta Y = x_{2i}\, p_{2i}^{\sigma}\,[\sum_{i=1}^{m} p_{2i}^{1-\sigma} + \sum_{j=1}^{m^{*}} p_{2j}^{*(1-\sigma)}] \tag{A.23}$$

Given equation (17) and solving for x_{2i} in equation (A.23), we obtain the demand functions in equations (18) and (19).

The amount of overhead expenses and variable cost for each identical firm in the monopolistically competitive market is given by the following:

$$F_{2} = wa_{LF} + ra_{KF} \tag{A.24}$$

$$v = (wa_{L2} + ra_{K2})x_{2} \tag{A.25}$$

Thus, price-average cost equality in sector 2 implies

$$p_{2} = wa_{L2} + ra_{K2} + \frac{(wa_{LF} + ra_{KF})}{x_{2}} \tag{A.26}$$

Substituting the value of $(wa_{L2} + ra_{K2})$ from equation (21) in the above expression (A.26), we obtain equation (22).

A2.2. Equations of Change

Taking the total derivative of equations (4) and (21) and arranging them in matrix form, we get

$$\begin{bmatrix} \theta_{L1} & \theta_{K1} \\ \theta_{L2} & \theta_{K2} \end{bmatrix} \begin{bmatrix} \hat{w} \\ \hat{r} \end{bmatrix} = \begin{bmatrix} 0 \\ (\dfrac{\sigma-1}{\sigma})\hat{p}_{2} \end{bmatrix} \tag{A.27}$$

Solving equation (A.27) using Cramer's rule, we obtain the *following* expressions:

$$\hat{w}(\hat{p}_{2}) = -\frac{\theta_{K1}}{|\theta|_{12}}(\frac{\sigma-1}{\sigma})\hat{p}_{2} \tag{A.28}$$

$$\hat{r}(\hat{p}_{2}) = \frac{\theta_{L1}}{|\theta|_{12}}(\frac{\sigma-1}{\sigma}) \tag{A.29}$$

where $|\theta|_{12} = \theta_{L1}\theta_{K2} - \theta_{K1}\theta_{L2} > 0$, $\theta_{L1} = a_{L1}w$, $\theta_{L2} = a_{L2}w/p_{2}$, $\theta_{K1} = a_{K1}r$, and $\theta_{K2} = a_{K2}r/p_{2}$.

Differentiating equations (22) and (6.1), we obtain

$$\hat{x}_{2}(\hat{p}_{2}) = \hat{p}_{2}\{(\frac{\sigma-1}{|\theta|_{12}})|\theta|_{1F} - 1\} \tag{A.30}$$

$$\hat{P}_3(\hat{p}_2) = (\frac{n\varepsilon}{n\varepsilon - 1})(\frac{\sigma - 1}{\sigma})\frac{|\theta|_{13}}{|\theta|_{12}}\hat{p}_2 \tag{A.31}$$

where $|\theta|_{1F} = \theta_{KF}\theta_{L1} - \theta_{K1}\theta_{LF} < 0$ and $|\theta|_{13} = \theta_{K3}\theta_{L1} - \theta_{K1}\theta_{L3} > 0$.

Taking the total derivative of equations (23) and (24) and represented in matrix form as follows:

$$\begin{bmatrix} \lambda_{L1} & \lambda_{L3} \\ \lambda_{K1} & \lambda_{K3} \end{bmatrix} \begin{bmatrix} \hat{X}_1 \\ \hat{x}_3 \end{bmatrix} = \begin{bmatrix} -(\lambda_{L2} + \lambda_{LF})\hat{m} \\ \eta_{KF}\hat{\bar{K}}_F + D\hat{p}_2 \end{bmatrix} \tag{A.32}$$

Solving equation (A.32) using Cramer's rule, we get

$$\hat{X}_1(\hat{m}, \hat{p}_2) = \frac{-\{\lambda_{L3}\eta_{KF}\hat{\bar{K}}_F + \lambda_{K3}(\lambda_{L2} + \lambda_{LF})\hat{m} + \hat{p}_2(\lambda_{L3}D + \lambda_{K3}B)\}}{|\lambda|_{13}} \tag{A.33}$$

$$\hat{x}_3(\hat{m}, \hat{p}_2) = \frac{\lambda_{L1}\eta_{KF}\hat{\bar{K}}_F + \lambda_{K1}(\lambda_{L2} + \lambda_{LF})\hat{m} + \hat{p}_2(\lambda_{L1}D + \lambda_{K1}B)\}}{|\lambda|_{13}} \tag{A.34}$$

where $\lambda_{L3} = \frac{na_{L3}x_3}{\bar{L}}$, $\lambda_{K3} = \frac{na_{K3}x_3}{\bar{K}}$, $\lambda_{L1} = \frac{a_{L1}X_1}{\bar{L}}$, $\lambda_{K1} = \frac{a_{K1}X_1}{\bar{K}}$, $\eta_{KF} = \frac{\bar{K}_F}{\bar{K}}$, and

$$A = \lambda_{L1}S_{LK}^1 + \lambda_{L2}S_{LK}^2 + \lambda_{L3}S_{LK}^3 > 0$$

$$B = \lambda_{L2}\{(\frac{\sigma - 1}{|\theta|_{12}})|\theta|_{1F} - 1\} + \frac{A}{|\theta|_{12}}(\frac{\sigma - 1}{\sigma})$$

$$C = \lambda_{K1}S_{KL}^1 + \lambda_{K2}S_{KL}^2 + \lambda_{K3}S_{KL}^3 > 0$$

$$D = \frac{C}{|\theta|_{12}}(\frac{\sigma - 1}{\sigma}) - \lambda_{K2}\{(\frac{\sigma - 1}{|\theta|_{12}})|\theta|_{1F} - 1\}$$

$$|\lambda|_{13} = \lambda_{L1}\lambda_{K3} - \lambda_{K1}\lambda_{L3} > 0$$

Total differentiating equation (25), we get

$$\hat{Y} = \lambda_L\hat{w} + \lambda_K\hat{r} + (1 - \lambda_L - \lambda_K)(\hat{P}_3 + \hat{x}_3) \tag{A.35}$$

where $\lambda_L(= w\bar{L}/Y)$ and $\lambda_K(= r\bar{K}_D/Y)$ are labour and domestic capital owners' share of income in total national income, respectively.

Substituting equations (A.28), (A.29), (A.31), and (A.34), the above equation (A.35) boils down to the following equation:

$$\hat{Y}(\hat{m}, \hat{p}_2) = E\,\hat{p}_2 + (1 - \lambda_L - \lambda_K)(\frac{\lambda_{L1}\eta_{KF}}{|\lambda|_{13}}\hat{K}_F + \frac{\lambda_{K1}(\lambda_{L2} + \lambda_{LF})}{|\lambda|_{13}}\hat{m}) \quad (A.36)$$

where

$$E = (\frac{\sigma - 1}{\sigma})\frac{(\theta_{L1} - \theta_{K1})}{|\theta|_{12}} + (1 - \lambda_L - \lambda_K)\{(\frac{n\varepsilon}{n\varepsilon - 1})(\frac{\sigma - 1}{\sigma})\frac{|\theta|_{13}}{|\theta|_{12}} + \frac{\lambda_{L1}D + \lambda_{K1}B}{|\lambda|_{13}}$$

Taking the total derivative of equation (17), we obtain

$$\hat{P}_2(\hat{m}, \hat{p}_2) = m(\frac{p_2}{P_2})^{1-\sigma}(\hat{p}_2 + \frac{\hat{m}}{1-\sigma}) \quad (A.37)$$

Taking the total derivative of equation (18) and using equation (A.30) and (A.37), we get the following expression:

$$G\hat{p}_2 - H\hat{m} = \frac{(1 - \lambda_L - \lambda_K)\lambda_{L1}\eta_{KF}}{|\lambda|_{13}}\hat{K}_F \quad (A.38)$$

where

$$G = (\sigma - 1)\frac{|\theta|_{1F}}{|\theta|_{12}} - m(\sigma - 1)(\frac{p_2}{P_2})^{1-\sigma} + \sigma - 1 - E$$

$$H = \frac{(1 - \lambda_L - \lambda_K)(\lambda_{L2} + \lambda_{LF})\lambda_{K1}}{|\lambda|_{13}} - m(\frac{p_2}{P_2})^{1-\sigma}$$

Taking the total derivative of equation (7),

$$I\hat{p}_2 + J\hat{m} = -\frac{\lambda_{L1}\eta_{KF}(\lambda_L + \lambda_K)}{|\lambda|_{13}}\hat{K}_F \quad (A.39)$$

where

$$I = (\frac{n\varepsilon}{n\varepsilon - 1})(\frac{\sigma - 1}{\sigma})\frac{|\theta|_{13}}{|\theta|_{12}} + \frac{\lambda_{L1}D + \lambda_{K1}B}{|\lambda|_{13}} - E$$

$$J = \frac{\lambda_{K1}(\lambda_{L2} + \lambda_{LF})}{|\lambda|_{13}}(\lambda_L + \lambda_K) > 0$$

Solving equations (A.38) and (A.39) simultaneously using Cramer's rule, we get

$$\hat{p}_2 = \frac{\eta_{KF}\lambda_{L1}\{J(1-\lambda_L)-\lambda_K H\}}{(GJ+HI)|\lambda|_{13}} \tag{A.40}$$

$$\hat{m} = -\frac{\eta_{KF}\lambda_{L1}\{I+(\lambda_L+\lambda_K)(G-I)\}}{(GJ+HI)|\lambda|_{13}} \tag{A.41}$$

Substituting the final values of $\hat{p}_2$ and $\hat{m}$ given in equations (A.40) and (A.41), respectively, in the earlier equations, the final values of the rest of the variables could be easily obtained.

Interventions

Chapter 8

Food Security in the Informal Sector: Interventions and Challenges for the SDGs

Bita Afsharinia[a] and Anjula Gurtoo[b]

[a]Centre for Society and Policy, Indian Institute of Science, Bangalore, India
[b]Department of Management Studies, Centre for Society and Policy, Indian Institute of Science, Bangalore, India

Abstract

The COVID-19 pandemic, starting in early 2020, has significantly compromised global commitment to the 2030 Agenda for Sustainable Development Goals, notably affecting areas like food security (SDG 2) and the economy (SDG 8). Informal economy platform employees have been among the most impacted. In India alone, 7.7 million workers in the informal economy have suffered, with nearly 90% of unskilled and semi-skilled workers experiencing income loss. The widespread income loss among a significant portion of the workforce has led to disruptions in demand and supply mechanisms, thereby worsening food insecurity. This study investigates the determinants of the food consumption score (FCS) to serve as an indicator of food security within informal-economy households. A longitudinal survey of 2,830 unskilled and semi-skilled employees, including drivers, domestic workers, delivery personnel, beauticians, street vendors, small business owners, and self-employed individuals, was conducted. The findings show a significant shift towards borderline household FCS during the pandemic, with a sharp decline in daily consumption of dairy products and non-vegetarian items, indicating reduced protein intake. Consuming two or fewer meals per day increases the likelihood of poor FCS, highlighting the need for systematic interventions to ensure three regular meals per day. Moreover, insufficient government support for adequate food intake in informal economy households calls for redesigned assistance programs.

Informal Economy and Sustainable Development Goals:
Ideas, Interventions and Challenges, 157–182
Copyright © 2024 by Bita Afsharinia and Anjula Gurtoo
Published under exclusive licence by Emerald Publishing Limited
doi:10.1108/978-1-83753-980-220241008

Policymakers should prioritize practical solutions, such as community-based food distribution centers and mobile food vans, to ensure the delivery of nutritious food to vulnerable populations in Bangalore.

Keywords: COVID-19; food consumption score; education; government support; number of meals per day; informal-economy households

1. Introduction

The sustainable development goals (SDGs) were adopted by the United Nations in 2015 as a universal call to action to end poverty, protect the planet, and ensure that by 2030 all people enjoy peace and prosperity. The 17 SDGs are integrated to balance social, economic, and environmental sustainability (United Nations, 2020b). However, the global crises caused by the COVID-19 pandemic since early 2020 can compromise the world's commitment to the 2030 agenda for sustainable development (Shulla et al., 2021).

The ongoing COVID-19 outbreak across the globe has resulted in significant adversities, accounting for 12% of all deaths globally (IISD, 2022). In March 2020, the World Health Organization (WHO) declared the COVID-19 outbreak a global pandemic (Cucinotta & Vanelli, 2020). It is believed that COVID-19 is spread via person-to-person contact through respiratory droplets. Hence, various preventive and safety measures, such as quarantine, travel restrictions, closure of educational and business institutions, diminished social distance, and restricted public access to shops, supermarkets, and recreation facilities, have been taken to restrain the spread of the virus (Swarna et al., 2022).

Despite lockdown measures taken by governments worldwide, over 266 million cases have been reported in over 200 countries, as of December 2022 (WHO, 2022). According to a joint report by ILO, FAO, IFAD, and WHO on the impact of COVID-19 on people's livelihoods, health, and food systems, nearly half of the world's 3.3 billion global workforce is at risk of losing their livelihoods (ILO et al., 2022). Studies have recognized that the COVID-19 pandemic has more explicit impacts on poverty (SDG1), food security (SDG 2), health and well-being (SDG3), and the economy (SDG8) (Baniya et al., 2021; Fenner & Cernev, 2021).

At the economic level, evidence reveals higher unemployment rates, job insecurity, and lower wages across countries (Bàrcena, 2020). Concerning health and well-being, prolonged periods of staying at home could lead to disturbing consequences such as sedentary activity and weight gain (Dor-Haim et al., 2021). Moreover, several studies have reported an increase in adverse emotional responses, including stress, anxiety, fear, and worry (Ho et al., 2020; Wang et al., 2020). Regarding food security, the pandemic, coupled with the disruption of supply chains and access to markets for the sale of agricultural produce, as well as labour shortages, hinders the flow of agricultural goods and services. Additionally, there has been an increase in overall food prices due to stay-at-home restrictions (Times of India, 2022). On the demand side, the pandemic has led to changing consumer behaviour linked to panic buying and stockpiling, which may affect food availability. Other challenges include issues related to food import–export restrictions (Daniel & Varier, 2022). Among all, studies have recognized that COVID-19 has affected the world's economic and food security more than other infectious diseases (Kakaei et al., 2022).

1.1. COVID-19 and Economic Hardship

The pandemic has had a profoundly negative impact on global economic growth for more than nearly a century. Lockdowns have notably affected the gross domestic product (GDP) of various nations, particularly in Asia, Europe, and South America. Recent declines in the GDP of these regions could potentially have severe consequences in the near future, significantly affecting the economic and social well-being of their populations in the post-pandemic era (Mishra et al., 2020).

Studies indicate that while the majority of businesses were impacted by the pandemic, smaller businesses expected more significant impacts, such as a decrease in profitability and sales. Small businesses are more likely to experience a year-over-year decrease in revenue and are less likely to be able to take on more debt or adopt various technologies (Tam et al., 2021). In 2021, during the post-pandemic period, JPMorgan Chase notes a 9% decline in revenues from pre-pandemic levels, with a significant drop of 40% observed in April 2020. Additionally, opportunity insights, analyzing Womply data, report a 38% decrease in revenues compared to pre-pandemic levels, with a peak drop of 50% in April 2020 (Theodos et al., 2021).

In 2020, Xiang et al. (2021) suggest that the virus reduced global economic growth to an annualized rate of −4.5% to −6.0% (Xiang et al., 2021). India's $2.9 trillion economy remained shuttered during the lockdown period, except for some essential services and activities. As shops, eateries, factories, transport services, and business establishments were shuttered, the lockdown had a devastating impact on slowing down the economy (Mahendra & Sengupta, 2020; Sarıışık & Usta, 2021). Evidence demonstrates that the informal sectors of the economy have been worst hit by the global epidemic. India's GDP contraction during April–June could well be above 8% if the informal sectors are considered (NITI Aayog, 2022).

Studies reveal that informal economy workers are particularly vulnerable due to the majority lacking social protection, access to quality healthcare, and losing access to protective assets in the COVID-19 pandemic (ILO et al., 2022). Particularly, households relying on the informal economy due to low and uncertain income do not have assured access to adequate and nutritious food relative to their formal counterparts (Bansal, 2021). A household-level economic and social condition of limited or uncertain access to adequate food forms household food insecurity (FAO, 2020). Studies demonstrate that household food insecurity leads to a reduction in the food supply, less dietary diversity intake, and discrepancies in intra-household food distribution (Kumari, 2022).

1.2. COVID-19 and Food Security

In 2020, between 720 million and 811 million individuals worldwide were experiencing hunger, approximately 161 million more than in 2019. Moreover, a staggering 2.4 billion people were moderately or severely food-insecure due to the lack of regular access to adequate food across the globe. The number of people going hungry and suffering from food insecurity had been gradually rising between 2014 and the onset of the COVID-19 pandemic. The COVID-19 crisis has pushed those rising rates even higher and has also exacerbated all forms of malnutrition, particularly in vulnerable populations (United Nations, 2020a).

Furthermore, the COVID-19 pandemic exposed the weakness of the global food system, with hunger becoming a critical issue in most countries. In the context of India, the pandemic interacted with undernutrition, exacerbating nutritional insecurities (Perappadan, 2021). Despite being self-sufficient in food production, India faces problems of hunger and food insecurity due to widespread economic distress, high unemployment, and high levels of inequality (WHO, 2021). According to the research, India carries a heavy burden of multiple forms of malnutrition that affect 14% of the population (Bijarnia, 2021).

The COVID-19 pandemic in the context of India has exacerbated existing food insecurity and disrupted food consumption patterns due to multiple shocks. These shocks manifest in five ways. Firstly, economic hardships related to layoffs and job insecurity impact people's shopping behaviour and willingness to spend, leading them towards food security risks (Kumar Mishra, 2021). Secondly, the pandemic, coupled with disruptions in supply chains, access to markets for the sale of agricultural produce, labour shortages, and an increase in overall food prices due to stay-at-home restrictions, hinders the flow of agricultural goods and services (Times of India, 2022). On the demand side, it leads to changing consumer behaviour linked to panic buying and stockpiling, affecting short-term food availability and presenting long-term challenges related to food import–export (Daniel & Varier, 2022). Thirdly, school closures due to COVID-19 have disrupted the normal distribution channels through which school meal programs operate, leaving many children without this vital source of food (Borkowski et al., 2021). Fourthly, evidence reveals changes in consumer preferences toward specific modes of shopping, such as online versus offline (Kaushal, 2022), and types of food consumed in households, such as pro-healthy diets based on plant-based foods as opposed to meat-based foods (Rawat et al., 2020). Fifthly, studies demonstrate the influence of lockdown on sedentary behaviours, anxiety, and boredom caused by home confinement, influencing motivation to eat, promoting eating disorders, changing lifestyle patterns, reducing diet quality (Chopra et al., 2020; Roy et al., 2020), and increasing alcohol consumption (Rawat et al., 2020).

Despite a rapidly emerging stream of academic research on the implications of the pandemic for food consumption, the analytical scope and geographical scale of existing studies have been limited (Kecinski et al., 2020). The geography of scholarly investigation has excluded some major global markets for food consumption, such as India.

In India, R. R. Kumar et al. (2020), Singh et al. (2021), and Phatak et al. (2022) have examined the eating behaviour of Indian residents during the national COVID-19 lockdown, primarily focusing on the health implications of behavioural changes (Kumar et al., 2020; Phatak et al., 2022; Singh et al., 2021). While seminal in their geographical coverage, these studies have not compared the food consumption patterns of the most affected population before, during, and after the lockdown. Singh et al. (2021) and Bhol et al. (2021) investigate the dietary habits of Indian consumers in daily screen time before and during the lockdown, discussing these in the context of diet quality, such as junk food consumption and changes in snacking patterns (Bhol et al., 2021; Singh et al., 2021). While advancing our understanding of food consumption patterns among Indian residents, these studies do not elaborate on the implications of their findings for future behavioural intentions. Similarly, Aneesh and Patil (2021) discuss the food choices of Indian households during the COVID-19 lockdown, focusing on dietary diversity alongside food availability and accessibility rather than food consumption patterns and the drivers behind their occurrence (Aneesh & Patil, 2021). Although previous research has explored the impact of the COVID-19 pandemic on livelihood expectations and food security risk perception, these studies fail to shed light on the determinants of changes in food consumption in households with different profiles affected by the pandemic.

Furthermore, it is alarming that the topic of food consumption in low- or non-income households in COVID-19-related research is underrepresented. For instance, in India, the informal economy has emerged as one of the world's largest countries for flexi-staffing (e.g. informal and platform work). The study estimates that in 2020–2021, 7.7 million Indian workers were engaged in the informal economy, expected to expand to 23.5 million workers by 2019–2030 (NITI Aayog, 2022). Lockdown orders forced most businesses to close down or substantially reduce their operations (Filimonau et al., 2020). Consequently, evidence reveals that among the sectors immensely impacted by the pandemic were the platform economy and geographically tethered on-demand gig workers or informal economy workers. Nearly 90% of Indian unskilled and semi-skilled employees lost income during the COVID-19 pandemic (Flourish Ventures, 2020). This outlines a bleak perspective for misclassified informal economy workers without access to paid sick leave, unemployment insurance, workers' compensation, company-provided personal protective equipment, or income predictability, facing a heightened risk of COVID-19 infection, food insecurity, and homelessness among these groups (Herrera et al., 2020).

Building on these broad views of informal sectors and food security at risk, countries in every region and at every development stage should identify the most vulnerable groups to understand how the pandemic affected their food consumption preferences and, further, shape bold, rapid interventions to optimize nutritional health status (David Fine et al., 2020).

The aim of this exploratory study is to provide a clear understanding of the food and nutrition status among unskilled and semi-skilled employee households with higher vulnerability to food insecurity due to the loss of jobs and income during the COVID-19 pandemic. To this end, the study contributes to the literature in three ways. Firstly, it determines the major food groups that have been dramatically changed, comparing food consumption before (2018–2019) and during the pandemic to detail variations in major food group intake. Secondly, it predicts changes in the consumption of the most affected food groups through seven mainstream human security indicators across the population with diverse profiles (earning/not earning, got loan/not got loan, Gov support/not getting support, inappropriate housing condition/appropriate housing condition) before and after the COVID-19 pandemic. Thirdly, the study discusses context-based policy implications to eradicate food insecurity within the present and future context in India.

The unique contribution of this study is, thus, that it covers the food consumption of the most vulnerable population, considering both the periods before (2018–2019) and during the pandemic. Given the focus of past research on the effects of COVID-19 on food consumption at home, the current study extends the scope of analysis to explore the impact of the pandemic on food consumption in the unskilled and semi-skilled employee context. Such analysis is more comprehensive and holds implications for food service providers, as it enables a better understanding of informal economy household preferences for food consumption in a post-pandemic future.

Data were collected from a representative sample of households in Bangalore, India, to study how the COVID-19 shock has affected their food consumption. The total sample size consisted of 2,832 individuals aged between 18 and 80 years old across unskilled and semi-skilled employees, using a longitudinal survey conducted in two durations: July–November 2018–2019 and December–January 2020–2021. After data cleaning, 2,830 responses were used for further analysis. In addition to socio-demographic factors, the information gathered from the survey includes livelihood factors such as children's education, food intake, clothing, medical care, housing, employment, and environmental impacts of the pandemic, among others.

The current study is organized into six sections. Section 2 presents the methods used for analysis, including the theoretical foundation and data analysis. Section 3 presents the results of the analysis, followed by a discussion of the key findings in Section 4. Section 5 presents the conclusion and implications derived from the study. Section 6 includes the limitations and future scope of the study.

2. Methods

2.1. Participants and Procedures

Participants engaged in a panel study to assess the impact of COVID-19 on unskilled and semi-skilled employees, encompassing drivers, domestic workers, delivery personnel, beauticians, street vendors, small business owners, and self-employed individuals. The longitudinal survey occurred in two phases, spanning from July to November 2018–2019 and December to January 2020–2021, targeting a low-income job representative sample in Bangalore, India. This aimed to comprehensively investigate COVID-19's impact on participants' livelihoods and food security.

A combination of random and snowball sampling techniques ensured a diverse and representative sample, facilitating inclusion from various backgrounds. The study collected a total of 2,832 responses, encompassing participants aged 18–80 years, thereby offering a diverse range of experiences for a comprehensive exploration of the study objectives. The data collection occurred in two distinct time periods: before and after the pandemic. Following the data cleaning process, the final sample size consisted of 2,830 responses from individuals who agreed to participate in both rounds of the interviews.

The decision to employ interviews for data collection, both before and during the pandemic, was motivated by the need for a qualitative approach to capture the nuanced experiences of informal-economy households. Interviews offer a platform for participants to express their perspectives in-depth, providing researchers with a rich understanding of the challenges faced by individuals and households in the informal sector. This qualitative method was essential in revealing the intricate details of daily lives, economic struggles, and food security concerns. Additionally, conducting interviews during both periods allowed for a longitudinal exploration, offering insights into the evolving dynamics within informal-economy households in response to the changing circumstances brought about by the COVID-19 pandemic. Overall, the choice of interviews enhanced the study's qualitative nature, providing a comprehensive and dynamic portrayal of participants' experiences over time.

Data collection involved in-depth, structured, face-to-face interviews, chosen to capture nuanced insights challenging to obtain through quantitative methods alone. This qualitative approach delved into FCSs variation before and during the pandemic, identifying key factors determining food insecurity among the population. The survey questionnaire, administered in Hindi, Kannada, and English, ensured participant confidentiality.

Volunteers from the community-based organization 'StreeJagrutiSamiti', under the umbrella of 'MitrSanketa', conducted interviews. These interviews, based on the United Nations Human Security framework, aimed to comprehensively understand multidimensional challenges to human survival and well-being (United Nations, 2016). The study utilized this model to organize the questionnaire and offer a community-based intervention addressing food and nutrition insecurity.

In conducting our research, we prioritized the longitudinal connection with participants to capture the nuanced evolution of their experiences. By reaching out to the same individuals, we sought to establish a direct link between their pre-pandemic circumstances and the subsequent challenges and adaptations during the pandemic. This strategic approach not only strengthens the validity of our findings but also enables a comprehensive exploration of the dynamic shifts within the studied population. Interviews continued until data saturation, with brief demographic surveys administered via interview to summarize participant characteristics.

2.2. Survey Design

The survey consisted of a structured questionnaire with eight sections. The first section included descriptive questions aiming to ascertain participants' socio-demographic characteristics, covering educational levels, age, and total family members. The second section comprised descriptive questions focusing on the economic status of informal-economy households over time, including inquiries about types of occupation, monthly earnings before and after the COVID-19 national lockdown, and the receipt of financial support such as loans during March–August 2020.

The third section involved single-choice questions to gauge the impact of COVID-19 on livelihood, covering aspects such as medical care, housing conditions, community engagement, and government support. The fourth section included single-choice questions assessing the environmental impact of COVID-19. The fifth section featured questions evaluating food affordability, variety, and frequency of food consumption at the household level before and after the lockdown.

The sixth section comprised questions to identify psychological issues among participants, including feelings such as anger and irritation. The seventh section included questions assessing personal thoughts, covering fears and apprehensions such as increased family violence in the locality, heightened harassment from landlords, and changes in the nature of the job or job security. The eighth section contained questions evaluating participants' opinions on vaccination, encompassing awareness, beliefs, trust in vaccines, and vaccine acceptance.

2.3. Measures

2.3.1. Outcome Measure

To understand the changes in dietary patterns observed during the COVID-19 pandemic, information pertaining to the consumption of various food groups and their frequency were categorized into five groups: not consumed, weekly, two to three times a week, and daily. The current study considers the FCS indicator, employed to categorize and track household food security over time, as the dependent variable.

The FCS aggregates household-level data on the diversity and frequency of food groups consumed over the previous seven days, which is then weighted according to the relative nutritional value of the consumed food groups. To calculate the FCS from these results, the consumption frequencies are summed and multiplied by the standardized food group weight (see the food groups and corresponding weights below). Households can then be further classified as having 'poor (0–21)', 'borderline (21.5–35)', or 'acceptable (>35)' food consumption by applying the World Food Programme (WFP) recommended cut-offs to the FCS (WFP, 2008).

2.3.2. Predictor Variables

The independent variables were classified according to the United Nations Trust Fund for Human Security (UNTFHS). Socio-demographic characteristics, such as educational level, were categorized along seven mainstream human security indicators, including health security (lack of access to basic healthcare and epidemics), economic security (income and access to credit, along with other economic opportunities such as taking loans), food security (hunger and food consumption patterns), environmental security (environmental conditions such as garbage disposal during lockdowns and resource depletion, such as access to drinking water and cooking gas), personal security (physical violence in all its forms), community security (food, financial, and healthcare support), and political security (human rights violations, lack of rule of law and justice) (United Nations, 2016).

According to the UNTFHS framework, the human security approach encompasses five fundamental principles (United Nations, 2016). Firstly, it is people-centred, taking into consideration a broad range of conditions that threaten the survival, livelihood, and dignity of people and communities, with a particular focus on vulnerable populations. Secondly, it is comprehensive, recognizing the complexity and interconnected nature of challenges faced by people in their aspirations to be free from want, fear, and indignity. Thirdly, it is context-specific, acknowledging that there is no 'one size fits all' solution to addressing challenges, considering differing capacities among people, civil society, and governments, as well as the root causes that may vary within and across countries. Fourthly, it is prevention-oriented, going beyond quick responses by delving into the real causes of challenges and building sustainable and resilient solutions. This involves developing early warning mechanisms to mitigate the impact of current threats and prevent the occurrence of future challenges. Lastly, it emphasizes protection and empowerment, integrating measures into a framework that can better address complex challenges to the human condition. This includes inherent responsibilities within each society, such as empowering people and their communities to articulate and respond to their needs and those of others (United Nations, 2016).

2.4. Statistical Analyses

We employed the Statistical Package for Social Sciences software program, version 25.0, for all analyses. The data in our study underwent a comprehensive analysis utilizing a combination of descriptive and inferential statistical methods. To provide an overview of our approach, we employed descriptive statistics to summarize the essential variables and characteristics of the sample. This entailed calculating means, standard deviations, and frequencies to delineate the demographics, FCSs, and other pertinent attributes within the unskilled and semi-skilled employee population under examination.

In addition to these descriptive statistics, we incorporated inferential statistical techniques, specifically Wilcoxon's signed rank test and multinomial logistic regression analysis, to investigate the relationships between specific factors and the variations in FCSs, particularly within the context of the COVID-19 pandemic. These analytical methods enabled us to pinpoint the pivotal factors contributing to food insecurity in this demographic.

The approach involved two primary steps: firstly, we employed the non-parametric Wilcoxon's signed rank test to assess significant differences in mean FCSs before (2018–2019) and during (2020) the COVID-19 pandemic. This test was instrumental in evaluating the test–retest reliability of the modified scores at a group level.

In conducting the Wilcoxon test, we utilized the same sample of participants across both time periods, before and after the pandemic. This strategic choice was made to ensure a direct and consistent comparison within the same cohort, thereby enhancing the internal validity of our study. Maintaining continuity in the sample allows us to discern meaningful changes over time and draw robust conclusions regarding the impact of the pandemic on the variables under investigation. This decision is pivotal for the thorough analysis of observed effects and contributes significantly to the overall rigor of the research methodology.

Secondly, we implemented a multinomial logistic regression model to predict categorical placements or the probability of category membership in a dependent variable based on multiple independent variables. Specifically, this model allowed us to discern the human security factors associated with the likelihood of experiencing poor and borderline FCS among informal-economy households. In this model, the acceptable FCS served as the reference category (Kwak & Clayton-Matthews, 2002).

The use of the multinomial regression model in our study is grounded in its appropriateness for analysing categorical dependent variables with more than two categories. In our case, the FCSs exhibit multiple categories representing different levels of food security. This model allows us to examine the relationships between various independent variables and the likelihood of categorical outcomes, providing a robust analytical framework for understanding the factors influencing different levels of food security among the informal-economy households. The decision to employ the multinomial regression model aligns with the complexity of our research question and enhances the depth of our analysis by allowing us to explore the nuanced associations among multiple variables and the diverse categories of food security.

In selecting the multinomial regression model for our study, we prioritized its suitability for analysing categorical outcomes, specifically the diverse levels of food security represented by FCSs. The categorical nature of our dependent variable aligns with the strengths of the multinomial regression model, providing a straightforward approach to assess the direct impact of various variables on different food security levels. While alternative models such as partial structural equation modelling offer a more comprehensive exploration of intricate relationships among regressors, our research question focused on understanding specific factors influencing distinct levels of food security within informal-economy households. By utilizing these statistical techniques, we were able to gain valuable insights into the factors influencing food security and draw meaningful conclusions within the scope of our study.

Furthermore, in our study, both factors such as the number of meals and monthly income are included as regressors in the model to capture the intricate relationship between food consumption patterns and economic well-being within informal-economy households. Despite the potential correlation between these variables, their distinct roles make them valuable contributors to our research objectives.

The number of meals directly reflects food security, while monthly income is a crucial economic determinant. We acknowledge the importance of addressing potential collinearity issues and will conduct diagnostic tests to manage any concerns. This strategic inclusion enhances the depth of our analysis, allowing us to provide a nuanced understanding of the multifaceted factors influencing food security in the informal sector.

3. Results

3.1. Descriptive Statistics

Table 8.1 provides a comprehensive summary of the participants' demographic characteristics, health status, economic conditions, food habits, environmental factors, personal security, community support, and political aspects.

In examining the age range of our participants, which extends from 18 to 80 years, a notable concentration was observed among middle-aged adults, with a mean age of 37 and a standard deviation of 10. Additionally, we have provided a detailed breakdown of the gender distribution, highlighting that our participant composition comprises 20% females and 80% males. It is noteworthy that due to the unequal gender distribution, a comparative analysis between male and female participants was not pursued. These insights contribute to a more nuanced understanding of the demographic characteristics within our study, shedding light on both age-related trends and gender distribution while acknowledging the limitation imposed by the uneven gender composition.

The educational status indicates that the majority of participants (22.3%) have a secondary level of education, while 21.9% have no academic education. During the COVID-19 lockdown, over half of the participants (58%) did not visit doctors, and only 6.9% reported being infected by the coronavirus.

The average monthly income, both before ($M = 14{,}605$, SD $= 11{,}950$) and during COVID-19 ($M = 3{,}038$, SD $= 6{,}619$), reflects a dramatic reduction in earnings. Consequently, the results show that 32.8% of individuals availed themselves of personal loans during the March–August 2020 lockdown. Moreover, 31.5% of participants reported the unaffordability of food for their families, 31.3% reported experiencing sleep hunger, and a significant 48.1% consumed less than two meals per day during the pandemic. About 35.1% of participants reported that cooking gas was not available during the lockdown, 27.6% reported that garbage was not taken care of and close to 30% reported not having access to drinking water as before the lockdown.

Notably, the largest number of participants (42%) received community food support during the pandemic. However, the community played a minor role in financial support (5.3%) and healthcare support (3.4%). Furthermore, the Indian government implemented multiple support packages in 2020 for people and businesses affected by the COVID-19 pandemic.

Table 8.1.   Descriptive Statistics of the Participants.

Variables	Before COVID-19		During COVID-19	
	Frequency	Percentage	Frequency	Percentage
Demographic characteristics				
Education level				
No education	619	21.9		
Primary (grades 1–5)	317	11.2		
Middle school (grades 6–8)	450	15.9		
Secondary (grades 9 and 10)	631	22.3		
High school/PUC (grades 11 and 12)	488	17.2		
College and above	325	11.5		
Health security				
Any of family members infected by COVID-19 – yes			194	6.9
Number of visit doctors – not visited			1,640	58.0
Economic security				
Take loan during March–August 2020 – yes			929	32.8
Monthly income of the participant				
≥ 78,063	8	0.2	1	0.0
39,033–78,062	107	3.6	16	0.5
29,200–39,032	242	8.4	23	0.8
19,516–29,199	621	27.7	60	2.1
11,708–19,515	664	22	185	4.3
3,908–11,707	571	12.4	607	19.1
≤ 3,907	222	4.5	212	4.4
Not earning	486	17.2	1,918	67.8
Food security				
Any food family need but cannot afford – yes			890	31.5
Did your family sleep hungry anytime during lockdown – yes			885	31.3
Number of meals consumed per day – less			244	8.6

Table 8.1.   (*Continued*)

Variables	Before COVID-19		During COVID-19	
	Frequency	**Percentage**	**Frequency**	**Percentage**
Number of meals consumed per day – same			13	0.5
Number of meals consumed per day – two meals			1,360	48.1
Number of meals consumed per day – three meals			1,089	38.5
Number of meals consumed per day – four meals			124	4.4
Environmental security			479	16.9
Was garbage taken care during lockdown – no			781	27.6
Easy access to drinking water as before pandemic – no			832	29.4
Cooking gas was available during lockdown – no			994	35.1
Personal security				
Family violence increased during lockdown – yes			391	13.8
Community security				
Received food support from community during lockdown – yes			1,211	42.8
Received financial support from community during lockdown – yes			151	5.3
Received healthcare support from community during lockdown – yes			95	3.4
Political security				
Received any types of support from Government				
No			974	34.4
Ration			1,186	41.9
Medical help			233	8.2
Financial/money			117	4.1
Help line to call if needed			173	6.1
Helpless			147	5.2

Source: Estimated by authors.

As the results show, the highest number of participants (41.9%) received government ration support, but 34.4% of participants did not receive any types of support packages, among other findings.

3.2. Food Consumption Score

The study compares the FCSs of participants before and during the pandemic. Table 8.2 presents the analysis items with common significance levels: P-value < 0.01 (1 chance in 100), P-value < 0.05 (1 chance in 20), and P-value < 0.1 (1 chance in 10).

The result suggests significant changes towards the borderline category of household FCS during the pandemic. Before COVID-19, the FCS indicated 15.7% poor, 3.8% borderline, and 80.9% acceptable. However, during the pandemic, the FCS changed to 10% poor, 19.8% borderline, and 70.2% acceptable.

Table 8.2 reveals the results of the Wilcoxon signed rank test, showing significant differences between means ($p > 0.05$) in overall FCS and across diverse food groups. Overall FCS ($p < 0.010$, before COVID-19 $M = 2.65$, SD = 0.737, and during COVID-19 $M = 2.60$, SD = 0.664) demonstrates a significant change across time. Comparing the frequency of consumption of major food groups before and during the pandemic shows statistically significant negative changes, particularly in daily consumption of dairy products ($Z = -15.976$, $p < 0.001$, before COVID-19 $M = 5.25$, SD = 2.853, and during COVID-19 $M = 4.29$, SD = 2.959, with a medium effect size $r = 0.300$). Descriptive statistics reveal a decrease in daily consumption of dairy products from 72.2% before the pandemic to 53.3% during the pandemic.

Furthermore, the outcomes depict a reduction in daily consumption of non-veg items ($Z = -11.371$, $p < 0.001$, before COVID-19 $M = 1.59$, SD = 1.823, and during COVID-19 $M = 1.21$, SD = 1.438, with a small effect size $r = 0.213$).

Table 8.2. The Wilcoxon Signed-Rank Test for Comparing Means Scores.

Food Consumption	Pre COVID-19		During COVID-19			
	Mean	SD	Mean	SD	Z	P-value
FCS	2.65	0.737	2.60	0.664	−1.640	<0.010
Starch staples	4.53	2.900	4.03	2.803	−7.747	<0.001
Dairy products	5.25	2.853	4.29	2.959	−15.976	<0.001
Pulses	4.36	2.934	3.86	2.818	−8.309	<0.001
Non-veg	1.59	1.823	1.21	1.438	−11.371	<0.001
Vegetables and fruits	2.69	2.522	2.20	2.138	−9.968	<0.001

Source: Estimated by authors.
Note: Effect size formula: The effect size r; by dividing the Z by sqrt(N) – where N is the total number of observations. Using Cohen (1988) criteria of 0.1 = small effect, 0.3 = medium effect, 0.5 = large effect.

Descriptive statistics show that 22.9% are not consumed, and the frequency of consumption of non-veg items at 2–3 times a week and daily intake dropped to 15.3% and 4.8%, respectively.

Overall, these statistics demonstrate a reduction in the daily consumption of major food groups and a change in the frequency of consumption, particularly in consuming dairy products and non-veg items, with a greater effect size.

3.3. Predictors of FSC

Multinomial logistic regression was conducted to explore the impact of socio-demographic characteristics and various human security factors, including health security, economic security, food security, environmental security, personal security, community security, and political security, on the FCS as an indicator of food security in informal-economy households in the context of the COVID-19 pandemic.

Table 8.3 outlines the association between the FCS and contributing factors. The results reveal a significant negative association between participants' educational status, ranging from no education (p-value < 0.05, 95% CI 0.418 − 0.913) to primary (p-value < 0.01, 95% CI 0.343 − 0.854), middle school (p-value < 0.01, 95% CI 0.296 − 0.679), and secondary education (p-value < 0.01, 95% CI 0.298 − 0.646), with borderline FCS. Existing literature suggests that higher education reflects more knowledge, influencing the perceived outcome of a healthy diet and promoting the regular consumption of a wider variety of foods (Nestle et al., 1998; Worsley et al., 2004).

Moreover, monthly income significantly increases the likelihood of poor FCS (p-value < 0.01, 95% CI 1.00 − 1.00). Not receiving financial support, such as taking a loan during lockdown, has a negative significant impact on poor FCS (p-value < 0.05, 95% CI 0.536 − 0.981). Access to financial loans for economically vulnerable populations helps cover daily personal expenses during lockdown, and lack of access to this financial support could increase the likelihood of poor FCS or food insecurity.

The results indicate that the consumption of fewer meals per day, such as the consumption of fewer meals (p-value < 0.01, 95% CI 9.469 − 2.149), consumption of the same meals as before the pandemic (p-value < 0.01, 95% CI 10.828 − 1.389), and two meals (p-value < 0.01, 95% CI 3.795 − 0.897), contributes to an increased probability of poor FCS as an indicator of overall food insecurity. Additionally, the results highlight the significant negative role of food unaffordability in the risk of borderline FCS (p-value < 0.01, 95% CI 3.87 − 0.614).

Most notably, the findings underscore the negative significant role of government support, including ration (p-value < 0.1, 95% CI 0.092 − 0.552), medical help (p-value < 0.1, 95% CI 0.115 − 0.783), and financial support (p-value < 0.1, 95% CI 0.092 − 0.792), in poor FCS among informal-economy households. Lastly, the results indicate that the lack of healthcare community support negatively impacts the likelihood of poor FCS (p-value < 0.01, 95% CI 0.283 − 0.804). This is because communities are known to play a particularly important role in providing social and psychological resources for residents' health and well-being (Bowe et al., 2022; Ehsan et al., 2019). Furthermore, the lack of community support potentially leads to health and food insecurity.

Table 8.3.   Regression Analysis of Factors Determining the FCS at Household Level.

Variables	Poor				Borderline			
	B	Exp (B)	95% CI for Exp (B)		B	Exp (B)	95% CI for Exp (B)	
			LB	UB			LB	UB
Demographic characteristics								
Educational level (no education – college and above[a])	−0.261	0.771	0.443	1.341	−0.482**	0.618	0.418	0.913
Educational level (primary – college and above[a])	−0.292	0.747	0.403	1.383	−0.615***	0.541	0.343	0.854
Educational level (middle school – college and above[a])	−0.473	0.623	0.341	1.136	−0.802***	0.448	0.296	0.679
Educational level (secondary – college and above[a])	−0.122	0.885	0.512	1.529	−0.824***	0.439	0.298	0.646
Educational level (high school/PUC – college and above[a])	0.235	1.264	0.706	2.266	0.553**	1.738	1.225	2.466
Economic security								
Monthly earning during lockdown	0.000***	1.000	1.000	1.000	0.000	1.000	1.000	1.000
Taken loan during lockdown (no – yes[a])	−0.321**	0.725	0.536	0.981	−0.010	0.991	0.775	1.267
Health security								
Did you or your family visited doctor during lockdown (no – yes[a])	−0.057	0.945	0.541	1.650	−0.249	0.780	0.503	1.209
Did any of family members infected by COVID-19 (no – yes[a])	0.386	1.472	0.718	3.018	−0.249	0.780	0.503	1.209

Food security

Number of meals consumed per day (less – four meals)	2.248***	9.469	2.149	41.728	2.169*	8.748	3.491	21.918
Number of meals consumed per day (same – four meals)	2.382**	10.828	1.389	84.403	1.155	3.174	0.579	17.403
Number of meals consumed per day (two meals – four meals)	1.334*	3.795	0.897	16.050	1.482**	4.401	1.838	10.538
Number of meals consumed per day (three meals – four meals)	0.895	2.448	0.573	10.461	0.906	2.475	1.030	5.952
Did your family sleep hungry anytime during lockdown (no – yes[a])	−0.275	0.760	0.536	1.076	0.105	1.111	0.839	1.470
Food affordability (no – yes[a])	0.279	1.322	0.945	1.850	−0.718*	0.488	0.387	0.614
Environmental security								
Easy access to drinking water as before pandemic (no – yes[a])	0.154	1.167	0.809	1.684	0.150	1.161	0.847	1.592
Cooking gas was available during lockdown (no – yes[a])	0.176	1.193	0.832	1.708	−0.172	0.842	0.627	1.132
Was garbage taken care during lockdown (no – yes[a])	0.423	1.526	1.097	2.124	−0.172	0.842	0.627	1.132
Political security								
Received Government support (no – helpless[a])	−0.908**	0.403	0.169	0.963	0.572	1.773	0.486	6.462
Received Government support (ration – helpless[a])	−1.492	0.225	0.092	0.552	1.088	2.968	0.812	10.849
Received Government support (medical help – helpless[a])	−1.205	0.300	0.115	0.783	0.914	2.495	0.657	9.472

(*Continued*)

Table 8.3.   (*Continued*)

Variables	Poor				Borderline			
	B	Exp (*B*)	95% CI for Exp (*B*)		*B*	Exp (*B*)	95% CI for Exp (*B*)	
			LB	LB			LB	UB
Received Government support (financial – helpless[a])	−1.308	0.270	0.092	0.792	1.422**	4.146	1.068	16.093
Received Government support (help line to call if needed – helpless[a])	−0.388	0.678	0.240	1.916	0.901	2.462	0.586	10.336
Community security								
Did you get healthcare support from community during lockdown (no – yes[a])	−0.740*	0.477	0.283	0.804	−0.257	0.773	0.459	1.302
Did you get food support from community during lockdown (no – yes[a])	0.265	1.304	0.926	1.835	−0.034	0.966	0.747	1.250
Did you get financial support from community during lockdown (no – yes[a])	−0.312	0.732	0.309	1.734	−0.661	0.516	0.273	0.978
Personal security								
Did family violence increase during lockdown (no – yes[a])	−0.09	0.91	0.61	1.36	−0.40	0.67	0.41	1.11

Source: Estimated by authors.
[a]Reference level.
CI indicates confidence interval.
Significance determined at ***$p < 0.01$, **$p < 0.05$, *$p < 0.1$.

4. Discussion

The COVID-19 pandemic brought about tangible changes in individuals' livelihoods. One of the primary adversities during the pandemic was hurdles in the availability and accessibility of nutritional food, particularly for those in informal-economy households who lost their occupations and jobs due to severe economic lockdowns and restrictions, experiencing a major impact on food consumption patterns. The current study aims to determine the variation in FCSs of informal-economy households in time periods before and during the pandemic. Subsequently, we investigate the human security factors responsible for the significant reduction in the consumption of influenced food groups.

The outcomes highlight a severe reduction in the FCS. We focus on factors with an odds ratio greater than 1.0, reflecting a greater likelihood of having the outcome (a greater likelihood of poor and borderline FCS). Consequently, two key factors, namely, (a) the number of meals consumed per day and (b) government support, stand out as noteworthy results in the wake of the pandemic. In general, these results bring out three aspects of human security, namely, food and political security, as significant contributors to the likelihood of food consumption reduction during the pandemic.

Under the aspect of food security, the findings suggest that consuming a smaller number of meals per day reduces the likelihood of poor FCSs in informal-economy households. Dieticians recommend three meals a day for healthy digestion and proper assimilation of nutrients (Paoli et al., 2019). Curtailing daily food intake or skipping one meal is analogous to moderate food insecurity, according to the World Bank (The World Bank, 2020). Existing evidence on food insecurity in India reveals that impoverished communities in the country are consuming fewer calories due to household financial restrictions on food spending (Tandon, 2022).

In terms of political security, the existing literature highlights the limited role of government support in providing ration, medical help, and financial support to encourage food consumption (Aman & Masood, 2020; Kim et al., 2018; Sinha, 2021). In contrast to previous findings, the results of the current study indicate that the government has not been successful in enabling the consumption of some major food groups (such as protein food groups) among underprivileged and informal-economy households. This, in turn, leads to poor food consumption and food insecurity across households. For instance, India's nutrition programs, through the public distribution system (PDS), have targeted the vulnerable population by providing subsidized food grains, including rice, wheat, and millets, under the National Food Security Act. However, evidence affirms that the recommended dietary allowance for protein and energy is unmet for low-income households with low access to food (Saxena & Mohan, 2021). A nutritional report shows the under-consumption of major food groups provided under most feeding programmes due to a lack of availability, affordability, and/or awareness of food groups, dietary adequacy, and frequency of consumption (Shoba Suri, 2020). Hence, a re-evaluation of the relevant system with a focus on major food groups in the daily diets of the vulnerable population needs to be considered to eliminate any gaps in balanced food consumption and boost food security.

In the context of the COVID-19 pandemic, it is important to acknowledge that the effects of job loss extended to individuals across all social classes (Bonal & González, 2020; Kalil et al., 2020; Niles et al., 2020). Our study, which primarily focused on unskilled and semi-skilled employees, offers valuable insights into their experiences during this challenging period. However, the pandemic's repercussions transcended these boundaries, impacting people from various socio-economic backgrounds. While our research provides a microcosmic view of the challenges faced by a specific group, its applicability extends to a broader population. Our findings shed light on the universal dynamics of job loss, food security, and human security during crises. We aim to highlight the relevance of our study to a wider range of socio-economic groups, contributing to a more comprehensive understanding of the pandemic's impact on diverse populations.

Moreover, recent studies reveal that as informal employees struggle to survive amid the crisis, the post-crisis period put additional pressure on the already fragile sector (ILO, 2020; ILO et al., 2022; Swarna et al., 2022). The impact of COVID-19 on informal employment continues, and with the crisis lasting a long time, the global economy is expected to reduce the need for things and services from informal businesses (Shekar & Mansoor, 2020).

While the current study aimed to investigate the influence of various security variables on FCSs, it is noteworthy that we observed non-significant results for health security, environment security, community security, and personal security. These findings can be attributed to several factors. Firstly, within the scope of our research, health security may not have exhibited a significant impact on FCS due to the primary focus on economic and food security aspects, which took precedence in our investigation. Secondly, the connection between environmental factors and FCSs in our study population may not have been as robust as other variables examined, possibly due to the multifaceted and nuanced nature of environmental influences on food security.

Moreover, our concentration on individual and household-level factors affecting food security may have contributed to the non-significant findings in community security, as the impact of community security on FCSs may operate indirectly and require a distinct approach or scale of analysis. Lastly, the multifaceted nature of personal security, encompassing a wide array of individual factors, could explain the lack of significant results, suggesting that the specific elements of personal security we assessed may not have demonstrated a strong direct relationship with FCS. These observations underscore the complexity of the factors influencing food security and warrant further exploration to comprehensively understand their dynamics.

5. Conclusion and Policy Implications

The present study provides a comprehensive analysis of the factors contributing to the likelihood of food insecurity in informal-economy households. We ascertained the human security aspects surrounding a population crucially impacting the reduction of food consumption during the COVID-19 pandemic in India.

Among the various factors, the number of meals consumed per day has the most significant impact on the likelihood of food insecurity in informal-economy households. The findings suggest that the consumption of two or fewer meals per day leads to a poor FCS. In order to address these interruptions, governments all over the world issued directives, including delivering packaged meals, food grains, and take-home meals, to ensure that meal services for millions of people were restored. However, evidence shows several barriers, such as a lack of human resources to deliver meals to remote students, logistics issues, increased fear among frontline workers facilitating meal services, and limited government support, challenged the school authorities and meal service organizations to innovate more creative ways to meet the necessity of children dependent on these meal services, requiring a strategy to fulfil.

Furthermore, the limited role of government support is a crucial factor in poor FCSs or food insecurity among informal-economy households during the pandemic. The Government of India has various safety net programs under the National Food Security Act, such as the Integrated Child Development Services, the Mid-Day Meal Scheme, PDS, Pradhan MantriGaribKalyan Anna Yojana, and Atmanirbhar Bharat Abhiyan, aiming to address food security concerns and mitigate the impact on the nutritional status of the population. However, as per the Global Nutrition Report in 2019, India had 6.2 crore more people living with food insecurity, marking a 3.8% increase between 2014 and 2019. In 2020, India remained home to nearly 200 million undernourished people (Ray & Suri, 2021). Given the importance of government support in enhancing food security and overall health outcomes, policymakers need to emphasize accessible approaches, such as community-based food distribution centres and the utilization of mobile food vans, to deliver nutritious food to the vulnerable population. These strategies offer practical ways to ensure that vulnerable populations have regular access to adequate and healthy meals.

6. Limitations and Future Scope

While the study provides valuable insights into the broader impacts of the COVID-19 pandemic on the informal group, it is important to acknowledge certain limitations. Firstly, due to the uneven gender distribution within our participant composition (20% females and 80% males), a detailed comparative analysis between male and female participants was not pursued, limiting the depth of our gender-related exploration. Additionally, while recognizing the vulnerability of women within the informal group, we were unable to provide detailed information on the well-fed status of women and the specific impacts on young children and the elderly. The constraints in obtaining granular data on these specific dimensions pose a limitation to our study.

Moreover, it is essential to note that our study was conducted primarily in Bangalore, a city known for having a substantial informal economy workforce. While this context provided rich insights into the challenges faced by informal workers, the generalizability of our findings to other cities in India may be influenced by regional variations in economic structures, government interventions, and social dynamics. Conducting similar studies in diverse urban settings across the country could offer a more comprehensive understanding of the nuanced challenges faced by informal economy workers in different contexts.

Furthermore, our research primarily focused on unskilled and semi-skilled employees within the informal sector, providing a microcosmic view of the challenges faced by this specific group. To enhance the depth of our understanding, future studies could explore the comparisons in various social classes within the informal economy. Examining the experiences of different social classes, such as skilled workers versus unskilled workers or those with varying income levels, could unveil distinct patterns and dynamics, contributing to a more nuanced understanding of the impacts of the pandemic on different strata within the informal economy.

Additionally, considering the evolving nature of the COVID-19 situation, it is crucial to acknowledge that our study primarily captures a snapshot during the pandemic. Future research could explore the post-COVID-19 effects on informal economy workers, investigating how the recovery process, policy interventions, and societal changes impact the well-being, employment status, and food security of individuals in the informal sector. This longitudinal approach would enable a comprehensive examination of the sustained impacts and adaptive strategies employed by informal workers in the aftermath of the pandemic.

References

Aman, F., & Masood, S. (2020). How nutrition can help to fight against COVID-19 pandemic. *Pakistan Journal of Medical Sciences, 36,* 121–123. https://doi.org/doi: https://doi.org/10.12669/pjms.36.COVID19-S4.2776

Aneesh, M., & Patil, R. S. (2021). Diet diversity of urban households in India during the COVID-19 lockdown. *Nutrition and Health, 28,* 685–691. https://doi.org/10.1177/02601060211019676

Baniya, B., Ghimire, A., & Mahat, A. (2021). Impacts of COVID-19 on world economy and sustainable development goal in Nepal. *COGNITION: A Peer Reviewed Transdisciplinary Research Journal, 3*(1), 27. www.un.org/sustainabledevelopment/sustainable-development-goals/

Bansal, V. (2021). India's godowns are overflowing. So why are people starving? | The Indian Express. *The Indian Express.* https://indianexpress.com/article/opinion/columns/indias-godowns-are-overflowing-so-why-are-people-starving-7440463/

Bàrcena, A. (2020). Coyuntura, escenarios y proyecciones hacia 2030 ante la presente crisis de Covid-19. *Cepal, 66,* 1–66. https://issuu.com/publicacionescepal/docs/covid-19sdgshortunds2030_30_03_2020

Bhol, A., Sanwalka, N., Kapasi, T. A., Piplodwala, S. Z., Ansari, L. M. A., Katawala, F. M., & Bhandary, T. A. (2021). Changes in snacking patterns during Covid-19 lockdown in adults from Mumbai City, India. *Current Research in Nutrition and Food Science, 9*(3), 970–979. https://doi.org/10.12944/CRNFSJ.9.3.24

Bijarnia, R. (2021). SubscriberWrites: How Covid increased malnutrition, especially in children, and is crisis of the future. *The Print.* https://theprint.in/yourturn/subscriberwrites-how-covid-increased-malnutrition-especially-in-children-and-is-crisis-of-the-future/667792/

Bonal, X., & González, S. (2020). The impact of lockdown on the learning gap: Family and school divisions in times of crisis. *International Review of Education, 66*(5–6), 635–655. https://doi.org/10.1007/s11159-020-09860-z

Borkowski, A., Ortiz Correa, J. S., Bundy, D. A. P., Burbano, C., Hayashi, C., Lloyd-Evans, E., Neitzel, J., & Reuge, N. (2021, January, 1–30). *COVID-19: Missing more than a classroom the impact of school closures on children's nutrition.* UNICEF Office of Research – Innocenti. https://www.unicef-irc.org/publications/1176-covid-19-missing-more-than-a-classroom-the-impact-of-school-closures-on-childrens-nutrition.html

Bowe, M., Wakefield, J. R. H., Kellezi, B., Stevenson, C., McNamara, N., Jones, B. A., Sumich, A., & Heym, N. (2022). The mental health benefits of community helping during crisis: Coordinated helping, community identification and sense of unity during the COVID-19 pandemic. *Journal of Community and Applied Social Psychology, 32*(3), 521–535. https://doi.org/10.1002/casp.2520

Chopra, S., Ranjan, P., Singh, V., Kumar, S., & Arora, M. (2020, January). Impact of COVID-19 on lifestyle-related behaviours – A cross-sectional audit of responses from nine hundred and ninety-five participants from India. *Diabetes & Metabolic Syndrome: Clinical Research & Reviews, 14*, 2021–2030. https://doi.org/10.1016/j.dsx.2020.09.034

Cohen, J. (1988). Statistical power analysis for the behavioral sciences. *Lawrence Erlbaum Associates, 2*(10), 567. https://www.utstat.toronto.edu/~brunner/oldclass/378f16/readings/CohenPower.pdf

Cucinotta, D., & Vanelli, M. (2020). WHO declares COVID-19 a pandemic. *Acta Biomedica, 91*(1), 157–160. https://doi.org/10.23750/abm.v91i1.9397

Daniel, A. S., & Varier, M. (2022). Changing consumer behaviour during the pandemic in India: The new normal. *Amity Journal of Management Research, 5*(1), 651–662. https://amity.edu/UserFiles/admaa/2d48aAJMR651-662.pdf

Fine, D., Klier, J., Mahajan, D., Raabe, N., Schubert, J., Singh, N., & Ungur, S. (2020). *How to rebuild and reimagine jobs amid the coronavirus crisis| McKinsey.* McKinsey. https://www.mckinsey.com/industries/public-and-social-sector/our-insights/how-to-rebuild-and-reimagine-jobs-amid-the-coronavirus-crisis

Dor-Haim, H., Katzburg, S., Revach, P., Levine, H., & Barak, S. (2021). The impact of COVID-19 lockdown on physical activity and weight gain among active adult population in Israel: A cross-sectional study. *BMC Public Health, 21*(1), 1–10. https://doi.org/10.1186/s12889-021-11523-z

Ehsan, A., Klaas, H. S., Bastianen, A., & Spini, D. (2019). Social capital and health: A systematic review of systematic reviews. *SSM – Population Health, 8*(April), 100425. https://doi.org/10.1016/j.ssmph.2019.100425

FAO. (2020, September, 1–24). *Impacts of COVID-19 on food security and nutrition: Developing effective policy responses to address the hunger and malnutrition pandemic* [HLPE Issues Paper]. https://doi.org/10.4060/cb1000en%0Awww.fao.org/cfs/cfs-hlpe

Fenner, R., & Cernev, T. (2021). The implications of the Covid-19 pandemic for delivering the sustainable development goals. *Futures, 128*(January), 102726. https://doi.org/10.1016/j.futures.2021.102726

Filimonau, V., Derqui, B., & Matute, J. (2020). The COVID-19 pandemic and organisational commitment of senior hotel managers. *International Journal of Hospitality Management, 91*(July), 102659. https://doi.org/10.1016/j.ijhm.2020.102659

Flourish Ventures. (2020). *The digital hustle.* https://flourishventures.com/wp-content/uploads/2020/10/FlourishVentures-GigWorkerStudy-India-FINAL-2020-09-29.pdf

Herrera, L., Justie, B., Koonse, T., & Waheed, A. S. (2020). *Worker ownership, COVID-19, and the future of the gig economy.* UCLA, Institute for Research on Labor and Employment. https://escholarship.org/uc/item/3h60d754

Ho, C. S., Chee, C. Y., & Ho, R. C. (2020). Mental health strategies to combat the psychological impact of COVID-19 beyond paranoia and panic. *Annals of the Academy of Medicine, Singapore, 49*(1), 1–3.

IISD. (2022). *World population data sheet 2022 highlights excess deaths due to COVID-19 | news | SDG knowledge hub | IISD.* SDG KNOWLEDGE HUB, IISD. http://sdg. iisd.org/news/world-population-data-sheet-2022-highlights-excess-deaths-due-to-covid-19/

ILO. (2020, April). *ILO monitor: COVID-19 and the world of work. Second edition: Updated estimates and analysis.* International Labour Organization. https://doi.org/10.18356/ ba5cc386-en

ILO, FAO, IFAD, & WHO. (2022). *Impact of COVID-19 on people's livelihoods, their health and our food systems.* International Labour Organization. http://www.ilo.org/global/ about-the-ilo/newsroom/statements-and-speeches/WCMS_757974/lang–en/index. htm

Kakaei, H., Nourmoradi, H., Bakhtiyari, S., Jalilian, M., & Mirzaei, A. (2022). Effect of COVID-19 on food security, hunger, and food crisis. *COVID-19 and the Sustainable Development Goals, 29,* 3–29. https://doi.org/10.1016/B978-0-323-91307-2.00005-5

Kalil, A., Mayer, S., & Shah, R. (2020). *Impact of the COVID-19 crisis on family dynamics in economically vulnerable households* [Working Paper 134]. University of Chicago, Becker Friedman Institute for Economics. https://bfi.uchicago.edu/wp-content/ uploads/2020/10/BFI_WP_2020143.pdf

Kaushal, A. (2022). Consumer cognition with respect to ecommerce during pandemic. *Journal of Public Relations and Advertising, 1*(1), 21–22. https://www.mcu.ac.in/ wp-content/uploads/2022/04/7-Consumer-Cognition-With-Respect-To-Ecom-merce-During-Pandemic.pdf

Kecinski, M., Messer, K. D., McFadden, B. R., & Malone, T. (2020). Environmental and regulatory concerns during the COVID-19 pandemic: Results from the pandemic food and stigma survey. *Environmental and Resource Economics, 76*(4), 1139–1148. https://doi.org/10.1007/s10640-020-00438-9

Kim, M. K., Lee, S. M., Bae, S. H., Kim, H. J., Lim, N. G., Yoon, S. J., Lee, J. Y., & Jo, M. W. (2018). Socioeconomic status can affect pregnancy outcomes and complications, even with a universal healthcare system. *International Journal for Equity in Health, 17*(1), 2. https://doi.org/10.1186/s12939-017-0715-7

Kumar, R. R., Dhanaraj, S. A., Sain, R., Kumari, P., Roy, P., & Paul, S. (2020). Impacts on dietary habits and health of Indian population during COVID-19 lockdown. *Public Health Review: International Journal of Public Health Research, 7*(6), 38–48. https:// doi.org/10.17511/ijphr.2020.i06.01

Kumar Mishra, S. (2021). *COVID-19 and informal labor in India. Crisis and Fragility: Economic Impact of COVID-19 and Policy Responses, 3*(1), 243–257.

Kumari, L. (2022). *The impact of Covid-19 pandemic over the state of food security and nutrition in India introduction to SDGs* (Vol. 70, Issue 65) National Human Rights Commission. https://nhrc.nic.in/sites/default/files/Group%205%20June.pdf.

Kwak, C., & Clayton-Matthews, A. (2002). Multinomial logistic regression. *Nursing Research, 51*(6), 404–410. https://doi.org/10.1097/00006199-200211000-00009

Mahendra, S. D., & Sengupta, R. (IGIDR). (2020). *COVID-19 impact on the Indian economy – Detailed analysis.* Indira Gandhi Institute of Development Research. http://www.igidr.ac.in/pdf/publication/WP-2020-013.pdf%0Ahttps://blog.smallcase. com/the-new-normal-analysis-of-covid-19-on-indian-businesses-sectors-and-the-economy/

Mishra, N. P., Das, S. S., Yadav, S., Khan, W., Afzal, M., Alarifi, A., Kenawy, E. R., Ansari, M. T., Hasnain, M. S., & Nayak, A. K. (2020). Global impacts of pre- and post-COVID-19 pandemic: Focus on socio-economic consequences. *Sensors International, 1*(July), 1–7. https://doi.org/10.1016/j.sintl.2020.100042

Nestle, M., Wing, R., Birch, L., DiSogra, L., Drewnowski, A., Middleton, S., Sigman-Grant, M., Sobal, J., Winston, M., & Economos, C. (1998). Behavioral and social influences on food choice. *Nutrition Reviews, 56*(5 II), 50–64. https://doi.org/10.1111/j.1753-4887.1998.tb01732.x

Niles, M. T., Bertmann, F., Belarmino, E. H., Wentworth, T., Biehl, E., & Neff, R. (2020). *The early food insecurity impacts of COVID-19.* MedRxiv. https://doi.org/10.1101/2020.05.09.20096412

NITI Aayog. (2022, June). *India's booming gig and platform economy.* https://www.niti.gov.in/sites/default/files/2022-06/Policy_Brief_India%27s_Booming_Gig_and_Platform_Economy_27062022.pdf

Paoli, A., Tinsley, G., Bianco, A., & Moro, T. (2019). The influence of meal frequency and timing on health in humans: The role of fasting. *Nutrients, 11*(4), 719. https://doi.org/10.3390/NU11040719

Perappadan, B. S. (2021). High levels of maternal and child under nutrition continue to plague India: UNICEF official – The Hindu. *The Hindu.* https://www.thehindu.com/sci-tech/health/high-levels-of-maternal-and-child-under-nutrition-continue-to-plague-india-unicef-official-arjan-de-wagt/article36734871.ece

Phatak, M., Sujiv, A., Kamble, P., Patil, A., & Deshmukh, P. (2022). Impact of lockdown on physical activity, sleep and eating habits in Central India. *Indian Journal of Physiology and Allied Sciences, 74*(1), 32–39. http://ijpas.org/index.php/ijpas/article/view/39

Rawat, D., Dixit, V., Gulati, S., Gulati, S., & Gulati, A. (2020). Impact of COVID-19 outbreak on lifestyle behaviour: A review of studies published in India. *Diabetes & Metabolic Syndrome: Clinical Research & Reviews, 15*, 331–336. https://doi.org/10.1016/j.dsx.2020.12.038

Ray, S., & Suri, S. (2021). *Global nutrition report 2021 – India's nutrition profile and how to meet global nutrition target | ORF.* ORF. https://www.orfonline.org/expert-speak/global-nutrition-report-2021/

Roy, A., Singh, A. K., Mishra, S., Chinnadurai, A., Mitra, A., & Bakshi, O. (2020). Mental health implications of COVID-19 pandemic and its response in India. *International Journal of Social Psychiatry, 103,* 431–438. https://doi.org/10.1177/0020764020950769

Sarışık, M., & Usta, S. (2021). Global effect of COVID-19. *COVID-19 and the hospitality and tourism industry: A research companion* (pp. 41–59). https://doi.org/10.4337/9781800376243.00008

Saxena, A., & Mohan, S. B. (2021). The impact of food security disruption due to the Covid-19 pandemic on tribal people in India. *Advances in Food Security and Sustainability, 6*(January), 65–81. https://doi.org/10.1016/bs.af2s.2021.07.006

Shekar, K. C., & Mansoor, K. (2020). *COVID-19: Lockdown impact on informal sector in India.* Azim Premji University. https://practiceconnect.azimpremjiuniversity.edu.in/covid-19-lockdown-impact-on-informal-sector-in-india/

Shoba Suri. (2020). *India's protein deficiency and the need to address the problem | ORF.* ORF. https://www.orfonline.org/expert-speak/indias-protein-deficiency-and-the-need-to-address-the-problem/

Shulla, K., Voigt, B.-F., Cibian, S., Scandone, G., Martinez, E., Nelkovski, F., & Salehi, P. (2021). Effects of COVID-19 on the sustainable development goals (SDGs). *Discover Sustainability, 2*(1), 2–15. https://doi.org/10.1007/s43621-021-00026-x

Singh, B., Jain, S., & Rastogi, A. (2021). Effects of nationwide COVID-19 lockdown on lifestyle and diet: An Indian survey. *Journal of Family Medicine and Primary Care, 6*(2), 169–170. https://doi.org/10.4103/jfmpc.jfmpc

Sinha, D. (2021). Hunger and food security in the times of Covid-19. *Journal of Social and Economic Development, 23*(S2), 320–331. https://doi.org/10.1007/s40847-020-00124-y

Swarna, N. R., Anjum, I., Hamid, N. N., Rabbi, G. A., Islam, T., Evana, E. T., Islam, N., Rayhan, M. I., Morshed, K. A. M., & Juel Miah, A. S. M. (2022, March). Understanding the impact of COVID-19 on the informal sector workers in Bangladesh. *PLoS ONE, 17*(3), 1–20. https://doi.org/10.1371/journal.pone.0266014

Tam, S., Sood, S., & Johnston, C. (2021). *Impact of COVID-19 on small businesses in Canada, first quarter of 2021.* StatCan COVID-19. https://www150.statcan.gc.ca/n1/pub/45-28-0001/2021001/article/00009-eng.htm

Tandon, A. (2022). Food-insecure Indians eating less, skipping meal: Govt study: The Tribune India. *The Tribune India.* https://www.tribuneindia.com/news/nation/food-insecure-indians-eating-less-skipping-meal-govt-study-76900

The World Bank. (2020). *Food security and COVID-19.* The World Bank. https://www.worldbank.org/en/topic/agriculture/brief/food-security-and-covid-19

Theodos, B., Hangen, E., González-Hermoso, J., Docter, B., & Davis, C. (2021). *Despite the pandemic's hit to sales, small businesses aren't experiencing dramatically higher delinquencies. But will that trend last?* Urban Institute. https://www.urban.org/urban-wire/despite-pandemics-hit-sales-small-businesses-arent-experiencing-dramatically-higher-delinquencies-will-trend-last

Times of India. (2022). Reimagining supply chains amidst COVID-19 – Times of India. *Times of India.* https://timesofindia.indiatimes.com/auto/cars/reimagining-supply-chains-amidst-covid-19/articleshow/89113808.cms

United Nations. (2016). *Human Security Handbook: An integrated approach for the realization of the sustainable development goals and the priority areas of the international community and the United Nations system.* United Nation. https://www.un.org/humansecurity/wp-content/uploads/2017/10/h2.pdf

United Nations. (2020a). *Goal 2: Zero hunger – United Nations sustainable development.* United Nations. https://www.un.org/sustainabledevelopment/hunger/

United Nations. (2020b). *Universal declaration of human rights | United Nations.* United Nations. https://www.un.org/en/about-us/universal-declaration-of-human-rights

Wang, C., Riyu, P., Xiaoyang, W., Yilin, T., Linkang, X., Cyrus, S. H., & Roger, C. H. (2020). Immediate psychological responses and associated factors during the initial stage of the 2019 coronavirus disease (COVID-19) epidemic among the general population in China. *International Journal of Environmental Research and Public Health, 17*(5), 1–25. https://www.ncbi.nlm.nih.gov/pmc/articles/PMC7084952/

WFP. (2008). *World food programme.* https://www.wfp.org/publications/technical-guidance-sheet-food-consumption-analysis-calculation-and-use-food-consumption-score-food-s

WHO. (2021). Despite being self-sufficient in food production, India faces problems of hunger and food insecurity due to widespread economic distress, high unemployment and high levels of inequality [Comment – INSIGHTSIAS]. INSIGHTSIAS. https://www.insightsonindia.com/2021/08/09/despite-being-self-sufficient-in-food-production-india-faces-problems-of-hunger-and-food-insecurity-due-to-widespread-economic-distress-high-unemployment-and-high-levels-of-inequality-comment/

WHO. (2022). *Coronavirus disease (COVID-19) pandemic.* World Health Organization. https://www.who.int/europe/emergencies/situations/covid-19

Worsley, A., Blasche, R., Ball, K., & Crawford, D. (2004). The relationship between education and food consumption in the 1995 Australian National Nutrition Survey. *Public Health Nutrition, 7*(5), 649–663. https://doi.org/10.1079/PHN2003577

Xiang, L., Tang, M., Yin, Z., Zheng, M., & Lu, S. (2021). The COVID-19 pandemic and economic growth: Theory and simulation. *Frontiers in Public Health, 9*(May), 1–14. https://doi.org/10.3389/fpubh.2021.741525

Chapter 9

The Role of Self-help Groups in Financial Inclusion in India

Debolina Saha and Razdan Alam

Department of Economics, RabindraBharati University, Kolkata, West Bengal, India

Abstract

This study attempts to evaluate the performance of women-dominated self-help groups (SHGs) in India and their contribution to financial inclusion. The two dimensions – spread and status of SHGs are considered to assess their performance level, where each of the dimensions has a few number of indicators. The study also constructs a composite financial inclusion index (FII) to calculate the FII values, which appear from the performance of SHGs, during the study period 2007–2021, in India. Finally, the study establishes a relationship between financial inclusion and human development since women's involvement in financial inclusion is also conducive to human development. The study comes to the conclusion that despite success in achieving financial inclusion through promoting SHGs, the government should keep a focus on the ever-increasing amount of non-performing assets (NPA) of the banks since a part of that is related to the functioning of SHGs. However, the promotion of SHGs is fundamental for women empowerment, human development, and thereby, to ensure sustainable development.

Keywords: Self-help group; microcredit; financial inclusion; human development; women empowerment; India

Introduction

Financial inclusion aims to offer affordable financial services to the privileged and underprivileged sections of the society in an incessant manner. It ensures

Informal Economy and Sustainable Development Goals:
Ideas, Interventions and Challenges, 183–202
doi:10.1108/978-1-83753-980-220241010

financial protection for the economically backward people and reduces their dependence on informal money lenders, or charity, which are not sustainable. Broadly, financial inclusion deals with three aspects – access to credit, wealth creation and contingency planning. Access to credit opens the doors for the poor people to create new job opportunities, expand their existing businesses, invest for their future consumption, education, health care services, etc. Since financial inclusion also helps savings of the disadvantaged groups, it reduces poverty, inequality in income distribution and promotes inclusive growth. In lots of research works (such as Chibba, 2009; Dahiya & Kumar, 2020; Park & Mercado, 2015), it is well reflected that financial inclusion has helped economic growth with fair distribution across society and creating opportunities to all. It is often seen that economically backward people are unaware of their retirement plans. Although access to credit helps improve their income and lifestyle in the present times, they do not possess enough funds which can be utilized exclusively in future when they get old. Financial inclusion deals with such contingency planning by providing retirement plans which might give good returns to the poor people in the later stages of their lives. The vulnerable section of the society for whom the financial inclusion primarily works for includes women and children, old and physically challenged people, people of unorganized sector, agricultural and small-scale industrial labourers, unemployed persons, etc.

The term 'Financial Inclusion' was first pioneered in India, in April 2005, by Y. Venugopal Reddy, the then Governor of the Reserve Bank of India (RBI). The people of *Mangalam* village in Puducherry were fortunate enough to reap its first benefits. Very soon, the concept started to spread in every corner of the country without ignoring any remote area. However, financial inclusion was commenced in India long back, through the Co-operative Society Act in 1904, under the British rule, to help the deprived rural people. Much later, the State Bank of India was established in 1955. In the subsequent phase, nationalization of commercial banks took place in 1969 and 1980, Regional Rural Bank set up in 1975, and National Bank for Agriculture and Rural Development (NABARD) was founded in 1982. The basic initiatives taken by the government for financial inclusion are of opening up bank branches in rural areas through Rural Infrastructure Development Fund; providing access to credit to the vulnerable groups; creating SHG–Bank linkage programmes; utilization of *Business Correspondents* for providing financial and banking services to the common people; creating funds for financial inclusion; introducing financial literacy programmes; promoting different plans and schemes such as National Rural Financial Inclusion Plan (NRFIP), Aadhar Card (Unique Identification Number) for the Indian Nationals, Swabhiman, Pradhan Mantri Jan Dhan Yojana (PMJDY), the National Strategy for Financial Inclusion (NSFI), etc. Therefore to assess financial inclusion, the role of banks and microfinance institutions (MFIs), several insurance and pension schemes are of important ones. However, this chapter only focuses on financial inclusion and informal workforce.

Informal workforce is widespread throughout the developed and developing nations where the women are more likely than men to work in the informal economy. Generally, the definition of employment in the informal economy includes both – those workers who work in such enterprises that are not officially registered and those workers who hold informal jobs which lack basic social or legal protection and employment benefits. Women are particularly overrepresented in the second group being home-based workers with a lack of opportunities to explore the outer world. However, evidence suggests that those women, who came under the umbrella of financial inclusion, had started their own businesses, earned income and also gained intra-household bargaining power. In fact, women's economic empowerment boosts their access to and control over productive resources, access to decent work and lifestyles, meaningful participation in economic decision-making, etc. Even financial inclusion initiatives support women to think of their children's independence, better education, access to better health care, etc.

Since financial inclusion with women empowerment insists on inclusive growth, so this chapter focuses on microcredit and the role of SHGs. Microcredit is a part of the broader concept of microfinance. Microfinance deals with credit and savings of the vulnerable society that are facilitated by the government and registered non-government agencies. It also includes micro insurance, micro pension and other financial services to the excluded people. In this system, scheduled commercial banks and cooperatives sanction credit and encourage the poor people to open savings account, whereas non-governmental organizations (NGOs) train them to utilize financial services. Microcredit as a subset of this microfinance is involved with an extremely small amount of loans given to groups of individuals to help them become self-employed or grow up small businesses. It targets the economically backward people in rural, semi-urban and urban areas and is also known as 'microlending' or 'microloan'.

The main feature of microcredit system is group lending. Though the group members come through self-selection, they should have some entrepreneurial skills which may enable them to repay loan and generate savings for future business expansion. Stiglitz (1990) opined that 'Peer monitoring is largely responsible for the successful financial performance of the Grameen Bank of Bangladesh and similar group lending programmes elsewhere'. Moreover, according to Ray (1998), lending sequentially to group members minimizes the contagion effect of an individual default in this system. Although this loan is collateral-free, the size of loan is very small because of the low rate of interest compared to normal banking system.

This microlending actually gave birth to SHGs in developing nations which typically means informal groups of people who come together to deal with their common problems and to do something for their betterment with the idea of mutual support. The SHG approach of financial inclusion also endorses the enjoyment of human rights for the marginalized group. In India, a large majority of women's group programmes are implemented through SHGs. India's SHG movement, which evolved almost three decades earlier than now, has reached into one of the world's largest institutional platforms of the marginalized group with the help of banks and NGOs. According to the World Bank report (2020), 67 million Indian women were the members of 6 million SHGs nationwide. National Rural Livelihoods Mission is one of the biggest flagship programmes in India to reduce poverty through mobilizing poor rural women into SHGs and building community institutions of the deprived section. SHGs also served for the nation in difficult times. In the last pandemic, the SHGs served for the society by distributing masks, developing community kitchens, resolving conflicts, running help desk for the elderly and quarantined people, etc.[1] Therefore, though micro-credit system and SHGs have certain drawbacks like posing threats to NPA, they also possess multidimensional impacts like the generation of employment and income, reducing inequality and poverty, empowerment of women, formation of social capital, etc., over and above bringing more people under the umbrella of financial inclusion.

In developing nations, financial inclusion assists in more stable financial system and mobilizes domestic resources for development activities through an increase in national savings. The SHGs play a significant role in generating savings of the unprivileged section, under the umbrella of financial inclusion, and thereby, help sustain economic growth which is also termed as *sustainable development*. It is agreeable that women's involvement in financial inclusion is conducive to human development, and thereby inclusive growth. The basic idea of sustainable development is aligned with transforming the world with no one leaving behind.

History of Microfinance with Its Different Forms of Operation

Lysander Spooner was the theorist who wrote about the benefits of small credit to entrepreneurs and farmers as a way of reducing poverty in the mid of 18th century. Friedrich Wilhelm Raiffeisen founded the first rural central bank named *Rhenish Agricultural Cooperative Bank* to support farmers in rural Germany.[2] The modern use of the term 'Microfinance' is rooted in the formation of Grameen Bank in Bangladesh by the microfinance pioneer Muhammad Yunus in the 1980s. In India, NABARD took this concept and initiated a microfinance system in India.

The different forms of MFIs operating in India are (a) joint liability groups (JLGs), (b) SHG, (c) Grameen Bank (GB) and (d) rural cooperatives (RCs). JLGs are informal groups which consist of 4–10 individuals per group in intentions with availing bank loan either individually or through the group mechanism against mutual guarantee. Here, the members in a group are from the same village with having the same socio-economic backgrounds. JLGs generally consist of tenant farmers, share croppers, small and marginal farmers who carry out agricultural activities for a period not less than one year. In addition to farm activities, the loan is also for off-farm and non-farm activities. While a JLG loan is regulated by the RBI, and NABARD, its terms and conditions vary from lender to lender.

In India, a large number of poor people from different regions are connected with SHG programmes. SHGs are economically homogeneous groups consisting of 10–20 members formed through a process of self-selection. NABARD started

[1]https://www.worldbank.org/en/news/feature/2020/04/11/women-self-help-groups-combat-covid19-coronavirus-pandemic-india.
[2]https://www.eacb.coop/en/others/events/raiffeisen-2018.html#.

promoting SHGs in 1991–1992, in India, on a large scale. The RBI allowed SHGs to open saving accounts in banks in 1993 to reap the facilities of banking services. SHG as a financial intermediary committee helps the marginalized section in getting timely loans at a reasonable rate of interest to foster financial inclusion. A loan granted by the bank to the SHG is purpose neutral as the group decides the purpose for which the loan is to be taken by the members. As indicated by RBI, the banks are expected to meet the entire credit requirements of SHG members for (a) income generation activities; (b) social needs like housing, education, marriage, etc. and (c) debt swapping. Thus linking of SHGs with banks is highlighted in the monetary policy statements of RBI and union budget announcements from time to time, and various guidelines are issued to banks in this regard.[3] Since SHGs are primarily women dominated, they help women to become financially self-reliant and to hold self-esteem and status in the society through upgrading their living standards. SHGs have well-defined rules and by-laws. They hold regular meetings, maintain records and retain savings and credit discipline.

The primary objective of the GB is to promote financial independence among the economically backward people in the villages. It targets the poorest of the poor in the society with particular emphasis on women. The loans disbursed by GBs are collateral free, and they encourage all the borrowers to become savers so that their deposits are converted into new loans for the more needy people in the villages. GBs create financial preconditions that enable the poor to receive further loans based upon the group performance over the prior loan. They also provide social development inputs like financial literacy and consciousness, health and nutrition training, etc., to the poor so as to make them individually and socially responsible. The GBs mobilize deposits primarily from rural and semi-urban areas and provide loans mostly to agricultural labourers, small and marginal farmers, rural artisans and other segments of priority sector to develop the rural economy. NABARD is the chief body set up to regulate the rural banking sector in India.

RCs are an important part of the Indian banking system and are regulated by RBI. Though NABARD is entrusted with the responsibility for conduct of statutory inspections of State Cooperative Banks, District Central Cooperative Banks and Regional Rural Banks under the Banking Regulation Act, 1949/(AACS), the regulatory powers continue to be vested with the RBI. RCs provide financial assistance to rural and low-income population across the country and protect them from exploitation by the wealthy individuals. They are often the main source of credit for agricultural and allied activities, small-scale industries and other small businesses. The co-operative banks are small-sized units which operate both in urban and non-urban centres.

Literature Review and Significance of the Present Study

Numerous literatures are there which throw light on the role of SHGs in economic and social development. The relevant literatures which match our study

---

[3]https://www.rbi.org.in/ScriptS/BS_ViewMasCirculardetails.aspx?id=11614.

objectives are discussed here. Elson (2009) pointed out that most of the women face gender inequalities in the developing societies, suffering from poverty which retards the process of economic growth and development. Although governmental authorities, NGOs, national and international businesses, charities, etc., have launched programmes to encourage and support female entrepreneurs, sometimes access to credit from the established banking system becomes a barrier to most of the aspiring businesswomen, and thereby, they resort to microfinance services (Kuzilwa, 2005). The primary goal of MFIs is to provide small-scale loans to especially rural women and educate them on how to utilize to get success (Vossenberg, 2013). Lots of work has been done on microfinance, in general, and channelling microfinance through SGHs, in particular.

Gurumoorty (2000) revealed that credit needs of the rural women can be accomplished through the SHGs. SHGs also help women to take an active part in the socio-economic progress of the society. Rao (2004) pointed out that since the existing formal financial institutions had failed to provide loans to landless and marginalized groups, SHGs encouraged savings and endorsed income-generating activities through small loans. Even this initiative helped the disadvantaged group from getting rid of the vicious circle of poverty. Galab and Rao (2003) revealed that participation of women in SHGs reduced their dependency on moneylenders and improved the access to credit and quality of employment. This not only reduced the level of poverty but also made the rural women aware of health and nutrition, the educational status of children, etc. As a result, gender inequalities were reduced to some extent and freedom of voice in the home front and society was established. The study also found that women-headed households, aged women and *Dalits* were benefited more in the process of empowerment.

Several studies also draw attention to such positive impacts of SHGs on women empowerment. Puhazhendi and Satyasai (2001), covering 11 states and 4 different regions – north, south, east and west in India, exposed that the SHGs contributed to economic and social empowerment of economically backward rural women. Jothy and Sundar (2002) were on the notion that women development depends upon creating awareness on the issues related to legal rights, functional literacy, health and hygiene, communication and leadership skills for self and mutual help, etc. The authors found that irrespective of caste, creed and religion, SHGs enabled Tamil Nadu women in India to perform the activities like having vigilance on the functioning of the ration shops, preventing brewing of illicit liquor, helping the needy people, etc. Ramalakshmi (2003) showed how the women SHG members were appointed as dealers for promotion of sale in well-known manufacturing companies in Andhra Pradesh of India, where the majority of the members made savings regularly and that boosted their self-confidence. Their self-esteem even voiced against social evils like child marriage, dowry, untouchability, etc. Sharma (2001) opined that SHGs have strong gender orientation. More than 85 per cent of the SHGs linked to banks were reported to be women in his study. The author confirmed that women empowerment through SHGs boosted economic activities and decision-making ability at household and societal levels which called for the rural development process to be participatory, democratic and sustainable in India. Vijayanthi (2002) opined that mobilizing women into SHGs in Tamil Nadu under the comprehensive community development programme made the women empowered. They could access and control resources and manipulate the systems those had an effect on their lives, individually or collectively. The study also found that SHGs enhanced awareness levels of women on the issues like women's rights, mother and child welfare, sanitation and health, etc., in addition to promoting income-generation programmes. In the study of Sarkhel and Mondal (2013), a large number of the SHG members stated that their economic positions were improved by joining the groups in Jangal-Mahal areas of the Bankura district of West Bengal in India, and therefore, SHG participation was a major cause of improvement in their societal status.

Women Entrepreneur means when women initiate, organize and operate a business enterprise. Nawaz (2018) opined that entrepreneurship is a useful means to create job opportunities where female entrepreneurs could play a vital role. Manimekalai and Rajeswari (2001) revealed that the provision of micro-credit and assistance of NGOs helped the SHG members to build up organi-zational skill and leadership ability in managing various activities of a business in Coimbatore, Perambalur and Tiruchirappalli districts of Tamil Nadu during 1993–2000. Borbora and Mahanta (2001) exposed that SHGs helped the rural women of Assam in India in establishing a number of micro-enterprises for income-generating activities. Although women's access to financial resources has substantially increased over the years, their ability to benefit from finance is influ-enced by gender-related disadvantages (Skarlatos, 2004). In contrast, some stud-ies also keep different views. Ahl and Marlow (2012) opine that the women are more aware of natural environment and sustainable resource utilization which help make long-term decisions for their families and businesses.

Among the other notable evaluative studies on SHGs in India, Srivastava (2005), through collecting a micro sample of women members of SHGs in the four Indian States – Bihar, Chattisgarh, Madhya Pradesh and Uttar Pradesh, exhibited that women were able to contribute to household finances through micro-finance-based entrepreneurship which even led to decision-making ability in household chores. Panda (2009), using a multistage random sampling method, collected 150 cross-sectional samples from Jharkhand, Chhattisgarh and Odisha states of India, to measure the impact of participation in the SHG-based micro-finance. The author formulated a quasi-experimental design under which the tar-get group was compared with a selected control group across a set of household variables like income, assets positions, consumption, savings, employment, migra-tion and literacy. The study found that participation of women in the SHG pro-gramme was strongly determined by the household income, saving, employment, migration and literacy level. Again, Sahu (2013) made an attempt to find out the relationship between financial inclusion and economic growth across states in India. The author considered the socio-economic indicators of the states like literacy, per capita income, population, number of bank branches, number of SHGs, per capita net state domestic product (PNSDP) and found that 34 per cent of the change in the FII was due to changes in PNSDP. Moreover, the study revealed a significant correlation between FII and per capita income. However, no in-depth assessment was done to explore the role of SHGs on financial inclusion considering the spread and status of SHGs.

SHGs benefit not only individual women member or women's group but also extend help for their families and community as a whole. It is an acceptable fact that women's leadership is critical to the growth and development of a nation. From the overview of existing literature on SHGs, it is clearly visible that any comprehensive study on the role of SHGs to ensure financial inclusion at all India level has not been done so far for the last 15 years. Since women's involvement in financial inclusion is also conducive to human development, so the assessment of the relationship between financial inclusion through SHGs and human development is also an important research agenda. These gaps of the existing literatures on SHGs provide the insight to do further research works.

Objectives of the Study

The aim of the present study is to analyse the role of SHGs in financial inclusion in India during 2007–2021. Our study considers two dimensions – spread and status to evaluate the performance of SHGs. At the same time, this research work attempts to throw light on how far SHG activities have helped promote financial inclusion in India. Subsequently, the study investigates whether there is any significant relationship between financial inclusion and human development. Hence, the major objectives of the present study are as follows:

1. To calculate the composite FII values during the study period through the construction of a FII and considering the spread and status of SHGs in India.
2. To find out the relationship between financial inclusion through SHGs and human development in India, since women's involvement in financial inclusion is favourable to human development, and thereby inclusive growth.

Data and Methods Used in the Study

The study primarily uses secondary data for analysis collected from NABARD, on an annual basis, for the time period 2007–2021. The annual data of RBI and Global Data Lab have also been used for the study. While assessing the role of SHGs in financial inclusion in India, the two major dimensions have been considered namely, (A) spread of SHGs and (B) status of SHGs. Each of the dimensions has several indicators which are as follows:

A. Indicators related to the spread of SHGs:

  a. Total number of SHG members.
  b. Total number of SHGs credit-linked.
  c. Amount of bank loan provided to SHGs (in millions as of 31st March of each year).

B.   Indicators related to the status of SHGs:

   a.   Total number of SHGs saving-linked.
   b.   Amount of savings of SHGs (in millions as of 31st March of each year).
   c.   Amount of outstanding loan of SHGs (in millions as of 31st March of each year).

From the indicators *b* and *c* of dimension A, average loan per SHG (in millions) is calculated on an annual basis. Similarly, from the indicators *a* and *b* of dimension B, average savings per SHG (in millions) on an annual basis is calculated. Hence in both the dimensions A and B, the three indicators of each are reduced into two indicators. The indicators which influence SHG activities are analysed through regression analysis.

In the subsequent phase, the compound annual growth rate (CAGR) of each indicator has been calculated over the study period, at all India level. The following method has been used to calculate CAGRs of the indicators:

For any given time period *t*, let the value of the dependent variable (*y*) be y_t[4]. If the initial value of *y* is y_0 and *y* grows at the annual compound rate *r*, then we can write

$$y_t = Y_0(1+r)^t \tag{i}$$

Taking log on both sides, equation (i) becomes

$$\ln y_t = \ln y_0 + t \ln(1+r) \tag{ii}$$

Defining $\beta_1 = \ln y_0$ and $\beta_2 = \ln(1+r)$, equation (ii) takes the form of an econometric equation like

$$\ln y_t = \beta_1 + t\beta_2 + U_t \tag{iii}$$

Here, β_1 is the intercept and β_2 is the slope coefficient which indicates relative change in the dependent variable (y_t) due to the absolute change in the independent variable (t). U_t is the random error term which is assumed to be independently, identically and normally distributed.

Therefore,

$$\text{Percentage change in } y_t = \hat{\beta}(100). \text{ absolute change in } t$$

This $\hat{\beta}$ or estimated β_2 is also called the instantaneous rate of growth. Since $\beta_2 = \ln(1+r)$, taking antilog on both sides,

$$\text{antilog } \hat{\beta} = \text{antilog}(\ln(1+r)) = (1+r)$$

---

[4]Indicator value in period t can be treated as y_t.

Therefore,

$$r = \text{antilog } \hat{\beta} - 1 = e^{\hat{\beta}} - 1$$

and

$$\text{percentage change in } r = (e^{\hat{\beta}} - 1).\ 100$$

This r is the CAGR of the indicator.

The study subsequently calculates composite FII values in the study period. The *max–min method of normalization* is applied to get the index values of financial inclusion of each indicator. The fundamental way to convert an indicator value (V) into an index value (I) is given by

$$I = \frac{(V - \text{Min.Value})}{(\text{Max.Value} - \text{Min.Value})}$$

In the formula, I is a relative index with a scale of 0 to 1, in which '1' is the ideal state for each dimension. Min. Value is the minimum admissible value or the lower bound and Max.Value is the maximum admissible value or the upper bound of the data to be studied under each dimension. The bounds have constant values because of the pre-determined time horizon for analysis, and therefore, any incorporation of input for normalization outside the original data range would encounter an error and distort the analysis. This approach of data normalization is used by the United Nations Development Programme (UNDP) for computation of some popular development indices like human development index (HDI), gender development index, human poverty index, etc. Since normalizing the data attempts to put an equal weight to all indicators, so in our study, equal weight is given to each indicator. Moreover, there is not yet any consensus in literature that which dimension or indicator is more important than another. Many former studies like Sarma (2012), Rahman (2012) and Saha and Alam (2022, 2021) have used this method to calculate FII values earlier. Finally, taking geometric mean of the indices values for the four indicators, assuming all the indicators have equal weights, the composite FII values for each year have been calculated.

The study also shows diagrammatic representation of the trends of financial inclusion through SHGs. Furthermore, with the help of correlation matrices, the relationship between FII values and HDI values has been established.

Results and Discussion

Financial inclusion encourages banks and non-bank financial institutions to assist the unbanked sections of the society, especially assisting the unprivileged section like women. Hence, many of these institutions provide special rates with exclusive discounts or other benefits to the women. Even many banks charge subsidized interest rates from women for their loan products. There are also scopes for women depositors to gain more interest on their deposits in certain financial institutions while compared to men. All these initiatives of the government have raised the number of SHGs, SHGs with credit-linked and savings-linked, loan disbursement by the banks for SHGs and savings of the SHGs over time.

It is already mentioned that the study considers several indicators to evaluate the role of SHGs in financial inclusion. Financing SHGs allows poor women to evade the challenges of exclusion from formal financial institutions. Therefore, this system reflects solidarity lending, extensively used by MFIs. Beyond their functions as savings and credit groups, SHGs display a place of harmony among poor women. The indicators which may influence SHG activities are analysed through regression analyses and the result of the log linear models for the four indicators, where log of total number of SHG members, log of average loan per SHG, log of average savings per SHG and log of amount of outstanding loans of SHGs are the dependent variables, and time point is the independent variable, are presented in Table 9.1.

From Table 9.1(a), it is evident that the value of F-statistic is 73.30 and the P-value associated with it is 0.000. The probability value of less than 0.01 ($P < 0.01$) indicates that overall the regression result statistically significantly predicts the outcome variable. Therefore, it is a good fit for the data. R^2 measures the goodness-of-fit for linear regression models. The estimated model shows that 85 per cent of the variation in the data of outcome variable is due to the variation in data of explanatory variable. The fitted model also shows that there is a positive association between absolute change in time point and rate of growth of total number of SHG members, and this claim is significant at 1 per cent level. Therefore, the study result clearly indicates that the number of SHG members has increased over time. Furthermore, the more the number of SHG members, the more will be the economic activities through their enrolment in financial institutions, and thereby, financial inclusion.

Table 9.1.   Estimates of Log Linear Regression Models for the Four Indicators at India Level.

(a) Estimates of log linear regression model for total number of SHG members

Number of observation = 15
$F(1, 13) = 73.30$
Prob > F = 0.0000
R-squared = 0.8494
Adjusted R-squared = 0.8378

Log Member	Coefficient	Standard Error	t Statistic	$P > |t|$
Time point	0.0574523***	0.0067104	8.56	0.000
_cons	17.90784***	0.0610114	293.52	0.000

(Continued)

Table 9.1.   *Continued*

(b) Estimates of log linear regression model for average loans per SHG

Number of observation = 15
$F(1, 13)$ = 83.80
Prob > F = 0.0000
R-squared = 0.8657
Adjusted R-squared = 0.8554

Log Loan	Coefficient	Standard Error	*t* Statistic	$P > |t|$
Time point	0.0877957***	0.0095908	9.15	0.000
_cons	11.28342***	0.0872009	129.40	0.000

(c) Estimates of log linear regression model for average savings per SHG

Number of observation = 15
$F(1, 13)$ = 303.03
Prob > F = 0.0000
R-squared = 0.9589
Adjusted R-squared = 0.9557

Log Savings	Coefficient	Standard Error	*t* Statistic	$P > |t|$
Time point	0.1165291***	0.0066941	17.41	0.000
_cons	8.702669***	0.0608635	142.99	0.000

(d) Estimates of log linear regression model for amount of outstanding loans of SHGs

Number of observation = 15
$F(1, 13)$ = 873.42
Prob > F = 0.0000
R-squared = 0.9853
Adjusted R-squared = 0.9842

Log o/s Loan	Coefficient	Standard Error	*t* Statistic	$P > |t|$
Time point	0.1379104***	0.0046664	29.55	0.000
_cons	12.03995***	0.0424279	283.77	0.000

Source: Estimated by authors. *Note*: *** denotes significant at 1 per cent level.

The similar log linear regression models are used to assess the influence of other three indicators in financial inclusion. The regression result of the log linear model for the second indicator-average loans per SHG, where log of average loan per SHG is the dependent variable and time point is the independent variable, is depicted in Table 9.1(b). It is evident that the value of F-statistic is 83.80 and the P-value associated with it is 0.000, which indicates that overall the regression result statistically significantly predicts the outcome variable. Therefore, it is a good fit for the data. The R^2 value in the estimated model shows that 86 per cent of the variation in the data of outcome variable is due to the variation in data of explanatory variable. The fitted model also shows that there is a positive association between absolute change in time point and growth rate of average loan per SHG, and the claim is significant at 1 per cent level. The quality of SHGs is always linked to credit linkage with banks and volume of loan. The study shows that the indicator-average loans per SHG have amplified over time, indicating more involvement of SHG members in financial affairs.

The regression result of the log linear model for the third indicator – average savings per SHG, where log of average savings per SHG is the dependent variable and time point is the independent variable, is depicted in Table 9.1(c). It is evident that the value of F-statistic is 303.03 and the P-value associated with it is 0.000, which indicates that overall the regression result statistically significantly predicts the outcome variable and it is a good fit for the data. The R^2 value in the estimated model shows that 95 per cent of the variation in the data of outcome variable is due to the variation in data of explanatory variable. The fitted model also shows that there is a positive association between absolute change in time point and growth rate of average savings per SHG, and the claim is significant at 1 per cent level. Therefore, in the study, increase in the number of bank accounts through enrolment of women in SHGs, credit availed and savings by the members – all the indicators confirmed expansion of economic activities, and thereby, financial insertion over time.

Finally, the regression result of the log linear model for the fourth indicator – amount of outstanding loans of SHGs, where log of amount of outstanding loans of SHGs and time point is the independent variable, is depicted in Table 9.1(d). It is evident that the value of F-statistic is 873.42 and the P-value associated with it is 0.000, which indicates that overall the regression result statistically significantly predicts the outcome variable. It is also a good fit for the data and the R^2 value in the estimated model shows that 98 per cent of the variation in data of the outcome variable is due to the variation in data of explanatory variable. The fitted model also shows that there is a positive association between absolute change in time point and growth rate of amount of outstanding loans of SHGs, and the claim is significant at 1 per cent level. It is often seen that SHGs fail to repay loans. The delay or non-payment of loans happens because of the inefficiency of group members or when the group takes loan beyond its repayment capacity. Our study reveals that amount of outstanding loans of all SHGs taken together have increased over time. Therefore, though an increase in SHG members or expansion of SHG activities has helped financial inclusion in India, continuous failure of repayment of loans shows the gloominess of picture regarding the performance of SHGs.

The combined results of regression analyses show all the four indicators are important to analyse SHG activities, and thereby, promoting financial inclusion. Thus, at the subsequent phase, CAGRs of the four indicators are estimated and presented in Table 9.2.

Table 9.2 shows that CAGR is highest for the indicator – amount of outstanding loan of SHGs, followed by the other indicators – average savings per SHG, average loan per SHG and total number of SHG members, respectively. The estimates signify that the spread of SHGs through their total number of members

Table 9.2.   Estimates of CAGRs of the Four Indicators at India Level.

CAGR (in per cent)	Indicators			
	Total Number of SHG Members	Average Loans per SHG	Average Savings per SHG	Amount of Outstanding Loans of SHGs
	5.91	9.18	12.37	14.8

Source: Estimated by authors.

and average amount of loan taken per SHG have increased over time in India. In addition, the study reveals that SHG activities greatly contributed to generate savings. However, while assessing the performance of SHGs through their status other than considering savings, it comes out that amount of outstanding loan of SHGs has increased over time and that might be a great threat to the viability of SHGs. This is a serious policy concern since the increase in NPA retards economic growth. Hence, focus should be on formulating such SHG policies which can check NPA, along with endorsing financial inclusion.

Since the study also aims to calculate composite FII values during the study period, so the index values of the four indicators are calculated first, as an annual basis, after normalization of data applying *Max–Min procedure to convert indicators into indices*, during 2007–2021, and are depicted in Table 9.3.

Subsequently, taking geometric mean of the indices values for the four indicators, the composite FII value has been calculated for each year during 2007–2021, and the trend of financial inclusion through SHGs is shown in Fig. 9.1.

Implications of the Study Results

The upward trend of FII in Fig. 9.1 clearly shows that SHG activities have increased over time in India, indicating a substantial contribution of SHGs in financial inclusion. However, disbursement of bank loans, and thereby investment, was disturbed many times in the Indian economy, during the study period, due to sudden economic events. The Global Financial Crisis in 2008 affected India's gross domestic product (GDP) to a large extent. But, financial regulations of the country and its large domestic market could make an upturn of GDP growth and soon it reached its peak in 2010. Even a fall in GDP growth during 2010–2012 was successfully controlled by the Indian government through different courses of action. As a consequence of low GDP growth, the rate of inflation increased after the Global Financial Crisis. Government's fiscal-monetary policy initiatives made the inflation manageable after 2010. But, again 2011 onwards, slowly inflation began to gain momentum and reached to its peak in 2013 (Data of World Bank).[5] Furthermore, in 2016, *demonetization policy* of the Indian

---

[5]https://data.worldbank.org/indicator/NY.GDP.MKTP.KD.ZG?locations=IN; https://data.worldbank.org/indicator/FP.CPI.TOTL.ZG?locations=IN.

Table 9.3.   Index Values of the Four Indicators at India Level.

Year	Total Number of SHG Members	Average Loans per SHG	Average Savings per SHG	Amount of Outstanding Loans of SHGs
2007	0.00	0.00	0.00	0.00
2008	0.24	0.02	0.05	0.04
2009	0.25	0.09	0.04	0.08
2010	0.43	0.22	0.06	0.11
2011	0.52	0.33	0.02	0.14
2012	0.44	0.44	0.11	0.17
2013	0.44	0.47	0.18	0.19
2014	0.43	0.44	0.21	0.26
2015	0.48	0.59	0.30	0.30
2016	0.56	0.60	0.35	0.33
2017	0.61	0.62	0.46	0.44
2018	0.79	0.65	0.49	0.52
2019	0.81	0.79	0.56	0.68
2020	0.97	0.58	0.80	0.64
2021	1.00	1.00	1.00	1.00

Source: Calculated by authors.

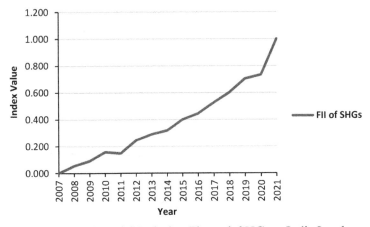

Fig. 9.1.   Trend of Financial Inclusion Through SHGs at India Level.
Source: Prepared by authors.

government adversely affected liquidity in the money market and caused a hike in inflation rate. Though the situation was getting improved from 2019 onwards, the pandemic since 2020 has begun to deteriorate the situation again. It is an acceptable fact that all these economic incidents had an adverse effect on investment, and thereby, loan disbursement for SHGs in different phases of time. Investment was cut down just after the Global Financial Crisis, adaptation of *demonetization policy* and during a pandemic.[6] Simultaneously, NPA amplified across regions as a result of sluggish growth in investment. But due to less economic activities in the pandemic situation, NPA did not affect much. Since 2022, the situation is getting better than before.

Our study result also reveals that despite several unfavourable events during the study period, the SHGs kept on moving and contributed largely to financial insertion in India. Sustainable development goals of the United Nations (UN) recognize financial inclusion as an integrated continuum to aim the goals like reducing poverty and inequality, ensuring impartial quality education, facilitating health and well-being to all, assisting decent work and growth of the economy, providing access to effective and inclusive institutions at all levels to put across justice, etc. (Saha & Alam, 2022). India being a member State of the UN, commenced to focus on escalating the accessibility of financial products and services to all types of citizens since the year 2015, to make the growth inclusive. Hence, it is comprehensible that SHG activities possess a vital role to play to achieve the Global Goals by 2030, through employment generation, livelihood promotion, empowerment of women, poverty alleviation, etc.

Relationship Between Financial Inclusion and Human Development

This sub-section deals with the second objective of the study which shows the relationship between financial inclusion and human development. The concept of human development was first developed by the economist Mahbubul Haq, followed by the economist Amartya Sen in 1990. Human development is a multidimensional concept which is defined as a process of assuring people's sovereignty and expanding opportunities to improve their well-being. Hence, human development deals with productivity, equity, empowerment and sustainability. The HDI is a summary composite measure of a country's average achievements in three basic aspects – education, health and standard of living. The HDI is published by the UNDP. There are several literatures which have established the positive relationship between financial inclusion, human development and growth of nations. Some of the recent notable works across countries include Nanda and Kaur (2016), Raichoudhury (2016), Ababio et al. (2021), Abdelghaffar et al. (2022), etc. A few research works have also been conducted at India level, which include Kuri and Laha (2011), Arora and Kumar (2021) and Saha and Alam (2022). However, while establishing the association between financial inclusion

---

[6]https://data.worldbank.org/indicator/NE.GDI.TOTL.ZS?locations=IN.

and human development, all these works dealt with banking data of India for financial inclusion. The present study finds a high correlation (0.84) between FII values and HDI values during the study period in India, while considering financial inclusion through SHG activities.

Pertaining to the relationship between financial inclusion and human development, it existed long back. In the 1930s, for the first time, the economist *Keynes* comprehensively evaluated the role of financial sector in reducing poverty. *Keynes* explained how the financial intermediaries could mitigate poverty through providing saving opportunities to the poor which might lead to higher income. Our study is not an exception of this *Keynesian* view.

Our study also shows that how financial inclusion is very particular about including women. It is seen in India that in many of the households, women are controlled by men and are not permitted to be involved in managing finance. Their works are confined to domestic chores which mainly constitute reproductive and caring services. Since financial inclusion targets this women population to be financially independent, so it helps empower women. It also intends to educate women by increasing financial awareness among them. Hence, they are taught in simple ways about how to get credit in the market, start a business and save money for future purposes. They are even taught how to take up training courses to plan for a start-up. As a result, nowadays, women are getting access to mobile phones for digital modes of payment and other financial operations which has accelerated their transactions. Since SHGs have strong gender orientation, so from one hand, microcredit through SHGs helps empowerment of women. From the other hand, it also contributes to income generation through livelihood promotion and reduction in poverty and, thereby, secures human development.

Conclusions

The study discusses the role of microfinance which provides microloans or microcredit to the economically backward people, especially women in the society, in an effective way for their livelihood protection and promotion. Our study result clearly indicates that this mode of financing has helped India in achieving financial inclusion extensively and in a cost-effective manner. Moreover, women empowerment through SHGs secures human development.

The study also highlights the fact that though government policies have helped raising the number of SHG members, SHGs with credit-linked, SHGs with savings-linked, loan disbursement for SHGs and savings of SHGs over time, special attention should be given on framing policies towards reduction in NPA; a part of which is related to the functioning of SHG. It is expected that proper policy design and development strategies can make the nation's growth sustainable and help achieving the Global Goals by 2030.

Although this kind of study is useful in developing nations with people possessing diversified socio-economic profile, expansion of time period or analysis at sub-national level might enhance the acceptability of the study.

Acknowledgement

We gratefully acknowledge Professor Swati Ghosh, Rabindra Bharati University, for her valuable comments.

Declarations

Funding: No specific funding has been received to carry out this piece of research.

Conflicts of interest: The secondary data used in the study are from authentic sources and are clearly mentioned in the chapter. So, there are no conflicts of interest.

References

Ababio, J. O.-M., Attah-Botchwey, E., Osei-Assibey, E., & Barnor, C. (2021). Financial inclusion and human development in frontier countries. *International Journal of Finance and Economics, 26*(1), 42–59.
Abdelghaffar, R. A., Emam, H. A., & Samak, N. A. (2022). Financial inclusion and human development: Is there a nexus?. *Journal of Humanities and Applied Social Sciences, 5*(3), 163–177. https://www.emerald.com/insight/content/doi/10.1108/JHASS-11-2021-0178/full/pdf
Ahl, H., & Marlow, S. (2012). Exploring the dynamics of gender, feminism, and entrepreneurship: Advancing debate to escape a dead-end?. *Organization, 19*(5), 543–562.
Arora, N., & Kumar, N. (2021). Does financial inclusion promote human development? Evidence from India. *Jindal Journal of Business Research, 10*(2), 163–184.
Borbora, S., & Mahanta, R. (2001). Micro finance through self help groups and its impact: A case of Rastriya Gramin Vikas Nidhi credit and savings programme in Assam. *Indian Journal of Agricultural Economics, 56*(3), 449–450.
Chibba, M. (2009). Financial inclusion, poverty reduction and the millennium development goals. *European Journal of Development Research, 21*(2), 213–230.
Dahiya, S., & Kumar, M. (2020). Linkage between financial inclusion and economic growth: An empirical study of the emerging Indian economy. *Vision, 24*(2), 184–193.
Elson, D. (2009). Gender equality and economic growth in the World Bank World Development Report 2006. *Feminist Economics, 15*(3), 35–59.
European Association of Co-operative Banks. (2018). *Raiffeisen Year 2018 – Celebration of the 200th Raiffeisen's anniversary*. https://www.eacb.coop/en/others/events/raiffeisen-2018.html#
Galab, S., & Rao, N. C. (2003). Women's self help groups, poverty alleviation and empowerment. *Economic & Political Weekly, 38*(12/13), 1274–1282.
GlobalDataLab. (2021). *Subnational HDI*. https://globaldatalab.org/shdi/table/shdi/IND/?levels=1&interpolation=0&extrapolation=0
Gurumoorty, T. R. (2000). Self help groups empower rural women. *Kurukshetra, 56*(4), 30.
Jothy, K., & Sundar, I. (2002). Self help groups under the women's development programme in Tamil Nadu: Achievements, bottlenecks and recommendations. *Social Change, 32*(3–4), 34–44.
Kuri, P., & Laha, A. (2011). Financial inclusion and human development in India: An inter-state analysis. *Indian Journal of Human Development, 5*(1), 61–78.
Kuzilwa, J. A. (2005). The role of credit for small business success. *The Journal of Entrepreneurship, 14*(2), 131–161.

Manimekalai, M., & Rajeswari, G. (2001). Nature and performance of informal self help groups – A case study from Tamil Nadu. *Indian Journal of Agricultural Economics, 56*(3), 453.

NABARD. (2021). *Status of microfinance in India 2020–2021.* https://www.nabard.org/auth/writereaddata/tender/SoMFI-2020-21.pdf

NABARD. (2020). *Status of microfinance in India 2019–2020.* https://www.nabard.org/auth/writereaddata/tender/NABARD%20SMFI%202019-20_compressed.pdf

NABARD. (2019). *Status of microfinance in India 2018–2019.* https://www.nabard.org/auth/writereaddata/tender/1207192354SMFI%202018-19.pdf

NABARD. (2018). *Status of microfinance in India 2017–2018.* https://www.nabard.org/auth/writereaddata/tender/SMFI%202017-18.pdf

NABARD. (2017). *Status of microfinance in India 2016–2017.* https://www.nabard.org/auth/writereaddata/tender/1307174808Status%20of%20Microfinance%20in%20India%202016-17.pdf

NABARD. (2016). *Status of microfinance in India 2015–2016.* https://www.nabard.org/auth/writereaddata/tender/1409165809Status%20of%20Microfinance%20in%20India%20-%202015-16.pdf

NABARD. (2015). *Status of microfinance in India 2014–2015.* https://www.nabard.org/auth/writereaddata/tender/3107172451SMFI-2015r.pdf

NABARD. (2014). *Status of microfinance in India 2013–2014.* https://www.nabard.org/auth/writereaddata/tender/3107172406SMFI_2013_14h.pdf

NABARD. (2013). *Status of microfinance in India 2012–2013.* https://www.nabard.org/auth/writereaddata/tender/3107172325Status_of_Microfinance_in_India_2012-13.pdf

NABARD. (2012). *Status of microfinance in India 2011–2012.* https://www.nabard.org/auth/writereaddata/tender/3107172233SMFI2012.pdf

NABARD. (2011). *Status of microfinance in India 2010–2011.* https://www.nabard.org/auth/writereaddata/tender/3107173809SMFI%202010-11.pdf

Nanda, K., & Kaur, M. (2016). Financial inclusion and human development: A cross-country evidence. *Management of Labour Studies, 41*(2), 127–153.

Nawaz, A. (2018). Challenges faced by women entrepreneurs in Pakistan: A qualitative study. *Management and Organizational Studies, 5*(2), 13.

Panda, D. K. (2009). Assessing the impact of participation in women self-help group based micro-finance: Non-experimental evidences from rural households in India. *International Journal of Rural Management, 5*(2), 197–215.

Park, C.-Y., & Mercado, R. V. (2015). *Financial inclusion, poverty, and income inequality in developing Asia* [ADB Economics Working Paper Series, 426], Asian Development Bank. https://www.adb.org/sites/default/files/publication/153143/ewp-426.pdf

Puhazhendi, V., & Satyasai, K. S. (2001). Economic and social empowerment of rural poor through self help groups. *Indian Journal of Agricultural Economics, 56*(3), 450–451.

Rahman, Z. A. (2012). *Financial inclusion in Malaysia: Tracking progress using index* [IFC Workshop on financial inclusion indicators], IFC Bulletin No. 38, Kuala Lumpur. https://www.bis.org/ifc/publ/ifcb38.pdf

Raichoudhury, A. (2016). Financial inclusion and human development: A cross country analysis. *Asian Journal of Business Research, 6*(1), 2463–4522.

Ramalakshmi, C. S. (2003). Women empowerment through self help groups. *Economic and Political Weekly, XXXVIII*(12–13), 1302.

Rao, V. M. (2004). Women self help groups: Profiles from Andhra Pradesh and Karnataka. *Kurukshetra, 51*(6), 26.

Ray, D. (1998). *Development economics.* Oxford University press.

Reserve Bank of India. (2019, July 01). *Master circular on SHG-bank linkage programme.* https://www.rbi.org.in/ScriptS/BS_ViewMasCirculardetails.aspx?id=11614

Saha, D., & Alam, R. (2021). Financial inclusion in India through banking activities over the time period 1990–2018. *NMIMS Management Review, XXIX*(1), 80–105.

Saha, D., & Alam, R. (2022). Revisiting financial inclusion with human development in India. *Indian Journal of Human Development*, *16*(3), 548–577.

Sahu, K. K. (2013). Commercial bank, financial inclusion and economic growth in India. *International Journal of Business and Management Invention*, *2*(5), 01–06.

Sarkhel, J., & Mondal, T. (2013). An overview of the self-help groups in tribal inhabited Jangal–Mahal and their role in women empowerment: A case study of Ranibandh block of Bankura district, West Bengal. *Business Spectrum*, *3*, 30–40.

Sarma, M. (2012). *Index of financial inclusion – A measure of financial sector inclusiveness* [Working Paper No. 07/2012, 1–34]. Berlin Working Papers on Money, Finance, Trade and Development. https://finance-and-trade.htw-berlin.de/fileadmin/HTW/ Forschung/Money_Finance_Trade_Development/working_paper_series/ wp_07_2012_Sarma_Index-of-Financial-Inclusion.pdf

Sharma, K. C. (2001). Micro financing through SHGs. *Indian Journal of Agricultural Economics*, *56*(3), 460–461.

Skarlatos, K. (2004). Microfinance and women's economic empowerment: Bridging the gap, redesigning the future. *Spring*, *1*, 66.

Srivastava, A. (2005). Women's self help groups: Findings from a study in four Indian states. *Social Change*, *35*(2), 156–164.

Stiglitz, J. (1990). Peer monitoring and credit markets. *The World Bank Economic Review*, *4*(3), 351–366.

The World Bank. (2020, April 11). In India, *women's self-help groups combat the* COVID-19 (coronavirus) pandemic. https://www.worldbank.org/en/news/feature/2020/04/11/ women-self-help-groups-combat-covid19-coronavirus-pandemic-india

The World Bank. (2021). *GDP growth (annual %) – India*. https://data.worldbank.org/indi-cator/NY.GDP.MKTP.KD.ZG?locations=IN

The World Bank. (2021). *Inflation, consumer prices (annual %) – India*. https://data.world-bank.org/indicator/FP.CPI.TOTL.ZG?locations=IN

The World Bank. (2021). *Gross capital formation (% of GDP) – India*. https://data.world-bank.org/indicator/NE.GDI.TOTL.ZS?locations=IN

Vijayanthi, K. N. (2002). Women's empowerment through self-help groups: A participatory approach. *Indian Journal of Gender Studies*, *9*(2), 263–274.

Vossenberg, S. (2013). *Women entrepreneurship promotion in developing countries: What explains the gender gap in entrepreneurship and how to close it?* Business, Economics. Sociology (Corpus ID: 155814102).

Chapter 10

Waste Management Practices in the Informal Settlement: Functionality of Local Assemblies

Anthony Nkrumah Agyabeng[a], James Kwame Mensah[b] and Anthony Acquah[c]

[a]*Department of Business Administration, University of Professional Studies, Accra (UPSA), Ghana*
[b]*Department of Public Administration, University of Ghana Business School, Accra, Ghana*
[c]*Department of Business Administration, Bluecrest University College, Accra, Ghana*

Abstract

Waste management has become a topical issue among scholars, practitioners, and industrialists. This study extends the debate on waste within informal communities, highlighting the functionalities of local assemblies in Ghana, a developing country context. This study utilized the desk research regime situated within the qualitative approach. Several sources of data, including key policy documents in context, were used to inform the conclusion reached. The results show a lack of independence of local assemblies to enforce waste management by-laws in informal communities. It further indicates that limited waste management departments within the metropolitan, municipal, and district assemblies (MMDAs) and a lack of funds are to blame for effectively managing waste and sanitation in the informal settlements. Being desk research, the findings of the study should be carefully interpreted to reflect similar settings and characteristics across national, regional, and international contexts. The study explored the nuance of waste and sanitation management and discovered some setbacks to effective waste management, as well as practical ways of addressing them. This research is one of the few to examine waste management and

Informal Economy and Sustainable Development Goals:
Ideas, Interventions and Challenges, 203–224
doi:10.1108/978-1-83753-980-220241011

sanitation-related issues within informal communities in a developing country context.

Keywords: Waste management; local assemblies; informal settlements; sanitation; stakeholders Ghana

Introduction

Waste management practices have become one of the most discussed issues among stakeholders such as academics, industry players, and environmental practitioners. Amplifying the discussion is the impact of human activities on the environment and its implications for climate change and global warming (Elbasiouny et al., 2020; Shen et al., 2020). Wastes are items or materials that are discarded, intended to be discarded, or are required to be discarded by the legislation of the country where they were created (Peiry, 2010). Every resident, organization, and human activity generates some type of waste; hence, the amount of waste produced is influenced by human activity, consumption, and population growth. On a broad spectrum, waste is generated from different sources, including households, municipal, industrial, agriculture, and animals.

Procedures for the collection, treatment, transportation, disposal, and maintenance of disposal sites are known as waste management. Urban authorities are embarking on intense efforts for a sustainable approach to the problem of solid waste because effective waste management methods help the environment, human health, socioeconomic production, and job security (Ezeah & Roberts, 2012). Studies by Ahmed and Ali (2006) and Shekdar (2009) have established that the poor solid waste management practices in developing nations are the root cause of urban sanitation issues. This study contributes to the ongoing waste management discussions within the informal communities by exploring the functionalities of local assemblies in the pursuit of waste management in Ghana.

The sustainable development goals (SDGs), which call for resilient and sustainable human settlements (SDG 11), safe cities for human habitation (SDG 6), and sustainable management of water and sanitation, are of special interest to the SDGs' global philosophy. The integrated 17 SDGs recognize the need to balance development efforts across social, economic, and environmental sustainability as well as the fact that decisions made in one area will have an impact on others. The "ethos" of the global goals is congruent with waste management in urban areas since it is essential for reducing poverty, preserving the environment, and ensuring environmental sustainability (United Nations, 2015). Universally, 2.01 billion metric tons of municipal solid waste are generated annually; this is expected to increase to 3.4 billion metric tons by 2050.

Multiple strategies and solutions have been used in Ghana throughout the years to mitigate the impact of waste management, but there is still much room for improvement. According to a report by the United Nations Development

Programme (UNDP), Ghana produces 12,710 metric tons of solid waste every day. By 2050, this amount is expected to reach 3.88 billion metric tons (United Nations Development Planning, 2022). Ghana's urban areas generate greater amounts of solid waste, industrial, and construction than the entire rural areas. Most of these wastes are sent to a few dumpsites, with the majority ending up in drains, streams, and open places. Essentially, the traditional approaches to waste management in Ghana revolve around open dumping, open burning, controlled burning, and tipping at dumpsites. Unfortunately, these approaches tend to create pressing sanitation problems as many towns and cities are overwhelmed with the management of municipal solid and liquid wastes. Dealing with sanitation and waste management issues within informal settlements is a greater concern. This is because the capacity of municipal governments to develop a structured waste management and sanitation system is being hampered by the rate of urbanization. As a result, issues with sanitation and waste management are made worse by the spillover population in the urban area, which continues to encourage the influx of rural residents looking for work to eke out a living in the informal settlement. According to the current Statistical Service report, out of the urban population of 31,072 million, informal settlements, or slum dwellers, occupy 5.5 million (Ghana Statistical Service GSS, 2021).

The President of Ghana, his excellency Nana Addo Dankwa Akuffo-Addo, promised to pursue policies for sanitation and waste management with all of his might in his inauguration speech to the 7th Parliament of the 4th Republic (Akufo-Addo, 2017). In line with this, he pledged to make Accra, Ghana's administrative capital, the cleanest city in Africa by the end of his second term in office. There have been less than two years in government, and there are still no obvious signs that even a fraction of that promise has been fulfilled. Even though the MMDAs have established and executed a number of initiatives, such as operation clean your frontage (OCYF), to deal with waste and sanitation, it seems more rhetoric than reality. Despite these approaches, the MMDAs and local assemblies' functionalities are not given sufficient weight when debating waste management and sanitation in the literature.

Indeed, it seems the functions of the local assemblies' role in against waste management and sanitation are least examined within academic field or mentioned in public discussions. This chapter examines the functions of local assemblies in tackling the menace of waste in informal settlements in Ghana. For this desk research, secondary data from the documentary review approach were mostly used. In addition to policy documents, reliable journals and databases were used to obtain empirical findings from previously published scholarly articles. The chapter proceeds as follows: After the introduction, the next section explains the concepts of waste management, informal settlements, and the structure of local assemblies and their structures. Next, we discussed an overview of waste management approaches in Africa and Ghana, focusing on the legislative framework for waste management in informal settlements. Followed by a discussion of challenges hindering effective waste management in the informal settlements. The last section details the conclusion and recommendations.

The Concepts of Waste Management, Informal Settlement, and Local Assemblies

Waste Management

Waste as a concept can be challenging to define because what is considered waste depends on the viewer or the person for whom the waste matters because it may be a resource for another person. Solid waste has been a major problem for urban authorities for nearly 6,000 years according to the World Bank Institute (2019). Waste is a relative concept in two important respects. First, something becomes wasteful when it no longer serves the user for the purpose for which it was created. As a result, the waste generated by one individual may be reused as raw material by another. Second, the definition of waste depends on where it is produced and the state of technology today (Pongrácz, 2002). While we do not intend to synthesize definitions of the concept, a revisit of some agencies definitions of waste is needed. According to the United Nations Environment Programme (UNEP, 2002), "waste" is defined as any substances or objects that are disposed of, are intended to be disposed of, or are required to be disposed of by national law.

The United Nations Statistics Division also describes it as materials that are not prime products for which the generator has no further use in terms of his or her own purposes of production, transformation, or consumption and of which he or she wants to dispose. The Public Services International Research Unit (2010) defined waste as any substance that the holder discards, intends to discard, or is compelled to dispose of. There are various forms and types, including municipal, residential, commercial, construction, demolition, and hazardous waste. Each of them has techniques, methods, or procedures for treating, collecting, transporting, and disposing of waste, often known as waste management. Therefore, "waste management" refers to the procedures and actions necessary to control waste from its creation to its ultimate disposal. The procedures cover the collection, transportation, treatment, and disposal of trash, as well as the supervision and control of the laws, technologies, and economic mechanisms that are associated with waste, as well as the waste management procedure.

Primarily, waste management aims to reduce the dangerous effects of such waste on the environment and human health. In this chapter, we focus on the household and municipal wastes, either solid or liquid, that emanate from the informal settlements and their disposal and management in Ghana. Contextually, waste is explained as undesirable materials, including but not limited to litter such as plastics, empty sachets, plastic bottles, wastewater, or any form or type of unwanted foreign material flying or lying on the open space. We are interested in understanding the practices used in the gathering, collecting, transporting, treatment, and disposal of waste by the responsible authorities in the informal settlements.

Informal Settlements

Informal settlements and slums are concepts often used interchangeably in academic scholarships (Mahabir et al., 2018). Informal settlements are defined as residential areas situated on illegally occupied land or where housing does not comply with planning and building regulations (UN-Habitat, 2003). In each local area, they face particular socioeconomic, environmental, institutional, and demographic constraints that are context-specific (Foppen & Kansiime, 2009; Lüthi et al., 2009). Slums, on the other hand, refer to residential areas characterized by high population density, poor infrastructure, and bad living conditions amid a lack of basic social amenities (UN-Habitat, 2016). Formal settlements are those that are recognized by the government, which, in turn, provides administration and management. Such settlements are expected to provide shelter over a longer period and access to basic services.

From the above definitions, it is instructive to highlight that whereas informal residents' dwell in areas classified as illegal by the state, slums do not follow that classification. The underlying commonality is that both of the settlements are endemic with abject poverty and face similar economic, environmental, infrastructural, and social amenities challenges. This chapter also uses the two terms informal settlements and slums in a similar fashion to mean neighborhoods whose setup, activities, and characteristics do not conform with the urban planning architecture. Urban Africa's developing economies are all experiencing a proliferation of informal settlements. Primarily, its emergence in African cities may be traced back to the colonial era when the city's planners divided the neighborhood into two exclusive zones. The colonial masters occupied the first zone with high infrastructure and services, while the indigenous settled in the second zone with marginal services (Myers, 2003).

Following Second World War, Africa experienced a surge of rapid urbanization, during which native citizens dominated urban growth. Hence, informal settlements were viewed as a barrier to developing modern cities in the 1960s when urbanization was addressed in the concept of modernization (Ono & Kidokoro, 2020). The dominant idea was that informal settlements should be eradicated from urban areas by the government, leading to the adoption of policies such as eviction and relocation (Sholihah & Chen, 2018) and self-help policies (Braathen et al., 2014), among others. The emergence of informal settlement in Ghana, particularly in the Greater Accra Region, can be traced back to the era of returnees, mostly soldiers, teachers, and traders, after the ruins of the First World War. The returnees first settled around Nima, and over time, their population increased, causing the need for more structures to accommodate the growing numbers. As history recalls, the ancestors who lived in Nima put up properties, and the generation that followed has sustained and continued.

Over time, the community attracted other tribes, mostly from the northern parts of Ghana and Togo, as well as missionaries from the sub-region. There were influxes of migrants into Nima, typically from West African countries, including Nigeria, Cameroon, and Niger, among others, for trading purposes. Some of the migrants, under the guise of missionaries and traders, rented houses; others constructed structures and shacks, accounting for the slums' spread into other parts of the country. Slum growth has created governance problems in the areas of education, health, water, sanitation services, and planning in general, especially in urban areas. This may be due to a lack of control and effective supervision of structural and physical development by the local assembly.

Structure of Local Assemblies

The local assemblies are the wheels through which decentralization, a pillar of democracy and good governance passes. Between national governments and grassroots communities, local assemblies act as a link and conduit through which services are rendered and resources distributed. According to the European Charter of Local Self-Government (1985), "local assemblies are the main foundations of democracy and safeguard citizens" rights to participate and directly exercise their franchise at the local level. The African Charter on the Values and Principles of Decentralisation (2014) indicates that local authorities should be accountable to local communities for the adoption and implementation of local development decisions and policies and the management of financial resources. Numerous international initiatives, such as the SDG and inclusive governance, have given cities more prominence as urbanization challenges African nations. African municipalities are twice as big as those worldwide, with an average population of more than 100,000 people Organization for Economic Cooperation and Development (OECD, 2016). Over 50% of Africans who live in cities, according to estimates, reside there. According to Henderson and Kriticos (2018), Ghana and South Africa both have issues with their largest cities having populations that are more than twice as large as the next largest agglomeration.

The central governance structure consists of ministries, departments, and agencies (MDAs). The ministries, being the highest decision-making body in the public sector organization, are responsible for formulating policies within the specific sector and implementing the business of the government to serve the public interest. The ministries delegate part of their responsibilities to the departments and agencies under their jurisdiction to perform under the supervision of the ministries. For effective administration, Ghana is further decentralized into 16 administrative regions across the four cardinal points, with the department and agencies operating in all the regions. The gaffers of the ministries and regions bear the title Ministers who are appointed by the President of the Republic to represent him in the various fields. With the advice of the Council of State, some of the ministers are appointed either directly from the people's representation in Parliament or from non-Parliament in accordance with the 1994 Constitution of Ghana. The point of decentralization, where control of an activity is transferred to local authorities rather than MDAs, starts with the MMDAs in line with the Local Governance Act, 2016 (Act 936).

Decentralization is explained as a management tool that is used in the administration and distribution of both public and private organizations. It involves the transfer of power, competencies, functions, and financial (and other) resources from central government MDAs to sub-national bodies, which are normally local authorities. The aim of decentralization is to enlarge the decision-making limit for greater stakeholder participation in the decision-making process to ensure efficiency and effectiveness in service delivery (Appiah-Agyekum et al., 2013). Governmental decentralization normally operates along the concept of subsidiarity, which assumes that national-level functions are performed at the center while local-level institutions perform sub-national functions. The Local Government

Act obligates the Local Government Service to secure effective administration and management of the decentralized local government system in the country. Act 1993, amended as Act 936 of 2016, recognizes the MMDAs as the highest public authority at the local assembly level. The MMDAs are decentralized across the 16 administrative regions in the four cardinal points of Ghana. Thus, depending on the population of a particular region, a number of MMDAs are assigned and are headed by the Chief Executive, who is appointed President of the Republic. The MMDAs are supervised by the Regional Coordinating Council (RCC) and made up of the local government structure and administration. The RCC serves as an intermediary between the central government and the local assemblies in the various regions. This means that while MDAs serve as a link between the ministries and the public in service delivery, the RCC coordinates the activities of the local assemblies and the central government in the regions.

This structure represents the decision flow and substantive fields within which public administrators work across the varied interests of government and public affairs. It also represents the vehicle within which the government exercises its policies and decisions to promote the well-being of its citizens. The structure of the local assembly is made up of a RCC and four-tier metropolitan and three-tier municipal and district assemblies. The Waste Management Department (WMD) is allocated only to metropolitan without the municipal and district assemblies. The RCC is responsible for handling all matters relating to human resource management and development, including capacity-building, professional standards, performance reporting, and service delivery standards. Additionally, it is responsible for issues relating to local government and decentralization policy, legislation, and finance, including the district composite budget. The structure of the local government system is determined by the layers of authority and the relationships between the various parts of the local assemblies.

In Ghana, the local assemblies are made up of an RCC and a four-tier metropolitan and three-tier municipal/district assembly structure. In Fig. 10.1, the metropolitan assemblies have a four-tier structure comprising the metropolitan assembly, the sub-metropolitan district councils, town councils, and unit committees. Municipal assemblies have a three-tier structure involving the municipal assemblies, zonal councils, and unit committees. Similarly, the district assemblies have a three-tier structure comprising the district assemblies, urban/town/area councils, and unit committees. While the metropolitan population size is over 250,000, the municipal population is over 95,000, and the district population is 75,000 and over.

The unit committees and regional co-coordinating councils, respectively, are at the bottom and highest levels of the structure. Inputs into the decision-making process originate with the unit committees to the metropolitan, municipal, and district assemblies. Policy directives emanate from the latter and are communicated bottom-up to the unit committees for implementation and feedback. On the other side, the RCCs are in charge of coordinating and harmonizing all of the regional assemblies' activities in accordance with the state's overall development agenda.

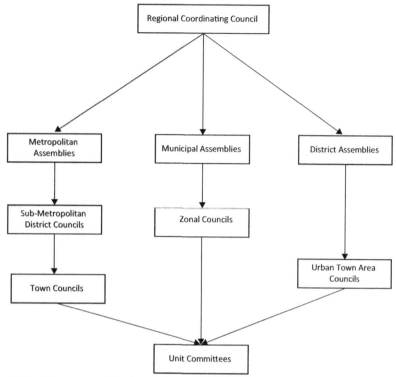

Fig. 10.1.   Structure of the Local Assemblies in Ghana. *Source*: Local Government Act 136 (2016).

Functions of Local Assemblies

The Local Government Act, 1993 (Act 462), Section 10, defines the roles of local assemblies and broadly construes the political and administrative responsibilities of local assemblies. They are required to perform executive, legislative, and deliberative duties, and they are responsible for supervising all other administrative authorities in the district. These functions make them the sole agents of development in the various communities, towns, and villages across all the regions of Ghana. To develop or not to develop, or the pace of development, rests on the shoulders of both elected and appointed officials that operate the assembly. The relationship between these two categories of public officials is, therefore, crucial since it is a function of an effective administrative and governance system that is development-oriented.

These functions are aimed at attaining its objectives and fulfilling its mission of improving the quality of life of its people. Generally, the three functions span planning, budgeting, formulation, and mobilization of resources for the overall development of the assemblies. Through the local government structure, the RCC provides some oversight and responsibility to the local assemblies in the execution of the functions. The local assemblies, which are generally made up of MMDAs, exercise political and administrative authority by promoting local economic development, providing guidance, giving direction, and supervising other administrative authorities in the district as may be prescribed by law. Within the broad functions of the assembly, undertake deliberative, legislative, and executive functions.

First, the executive function becomes the operational arm within which the entire assembly thrives. Specifically, they undertake auction sales, licensing, control and prevention of bushfires, provisions of criminal offenses relating to throwing rubbish in the street, and have the powers, rights, duties, capacities, liabilities, and obligations over all persons. They also formulate and implement plans, programs, and strategies for the effective mobilization of the resources necessary for the overall development of the assembly. Additionally, they coordinate sub-committee activities relating to development with the purpose of developing a comprehensive report for the whole assembly operation. All resolutions by the assembly and their implementation in collaboration with the gaffer of the assembly form part of the functions. Similarly, they oversee that all issues bordering on the approval of all plans relating to the various units, areas, and towns are executed. Overall, they are required to submit the assembly's programs to the RCC and the National Development Commission for budgetary approval by the Minister for Finance.

Second, the assembly coordinates, integrates, and harmonizes the execution of programs under approved development plans and other development promoted by ministries, departments, and other statutory bodies, including the non-governmental organizations in the district. It is also the responsibility of the assemblies to promote other persons to undertake projects under approved development plans, monitor the execution of projects, and assess their impact on the development of the district. They also initiate programs for the development of basic infrastructure and provide municipal works and services in the district. These include being responsible for the development, improvement, and management of human settlements and the environment in the district. Section 12 clause 6 (b) of the Local Government Act stipulates that the assemblies will be subject to the guidance and directives of the president on matters of national policy in the exercise of their functions.

It should be noted that within the broader and more specific functions of the local assemblies, sanitation and waste management issues did not surface, indicating less importance within the legislation. Of particular concern is that even though the assemblies are by law supposed to be independent in theory, in practice, they operate under the supervision of the RCC and the President of the Republic. In this narration, the paradox is that the local assemblies have been given powers to discharge deliberative, legislative, and executive functions by law and that the president has seemingly taken over the same law under the supervision of the RCC and his directives. The authors refer to this scenario as giving powers with the right hand through legislation and taking over the same powers with the left hand through supervision. This development would not only incapacitate the local assemblies to effectively discharge their functions if the waste management clause were written; the fact that the RCC and the President remain monitors of the assemblies is also a big issue.

Overview of Waste Management Approaches in Africa

Africa Perspective

Among the populous continents in the world, Africa has the second fastest growing population and is hugely drowning in waste management challenges. Available data show that 125 million metric tons of municipal waste were generated in Africa in 2012. Out of the total, 81 million metric tons were from Sub-Saharan Africa, and it is expected to grow to 244 million metric tons by 2025 (Scarlat et al., 2019). This is because the current approaches adopted by many African countries to the management of waste seem to have negative impacts on the economy, society, and environment. Research has shown that the African continent is not sited to confront the amount of harmful waste it produces; hence, much of the waste is openly dumped without treatment and in poorly functioning incinerators (Udofia et al., 2015).

Waste management, a product of environmental sustainability (Das et al., 2019; Pujara et al., 2019), has been recognized as the nerve center of sustainable development (Cobbinah et al., 2017). In fact, the concept of a green economy and business being the wheels on which the industrial revolution thrives will be mere rhetoric with little attention to waste management. In essence, pollution, poverty, food security, clean drinking water, and many more issues could hugely affect the African continent should waste management and sanitation issues be devalued. Waste can be both a resource and an environmental problem. According to the United Nations (2015), waste management that works poorly involves a considerable waste of valuable material that can affect the environment, health, sanitation, and water. In the wisdom of discourse, African countries have not discovered the full potential of waste as a resource despite its environmental predicament. According to research, six dominant methods for waste management have been established in Africa. Such practices include open dumping (Awodele et al., 2016; Bendjoudi et al., 2009), chemical disinfection (Awodele et al., 2016), landfilling (Mmereki et al., 2017), incineration (Awodele et al., 2016), and indiscriminate.

The above practices not only violate international best practices but also have detrimental effects on both the ecosystem as a whole and the socioeconomic wellbeing of people. For instance, airborne and land contamination from incineration and open dumping of waste risk the lives of communities against clean water and air pollution (Awodele et al., 2016; Mmereki et al., 2017). Additionally, lack of political will (Hettiarachchi et al., 2020), low public awareness, inadequate budgets, weak legislation, and a lack of appropriate skills and enforcement (Godfrey et al., 2019) are blamed for waste management challenges in Africa.

Sadly, the informal communities are often the worst off in every human-related endeavor, including waste management and sanitation, so progression in that scorecard may be far-fetched. Since the informal communities are already vulnerable, improving waste management and sanitation is crucial to achieving good health and sustainable livelihoods amidst increasing pressure from conditions and population growth. This is because the majority of domestic waste emanates from informal areas, where private and illegal dumping and uncontrolled burning dominate the methods of waste management (Rodseth et al., 2020). Coupled with the above, factors including social, economic, and behavioral have forced many to adopt porta-potties, plastic bags, and other existing materials within and outside the informal settlements for either defecating or discharging bucket contents and open defecation (Muanda et al., 2020). Commonly, waste is kept in an open fashion within the vicinity; waste containers are without lids and left uncovered, occasioning waste spillage and flying within and outside the vicinity.

Delays in lifting or transporting the waste in mostly unsuitable waste vans passing through residential areas can cause leakages and lead spillage. Such situations can form the basis for air pollution, the breeding of insects and flies, and the introduction of many rodents that affect health-related issues. Additionally, duping waste in open dumps or unsecured landfills can potentially transmit infections to scavengers.

The Ghanaian Context

Major cities in Ghana are still grappling with waste difficulties, including Accra, Kumasi, Sekondi-Takoradi, Tamale, and Wa (Amoah & Kosoe, 2014; Obeng et al., 2009). The production of waste is predicted to rise by 73% from 2020 levels to 3.88 billion metric tons in 2050 as a result of the world's fast urbanization and population growth. Just 10% of the 12,710 metric tons of material waste that are produced daily in Ghana are appropriately collected and disposed of. From Table 10.1, the estimated waste generation per population and actual tonnage collection per day from 2000 to 2030 in Accra are alarming.

This is despite a number of private sector waste management agreements in place. Generally, waste management in Ghana has broadly centered on open dumping, controlled dumping of waste, uncontrolled dumping, sanitary land filling, burning, and composting. Notably, victims of open dumping areas include the perimeters of major urban centers in open lots, wetland areas, or areas next

Table 10.1.   Projected Waste Generation in Accra, Ghana (2000–2030).

Year	Population	Waste Generation Tones Per Day	Waste Collection Tones Per Day	Residual Tones Per Day
2000	1,658,939	2,127	1,702	425
2015	1,960,797	3,369	2,695	674
2010	2,327,583	2,654	2,123	531
2020	3,237,730	3,390	2,712	678
2030	4,523,203	4,419	3,535	884

Source: Adapted from Oteng-Ababio (2014).

to surface water sources. Open dumps are commonly located based on access to collection vehicles rather than hydrological or public health considerations. Historically, waste management in the 1980s witnessed incinerators as the main technological drive for waste control and handling in the urban centers of Ghana. The sustainability of it was thwarted by financial constraints and technical know-whow, leading to the dumping of waste in uncontrolled locations, popularly known as "bola" in Ghanaian parlance, in 1985. With financial support from the German Agency for Technical Cooperation, the WMD was born to manage the waste in Ghana when incinerator technology failed. Using donkeys as the means of lifting waste under the WMD initiative from households and discarding it into central containers, dataset records for German technical cooperation agency (GTZ) project aided in improving waste management in Ghana. The WMD approach could not withstand the pressure of urbanization and the associated waste generated; hence, there was an establishment of the private sector initiative (PSI) in Accra and Tema, then Kumasi in the 1990s. Under the PSI, house-to-house and communal services were the centers of focus for waste lifting, with the lower middle-income areas receiving the communal service attention. The surge in population in the urban cities led to the expansion of PSI to other MMDAs across the regions and the inclusion of more private companies into the business of waste all over Ghana (Oduro-Kwarteng, 2011).

Although, as part of the decentralization process, waste management functions became a responsibility of the assemblies in 1988, for the management of waste and sanitation at the local and community levels, the district assemblies are essential institutions. However, a number of other institutions and organizations provide assistance in this pursuit. For instance, the Environmental Protection Agency provides technical assistance to the district assemblies by establishing environmental standards and guidelines for waste management, enforcing Environmental Assessment Regulations, carrying out environmental education and awareness campaigns, and observing environmental quality. Ghana Environmental Assessment Regulations, 1999 (LI 1652) make provisions for existing undertakings that are required to submit environmental management plans. Within the Ministry of Local Government and Rural Affairs, a National Environmental Sanitation Policy Coordination Council has been established to oversee the successful implementation of the policy's objectives. The institution responsible for waste management services at the national level is the Ministry of Local Government, Decentralization, and Rural Development (MLGDRD). It is mandated with the role of formulating waste and sanitation policies, providing oversight responsibility to the local assemblies, and providing subsidies for the provision of sanitation and waste management services. The MLGDRD ensures the supervision of local assemblies' activities and the various WMD responsible for effective solid waste management. The WMD is responsible for all the waste collection, disposal, and monitoring activities of companies engaged by the local assemblies for waste management. The policy framework that guides WMD operations and regulates solid waste management in Ghana is reflective of top-down legislation developed at the national level and decisions made in pertinent case law. Thus, in accordance with Act 462, which replaces the previous act enacted in 1988, the Central Government grants local assemblies some status.

Under the Local Government Act 2016 (Act 462), the local assemblies have a constitutional mandate to handle all sanitation and waste management. However, the independence of the local assemblies is questionable because the Central Government continues to exercise control over and give directives that affect the operations and independence of the local assemblies in spite of their status (Oduro-Kwarteng, 2011).

Legislative Frameworks for Waste Management in Ghana

The government to address waste management in Ghana has implemented various policies and regulatory frameworks. In this sense, the legislative frameworks refer to the different policies, programs, and laws that the Ghanaian government has approved and put into practice in order to guarantee efficient waste and sanitation management. For instance, the Local Government Act, 1993, as amended in 2016 (Act 462), mandates the local assembly to perform deliberative, legislative, and executive functions and effectively handle sanitation issues, which include solid-waste management. The assemblies under Article 243 are required to exercise political and administrative power and supervise the other administrative authorities under their jurisdiction. Act 29 of the Criminal Code of Ghana, which enjoins individuals to take full responsibility for the streets, drains, and space closer to their premises, reinforces this. It posits that whoever places or permits to be placed any refuse, rubbish, or unpleasant material on any yard, street, enclosure, or open space commits a criminal offense. The Environmental Assessment Regulations, 1999 (LI 1652), seek to protect the integrity of the environment against any form of nuisance, including poor waste management and sanitation. Article 2 of the legislation stipulates that no activity considered to have an adverse effect on the environment or public health shall be allowed until it is sanctioned by the Environmental Agency and a permit is issued by the Agency in respect of such activity. Consistently, the Water Resources Commission Act, 1996 (Act 522), is required to advise the government and other pollution control agencies on matters concerning the management and control of pollution of water resources and its adverse effect on citizens.

In 2022, an initiative dubbed OCYF aimed at compelling citizens, individuals, and households, including the informal settlements, to be responsive to waste management and sanitation, was launched in the Greater Accra Region. Championed by the RCC, the OCYF seeks to make it obligatory for all individuals and corporate entities to be responsible for the cleaning and greening of their immediate surroundings. It aimed at harmonizing all stakeholders' efforts in a collaborative manner to enforce the sanitation by-laws and sensitize the populace on the modalities of clean-up exercises in line with the ethos of the operation. The OCYF is meant to actualize the public pronouncement by the President of Ghana to make Greater Accra the cleanest city in Africa. The implementation of the legislation saw the deployment of 1,000 people, most of whom were national security personnel and leaders of the local assemblies, to enforce waste management and sanitation compliance in the informal settlements and catchments.

Additionally, through the exercise, the Environmental Health Officers take instant action against households and businesses that have not maintained a clean frontage and sanitized environment. In some cases, defaulters were cautioned with compliance notices issued once it was found that an individual frontage was not clean. It is interesting to note that despite the fact that all policy frameworks and programs in Ghana are focused on sustainable waste management and sanitation, some important issues are overlooked. First, no regulation from the past or present has addressed the informal settlements, where the majority of waste originates, in terms of spatial order. Second, it is well known that pollutants originating primarily from informal communities are liquid from open defecation and improper disposal. The issue of managing liquid waste is not specifically addressed by the various laws or in informal settlements.

Waste Management in the Informal Settlements

Waste management is a necessity for all humankind because a clean environment ensures sustainable development and prosperity. The view that proper waste management is next to godliness because the environment is the basis for the survival of all living and non-living beings cannot be underestimated. According to the World Commission on Environment and Development (WCED), sustainable development that meet the present generation (WCED, 1987). This is highlighted in the Brundtland report dubbed "Our Common Future," which placed environmental issues firmly on the political agenda – a discussion that addresses environment and development as one single issue (Brundtland, 1987). Waste management in informal settlements appears to be a tall order due to the congestion of the dwellings, human activities, and environmental pollution. Research has confirmed that the socio-economic activities undertaken by informal dwellers generate numerous wastes (Preko et al., 2021; Takyi et al., 2021). Activities such as the sale of sachet water, assorted drinks, processed and unprocessed foodstuffs, assisting shoppers (Kayayie), and scavenging for scraps and used metals create nuisances for the environment.

While such activities are necessary for slum dwellers' daily, sustainable livelihoods, the amount of waste associated with such undertakings and the pollutants they emit cannot be overlooked. Poor waste management practices, such as indiscriminately dumping waste, throwing plastics and filthy things in the open, and burning or burying waste, produce pollutants, which explain the exigencies of the phenomenon. The World Health Organization (WHO, 2021) indicates that overcrowding, poor sanitation, and deplorable living and environmental conditions in informal communities compromise the spread of infectious diseases such as tuberculosis, hepatitis, fever, pneumonia, cholera, and malaria.

Managing waste and providing sanitation services in informal settlements is complex on the basis that basic sanitation coverage is much lower compared to the average for urban areas (UN-Habitat, 2003). Predominantly, open defecation and indiscriminate waste disposal are common practices in informal settlements and promise to adversely affect the environment (Monney et al., 2013).

Unproductive waste collection, haphazard solid waste disposal, and environmental pollution have become major challenges for waste management in the informal sector (Kasala, 2014). In Ghana, it is more devastating due to the absence of accessible roads for waste collection, the lack of funding for waste management, and inadequate waste equipment. Thus, residents in the informal areas are left to dispose of waste through open burning and indiscriminate dumping of solid and liquid waste.

Sadly, in all the policy frameworks for waste and sanitation management reviewed, there were some nagging and rhetorical issues worth considering. For instance, all the past and present legislation is focused on spatial order without recourse to the informal settlements where most of the waste emanates from. Additionally, it is public knowledge that pollutants, which predominantly emanate from informal settlements, are liquid from open defecation and indiscriminate waste disposal. The issue of liquid waste management is not emphasized in the various legislations or specified in the informal settlements. Earlier research has shown that waste management planners in Ghana focus their attention on the collect and dispose strategy, focusing on the final disposition of waste rather than utilizing inclusive and sustainable waste management (Asomani-Boateng, 2007). This contradicts the argument that ensuring responsive waste management policies in informal settlements requires both top-down and bottom-up approaches. Collaboration between urban developers and other stakeholders, on the one hand, as well as community-based organizations and advocacy organizations, academics, and health experts, can provide effective waste management (Sinharoy et al., 2019). So, what are the impediments and hindrances bedeviling effective waste management in the informal sector? Answers to this rhetorical question are addressed in the next section of the chapter.

Challenges of Waste Management in Informal Settlements

Some constrains and challenges that vitiate effective management of waste in Ghana and by extension the informal settlements have been itemized in (Table 10.2). One, the independence of the local assemblies, is partly a challenge to effective waste management in the informal settlements. Central to the ethos of local governance and decentralization is the independence of the people to whom authority is devolved to be responsible and accountable to the masses who are to be served. This means leaders whom the indigenes trust to serve their interests and end their support should be selected by the commonalities to lead them. Even though the President appoints them with the prior approval of not less than a two-thirds majority of the assembly members, the heads tend to serve the interests of the master rather than the public. The appointment of the heads of the local districts into office in itself compromises the assemblies' determination to work effectively as a team. Section 20 of the Act charges the heads to be responsible for the day-to-day performance of the executive and administrative functions, be answerable for the supervision of the departments, and represent the Central Government in the district.

Table 10.2.   Constrains of Waste Management in Informal Settlements.

Serial	Constrains	Nature
1.	Lack of independence of the local assemblies	Heads of local assemblies are appointed by the President
2.	Protection of job security	Heads of assemblies serve the interest of the appointed
3.	Waste management given less priority	WMD are only limited at the metropolitan level without the municipal and district assemblies
4.	Lack of adequate resources to manage waste	Limited budgeting and financing allocation for effective waste and sanitation management
5.	Lack of attitudinal change and culture orientation	Informal residents have negative attitude toward the disposal of waste

Source: Generated-by-the-authors.

Waste management in informal communities requires effective engagement with the grassroots so that responsibilities and enforcement can be shared. For instance, individuals in the community can be assigned the responsibilities of community watchdogs against indiscriminate littering and defaulters of assembly by-laws on waste management. Because the watchdogs stay within the communities, they can effectively monitor the drivers of waste and provide tailor-made recommendations for effective waste management. Allowing the communities to select their leader rather than imposing a leader on them not only fulfills the ethos of good governance, but it will also foster community participation. The current system, which is predicated on the presidents imposing the gaffers of local assemblies on the communities, can be best described as centralized-decentralization system. It is impossible to dismiss the idea that decentralization is theoretically promoted as being embraced in Ghana, considering the fact that it is not effectively implemented there. It not only affects group efforts and grassroots involvement in assembly operations, but it additionally obligates the heads who are appointed to defend their own interests against those who must be served.

Two, waste management endeavors in informal settlements should be geared towards serving the interests of the entire community rather than individual job security. Thus, the view that an appointee by a president thinks of future appointments but not the interests of future generations cannot be absolved from looking at warm attitudes toward waste management in informal communities. The informal settlements are mostly described as lawless communities with residents tagged with suspicious behaviors, most of whom are used as political tools. In recognition of this fact, gaffers of the local assemblies see the informal communities as a "pool of electoral treasures" to be used for political gambling. In other words, due to the huge population of informal dwellers, urban managers pretend to be oblivious to how some of the people pollute the environment because of the election. The handlers of the local assemblies relax their enforcement of waste management and sanitation byelaws or surcharge offenders that flout instructions in the slums with the motive of protecting their current positions and future elections.

Additionally, apart from their emoluments charged to the Consolidated Fund in line with Article 71 of the Constitution, the President determines their tenure of office until death. This means leaders of the local assemblies are not accountable to the local residents, whom they superintend, a situation that compromises effective discharge of responsibilities. Such provisions also embolden them as special representatives of the President and make them too powerful to be approached by assembly members, community stakeholders, and the grassroots. Essentially, a lack of autonomy in local assemblies and protection of the self not only undermines collaborative efforts for an efficient waste management agenda in informal communities, but it also exacerbates the assemblies' practical ineptitude.

Three structural arrangements where waste management departments are only deployed at the metropolitan level without the municipal and district assemblies can explain the lack of an efficient approach to waste management at the local assemblies. This is because out of the 261 local assemblies, the metropolitans have the fewest, with 6 metropolises, 109 municipalities, and 146 districts. This means the authorities responsible for effective waste management across the 16 regions are only 6, leaving out 255 assemblies. Indeed, one would have expected that all 16 administrative regions be assigned a department of waste management, if not the entire 261 assemblies, to oversee and supervise waste and sanitation-related issues. Even though there has always been institutional collaboration in theory, the orphan assemblies without a department of waste management could take advantage. In practice, such collaborative arrangements remain a mirage not only at the local level of governance but also at the central level. Thus, such a structural arrangement clearly shows the low commitment of the state toward waste and sanitation management in the informal communities under the local assemblies.

Furthermore, according to studies, inadequate conditions are commonly observed in the solid waste sector across emerging economies. For instance, the operational trucks needed to transport solid waste are expensive to use, costly to acquire, and expensive to maintain. The United Nations Environment Programme predicted that 70% of the solid waste collection and transfer vehicles in West African municipalities might be inoperable due to operational issues that arise at any one moment. Transporting solid waste is an arduous task that necessitates effective and functional vehicles. Such vehicles frequently break down due to a shortage of replacement components, rendering collection impossible for a prolonged period in most cases. As a result, only a small number of the trucks will still be in usable condition after only a few months of operation due to factors like poor maintenance practices, a lack of dedication, and the poor quality of urban roads.

Four, the lack of funding restricts the extent to which assemblies' combat effective waste management in developing nations. This is because attaining an efficient solid waste management system necessitates heavy capital involvement, which may be beyond the capacity of municipal authorities and individual households.

Frequently, the assemblies fall short of the standards for delivering effective municipal services, which limits the attention that authority's accord to waste disposal and sanitation problems. For instance, budgeting and financing may make it more difficult to execute sanitation and waste management services effectively. Given the president's dedication to eradicating waste and improving cleanliness, it is reasonable to assume that a portion of the budget for local assemblies in Ghana will go toward solid waste management. Nevertheless, given that the situation appears to be getting worse by the day, further research is needed to determine whether the budget is adequate and how well it can cover the operating costs related to efficiency. Contractors might, therefore, be prevented from increasing the effectiveness of solid waste collection in the city if the assemblies and individual homeowners are unable to pay for it.

Fifth, besides the financial limitations, it is impossible to disregard and separate improper waste management from the attitudes and cultures of those who live in informal settlements. According to the UN-Habitat (2003) indicator, informal settlements are places where people live without decent housing, access to better water and sanitation, enough space for their needs, security of tenancy, and adequate living space. These indicators assume that residents have an extremely negative attitude toward the disposal of waste. It is known that households produce huge amounts of solid waste, which is then carelessly disposed of, choking natural waterways and sewers (Songsore, 2008). Poor waste management is a problem that affects most urban neighborhoods in Ghana as well as informal settlements, and it requires a comprehensive approach to be resolved. Especially in order to achieve sustainable environmental management, it is important for people to adopt attitudes that are in line with those practices.

Conclusion and Recommendations

Discourse on waste management and sanitation has received global attention in line with the integrated SDGs, climate change, and global warming. According to the World Bank Institute (2000), solid waste management has been a major problem for urban authorities for nearly 6,000 years. Developing countries, of which Ghana is a part, are not spared the quagmire of waste in informal settlements, in particular, and urban areas, in general. Several policy initiatives and programs have been implemented in response to effective waste and sanitation management over the years. Despite these approaches, what is less known and has the least emphasis, which this study explores, are the functionalities of the local assemblies toward waste management and sanitation. The local assemblies are the wheels on which decentralization traverses and the foundations through which citizens' rights are guaranteed to exercise their franchise at the local level.

Over the years, waste management in Ghana has broadly centered on open dumping, controlled dumping of waste, uncontrolled dumping, sanitary land filling, burning, and composting. Since the 1980s, a number of laws have been implemented in collaboration with the private sector to deal with the menace. The recent policy of waste management, dubbed OCYF, was implemented in response to the pledge of the President of the Republic of Ghana. The review of the extant literature shows some challenges bordering on structural, financial, socio-economic, and attitudinal that hinder effective waste and sanitation management in informal settlements.

First, there is a lack of independence in the local assemblies' due to the appointments or imposition of the heads of local assemblies and the structural flow of authority. This situation flies in the face of decentralization, which hinges on grassroots participation in decision-making and accountability for stewardship. The appointment of the heads of local assemblies by the president and structural arrangements tend to prevent effective engagement and collaboration toward a common pursuit of waste management legislation. In response to the above, it is suggested that the necessary legislative instrument be instituted to enable citizens to elect their preferred and qualified candidate to lead them for the purposes of effective teamwork and accountability.

Second, the current system of governance, where waste management departments are only based at the metropolitan assemblies, which constitute only 6 out of the 261 MMDAs, can only be described as a "tokenistic" approach to waste management. It again suggests a lack of nationalistic commitment toward waste management and sanitation in Ghana. The authors recommend the additional establishment of waste management departments in all 261 local assemblies so that there will be autonomy for effective waste management in each of the local assemblies. In addition, it is proposed that staff with the requisite skills and qualifications be recruited to operate the department.

Third, lack of funding to procure the required trucks to lift waste, maintenance culture, and commitment levels of the working force have been highlighted as major challenges. While financial constraint is a global phenomenon, poor waste management and sanitation can worsen the financial crisis and affect the entire ecosystem with sickness-related issues if not properly addressed. The study canvasses the need for priority expenditure by the government and the local assemblies to ensure a conducive environment for all humankind. It is recommended that the local assemblies be empowered to engage with the private sector for effective waste collection through a mutually beneficial agreement.

Conclusively, it is important to indicate that the attitudinal change and cultural reorientation of people domiciled in informal settlements require critical attention. This is because, while it is possible to solve the earlier highlighted challenges with some level of certainty, it is extremely difficult, if not impossible, to change people's attitudes and cultural orientations toward waste handling. The study recommends two pathways to address the issues of attitudes and cultures. Institute effective communication based on local dialects within associations, organizations, groups, religious groupings, and many others to educate people on proper waste management. Two, appoint effective community watchdogs, empower them, and provide them with some incentives, so they will be motivated to enforce waste management and sanitation by laws. These two arrangements, when implemented, will minimize improper waste disposal and sanitation issues in the slums.

References

Adarkwa, K. K. (2012). The changing face of Ghanaian towns. *African Review of Economics and Finance, 4*(1), 1–29.

African Charter on the Values and Principles of Decentralisation. (2014, June 27). *African Charter on the values and principles of decentralisation, local governance and local development*. Africa Union.

Ahmed, S., & Ali, S. (2006). People as partners: Facilitating people's participation in public–private partnerships for solid waste management. *Habitat International, 30*(4), 781–796.

Akufo-Addo. (2017, April 24). *President Nana Addo Dankwa Akufo-Addo has pledged to make Accra the neatest and best city in Africa by the end of his first term of office. I'll make Accra cleanest city in Africa*. Graphic Corporation.

Amoah, S., & Kosoe, E. (2014). Solid waste management in urban areas of Ghana: Issues and experiences from Wa. *Journal of Environment Pollution and Human Health, 2*(5), 110–117.

Appiah-Agyekum, N., Boachie-Danquah, N., & Sakyi, E. (2013). Local government finance in Ghana: Disbursement and utilisation of the MPs share of the District Assemblies Common Fund. *Commonwealth Journal of Local Governance, 12*, 90–109.

Asomani-Boateng, R. (2007). Closing the loop: Community-based organic solid waste recycling, urban gardening, and land use planning in Ghana, West Africa. *Journal of Planning Education and Research, 27*(2), 132–145.

Awodele, O., Adewoye, A., & Oparah, A. (2016). Assessment of medical waste management in seven hospitals in Lagos, Nigeria. *BMC Public Health, 16*(1), 1–11.

Bendjoudi, Z., Taleb, F., Abdelmalek, F., & Addou, A. (2009). Healthcare waste management in Algeria and Mostaganem department. *Waste Management, 29*(4), 1383–1387.

Braathen, E., Dupont, V., Jordhus-Lier, D., & Sutherland, C. (2014). Introduction: Situating the politics of slums within the 'urban turn'. In *The Politics of Slums in the Global South*. Routledge.

Brundtland, G. (1987). Our common future – Call for action. *Environmental Conservation, 14*(4), 291–294.

Cobbinah, P., Addaney, M., & Agyeman, K. (2017). Locating the role of urbanites in solid waste management in Ghana. *Environmental Development, 24*, 9–21.

Das, S., Lee, S., Kumar, P., Kim, K., Lee, S., & Bhattacharya, S. (2019). Solid waste management: Scope and the challenge of sustainability. *Journal of Cleaner Production, 228*, 658–678.

Elbasiouny, H., Elbanna, B., Al-Najoli, E., Al-Najoli, E., Alsherief, A., Negm, S., El-Nour, E. A., Nofal, A., Sharabash, S. (2020). Agricultural waste management for climate change mitigation: Some implications to Egypt. In A. M. Negm & N. Shareef (Eds.), *Waste management in MENA regions* (pp. 149–169). Springer Water.

Ezeah, C., & Roberts, C. (2012). Analysis of barriers and success factors affecting the adoption of sustainable management of municipal solid waste in Nigeria. *Journal of Environmental Management, 103*, 9–14.

Foppen, J., & Kansiime, F. (2009). SCUSA: Integrated approaches and strategies to address the sanitation crisis in unsewered slum areas in African mega-cities. *Reviews in Environmental Science and Bio/Technology, 8*, 305–311.

Ghana Statistical Service. (2021). *Population and housing census (PHC)*. StatsGhana.

Godfrey, L., Ahmed, M., Gebremedhin, K., Katima, J., Oelofse, S., Osibanjo, O., & Yonli, A. (2019). Solid waste management in Africa: Governance failure or development opportunity. *Regional Development in Africa, 10.5772*, 235.

Henderson, J., & Kriticos, S. (2018). The development of the African system of cities. *Annual Review of Economics, 10*, 287–314.

Hettiarachchi, H., Bouma, J., Caucci, S., & Zhang, L. (2020). Organic waste composting through nexus thinking: Linking soil and waste as a substantial contribution to sustainable development. In H. Hettiarachchi, S. Caucci, & K. Schwärzel (Eds.), *Organic waste composting through nexus thinking: Practices, policies, and trends* (pp. 1–15). Springer.

Kasala, S. (2014). Critical analysis of the challenges of solid waste management initiatives in Keko Machungwa informal settlement, Dar Es Salaam. *Journal of Environmental Protection, 5*(12), 1064.

Lüthi, C., McConville, J., & Kvarnström, E. (2009). Community-based approaches for addressing the urban sanitation challenges. *International Journal of Urban Sustainable Development, 1*(1–2), 49–63.

Mahabir, R., Croitoru, A., Crooks, A., Agouris, P., & Stefanidis, A. (2018). A critical review of high and very high-resolution remote sensing approaches for detecting and mapping slums: Trends, challenges and emerging opportunities. *Urban Science, 2*(1), 8.

Ministry of Local Government, D. a. (2016). *The councils of the local government service (LGS)*. Public Relations Unit.

Mmereki, D., Baldwin, A., Li, B., & Liu, M. (2017). Healthcare waste management in Botswana: Storage, collection, treatment and disposal system. *Journal of Material Cycles and Waste Management, 19*, 351–365.

Monney, I., Tiimub, B., & Bagah, H. (2013). Characteristics and management of household solid waste in urban areas in Ghana: The case of WA. *Civil and Environmental Research, 3*(9), 10–21.

Muanda, C., Goldin, J., & Haldenwang, R. (2020). Factors and impacts of informal settlements residents' sanitation practices on access and sustainability of sanitation services in the policy context of Free Basic Sanitation. *Journal of Water, Sanitation and Hygiene for Development, 10*(2), 238–248.

Myers, G. (2003). Colonial and postcolonial modernities in two African cities. *Canadian Journal of African Studies/Revue canadienne des études africaines, 37*(2–3), 328–357.

Obeng, A., Donkor, E., & Mensah, A. (2009). Assessment of institutional structures for solid waste management in Kumasi. *Management of Environmental Quality: An International Journal, 20*(2), 106–120.

Oduro-Kwarteng, S. (2011). *Private sector involvement in urban solid waste collection*. CRC Press/Balkema.

Ono, H., & Kidokoro, T. (2020). Understanding the development patterns of informal settlements in Nairobi. *Japan Architectural Review, 3*(3), 384–393.

Organization for Economic Cooperation and Development. (2016). *Subnational governments around the World structure and finance*. U.S. Department of State.

Oteng-Ababio, M. (2014). Rethinking waste as a resource: Insights from a low-income community in Accra, Ghana. *City, Territory and Architecture, 1*(1), 1–14.

Peiry, K. (2010). Basel convention on the control of transboundary movements of hazardous wastes and their disposal. *United Nations Audiovisual Library of International Law, 10*, 2–120.

Pongrácz, E. (2002). Re-defining the concepts of waste and waste management evolving the theory of waste management. *Acta Universitatis Ouluensis. Series C, Technica, 32*, 2–168.

Preko, A., Agyabeng, N., & Mensah, J. (2021). Slum dwellers' occupational activities and health implications. *Health Education, 121*(6), 632–648.

Public Services International Research Unit. (2010). *Waste management in Europe: Framework, trends*. PSIRU, Business School, University of Greenwich, Park Row.

Pujara, Y., Pathak, P., Sharma, A., & Govani, J. (2019). Review on Indian Municipal Solid Waste Management practices for reduction of environmental impacts to achieve sustainable development goals. *Journal of Environmental Management, 248*, 109238.

RECYCLING magazine. (2023, June). *Global Waste Index 2022 released.* Retrieved March 17, 2022, from https://www.recycling-magazine.com/2022/03/17/global-waste-index-2022

Rodseth, C., Notten, P., & Von Blottnitz, H. (2020). A revised approach for estimating informally disposed domestic waste in rural versus urban South Africa and implications for waste management. *South African Journal of Science, 116*(1–2), 1–6.

Scarlat, N., Fahl, F., & Dallemand, J. (2019). Status and opportunities for energy recovery from municipal solid waste in Europe. *Waste and Biomass Valorization, 10*(9), 2425–2444.

Schwerhoff, G., & Sy, M. (2017). Financing renewable energy in Africa–Key challenge of the sustainable development goals. *Renewable and Sustainable Energy Reviews, 75,* 393–401.

Self-Government, E. C. (1985). *Local self-government.* European Charter.

Shekdar, A. (2009). Sustainable solid waste management: An integrated approach for Asian countries. *Waste Management, 29*(4), 1438–1448.

Shen, M., Huang, W., Chen, M., Song, B., Zeng, G., & Zhang, Y. (2020). (Micro) plastic crisis: Un-ignorable contribution to global greenhouse gas emissions and climate change. *Journal of Cleaner Production, 254,* 120138.

Sholihah, P., & Chen, S. (2018). Improving living conditions of displaces: A review of the evidence benefit sharing scheme for development induced displacement and resettlement (DIDR) in urban Jakarta Indonesia. *World Development Perspectives, 20,* 100235.

Sinharoy, S., Pittluck, R., & Clasen, T. (2019). Review of drivers and barriers of water and sanitation policies for urban informal settlements in low-income and middle-income countries. *Utilities Policy, 60,* 100957.

Songsore, J. (2008). Environmental and structural inequalities in Greater Accra. *Journal of the International Institute, 16*(1), 1–8.

Takyi, S., Amponsah, O., Yeboah, S., & Mante, E. (2021). Locational analysis of slums and the effects of slum dweller's activities on the social, economic and ecological facets of the city: Insights from Kumasi in Ghana. *GeoJournal, 86,* 2467–2481.

The World Bank. (2019). *Solid waste management.* The World Bank.

Udofia, E., Fobil, J., & Gulis, G. (2015). Solid medical waste management in Africa. *African Journal of Environmental Science and Technology, 9*(3), 244–254.

UN-Habitat. (2003). *The challenge of slums: Global report on human settlements.* UN-Habitat.

UN-Habitat. (2016). *World cities report 2016: Urbanization and development – Emerging futures.* UN-Habitat.

United Nations. (2015). *Sustainable development in the 21st century.* United Nations.

United Nations Development Planning. (2022). *Ghana tackles urban waste management.* United Nations.

United Nations Environment Programme. (2002). *World summit on sustainable development.* United Nations.

WCED. (1987). World commission on environment and development. *Our Common Future, 17*(1), 1–91.

World Health Organization. (2021). *Global report on urban health: Equitable, healthier cities.* UN-Habitat.

Chapter 11

Inclusivity and Climate Action: City and Informal Waste Actors Collaboration in Accra

James Kwame Mensah[a] and Anthony Nkrumah Agyabeng[b]

[a]*Department of Public Administration, University of Ghana Business School, Legon, Ghana*
[b]*Department of Business Administration, University of Professional Studies, Accra, Ghana*

Abstract

The informal sector has become the most dominant sector in the Global South and can be seen in all sectors of the economy. The waste management sector is one of the major areas with many informal actors. This chapter examined how the collaboration of city authorities with informal waste actors (IWAs) can help improve the management of waste and address climate change issues. The study employed a qualitative case study where IWAs and leadership of the waste management department of the Accra Metropolitan Assembly (AMA) engaged in a workshop to gather information data. The findings showed that informal waste actors' valuable contributions have changed city authorities' perception of them from being a nuisance to key stakeholders in waste management. This recognition and collaboration go beyond seeing IWAs as partners in waste management but also as climate change mitigation agents.

Keywords: Informal actors; waste management; climate change; sanitation; Accra

Informal Economy and Sustainable Development Goals:
Ideas, Interventions and Challenges, 225–238
Copyright © 2024 by James Kwame Mensah and Anthony Nkrumah Agyabeng
Published under exclusive licence by Emerald Publishing Limited
doi:10.1108/978-1-83753-980-220241012

Introduction

Informality is a key issue for cities – especially cities in developing economies – dominating both housing and local economic development. Informality is well acknowledged at the global level, particularly by the post-2015 global agendas, especially the 2030 agenda, the Paris climate agreement, and the New Urban Agenda. The New Urban Agenda takes cognizance of the role played by informal livelihoods in cities, whose future will determine whether member states meet their pledge to 'leave no one behind and, indeed, leave no place behind'. The 2030 agenda has addressed the primary causes of socio-spatial and economic inequality through the sustainable development goal (SDG) 1. Other SDGs addressing informality include SDG 8 – decent work and economic growth, SDG 10 – reduced inequalities, and SDG 11 – sustainable communities and cities. These goals intend to safeguard and enhance the well-being of the vulnerable in society.

Within the context of climate change and environmental sustainability, finding modalities to collaborate with IWAs in developing nations takes on greater importance (Valencia, 2019; Velis, 2018). The IWA has a unique ability to complement the effort of city authorities in actions that reduce emissions as well as build resilience in the city. Workers in the informal waste sector participate actively in climate mitigation and adaptation as local agents of climate action. Thus, through the environmental services they provide, IWA helps to reduce greenhouse gas (GHG) emissions, keep cities clean, improve air quality in cities, and enhance the quality of urban life. Measures that are designed to promote environmental sustainability acknowledge the linkage between the informal waste economy and the environment (ILO, 2022).

Therefore, it becomes necessary for more inclusive governance in terms of the management of solid waste by recognizing and formalizing IWA into the overall agenda of implementing Accra's Climate Action Plan. Integrating IWA as a key stakeholder in managing waste and reducing emissions will make city authorities encourage and promote the creation of an environment that allows members of the IWA to promote local ownership of climate action, make a living as well, and reduce the cost of waste management incurred by city authorities (Gunsilius, 2010; Oduro-Appiah et al., 2020; Paul et al., 2012). For example, IWA indirectly saves AMA an amount of $20,192,640 every year in the cost of solid waste collection and disposal and the average income of the IWA per month is $300.00 (Oduro-Appiah et al., 2020, p. 8).

To be more precise, in order to combat unemployment, promote livelihood development, lessen vulnerability, and promote local ownership of climate action of which all targets at achieving the SDGs, city authorities must be more creative in how they approach the informal sector. Thus, the involvement and growth of the informal sector in managing solid waste in the cities should be acknowledged as a positive entry (Shaw, 2016) as such recognition has been shown to improve the recovery rate of waste, enhance collection coverage, and give jobs to city dwellers who cannot find work in the formal sector (Oduro-Appiah et al., 2019). In other words, there is a need to recognize, embrace, and support the informal waste sector (Mensah, 2023).

Despite this compelling evidence, the IWA is still extensively unexplored in the climate change literature. Previous studies paid little focus to the role and importance of collaboration between city authorities and IWA in contributing to climate action in the way they handle and manage solid waste (Mensah, 2023; Oduro-Appiah et al., 2020; Valencia, 2019; Velis, 2018). Meanwhile, a collaboration between city authorities and IWA has the potential to improve not only livelihoods but is also crucial for climate change mitigation and environmental sustainability (Onyanta, 2016). The seeming absence of research on this collaboration in the extant literature not only stops IWA from fully releasing their potential towards the modern management of solid waste but also keeps them constantly on edge about losing their sources of support for employment and survival (Oduro-Appiah et al., 2020; Sandhu et al., 2017). Indeed, Oteng-Ababio et al. (2017) call for more empirical research that focuses on creative ways of integrating IWA in the design, planning, and management of solid waste that aims at addressing climate change issues.

Against this backdrop, this chapter is aimed at examining how the collaboration of city authorities with IWA can help improve waste management and address climate change issues. The chapter is largely focused on the efforts of city authorities in collaborating with informal waste pickers, collectors, aggregators, recyclers, and processors as an environmental sustainability and climate change mitigation strategy. The chapter is of the view that IWA plays a critical role in the effective and efficient management of solid waste (World Bank Group, 2018) which helps in climate change mitigation, and as a result, an enhanced understanding of the recognition, collaboration, and structural cooperation between city authorities and IWA is important in closing apparent gaps in solid waste management and climate change mitigation literature.

The rest of the chapter proceeds as follows; the first section introduces the concept of informality in broad and Ghana in particular. The second is reviewed literature. The third section describes the methodology employed in the study. The fourth section provided a discussion of the findings. The fifth and sixth sections focused on the policy implications and conclusions, respectively.

Literature Review

The Concept of Informality

The interpretation and meaning of the term 'informality' have taken different dimensions. These different dimensions can be seen in how the term suffices like employment, sector, and economy (Mensah, 2023). ILO (2002) refers to the informal sector as all economic activities that are done by people that are not either captured at all or adequately covered by formal institutional governance. Chen (2012), in like manner, defined the informal economy to include all small, unregistered businesses that are not covered by the formal sector, however, produce goods and provide a source of livelihood to people.

The informal sector in Ghana has grown over the years since the 1970s when many Ghanaians were actively working and generating their income (Debrah, 2007).

Currently, about 88% of the active working population depends on the informal sector for a source of livelihood, making the informal sector contribute to 88% of the GDP of Ghana (GLSS 6, 2014). This shows how important the informal economy has become to bringing development to the country. Unlike previous years when the informal sector has been largely neglected in the formulation and implementation of policies to deal with the bottlenecks of the sector for better performance (Debrah, 2007), in recent years, the sector has been recognized and attracted policy response from key stakeholders.

Notable among these policies are the National Local Economic Development Policy (2014), the Ghana National Urban Policy (2012), and the Ghana National Poverty Reduction Strategy II (2006–2009). However, these policies have no clear plan for implementation (Mensah, 2023). It is, therefore, imperative that policy-makers fully acknowledge the informal sector, embrace it, and support it for it to realize its potential as it can address the solid waste menace in cities, thereby climate action.

Formal Waste and Informal Waste Management

IWAs refer to private individuals and small businesses that are engaged in the management of solid waste and recycling activities but are not always given recognition or support by formal waste actors (Oduro-Appiah et al., 2020; Scheinberg et al., 2010). Most cities in the global south including the city of Accra face the menace of waste management which further developed into serious human health and environmental challenges (Gutberlet et al., 2017; Onyanta, 2016). Due to the lack of capacity and resources to manage waste effectively and efficiently over time, the informal sector has emerged as a key stakeholder to strengthen the weak formal sector in order to perform better work (Ezeah et al., 2013). Apart from this reason, the informal waste sector also serves as a source of employment for those who get involved in it (Velis et al., 2012; Wilson et al., 2006).

The contribution of the informal waste sector has been critical to environmental sustainability thereby making cities habitable (Fahmi & Sutton, 2013). For example, according, to the results of a recent research commissioned by the Greater Accra Resilient and Integrated Development, 51% of the waste in the Greater Accra Metropolitan Area is collected by actors in the informal waste sector (Mensah, 2023). Despite these valuable contributions, the informal sector has not been fully integrated into the formal sector (Gutberlet et al., 2017). According to Tirado-Soto and Zamberlan (2013), this is regrettable because the operation of collaborative arrangements calls for assistance with storage, equipment, advertising of the collection services, and the removal of the collected solid waste from transfer stations or recycling facilities. As also noted by Joshi and Moore (2004), in order to improve waste management, policies to incorporate IWAs and more institutional changes are needed. These changes include empowering, developing skills, and fostering cooperative relationships among all stakeholders.

As stated clearly earlier, the literature argues that IWAs play a critical role in terms of addressing solid waste challenges. However, much research has not been done on how both the formal and the informal can collaborate to improve solid waste management, thereby addressing climate change and environmental sustainability issues in Accra. This study seeks to look further into that.

The Informal Waste Sector: The Engine for Combating Climate Change

The major activities of IWAs are basically divided into two: waste collection in places that the formal sector cannot serve and the recovery of waste materials that are recyclable from landfills, streets, and other public spaces (Onyanta, 2016). The contribution of IWA to sustainable development and climate change mitigation cannot be overemphasized. As noted by Oteng-Ababio (2011), it is challenging to quantify the environmental benefits made by the IWAs due to their informal operations, but it is reasonable to infer that they have good environmental effects.

One of the contribution areas of IWA is resource recovery. In this area, the performance of formal waste management systems is lower as compared to IWA (Paul et al., 2012). For example, in Egypt, after the privatization of solid waste management systems, there was a decline in the recovery rate of resources, meaning there was less role for the IWA to play (Gunsilius, 2010). According to Medina (2011), when there are high recovery rates of waste, it plays a crucial role by leading to the reduction of emissions like GHG as well as the generation of leachate and methane. These are relevant to climate change mitigation and a sustainable environment because of their role in atmospheric warming, especially methane which has a power greater than carbon dioxide.

Another way IWA contributes, as noted by Adama (2012) is through the technique of reusing part of the wastes generated during manufacturing in the process of production. According to Gunsilius (2010), the reuse of materials that cannot be recycled helps in the reduction of energy consumption as well as the emission of gases. For instance, from the research of Medina (2011), the energy consumption for the manufacturing of glass can be lowered by up to 35%, that of paper and steel by 50%, that of plastics by over 50%, and that of aluminium by more than 90%. This means that reusing secondary materials also lessens the use of natural resources and their depletion.

However, the negative effect of IWA's activities on the environment and people cannot also be overlooked. In their pursuit of recovering recyclable goods, waste pickers are said to be frequently littering the environment (Adama, 2012). Open burning, which releases harmful gases into the air but makes it easier to acquire recyclable materials, is prevalent. Monni et al. (2006) noted that an important source of carbon dioxide emissions in the waste industry is the burning of waste that contains fossil carbon. Another bad practice is the unauthorized disposal of waste in places like deserted lots and riverbanks, which threatens both environmental sustainability and human health (Wilson et al., 2006). Due to their extended contact with poisonous and dangerous chemicals, waste pickers are at risk for health problems themselves (Paul et al., 2012).

Methodology

The study was conducted in the AMA in the Greater Accra Region. It lies along the South-Eastern coast of Ghana and covers an area of 1,453.53 km. It is home to about 4.6 million residents and contributes about 25% of the gross national income of Ghana (Government of Ghana, 2017). It is considered the 11th largest metropolitan area in Africa and generates an estimated 3,293 metric tonnes of solid waste daily (Oduro-Appiah et al., 2020). The major components of solid waste that are biodegradable are metals (2–5%), grass cuttings (45–61%), cardboard and paper (5%), and plastics (14%) (Miezah et al., 2015). The AMA was chosen for this study because it represents the largest and oldest local government in Ghana.

The study used a qualitative approach based on the interpretative philosophical worldview. The reason for using the qualitative approach is because the study is interested in understanding the collaboration of city authorities with IWA which can help improve waste management and address climate change issues. As Creswell (2016) indicates, qualitative research seeks purposefully to select participants that will best help the researcher understand the problem and the research question. A case study within the research was considered suitable for this study, as case studies are the favourite strategy of inquiry when 'why' and 'how' questions are being asked as the focus of the study (Yin, 2009). A purposive sampling technique was adopted for this study, and the sample size was based on the principle of saturation, the point where additional information from participants does not give a fresh perspective on a particular subject (Babbie, 2013).

The city stakeholders were purposively selected based on their knowledge and involvement in the management of waste. Thus, the head and workers of the waste management department of AMA were purposively selected based on their knowledge and direct involvement with IWA. The IWAs such as pickers, aggregators, crushers, collectors, recyclers, and processors were interviewed during a workshop held at the AMA. This workshop was part of a bigger consultation effort of C40 cities to develop an inclusive waste management system for the AMA. The workshop brought together IWA and city authorities to brainstorm on inclusiveness and collaboration between the two actors as well as the challenges in the waste management sector.

The study combined primary and secondary data sources as this offers a unique strength to deal with a full variety of evidence – documents, artefacts, interviews, and observation (Yin, 2009) and serves as a way of triangulation. In total, 50 respondents were sampled for this study, consisting of three workshops and one focus group discussion. Thus, the study adopted a participatory and inclusive workshop approach to ensure an in-depth understanding of the collaboration between city authorities and IWA, the opportunities, and the challenges. Multiple stakeholders and respondents were used, which served to lessen data source biases and improve the validity and dependability of the research findings.

The interviews, which lasted between one hour and two hours and were audiotaped, were guided by an interview guide and were participatory and interesting. Interviews with practitioners and city authorities took place in English, while those with employees in the informal sector took place in Twi, a local dialect of Ghana, and were then translated into English. After being asked, the subjects gave their consent voluntarily to participate in the study. The audiotaped interviews were transcribed for the data analysis, where common themes emerged and varied as a result of the consideration of the data (Brockopp & Hastings-Tolsma, 1995). Additionally, verbatim statements were used to support the claims being made.

Findings

Demographic Characteristics of Respondents

Table 11.1 shows the demographic characteristics of the respondents of this study. The respondents are dominated by men, and the majority of them are waste collectors. Again, most of the respondents were Ghanaians. The IWAs are involved in waste collection, recycling, processing, crushing, and picking. However, the data showed that the majority of them are waste collectors.

The Emergence, Growth, and Work of Informal Waste Sector in Accra

Since the 1960s, AMA has been fully in charge of waste collection and management; nevertheless, this arrangement could not continue because it was costly for the city. As a result, public–private partnerships were used to collect waste in

Table 11.1.   Demographic Characteristics.

Sex	Frequency	Percentage
Male	38	76.0
Female	12	24
Category of waste actors		
Waste aggregators	8	16
Waste pickers	9	18
Waste collectors	13	26
Waste crushers	8	16
Waste recyclers	7	14
Waste processors	5	10
Country of origin		
Ghana	29	58
Nigeria	4	8
Liberia	7	14
Burkina Faso	10	20

Source: Field data.

the late 1990s and early 2000s (Oduro-Appiah et al., 2020). Before the informal waste sector in the city gained popularity over the past 10 years, some itinerant collectors collected 'waste glass bottles' from homes in exchange for money, demonstrating that the practice was, to some extent, accepted in communities. However, thoughtful consideration should be given to the possibility that the 'waste-for-cash' system might have provided a good incentive for the rapid growth of the sector. The IWAs in AMA consist of waste pickers, recyclers, aggregators, collectors, crushers, and processors. Recently, the number of IWAs, especially waste pickers in Ghana, is experiencing continuous growth because of rapid urbanization as well as serving as a source of livelihood for many people living in slums and poor communities. These categories of informal workers in one way or another have their work linked.

Waste collectors are a category of IWAs that go to establishments that produce waste such as homes and shops to collect waste. They either sell this to waste aggregators or directly send it to landfill sites or processing plants. Waste aggregators are also a group of IWAs who purchase waste from pickers and collectors, clean it, and then sell it to crushers, recyclers, and processers. Crushers also break down plastic waste into smaller pieces so that they can be purchased by recyclers. Recyclers, on the other hand, also purchase waste from pickers, collectors, aggregators, and crushers to turn plastic waste into new items.

While some of the IWAs operate individually, many of them have come together to form associations for representation. The department responsible for the management of waste in AMA reveals that there are 14 informal waste management associations in Accra currently, which makes it very clear that the informal sector is becoming permanent in the city as it continually expands. Out of the growing numbers in the informal sectors, statistics show that it is dominated by males and just a few are females who are involved in plastic bottles and sachet rubbers collection. Many of these actors are said to have migrated from the Northern regions of Ghana, with some coming from neighbouring countries like Nigeria, Liberia, and Burkina Faso. Their wages are dependent on the quantity of waste they can collect which is paid by the waste producers. These IWAs, however, play a crucial role as stakeholders in the management of solid waste in Accra.

Recognizing Informal Waste Sector: City Authorities Understand the Necessity

Results from the data collected in the area under study demonstrated that city authorities have recognized the informal sectors and understand the necessity of collaborating with them for the effective and efficient management of waste in the city. This recognition by city authorities was born out of the fact that the waste that slums and highly inhabited areas produce is not effectively managed by the formal waste sector, and as a result, poses a threat to the environment, making cities less habitable and sustainable. Therefore, recognizing and embracing them into the waste management systems will be an effective way to address this menace. City authorities further revealed that this understanding has deepened their relationship in a positive way over the past five years with the IWAs.

The interviews with IWAs confirmed that, indeed, their relationship with city authorities had improved in an appreciable manner as they now open their doors to them in a friendly way with the purpose of cleaning up the city and also maintaining law and order. One of the respondents captured it as 'there is some improvement in how they relate to us'. This due recognition of IWAs by city authorities has been in the form of giving them work permits as well as slums and densely populated places as areas of jurisdiction.

The IWAs further revealed that though their services are very important in keeping the city clean and reducing emissions and recognition has been given to them as key stakeholders, however, they are not taken into consideration in the planning process. Specifically, the Pure Water Waste Collectors Association indicated that they are affected as they are left out of discussions. These actors, therefore, call for integration into waste management especially at the planning stage. One of them said, 'we want to be fully integrated'.

Collaborating with IWAs to Address Climate Change Issues

In order to effectively address the menace of waste management in the city, there is a need for a collaborative effort by both the formal and the IWAs. Supporting the efforts of the city's informal waste players would enable them to provide the best possible services for maintaining city cleanliness and reducing emissions. City authorities in the interviews revealed that they are taking active roles in collaborating and supporting the work of IWAs in various ways such as training on road safety and traffic regulations, training in the area of sorting and weighing, capacity building and financial literacy, insurance and pension schemes for informal workers, environmental health and occupational safety, and plans to facilitate the acquisition of riding licences for tricycle operators.

In addition to this, city authorities have granted an office space to facilitate the activities of IWAs. This support given to IWAs is not only targeted at providing them with a source of livelihood but, most importantly, to address the waste menace in the city, thereby climate action. The IWAs also in an interview confirmed the assertion of the city authorities that training sessions have been organized for them from time to time on waste collection and segregation. These training sessions are targeted at the leaders of the various categories of informal workers who are also expected to implement the lessons with their teams.

Challenges of Collaborating and Supporting the Informal Waste Sector

Though great efforts are made to integrate IWA into the management of solid waste in the city, this attempt, however, is not without challenges. These challenges can be seen from both the city authorities and IWAs. From the viewpoint of the city authorities, the main challenge they face has to do with managing IWAs. There exist many associations in the informal waste management space, specifically about 14, and as a result, engaging them becomes challenging as every group tries to fight for its interest and might not necessarily be interested in the concerns that the city would have to ensure cordial interactions and best practices in waste management.

Secondly, the language barrier. To the city authorities, many of the IWAs do not understand the English language largely because they are uneducated and those coming from neighbouring countries cannot also speak any Ghanaian language. Communication becomes difficult, and eventually, they are unable to understand the best practices the city expects from them. Thirdly, threatened the source of livelihood. The IWAs believe that the city is on the side of the formal waste management businesses and will not hesitate to eject them from the area and hand over waste collection to formal businesses. Because they are concerned about losing their jobs, IWAs are frequently hesitant to cooperate when the city authorities call them.

However, on the part of the IWAs, the pressing issue for them is having not just an office but an officer at AMA who will be responsible for dealing with the challenges of the sector as well as taking into consideration their suggestions. To them, this will resolve the barrier of integration. Another challenge has to do with their negligence in decision-making AMA. They are of the view that the city authorities should frequently engage and seek their opinions on certain decisions as this makes it easier for them to perform services better. Lastly, they suggest that city authorities should visit them in the field to see what is happening. This would not only correct any mismanagement of waste that will be harmful to the environment and people, but these gestures would also encourage them to participate in the activities of AMA.

Discussion and Implications

To achieve the objective of managing waste effectively, reducing unemployment, as well as reducing emissions in order to contribute to SDGs, there is a need to collaborate with the informal waste sector. Therefore, the aim of the chapter was to examine how the collaboration of city authorities with IWAs can help improve the management of waste and address climate change issues. The findings of this study are discussed as follows.

Firstly, the findings revealed that there have been changes in approach towards the informal waste sector. Whereas there were no efforts previously to collaborate and address the issues of the informal waste sector, some significant progress has been seen in the past few years in AMA. Efforts have been made to ensure that the activities of the informal waste sector are recognized and supported by integrating them into Accra's Climate Action Plan. This is very crucial as the IWA could serve the purpose of addressing climate change issues by reducing emissions as well as creating employment opportunities for city dwellers. Indeed, it is evident that the contribution of the informal waste sector has been crucial in climate change and environmental sustainability in both developed and developing countries (Onyanta, 2016; Paul et al., 2012), and therefore, giving them social acceptance in AMA could improve upon the waste menace in the city.

Secondly, not only has recognition been given to IWAs as a stakeholder in waste management but also attempts have been made to provide support for them in order to perform services better. This support came in the form of providing training sessions on road safety and traffic regulation, facilitating the acquisition of licences for tricycle operators, and enrolling them in insurance and pension schemes. Clearly, these efforts demonstrate that city authorities are supporting and creating a good environment for integrating them as key stakeholders in addressing the waste menace in the city. According to Mensah (2023), efforts in recognizing and supporting the informal sector have important consequences for reducing poverty and fostering social development. Similarly, recognizing the informal sector is paramount as it contributes to environmental sustainability (Oguntoyinbo, 2012) and local economic development (Mensah, 2023).

Thirdly, the finding of the study demonstrates that collaborating with the informal sector has great potential to address climate change challenges. These collaborations will make the IWAs see themselves as not just struggling to make a living thereby doing everything to survive even if it will be harmful to the environment and people but will also give them some motivation and training to have the best practices in their work to safeguard the environment (Onyanta, 2016). The collaboration will give informal actors an appropriate dumping site for waste which is mostly done at illegal places such as riverbanks and vacant areas which endangers the environment and health of humans (Wilson et al., 2006). This collaboration will ensure that IWAs are provided with personal protective equipment which helps them deal with health challenges as a result of lengthy exposure to dangerous and harmful chemicals (Paul et al., 2012).

Lastly, several issues arise when attempting to recognize and collaborate with informal actors, including dealing with multiple associations of IWAs; therefore, organizing and regulating them becomes difficult. Due to their low level of formal education, interacting with them to follow due processes becomes another challenge. However, the IWAs accused the city authorities of harassing them regularly and not being willing to provide the needed support for them as expected. IWAs also noted that they have been left out of decision-making and that calls for the negligence of the directives of the AMA.

The implications of the study for policy and practice based on the findings are as follows: First, city authorities are to ensure that a friendly and conducive environment is created for the IWAs to perform superior services. Some of the roles they can play to create this enabling environment are putting in measures to address job security and dignity as most of the IWAs refuse engagement with them because they think they could be ejected and give their work to the formal waste sector. IWAs should be given full concessions in slums and highly populated areas where the trucks of formal waste sectors cannot navigate. City authorities should provide sorting centres, where materials can easily be recovered, and support with working equipment such as tricycles and personal protective equipment. This supportive environment will encourage IWAs to not just see their work as a source of livelihood but most importantly as a means of protecting the environment and making it habitable and sustainable.

Secondly, given the dynamics of the informal waste sector in AMA, there are some prospects for integration and formalization into the formal sector. The first step in doing this is to form a cooperative union to capture the various associations in the sector. This will help the least organized category of informal actors, specifically waste pickers to be on board for meaningful discourse. Collaboration is very crucial as it comes with benefits for both the city authorities and informal actors. The advantages that lie for informal actors include a decent job and better working conditions that lower health hazards, a consistent income, and access to recyclables. For city authorities, it will save them some costs in collecting, transporting, and disposing of waste because of the collaboration with the informal sector as access to and recovery of waste materials will increase. For climate action, there will be more recovery of recyclables from landfills and public spaces.

Furthermore, it has been acknowledged that informal waste is playing a critical role in waste management and providing job opportunities; however, city authorities have not given it a cogent and thorough policy response to which the challenges of integrating and managing the informal sector are linked. Therefore, it is crucial for city authorities to develop a cogent policy framework that gets rid of the informality's drawbacks while maintaining its ability to address the waste menace by contributing to climate change and environmental sustainability as well as creating a source of livelihood for the city dwellers. Critical areas that need policy response from the city authorities are health and environmental protection, livelihood improvement, fair income for work done (pricing policy), and social acceptance policies.

Conclusion

The findings of this study demonstrate that the informal waste sector has continued to experience growth in terms of numbers and activities. Their valuable contributions have been crucial and, as a result, have changed city authorities' perception of them from being a nuisance to key stakeholders in the management of solid waste, urban sustainability, and development, thereby climate action. The city authority has, therefore, recognized them and put measures in place to collaborate with them for the effectiveness and efficiency of waste management. This recognition goes beyond giving the IWAs a source of livelihood to include protecting the environment from emissions of gases such as GHG, methane, and ethane which cause warming in the atmosphere, making cities less habitable and sustainable.

Both national and local governments should embrace and integrate the informal waste sector in their attempts to achieve SDGs and Accra Climate Plan Action. To improve the performance of the IWAs, city authorities must identify the key challenges facing them and make intentional efforts to address them. This will go a long address the job insecurities facing them as well as promote environmental sustainability and climate action. However, this study is limited to only AMA which is just one of the municipalities in the Greater Accra Region of Ghana. The study is also limited to selected officials and leaders of IWA. Future studies can address these limitations by expanding the scope of this study.

References

Adama, O. (2012). Urban livelihoods and social networks: Emerging relations in informal recycling in Kaduna, Nigeria. *Urban Forum, 23*, 449–466.

Babbie, E. (2013). *The practice of social research* (13th ed.). Cengage Learning.

Brockopp, D. Y., & Hastings-Tolsma, M. T. (1995). *Fundamental of nursing research.* UNISA.

Chen, M. A. (2012). *The informal economy: Definitions, theories and policies* [Working Paper, Vol. 1, No. 26, pp. 90141-4]. WIEGO.

Creswell, J. W. (2016). *Qualitative inquiry and research design: Choosing among five approaches.* Sage Publications.

Debrah, Y. A. (2007). Promoting the informal sector as a source of gainful employment in developing countries: Insights from Ghana. *The International Journal of Human Resource Management, 18*(6), 1063–1084.

Ezeah, C., Fazakerley, J. A., & Roberts, C. L. (2013). Emerging trends in informal sector recycling in developing and transition countries. *Waste Management, 33*(11), 2509–2519.

Fahmi, W., & Sutton, K. (2013). Cairo's contested waste: The Zabaleen's local practices and privatisation policies. In M. J. Zapata & M. Hall (Eds.), *Organising waste in the city* (pp. 159–180). Policy Press.

Government of Ghana. (2017). *Enhancing Urban Resilience in the Greater Accra Metropolitan Area.* World Bank Group.

Gunsilius, E. (2010). *Role of the informal sector in solid waste management and enabling conditions for its integration: Experiences from GTZ* In Trans Waste Workshop on the Informal Sector, Geneva. Retrieved May 8, 2023, from http://www.transwaste.eu/file/001441.pdf

Gutberlet, J., Kain, J. H., Nyakinya, B., Oloko, M., Zapata, P., & Zapata Campos, M. J. (2017). Bridging weak links of solid waste management in informal settlements. *The Journal of Environment & Development, 26*(1), 106–131.

ILO. (2002). *Resolution concerning decent work and the informal economy.* International Labour Office.

ILO. (2022). *A double transition: Formalization and the shift to environmental sustainability with decent work.* International Labour Office.

Joshi, A., & Moore, M. (2004). Institutionalised co-production: Unorthodox public service delivery in challenging environments. *Journal of Development Studies, 40*(4), 31–49.

Mensah, J. K. (2023). Recognizing, supporting and embracing the urban informal economy in Ghana: A local economic development perspective. *Urban Research & Practice, 16*(1), 25–43.

Medina, M. (2011). The informal sector – A driving force for recycling management. In E. Gunsilius, S. Spies, & S. García-Cortés (Eds.), *Recovering resources, creating opportunities: Integrating the informal sector into solid waste management.* Retrieved December 18, 2023, from http://wiego.org/publications/recovering

Miezah, K., Obiri-Danso, K., Kádár, Z., Fei-Baffoe, B., & Mensah, M. Y. (2015). Municipal solid waste characterization and quantification as a measure towards effective waste management in Ghana. *Waste Management, 46*, 15–27.

Monni, S., Pipatti, R., Lehtilä, A., Savolainen, I., & Syri, S. (2006). *Global climate change mitigation scenarios for solid waste management* (Vol. 603, pp. 51–55). Espoo, Technical Research Centre of Finland. VTT Publications.

Oduro-Appiah, K., Afful, A., Kotey, V. N., & De Vries, N. (2019). Working with the informal service chain as a locally appropriate strategy for sustainable modernization of municipal solid waste management systems in lower-middle income cities: Lessons from Accra, Ghana. *Resources, 8*(1), 12.

Oduro-Appiah, K., Scheinberg, A., Miezah, K., Mensah, A., & de Vries, N. K. (2020). Existing realities and sustainable pathways for solid waste management in Ghana. In A. Pariatamby, F. Shahul Hamid, & M. Sanam Bhatti (Eds.), *Sustainable waste management challenges in developing countries* (pp. 115–143). IGI Global.

Oguntoyinbo, O. O. (2012). Informal waste management system in Nigeria and barriers to an inclusive modern waste management system: A review. *Public Health, 126*(5), 441–447.

Onyanta, A. (2016). Cities, municipal solid waste management, and climate change: Perspectives from the South. *Geography Compass, 10*(12), 499–513.

Oteng-Ababio, M. (2011). Missing links in solid waste management in the Greater Accra Metropolitan Area in Ghana. *GeoJournal, 76*(5), 551–560.

Oteng-Ababio, M., Owusu-Sekyere, E., & Amoah, S. T. (2017). Thinking globally, acting locally: Formalizing informal solid waste management practices in Ghana. *Journal of Developing Societies, 33*(1), 75–98.

Paul, J. G., Arce-Jaque, J., Ravena, N., & Villamor, S. P. (2012). Integration of the Informal Sector into municipal solid waste management in the Philippines – What does it need? *Waste Management, 32*(11), 2018–2028.

Sandhu, K., Burton, P., & Dedekorkut-Howes, A. (2017). Between hype and veracity; privatization of municipal solid waste management and its impacts on the informal waste sector. *Waste Management, 59*, 545–556.

Scheinberg, A., Simpson, M. H., Gupt, Y., Anschütz, J., Haenen, I., Tasheva, E., Hecke, J., Soos, R., Chaturvedi, B., Garcia-Cortes, S., & Gunsilius, E. (2010). Economic aspects of the informal sector in solid waste management; WASTE, SKAT, and city partners for GTZ (Deutsche Gesellschaft fur Technische Zusammenarbeit) and CWG (Collaborative Working Group on Solid Waste Management in Low-and middle-Income Countries), Eschborn, Germany.

Shaw, A. (2016). The informal sector in Kolkata metropolitan area: Appraisal and prospects for local economic development. In A. K. Dutt, A. G. Noble, F. J. Costa, R. R. Thakur, S. K. Thakur (Eds.), *Spatial diversity and dynamics in resources and urban development: Volume II: Urban development* (pp. 499–516). Springer.

Valencia, M. (2019). Informal Recycling Sector (IRS), contribution to the achievement of the SDGs, and a circular economy. *Journal of Cleaner Production, 415*, 137894.

Tirado-Soto, M. M., & Zamberlan, F. L. (2013). Networks of recyclable material waste-picker's cooperatives: An alternative for the solid waste management in the city of Rio de Janeiro. *Waste Management, 33*(4), 1004–1012.

Velis, C. (2018). No circular economy if current systemic failures are not addressed. *Waste Management & Research, 36*(9), 757–759.

Velis, C. A., Wilson, D. C., Rocca, O., Smith, S. R., Mavropoulos, A., & Cheeseman, C. R. (2012). An analytical framework and tool ('InteRa') for integrating the informal recycling sector in waste and resource management systems in developing countries. *Waste Management & Research, 30*(9 Suppl), 43–66.

Wilson, D. C., Velis, C., & Cheeseman, C. (2006). Role of informal sector recycling in waste management in developing countries. *Habitat International, 30*(4), 797–808.

World Bank Group. (2018). *Municipal solid waste management: A roadmap for reform for policymakers*. World Bank.

Yin, R. K. (2009). *Case study research: Design and methods* (2nd ed.). Sage Publications.

Chapter 12

Strengthening Sustainable Rural Development Through Entrepreneurship: An Indian Perspective

Kalpana Rajsinghot[a], Shashi Bala[b] and Puja Singhal[c]

[a]*Ministry of Communication, India*
[b]*VV Giri National Labour Institute, India*
[c]*NCSL-National Institute of Educational Planning and Administration, India*

Abstract

Rural entrepreneurship is an important vehicle to drive sustainable rural development in India. The process of planning, starting, and operating a new business is termed as entrepreneurship. It has been described as having the ability and willingness to create, plan, and manage a business enterprise while accepting any risks involved to generate a profit. In India's rural areas, enterprise and entrepreneurship are what fuel economic progress. A rural entrepreneur is someone who uses rural resources to develop products and establish enterprises that support the development of the rural economy and its growth potential. Although, these rural business owners encounter issues similar to those faced by urban business owners due to the rural setting in which they operate amplifies their difficulties. To reduce rural people's migration and to support rural upliftment, it is necessary to encourage entrepreneurship and new employment opportunities. Consequently, rural entrepreneurship has the potential to greatly increase employment in rural areas. It is a more effective method of eradicating poverty and hunger, sustainable health and well-being, enhancing gender equality, quality education, decent work conditions, promoting innovation in industries, and ultimately reducing the inequalities which are mapped with the important agenda of the United Nation's sustainable development goals (SDGs 2030). To bring about change, institutions must concentrate on the interactions between education, skill, entrepreneurship, and employment.

Informal Economy and Sustainable Development Goals:
Ideas, Interventions and Challenges, 239–256

This chapter explores the challenges and skills required for rural entrepreneurship in India, proposing a framework to enhance rural development through entrepreneurship.

Keywords: Sustainable development goals; rural development; entrepreneurship; skill development; quality education

1. Introduction

India is moving towards celebrating 100 years of independence in 2047, and Hon'ble Prime Minister of India, *Shri Narendra Modi* has been making various initiatives to uplift the rural population for inclusive sustainable development which aims at elevating the financial condition and purchasing power of the rural population. As our economic cycle is interconnected, this will also fuel the financial system of towns and cities of India. This also aligns with the idea of the Father of Nation *Mahatma Gandhi* about rural development which reflects that the progress of the nation lies in rural development. Therefore, his statement 'India lives in villages' is very apt as Indian society is centred in its villages, which are a true representation of the country. In India, according to the 2011 Census, 68.84% of the population resides in rural areas, and the urban population is increasing from 10.8% in 1901 to 31.2% in 2021 (Punyamurthy & Bheenaveni, 2023). There are numerous driving forces behind the movement of rural residents to urban areas. One such determining variable is unemployment. The majority of people in India depend on agriculture as their primary source of income. Raw materials for industries are also abundant in rural locations. Yet, due to the concentration of processing hubs in metropolitan regions, rural residents' income levels are lower than those of urban residents. Urban slums tend to congregate when employment possibilities are concentrated in one section of the city, which also leads to imbalanced growth. Rural regions will not become prosperous until they generate sustainable employment prospects within their borders. To end the cycle of poverty and to develop rural areas of the country, it is important to encourage rural entrepreneurship.

Economic development of rural areas also involves considerable social and environmental impacts such as ecological pollution, exhaustion of resources, damage to biodiversity, etc. This makes it necessary to create a balance between economic development, sustainability, and environmental protection to achieve the sustainable protection of the various ecosystems like agriculture, food, industries, and tourism as well as the natural and cultural heritage connected to the rural environment. In this sense, entrepreneurship must be developed into a key tool for rural communities to address current economic, environmental, and social concerns and help to meet the 2030 SDGs. Rural entrepreneurship can be viewed as an effort to develop risk-taking management that is relevant to opportunity and to mobilize people, material, and financial resources to complete projects in rural areas (Saxena, 2012). A rural entrepreneur can be defined as an individual who utilizes local rural resources to develop new products and establish enterprises in these areas to support the development of the rural economy and its growth potential (Petrin, 1992). Rural entrepreneurs play a significant role in closing the job gap, combating unemployment issues, and expanding the purchasing power and standard of living of the people by offering sustainable employment opportunities to people in rural areas.

In India, rural youth lack education and skills unlike urban youth. Lack of new, challenging, and better job opportunities in the agriculture sector, and financial constraint, limits the job opportunities for educated rural youth. To meet the needs of rural entrepreneurs and to generate ample employment prospects in rural areas, the ecosystem of skill development and entrepreneurship promotion in India needs to be strengthened. In this direction, the Government of India (GoI) has launched numerous vocational training courses, apprenticeship schemes, and programs to help young people develop their skills and encourage rural entrepreneurship. Improving the employability of young people is critical for maximizing the demographic dividend. To do this, the Ministry of Skill Development and Entrepreneurship (MSDE), GoI, has taken up the responsibility of organizing all national skill development initiatives. This entails eliminating the gap between the demand for and supply of skilled labour, creating a framework for vocational and technical education, and developing new skills and creative thinking for both existing and future job opportunities. Hence, India can enhance entrepreneurial abilities and employability by upskilling the rural youth through education programmes and skilling initiatives. In light of this, the chapter focusses on various GOI initiatives as well as institutional mechanisms for promoting entrepreneurship and skill development in rural regions. Furthermore, an attempt is made in this chapter to propose the framework for strengthening sustainable rural development through entrepreneurship and skills enhancement.

2. Major Objectives

1. To analyse the need to promote rural entrepreneurship in India.
2. To understand the current labour market trends promoting entrepreneurship in India.
3. To study government initiatives for enhancing the entrepreurial abilities of rural population.
4. To suggest a framework for sustainable rural development through entrepreneurship.

3. Methodology

The present chapter employs descriptive research and intends to analyse the possibilities of strengthening sustainable rural development through entrepreneurship. In this context, the study attempted to elaborate on various Indian government entrepreneurial initiatives and labour market trends. Various secondary qualitative and quantitative data have been analysed for the same, and a framework for sustainable rural development has been proposed.

4. Review of Literature

Sustainable development is always a prime concern for every government and policymaker, with a specific focus on rural areas for attaining SDGs. Entrepreneurial activity contributes significantly to economic growth and sustainable development (Chowdhury et al., 2019). Since the formation of the United Nations' SDG 2030, various research studies (George et al., 2016; Ricciardi et al., 2021) emphasized the role of entrepreneurship in addressing 'grand challenges' such as poverty, gender equality, quality education, etc. In emerging economies (Mishra, 2021), rural entrepreneurship contributes to the development of a sustainable and inclusive future that is essential for lowering inequality in rural areas with weak institutions and alleviating extreme poverty (Sutter et al., 2019). To put it briefly, rural entrepreneurship has the capacity to help rural business owners and organizations improve local economies and communities. To enhance women's and communities' quality of life and help them reach a sustainable level of subsistence, rural entrepreneurship offers various options for self-employment (Aggarwal et al., 2019). Additionally, it strengthens rural economic development and promotes sustainable development while meeting bottom-of-the-pyramid needs. However, rural entrepreneurial growth is constrained by several factors despite advancements in technology. Firstly, there is a dearth of fundamental resources like trained and skilled personnel, improved infrastructure, financial resources, limited availability of agricultural land, and more expansive market prospects. Next is the entrepreneurs' lack of confidence in their ability to take calculated risks and make the right decisions. If these factors could be improved, there might be more opportunities for these rural business owners to grow, thrive, and produce capital in these remote economic markets.

To be successful, entrepreneurs require abilities like innovation, problem-solving, and communication. Often, these abilities are developed through experience, heredity, and business failures – that aid an entrepreneur in developing a successful business. Programmes for entrepreneurship education, training, capacity building programmes, and vocational education that are especially geared towards business skills can also help to build these abilities. Such programmes place a strong emphasis on giving participants hands-on instruction and experiential learning that develops both soft skills, like communication and social intelligence, and hard skills, like accounting and money management. Increased entrepreneurial activity depends on several variables, including the standard of training, the sufficiency of the infrastructure, and the economic climate in the area (World Bank, 2013). However, increased access to quality entrepreneurship education can positively affect the success of rural entrepreneurs and, in turn, the creation and expansion of creative new enterprises in rural areas. Therefore, entrepreneurship education is crucial for rural development since it generates economic activity and can build regional sustainability (Hagebakken et al., 2021).

Governments and other institutions (such as employer associations, NGOs, and universities) have critical roles to play in enhancing rural entrepreneurship and implementing policies and programmes that reduce unemployment while encouraging economic growth. Collaboration between governments, the private sector, and educational institutions is also critical for mapping the supply and demand of skilled workforce while ensuring the system operates in a favourable policy environment, such as the German dual system of apprenticeship in which the government and the private sector work closely together, sharing the expense and responsibility for the creation of the training materials. This programme facilitates a smooth school-to-work transition that helps young students gain valuable work experience that will increase their employability. Such types of apprenticeship programmes are helpful for promoting entrepreneurship in rural areas as well. In India also various initiatives have been taken by the MSDE such as Pradhan Mantri Kaushal Vikas Yojana (PMKY), National Apprenticeship Promotion Scheme (NAPS), Start-up Village Entrepreneurship Programme (SVEP), Jan Shikshan Sansthan (JSS), etc. Niti Aayog Annual Report 2022–2023 emphasized the on-ground implementation of rural development programmes and documented good practices in public service delivery. To measure the progress at the national and sub-national levels achieving the 2030 SDG targets, NITI Aayog has developed the SDG India Index in collaboration with the Ministry of Statistics and Programme Implementation. In the latest SDG India Index Report 2020–2021, 16 goals comprising 70 targets and 115 indicators were taken. According to the report, 22 states/UTs belong to the category of front-runners (score in the range of 65–99, including both), and Kerala is at the top with a score of 75.

5. Need to Promote Rural Entrepreneurship

Rural entrepreneurship is the key factor in the socioeconomic development of developing economies. The fact that according to the Economic Survey 2020–2021, agriculture contributes only 20.19% of the Nation's gross domestic product despite employing 49% of the working-age population and approximately 55% of the total population and highlights the need to promote rural entrepreneurship in India. Demand for food and agricultural products also rises along with population growth, but supply remains constant due to low agricultural productivity. Employment opportunities are also very low in rural areas. Migrants from rural areas who are looking for work to earn a decent living are sometimes obliged to work low-paying jobs in cities to support themselves, and their situation gets worse as a result. Therefore, it is crucial to make investments in enhancing rural human resource capacity. According to various research studies like Shah et al. (2009) by developing the skills of rural entrepreneurs' various rural issues such as poverty, unemployment, and rural–urban migration can be resolved. The growth of local businesses will provide employment and lead to the creation of jobs in rural areas; therefore, the enterprise in the rural sector should be established, nourished, and promoted in India.

Rural entrepreneurship has received a lot of attention because it is thought to be the foundation of the rural economy in developing nations like India, for instance. Rural entrepreneurship not only generates income for the community but also helps to improve opportunities, mobilize resources, and stop the agricultural brain drain, all of which improve the quality of life for rural residents. The ability to innovate and embrace new technologies in rural development increases with education and skill, which also raises the income level of rural residents. However, the disparity between the available and needed talents is substantial, and this demand-supply gap of skilled labour must be bridged to make India the second-largest economy by 2050. There is a critical lack of qualified, skilled people in India right now. According to the National Policy for Skill Development and Entrepreneurship (2015), only 4.69% of the workforce in India has undergone formal skill training, compared to 80% in Japan, and 96% in South Korea, and this is primarily due to the existing skewed education system in India and the irrelevance of existing infrastructure as per industry needs. Due to the mismatch between the supply and demand for certain skills, skill gaps are enhancing. A key issue affecting the competitiveness of the Indian industry is the lack of trained, semiskilled, and unskilled personnel. As a result, rural entrepreneurs have access to a wide range of undiscovered prospects.

In addition, gender diversity is a significant concern for India, in particular, and for all emerging nations, in general, that should be addressed for rural development. As the female population in India makes up about half of the total population, and if their labour force participation rates (LFPRs) rise, they would be able to propel the nation's economy forward. Women must have equal access to productive resources as males, and this could increase total agricultural productivity in developing countries by 20–30% and decrease global hunger by 12–17%. Female entrepreneurship plays a pivotal role in empowering females (Bala & Singhal, 2020), and in rural areas, it can open various women's career options close to their homes. By honing their skills and potential, they can obtain a good wage and respectable employment as visualized in the SDG 2030 goal. In this way, they can play a significant part in contributing to the national economy. To encourage young people and women to enter nontraditional occupations, it is also necessary to replace traditional vocational courses with new technical ones. Therefore, there is a need for a paradigm shift in rural entrepreneurship that is 'from a rural livelihood sector to a modern business enterprise' by respecting diversity and adopting an inclusive approach.

6. Current Labour Market Scenario

The labour market, commonly referred to as the job market, is an essential part of every economy. It provides insightful information on employment and the economy overall and is closely connected to the markets for capital, goods, and services. Understanding the labour market is crucial and helpful since it reflects the perspectives, policies, and employment-related actions of businesses and the government. In labour market, the working population ratio (WPR) measures the percentage of the population that is employed, and the proportion of the population entering the labour market is indicated by LFPR. While, the unemployment rate (UR) measures the percentage of the labour force that is unemployed but available for work. According to the periodic labour force survey (PLFS) 2020–2021, in India, the LFPR for the age group of 15 years and over was 54.9%, with 57.54% in rural regions and 49.1% in urban areas (Table 12.1). In both rural and urban areas, the female LFPR was just one-third that of the male LFPR. Just 52.6% of the population entered the workforce, with 55.5% living in rural areas and 45.8% in urban areas, compared to 54.9% who entered the labour market. Both rural and urban areas have significantly low WPRs for females. It is interesting to note that in rural areas, 42% of youth (15–29 years age group) entered the labour force, compared to 39.9% in urban areas. Women in the age group 15–29 years in rural areas had a higher LFPR (22%), compared to those in urban areas (19%). Only 36.1% of young people enter the workforce, compared to 41.4% who enter the labour market. Youth unemployment (UR) was 12.9%, which is more than the rate for the productive population (15 years and above) which is 9.1%. Women in urban areas continue to have a greater UR (24.9%) than women in rural areas (8.2%) which may be due to the push factors working in rural areas. Probable push factors working in rural areas are because rural-dwelling women have to support their marginalized large and joint families and, therefore, cannot afford to be unemployed. In addition to the unpaid care/service work, they are engaged in the agricultural sector since the majority of jobs in the rural areas are available in the agriculture sector which lacks some elements regarding decent and productive work. Various research studies

Table 12.1.   Labour Market Indicators by Age and Area as per Usual Status (in percentage).

LFPR, WPR, and UR in usual principal status and subsidiary status (ps + ss) for persons of age 15–29 years in India

	Urban			Rural			Urban + Rural		
Indicators	**Male**	**Female**	**Person**	**Male**	**Female**	**Person**	**Male**	**Female**	**Person**
LFPR	59	19	39.9	60.6	22	42	60.1	21.1	41.4
WPR	49.2	14.3	32.6	53.6	20.2	37.5	52.3	18.5	36.1
UR (youth person)	16.6	24.9	18.5	11.6	8.2	10.7	13	12.5	12.9

LFPR, WPR, and UR in usual status (ps + ss) for persons of age 15 years and above in India

LFPR	74.6	23.2	49.1	78.1	36.5	57.4	77	32.5	54.9
WPR	70	21.2	45.8	75.1	35.8	55.5	73.5	31.4	52.6
UR[a]	8.6	16.3	10.2	7.8	10	8.3	8.1	12.6	9.1

Source: Annual report, PLFS (PLFS) 2020–2021.
[a]Educated (highest level of education secondary and above).

(Basu & Goswami, 1999; Dobrev & Barnett, 2005; Morrison, 2001) also indicated that due to push factors such as the inability to find a job in the mainstream sector, underemployment, facing discrimination in the labour market, underpayment, and the possibility of redundancy, individuals are pushed into entrepreneurship. Hence, in rural areas, entrepreneurship is a way to get dignified and decent work if it is adopted as a means of livelihood.

In the case of urban areas, female UR is high as various pull factors are working such as new opportunities, desire for independence, autonomy, education, personal wealth self-fulfilment, and family security (Gilad & Levine, 1986); therefore, they prefer to wait for right opportunity instead of indulging themselves into unproductive work, and they are moving towards opening their enterprises and startup as also envisioned in Sustainable Development Goal 5 of gender equality.

To increase workforce participation and reduce the UR, vocational/technical training plays an important role. Broadly, vocational/technical education provides knowledge and skills needed for the workplace. Making people employable for a wide range of employment in different industries and other economic sectors is the primary goal of vocational/technical education and training. As per NSS 68th round (July 2011–June 2012), formal vocational training refers to training that took place in structured educational/training institutions that led to government recognized certificates, diplomas, or degrees. Non-formal vocational training involves hereditary, self-learning, learning on the job, and other sources. The self-employment capacity or expertise in a vocation acquired by the succeeding generations or other members of the household is considered a 'hereditary' source while when a person learns through his/her effort without undergoing any training, it is termed as 'Self Learning'. Non-formal vocational training acquired through 'Learning on the job' refers to the expertise acquired by an individual working in past or current employment through informal training provided by the employer/organization. Whereas the cases where individuals developed vocational expertise from the household members or ancestors, provided the said vocation or trade different from the one relating to their ancestors is termed as other sources of non-formal vocational training. All these sources substantially raise the number of youth and adults with relevant technical and vocational skills for employment, decent jobs, and entrepreneurship as visualized in SDG 4.4.

According to the annual report of PLFS 2020–2021, formal vocational/technical received by the persons of age group 15–59 years in urban areas is only 6.2% for males and 5.3% for females, while in rural areas, only 2.5% of males and 1.9% of females can get such training (Table 12.2). Interestingly, in the category of other than formal training involving hereditary, self-learning, and learning on the job, in urban areas, males majorly benefitted through *'learning on the job'* (11.1%) and females through 'self-learning' (2.7%). While in rural areas, males and females both are mostly benefitted through *'heredity learning'*. Overall 83.1% of persons in the age group of 15–59 years did not receive any vocational training and only 16.9% can get this training.

Table 12.2. Distribution of Persons in the Age Group 15–59 years by the Status of Vocational/Technical Training Received (in percentage).

Category of Persons	Formal	Received Vocational Training (Other than Formal)					Total	Did Not Receive Vocational Training	Total
		Hereditary	Self-Learning	Learning on the Job	Others	Total (Other than Normal)			
Rural									
Male	2.5	7.2	4.7	6.6	0.6	19	21.5	78.5	100
Female	1.9	3.7	2.7	1.6	0.6	8.7	10.6	89.4	100
Person	2.2	5.5	3.7	4.1	0.6	13.9	16.1	83.9	100
Urban									
Male	6.2	1.9	5.2	11.1	1.1	19.2	25.5	74.5	100
Female	5.3	0.6	2.7	2.5	0.8	6.6	12	88	100
Person	5.8	1.3	4	6.8	0.9	13	18.8	81.2	100
Rural + urban									
Male	3.6	5.6	4.8	7.9	0.7	19.1	22.7	77.3	100
Female	2.9	2.8	2.7	1.9	0.7	8.1	11	89	100
Person	3.3	4.2	3.8	4.9	0.7	13.6	16.9	83.1	100

Source: Annual report, PLFS 2020–2021.

7. Government Initiatives for Enhancing the Entrepreneurial Abilities of Rural Population

Recognizing the importance of rural entrepreneurship, the Indian Government has taken several initiatives aimed at fostering entrepreneurship and increasing the capacity of rural youth, women, and farmers through different training programs focussed on self-employment and skill development. Some of the recent initiatives are discussed below.

Since 2015, the PMKV has been implemented by the MSDE to provide industry-ready workers and improve the employability of our youth. Several new elements are being incorporated into PMKY 4.0 to make the programme more pertinent to the changing economic landscape, including on job training, the addition of cutting-edge courses for Industry 4.0, and an extension of the skilling delivery network. As part of this effort, the MSDE has chosen to place skill hubs at specific institutions of national reputation schools, colleges, universities, technical institutions, etc., after consulting with the Department of Higher Education, Department of School Education, UGC, and AICTE.

To help rural poor youth and to make them self-employed by starting their self-employment units, the Ministry of Rural Development, GOI is operating Rural Self Employment Training Institutes (RSETIs) in collaboration with banks. In addition to giving the institutions infrastructural funding, this ministry reimburses the cost of the training delivered by the RSETIs to the rural poor youth through the State Rural Livelihoods Missions. Up till 30 June 2022, a total of 29.34 lakh youth have been settled and 41.93 lakh youth have received training since the programme's beginning. As a sub-scheme of the Deendayal Antyodaya Yojana-National Rural Livelihoods Mission, the ministry is also implementing the SVEP into action. Its goal is to assist the rural poor (from the SHG eco-system) in starting businesses at the village level in non-agricultural sectors. The project's functional unit is called Block. As per the information of Ministry of Rural Development (2022), under SVEP, one Block may not exceed a budget of Rs. 650.00 lakhs. 2,08,594 businesses in 29 states/UTs have received help thus far. This programme has covered nearly 9 crore women through 83 lakh SHGs. The centre recently set a goal of creating 2 billion Lakhpati Didis (women with yearly incomes of Rs. 1 lakh or more) by empowering SHG members with marketable skills like LED bulb manufacturing, drone operation, repair, and plumbing, among other things.

In addition, JSS scheme seeks to give vocational training to illiterates and school dropouts in rural areas. JSS's goal is to provide these rural people with vital skill training to improve their economic situation and open up new job prospects for the locals. The Indian Institute of Public Administration carried out a third-party impact evaluation of the JSS programme, and it was finished by July 2020. According to the study, women make up 79% of the population; rural areas make up 50%; employment for improved livelihoods has increased by 73.4%; beneficiary average income has increased by 89.1%; and 85.7% of resources have been mobilized. Till March 2023, the total number of beneficiaries trained under this scheme was 3,61,820.

Similarly, the NAPS encourages apprenticeship throughout the nation by offering financial incentives, technology, and advocacy assistance. NAPS has been successful in igniting interest in apprenticeship training among both business and young people, together with strong governmental support and policy advocacy. The apprentice has discovered that it is helpful to enhance the likelihood that young people in the nation will find a job. All 'Designated Trades' under the act for all establishments coming under the authority of the Central Government are implemented in respective areas by the Regional Directorates of Skill Development and Entrepreneurship (RDESE) under the Directorate General of Training (DGT).

To provide training in a variety of trades, the DGT, MSDE, and Union Government established Industrial Training Institutes (ITI) and Industrial Training Centres. According to the Tracer Study of ITI Graduates' final report, which the MSDE, GoI issued in January 2018, 63.5% of all ITI pass-outs found employment (wage + self, of which 6.7% are self-employed), while 36.4% remained unemployed and were looking for work. The comparable percentages for SCs (65%) and STs (69.8%) were greater than the proportion of all pass-outs in the (wage + self) employed even though the first figure for females was lower than that for males (65.1%). As per PMO (Prime Minister's Office), on 19 October 2023, 511 rural skill development centres located in rural areas of Maharashtra's 34 districts were launched with the agenda of training around 100 youths in at least two vocational courses. Youths will receive training for construction, modern farming, media, entertainment, and electronics jobs.

The National Institute of Entrepreneurship and Small Business Development (NIESBUD), which operates under the aegis of MSDE, has been promoting the advancement and development of women throughout the nation. For women who want to become independent or launch creative businesses, the institute offers entrepreneurial orientation, awareness, skill development programmes, and women's entrepreneurship development programmes (WEDP). With suitable incentives for women-owned firms under the public procurement process, the emphasis is on supporting female entrepreneurs. To instil entrepreneurial ideas, attitudes, and drive among rural women, NIESBUD has established entrepreneurship development programmes for them. The Ministry of Rural Development has empanelled NIESBUD as a National Resource Organization for the SVEP for non-farm livelihoods to assist states and UTs with programme implementation and capacity building. In addition, to promote women-led enterprises in India, in collaboration with Deutsche Gesellschaft fuer Internationale Zusammenarbeit GmbH, MSDE is implementing 'Economic Empowerment of Women Entrepreneurs and Start-ups by Women', and nearly 725 female entrepreneurs in all have received support through the project's incubation and acceleration support programmes.

The National Skill Development Corporation made a significant contribution to workforce mobility by employing strategic partnerships, focussed training initiatives, and digital and on-ground initiatives. A comprehensive digital platform called Skill India Digital aims to transform India's education, skill, entrepreneurial, and employment landscape. It is the convergence of initiatives like 'Digital India' and 'Skill India', which provide a multidimensional strategy to empower the nation's workforce and young. The portal offers career prospects, industry-relevant skill development courses, and support for entrepreneurship. It makes entrepreneurial endeavours more accessible and strengthens the bonds between businesses and job seekers. Its user interface is simple to use, versatile across different platforms, and mobile-first, acknowledging the reliance on smartphones. This guarantees continuous learning experiences via portable devices, revolutionizing conventional learning approaches.

8. Encouraging Rural Development Through Entrepreneurship in the Context of India

It is a well-known fact that rural entrepreneurship plays a significant role in rural development; however, in India, this needs to be strengthened. Rural areas are the backbone of an economy and support economic progress in developing nations like India. Even so, there are several drawbacks for rural areas compared to urban ones, particularly in terms of economic development. Less trained and unskilled labour is available due to issues like rural–urban migration and infrastructure development in semi-urban to fully developed urban areas. Many rural regions lack the resources necessary to assist beginning and emerging business owners. Despite this, rural business owners and the notable work they do in rural areas demonstrate considerable significance. Rural entrepreneurs not only contribute by starting their new firms but also optimally utilize the resources that are already accessible to them, providing employment opportunities for the local labour force. In light of this, the framework for strengthening sustainable rural development has been proposed in Fig. 12.1.

1. Creating a conducive environment for rural entrepreneurship
   a. Entrepreneurial skills development should be integrated with rural development policies of a nation like entrepreneurial, agricultural, education, employment, and research policies by strengthening convergence with other

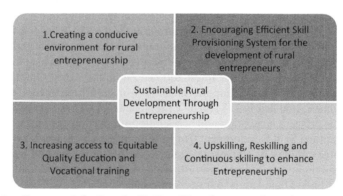

Fig. 12.1.   Framework for Sustainable Rural Development Through Entrepreneurship in the Context of India. *Source*: Authors creation.

ministries such as the MSDE, Ministry of Education, Ministry of Rural Development, Ministry of Labour and employment, etc., and national organizations, institutes, community groups, and NGOs.

b. For skill development in rural areas, innovative formal, non-formal, and informal vocational/technical training programmes should be integrated with national training programmes.

c. Analyse the data disaggregated based on diverse dimensions such as by gender, age, ethnicity, disability, economic prospects, and labour market needs in the context of rural development for appropriate designing and implementation of capacity-building programmes of entrepreneurial skills requirement.

2. Encouraging efficient skill provisioning system for the development of rural entrepreneurs

a. To build the capacities of entrepreneurs in rural areas, it is necessary to develop an integrated skill provisioning system that can provide varied skills, use innovative pedagogies, and optimally utilize pre-existing social organizations.

b. At the same time, there is a need to connect formal and informal training or fuse institution-based education with work-based learning, by creating creative community-based training programmes. For those young men and women who are not able to attain training through formal structure, apprenticeship systems are the feasible solution for that. However, it should be upgraded in terms of its equity in accessibility, technology, and entrepreneurship skills in the Indian rural context.

c. Entrepreneurship training must provide recent information on micro-credit schemes, financial schemes, rural development policies, and new technological know-how. In the current digital era, knowledge of e-commerce is also beneficial for rural entrepreneurs. Apart from this, training programmes also focus on other dimensions of skills such as technical skills, business skills, personal entrepreneurial skills, behavioural skills, communication skills, listening skills, and soft skills for the holistic development of an entrepreneur.

d. There are threats to rural livelihoods from environmental degradation and climate change that need to be controlled and reduced. This demands learning of new environmentally friendly technologies and skills which help in attaining SDGs.

3. Increasing access to equitable quality education and vocational training

a. The key to prepare today's youth for high-skill jobs is to provide them with quality inclusive education with future-oriented pedagogy and curricula that monitor progress at all levels and take corrective action to improve fundamental literacy, numeracy, and digital literacy proficiency for improved access and learning. Such education is also a major contributor to Sustainable health and well-being, gender equality, and climate mitigation (UN Report, 2023).

    b. Accessibility of equitable quality education should be extended to rural areas and vocational education should be integrated with general education. As education is the base of all skills, it should be free of cost till higher education.

    c. An inclusive approach should be adopted in accessing quality education and vocational/technical training by including all socially and economically disadvantaged groups (NEP, 2020, pp. 24–25).

    d. National Curriculum Framework 2022 for schools based on the National Education Policy (NEP) 2020 recommends scientific need and skill-based education for all and 'skill' being offered as a regular course. As emphasized by NEP 2020, pre-vocational education (classes 6–8) and vocational education (classes 9–12) must include business knowledge and skills that inculcate entrepreneurial acumen among students through the formal education system.

    e. Gender-responsive learning systems should be encouraged in vocational learning and there is a need to increase the participation of girls and boys in non-gender stereotypical trades such as girls in the technology trade and boys in the beauty and wellness trade.

    f. The societal mindset should be changed regarding vocational education and must give equal preference to general education and vocational education.

    g. ITI plays an important role in encouraging an entrepreneurship mindset with limited resources. Hence, accessibility of government ITIs in rural areas needs to be strengthened, this will also help in promoting startup in rural areas.

4. Upskilling, reskilling, and continuous skilling to enhance entrepreneurship

    a. Entrepreneurial skills can be boosted with the help of organizing capacity building programmes for rural entrepreneurs. Various institutes such as the NIESBUD, V.V. Giri National Labour Institute (VVGNLI), Mahatma Gandhi National Council of Rural Education, National Institute of Rural Development and Panchayati Raj, or local organizations such as Panchayati Raj institutions are organizing such programmes to build the capacities of entrepreneurs. In order to disseminate these skills at the grassroot level, such national level institutions must prepare master trainers. These institutions must focus on social and eco-entrepreneurship as well for sustainable rural development.

    b. Producer associations and rural cooperatives must be upskilled according to the demand of the market as these associations assist their members in unrestricted access to market information, markets, and institutions that provide inputs and know-how while also offering effective ways to improve their technical and entrepreneurial skills.

    c. Assist small-scale manufacturers in gaining access to markets, cutting-edge technology, and value chains that may be used to transfer expertise and improve networking. By combining formal and informal methods, rural extension services can reach a wider audience. These services can significantly improve the technical expertise of small-scale farmers and help them engage in environmentally friendly farming practices.

Enhancement of entrepreneurial skills is vital to improve employability and livelihood opportunities, lessen poverty, improve productivity, and promote environmentally sustainable development of rural areas. Sarpanch, Gram Sabha members, and self-help groups should be involved in the process of creating an entrepreneurial ecosystem in rural areas. Hence, above framework indicates that for sustainable rural development, coordinated efforts are required to develop an integrated approach that improves access to relevant quality education and training for all rural women and men.

9. Discussion and Policy Implications

Rural entrepreneurship is one of the best tools for rural development and rural entrepreneurs are the key agent of this process. It is crucial to train rural youth through education programmes and skill-building efforts to improve their employability, financial independence, and entrepreneurial skills for sustainable rural development and attaining SDGs. Due to the situation of saturation in agricultural work, there is a growing trend in rural-to-urban migration for employment and that creates excessive strain on the civic infrastructure in urban and semi-urban areas. This results in unsustainable living conditions and impedes the achievement of SDG 11 (sustainable cities and communities). Therefore, to reverse the migration trend, rural entrepreneurship is significant. Next, a significant fraction of young people from rural areas who aspire to work in white-collar positions but lack access to professional education contribute to the nation's unemployment problems, which call for quick solutions. Such unpaid work frequently results in societal problems including engaging in antisocial behaviour to make ends meet, which affects SDG 16 (peace, justice, and strong institutions), and entrepreneurship is the best solution to engage such talent in rural areas. Furthermore, SDG 8 (decent work and economic growth) and SDG 9 (industry, innovation, and infrastructure) may be advanced as a result of the gradual transition in rural India from agrarian skills to entrepreneurial training for more complex goods and services. The necessary skills, the inputs of physical and human capital, and the institutional frameworks required for the production processes all influence these kinds of transformations.

India's rural economy is undergoing a socioeconomic transition, with women at its core. Skill-building initiatives must ensure that rural women have equal access to entrepreneurial resources, technology, and education, which support self-reliance and empower them. Thus, promoting women's entrepreneurial endeavours aids in achieving SDG 5 (gender equality) as well as reducing unemployment and improving financial independence. This substantially promotes SDG 4.4 which talks about the increase in the number of young people and adults with the necessary skills – technical and vocational for employment, decent occupations, and entrepreneurship. Rural entrepreneurship goes hand in hand with depreciation in poverty (SDG 1), and hunger (SDG 2) and promoting good health, and well-being for all at all ages (SDG 3) as it improves income opportunities and better chances of livelihood.

In India, SDG localization at the rural level would also help to strengthen sustainable rural development as the Ministry of Panchayati Raj advised rural local governments on integrating SDGs in local level plans (Gram Panchayat Development Plans or village development plans). Localization refers to both how subnational and local governments can work together to support the SDGs' implementation from the bottom up and SDGs can serve as a framework for regional development strategies (NITI Aayog, 2019). Rural entrepreneurship and skilling should be integrated with participatory planning, execution, and assessment in rural areas. This would be helpful in creating a conducive environment for rural entrepreneurs.

10. Conclusion

A powerful subset of rural entrepreneurship is social entrepreneurship, which aims to build a safe, sustainable, and inclusive future. This covers several types of entrepreneurship, including those carried out by women, women's empowerment, youth, and indigenous groups. In this way, social entrepreneurship can support sustainable livelihood solutions through group-based organizations and offer options for reducing poverty that are founded on the initiative and resilience of farmers. These types of entrepreneurship require the support of governments, especially in the early stages.

Eco-entrepreneurship which may involve tourism has the potential to serve as a means of fostering economic growth and providing fair and just benefits to local communities, so they can meet their basic needs. Agritourism, rural tourism, and sustainable tourism are three approaches to achieving sustainable rural livelihoods. These approaches call for modern tourism affairs, tourism strategies, and eco-innovations which may be supported by educational and entrepreneurial initiatives of government and other local eco-entrepreneurs. Development of diverse skills and upskilling and reskilling of local entrepreneurs are also helpful in this regard.

The government and other local organizations ought to provide quality education, vocational training, and ongoing support networks that offer all the help required to encourage young people in rural areas to pursue careers in entrepreneurship. Increasing community access and bridging gaps in specific areas, such as offering industry experts' mentoring, setting up incubation centres, and holding ideation workshops, hackathons, and other events in rural areas to encourage innovation and entrepreneurial mindsets, are other fundamental ways to promote rural entrepreneurship. To support rural entrepreneurs, standardization and grading should be encouraged. Promotional activities should also be strengthened. Despite numerous strategic initiatives from the government to encourage entrepreneurship in the rural sector and provide reasonable living standards, India is still regarded as a developing industrial nation. These government programmes are not widely known by the rural people. Therefore, it is important to educate rural residents about government initiatives and programmes that support rural entrepreneurship. State and central governments can take the initiative to spread more awareness and can organize special training programmes throughout the calendar.

The need for highly skilled labourers is growing as technology advances. People in rural areas lack digital and technological skills. Gender digital gap is also widening due to the disparity in the usage of information technologies (Bala & Singhal, 2018). To close this gap, it is important to focus on strengthening digital infrastructure in rural areas. Without access to quality digital infrastructure, rural entrepreneurs are restricted in their capability to innovate and apply new expertise to renovate their processes. Skill India Digital initiative is helpful in this regard as it empowers Indian youth to explore different learning paths digitally. Rural youth can also take advantage of this digital platform, but they must be sensitized about this initiative through local organizations.

In addition to the GOI, civil society organizations and NGOs play a significant role in institutionalizing assistance systems through their engagement and active participation. These days, an education in entrepreneurship aids entrepreneurs not only to fulfil their personal needs but also to help in the economic contribution of the nation. In addition to generating new jobs and boosting the national revenue, rural entrepreneurship contributes to long-term sustainable economic growth. Therefore, the synergies between education, skilling, entrepreneurship, and employability for the rural youth play a vital role in driving India to attain the SDG 2030 goals of the United Nations. For this conducive environment for rural entrepreneurship, an efficient skill provisioning system, equitable access to vocational and quality education, and reskilling, upskilling continuous skilling are essential. Hence, an inclusive and equitable approach is required for strengthening rural development in India where diversity should be respected.

> Today India is preparing skilled professionals for the world, not just for itself. (Prime Minister, Shri Narendra Modi, *Economic Times*, 21 October 2023)

References

Aggarwal, S., Pahuja, A., & Sharma, R. (2019). Samriddhii: A case of integrated social entrepreneurship in Bihar. *International Journal of Indian Culture and Business Management*, *19*, 22–36.

Bala, S., & Singhal, P. (2018). Gender digital divide in India: A case of inter-regional analysis of Uttar Pradesh. *Journal of Information, Communication and Ethics in Society*, *16*(2), 173–192.

Bala, S., & Singhal, P. (2020). *Female entrepreneurship: Comparison of OECD and BRICS nations*. Inclusive Development in India. ISBN-978-81-921023-9-9

Basu, A., & Goswami, A. (1999). South Asian entrepreneurship in Great Britain: Factors influencing growth. *International Journal of Entrepreneurial Behaviour & Research*, *5*(2), 123–134.

Census of India. (2011). *Population finder*. Government of India. https://censusindia.gov.in/

Chowdhury, F., Audretsch, D. B., & Belitski, M. (2019). Institutions and entrepreneurship quality. *Entrepreneurship: Theory and Practice*, *43*(1), 51–81.

Dobrev, S., & Barnett, W. (2005). *Organisational roles and transition to entrepreneurship*. *Academy of Management Journal*, *48*(3), 433–449.

Economic Times. (2023, October 21). Skilling is empowering, promotes justice: Modi. *The Economic Times*, New Delhi, 20 October 2023.

George, G., Howard-Grenville, J., Joshi, A., & Tihanyi, L. (2016). Understanding and tackling societal grand challenges through management research. *Academy of Management Journal*, *59*(6), 1880–1895.

Gilad, B., & Levine, P. (1986). A behavioral model of entrepreneurial supply. *Journal of Small Business Management*, *24*(4), 45–54.

Hagebakken, G., Reimers, C., & Solstad, E. (2021). Entrepreneurship education as a strategy to build regional sustainability. *Sustainability*, *13*(5), 2529.

Ministry of Rural Development. *Government of India. Entrepreneurial Culture in Rural Areas*, PIB Delhi, August. https://rural.gov.in/

Ministry of Skill Development and Entrepreneurship. *Government of India*. Tracer study of ITI graduates' final report, New Delhi, January. https://www.msde.gov.in/

Ministry of Statistics and Programme Implementation (2020–2021), National Statistical Office, Government of India. *Annual Report, Periodic Labour Force Survey (PLFS) July 2020–June 2021*. https://dge.gov.in/dge/sites/default/files/2022-11/Annual_Report_PLFS_2020-21_0_0.pdf

Mishra, O. (2021). Principles of frugal innovation and its application by social entrepreneurs in times of adversity: An inductive single-case approach. *Journal of Entrepreneurship in Emerging Economies*, *13*, 547–574.

Morrison, A. (2001). Entrepreneurs transcend time: A biographical analysis, *Management Decision*, *39*(9), 784–790.

NEP. (2020). Ministry of Human Resource Development, Government of India, National Education Policy 2020, New Delhi, Retrieved from https://www.education.gov.in/sites/upload_files/mhrd/files/NEP_Final_English.pdf

NITI Aayog. (2019). *Localising SDG's early lessons from 2019*. NITI Aayog, Government of India, New Delhi, India. Retrieved from https://www.niti.gov.in/sites/default/files/2020-07/LSDGs_July_8_Web.pdf

Petrin, T. (1992, October 13–16). *Partnership and institution building as factors in rural development* [Paper presentation]. The sixth session of the FAO/ECA working party on women and the agricultural family in rural development, Innsbruck, Austria (Vol. 6, No. 2, pp. 1–6).

Punyamurthy, C., & Bheenaveni, R. S. (2023). Urbanization in India: An overview of trends, causes, and challenges. *International Journal of Asian Economic Light*, *11*, 9–20.

Ricciardi, F., Rossignoli, C., & Zardini, A. (2021). Grand challenges and entrepreneurship: Emerging issues, research streams, and theoretical landscape. *International Entrepreneurship and Management Journal*, *17*, 1673–1705.

Sah, P., Sujan, D. K., & Kashyap, S. K. (2009). *Role of agripreneurship in the development of rural area*. Paper presentation in ICARD at Banaras Hindu University, Varanasi.

Saxena, S. (2012). Problems faced by rural entrepreneurs and remedies to solve it. *IOSR Journal of Business and Management*, *3*(1), 23–29.

Sutter, C., Bruton, G., & Chen, J. (2019). Entrepreneurship as a solution to extreme poverty: A review and future research directions. *Journal of Business Venturing*, *34*, 197–214.

United Nations. (2023). *The sustainable development goals report 2023: Special edition – July 2023*. New York: UN DESA. © UN DESA. Retrieved from https://unstats.un.org/sdgs/report/2023/

World Bank. (2013). *Doing business 2013: Smarter regulations for small and medium size enterprises*. World Bank.

Challenges

Chapter 13

Flexibility, Vulnerability, and Inclusiveness in the Gig Economy: A Review of India's Experience in the Context of Informalisation

K. Jafar, U. G. Unnimaya and Umanath Malaiarasan

Madras Institute of Development Studies, Chennai, Tamil Nadu, India

Abstract

The emergence of the gig economy, with the growth of technology and increased use of digital solutions, has been transforming the nature of work and its organisation in different ways. The differences in technical infrastructure, access to the internet, availability of cloud computing, and ownership of digital devices influence how countries manage this transition. Besides promoting economic growth and employment opportunities, the expansion of gig work offers wider possibilities for addressing some of the structural problems that the Indian economy has faced in recent years. In this chapter, we review the nature of the gig economy in the context of informalisation, flexibility, and vulnerability associated with gig work. In many contexts, gig workers are neither formal nor informal; they are independent contractors, enjoying no benefits as formal or informal workers do. We explore the links between gig workers and those workers engaged in the informal economy; both operate with a certain degree of flexibility but are vulnerable to many risks associated with occupation, health, and social problems. The discussion also highlights the importance of making gig work more inclusive by extending its flexible employment options to more women, persons with disabilities, and those from marginalised backgrounds and utilising the gig economy in formalising the economy in general.

Keywords: Gig economy; gig work; flexibility; vulnerability; informal economy

Informal Economy and Sustainable Development Goals:
Ideas, Interventions and Challenges, 259–272
Copyright © 2024 by K. Jafar, U. G. Unnimaya and Umanath Malaiarasan
Published under exclusive licence by Emerald Publishing Limited
doi:10.1108/978-1-83753-980-220241014

1. Introduction

The digitisation process pushes technology and technical solutions into almost all areas of everyday life and the economy. It plays a critical role in reshaping the economy and society in multiple ways. Other forces like globalisation and technological advances in communication, transport, production, and marketing also complement this process. Artificial intelligence and robotics technology advancements are blurring the lines between the physical, digital, and biological spheres associated with the new waves of industrialisation. The digital revolution and the development of a platform-mediated gig economy can be identified as important features of the fourth industrial revolution, or Industry 4.0. Within a short time, gig economy has marked its active presence in traditional and modern sectors worldwide. It promises new prospects for increased productivity and growth in key sectors of the economy and opens new opportunities in the labour market. In countries like India, gig work promises great potential for addressing some structural issues like unemployment and dependence on informal work arrangements. Its realisation depends on India's ability to improve its technical infrastructure, access to the internet, availability of cloud computing, reducing the digital divide, and unequal access to digital devices across regions and groups. It is important to know how different regions, sectors, and actors responded to the new model and see its impact on them. This chapter reviews the larger context, tries to map the global and national experience with the development of gig economy, and attempts to link this transition with informalisation.

2. Methodology

The chapter reviews platform-based gig work globally and looks at its evolution in India, utilising the body of available literature. While doing this, it also tries to link the broad structure of the Indian economy, inter alia, the active presence of the informal economy, in a way that could affect how the country responds to the emergence of the gig economy. The secondary evidence is partially supplemented with some preliminary observations made in the urban context of India.

3. Emergence of Gig Economy: A Review

The gig or platform economy has changed work worldwide. It represents rapidly growing labour platforms that connect 'workers' and 'requesters' for on-demand work. This need not follow traditional frameworks and understanding of new work, its nature, and organisation. Digital labour platforms, such as crowd-work or location-based apps, connect workers to work. They allow platform operators to become intermediaries and workers to become independent contractors. Companies allow requesters to order a defined task or project from an available service worker, usually charging a fee or commission. However, workers accept 'gigs'/'tasks' without guaranteeing future employment. These patterns are growing rapidly in India, especially in urban and semi-urban areas, like many other developing economies. This economy has two operating models. Firstly, the digital gig economy involves online labour like freelance, crowdsourced, or microwork. Secondly, the physical gig economy involves work-on-demand via apps.

An online platform matches labour supply and demand for piece-rate gig work, and each engagement is a separate contract (De Ruyter et al., 2018). The economy already had piece-rate payment methods and gig or freelance employment contracts, but platform gig work was a new entry due to its extensive use of digital intermediation. For commissioning, delivery, payment, and supervision, digital intermediation is used (Standford, 2017). Modern gig work includes microwork, crowd work, online freelancing, outsourcing, and on-demand location-based service delivery (Heeks, 2017). In spite of the fact that a digital intermediary is a binding element, each work arrangement is unique. Service-based gigs use low- to semi-skilled labour, while knowledge-based gigs like freelancing use high-skilled labour (Korde et al., 2021).

The gig economy promises new jobs and growth in many ways. Countries with high unemployment and disguised unemployment hope platform gig work will help (Wood et al., 2019). Gig work in these countries takes advantage of cheap labour and deregulated labour laws. Thus, gig work is hailed as 'the revolution' that lifts masses out of poverty and the 'ramps' to formalisation in the global south, benefiting both job providers and job seekers (Kuek et al., 2015; Randolph et al., 2019). Because low-income countries have historically lacked standard employment practices, policymakers are optimistic about platform gig work. Gig platforms democratise job access and improve livelihood generation, according to India's top public policy think tank, NITI Ayog (2022).

Several factors could affect how a country handles platform economy growth and opportunities. Strengthening digital infrastructure through large-scale investment and promotion of the digital economy plays a critical role in supporting platform gig work. High-speed internet, cloud computing, computer services, smartphones, etc., are essential for platform-based gig work. However, the global South faces a significant digital divide (Rani & Gobel, 2022). Developing countries need to invest heavily in digital infrastructure to capitalise on Industry 4.0's economic potential. The Indian Union Government launched digital India in 2015 to address this issue (GOI, 2023). India had 560 million internet subscribers, 354 million smartphones, and 0.1% of per capita monthly income for GB data in 2019 (GOI, 2019). By 2025, India's digital economy will generate $9.8 billion (Khurana, 2021). Platform-based gig work employs 77 lakh people, or 2.6% of the non-farm workforce and 1.5% of the total workforce. Currently, 47% of gig work is medium-skilled, 22% high-skilled, and 31% low-skilled (NITI Ayog, 2022).

3.1. Transformation of Work and Worker in Gig Economy?

Platform gig work has changed industries and created new ones. The service sector continues to use digital solutions and promote gig economy apps for various reasons. Initially, it focused on transportation, communication, hospitality, etc., but later expanded to personal and home care. Uber, Ola, Rapido, etc., transformed the taxi service. Amazon Mechanical Turk and food and parcel delivery services (Swiggy, Zomato, Deliveroo, Flipkart, Amazon, etc.) created a large low/semi-skilled job market in India. The organisation's flexibility and gradual expansion created new business models and opportunities. The owner of an extra room in the house made money (Airbnb); freelancers found a global market (Upwork) and brought wellness services to our doorsteps (Urban Company). Platform gigs offered consumers convenience and more options. Platform gig work and the services provided by gig workers have greatly influenced urban middle class lifestyles. The following section reviews India's experience with gig work against the key features of the economy.

3.1.1. Flexibility Versus Vulnerability in the Gig Economy

The digital platform and gig economy's flexible work arrangements can improve consumer well-being, productivity, growth, job creation, regional and national entrepreneurship, and business innovation. Gig work's flexible hours and autonomy can attract marginalised workers like women and people with disabilities. Noronha (2016) finds that Indian freelancers value a neutral algorithm's merit assessment. Platform gig work can create crowd capitalism where everyone is a capital owner and self-employed, changing employment forever (Sundararajan, 2018). With the COVID-19 pandemic and new mobility restrictions, remote work and digital solutions took off. Flexible and organised work allowed millions to continue working, and gig work expanded during the crisis.

While it opens new opportunities and flexible work arrangements, gig workers are found vulnerable and working in precarious conditions. The workers involved in gig markets are more vulnerable to various occupational, social, and health issues. In fact, gig work is referred to as non-standard, flexible, atypical, contingent, temporary, informal, and precarious, in particular, as a commonly identified feature in the social inequalities and occupational health literature, in general. As the quality of gig work can vary depending on the specific platform, industry, and individual circumstances, it is important to understand the kinds of vulnerabilities of gig work in different environments, like home, workplace, etc.

Under the excitement and predictions of the digital revolution transforming work lie rising precarious labour conditions in post-Fordist times. Measuring platform gig work precarity helps determine the social cost of expanding gig work (Lewchuk, 2017). Platform gigs range from highly skilled freelance to low/semi-skilled, while on-demand delivery work is characterised by time pressure, standardisation, algorithmic surveillance, and precarious working conditions (Altenried, 2019; De Ruyter et al., 2018; Wood et al., 2019). Work is precarious because there is no contract or social security, there is a constant risk of not getting work, and workers are not recognised. The terms freelancers, independent contractors, delivery executives, delivery partners, etc., distance workers from the labour process. Commercialising their smartphones, two- or four-wheelers, laptops, etc., and calling them 'capital owners'. Platform gig work is the latest example of workplace fractures and blurred organisational boundaries (Rani & Furrer, 2021). The isolated workplace makes unionisation and collective bargaining difficult; disempowerment to demand better wages is seen, especially in developing countries where competition forces lower wages (Heeks, 2017).

3.1.2. Nature of Vulnerability in the Gig Economy

The digital economy has led to unstable employment and a lack of social and labour rights for relevant practitioners (Chen et al., 2020). Gig workers cannot sue their employers for problems or demand higher prices. There is no employer-employee relationship or labour law compliance in gig businesses. No health or workers' compensation benefits like insurance are offered by most. Gig workers must accept virtually all terms to access tasks unlike independent contractors. Although they may not want to leave, most employees can be fired for any reason (Tran & Sokas, 2017). Deactivating gig workers from the platform is enough to let them go since gig workers and employers do not have contracts (Bartkiw, 2014).

3.1.3. Occupational Safety

The higher fatal and non-fatal injury rates in gig work may be due to training and job insecurity compared to construction or agriculture (Foley et al., 2014). The business platform may also make gig workers vulnerable to the inability to negotiate and fix prices and workflow, work-related stress, and psychological problems due to company monitoring and surveillance. Transportation and service industries have more occupational risk (Jakobsen et al., 2023). Such risks are especially serious in the gig economy, with effects like fatigue, distraction, speeding, high mileage, and poor weather exposure (Christie & Ward, 2019). The more gig workers enter the market, the longer they must work and drive to earn a stable income, especially since they must pay for vehicle operating costs. Job hunting increases risk (Christie & Ward, 2018).

Also, entering unfamiliar locations to provide maintenance and cleaning services may be difficult. Food delivery riders with occupational injuries are less likely to continue working according to Zheng et al. (2023). Gig work may pose greater health and safety risks due to the lack of public workplace protection (Rockefeller Foundation, 2013). Tran and Sokas (2017) noted that road traffic safety, public interaction, household cleaning agents, and intensive keyboard activity at poorly arranged workstations are known hazards with preventive measures, but the regulatory framework does not apply without an employment relationship. Workers are vulnerable to the social and economic demands of providing their tools and equipment (Bajwa et al., 2018), including limited career-development opportunities like training, low wages, no job and income security, and wage discrimination.

3.1.4. Health Issues

Discussing the gig economy's health effects on workers is another important topic for understanding the transitional labour market. The health risks and psychological disorders (Glavin & Schieman, 2022; Griesbach et al. 2019; Ravenelle 2019) of gig workers include insomnia, fatigue, and distress. Working long hours, high physical and mental demands, high mileages, long commutes, and circadian lows can fatigue gig workers (Christie & Ward, 2019; Davis, 2015; Prabhat et al., 2019). Choudhary and Shireshi (2022) noted that gig drivers' long hours and fierce peer competition lowered their quality of life. While gig workers are encouraged to work to satisfy customers' appetites or deliver food and other goods quickly, a perfect storm of risk factors affecting gig workers' health and safety and road users' is inevitable.

3.1.5. Social Vulnerabilities

Gig-work platforms encourage those in need of immediate income to pursue unstable employment that isolates them from traditional social support by forcing them to choose between flexibility and infrastructural benefits (Cant, 2019). The majority of gig workers use unofficial digital platforms and operate as unregistered self-run businesses, so they are excluded from traditional worker benefits and the social protection system (Uchiyama et al., 2022). Traditional jobs offer bonuses, paid time off, insurance, travel and housing benefits, retirement savings, and more. However, gig workers cannot receive all social benefits. Many countries' social safety nets are for permanent workers, not gigs (Friedman, 2014).

The nature of gig work seems to affect workers' engagement with the society in specific ways; it may prevent workers from building meaningful relationships with family and friends and restrict them from inter-relational and instrumental support (Machielse, 2006). Platform-based work isolates gig workers who deliver and affects how they interact with peers, friends, and families (Seetharaman et al., 2021). This social isolation affects gig workers' well-being and social integration (Cohen & Syme, 1985; Sarason et al., 1990). A study in India found that young men doing restaurant delivery and app-based delivery spend most of their time on the road without a formal home base, resulting in fewer opportunities to see and interact with friends and families because work incentives like more orders and bonus pay take precedence over rest (Seetharaman et al., 2021). A recent survey indicates that 74% of respondents did not have face-to-face contact with each other who used platforms and never or rarely communicated with themselves (Graham et al., 2017). The isolation of gig workers and weak communication among the gig workers and from other workers reduce the possibilities of collective bargaining and workers' ability to voice concerns on issues they face.

3.2. Towards an Inclusive Gig Economy?

Many workers avoid traditional labour markets due to a lack of information, education, training, skill development, and capital. Personal markers like gender, disability, and identity may affect a person's labour market access, along with social and economic factors. The flexible nature of gig work can help address these issues and make the gig economy more inclusive.

3.2.1. Participation of Women and Persons with Disabilities

Women and people with disabilities are underrepresented in the workforce worldwide for many reasons (Ali et al., 2011; Blanck, 2020; Chaudhary, 2021). Digital labour platforms can expand their gig economy labour market participation by creating new opportunities and modes of work. Flexibility and high earnings are driving their gig economy participation according to evidence. Women and disabled workers face the same risks as others, but they also face discrimination, harassment, and the inability to access basic rights (Hunt et al., 2019; Kasliwal, 2020; Sannon & Cosley, 2022). Women work in domestic, care, beauty, and wellness, and big, multi-service aggregator platforms like Urban Company and Housejoy hire beauty and wellness service providers. The gig economy and gig work have given women new and flexible paid work opportunities. This may have increased women's work participation. However, lack of digital economy access and security and safety concerns limit women's gig work (Chaudhary, 2021). According to Fair Work India 2023's annual report, some platforms discourage women from working after 6 p.m. for security reasons. However, some platforms assign remote deliveries to women without considering safety. The difference in digital technology access may also affect women's gig-work participation. In India, women and girls have lower access to digital devices like computers, the internet, and smartphones. The digital divide affects women more than men (Bailur, 2020).

3.2.2. Participation of Persons with Disabilities and from Marginalised Groups

The flexibility and ease of managing gig jobs as self-independent contractors and creating individualised disability-accessible work systems make platform-based gig work comfortable for disabled workers (Harpur & Blanck, 2020; Yamamoto et al., 2011). The gig platform can offer greater control over when and how tasks should be performed than traditional jobs, as the flexible work schedules can benefit disabled people by reducing or eliminating the need to disclose them to an employer, reducing stigma and bias (Harpur & Blanck, 2020). Gig work is not a panacea for disabled workers; they may face additional challenges (Hara et al., 2019; Lee et al., 2019; Zyskowski et al., 2015). Sannon and Cosley (2022) found that gig work can provide income for workers who cannot work. Workers face many new disability-related challenges on gig platforms. However, little is known about disabled workers' economic and personal reasons for gig work and their challenges (Harpur & Blanck, 2020). We must understand the many challenges women and disabled workers face, including work precarity and other risks, to make the gig economy more inclusive. Vulnerable social groups are underrepresented in formal job markets for various reasons. Expanding gig economy opportunities can make it more inclusive and solve structural problems in India.

4. Gig Economy and Informality: The Indian Experience

For various reasons, the growth of employment and opportunities remain limited in the formal sector. This leads to excessive dependence on the informal sector[1] for employment and livelihoods. In many cases, formal sector opportunities are

---

[1]ILO defined 'all jobs in informal sector enterprises, or all persons who, during a given reference period, were employed in at least one informal sector enterprise, irrespective of their status in employment and whether it was their main or a secondary job' as informal sector employment. The new definition extends its coverage to formal and informal sectors and economic activities under organised and unorganised nature.

shrinking, while the informal sector is growing. Only 10% of Indian workers are in the formal sector; 90% work informally. Formal sector employment is scarce and promotes informalisation for various reasons. The rise of informality in formal sectors worries scholars (Anand & Khera, 2016; Chandrasekhar & Ghosh, 2014; Sharma, 2014). Close to 58% of formal sector workers in India are informally employed, and employment growth has been linked to this (Sharma, 2014; Srivastava, 2012).

Informality and informal sectors in India have been studied for their effects. Some see it as a way out of poverty (Deshingkar, 2006; Deshingkar & Farrington, 2009), while others see it as a trap (Grant, 2008; Mitra, 2010). Informal workers are vulnerable to exploitation and uncertainty in the workplace and outside due to their lack of employer-provided social security and safety nets. Informalisation gives employers flexibility in organising economic activities and can reduce their costs and responsibilities. Various estimates show that the informal economy accounts for nearly 90% of Indian employment and over 50% of output. Informalisation's response to globalisation, technological progress, and large-scale technical solutions' changes in work is crucial.

4.1. Convergence Between Gig Economy and Informalisation?

Traditional employment has changed with the gig economy. It follows the formal process for recruiting, service delivery, and compensation but often makes the work informal. Contractual work reduces the benefits of self-employment for self-employed workers. Companies may find it easier to enter and operate informally with minimal cost and procedure, and workers may be drawn to gig economy opportunities for various reasons. Sometimes, informalisation and promotion of gig work go together or reinforce each other. Their work and working conditions are more flexible, vulnerable, and precarious than those of formal workers.

In some ways, gig economy resembles informal economy or informalisation in India and elsewhere. Workers engaged in the gig economy and informal sector face similar issues. Thus, gig work has normalised poor working conditions, and gig workers live in poverty and face significant financial and personal risk (Funnell, 2016; Myhill et al., 2021). Workers are generally at risk due to job insecurity and a lack of control over their working conditions. Lack of job security and uncertain employment status turned 35% of women away from the gig economy (Chapman et al., 2018). Discrimination and exploitation against vulnerable domestic workers are also creating unequal power relations (Hunt & Machingura, 2016). In many countries, men and women earn different salaries. The monthly salary gap between male and female delivery executives in India is 9–10% (Kar, 2019), and Uber in the United States paid men more for similar tasks (Cook et al., 2021). Women in low-income countries work mostly in low-paying, low-skilled gig work rather than high-skilled, high-income freelancing gig work (Chami, 2021), limiting their access to high-end data and AI jobs. These issues suggest that gig workers face the same flexibilities, vulnerabilities, and discrimination as informal economy workers. The nature of flexibility, vulnerability, inclusion, access, and other characteristics indicate the possibility of convergence between workers across these two groups.

5. Conclusion and Policy Recommendations

The gig economy and gig workers in India have grown steadily due to various factors. The gig workforce in India is expected to reach 2.35 crore by 2029–2030 accounting for 6.7% of the non-agricultural workforce and 4.1% of total livelihoods (NITI Ayog, 2022). COVID-19 challenges accelerated digital solutions and gig economy adoption. Given the new gig economy opportunities, the policy may promote and protect gig workers and access to flexible gig work for women, people with disabilities, and vulnerable socio-economic groups by prioritising their occupational safety, health, inclusion, and social well-being. Workers in the gig economy and informal economy share some common features in terms of vulnerability and limited access to social security. At the same time, gig economy adheres to the formal system for hiring gig workers and compensating them. Policymakers propose that India could leverage the digital economy and gig economy to formalise the informal sector and strengthen the formal economy.

While gig work is expanding in all key economic sectors, its nature and scope vary by sector and subsector. Such differences require sector-specific policies. For instance, industries like transportation and service delivery opened the gig work from the early phases. The experience highlights the importance of developing mechanisms for empowering gig workers to negotiate equitable prices, workflow, and overall working conditions. Policy interventions should ensure decent wages, positive working conditions, and social security in gig work, given its growing potential. Platform aggregators and government agencies should work closely to develop policies for the future of gig work in the country.

Based on the above discussion, we identify some key steps towards improving the quality of gig work and the organisation of work in India's gig economy.

- Beyond ensuring the minimum wage, policies can encourage companies to cover work-related expenditures like petrol, vehicle maintenance, and uniforms while ensuring reasonable compensation (paying a living wage) and incentives.
- Policy initiatives should ensure occupational safety and protection against health risks associated with gig work, especially those caused by prolonged working hours, physical and mental tasks, and long commutes. Promoting awareness campaigns that underscore the significance of maintaining a healthy work-life balance, specifically related to mental health assistance and practicing self-care, is crucial for improving the overall well-being of gig workers.
- By supporting women and people with disabilities and addressing discrimination, harassment, and limited access to digital devices and platforms, policies can make gig work more inclusive and viable. Customising training and support programmes to engage marginalised workers will improve this. Adding safety and anti-discrimination features to the app and guidelines can make gig work a viable option for women, people with disabilities, and others with personal challenges.

- Regardless of the specific gig job or platform, social protection measures, including healthcare coverage, insurance, retirement savings, and financial assistance during periods of unemployment or emergencies, should be prioritised for gig workers. The existing policies for ensuring decent working conditions and social security for gig workers at the national and state levels can play critical roles in this direction. For instance, the Code of Social Security 2020 and Motor Vehicle Aggregator Guidelines 2020 intend to regulate the condition of platform workers in India. Similarly, the Rajasthan Platform-Based Gig Workers (Registration and Welfare) Act, 2023, passed by the state of Rajasthan in July 2023, mandates compulsory registration of all digital intermediaries (platforms) operating in the state, along with the details of the workers and the transactions taking place on the platform.
- Policies should promote social bonds among gig workers; platforms can enable gig workers to engage with peers, friends, and families through virtual communities, networking events, and support groups. In order to manage the balance between work and personal life, companies should allow flexible work arrangements.
- Ultimately, workers' voices must be empowered. It can help to express their concerns, to offer feedback, and to participate in decision-making processes concerning their working conditions and rights. Trade unions and workers' collectives traditionally function in these roles, while modern work arrangements, including gig work, could find some alternate forms of associations facilitating collective bargaining and representation in India.
- The design, application, and technical requirements could be revised to address the concerns of gig workers about data privacy, transparency, and operation. Making the application more interactive and facilitating feedback and communication across the teams in regular mode can improve collective work. Periodic meetings with the workers' representatives and fair representation of workers in decisions regarding changes in wages, work arrangements, etc., may be very helpful.

The existing literature is not enough to assess the problems and policies concerned here and lacks clarity regarding the conceptual framework and methods used in exploring the impact of the gig economy on the welfare of workers. We need to take a closer look at the issues surrounding the productivity and profitability of gig works as well as the job quality of platform-based on-demand gig workers, their level of livelihood security, the main socio-economic and household factors that influence their participation in the not-so-easy-to-work gig works, their health and social problems, and gender disparity. It is also important to pay attention to how many workers can face complicated, intersectional challenges based on multiple marginalised identities in addition to disability, such as race, gender, sexual orientation, caste, religion, ethnic groups, status of migration, socio-economic status, etc. The chapter reviews some key studies on issues faced by gig workers in India and emphasises the need for systematic empirical studies on the nature of gig work in key sectors of the country and supporting evidence-based policymaking.

References

Ali, M., Schur, L., & Blanck, P. (2011). What types of jobs do people with disabilities want?. *Journal of Occupational Rehabilitation, 21*, 199–210.

Altenried, M. (2019). On the last mile: Logistical urbanism and the transformation of labour. *Work Organisation, Labour & Globalisation, 13*(1), 114–129.

Anand, R., & Khera, P. (2016). *Macroeconomic impact of product and labor market reforms on informality and unemployment in India.* International Monetary Fund.

Bailur, S. (2020). *Female livelihoods in the gig economy.* Caribou Digital. https://medium.com/caribou-digital/female-livelihoods-in-the-gig-economy-tensions-andopportunities-f14982b6aaad

Bajwa, U., Knorr, L., Di Ruggiero, E., Gastaldo, D., & Zendel, A. (2018). Towards an understanding of workers' experiences in the global gig economy. *Globalization and Health, 14*(124), 2–4.

Bartkiw, T. J. (2014). *The fissured workplace: Why work became so bad for so many and what can be done to improve it.* David Weil.

Blanck, P. (2020). Disability inclusive employment and the accommodation principle: Emerging issues in research, policy, and law. *Journal of Occupational Rehabilitation, 30*, 505–510.

Cant, C. (2019). *Riding for Deliveroo: Resistance in the new economy.* John Wiley & Sons.

Chami, A. G. (2021, February). *The urgency of gender justice in the digital economy.* Retrieved April, 2021, from Social Europe: https://www.socialeurope.eu/the-urgency-of-genderjustice-in-the-digital-economy

Chandrasekhar, C. P., & Ghosh, J. (2014). *Growth, employment patterns and inequality in Asia: A case study of India.* ILO.

Chapman, T., Saran, S., & Sinha, R. K. (2018). *The future of work in India: Inclusion, growth and transformation.* ORF

Chaudhary, R. (2021). India's emerging gig economy: Shaping the future of work for women. *Georgetown Journal of Asian Affairs, 7*, 50–57. https://repository.library.georgetown.edu/bitstream/handle/10822/1061300/GJAA_Chaudhary.pdf?sequence=1

Chen, B., Liu, T., & Wang, Y. (2020). Volatile fragility: New employment forms and disrupted employment protection in the new economy. *International Journal of Environmental Research and Public Health, 17*(5), 1531.

Choudhary, V., & Shireshi, S. S. (2022). Analysing the gig economy in India and exploring various effective regulatory methods to improve the plight of the workers. *Journal of Asian and African Studies, 57*(7), 1343–1356.

Christie, N., & Ward, H. (2018). *The emerging issues for management of occupational road risk in a changing economy: A survey of gig economy drivers, riders and their managers.* UCL Centre for Transport Studies.

Christie, N., & Ward, H. (2019). The health and safety risks for people who drive for work in the gig economy. *Journal of Transport & Health, 13*, 115–127.

Cohen, S. E., & Syme, S. I. (1985). *Social support and health.* Academic Press.

Cook, C., Diamond, R., Hall, J. V., List, J. A., & Oyer, P. (2021). The gender earnings gap in the gig economy: Evidence from over a million rideshare drivers. *The Review of Economic Studies, 88*(5), 2210–2238.

Davis, J. (2015). Drive at your own risk: Uber's misrepresentations to UberX drivers about insurance coverage violate California's unfair competition law. *Boston College Law Review, 56*(3), 1097–1142.

De Ruyter, A., Brown, M., & Burgess, J. (2018). Gig work and the fourth industrial revolution. *Journal of International Affairs, 72*(1), 37–50.

Deshingkar, P. (2006). *Internal migration, poverty and development in Asia* [Briefing Paper 11]. Overseas Development Institute.

Deshingkar, P., & Farrington, J. (2009). *Circular migration and multi locational livelihood strategies in rural India*. Oxford University Press.

Fairwork. (2023). *Fairwork India ratings 2023: Labour standards in the platform economy*. https://fair.work/wp-content/uploads/sites/17/2023/11/Fairwork-India-Report-2023.pdf

Foley, M., Ruser, J., Shor, G., Shuford, H., & Sygnatur, E. (2014). Contingent workers: Workers' compensation data analysis strategies and limitations. *American Journal of Industrial Medicine, 57*(7), 764–775.

Friedman, G. (2014). Workers without employers: Shadow corporations and the rise of the gig economy. *Review of Keynesian Economics, 2*(2), 171–188.

Funnell, A. (2016). *The contingent workforce and the growth of digital Taylorism*. ABC. https://www.abc.net.au/radionational/programs/futuretense/future-employment—going-back-to-square-one/7700584

Glavin, P., & Schieman, S. (2022). Dependency and hardship in the gig economy: The mental health consequences of platform work. *Socius, 8*, https://doi.org/10.1177/23780231221082414

GOI. (2019). *Report on India's trillion dollar digital opportunity*. Ministry of Electronics & IT. Retrieved August 30, 2019, from http://pib.gov.in/PressReleaseIframePage.aspx?PRID=1565669

GOI. (2023). *Digital India*. Common Service Centre. Retrieved July 11 from https://csc.gov.in/digitalIndia#:~:text=Digital%20India%20is%20a%20flagship,Prime%20Minister%20Shri%20Narendra%20Modi

Graham, M., Lehdonvirta, V., Wood, A., Barnard, H., Hjorth, I., & Simon, P. (2017). *The risks and rewards of online gig work at the global margins*. Oxford Internet Institute.

Grant, U. (2008). *Opportunity and exploitation in urban labour markets* [Briefing Paper 44]. Overseas Development Institute.

Griesbach, K., Reich, A., Elliott-Negri, L., & Milkman, R., (2019). Algorithmic control in platform food delivery work. *Socius, 5*, https://doi.org/10.1177/2378023119870041

Hara, K., Adams, A., Milland, K., Savage, S., Hanrahan, B. V., Bigham, J. P., & Callison-Burch, C. (2019). Worker demographics and earnings on amazon mechanical Turk: An exploratory analysis. *In CHI conference on human factors in computing systems proceedings (CHI 2019)*, (p. 12). May 4–9, Glasgow. https://ink.library.smu.edu.sg/sis_research/4402

Harpur, P., & Blanck, P. (2020). Gig workers with disabilities: Opportunities, challenges, and regulatory response. *Journal of Occupational Rehabilitation, 30*, 511–520.

Heeks, R. (2017). *Decent work and the digital gig economy: A developing country perspective on employment impacts and standards in online outsourcing, crowdwork, etc.* [Working Paper 71]. Development Informatics.

Hunt, A., & Machingura, F. (2016). *A good gig? The rise of on demand domestic work* [Working Paper 7]. ODI Development Progress.

Hunt, A., Samman, E., Tapfuma, S., Mwaura, G., Omenya, R., Kim, K., Stevano, S., & Roumer, A., (2019). *Women in the gig economy: paid work, care and flexibility in Kenya and South Africa*. Overseas Development Institute.

Jakobsen, M. D., GliesVincentsSeeberg, K., Møller, M., Kines, P., Jørgensen, P., Malchow-Møller, L., Andersen, A. B., & Andersen, L. L. (2023). Influence of occupational risk factors for road traffic crashes among professional drivers: Systematic review. *Transport Reviews, 43*(3), 533–563.

Kar, S. (2019). Women bag frontline roles in gig economy, but lag behind in wages. *The Economic Times*.

Kasliwal, R. (2020). Gender and the gig economy: A qualitative study of gig platforms for women workers. *ORF Issue Brief, 359*, 1–14.

Khurana, R. (2021). JioFiber: Disrupting the digital market in India. *Journal of Information Technology Case and Application Research, 23*(2), 115–138.

Korde, R., Agarwal, P., Adimulam, D., & Gandhi, M. (2021). *Gig Economy India: 2020–2021.* FLAME University.

Kuek, S. C., Paradi-Guilford, C., Fayomi, T., Imaizumi, S., Ipeirotis, P., Pina, P., & Singh, M. (2015). *The global opportunity in online outsourcing.* World Bank.

Lee, S., Hubert-Wallander, B., Stevens, M., & Carroll, J. M. (2019). Understanding and designing for deaf or hard of hearing drivers on Uber. In *CHI conference on human factors in computing systems proceedings (CHI 2019)*, (p. 12). May 4–9, Glasgow. https://doi.org/10.1145/3290605.3300759

Lewchuk, W. (2017). Precarious jobs: Where are they, and how do they affect well-being? *Economic and Labour Relations Review, 28*(3), 402–419.

Machielse, A. (2006). Theories on social contacts and social isolation. In R. Hortulanus, A. Machielse, & L. Meeuwesen (Eds.), *Social isolation in modern society* (pp. 13–36). Routledge.

Mitra, A. (2010). Migration, livelihood and well-being: Evidence from Indian city slums. *Urban Studies, 47*(7), 1371–1390.

Myhill, K., Richards, J., & Sang, K. (2021). Job quality, fair work and gig work: The lived experience of gig workers. *The International Journal of Human Resource Management, 32*(19), 4110–4135.

NITI Ayog. (2022). *India's booming gig and platform economy: Perspectives and recommendations on the future of work.* https://www.niti.gov.in/sites/default/files/2022-06/25th_June_Final_Report_27062022.pdf

Noronha, P. D. (2016). Positives outweighing negatives: The experiences of Indian crowdsourced workers. Work Organisation. *Labour and Globalisation, 10*(1), 44–63.

Prabhat, S., Nanavati, S., & Rangaswamy, N. (2019). India's "Uberwallah" profiling Uber drivers in the gig economy. In *Proceedings of the tenth international conference on information and communication technologies and development.* January. https://doi.org/10.1145/3287098.3287139

Randolph, G., Galperin, H., & Khan, L. (2019). *New opportunities in the platform economy: On-ramps to formalization in the global south.* Just Job Network.

Rani, U., & Furrer, M. (2021). Digital labour platforms and new forms of flexible work in developing countries: Algorithmic management of work and workers. *Competition & Change, 25*(2), 212–236.

Rani, U., & Gobel, N. (2022). *Labour in the gig economy. The Routledge handbook of the gig economy.* Routledge.

Ravenelle, A. J. (2019). *Hustle and gig: Struggling and surviving in the sharing economy.* University of California Press.

Rockefeller Foundation. (2013). *Health vulnerabilities of informal workers.* Retrieved July 16, 2023, from https://www.rockefellerfoundation.org/report/health-vulnerabilities-of-informal-workers/

Sannon, S., & Cosley, D. (2022). Toward a more inclusive gig economy: Risks and opportunities for workers with disabilities. *Proceedings of the ACM on Human-Computer Interaction, 6*(CSCW2), 1–31.

Sarason, B. R., Sarason, I. G., & Pierce, G. R. (1990). *Social support: An interactional view.* John Wiley & Sons.

Seetharaman, B., Pal, J., & Hui, J. (2021). Delivery work and the experience of social isolation. *Proceedings of the ACM on Human-Computer Interaction, 5*(CSCW1), 1–17.

Sharma, A. N. (2014). *India-labour and employment report 2014: Workers in the era of globalisation* (Institute for Human Development, New Delhi). Academic Foundation.

Srivastava, R. (2012). Changing employment conditions of the Indian workforce and implications for decent work. *Global Labour Journal, 3*(1), 63–90.

Standford, J. (2017). The resurgence of gig work: Historical and theoretical perspective. *Economics and Labour Relation Review, 28*(3), 382–401.

Sundararajan, A. (2018). Crowd-based capitalism, digital automation, and the future of work. *University of Chicago Legal Forum, 2017*(1), 19.

Tran, M., & Sokas, R. K. (2017). The gig economy and contingent work: An occupational health assessment. *Journal of Occupational and Environmental Medicine, 59*(4), e63.

Uchiyama, Y., Furuoka, F., & Akhir, M. N. M. (2022). Gig workers, social protection and labour market inequality: Lessons from Malaysia. *Jurnal Ekonomi Malaysia, 56*(3), 165–184.

Wood, A. J., Graham, M., Lehdonvirta, V., & Hjorth, I. (2019). Good gig, bad gig: Autonomy and algorithmic control in the global gig economy. *Work, Employment and Society, 33*(1), 56–75.

Yamamoto, S., Unruh, D., & Bullis, M. (2011). The viability of self-employment for individuals with disabilities in the United States: A synthesis of the empirical-research literature. *Journal of Vocational Rehabilitation, 35*(2), 117–127.

Zheng, Q., Zhan, J., & Feng, X. (2023). Working safety and workloads of Chinese delivery riders: The role of work pressure. *International Journal of Occupational Safety and Ergonomics, 29*(2), 869–882.

Zyskowski, K., Morris, M. R., Bigham, J. P., Gray, M. L., & Kane, S. K. (2015, February). Accessible crowdwork? Understanding the value in and challenge of microtask employment for people with disabilities. In *Proceedings of the 18th ACM conference on computer supported cooperative work & social computing* (pp. 1682–1693). https://doi.org/10.1145/2675133.2675158

Chapter 14

Reconnoitring Vulnerabilities of Migrant Women Workers in the Urban Informal Labour Market[*]

Nomita P. Kumar and Achala Srivastava

Giri Institute of Development Studies, Lucknow, Uttar Pradesh, India

Abstract

The present chapter attempts to highlight the vulnerabilities of female migrants as compared to non-migrants in the unorganized urban labor market. Informal female migrants working in construction, as domestic workers, tailors/boutiques, and garment workers in the urban unorganized sector of Uttar Pradesh's selected urban locations, are covered in this chapter. Though the fact prevails that workers in the unorganized labor markets are confronted with various livelihood crunches, still those who are migrants and swelling the urban labor markets are more prone to different vulnerabilities. There is scanty literature on the situation and condition of migrants particularly female migrant workers in India, whereas we know more about the condition of international migrants, mainly migrant workers in the Gulf and other regions. The study is based on interviews with 174 female informal workers who have migrated and 222 non-migrants from various regions of the state to the urban locations of selected cities. Our study also attempts to do an in-depth, qualitative exploration of these vulnerable women's lives and perceptions and tries to capture layered vulnerabilities, risks, and rewards confronted due to both migration and work in the informal sector. Specifically, the findings reflect upon the fact that how strong societal norms may actually prevent women from acknowledging or articulating the true reasons for their migrations.

Keywords: Migrants; vulnerabilities; urban informal labor market; women migrants; social security

---

[*] This chapter is a part of larger study sponsored by ICSSR, New Delhi.

Informal Economy and Sustainable Development Goals:
Ideas, Interventions and Challenges, 273–296

1. Introduction

The urban informal sector continues to play a crucial role in providing sources of livelihood, particularly to rural migrants and other low-income households (Mehta & Awasthi, 2022). Female migration from rural to urban areas is an important component of labor migration. The average annual growth rate of the migrant population over the last 30 years (1971–2001) was 2.12% – female migration showed a growth rate of 2.24% compared to 1.85% for males during the same period. Rural females were most mobile although urban females have picked up over the decades (Banerjee & Raju, 2009). Unemployment and low wages prevailing in the rural labor market push female workers to look for better employment in the urban informal sector. In the urban market, migrant workers provide essential services to the places where they go, contributing to the wealth of aging societies and the sustainability of these countries' welfare and employment systems. Yet, migrant workers can be confronted with additional vulnerabilities, leading to violations of their labor rights. Women migrants in the informal urban labor market are likely to be more vulnerable than their male counterparts in the workplace regarding health, physical safety, job security, social protection, and so on. As pointed out by Banerjee and Raju (2009), many women migrant workers face discrimination, violence, health risks, and exploitation at all stages of migration, deriving in large part from gender in addition to social class, ethnicity, and immigration status. The preference for migrant women workers on the part of employers is mainly because women accept lower wages, are not unionized, and do not protest much against unpleasant working conditions. Their vulnerabilities are often linked to insecure recruitment, the social and cultural isolation they can face at their workplace due to poor economic conditions and cultural differences, a lack of advance and conditions of employment, the absence of labor law coverage, and restrictions on freedom of movement and association, among other things.

The majority of unskilled women migrant workers live on worksites in temporary huts or on roads and in slum areas. In this background, an attempt has been made in this chapter to explore the adversities faced by women migrants in the informal sector of the economy of Uttar Pradesh.

The main objective of this chapter is to examine the migration pattern, causes of migration, and socio-economic and health vulnerabilities of female migrants working in the informal sector in selected districts of Uttar Pradesh. To examine this objective, the chapter is organized as follows: Section 2 deals with the review of literature and data and the methodology of the chapter is presented in Section 3, and Section 4 presents migration patterns of female informal workers. Section 5 provides detailed information related to socio-economic characteristics of female migrant workers. Section 6 discusses the background of migrant workers prior to their migration, Section 7 discusses the paradoxical question of migrant workers' workplace vulnerabilities and access to social security benefits, Section 8 explores the factors responsible for female migration followed by Section 8 which discusses the causes of female migration, and Section 9 transcribes determinants of income vulnerabilities for migrants and non-migrants followed by Section 10, the last section provides conclusions and policy implications/suggestions.

2. Review of Literature

There is scanty literature on the situation and condition of migrants particularly. Female migrant workers in India, whereas we know more about the condition of international migrants, mainly migrant workers in the Gulf and other regions. In India, as in most countries, there are generally no restrictions on internal movement. The number of internal migrants in India was 450 million as per the most recent 2011 census (De, 2019). Internal migrants, mainly absorbed within the informal economy, contribute to high-growth sectors of construction, manufacturing, and urban services at destination sites. Women outnumber men in internal migration in India, and it is often identified as part of marriage or associational migration (Mazumdar et al., 2013; Rajan & Sumeetha, 2020; Srivastava, 2012). Rajan and Sumeetha (2020) argues that among circular migrants, the vulnerability of women falls into several categories, first; where single male migrants leave women and children behind, and the major responsibility of economic and social reproduction falls on these women, second; where women migrate with men, joining the labor force or taking up care responsibilities at home, and third; where women migrate singly to join the workforce. In each of the last two cases, women workers are part of the lower end of the informal economy, where their contribution as workers remains invisible and unrecognized, and their access to social protection entitlements remains weak. The paper of Ajith Kumar (2011) examines the dimensions of vulnerability of migrant laborers in Kerala, one of the few states which has had proactive policy for labor migrants (Srivastava, 2020). His paper examines how the state responded to reduce the vulnerability of inter-state migrant workers. The paper also makes an assessment of a pioneering welfare scheme for inter-state migrant workers introduced by the Kerala government. The paper points out that due to limitations in portability of entitlements, the inter-state migrants are not able to enjoy some of the entitlements/benefits from central and state governments they had enjoyed before migration. Migrant workers face unique challenges due to their high levels of mobility, as they are unable to settle in their work destinations, therefore falling outside the state's purview in both their source and their destination regions. They also include economically vulnerable and socially marginalized populations, including women and children, who are absorbed into highly informal, invisible, and exploitative work arrangements at the lowest ends of the labor markets (ILO, 2020). The paper by Jayaram and Varma (2020) analyzes the conditions of migrant workers in industrialized Gujarat with a focus on two cities – Surat and Ahmedabad – and three sectors – construction, textiles, and hotels. Similarly, paper by Das (2020) focuses on two important sectors: domestic workers and construction workers to analyze the situation of informal women migrant workers who work in the lowest rungs of the informal economy. Her fieldwork is based in the National Capital Region of Delhi, where a large number of circular labor migrants are employed. Her paper examines how migrant women workers organized their productive–reproductive responsibilities as construction workers and domestic workers. Of the women on whose narratives this paper is based, most had migrated from villages, and two from small villages and four-fifth were from scheduled castes (SCs) or were Muslims. For most of the women, the migration to the NCR is as what is described as associational migration. Migrant women are largely concentrated in sectors where they are not identified as workers. They are employed as helpers to carry and lift materials in the construction sector along with their spouses or male relatives (Jayaram et al., 2019). Banerjee and Raju (2009) focus on the changing work profile of migrant women and the avenues available to them. The central question is whether women's post urban continuation in the workforce and fresh work status destabilizes any of the established stereotypical gendered codes woven around familial and domestic responsibilities and if caste, class, and accessibility to human resources (education in particular) intersect with such codes.

3. Data and Methodology

The database of the study is drawn from the primary survey (2018–2019) carried out in four districts of Uttar Pradesh, where the concentration of women migrants in the urban labor market could be traced to canvass the vulnerabilities of unorganized sector women workers. The empirical base of the current study is based on the primary data collected through interviews with 396 informal workers in the unorganized sector of Uttar Pradesh (174 migrants and 222 non-migrants). Females who had migrated to work in construction jobs as domestic workers, tailors/boutique workers, and workers in the garment sector in different urban cities were covered. The study was conducted between August 2018 and January 2019. For selecting the sample, a multistage stratified random sampling design was adopted. In the first stage, four districts from different regions of Uttar Pradesh were selected. According to Uttar Pradesh Economic Census 2011–2012, Lucknow district had a predominantly service sector-based economy, and being the capital of the state, recorded the fastest growth of female migrant workers. The districts of Ghaziabad, Jhansi, and Varanasi showed higher number of female workers in the non-agricultural sector. So, considering the large availability of female workers who belong to the 15–59 age groups were selected from these four districts. The second stage encompassed the selection of urban areas of the selected districts to conduct a survey. The third stage consisted of selecting the respondents or women who were migrants to the cities selected randomly from the selected areas. A self-formulated interview schedule was used for primary data collection among women who migrated and are mostly destitute, landless, and belong to marginal households living temporarily in makeshift houses. Due to the difficulties of accessing this vulnerable population, a convenience sampling approach was utilized at the construction site, and domestic workers/tailors and garment workers who were willing and equipped to offer their time to answer the questions were included in the survey. Some of them were interviewed personally at the place of their work. Hence, a purposive random sampling design was adopted, and the questionnaire was canvassed as per the convenience of the respondents to preserve the interests of all parties (respondent, employer, and questioner) so that migrants who migrated from the different districts to the cities of Lucknow, Ghaziabad, Varanasi, and Jhansi could speak more freely about their work conditions. The study based on migrant and non-migrant female workers to access comparative status in urban labor market. In the course of our study, field staff also gathered relevant information in qualitative terms, considering previous empirical studies. Before collecting the final data, a pilot questionnaire was canvassed, and based on that, a final questionnaire with a more structured format was prepared. For identifying the factors affecting migrant and non-migrant workers' income, ordinary least square (OLS) regression has been used. We have also carried out mean comparisons of the selected variables to highlight the basic differences between migrants' and non-migrant workers' socioeconomic and demographic characteristics.

Numerous studies are available based on women migrant workers at the national level (Agrawal, 2006; Banerjee & Raju, 2009; Srinivasan & Illango, 2012), but in the state of UP, little attention has been given to the vulnerable populations of migrant women workers. This study is proposed to fill this gap in the available literature. Although some studies that have explored the issue of female migrants at the national and state levels, we could not find any studies on the condition and status of the women migrant workers in Uttar Pradesh in the unorganized sectors.

4. Migrants Throng the Exploitative Informal Sector

Since the end of the colonial era, India has had a long history of migration to escape the exploitative practices of landlords toward farmers who were observed leaving their land after their rights were terminated and losing it to landlords because they were unable to pay rent. Even now, people still migrate for work when they lose their primary source of income in rural areas or villages due to decreased agricultural productivity, the division of members' land among themselves, landlessness, or other socioeconomic obstacles. People have even been motivated to migrate to metropolitan regions and assisted in finding employment by social capital, caste, and familial ties (see Banerjee, 1986, 1991; Banerjee & Bucci, 1994; Mitra, 1994; Sovani, 1964). Long-term or seasonal workers in the unorganized sector swarm cities, which eventually aids in the advancement of economic development.

The question of "How does a worker get over exploit in the informal sectors?" was correctly brought up by Das (2020), and he expresses his concern about the matter in a very pertinent way, pointing out that it is a well-known truth that faster economic development rates do not necessarily result in more jobs, particularly in a developing nation like India's formal sectors. However, when it comes to creating jobs, India's informal sector functions as a "absorbent sector" in comparison to the formal sector (ILO-WTO, 2009). Given the recent growth in the number of migrant workers in India's informal sectors and the country's greater percentage of informal labor force participation, it is important to comprehend how the informal sector exploited labor after globalization and liberalization.

Marjit and Beladi (2008) rightly stated that as cited in Das (2020, p. 4) that

> Globalization would increase the size of the informal sector. This probably happens through the presence of liberal trade policy, especially in the form of declining tariff rates that would reduce open unemployment and an increase in informal wage and informal employment if capital is more mobile between the formal and informal sectors.

The capitalist resort of today is driven by market competition to maximize profits by increasing the informalization of labor and employing wage-cutting tactics in conjunction with longer labor hours. In the market, coercive techniques are often used to optimize production relative to profits by selling at higher prices. Such a drastic shift in the labor market, coupled with informalization, emphasizes unequal production relations and widens social hierarchical disparities. Das (2020) correctly points out that workers lack significant union or political representation in their fight against this increased informalization. The deplorable working circumstances of informal laborers are made much more precarious when they are employed as migrants and are unable to obtain legal assistance because of their informal status.

Mundle (1993) argued about informal sector, "Increased competition in the world would force firm to cut their work force and shift towards more capital-intensive advanced technology, there by restricting employment and lead to casualization or in formalization of work force." In our sample, we find that among the migrant workers 40.00% are male migrant workers and 43.94% are female migrant workers. In all, the migrant workers account for 42.75% of the total informal workers.

In our sample, we find that among the migrant workers, 40.00% are male migrant workers, and 43.94% are female migrant workers. Overall, migrant workers account for 42.75% of the total informal workers. Of the total female migrant workers, majority of females (37.36%) were employed as the construction workers, followed by 23.56% working as domestic workers and 13.79% as tailoring workers (Table 14.1). Other occupations reported were garment/textile workers, nursing personnel, teachers, workers in private enterprises, and sales workers. As expected in a low-income setting, no female respondent was engaged in formal-jobs in informal sector. Contrary to this, a large number of non-migrant workers (20.96%) were engaged as tailors and 20.20% in garment and textile factories as low-paid workers. Thus, it has been observed that urban areas have attracted numerous migrants from rural areas in the hope of a better life. However, most of the female informal workers have been working in the domestic (20.45%) and construction sectors (19.44%) in urban areas.

5. Socio-Demographic Background

Socio-economic and demographic characteristics of migrant workers have been discussed in the following section in terms of sex, marital status, caste, education,

Table 14.1. Occupational Structure of Migrants/Non-migrants.

Occupation	Migrants			Non-migrants			Total		
	Female	%	Average Income (Rs)	Female	%	Average Income (Rs)	Female	%	Average Income (Rs)
Construction workers	65	37.36	6,271	12	5.41	6,600	77	19.44	6,322
Garment/textile workers	18	10.34	4,439	62	27.93	4,930	80	20.2	4,926
Domestic workers	41	23.56	3,927	40	18.02	4,275	81	20.45	4,099
Tailors	24	13.79	6,000	59	26.58	6,892	83	20.96	6,258
Nursing personnel's	9	5.17	7,000	12	5.41	8,625	21	5.3	7,929
Teachers	6	3.45	6,909	11	4.95	12,333	17	4.29	8,824
Private enterprise (worker)	4	2.3	9,364	11	4.95	14,000	15	3.79	10,600
Mall/superstore (sales worker)	7	4.02	6,429	15	6.76	8,995	22	5.56	8,178
Total	174	100	4,025	222	100	6,008	396	100	5,137

Source: Primary Survey, 2018–2019.

and income. Taking cues from the body of research demonstrating that migrant workers' transitional and informal employment places them in double jeopardy and causes their socioeconomic status to fall well below the desired level. In addition, immigrants' economic and social lives in new urban settlements are considerably more precarious due to their lack of education and competence. Additionally, it appears that workers' free will to explore opportunities in the labor market is severely limited in this new setup due to the influence of middlemen like labor brokers, who limit their ability to obtain decent-paying jobs that include social security.

Age of the migrant women worker is one of the most important factors for out-migration. Most often, it is the reproductive and productive age group between 21 and 35 years who chose to migrate. A significantly higher proportion about 55.75% of these migrant women was from the age group 21–35 years (Appendix). However, when all age groups were taken into account, next significant age group of women migrants (i.e., 31.03% workers) was found in the age cohorts of 36–50, migrated in urban areas due to family reasons (marriage and family immigration) and for economic reasons (employment, business, and education).

Demand for women-centric services, such as full-time home caretakers, childcare providers, and domestic help, has increased due to the rise of nuclear families, the increased involvement of educated women in the labor market, and shifting consumption patterns (Majumdar, 1980; Martin, 2004; Pillai, 2007). Marriage is the main factor contributing to the increased number of women among the migrants. Correctly noted, the gender-specific labor migration pattern is another factor contributing to this growth (Ghosh, 2002; Sassen-Koob, 1984; Shanti, 1991). Men are moving abroad in search of work, and their spouses are moving abroad as well. According to the survey, the majority of migrant workers' wives – 72.99% – are married, while 20.69% are single or have never married. The Appendix shows that 6.32% of the population was widowed; most of them lived with parents or other family members, but some of them also lived alone or with friends. Researches show that socio-cultural factors are important when making decision to migrate. It is true that those who are poor and/or belong to lower castes/tribes tend to be more likely to migrate (Breman, 1996; Deshingkar & Start, 2003; Rogaly, 1999; Singh, 1978). However, little is known about how caste locations affect people's ability to migrate and obtain paid employment (Banerjee & Raju, 2009).

Our current study categorized social groups into SC, other backward caste (OBC), and general (GEN) – this social composition of the migrant population corroborates the overall social composition of the population in Uttar Pradesh. It has been observed from the Appendix that among the women migrant workers majority (48.85%) of workers belong to SC followed by OBCs (31.61%) and GEN (19.54%) caste, indicating the fact that informal labor market is largely dominated by lower caste females who have migrated from the rural areas. Misra and Alma (2014) discovered in their research that a significant proportion of migrants belong to historically marginalized communities, including SCs, scheduled tribes, and OBCs. There were significant differences in the educational distribution across the category of workers. A fair proportion of women migrant workers were uneducated (44.83%). Less than 24.71 were literate up to primary level and 13.22% had completed secondary-level education. Due to illiteracy, they were left with no choice but to do unskilled work in the informal sector. According to the survey results, the majority of female migrants who are relocating to urban areas are either illiterate or only somewhat literate. In contrast to nations in Southeast and East Asia, the majority of India's migrant labor force is poorly or never educated (Srivastava, 2003).

Due to migration, a sizeable proportion of the increased work force in the informal sector is likely to be absorbed in the informal work where they get low wages and less facilities. On an average, 40.80% female migrants reported earnings of about 5,000 rupees per month; 52.30% respondents earned more than 5,000 rupees (i.e., 5,000–10,000 rupees) per month (Appendix). Semi-skilled workers with some education and skills such as those in tailoring and garment factories get slightly higher wages as compared to illiterate and less educated domestic workers be it migrants or non-migrants. As Table 14.1 shows that migrated workers, who belonged to tailoring work (Rs 6,000), non-migrants got higher wages (i.e., Rs 6,892). Therefore, in informal sector, migrated females who join the workforce often end up earning lower than the minimum wages.

No significant difference seems to exist between the average wages of women migrant workers in any occupation whatever differences are there it is all because of education and skills. As shown in the Appendix that lowest average wage has been paid to domestic workers as they were getting less wage, that is, 136.63 rupees per day (4,099 per month) as compared to their counterparts engaged in other occupations both for migrants and for non-migrants. Among the different occupational categories, highest average wage has been received by female workers engaged in private enterprises and teachers followed by tailoring job followed by garment and construction sector (Appendix). The tasks completed, the number of hours worked, the worker's social standing, their skill set, the requirement for flexibility, and other aspects of the labor market all affect how much an informal worker gets paid. Nature of wage is mostly of daily as reported by 14.65% respondents. Whereas, 22.14% respondents reported that they have got weekly payment. 75.51% reported that they have received monthly payment (of which 48.74% were non-migrants and only 26.77% were migrants). The vulnerability of migrants can be gauged from the fact that women who migrated were employment on as daily wagers as compared to non-migrants. However, the average income was same for all categories of workers. Majority of female workers (66.67%) had been getting time – wage followed by 27.53% women workers, who were getting piece – rate wage (Appendix). Only, 4.29% migrant workers reported about contract wage. Verite (2010) observed in his study that workers in India are typically migrants from impoverished backgrounds and marginalized communities of rural areas.

Along the whole garment supply chain, from massive factories to tiny home-based businesses, they are hired as piece rate workers, daily wage workers, and assistants. Therefore, it is necessary to implement migration policies that prioritize the education and economic advancement of women, as female education plays a critical role in enabling women to make the decision to migrate and/or pursue better employment opportunities. Establishing pay should follow established guidelines, regardless of whether it is hourly, weekly, time- or piece-rated, or full-time.

6. Background of Migrant Workers Prior to Migration

We also examined the pre-work status of migrant workers before migration across selected occupational categories in Table 14.2. Service, agriculture, and trade have been reported to be the main economic activities of workers before their migration and settlement for present activities. Nearly 5.05% of workers have reported that they were engaged in agriculture before migrating to the present location. Those engaged in trade or business before migration had been reported to be 0.25%. However, the majority of migrant workers (38) were engaged in studies. Table 14.2 depicts that 26.77% female workers were studying before migration, and only about 0.25% of migrant workers were engaged in service work before migration.

In all occupational categories, the majority of workers were studying and carrying out agriculture, trade, and service work before migration. However, 18.43% of female migrants were found unemployed before migration. The above analysis, therefore, implies that there is a clear economic gain for informal sector female workers (migrants) after migration, as most of the unemployed workers (18.43%) and students (9.60%) were able to get jobs in different segments of this sector.

Table 14.2.   Pre-work Status of Migrants and Non-migrants.

Work Status	Migrants		Non-migrants		Total	
	Female	%	Female	%	Female	%
Agriculture	20	5.05	3	0.76	23	5.81
Trade/business	1	0.25	3	0.76	4	1.01
Service	1	0.25	22	5.56	23	5.81
Students	38	9.6	68	17.17	106	26.77
Unemployed	73	18.43	45	11.36	118	29.8
Others	41	10.35	81	20.45	122	30.81
Waiting period for getting jobs						
1–10 days	92	23.23	103	26.01	195	49.24
10–20 days	30	7.58	48	12.12	78	19.7
20–30 days	12	3.03	15	3.79	27	6.82
1–6 months	20	5.05	42	10.61	62	15.66
More than 6 months	20	5.05	14	3.54	34	8.59
Total	174	43.93	222	56.06	396	100

Source: Primary Survey, 2018–2019.

6.1. Waiting Period for Job

We now examine the waiting period (Table 14.2) of migrant workers for jobs. About 23.23% of respondents reported that they had to wait only for a few days (1–10 days) or their job was fixed after a few days of their arrival or departure. About 7.58% of migrant workers reported that they had to wait for 20 days, and 3.03% reported that they had to wait for almost 20 days to 1 month (Table 14.2). Only 5.05% reported that they had to wait for a job for one month to six months, and 5.05 migrants had to wait for more than six months, respectively. Thus, the maximum number of workers (23.33% migrant and 26.01% non-migrants) waited only up to 10 days in the informal sector. This finding confirms that to enter the urban informal sector, women workers require only ten days to get low-paid jobs such as domestic servants, garment workers, construction laborers, and tailors.

7. The Paradoxical Question of Migrant Workers' Workplace Vulnerabilities and Access to Social Security Benefits

7.1. Stress

A considerable proportion of women migrants was facing problems of physical and mental stress and health, overtime work, absence of leave, and social security facilities at the workplace, which were possibly caused by the stress of earning a living in addition to managing household chores and trying to adjust in a different socio-cultural environment. Migrant workers mostly live/work in areas where the living/working conditions are even worse than what they left behind in their native place.

Due to the prevailing stress among the migrant workers, health-related vulnerabilities were observed. A significant proportion, that is, 6.06%, of migrants had blood pressure (Table 14.3). Out of total migrant workers, 7.32% reported that they are always stressed, and 24.24% of women workers were of the view that, to some extent, they have to bear stress and anxiety. However, 12.37% of female migrants reported that they had never faced stress at the workplace (Table 14.3). More than 30% of female migrants (33.08%) reported problems related to weakness and fatigue. Thus, the most reported problems were fatigue and weakness. Thus, health problems due to stress and high workloads are of great concern for women migrants, mainly in the informal sector. To some extent, migrant women also bear the risk of sexual harassment and abuse at the workplace.

7.2. Working Overtime

When asked about overtime work, some migrant women workers said that they are required to work overtime if they cannot complete the assigned production targets in the predetermined time period. Overtime work in the informal sector

Table 14.3.   Extent/Nature of Stress and Payment for Overtime Work at Workplace.

	Migrants		Non-migrants		Total	
Stress	**Female**	**%**	**Female**	**%**	**Female**	**%**
Always	20	7.32	12	4.40	32	12.12
To some extent	96	24.24	89	22.47	185	46.72
Never	49	12.37	114	28.79	163	41.16
Total	174	43.94	222	56.06	396	100.00
Nature of stress						
Anger	6	1.52	9	2.27	15	3.79
Fatigue/weakness	131	33.08	193	48.74	324	81.82
High BP	24	6.06	12	3.03	36	9.09
Irritation	13	3.28	8	2.02	21	5.30
Total	174	43.94	222	56.06	396	100.00
Payment for overtime work						
Yes	16	4.04	21	5.30	37	9.34
No	8	2.02	7	1.77	15	3.79
Total	24	6.06	28	7.07	52	13.13

Source: Primary Survey, 2018–2019.

of Uttar Pradesh was minimal, as very few women workers, that is, 13.13%, had reported overtime work (Table 14.3). Though, according to the wage law, overtime work must be remunerated at double the standard wage rates, workers are often paid less in the informal labor markets. Average working hours and days were greater for these workers. They earned low wages, worked very long hours without any overtime benefits, and were almost without any leave or social protection. In contrast, in the state of Karnataka (Bengaluru), most workers are usually paid at the stipulated rate, which is double the standard rate for all hours of overtime (Gangly, 2013).

7.3. Migrant Workers' Access to Social Security Benefits

Migrant workers' accessibility to social security benefits forms a paradoxical question because the migration of labor has been identified by Mitra et al. (2017) as the primary means through which industry accumulates profits in the contemporary capitalist economy. Jain and Sharma (2018) corroborated their vulnerability by classifying migrant workers as a "super-exploited" workforce, deprived of the entire gamut of labor legislation and labor regulatory institutions, which eventually allows employers to increase their profits by cutting costs associated with compliance with labor regulations and social security benefits. Even NCEUS (2007) stated that, on the one hand, migrant workers are economically vulnerable and socially marginalized groups representing rural populations who are dispossessed of their subsistence-based livelihoods, along with the loss of resources to rural elites and corporations, as Prasad (2016) put it. Academia notes that in India, economic growth has been triggered in large urban towns, where huge investments are made in the services and manufacturing sectors, along with a booming construction sector and the real estate boom (Das, 2015). Rural–urban migration plays a critical role in this urban-led economic growth model, with surplus rural workforces undergoing distress migration by fleeing to urban areas as wage-earners and footloose workers (Breman, 2013), keeping aside their garb of agricultural workers. Urban sectors prefer employing migrant workers because these marginalized workers are pushed to work for adverse terms and conditions, thus forming a cheap workforce that can be hired and fired at will, as the Aajeevika Bureau (2020) puts it.

Jain and Sharma (2018) illustrated that these workers get trapped in a vicious cycle of vulnerability being transferred from one lot to another, causing the intergenerational transfer of poverty. Shyamsundar and Sapkal (2020) refer to them as "job thieves" and are excluded from social support or platforms for collective bargaining, such as trade unions and local workers' mobilization (Sharma et al., 2014). The vulnerability merely gets aggravated when migrant workers land up in an unorganized sector as employers try to maximize their profits by exploiting workers on wages as well as working conditions.

There are various forms of discriminatory practices against women migrants as compared to non-migrants in the informal sector. In addition to problems like relatively lower wages, women are not given maternity leave or social security facilities in terms of PF, pension, gratuity, etc., at the workplace. The social security benefits of female migrants were assessed through their access to social security schemes (Table 14.4). Overall, no female migrant had accessed a social security facility or a maternity leave facility. However, access was slightly higher among non-migrants (Table 14.4).

Hence, discrimination against migrant women workers takes numerous forms, ranging from the absence of social security to the absence of maternal leave benefits at the workplace. In general, migrants live in deplorable conditions and have extremely poor health status. They do not enjoy basic health benefits like maternity leave and social security benefits. In addition, for migrants, the tenure of work in industries like construction is very unpredictable, which leaves them with a sense of insecurity about their income and work (Solanki, 2002, cited in Misra & Alma, 2014).

7.4. Saving Pattern

There were significant differences between female migrants and non-migrants in the informal sector in Uttar Pradesh. About half of the migrants had bank accounts in contrast to only one-fifth of the migrants having Bima (Table 14.4). The use of informal channels like employers, mahajans, and sahukars for saving

Table 14.4.   Social Security Benefits.

Types of Social Security	Migrants		Non-migrants		Total	
	Female	%	Female	%	Female	%
PF	8	2.02	10	2.53	18	4.55
Maternity leave	3	0.76	5	1.26	8	2.02
Gratuity	6	1.52	6	1.52	12	3.03
All of the above	2	0.51	8	2.02	10	2.53
None of these	155	39.14	193	48.74	348	87.88
Total	174	43.94	222	56.06	396	100.00
Source of saving						
Bank	66	51.97	102	58.62	168	55.81
Bima	22	17.32	35	20.11	57	18.94
PO	24	18.90	27	15.52	51	16.94
Other	15	11.81	10	5.75	25	8.31
Total	127	100	174	100	301	100

Source: Primary Survey, 2018–2019.

money was also popular among them (about 11.81%). Female migrants had saved money by keeping to themselves.

According to these migrants, they were saving money for financial emergencies. However, they have also reported that they could neither save much to improve their conditions nor save enough to live comfortably in a new place. Over half of unorganized workers (i.e., 55.81%) had bank accounts; among them, 51.97% were migrant workers. Contrary to this, 23.99% of female unorganized workers reported that they were unable to save money.

8. Causes of Female Migration

The section argues that academia has delineated the contours of female labor migration based on a preconceived approach to migration, which prodigiously beckons social over economic reasons for female migration. Very pertinently, studies have stated that the female migration data have hitherto been dismissed as irrelevant to development-oriented analysis of migration in India because the proportions of women identified as moving for employment-related reasons are exceedingly small (Mazumdar & Agnihotri, 2013). Notwithstanding the fact that the majority of women are shown as migrating for marriage, unlike men, who are shown as moving predominantly for employment-related reasons (Mazumdar & Agnihotri, 2013). Strikingly, decades of data on migration have, thus, presented a largely unchanging picture of women migrating for mainly social reasons and men for economic reasons. The net result has been an established tendency among policymakers and analysts to maintain a complete statistical silence on the scale, dimensions, and patterns of female labor migration. This section attempts to lay bare the key gendered features of labor migration and examine major reasons for migration among women unorganized workers. There are certain traditional push factors, such as low wages, large families, a lack of sources of income, seasonal employment, a lack of basic facilities, etc., that affect the rate of migration to a very significant extent. Mitra and Gupta (2002) stated that the decision to migrate involves contextual factors such as push factors, which force migrants out of rural areas, and pull factors, which attract migrants to urban areas (cited in Misra & Alma, 2014). It would imply that expectations of high earnings and better job opportunities have pushed female workers into the informal urban sector. Generally, poor job prospects have been stated as the primary cause of migration for workers. Fig. 14.1 reveals that poor job prospects (54.02%), low income (36.78%), and availability of poor work opportunities (42.53%) were the most frequently reported push factors by the migrant workers. Beside this, small size of agricultural land (9.20%), poverty (13.79%), and family movement, viz., husband's job (8.05%) were some other reported push factors.

The most frequently cited reasons to migrate (pull factor) in urban areas were better income, good job prospects, and availability of better job opportunities. Lack of basic facilities, large families, and poverty were infrequently reported as push factors for migrating from their native places (Fig. 14.1). Thus, we find employment-oriented migration of females from their native places to the urban informal sector.

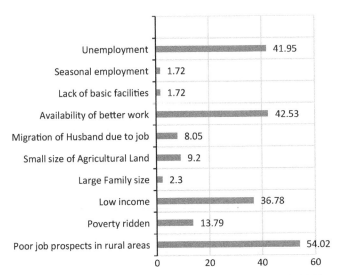

Fig. 14.1.   Causes of Migration. *Source*: Primary Survey, 2018–2019.

9. Determinants of Income Vulnerabilities for Migrants and Non-migrants

As mentioned earlier, in the present chapter, an attempt has been made to highlight the vulnerabilities of female migrants as compared to non-migrants in the unorganized urban labor market. The above examination reveals that unemployment and low wages, that is, income vulnerability, and a few other reasons discussed above, prevailing in the rural labor market, push female workers to seek better employment in the urban informal market. Due to income or financial vulnerability, workers in poorer areas often look for higher wages and better employment opportunities, which can usually be found in well-developed urban cities (Simpson Nicole, 2022). In the informal urban market, migrant workers provide essential services to the places where they work. They also contribute to the wealth of aging societies and the sustainability of these areas' welfare and employment systems. However, migrant workers can be confronted with additional vulnerabilities. Women migrants are more vulnerable financially than their non-migrant counterparts. Hence, in the present section, we have tried to find out the differences in factors related to the income vulnerability (low income) of migrant workers and non-migrant workers. For identifying the factors affecting migrant and non-migrant workers' income, OLS regression has been used. We have also carried out mean comparisons of the selected variables to highlight the basic differences between migrants' and non-migrant workers' socioeconomic and demographic characteristics.

Our dataset covers 396 female informal workers, consisting of 174 migrants and 222 non-migrant workers. Comparisons of the means for the selected variables show clear differences between migrants and non-migrants. It is clear that migrant workers are comparatively poorer or more vulnerable than non-migrant workers, as average monthly income was found to be significantly higher for non-migrant workers. These workers also have fewer dependents, and the number of average earners per family is higher than that of migrants. On the contrary, migrant workers have a larger family size, and the number of dependents is also high.

To find out the difference in socioeconomic determinants of income vulnerabilities of migrant and non-migrant workers, the results of the coefficient and t-statistics were used. Table 14.5 shows the estimates of the determinants of income (monthly) of migrants and non-migrators using the following regression equation:

$$\text{Ln (MI) } y = a + b1X1 + b2X2 + \ldots + bnXn + \epsilon i$$

where y = log monthly income (dependent variable) and $b1x1, b2x2, \ldots bnxn$ are regression coefficients of selected variables (independent).

Hence, we have estimated a multivariate linear regression model where monthly income (log) is taken as the dependent variable, and the independent variables considered are age, age^2 (proxy for experience), union membership

Table 14.5. Results of OLS Regression.

Variables	Migrants			Non-migrants		
[Monthly Income (Log) (DV)]	Coef.	*t*	*P > t*	Coef.	*t*	*P > t*
Age	0.0060	0.03	0.97	−0.1442	−3.89	0.00
Age² (proxy for experience)	−0.0004	−0.17	0.87	−0.0008	−3.11	0.00
Union membership	−0.5600	−4.53	0.00	−0.5600	−4.53	0.00
Participation in voting	0.3494	0.59	0.55	0.1039	1.57	0.12
Awareness about labor laws	0.1075	1.62	0.11	1.3740	2.42	0.02
OBC	−1.8702	−2.51	0.01	−0.4057	−6.01	0.00
SC	−2.4404	−3.89	0.00	−0.1489	−1.52	0.13
Literate	0.4808	1.00	0.32	0.5966	5.51	0.00
Secondary	1.4808	2.55	0.01	0.1942	2.97	0.00
Higher-secondary	2.1427	2.54	0.01	0.5293	7.27	0.00
Graduate and above	2.4850	3.64	0.00	0.6025	8.75	0.00
Married				−0.6255	−5.72	0.00
Unmarried	3.0019	4.97	0.00	0.2560	2.47	0.01
Constant	−4.1035	−1.32	0.19	9.3623	38.59	0.00
Prob > *F*	0.00			0.00		
R-squared	0.5081			0.5821		
Adj *R*-squared	0.4681			0.5558		
Number of observation	174			222		

Source: Based on Primary Survey, 2018–2019.

(1 if member, 0 if otherwise), participation in voting (1 if participated in the last election, 0 if otherwise), awareness about labor laws (1 if aware, 0 if otherwise; the caste status of the worker is captured by a dummy variable that assumes values 1 for the SC, OBC, and GEN caste worker and 0 for otherwise); education has a powerful impact on reducing the vulnerability of workers, as it improves the potential for earnings in the job market and further contributes toward making themselves less vulnerable. The education level of the worker is denoted by a dummy variable that assumes values 1 for the literate worker and 0 for the illiterate worker: secondary (1 for secondary, 0 for otherwise), higher-secondary (1 for higher-secondary, 0 for otherwise), graduate and above (1 for

graduate and above, 0 for otherwise), married (1 for married, 0 for otherwise), and unmarried (1 for unmarried, 0 for otherwise).

A one-year increase in age will decrease the monthly income of non-migrant workers by 14.42%. Contrary to this, it is not significant in the case of migrant workers. A 1% increase in union membership will further increase the monthly income of migrants by 40.59%. However, the significant ($t = -4.53$) but negative impact of union membership in the case of non-migrant workers indicates that there is no relationship between income and union membership. Regression results confirm that people with larger (higher) monthly incomes reported lower levels of experience both in the case of migrant and non-migrant workers; however, this relationship is significant in the case of non-migrant workers (values of $P < 0.00$). So, it can be asserted that there is no relationship between experience (work) and income (vulnerability). Furthermore, the coefficients on education dummies are positive and highly significant in the case of those migrant workers who were literate (secondary, higher secondary, graduation, and above), indicating an increase (by 14.81%, 21.42%, and 24.85%, respectively) in the income of migrant workers after a 1% increase in secondary, higher secondary, and graduation levels of schooling. This implies that prevailing illiteracy among female workers in the informal sector has a significant effect on vulnerability in terms of income (income vulnerability). Similar results have been noticed in the case of non-migrant workers. This clearly exhibits the significant effect of education on income. Unmarried female migrant workers have a 30.02% higher monthly income than married females, implying that unmarried female migrant workers are less vulnerable as compared to married and widowed females. Similarly, the negative effect of income on married non-migrant workers reveals that non-migrant workers who are married have 62.55% lower monthly income, indicating the vulnerability of married females in the informal urban market. This is possibly because the married female (compared to unmarried and widowed females) has no problem regarding the type of job or sector they engage themselves in to earn a living. No significant impact of awareness of employment laws has been noticed on the income of migrant workers; however, 1% increase in awareness of employment laws among non-migrant workers will increase their monthly income by 13.74%. There is a negative and significant relationship between caste (OBC and SC) and the income vulnerability of informal workers (Table 14.2). Workers (migrants) who belong to the lower caste (SC/OBC) are more likely to work in low-income jobs, showing the disadvantaged position of women in the labor market.

Hence, the above analyses highlight interesting differences between the determinants of migrant and non-migrant workers. However, one common characteristic of migrant and non-migrant workers is that they are far from their socio-economic development and well-being, as both of these groups belong to the informal labor market.

10. Conclusion and Policy Implications

Female migrants are more vulnerable to discrimination and exploitation in the informal sector of the economy because many of them are poor, illiterate, and live in slums and hazardous locations. Beside this, female migrants are vulnerable due to gender-based discrimination in wages and job status. They mostly work in the informal sector and get a very low wage. They have to face unhealthy, stressful, and dangerous working conditions at the workplace. The real solution to this issue would be to enforce all relevant labor laws for migrant workers so that segmentation of the labor market becomes weak and workers get a rational and equal right and status in the labor market. However, with the modernization and increasing autonomy of women, it is expected that the volume and rate of female migration will increase in the future, mostly for economic reasons. Therefore, female migration is an area that needs further exploration and research to understand it better.

Over time, several laws have been enacted to give protection for migration workers' rights by the government, such as the Inter-State Migrant Workmen (Regulation of Employment and Conditions of Service) Act, 1979, which extends the provision of minimum wages and several welfare allowances like journey allowance, displacement allowance, allowances for residential accommodations, medical allowance, protective clothing, and so forth (Das, 2020). Women migrant workers' deplorable conditions point towards the failure of the current welfare policies of the government and violations of the basic human rights of workers. The government needs to revamp their welfare schemes along with other administrative and economic efforts that could meet the aspirations of the workers in the informal sector of the urban economy. Very pertinently, Das (2020) has stated to focus on the ardent welfare approach, pinning them with cash benefits along with job security. It is time to build a strong center–state relationship to ensure the rights of migrated workers, thus following the recommendations of the first taskforce, "Working Group on Migration under the Ministry of Housing and Urban Poverty Alleviation," in 2015. The government should boost the social protection of these workers through self-registration, hence promoting the digitization of registration records so that it can deliver benefit to workers across India, overcoming inter-state barriers.

References

Aajeevika Bureau. (2020). *Unlocking the Urban: Reimagining migrant lives in cities Post-COVID-19.* https://ruralindiaonline.org/en/library/resource/unlocking-the-urban-reimagining-migrant-lives-in-cities-post-covid-19/

Agrawal, A. (2006). *Migrant women and work.* Sage Publication.

Ajith Kumar, N. (2011). *Vulnerability of migrants and responsiveness of the state: The case of unskilled migrant workers in Kerala, India* [Paper presentation]. The international conference on "Changing nature of forced migration: Vulnerabilities in South and South-east Asia", 22–24 September 2011, Asian University for Women, Chittagong, Bangladesh.

Banerjee, A., & Raju, S. (2009). Gendered mobility: Women migrants and work in urban India. *Economic & Political Weekly, xliv,* 28.

Banerjee, B. (1986). *Rural to urban migration and the urban labour market: A case study of Delhi.* Himalaya Pub. House.

Banerjee, B. (1991). The determinants of migrating with a pre-arranged job and of the initial duration of urban unemployment: An analysis based on Indian data on rural-to-urban migrants. *Journal of Development Economics, 36*(2), 337–351.

Banerjee, B., & Bucci, G. A. (1994). On-the-job search after entering urban employment: An analysis based on Indian migrants. *Oxford Bulletin of Economics and Statistics, 56*(1), 33–47.

Breman, J. (1996). *Footloose labour: Working in India's informal economy.* Cambridge University Press.

Breman, J. (2013). *At work in the informal economy of India.* Oxford University Press.

Das, D. (2020). Regional disparities of growth and internal migrant workers in informal sectors in the age of COVID-19. *Journal of Public Affairs, 20*(4), e2268. https://doi.org/10.1002/pa.2268

Das, U. (2015). Can the rural employment guarantee scheme reduce rural out-migration: Evidence from West Bengal, India. *The Journal of Development Studies, 51*(6), 621–641. https://doi.org/10.1080/00220388.2014.989997.

De, S. (2019). *Internal migration in India grows, but inter-state movements remain low.* https://blogs.worldbank.org/peoplemove/internal-migration-india grows-inter-state-movements-remain-low

Deshingkar, P., & Start, D. (2003). *Seasonal migration for livelihoods in India: Coping, accumulation and exclusion* (Vol. 111). Overseas Development Institute.

Ganguly, A. (2013). *Wage structures in the Indian Garment Sector.* Society for Labour and Development and Asia Floor Wage Alliance. http://asia.floorwage.org/resources/wage-reports/wage-structures-in-the-indian-garment-industry.

Ghosh, J. (2002). Globalisation, export-oriented employment for women and social policy: A case study of India. *Social Scientist, 30*(11/12), 17–60.

ILO-WTO (2009). *Joint study on trade and informal employment: Globalization and informal jobs in developing countries,* 12 January. https://www.ilo.org/publications/globalization-and-informal-jobs-developing-countries-joint-study

Jain, P., & Sharma, A. (2018). Seasonal migration of Adivasis from Southern Rajasthan: A political economy view of labour mobility. *Journal of Interdisciplinary Economics, 31*(1), 63–99.

Jayaram, N., Jain, P., & Sugathan, S. S. (2019). No city for migrant women: Construction workers' experiences of exclusion from urban governance and discrimination in labour markets in Ahmedabad. *Gender & Development, 27*(1), 85–104.

Jayaram, N., & Varma, D. (2020). Examining the 'labour' in labour migration: Migrant workers' informal work arrangements and access to labour rights in urban sectors. *The Indian Journal of Labour Economics, 63,* 999–1019. https://doi.org/10.1007/s41027-020-00288-5.

Majumdar, A. (1980). *In-migration and informal sector: A case study of urban Delhi.* Vision Books.

Marjit, S., & Beladi, H. (2008). Trade, employment and the informal sector. *Trade and Development Review, 1*(1), 453–461.

Martin, P. L. (2004). Labour migration in Asia. *Inter-national Migration Review, 25*(1), 176–193.

Mazumdar, I., & Agnihotri, I. (2014). Traversing myriad trails: Tracking gender and labor migration across India. In T. D. Truong, D. Gasper, J. Handmaker, & S. Bergh (Eds.), *Migration, gender and social justice: Perspectives on human insecurity* (pp. 123–151). Springer.

Mehta, B. S., & Awasthi, I. C. (2022). Dynamics of urban labour market and informality. *The Indian Journal of Labour Economics, 65,* 19–37. https://doi.org/10.1007/s41027-022-00354-0.

Misra, P., & Alma, S. (2014). Urban informal sector & migrants. *International Journal of Business and Administration Research Review, 2*(4), 72–79.

Mitra, A. (1994). *Urbanisation, slums, informal sector employment, and poverty: An exploratory study, Delhi.* BR Publishing Corporation.

Mitra, A., & Gupta, I. (2002, January 12). Rural migrants and labour segmentation – Micro-level evidence from Delhi slums. *Economic and Political Weekly, 37*(02) 163–168.

Mitra, I., Samaddar, R., & Sen, S. (2017). *Accumulation in post-colonial capitalism.* Springer.

Mundle, S. (1993). Unemployment and financing of relief employment in a period of stabilisation: India, 1992–94. *Economic and Political Weekly, 28*, 173–181.

NCEUS. (2007). *Report on conditions of work and promotion of livelihoods in the unorganised sector.* https://dcmsme.gov.in/condition_of_workers_sep_2007.pdf

Pillai, N. (2007). *Female employment in service sector: Trends and patterns* [Paper presentation]. Seminar on 'Making growth inclusive with reference to employment generation', 28–29 June 2008, CESP-JNU and IIAS, Shimla.

Prasad, A. (2016). Adivasi women, agrarian change and forms of labour in neo-liberal India. *Agrarian South: Journal of Political Economy, 5*(1), 20–49.

Rajan, S. I., & Sumeetha, M. (2020). Women workers on the move. In S. I. Rajan & M. Sumeetha (Eds.), *Handbook of internal migration in India* (pp. 408–414). Sage.

Rogaly, B. (1999). Dangerous Liaisons? Seasonal labour migration and agrarian change in West Bengal. In B. Rogaly, B. Harris-White, & S. Bose (Eds.), *Sonar Bangla: Agricultural growth and agrarian change in West Bengal and Bangladesh* (pp. 357–380). Sage Publications.

Sassen-Koob. (1984). Notes on incorporation of third world women into wage labour through immigrations and off-shore production. *International Migration Review, 18*(4), 1144–1167.

Shanti, K. (1991). Issues relating to economic migration of females. *The Indian Journal of Labour Economics, 34*(4), 335–346.

Sharma, A., Poonia, S., Ali, Z., & Khandelwal, R. (2014). *Their own country: A profile of labour migration from Rajasthan.* Aajeevika Bureau.

Shyamsundar, K. R., & Sapkal, R. (2020). Changes to labour laws by state governments will lead to anarchy in the labour market. *Economic and Political Weekly, 55*(23), 205.

Simpson Nicole, B. (2022). *Demographic and economic determinants of migration-push and pull factors drive the decision to move or stay* [IZA World of Labor] 373v2. https://doi.org/10.15185/izawol. 373.v2 | Nicole B. Simpson © | July 2022 [Previous version June 2017] | wol.iza.org

Singh, A. M. (1978). Rural–urban migration of women in among urban poor in India: Causes and consequences. *Social Action, 28*(4), 326–356.

Sovani, N. V. (1964). The analysis of "over-urbanization". *Economic Development and Cultural Change, 12*(2), 113–112.

Srinivasan, S., & Illango, P. (2012). A study on the problems of migrant women workers in Thuvakudi, Trichy district. *IOSR Journal of Humanities and Social Science (JHSS), 4*(4), 45–50. www.Iosrjournals.Org www.iosrjournals.org

Srivastava, R. (2003). *An overview of migration in India, its impacts and key issues* [Paper presentation]. The regional conference on migration, development and Pro-poor policy choices in Asia, 22–24 June 2003, Dhaka, Bangladesh.

Srivastava, R. (2012). *Internal migration in India: An overview of its features, trends, and policy challenges* (pp. 1–47) [National workshop on internal migration and human development in India workshop compendium Vol. II: Workshop papers October 2012]. United Nations Educational, Scientific and Cultural Organisation, and UNICEF India Country Office, New Delhi. ISBN 978-81-89218-45-4.

Srivastava, R. (2020). Labour migration, vulnerability, and development policy: The pandemic as infexion point? *The Indian Journal of Labour Economics, 63*, 859–883. https://doi.org/10.1007/s41027-020-00301-x

Srinivasan, S., & Illango, P. (2012). A study on the problems of migrant women workers in Thuvakudi, Trichy district. *IOSR Journal of Humanities and Social Science, 4*(4), 45–50. www.Iosrjournals.Org www.iosrjournals.org

Verite. (2010). *Indian workers in domestic textile production and middle east – Based manufacturing, infrastructure and construction.* http://digitalcommons.ilr.cornell.edu/cgi /viewcontent.cgi?article=2176&context=globaldocs.

Appendix: Socio-economic and Demographic Characteristics of Migrant and Non-migrant Workers

Variables	Migrants		Non-migrants		Total sample	
F/M>	F	%	F	%	F	%
Caste						
General	34	(19.54)	71	(31.98)	105	(26.52)
OBC	55	(31.61)	93	(41.89)	148	(37.37)
SC	85	(48.85)	58	(26.13)	143	(36.11)
Education						
Illiterate	78	(44.83)	36	(16.22)	114	(28.79)
Up to primary	43	(24.71)	61	(27.48)	104	(26.26)
Secondary	23	(13.22)	72	(32.43)	95	(23.99)
Higher secondary	30	(17.24)	53	(23.87)	83	(20.96)
Religion						
Hindu	143	(82.18)	173	(77.93)	316	(79.80)
Muslim	30	(17.24)	47	(21.17)	77	(19.44)
Sikh	1	(0.57)	2	(0.90)	3	(0.76)
Christian		(0.00)	0	(0.00)	0	(0.00)
Marital status						
Married	127	(72.99)	129	(58.11)	256	(64.65)
Unmarried	36	(20.69)	77	(34.68)	113	(28.54)
Divorced/widow	11	(6.32)	16	(7.21)	27	(6.82)
Age						
Below 21	20	(11.49)	34	(15.38)	54	(13.64)
21–35	97	(55.75)	120	(54.30)	217	(54.80)
35–50	54	(31.03)	62	(27.80)	116	(29.29)
50 and above	3	(1.72)	6	(2.71)	9	(2.27)
Monthly income						
Below 5,000	71	(40.80)	114	(51.35)	185	(46.72)
5,000–10,000	91	(52.30)	95	(42.79)	186	(46.97)
11,000–15,000	9	(5.17)	11	(4.95)	20	(5.05)
16,000–20,000	1	(0.57)	1	(0.45)	2	(0.51)

(Continued)

Variables	Migrants		Non-migrants		Total sample	
F/M>	F	%	F	%	F	%
Above 20,000	2	(1.15)	1	(0.45)	3	(0.76)
Mean monthly income	4,025.14		6,008.20		5,136.84	
Nature of employment						
Full time	151	86.78	209	94.14	360	90.91
Part time	23	13.22	13	5.86	36	9.09
Nature of wage						
Daily	42	10.61	16	4.04	58	14.65
Weekly	26	6.57	13	3.28	39	9.85
Monthly	106	26.77	193	48.74	299	75.51
Type of wage						
Time-wage	100	25.25	164	41.41	264	66.67
Piece-rate wage	57	14.39	52	13.13	109	27.53
Contract wage	17	4.29	6	1.52	23	5.81
Total (sample)	174	43.94	222	56.06	396	100.00

Source: Primary Survey, 2018–2019.

Chapter 15

Informal Employment, Gender Patterns and Policies in MENA Countries

Philippe Adair[a], Shireen AlAzzawi[b,c] and Vladimir Hlasny[d]

[a]*University Paris-Est Créteil, France*
[b]*Santa Clara University, USA*
[c]*Economic Research Forum, Egypt*
[d]*Ewha Womans University, Korea*

Abstract

Middle East and North African (MENA) countries notoriously exhibit high prevalence of unemployment and informality among a large fraction of population and, at the same time, gender gaps in labour force participation and job mobility. Why is there such persistent labour market segmentation? What is the impact and potential of various formalisation policies in several MENA countries (Egypt, Jordan, Lebanon, Morocco, Palestine and Tunisia)? An overview of the informal economy is provided with respect to taxonomy, coverage and drivers. Transition matrices and multinomial logistic regressions are applied to longitudinal microdata from labour market panel surveys (LMPS) (in Egypt, Jordan and Tunisia), focusing on workers' occupational mobility regarding their pre-existing status, age cohort, gender and other demographics. Persistent segmentation and low occupational mobility in all countries suggest that informal employment is not driven by choice on the labour supply side but by structural constraints on the demand side. Existing formalisation policies encapsulating distinct stick and carrot strategies and targeting business versus workers achieve rather modest impacts. Promoting social and solidarity enterprises and extending microfinance to informal enterprises are promising policies for the creation of decent jobs.

Keywords: Dualism; formalisation policies; gender; informal employment; MENA countries; logistic regressions; occupational mobility; labour force segmentation; transition matrices

Informal Economy and Sustainable Development Goals:
Ideas, Interventions and Challenges, 297–316
Copyright © 2024 by Philippe Adair, Shireen AlAzzawi and Vladimir Hlasny
Published under exclusive licence by Emerald Publishing Limited
doi:10.1108/978-1-83753-980-220241016

1. Introduction

In his pioneering paper, Lewis (1954) suggested that the phenomenon that would be later on coined as the informal economy (henceforth informality) was rather an outdated form of dualism that could go away with growth. In contrast, Harris and Todaro (1970) paved the way for a probabilistic analysis that left room for the plausibility that informality would persist.

In the 1970s, two distinct approaches loosely identified informality according to either a business definition (Hart, 1973) or the job definition of the International Labour Office (ILO, 1972), and this bifurcation prevails in multi-criteria analysis even 50 years on (Charmes & Adair, 2022). Statistical guidelines from the ILO in 1993 first restricted the definition of informality to businesses and the informal sector, before extending the definition in 2003 to informal jobs. The ILO *Manual* (ILO, 2013) ultimately encapsulated both of these distinct definitions. Admittedly, data collection on informality is challenging (Ackrill & Igudia, 2023).

Meanwhile, informality became progressively a major concern in as much as informal jobs together with informal businesses prove pervasive, or almost 'normal'. Informality was part of the questionnaire in cross-sectional surveys such as labour force surveys (LFS), which nurtured databases such as ILOSTAT, whereas panel data surveys started collecting data on informal employment including the gender issue only in the 2000s (ILO, 2002). First policy assessments were launched in the 2010s, without much link with the contrasted theories addressing distinct sides of the labour and commodity markets, namely, dualism (segmentation), structuralism and institutionalism.

Existing empirical literature on the MENA region has tried to tackle these problems largely within individual countries, without using a cross-country or regional perspective. The literature also typically stops at reviewing the gender gaps statically and putting less emphasis on the different dynamics of men's and women's transitions into/from informality or economic inactivity. In light of these limitations in the extant literature, this chapter addresses the following questions: Why do MENA countries face persistent labour market segmentation? What are the gender patterns in occupational mobility in this respect? What is the impact of various formalisation policies on informality? We evaluate the conditions in six middle-income, oil-importing MENA economies: Egypt, Morocco and Tunisia in North Africa and Jordan, Lebanon and Palestine in the Middle East. These countries share many pervasive labour-market characteristics: dramatically low female participation rate, high youth unemployment, micro and small-size informal businesses providing most jobs and operating in low-productivity industries and informal employment constituting one-half of the labour force (Charmes, 2019).

The rest of the chapter is organised as follows. Section 2 addresses informality as regards the definitions and coverage in middle-income MENA countries. Section 3 starts out with selected stylised facts across Egypt, Jordan, Lebanon, Morocco, Palestine and Tunisia and then evaluates occupational status and mobility according to workers' initial position, age cohort and gender, using transition tables and multinomial logistic regressions applied to the available LMPS, in Egypt, Jordan and Tunisia. Section 4 assesses existing formalisation policies in the middle-income MENA countries, including distinct stick and carrot strategies, and business and worker targeting approaches. Section 5 concludes taking stock of the status quo and the policy responses in place and proposes ways forward towards a more equitable and sustainable state. In this respect, fostering social and solidarity enterprises and extending microfinance funding to informal enterprises appear to hold promise for decent jobs creation.

2. Literature Review

2.1. Transitions from School to Work: Entering the Labour Market or Else?

Mansuy and Werquin (2018), using data from one region, point out that informal employment predominates among young people in Morocco. The least educated have few occupational choices; they are essentially relegated into jobs that are neither paid nor protected by labour legislation. For young women, entry into the labour force is strongly dependent on their local environment and family context, whereas they are considerably more vulnerable to unemployment.

Barsoum et al. (2016) provide an overview of the school-to-work transition survey (SWTS), a household survey of young people aged 15–29 diagnosing labour market dynamics and monitoring policies in Egypt. The main findings are as follows: Gender disparity is key in as much *as* almost one-third of female working youth (28.9%) are unpaid family workers compared to 14.2% of male working youth. Egypt has very few young entrepreneurs: the self-employed constitute 26.1% of employed youth, including unpaid family workers (17.2%), own-account workers (6.3%) who are mostly males and employers (2.6%). Almost three-quarters of employed youth (73.9%) are wage-workers.

Mansuy and Werquin (2015) examine the quality of education, in terms of learning outcomes, as well as its ability to meet the needs of the private economic sector using SWTS micro data for Tunisia. They observe that vocational training is often informal in nature and undertaken on-the-job, which may explain the labour market mismatch.

Dimova et al. (2016) provide an overview on SWTS in the MENA region, implemented in 2012–2013 and 2014–2015, two rounds in Egypt, Jordan and Palestine, and one round in Lebanon and Tunisia. The paradox of gender disparities already observed in country reports is emphasised: Rising levels of educational attainment, especially among women, accompanied by insufficient demand for skilled workers – which particularly affects female workers – in the services sector-dominated economies of these countries are among the primary obstacles to the labour market transitions of youth. Low levels of entrepreneurship and the reluctance of youth to engage in vocational education (to acquire the skills requested in occupations) slow down the transitions from school to work.

According to Solati (2017), the rate of female labour force participation in the MENA region is the lowest in the world, primarily due to the strong institutions of patriarchy. Patriarchy makes female economic activities invisible to official labour statistics, driving many women to work in the informal sector or work as unpaid family workers. Thus, it is somewhat of an illusion that women in the region are not economically active.

The SWTS point out what happens before or when youth enter the labour market. SWTS could not take full advantage of two rounds, given the short time span between the rounds. Actually, their purpose has never been to explore where youth enter the labour market, with respect to the various segments of the labour market such as formal and informal sectors, or wage-employment versus self-employment, or to capture the gender patterns and the dynamics of occupational mobility. These issues are within the reach of the analyses of longitudinal surveys presented in this chapter.

2.2. Definitions and Theories of Informality: A Fuzzy Set and Happy Heuristics

Extant research over half a century suggests that the concept of informal economy aligns with happy heuristics but encapsulates diverse theories and distinct methodologies lacking consensus. Informality is, thus, better thought of as a 'fuzzy set' at the intersection of multi-criteria assessments of the informal economy, the non-observed economy and the shadow economy. This fuzziness affects the precision and adequacy of policies and regulations relating to informality in developing countries (Adair et al., 2022).

Informality encapsulates three key components: the informal sector, and informal activities within the formal sector and in households. The informal sector encompasses the unincorporated enterprises made up of unregistered own-account workers and employers with fewer than five permanent paid employees. Informal employment encompasses all precarious jobs carried out both in the informal sector (the largest component) and within formal enterprises and households. It includes domestic workers and household members producing goods and services for their own final use, where workers are not subject to labour regulations, income taxation or employer-provided social protection (Charmes, 2019).

According to Chen and Carré (2020), there is gender segmentation of informal employment according to status and income. The vulnerability to poverty risk is uneven between genders. In a five-prong classification of informal workers – as employers, regular informal employees, own-account workers, casual/irregular employees and unpaid family workers – men are over-represented among the three upper categories, whereas women concentrate in the two bottom categories wherein higher poverty risk prevails.

The stratification of regional formal and informal labour markets has attracted various explanations. A threefold spectrum of theories has tackled the emergence of informality, namely dualism, structuralism and institutionalism. According to a less optimistic interpretation of dualism (Lewis, 1954), persistent informality is due to labour market segmentation, namely barriers to entry in the formal economy affecting labour market supply (i.e. workers).

Labour market segmentation into formal versus informal jobs is not congruent with structuralism (Castells & Portes, 1989), given that the informal economy is not separated but rather subsumed by the formal economy under subcontracting arrangements (Chen, 2014). Such arrangements have been used in the region, for instance, to shrink production costs in the textile industry or in call centres in Tunisia and Morocco.

The institutionalist approach (De Soto, 1986) assumes that informality stems from inadequate regulation, and excessive bureaucracy and taxation, driving small firms and marginal workers to voluntarily step outside or being excluded from the formal economy. This is prevalent in Tunisia and other North African countries (De Soto, 2012). Hence, this viewpoint advocates removing constraints on informal entrepreneurs, and diminishing the costs borne by start-ups. The emphasis from the World Bank on lowering barriers to entry and to business activity, and levelling the competitive field, is consistent with institutionalism together with structuralism, as they focus on the labour demand side and the goods supply side (i.e. businesses).

La Porta and Shleifer (2014) provide a convincing comparative analysis supporting Lewis' dualistic theory and dismissing the two other theories. The authors contend that the size of the informal economy, as measured by the share of self-employment in total employment, declines with per capita income. This rather optimistic view suggests a spillover of growth and development. However, it does not preclude the implementation of adequate formalising policies. Notably, their definition of the informal economy is restricted to the employment in the informal sector and perhaps in households but overlooks the component of informal employment within the formal economy.

3. Methodology: Investigating Informal Employment in MENA Countries

3.1. Stylised Facts at the Aggregate Level

The common threads in literature on the MENA region labour markets are fragmentation; a duality between formal and informal private employment (Hlasny & AlAzzawi, 2020); and a growing trend of vulnerable employment, particularly among youths (aged 15–29). Once the rush associated with the school-to-work transition drives workers into informal jobs, they are at pain transitioning to formal employment later in their careers. Despite higher learning attainment, noteworthy is that female labour force participation in the MENA region (the lowest worldwide) has been rising very slowly from 2000 (19%) up to 2019 (20%) and even receded during 2016–2019 (ILOSTAT retrieved in World Bank Data Bank, 2022).

At the aggregate level, three stylised facts about MENA labour markets are noteworthy. Firstly, average (non-agricultural) informal employment is a structural phenomenon, standing around 50% of the work force throughout the 2000s and the 2010s. Secondly, informal employment has been counter cyclical, rising with economic slowdowns until the late 2000s, contracting with upswings of economic growth and experiencing a trend reversal in the early 2010s. The levels and trends of informal employment differ across countries according to the impact of economic shocks and policies designed to absorb these. Throughout the 2010s, the trend was rising in Egypt and Tunisia. Thirdly, informal employment is related negatively to GDP per capita, due to low factor productivity and value added in the informal sector, which can be measured (Charmes, 2019).

Unemployment and informality are not distributed uniformly across the MENA population and industries. Youth unemployment and informality, in particular, have been pervasive (Fehling et al., 2016; Suleiman, 2022). Fresh graduates, if they succeed at finding employment, land in informal jobs leaving workers with limited prospects for transition to decent work later in their careers. The informal sector, and micro and small enterprises (MSEs) lag behind the formal sector and conglomerates in factor productivity, value-added and fiscal receipts, in part, due to a mismatch between skill supply and demand, in a state where workers have few opportunities for lifetime vocational up skilling or retraining, and employers fail to invest in them.

Job creation in the region over the past decade has favoured manufacturing, building and construction, with an outsized share of informal workforce, while skilled services relying on formal workforce have stagnated. Public sector has also scaled down recruitment since the 2000s as part of macroeconomic and public sector reforms (Shahen et al., 2020).

3.2. Sources and Coverage of Informality in MENA Countries

Data on labour informality are patchy, and coverage remains poor, not least in the MENA. Data also vary in quality across MENA countries. Morocco is the only country with three representative surveys devoted to the informal sector (1999, 2007 and 2013). These surveys show that three in four Moroccan businesses consist of own-account micro-enterprises with only one worker (HCP, 2016; Lopez-Acevedo et al., 2021). In Egypt, the 2012 and 2018 representative surveys of household firms conducted by the Central Agency for Public Mobilization and Statistics and the Economic Research Forum (ERF) revealed that 62.5% of firms in 2018 consisted of the self-employed (1-person firms) and 31% were microenterprises (2–4 workers). The absence of national household surveys devoted to informal employment or enterprise surveys devoted to the informal sector is an ongoing challenge in much of the region including Jordan, Lebanon and Palestine.[1]

Informal employment in the region as scoped from the LFS or LMPS use relevant questions regarding social protection coverage although criteria across countries prove disparate. In the selected countries, the share of informal employment (including agriculture) has been highest in Morocco (77.22%) and lowest in Tunisia (44.80%), the two countries that do not avail of their LFS data through ILOSTAT.

---

[1]In Tunisia, the threshold for microenterprises (below six employees) is inconsistent with the definition (below five) used by the International Labour Organisation (ILO) and the World Bank Enterprise Surveys (WBES).

Table 15.1 displays statistics – on self-employed, wage employed, and vulnerable workers – by gender. Self-employment overlaps to a large extent with informal and most vulnerable forms of work, such as male own-account workers and female contributing family workers or casual/irregular workers.

The 2016 *Sahwa* youth survey covering 7,816 individuals aged 15–29 from 4 MENA countries (Algeria, Morocco, Tunisia and Egypt) provides additional evidence of gender gaps (Weber et al., 2021). Despite an even distribution for young males and females in the sample, participation rate among 3,027 active people is over twice as high for males (54.5%) than for females (23.1%), a result in line with that of larger non-weighted samples in LFS (ILOSTAT). One-quarter of the labour force is unemployed, disproportionately affecting women. Two in three men and one in three women are informal (Gherbi & Adair, 2020). These high prevalence rates of informal employment without social protection among youths of both genders (Merouani et al., 2018) are consistent with a U-shaped lifecycle pattern: informality declines from youth to maturity (Gatti et al., 2014) and rises again among the older age group.

Evidence from the *Sahwa* survey also shows substantial income gaps between informal/formal jobs and across genders. This supports the segmentation theory. The formal/informal employee income ratio is similar for females (43.77%) and for males (43.65%), just as the formal/informal self-employed income ratio (55.33% and 54.51%, respectively). In contrast, gender pay gap is lower among formal workers (21.82%) than among informal workers (24.05%), illustrating the absence of safeguard mechanisms in the informal sector.

This study relies on the LMPS, currently available for Egypt (2012, 2018), Jordan (2010, 2016) and Tunisia (2014). LMPS are harmonised, administered and disseminated by national statistical offices in partnership with a large think

Table 15.1. Distribution of Workforce Status and Vulnerability in Six MENA Countries by Gender, 2019 (%).

Country	Self-employed[a]			Wage Employees			Vulnerable[b]		
	Female	Male	Total	Female	Male	Total	Female	Male	Total
Egypt	*31.3*	30.18	30.43	68.63	*69.82*	*69.57*	*27.73*	15.41	17.97
Jordan	2.30	16.24	13.92	*97.70*	*83.76*	*86.08*	1.58	12.37	10.58
Lebanon	15.01	*44.39*	*37.48*	84.99	55.61	62.53	13.84	*35.73*	*30.58*
Morocco	*57.11*	*45.89*	*48.56*	42.89	54.11	51.44	*56.29*	*42.91*	*46.10*
Tunisia	14.27	28.61	25.16	*85.73*	*71.39*	*74.84*	11.47	21.29	18.93
Palestine	22.72	29.66	28.57	*77.28*	*70.34*	*71.44*	20.00	22.42	22.04
Average[c]	*23.80*	*32.49*	*30.69*	76.20	67.50	69.32	21.82	25.02	24.37

Source: Authors' compilation of modelled estimates in the ILOSTAT.
[a]Employers, own-account workers and contributing family workers.
[b]Self-employed (excluding employers), such as own account workers and contributing family workers, as a percentage of total employment.
[c]Figures in italics are above average.

tank, namely the ERF (OAMDI, 2019). These surveys are suitable for examining the dynamics governing individual workers' employment statuses, in as much as they track the same workers and their employment status over the span of six or so years between survey waves. LMPS also include recall modules screening workers' past occupations, supplementing the information on workers' contemporaneous labour market statuses from across multiple survey waves and providing multiple snapshots even in unbalanced-panel or cross-sectional settings. The available surveys appear to be of adequate quality and representative of the labour market at large, and there is limited indication that the data suffer from measurement errors or bias-inducing attrition. For example, in the 2018 Egyptian LMPS, attrition rate was 15%, but this was concentrated primarily among disabled, retired and other economically inactive workers. While the Egyptian LMPS oversampled poor rural and high-migration communities, the stratified sample design and population expansion weights mitigated the consequences for survey representativeness (Assaad et al., 2021). Finally, although the employment distribution among marginal demographic groups (such as rural subsistence workers or female youths) showed some discrepancies against LFS and Census figures, employment transitions and their drivers are not thought to be biased.

LMPS survey workers' current occupation type, status as (ir)regular and (in)formal in/outside establishment, and contract and social insurance coverage.

4. Results and Discussions

4.1. Persistent Informality and Declining Occupational Mobility

Assessments of the composition of labour force across subsequent survey waves reveal that occupational mobility has been deteriorating over time. For instance, mobility proved stronger in Egypt over 1996–2006 due to the contribution of the public sector, whereas most individuals remained in their initial labour market segments over 2006–2012 (Tansel & Ozdemir, 2019). Over the past decade, employment vulnerability of youth rose in Egypt. In Jordan, while youth men's vulnerability dropped from 40% to 34% between 2010 and 2016, that of youth women and non-youth men increased, for an overall increase in informality.

4.1.1. Egypt

Dynamic analysis using LMPS confirms that, across the three countries, youths starting in vulnerable jobs are unlikely to move to better quality jobs over time (AlAzzawi & Hlasny, 2022). In Egypt, two-in-three young men were self-employed or informal in 2012, and they had less than a one-in-ten prospect of transitioning to formal jobs in 2018. By contrast, one-in-four young women were self-employed or informal in 2012, and nearly three-in-four of them remained in this status by 2018. Young women were more likely to exit the labour force than to stay self-employed/informal or secure a formal job.

Adult men (30–44), less than one-half of whom were self-employed or informal in 2012, had a slightly higher chance of over one-in-six of transitioning to formal jobs. Adult women (30–44), less than one-in-three of whom were self-employed or informal in 2012, had a miniscule chance of transitioning to formal jobs of less than one in twenty. As with youths, adult women were far more likely to exit the labour force, and those formally employed in 2012 were likely to remain in that status by 2018.

Among the older cohort (45–59), moving out of the labour force becomes more prevalent for both genders, regardless of their status in 2012. Men, over one-in-four being self-employed or informal in 2012, had a less than one-in-ten chance of transitioning to formal jobs. Women, less than one-third being self-employed or informal in 2012, had almost no chance of transitioning to formality. Those formally employed in 2012 – roughly two-thirds for both genders – are most likely to remain in that status by 2018.

Hence, informality is strongly persistent although lessening over workers' lifetime. Occupational mobility from informality towards formal jobs is modest and shrinks from youth to maturity. Meanwhile, formal workers cling to their status. This threefold pattern is consistent with segmentation theory.

Unsurprisingly, the wage gap between formal and informal employees in Egypt favours the former group. Table 15.2 reports that formal/informal average wage gap was usually wider for women than for men in both 2012 and 2018. Without accounting for differentials in worker characteristics, the formal/informal wage gap hovered around 31% in 2012, and 38% in 2018, broadly consistent with the gaps across North Africa according to the *Sahwa* survey in 2015. For all countries, in accordance with segmentation theory, 'insiders' within formal employment benefit from higher social protection and income from entry barriers, whereas 'outsiders' in informal jobs miss out on these advantages.

4.1.2. Jordan

In Jordan, one in two young men was formally employed in 2010, and most of them (roughly two in three) remained formal by 2016. Of those who did not, the majority transitioned out of the labour force by 2016. Young men who were self-employed or informal in 2010, about one in four, were less likely to transition to formal jobs in 2016. They had a relatively high propensity to exit the labour force altogether – about one-fifth of the self-employed and slightly less of those informally employed. Far fewer young women, less than one-tenth, were self-employed or informal in 2010. Almost one-half were formal, and the majority of them remained in this status. According to the transition matrix, young women are more likely to transition out of the labour force or become unemployed rather than stay self-employed/informal or attain formality.

Adult men (30–44), about one-quarter of whom were self-employed or informal in 2010, had a similar chance of transitioning to formal jobs as young men, of over one-third. Adult women, less than one-fifth of whom were self-employed or informal in 2010, had a less than one-in-twenty chance of transitioning to formal jobs and were far more likely to exit the labour force. By contrast, women formally employed in 2010 were most likely to remain in that status by 2016.

Table 15.2.   Formal/Informal Employees Real Monthly Wage and Wage Gap in Egypt (2012–2018).

Year	Informal Employees		Formal Employees		Formal/ informal	Formal/ informal
	2012	2018	2012	2018	Wage Gap (2012)	Wage Gap (2018)
Youth men	2,085	2,267	2,791	2,894	(25.29)	(21.66)
Youth women	1,376	2,323	1,979	2,002	(30.46)	(−16.03)
Adult men, 30–44	2,414	2,180	3,561	4,812	(32.21)	(54.69)
Adult women, 30–44	1,211	2,757	2,335	2,629	(48.13)	(−4.86)
Adult men, 45–59	2,452	2,038	3,671	3,051	(33.20)	(33.20)
Adult women, 45–59	1,360	1,503	3,179	2,911	(57.22)	(48.36)
Total	2,193	2,224	3,195	3,582	(31.36)	(37.91)

Source: Authors' calculations from Egypt LMPS for 2012 and 2018.
Notes: All wages are in 2018 EGP currency, deflated using the CPI. Wage gap in percentage.

Among older workers (45–59), moving out of the labour force by 2016 was again highly prevalent among both genders, regardless of their status in 2010. Over one-in-three men in the older cohort were self-employed or informal in 2010, and had a less than one-tenth chance of transitioning to formal jobs. Women (less than one-quarter of whom were self-employed or informal in 2010) had essentially no chance of transitioning to any job, with the vast majority exiting the labour force by 2016. Those formally employed in 2010 – roughly two in five among men and less than one-fifth of women – are most likely to remain in that status by 2016.

Labour supply behaviour differs in Jordan as compared to Egypt. Across most initial employment statuses and regardless of age cohort and gender, Jordanian workers were far more likely to exit the labour force than their Egyptian counterparts were. In 2016, young Jordanians were also more likely to be formally employed than Egyptians were in 2018, and if they were not, they either exited the labour force or remained unemployed.

Informality is strongly persistent in Jordan even though the trend diminishes from workers' youth to their maturity. Occupational mobility from informality towards formal jobs is rather modest and falls over workers' lifetime, as their propensity for exiting the labour force increases. As in Egypt, Jordanian formal workers typically manage to cling to their status. The threefold pattern is once again consistent with segmentation theory.

4.1.3. Tunisia

For Tunisia, a single survey round is available, but workers' employment mobility can be inferred using retrospective data on past jobs. We examined workers' employment status in 2008, 6 years before the survey year, and how their status evolved by 2014. For youths, one-in-four young men were formally employed in 2008, and most of them (roughly four in five) remained formal by 2014. Young men, one-half being self-employed or informal in 2008, had a less than one-in-ten chance to transition to formal jobs in 2014. Far fewer young women (less than one in three) where self-employed or informal in 2008 and over one-half were formal, whereas slightly less than one-half remained in this status in 2014. Young women were more likely to exit the labour force or become unemployed rather than stay self-employed/informal or attain formality.

Among adult men, over one-half were self-employed or informal in 2008 and had a very low chance (less than 10%) of transitioning to formal jobs by 2014. Adult women, less than one-third of whom were self-employed or informal in 2008, had only a 1% chance of transitioning to formal jobs. Instead, they were far more likely to exit the labour force. By contrast, women formally employed in 2008 were most likely to keep that status by 2014.

Among the older cohort, moving out of the labour force in 2014 was again far more prevalent for both genders regardless of their 2008 status. Among older men, over two in five were self-employed or informal in 2008 and had less than one-tenth of a chance of transitioning to formal jobs. Somewhat similarly, one in two women were self-employed or informal in 2008 and had essentially no chance of transitioning out, with the vast majority remaining in their status. Roughly two in five men and less than one-fifth of women were formally employed in 2008 and were most likely to remain so by 2014. Thus, for Tunisia, the data from the transition matrix suggest relatively lower occupational mobility across age groups and genders regardless of their 2008 status.

4.2. Drivers of Informality: Evidence from Multinomial Logistic Regressions

To investigate factors behind workers' employment status, and sources of the youth/non-youth gaps, we turn to multinomial logistic regressions. The regressions estimate the probability that a worker will attain a particular employment type (i.e. formal, informal/irregular, self-employed/unpaid family worker, unemployed) relative to the probability of the baseline option of remaining out of the labour force. The results of the regressions allow us to calculate the (conditional) propensities of workers to attain each employment outcome. The model takes the values of explanatory variables (x), estimates the j-outcome specific coefficients on those explanatory variables (β_j) using maximum likelihood and calculates the probabilities of all possible outcomes relative to the baseline outcome.

$$\Pr(y = j) = \frac{\exp(\beta_j x)}{\sum_{k \in J} \exp(\beta_k x)} \tag{1}$$

Workers' employment outcomes are made a function of workers' demographics (age, gender, education), household characteristics (gender of household head, highest education in household, location of residence) and father's social status (education, employment status). Three age cohorts are distinguished: youth (15–29), ascending to prime working age (30–44) and prime working age (45–59). In equation (1), we, thus, use

$$\beta x = \beta_0 + \beta_1 \text{youth} + \beta_2 \text{ascending} + \beta_3 \text{age} + \beta_4 \text{age}^2 + \beta_5 \text{female}$$
$$+ \sum_l \beta_l \text{edu}_l + \sum_m \beta_m \text{edu}_m \times \text{female} + \beta_6 \text{wealth} + \beta_7 \text{HH head} \tag{2}$$
$$+ \beta_8 \text{HH highest ed} + \sum_r \beta_r \text{father ed}_r + \sum_k \beta_k \text{father employment}_k + \beta_9 \text{rural}$$

The results of these regressions, and selected tests of their robustness, are presented in the next sub-section. The main findings from the regressions are that family wealth and father's education and employment are important determinants of employment outcomes, and these associations persist even after a long span of work experience. Opportunities for upward mobility deteriorated over the past decade in all three countries evaluated (Egypt, Jordan and Tunisia). Educational attainment in particular is a critical factor that allows workers to transition to better employment statuses, and thus a crucial means for improving social mobility (AlAzzawi & Hlasny, 2022).

Fig. 15.1 shows the estimated probabilities of workers' employment status – separately by gender – derived from the multinomial logistic regressions. Among men, the prospects of formal employment are found to increase monotonically with age in Egypt and Tunisia but have an inverse-U dynamic in Jordan, peaking in the 30–44 age group. Formal employment is the predominant employment category among higher age groups – above the age of 40 in Egypt, above 30 in Tunisia, and only in Jordan they show a temporary dip in the 45–59 year age group. Youth workers – in their early 20s in Egypt and Jordan, but as far as until 30 in Tunisia – are predominantly economically inactive.

Unemployment is also notably high among youth in all three countries. Informality and irregular employment take the highest share of all employment among Egyptian men aged 22–40 and are a consistent risk among Tunisian men of all ages (around 15% for Tunisian men in their 20s, 20% in their thirties and again 15% in the 45- to 59-year age group).

Among women, being economically inactive is the singly predominant status across all ages. In all three countries, the probability of being inactive starts very high in women's youth gradually declines until the age of 45 and jumps up again among the 45- to 59-year age cohort. Being unemployed and searching for jobs is the second most dominant status among young women up to their late 20s in Jordan and Tunisia, and as far as late 30s in Egypt. In all three countries, women in their 30s and early 40s then have a moderate chance, 10–20%, of holding formal employment, before this prospect again fades away.

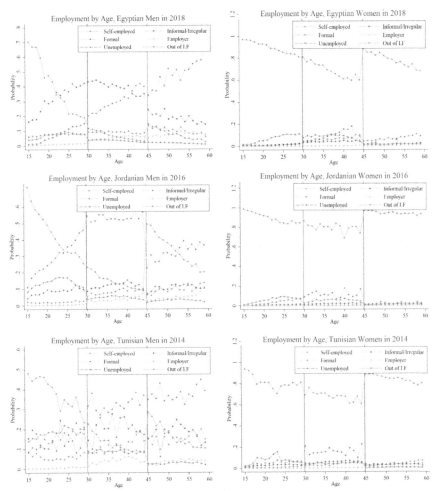

Fig. 15.1.   Predicted Probability of Employment Status: Gender and Age in Egypt, Jordan and Tunisia. *Source*: Authors' calculations based on ELMPS 2018, JLMPS 2016, TLMPS 2014.

4.3. Robustness Checks

The multinomial logistic models that were applied[2] have a number of theoretical and empirical merits, but some limitations and potential pitfalls should be acknowledged.

Most saliently, while the majority of explanatory variables in multinomial logit regressions are significant when evaluated jointly across the columns, meaning

---

[2]Due to limited space, tables were removed, but remain available on simple request.

that the variables belong in the model, many of the average marginal effects are insignificant individually, meaning that the corresponding variables may have positive or negative effects on particular employment outcomes. One explanation for the weak results is the heterogeneity of the sample. The inclusion of both age groups and genders in the same models likely confounds the differential impacts on prime-age workers and recent graduates. For alternative specifications, we have evaluated models disaggregated along important demographic fault lines, separately for two age groups as well as separately for those starting in formal, informal or inactive employment statuses. Interaction terms of education/experience with the cohort and gender indicators were also evaluated. The pitfall of these models is their lower degrees of freedom. These models produced consistent but generally less significant results.

Two, the specifications are static, without any direct controls for panel dynamics (beside the large set of time-varying controls). Regressions with worker fixed effects were estimated, but produced less interesting results due to the mechanics of fixed-effect estimation. One issue is that the fixed effects absorb a large share of variation in the dependent variables at the expense of other factors such as education, which may be causally more responsible for employment outcomes. For completeness, models with lagged dependent variables were also estimated. These specifications again broadly validate our main models, although they are considered less valid, due to the lost degrees of freedom and lost ability to attribute differences in job outcomes (which are near time-invariant) to stagnant socio-demographic factors.

Three, a critical assumption for the validity of the multinomial logistic model is independence of irrelevant alternatives (IIA) – the ratio of the probabilities of any two statuses should be independent of the set of possible options. Clear violations of this assumption can be identified using the Hausman tests. In our case, these tests fail to reject the IIA assumption in each country's model, implying that the estimates are not systematically affected by the exclusion of any one of the outcomes from the analysis.

5. The Root Causes of Informalisation and the Formalisation Drive

The first main cause of persistent or rising informality is the inability of the formal economy (including the public sector) to absorb increasing labour force (Chen & Harvey, 2017). The IMF (Balima, 2021) suggests that 85% of all informal workers are in precarious employment not through choice but due to lacking opportunities in formal (private or public) employment. The other main cause is inadequacy of regulatory frameworks and weak enforcement of contracts by labour and social security inspectorates, attributable to capacity weaknesses and corruption, which keep the informal sector and microenterprises operating effectively outside the purview of formal regulations. According to Angel-Urdinola and Kuddo (2011), although labour legislation in MENA is rigid *de jure*, it is *de facto* widely evaded and law enforcement remains weak.

Chen (2012) was among the first to sketch out a comprehensive policy response to the informal economy based on four main pillars: increase formal jobs creation, regulate informal enterprises and informal jobs, extend state protections – social and legal – to the informal workforce and raise the productivity of informal enterprises and the incomes of informal workers.

Over the past decade, a broad range of formalisation policies has been introduced to address the heterogeneity of informality, but impact assessments provide mixed evidence. A relevant distinction is between policies explicitly tackling informality versus policies that prove influential though without explicitly aiming at formalisation, such as active labour market policies (ALMPs). The former policies target categories of businesses (e.g. microenterprises), or workers (e.g. domestic work), and the component of informality (e.g. undeclared work in formal enterprises). ALMPs have been applied in the following areas: (i) Skills training in Tunisia (Almeida et al., 2012) and in Morocco (Kluve et al., 2014); (ii) support for enterprise development including microfinance services; (iii) employment services in Jordan, even though they were found to have little impact on employment outcomes (Groh et al., 2012) and (iv) subsidised public employment and wage subsidies in Jordan and Tunisia (Barcucci & Mryyan, 2014) even though they failed to create jobs in the long run.

Microcredit has had significant positive impacts in the short term, mainly for already established businesses in Egypt (Amer & Selwaness, 2021) as well as in Morocco (Crépon et al., 2015), but no impact on the probability of establishing new businesses. Positive effects have been found to vanish in the long run, perhaps because the loan amounts were too low to spur investment, thus calling for a more robust and sustainable approach.

Formalisation policies have addressed the informal sector more than those informally employed although formalisation targeting the latter has proved more effective than targeting the former (Jessen & Kluve, 2019). Enacting laws alone does not ensure the transition of workers from informal to formal jobs – beyond design and implementation, monitoring and assessment are crucial steps in the policy cycle. This applies to the law on self-employed entrepreneurship and the law on domestic employment that Morocco adopted, respectively, in 2015 and 2016 (Cherkaoui & Benkaraach, 2021).

Formalising businesses using incentives (carrot) is threefold. Firstly, information campaigns on the procedures and benefits of registration, alone, remain ineffective. Secondly, mechanisms that have proven effective include one-stop shops bringing together several procedures, relevant agencies simplifying business registration and incentives for reducing taxes as well as social security contributions. Thirdly, shrinking of registration costs for start-ups and providing of bonuses to businesses willing to register can be effective depending on the scale of support. Eliminating one-half, the entry cost has been projected to decrease the informal sector by 5%, whereas shrinking the payroll tax by one-half would lower informal employment by 13% (Balima, 2021).

Formalising businesses using penalty (stick) includes, as a fourth approach, law enforcement by the labour inspectorate, which has been found to have a minor but significant impact on the formal employment of workers persisting several years (Gaarder & van Doorn, 2021).

We contend that a concerted effort towards labour-market formalisation would increase firms' factor productivity and performance, which would, in turn, encourage retention of high-quality workers and acquisition of complementary capital, leading to further performance gains and incentives to curtail labour attrition and turnover. The availability of the bulk of currently underutilised youths (in the informal sector, or unemployed) and women (economically inactive) presents an untapped opportunity to for-profit as well as social entrepreneurs.

6. Conclusions

As emphasised in this study, informality is a dynamic concept that looks to the future while remaining grounded on achievements made to this day. Informality remains more topical than ever, conceptually (linking informality to value added), metrically (calculating its scope and trend) and politically (better integrating and formalising it). Informality requires both ongoing thorough investigation and taking stock of evolving stylised facts. Quarterly surveys that were disrupted in several countries by the Covid-19 pandemic must resume data collection for assessment. This is a pre-requisite for policies addressing the formalisation of informality.

The International Labour Organisation (ILO, 2013) has provided a comprehensive overview of the informal economy and recommended policy approaches to achieve transition and integration into the formal economy. The World Bank has also advocated and assessed formalisation policies targeting the inefficiencies and inequities in the informal sector. The persistence of informality reveals contradictory patterns of narrow short-term advantages and general disadvantages. Hurdles in the formalisation drive include deep-rooted bare-knuckles competition between informal MSEs and formal firms; erosion of the fiscal tax bases limiting the public sectors' capacity; entrapment of informal workers in subsistence jobs without employment protection or prospect for up skilling. Furthermore, legislation lacking standards and guarantees of equal treatment across different classes of workers and the general weakness of incentives for investment in human capital, technology and infrastructure should be added. Successful formalisation drive should reconcile the promotion of sustainable entrepreneurship advocated by the World Bank, with the ILO-supported organic expansion of social protections for informal and other non-covered workers (Adair et al., 2022).

Formalisation policies should be judged by the minimal standards of whether they increase employment and general welfare. Their major component of promoting job creation should take place within formal sustainable organisations. In this respect, for-profit cooperatives and not-for-profit social and sustainable institutions (SSEs) including microfinance institutions (MFIs) could play a key role (Adair et al., 2022). In the MENA region, SSEs were spearheaded in Morocco decades ago and were recently adopted by Tunisian, Egyptian and other governments (Prince et al., 2018). Female workers, being typically disadvantaged compared to their male counterparts, should be assigned priority.

Formalisation should target both informal businesses and workers, using both incentives and penalties. Specific tax and public procurement policies addressing informal workers who are establishing or joining formal sustainable organisations should be promoted.

MFIs will enable formalisation by supporting and incentivising informal businesses and workers to take steps towards inclusivity and sustainability. According to Adair et al. (2022), as a paragon to emulate and to benchmark against, the Alexandria Business Association, an Egyptian MFI, managed to triple the number of fully formalised clients between 2004 (6%) and 2016 (18%).

Innovative formalisation approaches are advocated to stimulate decent job creation, tackle the fragmentation of MENA labour markets and promote occupational mobility and human capital development. This will lead to a better matching of employer needs and worker skills, and productivity growth across various sectors of the regional labour markets and underrepresented segments of society. Ultimately this will foster a more sustainable and inclusive trajectory of development.

With respect to practical implications, the recommendations advocated above must be designed and implemented as well as assessed and enforced. International cooperation, especially with the European Union, can prove effective for design. Implementation requires the participation of public and private stakeholders. Monitoring is crucial and the stick and carrot policy must resist cronyism and corruption. Assessments need public disclosure.

There are limitations in this study. As aforementioned, data for Tunisia are not panel data and, therefore, strictly speaking, do not compare with that of Egypt and Jordan. A thorough review on extended social protection to informal workers would show that this policy addresses a relevant issue of formalising informality and its implementation may prove not so expensive with respect to labour costs. This could be the topic of a future research.

Acknowledgements

The authors gratefully acknowledge the comments from two referees, which helped improve this chapter. The usual disclaimer applies.

References

Ackrill, R., & Igudia, E. (2023). Analysing the informal economy: Data challenges, research design, and research transparency. *Review of Development Economics*, forthcoming.

Adair, P., Hlasny, V., Omrani, M., & Sharabi-Rosshandler, K. (2022). *Assessing the job creation potential of the social economy in the MENA region* [EuroMeSCo policy study 26]. IEMed.

AlAzzawi, S., & Hlasny, V. (2022). Youth labor market vulnerabilities: Evidence from Egypt, Jordan and Tunisia. *International Journal of Manpower*, 43(7), 1670–1699.

Almeida, R. K., Barouni, M., Brodmann, S., Grun, R., & Premand, P. (2012). *Entrepreneurship training and self-employment among university graduates: Evidence from a randomized trial in Tunisia* [Policy research working paper series 6285]. The World Bank.

Amer, M., & Selwaness, I. (2021). *Unleashing the employment potential in the manufacturing sector: developing SME finance and the way forward* [Alternative policy solutions policy paper]. American University in Cairo.

Angel-Urdinola, D. F., & Kuddo, A. (2011). *Key characteristics of employment in the Middle East and North Africa* [MNA Knowledge and Learning Fast Brief 84]. The World Bank.

Assaad, R., Krafft, C. G., & Rahman, K. W. (2021). Introducing the Egypt labor market panel survey 2018. *IZA Journal of Development and Migration, 12*(1), 20210012. https://doi.org/10.2478/izajodm-2021-0012

Balima, H. (2021, October 13). *Informality and development in North Africa* [Speech at the IMF 2021 Annual Meetings]. International Monetary Fund.

Barcucci, V., & Mryyan, N. (2014). *Labour market transitions of young women and men in Jordan* [Work4Youth Publication Series No. 14]. International Labour Office.

Barsoum, G., & Ramadan, M., & Mostafa, M. (2016). *Labour market transitions of young women and men in Egypt* [Work4Youth Publication Series, No. 16]. International Labour Office.

Castells, M., & Portes, A. (1989). World underneath: The origins, dynamics, and effects of the informal economy. In A. Portes, M. Castells, & L. A. Benton (Eds.), *The informal economy: Studies in advanced and less developed countries* (pp. 11–40). Johns Hopkins University Press.

Charmes, J. (2019). *Dimensions of resilience in developing countries: informality, solidarities and carework* [Series: Demographic Transformation and Socio-Economic Development, 10]. Springer.

Charmes, J., & Adair, P. (2022). Après un demi-siècle, l'économie informelle reste un concept heuristique et un ensemble flou [The informal economy is fifty: A heuristic concept and a fuzzy set]. *Mondes en développement, 50*(3–4), 199–200, 255–274.

Chen, M. (2012). *The informal economy: Definitions, theories and policies* [WIEGO working paper no. 1]. Women in Informal Employment: Globalizing and Organizing (WIEGO), Kennedy School, Harvard University.

Chen, M. (2014). Informal employment and development: Patterns of inclusion and exclusion. *The European Journal of Development Research, 26*, 397–418.

Chen, M., & Carré, F. (Eds.). (2020). *The informal economy revisited examining the past, envisioning the future.* Routledge.

Chen, M., & Harvey, J. (2017). *The informal economy in Arab nations: A comparative perspective.* Women in Informal Employment: Globalizing and Organizing (WIEGO), Kennedy School, Harvard University.

Cherkaoui, M., & Benkaraach, T. (2021). Striving for formalisation: Gender and youth aspects of informal employment in Morocco. In J. Ghosh (Ed.), *Informal women workers in the global south. Policies and practices for the formalisation of women's employment in developing economies* (Chapter 5, pp. 137–173). Routledge.

Crépon, B., Devoto, F., Duflo, E., & Parriente, W. (2015). Estimating the impact of microcredit on those who take it up: Evidence from a randomized experiment in Morocco. *American Economic Journal: Applied Economics, 7*(1), 123–150.

De Soto, H. (1986). *The other path: The invisible revolution in the third world.* Harper and Row.

De Soto, H. (2012). *L'économie informelle: comment y remédier? Uneopportunité pour la Tunisie* [*The informal economy: how to remedy it? An opportunity for Tunisia*]. UTICA and Instituto Libertad y Democracia. Ceres Edition.

Dimova, R., Elder, S., & Stephan, K. (2016). *Labour market transitions of young women and men in the Middle East and North Africa* [Work4Youth Publication Series, No. 44]. International Labour Organization.

Fehling, M., Jarrah, Z. M., Tiernan, M. E., Albezreh, S., VanRooyen, M. J., Alhokair, A., & Nelson, B. D. (2016). Youth in crisis in the Middle East and North Africa: A systematic literature review and focused landscape analysis. *Eastern Mediterranean Health Journal, 21*(12), 916–930.

Gaarder, E., & van Doorn, J. (2021). *Enterprise formalization: Simplifying and facilitating business start-up and compliance.* International Labour Office.

Gatti, R., Angel-Urdinola, D. F., Silva, J., & Bodor, A. (2014). *Striving for better jobs – The challenge of informality in the Middle East and North Africa.* The World Bank.

Gherbi, H., & Adair, P. (2020). *The youth gender gap in North Africa: Income differentials and informal employment* [Erudite working paper series 06-2020]. RePEc.

Groh, M., Krishnan, N., McKenzie, D., & Vishwanath, T. (2012). *Soft skills or hard cash? The impact of training and wage subsidy programs on female youth employment in Jordan* [Policy research working paper 6141]. The World Bank.

Harris, J. R., & Todaro, M. P. (1970). Migration, unemployment and development. A two-sector analysis. *American Economic Review, 60,* 126–142.

Hart, T. K. (1973). Informal income opportunities and urban employment in Ghana. *Journal of Modern African Studies, 11*(1), 61–89.

Haut Commissariat au Plan (HCP). (2016). *Enquête nationale sur le secteur informel 2013/2014.* Haut Commissariat au Plan.

Hlasny, V., & AlAzzawi, S. (2020). *Informality, market fragmentation and low productivity in Egypt.* ERF Forum.

ILO. (1972). *Employment, incomes and equality. A strategy for increasing productive employment in Kenya.* International Labour Office.

ILO. (2002). *Women and men in the informal economy: A statistical picture.* International Labour Office.

ILO. (2013). *Measuring informality: A statistical manual on the informal sector and informal.* International Labour Office.

ILOSTAT. (n.d.). *Labour statistics database.* International Labour Office.

Jessen, J., & Kluve, J. (2019). *The effectiveness of interventions to reduce informality in low- and middle income countries* [IZA discussion paper 12487]. IZA.

Kluve, J., Dyer, P., Gardiner, D., & Mizrokh, E. (2014). *Boosting youth employability in Morocco – II randomized controlled trial baseline report December.* International Labour Office.

La Porta, R., & Shleifer, A. (2014). Informality and development. *Journal of Economic Perspectives, 28*(3), 109–126.

Lewis, A. (1954). Economic development with unlimited supplies of labour, *Manchester School of Economic and Social Studies, 22*(2), 139–191.

Lopez-Acevedo, G., Betcherman, G., Khellaf, A., & Molini, V. (2021). *Morocco's jobs landscape: Identifying constraints to an inclusive labor market, international development in focus.* The World Bank.

Mansuy, M., & Werquin, P. (2015). *Labour market entry in Tunisia: The gender gap.* International Labour Office.

Mansuy, M., & Werquin, P. (2018). Moroccan youth and employment: Gender differences. *Journal of Education and Work, 31*(5–6), 545–562.

Merouani, W., El Moudden, C., & Hammouda, N.-E. (2018). *Social security entitlement in Maghreb countries: Who is excluded? Who is not interested?* [ERF working paper no. 1264]. Economic Research Forum.

Open Access Micro Data Initiative (OAMDI). (2019). *Version 2.0 of licensed data files; labor market panel surveys (LMPS), ELMPS 1998, 2006, 2012, 2018 Panel v.2.0; JLMPS 2010, 2016 Panel v.1.1; TLMPS 2014 v.2.0.* Open Access Micro Data Initiative, Economic Research Forum (ERF). http://erf.org.eg/data-portal/

Prince, H., Halasa-Rappel, Y., & Khan, A. (2018). *Economic growth, youth unemployment, and political and social instability: A study of policies and outcomes in post-Arab Spring Egypt, Morocco, Jordan and Tunisia* [UNRISD working paper 2018-12]. United Nations Research Institute for Social Development.

Shahen, M. E., Kotani, K., Kakinaka, M., & Managi, S. (2020). Wage and labor mobility between public, formal private and informal private sectors in a developing country. *Economic Analysis and Policy, 68*, 101–113.

Solati, F. (2017). *Women, work, and patriarchy in the Middle East and North Africa*. Springer.

Suleiman, H. (2022). *Youth unemployment in the south of the Mediterranean: A chronic challenge to development and stability* [EuroMeSCo paper 48]. EuroMeSCo – European Mediterranean Scientific Cooperation, European Institute of the Mediterranean.

Tansel, A., & Ozdemir, Z. A. (2019). Transitions across labor market states including formal/informal division in Egypt. *Review of Development Economics, 23*(8), 1–22.

Weber, W., Queralti Sans, T., Bourekba, M., & Sanchez-Montijano, E. (2021). *SAHWA youth survey 2016 dataset (2021)* [Data file edition 4.0]. Barcelona Centre for International Affairs (CIDOB).

Chapter 16

Employment Status of Women in the Power Loom Sector: A Case Study of Varanasi, Uttar Pradesh

Nandani Yadav and Priyabrata Sahoo

Department of Economics, Banaras Hindu University, Varanasi, India

Abstract

The chapter examines the employment status of women in the power loom sector by assessing their participation in this sector as well as in different major activities aside from power loom activities. The objective is to understand the time allocation of individuals who are related to the power loom sector and to evaluate the factors that affect the time spent in the sector. It has focused on women's contribution to the power loom sector and discusses gender inequality in unpaid domestic chores. The study is based on primary data collected through in-depth interviews in the rural area of Benipur, Varanasi, Uttar Pradesh. This study found that women participate less than men across all age groups in the power-loom sector in the rural area of Benipur. Women have lower education qualifications than men at each level; however, they are more involved in education than men in their initial years of schooling. Women's involvement in education declines with age, while men's involvement does not. Due to low educational attainment, they face many difficulties in understanding this new technology of power loom. Domestic involvement of women might be a major reason behind their low participation in education as well as the power loom sector. Even today, 'farming or agriculture' is the most important major alternate activity for the livelihood of the people who are related to the power-loom sector. The key contribution of this chapter is to understand the employment status of women and evaluate the women's contributions to the power loom sector.

Keywords: Power loom sector; women; domestic activities; farming; rural area; Varanasi; India

Informal Economy and Sustainable Development Goals:
Ideas, Interventions and Challenges, 317–333
Copyright © 2024 by Nandani Yadav and Priyabrata Sahoo
Published under exclusive licence by Emerald Publishing Limited
doi:10.1108/978-1-83753-980-220241017

1. Introduction

The textiles and clothing industry is considered to be a crucial pillar of the Indian economy. India holds the third position as a leading exporter of textiles and apparel globally. Handloom constitutes a notable economic endeavour, serving as one of the principal sources of employment, second only to agriculture in India. With an engagement of over 35 lakh individuals, it has emerged as one of the largest unorganised sectors in the country. The industry involves more than two and a half million female weavers and affiliated labourers, rendering it a crucial driver of women's economic empowerment (Ministry of Textiles, Government of India, 2022–2023). Less educated women contribute more towards unpaid activities such as domestic, care, etc. (Chakraborty, 2019; Singh & Pattanaik, 2020). This highlights the societal and individual constraints that have led workers to the informal sector due to gender discrimination, patriarchal norms, lack of education, old age, and economic struggles. Women are expected to take care of children and the home, whereas men are not required to share household burdens indicating gender inequality in domestic chores. This has caused some women to give up paid work due to a lot of burden of housework and switch to unpaid activities. The sector is significant for employment, and it creates jobs and supports many, including women and rural communities (Dadheech & Sharma, 2023). Uttar Pradesh is one of the mega handloom clusters among nine mega handloom clusters in India (Ministry of Textiles, Government of India, 2022–2023). However, a reduction in the percentage of handloom weavers' participation in the overall textile output of the nation has been observed, and most of the workers are shifting away from handlooms towards power looms (Kumar, 2016; Ministry of Textiles, Government of India, 2019–2020). Dev et al. (2008) also evaluated the difficulties of the handloom sector and its prospects in Andhra Pradesh. As a consequence of certain inherent constraints within the handloom industry, characterised by comparatively slower production rates and elevated costs (Kumar & Sulaiman, 2017), it created an opportunity for power loom to emerge as a third foundational element of the textile industry. Presently, approximately 60% of Indian fabric production is attributed to the decentralised power loom sector (Patali, 2020). As of April 2022, India possessed a total of 385,596 power looms. Several states in India, including Maharashtra, Andhra Pradesh, Gujarat, Uttar Pradesh, Karnataka, and Tamil Nadu, are primary producers of power loom textile products (Ministry of Textiles, Government of India, 2022–2023).

1.1. Significance of Study

Varanasi serves as the prominent handloom production hub in the northern Indian state of Uttar Pradesh. The majority of power loom units in the country are predominantly concentrated in semi-urban and rural locales (Shende & Musam, 2020). Within these areas, a significant concentration of handloom weaver's cooperative societies also exists, with a large population of weavers being present (Olive et al., 2022; Rai, 2022). Most of the workers are shifting away from handlooms towards power looms (Ministry of Textiles, Government of India,

2019–2020; Dhonde & Patel, 2020; Mishra et al., 2023). Though, official figures are significantly underestimated because the large number of power looms are not registered (Deshpande, 2018). Therefore, the development of the power loom sector in small villages and remote areas can be attributed to several advantageous factors such as affordability, and ease of installment, among others, which have facilitated the involvement of small entrepreneurs in the industry (Patali, 2020; Mishra et al., 2022; Mahiat et al., 2023). However, most of the studies are conducted in the urban areas. Thus, this study focuses on the workers in the weaving industry in the rural area of Benipur in the Varanasi district.

1.2. Objectives of Study

a. To discuss the current employment status of women in the power looms sector.
b. To examine the different major activities of people who are associated with this sector and its impact on the time spent in the power looms.
c. To highlight the time allocation of power loom workers and factors that affect the time spent in the power looms sector.

1.3. Research Questions

This study has attempted to answer the following questions:

a. What is the employment status of women in the power loom sector?
b. What are the different major activities[1] of the workers engaged in the power loom and their participation in these activities?
c. How much time is spent by the workers in power loom and different major activities?
d. What are the factors that affect the time spent in the power loom sector?

The study consists of nine sections, including introduction, review of literature, data sources and methodology, demographic characteristics, the employment status of women, different major activities of people, time allocation of people, results and discussions, and conclusions and policy implications.

2. Review of Literature

In the context of India's textile industry, the power loom sector has emerged as the predominant entity in the realm of weaving (Prusty & Mallick, 2022; Gautam, 2022). According to recent data from the Ministry of Textiles, Government of India (2022), the power loom industry has emerged as a noteworthy player in the fabric manufacturing landscape, responsible for generating a

---

[1]Apart from the power loom activities, those major activities in which people (associated with power loom sector) spend most of their time.

substantial proportion of the country's textile production, estimated at approximately 58.4% of the total output. With a total of 59,038 power loom units, the state of Uttar Pradesh ranks third highest among the various states. The state of Maharashtra boasts the largest number of power loom units with a total of 1,49,613 units, while Tamil Nadu ranks second with a total of 89,449 power loom units. As per the assessment conducted by the Directorate of Handloom and Textiles under the Government of Uttar Pradesh, the state of Uttar Pradesh is home to approximately 5,00,000 power loom weavers and 1,99,000 handloom weavers.

Most of the literature highlights the plight of workers, especially women in the weaving industry (Singh & Pattanaik, 2020; Tasnim, 2020), the problems related to the health of workers (Joshi & Padole, 2016; Das, 2018; Zara et al., 2022), and the wealth condition of weavers in the power looms sector (Mugilan & Muthukumar, 2021). Shende and Musam (2020) have analysed the performance of the power loom industry and the impact of dominant factors such as finance, technology, labour, marketing practices, raw material, the structure of ownership, and government policy on its performance in Maharashtra.

Furthermore, Prusty and Mallick (2022) conducted an in-depth personal interview in Siminoi village in the Dhenkanal district of Odisha and found that the downfall in the power loom cluster is caused by a lack of planning, education, government support, competition, product diversification, infrastructure bottlenecks, and marketing. A considerable proportion of weavers are socioeconomically disadvantaged, necessitating the involvement of additional family members, particularly women, children, and elderly individuals, in preliminary weaving activities (Sultana & Nisa, 2016; Kolgiri and Hiremath, 2019). Many weavers are quitting and seeking alternative occupations due to unfair trading practices with *Mahajana.*[2] They are forced to sell their products at lower rates, resulting in losses for the weavers (Prusty & Mallick, 2022). Due to all these issues of weavers, there is a need to study the status of this sector. Through the peer review of the literature, it was found that very few studies have been done on the time distribution of people who are related to power loom sector in the various major activities and on the dominant factors that affect the time spent in power loom sector of Benipur in Varanasi district of Uttar Pradesh. Therefore, this study fills this gap by studying the participation of women in the power loom sector and different major activities.

3. Data Sources and Methodology

The study of this chapter is based on primary data collected through in-depth interviews with 387 people in the rural area of Benipur in the Varanasi districts of Uttar Pradesh. Through a pilot survey, we found that the concentration of power loom in Benipur is the highest among the all-rural areas of Varanasi. A significant portion of the labour force residing in the Benipur village has returned to their place of origin from Surat, primarily owing to the impact of

---

[2]Middleman who acts as a mediator between weavers and shopkeepers or big dealers of textiles.

the prevailing pandemic. The locality of Benipur is classified as a Census Town within the Varanasi district of the Indian state of Uttar Pradesh. According to the Census Report of India 2011, the census town situated within the jurisdiction of the Benipur gram panchayat displays a population of 12,470 individuals. Of this cohort, 6,534 individuals are classified as male, while the remaining 5,936 are classified as female ("Demography" census report of India, 2011).

The sample size for the present study includes only those people who are associated with the power loom sector. Thus, the data of this study are based on the purposive sampling method. This method is suitable for studies of small sample sizes. For such a deep study, we need both qualitative and quantitative data. Therefore, open-ended questionnaires were prepared, and interviews were scheduled among workers in Benipur. The participation of women in this sector is shown in percentage, while the time distribution of people in different major activities is expressed in hours. Furthermore, we would also know how much time is spent by people in the power looms sector and how it is influenced by some variables such as age, gender, education level, marital status, and different major activities. For this, we used a regression approach to capture the impact of these variables on the targeted variable, that is, time spent in the power looms sector. Let's assume that the time spent in the power loom sector is the function of age, education level, different major activities, gender, and marital status.

Time spent in the power loom $= f$ (age, education level, different major activities, gender, marital *status*)

But in this function, we have two qualitative variables, that is gender and marital status. Therefore, we have constructed dummy variables like one dummy D1 for gender and two dummy D2 and D3 for marital status. We used the following regression model to see the impact of some independent variables such as age, education level, different major activities, gender, and marital status on the dependent variable which is the time spent in the power loom sector.

$$T_s = \beta_0 + \beta_1 X_1 + \beta_2 X_2 + \beta_3 X_3 + \beta_4 D_1 + \beta_5 D_2 + \beta_6 D_3 + \varepsilon \tag{1}$$

where T_s = The time spent in the power looms sector daily; D_1 = 1 if the gender is male, D_1 = 0 otherwise (i.e. female); D_2 = 1 if the marital status is unmarried, D_2 = 0 otherwise; D_3 = 1 if the marital status is widowed, D_3 = 0 otherwise.

β_0 is the constant term, that is it represents the mean value of time spent in the power loom sector or dependent variable when all independent variables like age, education level, different major activities, gender, and marital status are equal to zero. X_1, X_2, and X_3 represent age, education level, and different major activities, respectively. β_1, β_2, β_3, β_4, β_5, and β_6 are slope coefficients for each explanatory variable. β_1 measures the variation in the mean value of time spent in the power loom per unit change in age keeping other variables constant. Similarly, β_2, β_3, β_4, β_5, and β_6 measure the variation in the mean value of time spent in the power loom per unit change in the education level, different major activities gender, and marital status, respectively, holding others as constant. ε is the error or residual term.

4. Demographic Characteristics

We have taken some variables such as age, education level, gender, and marital status for the demographic. Let us discuss these demographic variables in detail. Fig. 16.1 represents the education level of people who are associated with the power loom sector and the education level is represented by age groups. We have categorised age groups into three: children group (under 15 years old), working-age group (15–59), and elder group (60 plus). 30.77% of female children and 40.00% of male children have no educational qualification. 38.46% of female children and 37.78% of male children are enrolled in the primary level of education. 30.77% of female children and 22.22% of male children are enrolled at the secondary level. From these data, we can observe that female children are more enrolled in education than male children at each level (i.e. primary and secondary).

When we look at the education level among the working age group, we found that 32.03% of females and 6.29% of males have no educational qualification. 7.03% of females and 13.29% of males are educated only at the primary level. 20.31% of females and 31.47% of males are educated at the secondary level. 21.88% of females and 23.78% of males are educated at the higher secondary level. 18.75% of females and 25.17% of males are educated at the graduate level and above. From these data, we found that females have lower educational qualifications than males at each level. Among elder people, 81.82% of females and 76.19% of males are illiterate. 18.18% of females and 9.52% of males are educated at the primary level. Elder females are not educated at secondary, higher secondary, and graduate and above, but elder males are educated at the graduate level and above. These data reveal that females are less educated than males but are more enrolled in education than males in their initial age. This indicates that women's involvement in education decreases with age, but this does not happen in

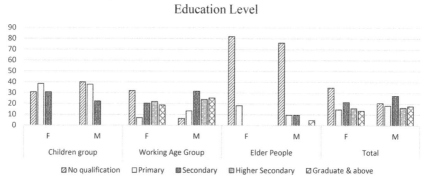

Fig. 16.1.   Education Level of People in the Power Looms Sector (in %).
Source: Authors' estimation using the field survey data.

the case of men. Domestic chores might be the main reason behind females' low participation in education (Chakraborty, 2019; Singh & Pattanaik, 2020).

Fig. 16.2 represents the age distribution, gender profile, and marital status. Among 387 people, 21.71% are children, 70.03% are those people who belong to the working age group, and 8.27% are elder people. The percentage of participants in the working age group is more than any other age group. In the selected sample of 387 people, the percentage of the male population is 54.01%, while the percentage of the female population is 45.99. Furthermore, 57.62% of people are married, 41.60% of people are unmarried, and 0.78% of people are widowed. The percentage share of married people is higher in the sample. However, we know that power looms activities involve an entire household, and it is not a work of an individual. Family members are involved in power loom-related activities directly or indirectly within each household associated with power loom.

5. The Employment Status of Women in Power Looms

To assess the current employment status in the power looms sector, we have used the information of all those people who are directly or indirectly associated with power looms whether paid or unpaid. Fig. 16.3 expresses the percentage share of people in power loom-related activities by gender and age categories. When we compared the participation of females and males in the power looms sector by age category, we found that 5.13% of female children and 13.33% of male children are engaged, while 94.87% of female children and 86.67% of male children are not engaged in power looms. The participation of female children is less than the participation of male children in power looms. From the working age group, 41.41% of females and 65.73% of males participate in the power loom sector, while 58.59% of females and 34.27% of males do not. 9.09% of elder females and 38.10% of elder males participate in the power loom sector, while 90.91% of elder females and 61.90% of elder males do not. Overall, 31.46% of total females and 51.67% of total males participate in the activities of the power loom sector, while

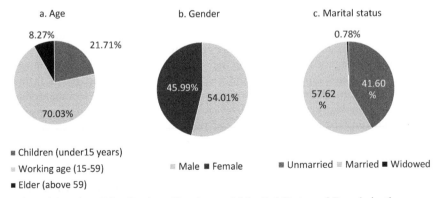

Fig. 16.2.   Age Distribution, Gender, and Marital Status of People in the Power Looms Sector. *Source*: Authors' estimation from the field survey data.

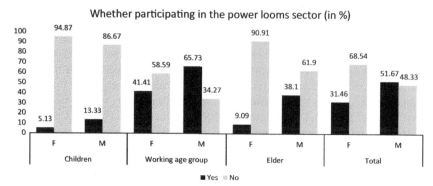

Fig. 16.3. Participation of People in the Power Looms. *Source*: Authors'
estimation from the field survey data.

68.54% of total females and 48.33% of total males do not. From all the above-
mentioned information, we concluded that female participation is less than male
participation in power loom-related activities among all age categories, and the
participation of both males and females together is highest in the working age
group while least in the children group.

6. Different Major Activities of People

Through in-depth interviews, this study also found that many workers have started
to search the alternate work or jobs for their livelihood during the pandemic time.
Furthermore, we discuss different major activities (other than power looms) of
the people in this village. The description of these major activities and people's
participation in them is mentioned in Table 16.1. It also shows how many people
are not involved in these different major activities. We found different major
activities like 'farming', 'study', 'domestic work', 'farming & domestic', 'study &
domestic', 'private job', 'tailoring', 'farming & study', 'farming & domestic and
study', 'labour', and 'others' at the time of the survey. If we see farming activities, both male and female children are not engaged in the 'farming' activities but
7.03% of females and 29.37% of males from the working age group, and 45.45%
of elder females and 38.10% of elder males are engaged.

Females belonging to the working age group are less engaged in 'farming'
activities than males; on the other hand, elder women are more engaged in 'farming' activities than elder men. 38.46% of female children and 57.78% of male children in the sample are 'studying'. 20.98% of males from the working age group
are still pursuing their studies but none of the females from the same group are
involved in 'studying'. This information indicates that women's education is not
being given much importance in this village. The participation of children groups,
as well as males of all age groups, is negligible in 'domestic chores'. On the contrary, 35.94% of females from the working group and 9.09% of elder females are
giving vital contributions to 'domestic chores'. Similarly, 36.72% of females from
the working age group and 9.09% of elder females are doing both 'farming &

Table 16.1. Participation of People in Different Major Activities (in %).

Different Major Activities	Children		Working Age Group		Elder		Total	
	F	M	F	M	F	M	F	M
1. Farming	0.00	0.00	7.03	29.37	45.45	38.10	7.87	23.92
2. Study	38.46	57.78	0.00	20.98	0.00	0.00	8.43	26.79
3. Domestic work	0.00	0.00	35.94	0.00	9.09	0.00	26.40	0.00
4. Farming and domestic	0.00	0.00	36.72	0.00	9.09	0.00	26.97	0.00
5. Study and domestic	20.51	0.00	16.41	0.00	0.00	0.00	16.29	0.00
6. Private job	0.00	0.00	0.00	7.69	0.00	0.00	0.00	5.26
7. Tailoring	0.00	0.00	0.78	0.00	0.00	0.00	0.56	0.00
8. Farming and study	0.00	2.22	0.00	10.49	0.00	0.00	0.00	7.66
9. Farming and domestic and study	7.69	0.00	2.34	0.00	0.00	0.00	3.37	0.00
10. Labour	0.00	0.00	0.00	1.40	0.00	0.00	0.00	0.96
11. Other	0.00	0.00	0.00	0.70	0.00	0.00	0.00	0.48
12. No other activities	33.33	40.00	0.78	29.37	36.36	61.90	10.11	34.93
Total	100.00	100.00	100.00	100.00	100.00	100.00	100.00	100.00

Source: Authors' estimation from the field survey data.

domestic activities' but males of all age groups and female children have no role in these activities.

Overall, male participants of all age groups have no contribution in 'private jobs', 'tailoring', 'study & domestic work', and 'farming & domestic work and study'. Equivalently, female children's participation is negligible in 'private jobs', 'tailoring', 'farming & study', 'labour', and 'others'. 20.51% and 7.69% of female children are engaged in 'study & domestic activities', and 'farming & domestic activities and study', respectively, while male children's engagement is negligible in both but 2.22% of male children are engaged in 'farming & study'. Hence, the data denote the inequality of the domestic burden between male children and female children. Female members of a household have to bear the burden of domestic chores. Considering the differences between these major activities by gender, the results show that the highest difference between female children and male children is in the 'study & domestic activities'. Similarly, the highest difference between the major activities of females and males (from both the working group and elder age group) is in 'farming & domestic' followed by 'domestic work'. Therefore, we could conclude that mostly female children are engaged in 'study' followed by 'study & domestic work'. On the other hand, male children are mostly involved in 'study' followed by 'farming & study'. The most common major activity of children is 'study'. Furthermore, the most common major activity of the working age group and the elder group is 'farming', but they differ in 'domestic chores' likewise the children group. Even today, 'farming' is the most important major alternate activity for the livelihood of the people who are related to the power looms sector.

7. Time Allocation of the People

Usually, we know that the role of children, females, and old people is crucial in any informal sector. However, their contributions are not well recognised, and mostly these people contribute without taking remuneration. Similarly, these people also work in the power loom sector without any remuneration. They participate more in preparatory activities[3] without any remuneration in the power looms sector. Hence, it is not easy to evaluate the contribution of children, females, and old people in monetary terms. Therefore, this study tries to assess the contribution of unpaid family members of each power looms household in the time aspect.

The time allocation of people in the power loom sector is presented in Table 16.2. We found that 94.87% of female children and 86.67% of male children don't spend any time in the power loom sector. 5.13% of female children and 13.33% of male children spend approximately 1–5 hours daily in power loom-related activities, while female children have less participation in the power looms sector than male children. From the working age group, 58.59% of females and 34.27% of males don't spend any time in the power

---

[3]Preparatory activities are those initial preparations that have been done before weaving for example choosing the yarn's quantity, washing, dyeing, winding, etc.

Table 16.2.   Time Allocation of People in the Power Loom Sector Daily (in %).

Time Spent in the Power Loom Sector in Hours	Children Group		Working Age Group		Elder People		Total	
	F	M	F	M	F	M	F	M
0	94.87	86.67	58.59	34.27	90.91	61.90	68.54	48.33
1–5	5.13	13.33	31.25	7.69	9.09	4.76	24.16	8.61
6–10	0.00	0.00	3.91	15.38	0.00	23.81	2.81	12.92
More than 10	0.00	0.00	6.25	42.66	0.00	9.52	4.49	30.14
Total	100.00	100.00	100.00	100.00	100.00	100.00	100.00	100.00

Source: Authors' estimation using the field survey data.

loom sector. 31.25% of females and 7.69% of males spend 1–5 hours daily in the power loom sector. 3.91% of females and 15.38% of males spent 6–10 hours, while 6.25% of females and 42.66% of males spent more than 10 hours daily in this sector. Overall, most of the females spend 1–5 hours and most of the males spend more than 10 hours daily in the power looms sector. 90.91% of elder females and 61.90% of elder males don't spend any time in the power loom sector. On the other hand, 9.09% of elder females and 4.76% of elder males spend 1–5 hours daily in the power loom sector. 23.81% of elder males spend 6–10 hours and 9.52% of elder males spend more than 10 hours in this sector. We found that females spend less time in the power loom sector in comparison to males. Although we also found that most of the female members of all households are more engaged in 'domestic activities' (from Table 16.1) and when they have finished their 'domestic chores', they help in the family business even though the time spent by them is less in comparison to men. Most unmarried women are either doing 'domestic work' or 'farming & study'. Thus, a female who belongs to a rural household related to power looms faces more burden than any other female who belongs to any other household which does not relate to power looms.

From the regression results in Table 16.3, we found that the time spent in the power looms sector is negatively related to age and the time spent in different major activities while it is positively related to education. As age increases by one unit, time spent in the power loom sector decreases by 0.0525273 hours, and as the education level increases by one unit, time spent in the power loom sector increases by 0.1488056 hours. Despite this positive relationship, the quality of education of the people in Benipur is not in good condition. They have been admitted to schools and colleges, but they engage again in power loom activities after school that affect their studies. Furthermore, when people increase their time in different major activities except for power looms by an hour, the time spent in power looms reduces by 0.4277095 hours. We already mentioned in the methodology part that D1, D2, and

Table 16.3.   Factors Affecting Time Spent in the Power Loom Sector.

Time spent in the Power Loom Sector	Coefficients	Standard Error	t	P > |t|	|95% Confidence Interval|	
Age	−0.0525273	0.0179802	−2.92	0.004	−0.0878803	−0.0171742
Education level	00.1488056	0.0357118	4.17	0.000	0.0785881	0.2190232
Time spent in major activities	−0.4277095	0.1023843	−4.18	0.000	−0.6290202	−0.2263987
D1 (male)	3.454141	0.4599116	7.51	0.000	2.54985	4.358431
D2 (unmarried people)	−5.876883	0.6655931	−8.83	0.000	−7.18559	−4.568177
D3 (widowed people)	−1.543481	2.314111	−0.67	0.505	−6.093548	3.006585
Constant	5.50593	0.8438563	6.52	0.000	3.846717	7.165142

Source: Authors' estimation using the field survey data.

D3 are dummies for gender and marital status. We have taken females as a reference point for gender and married people as a reference point for marital status. So, we found the values of time spent by males, unmarried people, and widowed people by comparing the values of dummies with the reference point. Therefore, the time spent by females is 5.50593 hours, while the time spent by males is 8.960071 hours daily in the power loom sector. Married people spend 5.50593 hours, unmarried people spend 0.370953 hours, and widowed people spend 3.962449 hours. Additionally, the probability values of all variables are less than 0.05; thus, all values are significant except D3 (widowed people). Moreover, most of the workers belong to the middle class in Benipur village, and they continuously try to reduce poverty and enhance their income but do not focus on improving the quality of their education. Due to their family power loom businesses, the participants do not get much time for their studies, especially in the case of females. The patriarchal norms (i.e. only females should be in the kitchen not males) are pushing a female to do domestic work from her childhood. They have to learn all the domestic chores as well as have to take care of the family members; thus, their educational qualification is badly injured. With a busy schedule, a female contributes to her family business without any remuneration.

During survey time, many observations were made regarding female participants. If even one female member of a household is available for making food or doing household chores, then other female members have a chance to contribute to power looms activities without any salary. Most of the females do preparatory activities, while the main work like handling the machines is the work of males. Likewise, children and old people also do a little bit of the preparatory activities without any remuneration. We also found that some females are engaged in tailoring, some males joined private jobs, some family members work as daily wage labour, etc. The workers in the power loom need much time to produce a greater number of units because one saree can take up to 5–6 hours to produce. They rarely have time to engage in other kinds of activities or jobs. However, we found that most people pursue farming as an alternative activity to power loom, and it was the only means of livelihood during the COVID-19 pandemic. Therefore, workers engage in farming activities seasonally, and many workers stop their weaving work during harvesting.

8. Results and Discussions

In all the discussion at hand, it can be said that in Benipur village, women are less likely than men to participate in the power loom sector. Female children are more enrolled than male children in education at each level, but women belonging to the working age group have lower education qualifications than men at each level. This indicates that women's involvement in education decreases with age, but this does not happen in the case of men. We also observed that the female participants were more involved in education than male participants at their initial age. However, their involvement falls as they grow as compared to men. This demonstrates that women's education is not being given much importance in rural areas of Benipur. Due to lower educational qualifications, women are not aware of this new technology of power loom (Sultana & Nisa, 2016). Hence, female participation is less than male participation in the power looms sector among all age categories, and the participation of both males and females together is comparatively highest in the working age group while least in the children group. The participation of female children and males of all age groups is negligible in 'domestic chores'. On the contrary, females from the working age group and elder females are more involved in 'domestic chores'. Similarly, females from the working age group and elder females are engaging in 'farming & domestic activities', but male participants of all age groups and female children have no role in both of these activities. We can conclude that this study shows gender inequality in the education and burden of 'domestic chores'.

Furthermore, this study found that the participants are involved in various major activities other than the power loom activities such as 'farming', 'study', 'domestic chores', 'farming & domestic', 'study & domestic', 'private job', 'tailoring', 'farming & study', 'farming & domestic and study', 'labour', and 'others'. Even today 'farming or agriculture' is the most important major alternate activity for the livelihood of the people who are related to the power looms sector. In addition, workers are making a profit now, but not as much as before the pandemic. The main problem for weavers is high raw material prices, high electricity bills, and not being able to get a fair price on their finished products. Through the in-depth interviews, this study has found that before the pandemic, workers were getting high profits from power looms, but after the pandemic or at the time of the pandemic, workers were facing huge losses (Maheshwari & Singh, 2023). The demonetisation and high rate of Goods and Services Tax may have contributed to the increase in the cost of raw materials. The profitability level will continue to fall unless there is a simultaneous increase in the fabric price (Shende & Musam, 2020). During the pandemic time, many power loom workers started to search for other jobs except power looms for livelihood and a few workers even mentioned to have stopped weaving work due to lots of problems (Dharmaraju, 2006; Kumudha & Rizwana, 2013; Kudachimath, 2019; Badkar & Benal, 2022). Weavers, who have *bunkar*[4] cards, are also not satisfied. The government provided them with a subsidy on electricity through *bunkar* cards, yet they are not entertaining any type of subsidy on electricity at present. Despite all the issues highlighted, most of the workers are continuing to weave in power looms due to their adherence. On the contrary, most of the workers in the power looms sector started to find alternate options for their bread earnings during the pandemic. Few workers stopped doing weaving work due to lots of problems (Srivastava, 2023). Many workers who are bearing loans are not able to pay them back. Furthermore, weavers are making a profit even in the present time but not as much as they gained earlier and many workers are disappointed with this sector because they do not find the appropriate prices for their products in the market. Moreover, the prices of raw materials are continuously increasing (Tanusree, 2015). They are using expensive raw materials in the weaving but do not get desirable prices. According to the responses of a few power loom weavers, one of the main reasons for not getting the desired profit is the involvement of middlemen. Middleman acts as a mediator between weavers and shopkeepers. Weavers sell their produced items to a middleman first and then that middleman sells those produced items to all shops, malls, etc. Middlemen used to buy produced items at low prices. Hence, the number of middlemen should be reduced, and if the weavers are directly connected with shops, stores, malls, consumers, etc., then the condition of the weavers could be improved. Otherwise, if the condition of weavers is not improved, many weavers of power looms would cease weaving permanently and they would not take this sector as their children's occupation. Many people do not want their children to learn weaving due to various issues associated with working in the sector.

9. Conclusions and Policy Implications

Based on the major findings of this study, we suggest that, firstly, the weavers in the power loom, especially women workers, should be provided with a significant amount of subsidy to motivate and encourage them to work efficiently and to their full potential. Secondly, the increasing cost of raw materials is the major

---

[4]The government provides financial support to weavers through this card, like subsidies on electricity bills, pensions, etc.

concern of the workers in Benipur which affects the sale of the products and their profit margin. Specific measures and policies should be implemented, and the sale of products made through weaving should be marketed. Thirdly, the government should also focus on encouraging various enterprises to invest in the weaving industry in rural areas and purchase their products so that the sale of their products will increase their profits. Fourthly, the power loom workers should be given special training to market their products through various channels. However, this study has not discussed the impact of the decision-making power of women in the time spent in the power loom sector due to time limitations.

References

Badkar, P. S., & Benal, M. M. (2022). Estimation of damping ratio of silicone rubber using half power bandwidth method. *Materials Today: Proceedings, 59*(5), 679–682. https://doi.org/10.1016/j.matpr.2021.12.219

Chakraborty, S. (2019). Contribution of the unpaid family labour in the handloom sector of textile industry in West Bengal. *The Indian Journal of Labour Economics, 62*, 693–713. https://doi.org/10.1007/s41027-019-00185-6

Dadheech, R., & Sharma, D. (2023). Home-based work or non-home-based work? Factors influencing work choices of women in the informal sector. *International Journal of Sociology and Social Policy, 43*(1/2), 89–106. https://www.emerald.com/insight/0144-333X.htm

Das, S. (2018). Present scenario and some problems of handloom industry a study with handloom weavers' in Tufanganj block-i of Cooch Behar district West Bengal. *International Journal of Research in Humanities, Arts and Literature, 6*(9), 153–170. https://www.impactjournals.us

"Demography". (2011). Census of India website. *Benipur Census Town City Population Census 2011–2024 | Uttar Pradesh*. November 1, 2021. https://www.census2011.co.in/data/town/209729-benipur-uttar-pradesh.html#google_vignette

Deshpande, N. (2018, August 7). Weavers bear the brunt as powerlooms displace the handloom sector. The Wire. https://thewire.in/labour/weavers-bear-the-brunt-as-power-looms-displace-the-handloom-sector

Dev, S. M., Galab, S., Reddy, P. P., & Vinayan, S. (2008). Economics of handloom weaving: A field study in Andhra Pradesh. *Economic and Political Weekly, 43*(21), 43–51.

Dharmaraju, P. (2006). Marketing in handloom cooperatives. *Economic and Political Weekly, 41*(31), 3385–3387.

Dhonde, B., & Patel, C. R. (2020). Characterization of freight trip from textile powerloom units – A case study of Surat, India. *Transportation Research Procedia, 48*, 428–438. https://doi.org/10.1016/j.trpro.2020.08.050

Directorate of Handloom and Textiles under the Government of Uttar Pradesh. (2023). https://handloom.upsdc.gov.in/

Gautam, N. (2022). Addressing the gap areas crucial for survival by focusing on the key growth determinants of micro, small and medium enterprises in India: A critical analysis pertaining to textile sector MSMEs. *The Indian Economic Journal, 70*(4), 577–596. https://doi.org/10.1177/00194662211062423

Joshi, P. P., & Padole, D. N. (2016). Powerloom industry in Solapur: Challenges and barriers in growth. *International Journal in Management & Social Science, 4*(4), 76–79.

Kolgiri, S., & Hiremath, R. (2019). Sustainable postural research for women workers from power-loom industry Solapur City, Maharashtra, India. *International Journal of Innovative Technology and Exploring Engineering (IJITEE)*, *8*(11), 377–382. https://doi.org/10.35940/ijitee.K1068.09811S19

Kudachimath, B. (2019). Determinants of turnover intention: A context of decentralized power loom sector in North Karnataka. *Journal of Advanced Research in Dynamical & Control Systems*, *11*(9), 690–699. https://doi.org/10.5373/JARDCS/V11/20192623

Kumar, I. V. S., & Sulaiman, E. (2017). Crisis of handloom units in Kerala and Tamil Nadu: An empirical study on the problems and challenges. *Journal of Rural and Industrial Development*, *5*(1), 22–34.

Kumar, N. (2016). The weavers of Banaras. *Economic and Political Weekly*, *51*(53), 59–63.

Kumudha, A., & Rizwana, M. (2013). Problems faced by handloom industry – A study with handloom weavers' co-operative societies in erode district. *International Journal of Management and Development Studies*, *2*(3), 50–56.

Maheshwari, K., & Singh, C. (2023). Sustainability of artists and craft persons during COVID-19: A case study of Kalakriti creations. In S. K. Dixit & S. Piramanaygam (Eds.), *Teaching cases in tourism, hospitality and events* (pp. 276–287). CABI.

Mahiat, T., Alam, M. A. A., Argho, M., Corlett, J., Chowdhury, R. B., Biswas, K. F., Hossain, M. M., & Sujauddin, M. (2023). Modeling the environmental and social impacts of the handloom industry in Bangladesh through life cycle assessment. *Modeling Earth Systems and Environment*, *9*(1), 239–252. https://doi.org/10.1007/s40808-022-01491-7

Ministry of Textiles, Government of India. (2019–2020). Fourth all India – Handloom census, 2019–2020. https://handlooms.nic.in/assets/img/Statistics/3736.pdf

Ministry of Textiles, Government of India. (2022). *Press information bureau*. Retrieved February 2, 2023, from https://pib.gov.in

Ministry of Textiles, Government of India. (2022–2023). *Annual report: 2022–23*. https://texmin.nic.in/sites/default/files/English%20Final%20MOT%20Annual%20Report%202022-23%20%28English%29_0.pdf

Mishra, A., Mohapatra, C. K., Pattnaik, P. K., & Satpathy, S. P. (2022). Issues and challenges of the Indian handloom sector: A legal perspective. *Rupkatha Journal on Interdisciplinary Studies in Humanities*, *14*(3), 1–11. https://doi.org/10.21659/rupkatha.v14n3.15

Mishra, T., Chatterjee, S., & Thakkar, J. J. (2023). Effect of coronavirus pandemic in changing the performance barriers for textile and apparel industry in an emerging market. *Journal of Cleaner Production*, *390*(136097), 1–14. https://doi.org/10.1016/j.jclepro.2023.136097

Mugilan, G., & Muthukumar, K. (2021). Study of physical hazard faced by the workers in power-loom. *International Research Journal of Engineering and Technology (IRJET)*, *8*(01), 589–593.

Olive, P. F., Mahendran, K., Lavanya, S. M., & Kumar, D. P. (2022). Status of handloom sector in India and Tamil Nadu State and Government initiatives for its promotion. *Asian Journal of Agricultural Extension, Economics & Sociology*, *40*(2), 29–35. https://doi.org/10.9734/AJAEES/2022/v40i230843

Patali, S. (2020, May 9). *Power loom cluster in India*. Textile Value Chain. https://textilevaluechain.in/in-depth-analysis/articles/textile-articles/power-loom-cluster-in-india/

Prusty, J. R., & Mallick, S. (2022). Powerloom in textile industry: A study of Siminoi powerloom cluster of Dhenkanal district in Odisha. *Journal of Asian and African Studies*, *59*(4), 1117–1134. https://doi.org/10.1177/00219096221130351

Rai, S. K. (2022). Handloom cloth production in colonial united provinces: The response to industrial competition. *Studies in People's History*, *9*(1), 46–58. https://doi.org/10.1177/23484489221080908

Shende, A. H., & Musam, P. (2020). Factors affecting performance of powerloom industry in Maharashtra – A review of literature. *Studies in Indian Place Names, 40*(75), 138–144.

Singh, P., & Pattanaik, F. (2018). Economic status of women in India: Paradox of paid–unpaid work and poverty. *International Journal of Social Economics, 46*(3), 410–428. https://doi.org/10.1108/IJSE-05-2018-0277

Singh, P., & Pattanaik, F. (2020). Unfolding unpaid domestic work in India: Women's constraints, choices, and career. *Palgrave Communications, 6*(1), 1–13. https://doi.org/10.1057/s41599-020-0488-2

Srivastava, J. (2023). The problems and challenges of the handloom co-operative societies in Varanasi district. *International Journal for Multidisciplinary Research, 5*(2), 1–9.

Sultana, F. M., & Nisa, M. (2016). Socio-economic condition of power loom weavers: A case study of Mau City. *International Journal of Humanities and Social Science Invention, 5*(11), 31–36.

Tanusree, S. (2015). A study of the present situation of the traditional handloom weavers of Varanasi, Uttar Pradesh, India. *International Research Journal of Social Sciences, 4*(3), 48–53.

Tasnim, G. (2020). Making women's unpaid care work visible in India: Importance and challenges. *Journal of International Women's Studies, 21*(2), 28–35.

Zara, B., Pervaiz, M., Aamir, M., Hamza, M., Yasir, I., & Naz, F. (2022). Prevalence and pattern of respiratory health problems among power loom workers in Mohallah Hajiabad, Faisalabad. *Pakistan Journal of Medical & Health Sciences, 16*(1), 374–376. https://doi.org/10.53350/pjmhs22161374

Chapter 17

Identifying Wage Inequality in Indian Urban Informal Labour Market: A Gender Perspective

Shiba Shankar Pattayat and Sumit Haluwalia

Department of Economics, CHRIST (Deemed to be University), Bangalore, Karnataka, India

Abstract

This chapter elucidates the wage differential between male and female informal workers in urban labour market by using employment and unemployment survey 61st (2004–2005) round, 68th (2011–2012), and Periodic Labour Force Survey 2019–2020 data of National Sample Survey Office (NSSO) unit level data. This study found that gender inequality not only increased during getting job but also persists after getting job during wage distribution. Based on the Oaxaca–Blinder (OB) decomposition, it is revealed that gender wage inequality is more in the labour market due to the labour market discrimination, that is, unexplained components. Hence, this study helps researcher, policy makers and government to fix the gender wage discrimination issues exist in the Indian labour market. This will enhance economic growth through the rise of the women labour force participation.

Keywords: Gender; informal employees; urban; Oaxaca–Blinder decomposition; labour market

Informal Economy and Sustainable Development Goals:
Ideas, Interventions and Challenges, 335–357
Copyright © 2024 by Shiba Shankar Pattayat and Sumit Haluwalia
Published under exclusive licence by Emerald Publishing Limited
doi:10.1108/978-1-83753-980-220241018

1. Introduction

The phenomenon of wage differential in labour markets has witnessed a significant increase over the past two or three decades due to various factors. In the
Indian labour market, unequal wage distribution is a major contributor to overall
income inequality. Consequently, treating workers fairly and without discrimination based on gender, caste, or job contracts is a moral and social imperative.
Eliminating wage discrimination can also lead to increased efficiency of labour
and growth in the overall economy. Numerous studies, such as Edgeworth (1922),
Becker (1957), and Arrow (1973), have explored the economics of labour market
discrimination from a theoretical perspective. In developing countries like India,
sociologists and anthropologists, including Berreman (1979), Beteille (1969),
Bhattacharya (2011), Cox (1959), and Wadhawa (1975), have undertaken empirical analyses of labor market discrimination. However, these empirical studies
mainly focused on caste discrimination in general, rather than specifically on
labour market discrimination.

In India, there have been other studies that have examined wage discrimination using data from the NSSO and the India Human Development Survey, conducted by the National Council of Applied Economic Research. Gender-based
wage discrimination in India has garnered significant academic attention since the
mid-1990s when the gender wage gap became evident. Researchers like Bhaumik
and Chakrabarty (2008), Deshpande and Deshpande (1997), Divakaran (1996),
Kingdon (1997, 1998), Kingdon and Unni (2001), and Sengupta and Das (2014)
have delved into this subject. Moreover, certain studies, such as Banerjee and
Knight (1985) and Madheswaran and Attewell (2007), have utilized NSSO data
to investigate caste-based wage discrimination in urban labour markets. Other
researchers like Gaiha et al. (2007), Ito (2009), Kijima (2006), Deshpande (2001),
Das and Dutta (2007), and Agrawal (2014) have examined the same issues in rural
labour markets.

A separate line of research represented by Gustafsson and Li (2000),
Schober and Winter-Ebmer (2011), and Taniguchi and Tuwo (2014) argues
that wage discrimination is determined by productivity differences among
workers. These productivity differences can be attributed to a growing mismatch between skill demand and supply (Blau & Kahn, 2017; Filippin & Ichino,
2005; Petreski et al., 2014).

The empirical research conducted in India (Agrawal, 2014; Ara, 2021;
Bhaumik & Chakrabarty, 2008; Chakraborty, 2020; Duraisamy & Duraisamy,
2016; Dutta & Reilly, 2008; Kingdon & Unni, 2001; Kijima, 2006; Kumar &
Hashmi, 2020; Lama & Majumder, 2018; Madheswaran & Attewell, 2007;
Madheswaran & Singhari, 2016; Singhari & Madheswaran, 2017; Singh &
Parida, 2020; Singh et al., 2020; Unni, 2005; Pattayat et al., 2023) has consistently found that women generally earn less than their male counterparts
due to existing anomalies and discriminatory practices in the labour market.
Furthermore, Deshpande (2017), Deshpande et al. (2018), and Pattayat et al.
(2023) have uncovered a 'sticky floor' phenomenon affecting female employees, contributing to gender wage disparities in urban India. Madheswaran

(2010) also identified a gender wage gap among regular salaried workers in urban labour markets caused by both the glass ceiling and sticky floor effect. While some studies have explored caste-based wage discrimination in informal labour markets (Singhari & Madheswaran, 2017), there have been limited investigations into gender wage disparities within this sector. Abraham (2019) and Kumar and Pandey (2021) conducted a study on gender wage discrimination in the informal labour market using NSSO data.

Given the scarcity of recent research on gender earning differences among informal employees in urban India, this study aims to address this research gap by estimating gender wage differentials in the urban informal labour market. Additionally, the study will explore the determinants of wages in urban informal labour market using Mincerian earning equation. Moreover, this study also tries to identify the factors of gender wage gap by employing the OB (average) decomposition method where it analyses the explained and unexplained components of wage discrimination. The findings of this research may aid policymakers in designing effective strategies to enhance women empowerment through women's work participation rate in Indian labour market.

This chapter is structured into four main sections. The second section of this study focuses on detailing the data and methodology. In Section 3, the results and discussions are presented. This section is further divided into four subsections. The first subsection offers an initial discussion on the workforce participation of men and women as well as their employment types and shares in informal sector jobs in urban India. Section 3.2 of this section covers the findings of the average wage differentials (Mean and Median). In the Section 3.3, an examination of the determinants of wages for both regular and casual workers is conducted, utilizing Heckman earning equation. Section 3.4 involves a thorough discussion of the OB decomposition results. Finally, in Section 4, the chapter concludes with policy suggestions based on the research findings.

2. Data and Methodology

2.1. Sources of Data

This study is based on secondary data. We have used both employment and unemployment survey data (61st round data in 2004–2005 and 68th round in 2011–2012) and the annual Periodical Labour Force Survey (PLFS) data conducted during 2019–2020. These two separate data rounds are comparable because these surveys use a similar interview schedule and they cover an equally large number of households across the states of India using a multi-stage stratified random sampling method (PLFS, 2019). Although in the PLFS, second-stage stratification is based on education (the number of household members having secondary and above level of education) criterion instead of the monthly per capita spending of the households, the selection of first stage units (villages and urban wards) and the hamlet groups (sub-blocks of large First Stage Sampling Units [FSUs]) in both these surveys are based on same population size criteria (see Mehrotra & Parida, 2019; Pattayat et al., 2022).

The employment status of a person is defined by combing the usual principal activity status[1] and usual subsidiary activity status.[2] The combination of these two activity status of persons is called as the usual principal and subsidiary status (UPSS). The employment indicators are calculated using the UPSS employment status of the persons. While the wage/earning information of the persons are estimated from the current weekly activity status file. The mean and median values of wage (for casual labour) and salary (for regular salaried workers) are computed for both men and women for comparison.

To estimate the informal sector employment, this study follows the definition of informal employment as proposed by National Commission on Enterprises in the unorganized sector (NCEUS) under Government of India. According to NCEUS (2007), 'Unorganized workers consist of those working in the unorganized enterprises or households, excluding regular workers with social security benefits, and the workers in the formal sector without any employment/social security benefits provided by the employers'. In this study, informal sector employment is taken into consideration and tries to examine the gender wage difference among informal sector employment in urban India.

The National Industrial Classification codes for 1998 and 2008 are used after due concordance to identify different sectors such as agriculture, manufacturing and services. To find out the broad occupation categories, we have used the National Classification Occupation code-200. Having the above information, dummy variables are created for important indicators which are used for the Mincerian earning equation (see Section 3).

2.2. Empirical Methods

An augmented Mincerian earning equation[3] (see Chiswick, 2003; Heckman et al., 2003) is estimated to determine the factors affecting informal sector wage. It is expressed as

$$\log(W_i) = X_i\beta + Y_j\gamma + \theta C + \varepsilon \tag{1}$$

---

[1]The UPS status of a person is determined on the basis of the major time or major occupation criteria. It includes that activity of a person, in which he/she has been engaged in most of the times (normally more than 180 days) during the last 1 year (or the 365 days preceding the date of survey).

[2]The USS is the activity in which a person is engaged for a period of at least 30 days, but less than 180 days during the reference year (last 365 days preceding the date of survey). Those persons, who report that they have not been engaged in any work-related activities for a period of 180 days and more, will have only a USS. But, persons, who are engaged in multiple activities, will also have USS along with their UPS (these persons's USS is not considered during calculation of UPSS to avoid double counting).

[3]This equation is important for this study because it helps researcher to find the earning of the worker based on their level of education and labour market experience.

where log (W_i) is the natural logarithm of daily wages/earning. Y_j is a vector of occupational characteristics, X_i is a vector of individual-level factors, C is the social group dummy (takes 1 for STs and SCs, OBC and 0 otherwise) (see details in the Appendix). We assume that these are all exogenous factors. And β, γ, δ, and θ are vectors of constant parameters to be estimated, and ε is an unobserved error term. This study has restricted the sample to only wage workers (both regular salaried and casual labour) for which actual daily wage is reported. This eliminates the issue of self-selection bias in our estimation.

For decomposing the average (mean) gender wage differential, the OB decomposition method (Blinder, 1973; Oaxaca, 1973) is used. The simplest form of the OB decomposition is as follows:

$$\log(W_M) - \log(W_F) = \sum (X_M \beta_M - X_F \beta_F) + \sum (Z_M \gamma_M - Z_F \gamma_F) \quad (2)$$

The subscripts M indicate male and F indicate female. The wage differential is to be estimated[4] using the above equation. The modified versions of OB decomposition, as suggested by Reimers (1983), Cotton (1988), Neumark (1988), are also used to show the twofold decomposition[5] (productivity and discrimination components) of wage differentials (see Table 17.3).

3. Results and Discussion

3.1. Workforce Participation and Gender

This chapter starts discussion with the workforce participation (WPR) of both male and female in Indian informal labour market. It is witnessed that WPR of females is quite lower as compared to their male counter parts in Indian informal labour market. This result is similar to the study of Pattayat et al. (2023) which indicates that WPR of female is lower than the male in Indian labour market due to individual and household factors. It is also noticed that WPR of female has been declining over the period of time (see Table 17.1). Consequently, this gender disparity is found in both rural and urban labour markets. However, urban labour market shows more gender disparities as compared to rural labour market (see Table 17.1). It is clearly reflected through a relatively higher WPR ratio (male/female).

Although the gender inequality in access to jobs, measured through the WPR, in urban India had increased during 2004–2005 and 2011–2012 from 3.39 to 3.99, it had declined substantially during 2011–2012 and 2019–2020 from 3.99 to 3.56. This is, indeed, a good sign. Nonetheless, the gender inequality in access to job has risen in rural Indian informal labour market. It is clearly witnessed from the

---

[4]For the detail derivation of equations, see Madheswaran and Attewell (2007).

[5]For the detail discussion and derivation of two- and three-fold equations, see Jann (2008).

Table 17.1.   Sector-wise Workforce Participation Rate (%) of Men and Women in Indian Informal Labour Market.

Year	Male	Female	Total	Male/Female
		Rural areas		
2004–2005	53.7	32.4	43.2	1.66
2011–2012	53.3	24.4	39.1	2.18
2019–2020	52.5	23.4	38.1	2.24
		Urban areas		
2004–2005	49.5	14.6	32.0	3.39
2011–2012	49.5	12.4	30.9	3.99
2019–2020	48.1	13.5	30.5	3.56
		Rural + urban areas		
2004–2005	52.7	28.0	40.5	1.88
2011–2012	52.3	21.1	36.8	2.48
2019–2020	51.3	20.5	35.9	2.50

Source: Author's estimation using NSS and PLFS unit level data.

ratio of male to female where the ratio increased from 1.66 to 2.18 during 2004–2005 and 2011–2012 and reached to 2.24 during 2019–2020.

Furthermore, the percentage share of female workforce in the urban informal labour market shows a very grim picture in Fig. 17.1. It is clearly visible that women workers had occupied only about 22.9% of the total urban informal sector jobs during 2004–2005 but have declined further to 20% during 2011–2012 and increased again to 22.6% during 2019–2020. The share of female WPR declined because female were being pushed out of the agriculture sector due to mechanization (Mehrotra et al., 2014; Pattayat et al., 2022), participation in education (Hirway, 2012) and rising standard of living and social constraints (Klasen & Pieters, 2015; Mehrotra & Parida, 2017). This is very worst and worrying case in Indian labour market.

The occupational distribution between genders in urban informal labour market reveals that a major chunk of urban informal workers are engaged as self-employed (own account worker, employer and unpaid domestic worker[6]) and casual workers. The self-employed workers and casual workers together contributed 73.6% workforce during 2004–2005 (see Table 17.2). However, it has substantially increased to 97.6% during 2019–2020. It indicates large number of people working as low skilled as unpaid domestic worker in urban Indian informal labour market.

---

[6]See NSSO and PLFS schedule where it mentioned that worker worked as helper in household enterprises is called unpaid family worker.

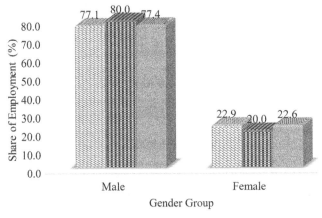

Fig. 17.1.   Gender-wise Distribution Informal Employment in Urban India, 2005–2020. *Source*: Author's plot using NSS and PLFS unit level data.

The gender inequality based on types of employment (favouring men) is also noted where large chunks of man are working as own account worker, while majority of female workers are working as unpaid domestic worker in urban informal sector in India (see Table 17.2). This is a clear reflection of the societal setting in India, in which women normally do engage themselves in almost all the

Table 17.2.   Distribution of Informal Workers by Their Type of Employment and Gender, 2005–2020.

	2004–2005			2011–2012			2019–2020		
	Male	Female	Total	Male	Female	Total	Male	Female	Total
Own account worker	41.5	27.5	38.3	39.5	31.2	37.8	38.6	29.5	3.9
Employer	3.6	0.9	2.9	3.3	0.5	2.8	5.5	1.0	0.0
Unpaid domestic work	10.5	27.1	14.3	8.5	20.3	10.8	5.2	14.4	93.7
Regular wage employee	26.7	25.2	26.4	30.6	30.7	30.6	33.0	41.0	0.0
Casual worker	17.8	19.3	18.1	18.1	17.2	17.9	17.7	14.2	2.4
Total	100	100	100	100	100	100	100	100	100

Source: Author's estimation using NSS and PLFS unit level data.

activities of their family. They not only cook foods for the family, take care of the kids and elderly, and do other household chores, but they also found shouldering their spouse (or the main bread winner) in running family business. However, in case of regular employees in urban informal sector, more female are working as compared to male. It may be due to the informality nature of work where low-skilled female worker agree to work without any social security. On the other workers in our patriarchy society, female has less bargaining power as compared to male worker. As a result, female workers are paid low wage rate without any social security benefit.

However, despite all these contributions, women are still restricted only to domestic chores and allowed to participate in education. But they are not found in the wage employment activities. In this context, it is argued that availability of skilled job opportunities in urban areas near to their vicinity could be one of the major reasons behind the low female work participation in urban informal sectors. This aspect of urban informal labour market could be partly revealed through the wage distribution of the both men and women.

3.2. Mean Wage Differential by Gender Groups in Urban Informal Sector

This section of the study discusses about the mean wage differences by male and female (see Fig. 17.2). The log of daily wage distributions of female employees

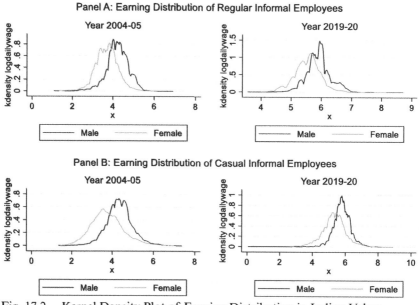

Fig. 17.2.   Kernel Density Plot of Earning Distribution in Indian Urban Informal Sector Employment by Gender. *Source*: Author's estimation using NSS and PLFS unit level data.

is placed towards the left of the wage distribution of their male counterparts within the urban informal labour market (see Fig. 17.2). This implies that female workers earn relatively less as compared to their male counterparts throughout the wage distribution. This is noted in both regular salaried employees and casual workers during 2004–2005 and 2019–2020. Panel A of Fig. 17.2 indicates the mean wage difference male and female among regular salaried worker while panel B indicates for casual worker (Fig. 17.2, panels A and B). This finding is consistent with earlier studies like Duraisamy and Duraisamy (2016), Deshpande et al. (2018), Chakraborty (2020), Singh et al. (2020), Ara (2021), and Poddar and Mukhopadhyay (2019) which have found that the gender wage difference prevails in urban India and within regular salaried employees.

Beginning with casual employees, we find that both mean and median wage of male and female employees are rising during 2004–2005 and 2011–2012. However, the average wage rate for casual workers declined during 2011–2012 and 2019–2020. The mean wage difference between male and female casual employees increased from about ₹22.54 to about ₹59.7 during 2004–2005 and 2011–2012 and declined to about ₹39.22 during 2019–2020. Similarly, the median wage difference between casual employees in the urban informal sector increased from about ₹25 to about ₹60 during 2004–2005 and 2011–2012 (Table 17.3).

In the case of regular salaried employees, we observed that the mean wage difference between male and female employees has been rising over the period of time during 2004–2005 and 2019–2020. It is also noted that while the mean wages of female regular employees have consistently been rising during 2011–2012 and 2019–2020 (Table 17.3). This is the main reason for the declining mean gender wage gap among urban non-farm sector regular employees in India. The median wage gap also revealed a similar pattern of decline. Although male workers earned about two times higher than their female counterparts during 2004–2005, this has declined to less than one and half times during 2019–2020. Although reducing the gender wage gap is desirable, it should not be at the cost of male wage rates. In order to attract more females into the non-farm regular jobs, the average wage rate of females needs to be increased. But a reduction in the male wage rate in the non-farm sectors may discourage many educated urban males from participating in the labour market.

To further explore the factors determining the gender wage gaps in regular and casual employment in the urban informal sectors, we have estimated the earning functions of both regular and casual employees separately.

3.3. Determinants of Wages of Male and Female Workers

The factors determining wages of regular and casual employees in urban informal sector can be classified into two broad categories, viz. endowment variables and occupational variables. The endowment variables include personal characteristics of employees such as age, gender, marital status, education (both general and technical education), vocational training, job market experience, social groups, and religion. On the other hand, the occupational variables include employment

Table 17.3.   Average Daily Wage of Informal Workers by Gender Groups in Urban India.

	Mean Wage (Rupees)			Median Wage (Rupees)		
	2004–2005	2011–2012	2019–2020	2004–2005	2011–2012	2019–2020
Regular salaried employees						
Male	94.01	246.41	384.62	75.00	200.00	333.33
Female	57.07	154.75	247.79	40.00	107.14	200.00
Difference (male–female)	36.94	91.67	136.83	35.00	92.86	133.33
Ratio (male/female)	1.65	1.59	1.55	1.88	1.87	1.67
Casual labour						
Male	46.00	127.00	43.71	45.00	120.00	0.00
Female	23.47	67.27	4.49	20.00	60.00	0.00
Difference (male–female)	22.54	59.73	39.22	25.00	60.00	0.00
Ratio (male/female)	1.96	1.89	9.74	2.25	2.00	0.00

Source: Author's estimation using NSS and PLFS unit level data.

dummies in urban informal sector (manufacturing, non-manufacturing and service sector) and occupational dummies (professional, administrative, clerical, sales worker and agriculture and associated worker). Two Heckman regression equations (for both male and female) are estimated for the comparison in urban informal labour market (see Table 17.4). The result of the first- and second-stage equations is given below in Table 17.4. It is witnessed that the inverse Mill's ratio is statistically significant in both male and female equations. There would have been biased estimates, if self-selection had not been corrected.

To begin the discussion with the coefficient of age, we found positive and statistically significant coefficient of age. It indicates that determination of wage of a worker those are working in urban informal labour market depends on the age. The physical capability of the youth (15–29 years) population is greater as compared to other age groups people.

As expected, we found the positive significant coefficient of job experience and the statistically significant negative coefficient for job experience square. This is found in both male and female equations (see Table 17.4). This reflects the true labour market features. It indicates that there are positive returns to the job

Table 17.4. Determinants of Wages in Urban India (Heckman's Selection Regression Results).

Indicators	Male Equation				Female Equation			
	Stage 1		Stage 2		Stage 1		Stage 2	
	Coefficient	Z-value	Coefficient	Z-value	Coefficient	Z-value	Coefficient	Z-value
Age	0.084	175.6***	—	—	0.017	44.74***	—	—
Household size	-0.015	-8.16***	—	—	-0.054	-28.68***	—	—
Job experience	—	—	0.256	42.38***	—	—	0.125	28***
Job experience square	—	—	-0.003	-25.56***	—	—	-0.001	-13.92***
Log MPCE	-1.079	-13.01***	—	—	-0.923	-14.55***	—	—
Log MPCE square	0.052	9.64***	—	—	0.049	11.91***	—	—
Social groups dummies (reference category: scheduled tribe)								
SC	0.175	8.17***	—	—	-0.14	-7.54***	—	—
OBC	0.099	5.11***	—	—	-0.147	-8.86***	—	—
Other caste	0.06	3.11***	—	—	-0.298	-17.68***	—	—
Religion groups dummies (reference category: other religion)								
Hindu	0.045	2.04**	0.198	2.72***	-0.025	-1.24	0.041	0.49
Muslim	0.156	6.36***	-0.034	-0.43	-0.221	-9.79***	-1.118	-11.4***
Christian	-0.039	-1.36	0.111	1.24	0.351	14.09***	1.276	12.15***

(Continued)

Table 17.4.   (*Continued*)

Indicators	Male Equation				Female Equation			
	Stage 1		Stage 2		Stage 1		Stage 2	
	Coefficient	Z-value	Coefficient	Z-value	Coefficient	Z-value	Coefficient	Z-value
Level of education dummies (reference category: illiterate)								
Primary	0.049	2.55**	0.951	17.34***	−0.189	−16.38***	−0.234	−4.43***
Secondary	−0.275	−13.42***	1.048	17.01***	−0.427	−28.81***	−0.72	−9.38***
Higher secondary	−0.425	−20.3***	1.144	17.24***	−0.404	−25.3***	−0.211	−2.54**
Graduate	0.117	5.11***	2.809	38.89***	0.074	4.65***	1.933	25.79***
Post graduate and above	0.469	14.02***	4.202	44.29***	0.475	22.18***	3.862	39.44***
Technical education dummies (reference category: no technical education)								
Tech below graduate	0.139	5.52***	0.621	8.31***	0.403	16.17***	1.445	14.53***
Tech graduate and above	−0.019	−0.52	0.282	2.5**	0.387	11.29***	1.078	8.08***
Vocational education dummies (reference category: no formal education)								
Formal vocational education	0.185	9.42***	0.242	3.76***	0.636	35.57***	1.474	17.17***
Informal vocational education	1.249	58.85***	1.216	25.22***	1.075	67.97***	2.641	26.27***
Marital status dummies (reference category: unmarried)								
Currently married	—	—	0.244	6.9***	—	—	−0.448	−11.79***
Widow	—	—	0.209	1.33	—	—	0.435	7.63***
Divorced/separated	—	—	0.134	0.62	—	—	0.285	3.09***

Industrial sector dummies (reference category: agriculture)								
Manufacturing	0.473	4.74***	—	—	–1.002	–14.26***	—	—
Non-manufacturing	0.713	7.08***	—	—	0.814	9.62***	—	—
Service	0.354	3.63***	—	—	0.227	3.24***	—	—
Occupation dummies (reference category: elementary worker)								
Professional	0.157	3.2***	—	—	0.475	9.38***	—	—
Administrative work	–1.628	–37.46***	—	—	–1.386	–28.56***	—	—
Clerical	1.216	18.8***	—	—	1.346	19.71***	—	—
Sales worker	–0.665	–17.22***	—	—	–0.624	–14.66***	—	—
Agriculture and associated work	–1.723	–16.56***	—	—	–2.264	–30.69***	—	—
Year dummies (reference category: 2004–2005)								
2011–2012	–0.009	–0.67	—	—	0.017	1.27	—	—
2019–2020	–0.288	–19.49***	—	—	–0.143	–9.52***	—	—
Constant	3.464	11.07***	–3.137	–19.05***	3.351	13.86***	–4.065	–20.13***
Lambda		4.88	50.92***	—		4.084	36.71***	—
Rho	1				1			
Sigma	4.88				4.084			
Observation	148,335				146,641			
Selected	108,536				31,452			
Non-selected	39,799				115,189			
Wald chi2 (25)	9,821.63***				13,329.51***			

Source: Authors estimation using NSSO and PLFS unit level data.
Note: ***, **, and * implies 1%, 5%, and 10% level of significance.

experience. But after a threshold level, it turns out to be negative as job experience continued to rise. Because, after threshold level (it may be the case when workers tend to attend their retirement age or they become older), the worker's productivity tends to decline. If workers are paid according to their productivity, their average wage is likely to decline after this threshold age is reached. This phenomenon is reflected by their mean log wage. This result is similar with previous studies like (Pattayat et al., 2022, 2023), where they discussed that after a certain age productivity of a worker will decline which leads to decline of their wage.

The other important factor of wage determination is level of education. It plays a very important role in determining the wage rate of regular informal employees in the urban labour market in India. It's as we expected: positive and significant effects have been obtained for certain level of general education dummies, whereas negative and significant effects have been obtained for other certain level of general education. It is clearly visible from urban informal labour market that higher level of education (graduate, post-graduate and above) have positive impact on the wage rate. However, lower level of education (illiterate, primary and secondary) has negative impact on wage rate. This result is consistent with Kingdon (1998) and Pattayat et al. (2023), where it argued that level of education reduces the gender wage discrimination and helps to increase rate of returns, that is, higher earnings. The statistically significant education dummies coefficients in both male and female equations also support Mincer's argument.

Similarly, the coefficients of technical education dummies (below graduate level and above graduate level) show that log wage is positively influenced by technical training education. On an average, workers without technical qualifications tend to earn a relatively lower wage rate in the urban informal sector as compared to workers with technical education degree. This result is consistent with the findings of Singh et al. (2020), Dhanaraj and Mahambare (2019), and Pattayat et al. (2022, 2023). Moreover, holding a graduate-and-above level technical degree significantly affects female employees' wage rates (see Table 17.4).

Holding vocational degree in urban informal labour market determines the wage rate of a worker. This is also an important factor for the wage determination in urban informal sector in India. The returns to vocational education found positive and significant result for both male and female workers. It indicates workers with vocational degree are getting more salary/wage as compared to workers without any vocational degree (Mehrotra & Parida, 2020; Pattayat et al., 2022).

After examining the sectors of employment dummies, we found negative significant coefficient for women those are engaged in manufacturing sector while opposite result we found their male counterparts (see Table 17.4). It indicates that females engaged in the manufacturing sector earn, on average, less than those involved in the agriculture, non-manufacturing and service sectors. If we see the gender disparities within urban manufacturing sectors, female are on an average earn lower wages than their male counter parts (see Table 17.4).

Furthermore, it is observed positive and significant coefficient for both male and female workers who are engaged in both non-manufacturing and service sector dummies. However, gender disparities also exist within these two sectors.

Male are getting higher wages as compared to their female counter parts in urban informal labour market. This result is consistent with Pattayat et al. (2023).

The observation from the result of occupational dummies indicates that the worker engage in urban informal sector as an administrator or engaged in administrative activities on an average earn less wages as compared to worker engaged in other occupation like professional, clerical, etc. It may be due to the informality nature of work. For example, being a receptionist is one kind of administrative work. Those working as receptionists are used to getting lower payments. The positive and statistically significant coefficient of occupational dummies like professional and clerical indicates that informal workers who engaged as professional workers and clerks earn more wages than other occupational dummies. This is because professional workers and clerks belong to skilled workers. According to human capital theory, skill is the most important factor for determining the wage rate of any individual. Hence, people engaged in that sector get higher wages. However, we found a negative and statistically significant coefficient for sales workers, agriculture, and associated work, which reflects the wage disparities across the occupations. On average, those working in these sectors earn less than other occupations. For this occupation, low-skilled workers are required. Hence, the wage rate is less.

Finally, we have noticed that the individual's social group and religious categories significantly determine the wages of males and females. This is as expected since the informal labour market in urban India and various socio-cultural norms often prejudice it.

3.4. OB Decomposition Results

In this section, we try to explain the gender wage differences among the workers in the urban informal labour market. The OB decomposition method splits the wage differential into explained and unexplained components. While the described component of wage differential can be considered endowment differences, the unexplained part can be termed pure discrimination in the labour market (Madheswarn & Attewell, 2007). Moreover, we further decomposed using the methods of Reimers (1983), Cotton (1988), and Neumark (1988). These methods have been used to determine the counterfactual wage differentials (see Table 17.5).

First, we consider the regular salaried employees in the urban informal sector. The twofold decomposition results suggest the wage differential between males and females in the urban informal sector due to both endowment and unexplained differences.

When women are paid as per their wage rate (or salary) structure (i.e. $D = 0$), there is about a 0.3% wage difference owing to the difference in their human capital endowments (productivity differences). Nearly 100% of the wage differences are because of discrimination against female employees during 2004–2005. In sharp contrast, the labour market discrimination against regular women workers in urban informal sectors has declined to 96% during 2019–2020. This is a good sign for women, but this percentage is still high (see Table 17.5).

Table 17.5.   Earning Decomposition Results by Gender Groups in Urban Informal Labour Market (OB Method).

	Regular Worker			Casual Worker		
	2004–2005	2011–2012	2019–2020	2004–2005	2011–2012	2019–2020
Mean prediction high (H):	4.21	5.31	5.71	2.72	3.75	5.87
Mean prediction low (L):	3.74	4.75	5.21	2.22	3.12	5.49
Raw differential (R) {H-L}:	0.47	0.56	0.51	0.50	0.63	0.38
Due to endowments (E):	-0.002	-0.03	0.02	-0.04	-0.08	0.010
Due to coefficients (C):	0.47	0.58	0.51	0.40	0.65	0.37
Due to interaction (CE):	0.003	0.012	-0.021	0.14	0.06	-0.001
	Oaxaca (1973) and Blinder (1973) $D = 0$					
Unexplained difference	0.474	0.589	0.485	0.542	0.704	0.368
Explained difference	-0.002	-0.028	0.02	-0.042	-0.076	0.01
% unexplained	100.3	105	96.1	108.5	112	97.5
% explained	-0.3	-5	3.9	-8.5	-12	2.5
	Oaxaca (1973) and Blinder (1973) $D = 1$					
Unexplained difference	0.471	0.577	0.506	0.403	0.648	0.369
Explained difference	0.001	-0.017	-0.001	0.096	-0.019	0.008
% unexplained	99.7	103	100.2	80.8	103	97.8
% explained	0.3	-3	-0.2	19.2	-3	2.2

Reimers (1983) $D = 0.5$

Unexplained difference	0.473	0.583	0.496	0.473	0.676	0.369
Explained difference	0	−0.022	0.009	0.027	−0.047	0.009
% unexplained	100	104	98.2	94.6	107.5	97.7
% explained	0	−4	1.8	5.4	−7.5	2.3

Cotton (1988) D = sample proportions

Unexplained difference	0.472	0.58	0.501	0.424	0.658	0.369
Explained difference	0.001	−0.019	0.004	0.075	−0.03	0.008
% unexplained	99.8	103.4	99.2	85	104.7	97.8
% explained	0.2	−3.4	0.8	15	−4.7	2.2

Neumark (1988) D = pooled

Unexplained difference	0.417	0.525	0.437	0.368	0.62	0.34
Explained difference	0.056	0.036	0.068	0.131	0.009	0.037
% unexplained	88.2	93.7	86.5	73.7	98.6	90.1
% explained	11.8	6.3	13.5	26.3	1.4	9.9

Source: Author's estimation using NSS and PLFS unit level data.

The counterfactual decomposition results suggest that if female regular employees in urban informal sectors were paid based on the men's wage structure (i.e. $D = 1$), wage discrimination still persists. About 99.7% of wage discrimination exists in the urban informal labour market. It is due to unexplained factors, that is, purely due to labour market discrimination. Then, this discrimination increased to 103% during 2011–2012 and further declined to 100% during 2019–2020. Moreover, if females were paid based on male–female average wage structure (i.e. $D = 0.5$), discrimination still persists among regular employees in the urban informal sector during 2004–2005, 2011–2012, and 2019–2020. Similarly, if females were paid according to the sample proportions (D = sample proportions), women are still discriminated against due to labour market discrimination. Hence, women are getting lower salaries than their male counterparts in the Indian urban informal labour market. However, we found a few good results; if females were paid based on the pooled wage rate structure (D = pooled), gender wage discrimination exists in the labour market. However, labour market discrimination due to unexplained factors declined from 88.2% in 2004–2005 to 86.5% in 2019–2020. Only 13.5% of wage discrimination is due to explained factors, that is, productivity differences among male and female workers.

The wage decomposition results of casual labour show a similar pattern (see Table 17.5). It indicates that the wage gap between men and women workers in the urban informal, casual labour market is primarily due to existing labour market discrimination or unexplained factors. This result is consistent with the studies like Ara (2021), Chakraborty (2020), Deshpande et al. (2018), and Duraisamy and Duraisamy (2016), which have found that the gender wage differentials are mainly owing to the existing labour market discriminations. Evidently, the skill level of men and women casual, informal workers in urban areas is not much different. Still, due to labour market discrimination, women workers suffer a lot.

4. Concluding Remarks and Policy Suggestion

From the above observation, it can be stated that gender inequality is not only an exit for getting jobs in the labour market but also persists after getting jobs, that is, during wage distribution in both urban and rural labour markets. The degree of gender wage discrimination has been increasing in the last two and three decades. This wage disparity is increasing in the urban labour market, which may be due to skill mismatch of workers, a large share of low-skilled migration from rural to urban areas and social stigma. The result clearly shows that the average (mean and median) earning gap between males and females increased during 2004–2005 and 2019–2020. From the regression result, we found that individual, household, industrial sector and occupation factors are responsible for the wage determination in the urban labour market. The level of education (general, technical and vocational) is the most important factor for the higher wage rate. The OB decomposition result reveals that a higher percentage of gender wage disparity among informal employees is due to existing labour market discrimination or unexplained factors.

Hence, the outcomes of this study help researchers, policymakers and the government fix the gender wage discrimination issues in the Indian labour market.

Moreover, policymakers and government officials should focus on enhancing the skill level of women workers, which can reduce gender wage inequality. Furthermore, the government should adopt a suitable and sustainable policy for providing minimum social security benefits to informal workers. This will enhance economic growth by increasing women's labour force participation.

Limitations: This study can be conducted for rural labour markets as well as state-specific labour markets. Only micro-level data are used.

Conflict of Interest

There is no conflict of interest.

References

Abraham, R. (2019). Informal employment and the structure of wages in India: A review of trends. *Review of Income and Wealth, 65*, S102–S122.

Agrawal, T. (2014). Gender and caste-based wage discrimination in India: Some recent evidence. *Journal for Labor Market Research, 47*(40), 329–340.

Ara, S. (2021). Gender pay gap in India: Evidence from urban labour market. *The Indian Journal of Labour Economics, 64*(2), 415–445.

Arrow, K. J. (1973). The theory of discrimination. In O. Ashenfelter & A. Rees (Eds.), *Discrimination in labour markets* (pp. 3–33). Princeton University Press.

Banerjee, B., & Knight, J. B. (1985). Caste discrimination in the Indian urban labor market. *Journal of Development Economics, 17*(3), 277–307.

Becker, G. S. (1957). *The economics of discrimination*. University of Chicago Press.

Berreman, G. D. (1979). *Caste and other inequities*. Folklore Institute.

Beteille, A. (1969). *Castes old and new essays in social structure and social stratification*. Asia Publishing House.

Bhattacharya, P. C. (2011). Informal sector, income inequality and economic development. *Economic Modelling, 28*(3), 820–830.

Bhaumik, S. K., & Chakrabarty, M. (2008). Does move to market have an impact on earnings gap across gender? Some evidence from India. *Applied Economics Letters, 15*(8), 601–605.

Blau, F. D., & Kahn, L. M. (2017). The gender wage gap: Extent, trends, and explanations. *Journal of Economic Literature, 55*(3), 789–865.

Blinder, A. S. (1973). Wage discrimination: Reduced form and structural estimates. *Journal of Human Resources, 8*(4), 436–455.

Chakraborty, S. (2020). Gender wage differential in public and private sectors in India. *The Indian Journal of Labour Economics, 63*(3), 765–780. https://doi.org/10.1007/s41027-020-00246-1

Chiswick, B. R. (2003). Jacob Mincer, experience and the distribution of earnings. *Review of Economics of the Household, 1*(4), 343–361.

Cotton, J. (1988). On the decomposition of wage differentials. *The Review of Economics and Statistics, 70*(2), 236–243. https://doi.org/10.2307/1928307

Cox, O. C. (1959). *Caste, race and class. A study in social dynamics*. Monthly Review Press.

Das, M. B., & Dutta, P. V. (2007). *Caste matter for wages in the Indian labor market: Caste pay gaps in India*. The World Bank, Human Development Unit.

Deshpande, A. (2001). Caste at birth? Redefining disparity in India. *Review of Development Economics, 5*(1), 130–144.

Deshpande, A. (2017). Interview with Ashwini Deshpande: "Sticky floors are becoming stickier for women in the Indian labor market." *Journal of Economic Sociology, 18*(4), 188–193.

Deshpande, A., Goel, D., & Khanna, S. (2018). Bad karma or discrimination? Male–female wage gaps among salaried workers in India. *World Development, 102*, 331–344. https:// doi.org/10.1016/j.worlddev.2017.07.012

Deshpande, S., & Deshpande, L. K. (1997). Gender-based discrimination in the urban labour market in India. *Indian Journal of Labour Economics, 40*(3), 545–562.

Dhanaraj, S., & Mahambare, V. (2019). Family structure, education and women's employment in rural India. *World Development, 115*, 17–29.

Divakaran, S. (1996). Gender based wage and job discrimination in urban India. *Indian Journal of Labour Economics, 39*(2), 235–257.

Duraisamy, M., & Duraisamy, P. (2016). Gender wage gap across the wage distribution in different segments of the Indian labour market, 1983–2012: Exploring the glass ceiling or sticky floor phenomenon. *Applied Economics, 48*(43), 4098–4111. https://doi. org/10.1080/00036846.2016.1150955

Dutta, P. V., & Reilly, B. (2008). The gender pay gap in an era of economic change: Evidence for India, 1983 to 2004. *Indian Journal of Labour Economics, 51*(3), 341–366.

Edgeworth, F. Y. (1922). Equal pay to men and women for equal work. *Economic Journal, 32*(128), 431–457.

Filippin, A., & Ichino, A. (2005). Gender wage gap in expectations and realizations. *Labour Economics, 12*(1), 125–145.

Gaiha, R., Thapa, G., Imai, K., & Kulkarni, V. S. (2007). *Disparity, deprivation and discrimination in rural India* [BWPI Working Paper 13]. Brooks World Poverty Institute, University of Manchester.

Gustafsson, B., & Li, S. (2000). Economic transformation and the gender earnings gap in urban China. *Journal of Population Economics, 13*(2), 305–329.

Heckman, J. J., Lochner, L., & Todd, P. E. (2003). *Fifty years of Mincer earnings regressions* [Working Paper 9732] National Bureau of Economic Research (NBER). https:// www.nber.org/papers/w9732

Hirway, I. (2012). Missing labour force: An explanation. *Economic and Political Weekly, 47*(37), 67–72. http://www.jstor.org/stable/41720140

Ito, T. (2009). Caste discrimination and transaction costs in the labor market: Evidence from rural north India. *Journal of Development Economics, 88*(2), 292–300.

Jann, B. (2008). A stata implementation of the Blinder–Oaxaca decomposition. *Stata Journal, 8*(4), 453–479.

Kijima, Y. (2006). Caste and tribe inequality: Evidence from India, 1983–1999. *Economic Development and Cultural Change, 54*(2), 369–404.

Kingdon, G. G. (1997). Labor force participation, returns to education, and sex discrimination in India. *The Indian Journal of Labour Economics, 40*(3), 507–526.

Kingdon, G. G. (1998). Does the labour market explain lower female schooling in India. *Journal of Development Study, 35*(1), 39–65.

Kingdon, G. G., & Unni, J. (2001). Education and women's labour market outcomes in India. *Education Economics, 9*(2), 173–195.

Klasen, S., & Pieters, J. (2015). What explains the stagnation of female labor force participation in urban India? *The World Bank Economic Review, 29*(3), 449–478.

Kumar, A., & Hashmi, N. I. (2020). Labour market discrimination in India. *The Indian Journal of Labour Economics, 63*(1), 177–188. https://doi.org/10.1007/s41027-019-00203-7

Kumar, M., & Pandey, S. (2021). Wage gap between formal and informal regular workers in India: Evidence from the national sample survey. *Global Journal of Emerging Market Economies, 13*(1), 104–121.

Lama, S., & Majumder, R. (2018). Gender inequality in wage and employment in Indian labour market. *Journal of Academic Research in Economics, 10*(3), 482–500.

Madheswaran, S. (2010). Labour market discrimination in India: Methodological developments and empirical evidence. *Indian Journal of Labour Economics, 53*(3), 457–480.

Madheswaran, S., & Attewell, P. (2007). Caste discrimination in the Indian urban labor market: Evidence from the National Sample Survey. *Economic and Political Weekly, 42*(41), 4146–4153.

Madheswaran, S., & Singhari, S. (2016). Social exclusion and caste discrimination in public and private sectors in India: A decomposition analysis. *The Indian Journal of Labour Economics, 59*(2), 175–201.

Mehrotra, S., & Parida, J. K. (2017). Why is the labour force participation of women declining in India? *World Development, 98*, 360–380.

Mehrotra, S., & Parida, J. K. (2019). *India's employment crisis: Rising education levels and falling non-agricultural job growth* [Working Paper No. 4]. CSE. http://publications.azimpremjifoundation.org/2119/1/Mehrotra_Parida_India_Employment_Crisis.pdf

Mehrotra, S., & Parida, J. (2020). *What it would cost to provide social security to unorganized workers in India?* Mimeo.

Mehrotra, S., Parida, J., Sinha, S., & Gandi, A. (2014). Explaining employment trends in the Indian economy: 1993–94 to 2011–12. *Economic & Political Weekly, 49*(32), 49–57.

National Commission for Enterprises in the Unorganized Sector. (2007). *Report on the condition of work and promotion of livelihoods in the unorganized sector.* http://dcmsme.gov.in/Condition_of_workers_sep_2007.pdf

Neumark, D. (1988) 'Employers' discriminatory behavior and the estimation of wage discrimination. *The Journal of Human Resources, 23*(3), 279–295. https://doi.org/10.2307/145830

Oaxaca, R. L. (1973). Male–female wage differentials in the urban labour market. *International Economic Review, 14*, 693–709.

Pattayat, S. S., Parida, J. K., & Awasthi, I. C. (2022). Reducing rural poverty through non-farm job creation in India. *The Indian Journal of Labour Economics, 65*(1), 137–160.

Pattayat, S. S., Parida, J. K., & Paltasingh, K. R. (2023). Gender wage gap among rural non-farm sector employees in India: Evidence from nationally representative survey. *Review of Development and Change, 28*(1), 22–44.

Petreski, M., Blazevski, N. M., & Petreski, B. (2014) Gender wage gap when women are highly inactive: Evidence from repeated imputations with Macedonian data. *Journal of Labor Research, 35*(4), 393–411.

Poddar, S., & Mukhopadhyay, I. (2019). Gender wage gap: Some recent evidences from India. *Journal of Quantitative Economics, 17*(1), 121–151.

Reimers, C. W. (1983). Labor market discrimination against Hispanic and Black Men. *The Review of Economics and Statistics, 65*(4), 570–579. https://doi.org/10.2307/1935925

Schober, T., & Winter-Ebmer, R. (2011) Gender wage inequality and economic growth: Is there really a puzzle? – A comment. *World Development, 39*(8), 1476–1484.

Sengupta, A., & Das, P. (2014). Gender wage discrimination across social and religious groups in India estimates with unit level data. *Economic and Political Weekly, 49*(21), 71–76.

Singh, S., & Parida, J. K. (2020). Employment and earning differentials among vocationally trained youth: Evidence from field studies in Punjab and Haryana in India. *Millennial Asia, 13*(1), 47–51. https://doi.org/10.1177/0976399620964308

Singh, S., Parida, J. K., & Awasthi, I. C. (2020). Employability and earning differentials among technically and vocationally trained youth in India. *The Indian Journal of Labour Economics, 63*(2), 363–386. https://doi.org/10.1007/s41027-020-00222-9

Singhari, S., & Madheswaran, S. (2017). Wage structure and wage differentials in formal and informal sectors in India: Evidence from NSS data. *The Indian Journal of Labour Economics, 60*, 389–414.

Taniguchi, K., & Tuwo, A. (2014). *New evidence on the gender wage gap in Indonesia* [Economics Working Paper Series No. 404]. Asian Development Bank.

Unni, J. (2005). Wages and incomes in formal and informal sectors in India. *The Indian Journal of Labour Economics, 48*(2), 311–317.

Wadhawa, K. K. (1975). *Minority safeguards in India.* Thomson Press.

Appendix: Summary of Statics of Variables Used in the Regression Models

	Male					Female				
	Observation	Mean	Std. Dev.	Min	Max	Observation	Mean	Std. Dev.	Min	Max
logdailywage	303,598	1.8	2.7	0.0	11.5	281,795	0.5	1.5	0.0	8.9
Age	303,598	29.5	18.8	0.0	110.0	281,795	30.1	19.1	0.0	110.0
Household size	303,598	5.3	2.6	1.0	34.0	281,795	5.4	2.5	1.0	34.0
Currently married	303,571	0.5	0.5	0.0	1.0	281,776	0.5	0.5	0.0	1.0
Widow	303,571	0.0	0.1	0.0	1.0	281,776	0.1	0.3	0.0	1.0
Divorced/separated	303,571	0.0	0.1	0.0	1.0	281,776	0.0	0.1	0.0	1.0
SC	303,544	0.1	0.3	0.0	1.0	281,746	0.1	0.3	0.0	1.0
OBC	303,544	0.4	0.5	0.0	1.0	281,746	0.4	0.5	0.0	1.0
Other caste	303,544	0.4	0.5	0.0	1.0	281,746	0.4	0.5	0.0	1.0
Hindu	303,598	0.7	0.4	0.0	1.0	281,795	0.7	0.4	0.0	1.0
Muslim	303,598	0.2	0.4	0.0	1.0	281,795	0.2	0.4	0.0	1.0
Christian	303,598	0.1	0.3	0.0	1.0	281,795	0.1	0.3	0.0	1.0
logmpce	303,598	7.3	0.8	0.0	17.7	281,795	7.3	0.8	0.0	17.7
Logmpce square	303,598	53.6	11.9	0.0	314.3	281,795	53.4	11.9	0.0	314.3
Job experience	303,598	16.6	17.4	0.0	104.0	281,795	18.3	19.0	0.0	104.0
Job experience square	303,598	577.7	930.8	0.0	10,816.0	281,795	695.0	1,092.9	0.0	10,816.0
Primary	303,374	0.4	0.5	0.0	1.0	281,593	0.4	0.5	0.0	1.0
Secondary	303,374	0.1	0.3	0.0	1.0	281,593	0.1	0.3	0.0	1.0

Higher secondary	303,374	0.1	0.3	0.0	1.0	281,593	0.1	0.3	0.0	1.0
Graduate	303,374	0.1	0.3	0.0	1.0	281,593	0.1	0.3	0.0	1.0
Post graduate and above	303,374	0.0	0.2	0.0	1.0	281,593	0.0	0.2	0.0	1.0
Tech below graduate	303,598	0.0	0.2	0.0	1.0	281,795	0.0	0.1	0.0	1.0
Tech graduate and above	303,598	0.0	0.1	0.0	1.0	281,795	0.0	0.1	0.0	1.0
Formal Voc. Edu	163,631	0.1	0.2	0.0	1.0	152,826	0.0	0.2	0.0	1.0
Informal Voc. Edu	163,631	0.1	0.3	0.0	1.0	152,826	0.0	0.2	0.0	1.0
Manufacturing	159,154	0.2	0.4	0.0	1.0	47,971	0.2	0.4	0.0	1.0
Non-manufacturing	159,154	0.1	0.3	0.0	1.0	47,971	0.0	0.2	0.0	1.0
Service	159,154	0.6	0.5	0.0	1.0	47,971	0.5	0.5	0.0	1.0
Professional	163,742	0.1	0.3	0.0	1.0	48,932	0.2	0.4	0.0	1.0
Administrative work	163,742	0.1	0.3	0.0	1.0	48,932	0.1	0.3	0.0	1.0
Clerical	163,742	0.1	0.2	0.0	1.0	48,932	0.0	0.2	0.0	1.0
Sales worker	163,742	0.2	0.4	0.0	1.0	48,932	0.2	0.4	0.0	1.0
Agriculture and associated work	163,742	0.1	0.3	0.0	1.0	48,932	0.1	0.4	0.0	1.0
2011–2012	303,598	0.3	0.5	0.0	1.0	281,795	0.3	0.5	0.0	1.0
2019–2020	303,598	0.3	0.5	0.0	1.0	281,795	0.3	0.5	0.0	1.0

Source: Author's estimation using NSSO and PLFS data.

Chapter 18

Gender Disparity in the Informal Sector Employment in India

B. S. Sumalatha and V. P. Nirmal Roy

Gulati Institute of Finance and Taxation, Thiruvananthapuram, Kerala, India

Abstract

India experiences enormous informalisation of employment which has become a global phenomenon in recent times. The quality of work, conditions of work and social security protection are important concerns in the growing informal sector. One of the sustainable development goals (SDGs) deals with 'decent work' for all. It is also reported that the inequalities and disparities in work participation and wage payment are high in the informal employment than the formal. Under this context, this study examined the status of informal employment in India by analysing different categories of informal employment, labour force participation rate (LFPR) and wage payments in detail. The aim of the study is to highlight the gender gap in these indicators of employment. The findings of the study show that there is an increase in the LFPR in both the usual and current weekly status (CWS) statuses in the course of all the periodical labour force surveys (PLFSs). The gender gap was prevalent not merely in the rural areas, but in the urban areas as well. The informal sector constitutes the highest share of employment in India, with self-employed individuals contributing the most. Half the workforce is not eligible for paid leave and other social security benefits, and wage disparities exist between rural and urban regions. This difference is found among both female and male wage workers in both the rural and urban regions. Female employees are much more vulnerable as there is a gender gap and a regional gap in wages paid to the regular employees.

Keywords: Informal employment; labour force participation rate; gender; wages; India

Informal Economy and Sustainable Development Goals:
Ideas, Interventions and Challenges, 359–371
Copyright © 2024 by B. S. Sumalatha and V. P. Nirmal Roy
Published under exclusive licence by Emerald Publishing Limited
doi:10.1108/978-1-83753-980-220241019

Introduction

The informalisation of employment is seen worldwide mainly after the economic reforms and liberalisation policies that were introduced by various nations. The informal employment constitutes more than 90% of India's total workforce working as self-employed and casual workers in India. The informal sector also contributes to nearly 50% of the national income in the country (Government of India, 2013–2014). There is also an increasing trend of informal employment within the organised sector (Abraham, 2019). The eighth goal of the SDGs of United Nations is to ensure not only productive employment but decent work for all. Inclusive and sustainable employment is an important factor for achieving SDGs (Rai et al., 2019). Though the government has adopted several policy measures for achieving SDGs, the issues and challenges pertaining to the informalisation of employment are yet to be considered (Srija & Shirke, 2012). LFPR is a wisely used indicator to analyse the employment rate of an economy. The gender gap in the LFPR and other indicators of employment are important issues that need high attention in the research and policy-making endeavours. The gender gap in the labour force participation is reported high in the Middle East, North African and South Asian countries. The female LFPR ranges from 21% in North Africa and Middle East to 71% in the Pacific region and East Asia during 2010. In India, the overall LFPR is 40%, and for females, it is 23% during the same period (Sanghi et al., 2015). The differences in economic development, literacy levels, fertility rates, access to childcare, prevailing social norms and other supportive mechanisms contribute to the varying levels of female labour force participation across countries.

It is also observed that there is a decline in the female labour force participation in India, in general, and among rural females, in particular. Besides the level of education, increased income, lack of quality jobs, the role of women as primary caregivers in the family and mechanisation of agriculture are the reasons reported by the literature to establish the declining female LFPR (CII Discussion paper, 2018; Kapsos et al., 2014; Mehrotra & Parida, 2017). The non-availability of non-farm jobs in the rural areas has resulted in women staying away from the labour market (Sanghi et al., 2015). The increased unpaid household activities make the females to take a decision of not taking up paid jobs outside (Ferrant et al., 2014). Absorbing female workers is important considering the huge potential of demographic dividend and female population which account for half of the population that our country is endowed with (Sanghi et al., 2015). Given this background, this study tries to look into the current scenario of gender disparity in informal employment in India by dealing with LFPR, categories of informal employment, various sectors of employment and wage payment using the latest data.

Review of Literature

According to the definition provided by The National Commission for Enterprises in the Unorganised Sector (NCEUS), 'the informal or unorganised sector is the unincorporated private enterprises owned by individuals or households which engage in the sale and production of goods and services operated on a proprietary or partnership basis with less than ten workers' (Srija & Shirke, 2012). As per the NCEUS definition,

> Informal workers consist of those working in the informal sector or households, excluding regular workers with social security benefits provided by the employers and the workers in the formal sector without any employment and social security benefits provided by the employers. (Srija & Shirke, 2012, p. 41)

Informality in employment is persisting in India with around 90 percentage of workers who are employed under the informal sectors and nearly 80 percentages in urban areas (Mehrotra, 2019; Raveendran & Vanek, 2020). Informality in employment is also seen within the formal enterprises (Abraham, 2019). Workers' education, gender and vocational training determine the participation in informal employment (Sheikh & Gaurav, 2020).

The female workforce participation rate in India is on the decline (Chakraborty, 2020). While in rural areas, female workers constitute less than half of male workers, and it is one-third in urban areas. Majority of the female workers in rural areas are self-employed or casual workers and agricultural workers. Though most of the female workers in urban areas engage in regular jobs, they are largely involved in low productive and low skilled employment of the informal sector (IWWAGE, 2021). There also exists gender and caste-based inequalities in employment in India (Neetha, 2014). A better working environment is a key to enhance women's participation in the labour market by promoting gender equality and non-discrimination at work (Shankaran & Madhav, 2011). Labour market inequality mainly consists of sector wise wage inequality, inequality in terms of quality of work, labour market access and inequalities between unorganised and organised sectors. In order to reduce these inequalities, investments in social sector infrastructure such as health, education and public service provisioning are mandatory (Dev, 2018). Wage disparity exists between the informal and formal sectors in terms of gender, religion and caste (Singhari & Madheswaran, 2017). Gender wage discrimination is found to be higher in informal employment than the formal (Deininger et al., 2013). The impartial labour market outcome at the lower section of the population can be attained with the appropriate labour market regulation, social protection mechanisms and anti-discrimination policies in place (Srivastava, 2019).

Sita and Rajarshi (2018) analysed the forms in inequality and workers conditions across formal and informal sectors using the National Sample Survey Organisation (NSSO) data. The study finds that there is a disparity in the LFPR and wages among workers of different sectors, regions and genders. The employment growth in rural India is distress driven and poverty-pushed, and the feminisation of work, higher underemployment rate and high dependence on unpaid household work are also seen in the agricultural distress regions (Abraham, 2009). Growing income and rising social mobility in the Indian patriarchal society resulted in the withdrawal of female labourers from paid work and confining to do unpaid domestic work including cooking, cleaning and babysitting. Female population belonging to the lower strata of the population face multiple vulnerabilities of class, caste and gender hierarchies and remain within the informal sector labour force for their subsistence (Abraham, 2013; Neetha, 2014). The factors such as demographic characteristics, education, labour market flexibility and other state policies determine the female labour force participation in India (Sorsa et al., 2015). Given this background, this study tries to look at the recent status of gender gap in employment and wages in the informal sector in India using the latest PLFS.

Data and Methods

This study is based on secondary data and information. The data pertaining to LFPR, informal sector employment, wages paid to different categories of informal workers are taken from the PLFS conducted during the period 2017–2018 and 2020–2021 by the Ministry of Statistics and Programme Implementation, Government of India. Simple techniques such as cross tables and figures are used to present the data.

Analysis and Discussion

This section details not only data analysis and inferences drawn from different data on various aspects of employment such as sector wise, category wise and state/union territory wise LFPR but also informal employment and category wise average earnings of informal workers. The detailed discussion on these aspects is presented in the following sections.

Labour Force Participation Rate in India

This section analyses the LFPR according to different employment statuses, distribution of workers by the category of employment, industry wise distribution of workers in usual status, social group wise LFPR and the state/union territory wise LFPR in India.

Concepts

The LFPR is defined as the 'percentage of persons in the labour force amongst the persons in the population' (Government of India, 2020–2021, p. 47).

> The workforce in the usual status (principal status + subsidiary status) is obtained by considering the usual principal status and subsidiary status together. The workforce in the usual status (principal status + subsidiary status) includes (a) the persons who worked for a relatively long part of the 365 days preceding the date of survey and (b) the persons from among the remaining

population who had worked for at least for 30 days during the reference period of 365 days preceding the date of survey.

The workforce measured in the Current Weekly Status (CWS) gives the average picture of the workforce in a short period of one week during the survey period. The estimate of workforce in the CWS is derived by considering those who worked for at least an hour on any day during the 7 days preceding the date of survey. (Government of India, 2020–2021)

Employment Category, Status and Sector Wise Labour Force Participation Rate

As per the data given by the Periodic Labour Force Survey Annual Report, 2020–2021, Government of India, it can be seen that there is an increase in the LFPR in both the usual status (increased from 36.9% to 41.6% from 2017–2018 to 2020–2021) and CWS (35.9% to 39.2% from 2017–2018 to 2020–2021) during all the PLFSs. The situation is identical for rural and urban areas. If we look at the gender wise LFPR, we can see that there is an increase in the LFPR for both males and females in both the categories in all the PLFSs. The gender gap in LFPR is visible for the usual status and CWS in all the PLFSs. During the period of 2020–2021, the male LFPR in usual status was 7.5%, whereas it was only 25.1% for females. In the case of CWS, male LFPR is 56.5% and 21.2% for females during the same period. The gender gap in LFPR is more in the urban region compared to the rural in the case of both usual status and CWS. Despite having several policies to encourage labour market participation, the gender gap remains high in the Indian context.

It can be noted from the data that the workers engaged in the category of self-employed have increased from 57.8% to 61.3% in rural areas and 38.3% to 39.5% in urban areas. Workers who engage in the regular wage and casual labour categories have seen a decline in the case of both rural and urban areas. It is also important to see that there exists a gender gap in different categories of employment. In the case of self-employed, it is the females who are engaged more compared to males in the rural areas. This is mainly due to the reason that in rural areas men largely participate in casual labour and females in self-employment and on the other hand in urban areas, both men and women engage more in regular wage employment followed by self-employment. Men engage more in the regular wage/salary employment and casual labour than the female in the rural areas. In the case of regular wage and casual labour employment in urban areas, females engage more in the former and males engage more in the latter case (Periodic Labour Force Survey Annual Report, 2020–2021, Government of India).

According to the data given, the agriculture sector constitutes the highest employment share in the rural areas followed by construction, trade, hotel and restaurant. In the case of urban areas, it is the trade, hotel and restaurant and other services that constitute the highest employment followed by manufacturing and construction. During the period of PLFS 2020–2021, overall, the agriculture sector provides 46.5% of employment followed by trade, hotel and restaurant (12.2%), construction (12.1%) and manufacturing (10.9%). If we look at the female–male composition, we can see that in the rural areas, female workers are engaged more in the agriculture sector (75.4%) followed by manufacturing (7.4%) and construction (5.9%). While in the urban areas, female workers are engaged more in other services (41.6%) and agriculture (10.4%). Though in the rural areas male workers are engaged more in the agriculture sector, their engagement in construction, trade, hotel and restaurant are relatively more compared to rural female workers. Urban male workers are more engaged in trade, hotels and restaurant, other services and the manufacturing sector (Periodic Labour Force Survey Annual Report, 2020–2021, Government of India).

The data also indicate that in the entire social groups, male persons' work participation is higher compared to their female counterparts during the PLFS (2020–2021) and PLFS (2017–2018) for both urban and rural areas. This is again a clear indication of the existing gender gap in the LFPR in India. Male work participation is higher among the 'other' category and STs in rural areas and high among the SCs in urban areas. The gender gap in work participation rate is very high in the rural and urban areas in both the periods of the survey. The female work participation rate is high among STs followed by SCs and OBCs in both the rural and urban areas. This may be due to the fact that the 'other' category females engage largely in the regular wage employment compared to the rest of the groups (Periodic Labour Force Survey Annual Report, 2020–2021, Government of India).

The state/union territory wise LFPR according to the usual status for the age group 15–59 years during 2020–2021 is provided by the PLFS Annual Report, 2020–2021. Overall, the LFPR is high in the states of Andhra Pradesh, Jharkhand, Madhya Pradesh, Tamil Nadu and Telangana and low in the case of Arunachal Pradesh, Bihar, Uttar Pradesh and Lakshadweep. It is very clear from the data that female work participation rate is much lower compared to their male counterparts in all the states and union territories. The male work participation rate is high in the state/union territories of Puducherry, West Bengal, Tripura and Himachal Pradesh and low in Bihar, Mizoram and Ladakh. While the female work participation rate is high in the state/union territories of Chhattisgarh, Himachal Pradesh, Sikkim and Tamil Nadu, it is low in Bihar, Haryana, Delhi and Lakshadweep. In the rural areas, male work participation is high in Himachal Pradesh, Chandigarh and Puducherry and low in Bihar, Goa and Ladakh. Similarly, the female work participation rate is high in Ladakh, Telegana and Meghalaya and low in Bihar, Delhi and Haryana in the rural areas. In the urban areas, male work participation rate is high in Ladakh, Uttarakhand and Sikkim and low in Mizoram, Manipur and Bihar. On the other hand, in the urban areas, the female work participation rate is high in Mizoram, Sikkim, Karnataka and Himachal Pradesh, and it is low in Bihar, Gujarat and Haryana (Periodic Labour Force Survey Annual Report, 2020–2021, Government of India). The state wise variations in the labour force participation are due to the various socio-economic factors including economic development, social development, educational attainments, social norms and falling fertility rates.

Fig. 18.1 provides the state/union territory wise gender gap in the LFPR (percentage difference) for the period 2020–2021. It is important to note that for majority of the states/union territories, the gender gap is nearly half of the LFPR in percentage. The percentage difference of gender gap in the LFPR is high for the states/union territories such as Bihar, Delhi, Punjab, West Bengal and Lakshadweep, whereas, it is low for Himachal Pradesh, Meghalaya and Sikkim.

Employment in the Informal Sector

Besides the details of informal and formal employment and category wise status of informal workforce, this section provides the sectoral distribution of formal and informal employment, category wise details of work contracts, leave availability and other social security benefits. The employment status and gender wise average wage earnings of the workers in India are also dealt with.

Category, Status and Sector Wise Informal Employment and Payment

The data provided by Srija and Shirke (2012) show that there is an increase in informal and formal employment from 426.2 million to 435.66 million and 33.41 million to 38.56 million, respectively, from 2004–2005 to 2011–2012. Informal sector constitutes the highest share of employment to the total employment in India (it is 92% in 2011–2012 period). The category wise status of informal workforce is given in Table 18.1. The self-employed category of employment (56%) is the highest among the informal workforce followed by casual workers (33%) and regular wage workers (11%) in 2011–2012. There is an increase in the regular wageworkers from 36.19 million to 48.79 million and casual workers from 132.81 million to 141.91 million from the period 2004–2005 to 2011–2012. A marginal decline in the workforce (4%) in the self-employed category of informal workforce (257.16 million to 244.97 million) is seen during the period 2004–2005 to

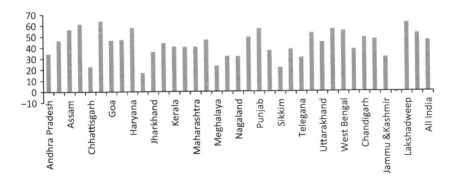

Fig. 18.1. State/Union Territory Wise Gender Gap in LFPR (Percentage Difference). *Source*: Drawn by calculating the gender gap in LFPR (percent) using Periodic Labour Force Survey Annual Report 2020–2021, Government of India.

Table 18.1. Category Wise Status of Informal Workforce (in Million).

Status	2004–2005	2011–2012
Self-employed	257.16 (60%)	244.97 (56%)
Regular wage/salaried	36.19 (8%)	48.79 (11%)
Casual worker	132.81 (31%)	141.91 (33%)
Total informal workforce	426.16 (100%)	435.66 (100%)

Source: Adapted from Srija and Shirke (2012).

2011–2012. The reason for this decline can be attributed to the rise in the workforce in regular wage and casual worker categories of employment.

Informal employment contributes the highest share to the total employment in agriculture, manufacturing, non-manufacturing and services sectors. Agriculture sector has the highest share of informal employment (48.85%) followed by services (21%) and manufacturing (11% and non-manufacturing (10.95%) during 2011–2012. The similar trend was seen during the 2004–2005 period. It is important to note that informal employment has increased in the service sector. The service sector includes trade, hotels, transportation, communications, financial services, real estate, professional services, etc. (Srija & Shirke, 2012).

The details of regular wage employees who are neither eligible for paid leave, not for any social security benefits and have no written job contracts in usual status in non-agricultural sector during PLFS 2017–2018 and 2020–2021 are given in Table 18.2. The percentage of regular wage employees who had no written job contracts in rural and urban areas is 66.3% and 63%, respectively. The gender difference in the percentage of regular wage employees who had no written job contracts is minimal in both the rural and urban areas. It shows that nearly half of the workforce is not covered under the employment benefits. Half of the workforce in both the rural and urban regions is not eligible for paid leave and other social security benefits. In the case of availing of paid leave and social security benefits, not much difference is seen among the rural–urban and female–male.

Table 18.3 indicates the average wage earnings during the previous calendar months by the regular wage employees in CWS during the survey period 2020–2021. It is important to note from the data that there is a huge difference in the wages of regular wage employees in the rural and urban regions. Rural wages is only half of the urban wages. This difference is found among female and male wages in both the rural and urban regions. Female employees are much vulnerable as there is a gender gap and regional gap in wages provided to the regular wage employees.

The casual labourer's average earnings per day in works other than public works during the PLFS period 2020–2021 is presented in Table 18.4. Both male and female workers are getting higher earnings in urban regions compared to their rural counterparts. There is a gender gap in the average earnings of casual labourers in both the urban and rural regions. The female workers are paid less compared to their male counterparts in both the rural and urban regions.

Table 18.2.   Regular Wage Employees Who Are Neither Eligible for Paid Leave Nor Eligible for Any Social Security Benefits and Had No Written Job Contracts in Usual Status (ps + ss) in Non-agriculture Sector During PLFS (2017–2018) and PLFS (2020–2021).

Category of Regular Wage/Salaried Employees	No Written Job Contract		Not Eligible for Paid Leave		Not Eligible for Any Social Security Benefit	
	PLFS (2020–2021)	**PLFS (2017–2018)**	**PLFS (2020–2021)**	**PLFS (2017–2018)**	**PLFS (2020–2021)**	**PLFS (2017–2018)**
Rural						
Male	68.7	71.7	55.5	58.1	59	51.9
Female	58.1	58.5	41.8	47.9	59.3	55.1
Person	66.3	69.2	52.3	56.2	59.1	52.5
Urban						
Male	62.8	72.7	45	53.1	49	47
Female	63.6	71.4	44.9	51.8	53.5	50.1
Person	63	72.4	44.9	52.8	50.1	47.7
Total						
Male	65.2	72.3	49.3	55.2	53.1	49
Female	61.5	66.8	43.7	50.4	55.8	51.8
Person	64.3	71.1	47.9	54.2	53.8	49.6

Source: Periodic Labour Force Survey, Annual Report, 2020–2021, Government of India.

The situation is similar throughout the reference period of the survey when the data were collected.

Table 18.5 presents the average gross earnings during the last 30 days in CWS status during the PLFS 2020–2021. Like in the case of other categories of employment, there is a higher wage rate for both the male and female workers in urban regions in comparison with their rural counterparts. This is a clear indication of the rural–urban gap in wage payment. The female workers get only half of the earnings of their male counterparts in both the rural and urban areas. There is a regional and gender gap in the average gross earnings of self-employed workers during all the reference periods of the survey.

It is understood from the existing research studies and data that female LFPR is much lower in all types of employment compared to males. The major reasons reported by the research studies include the income effect and no substitute available for doing household activities. The rural women engage in domestic duties has increased from 88% to 92% from 1993–1994 to 2011–2012. Out of the females who have reported that they spend most of their time in domestic duties, 60% of them reported that they do not have other people to engage domestic

Table 18.3.   Regular Wage Employees' Average Wage Earnings (in Rs) During the Preceding Calendar Month in CWS During PLFS 2020–2021 (All India).

Survey Period 2020–2021	Rural			Urban			Total		
	Male	Female	Person	Male	Female	Person	Male	Female	Person
July–September 2020	14,288	9,409	13,120	21,068	16,701	20,030	18,328	13,737	17,234
October–December 2020	15,962	10,009	14,707	21,447	16,568	20,285	19,103	14,014	17,950
January–March 2021	16,127	9,588	14,496	21,095	16,022	19,870	19,004	13,248	17,594
April–June 2021	15,449	10,672	14,266	21,139	16,599	20,062	18,653	13,927	17,509

Source: Periodic Labour Force Survey, Annual Report, 2020–2021, Government of India.

Table 18.4.   Average Earnings of Casual Labour During PLFS 2020–2021 (All India) (Rs Per Day).

Survey Period 2020–2021	Rural			Urban			Total		
	Male	Female	Person	Male	Female	Person	Male	Female	Person
July–September 2020	328	212	302	406	266	385	340	218	314
October–December 2020	326	216	297	413	266	391	341	221	311
January–March 2021	339	224	310	416	273	394	352	229	322
April–June 2021	348	229	317	413	281	394	357	233	327

Source: Periodic Labour Force Survey, Annual Report, 2020–2021, Government of India.

Table 18.5. Average Gross Earnings of Self-employed Workers During the Last 30 Days in CWS During PLFS 2020–2021 (All India) (in Rs).

Survey Period 2020–2021	Rural			Urban			Total		
	Male	Female	Person	Male	Female	Person	Male	Female	Person
July–September 2020	9,829	4,622	9,049	15,903	7,167	14,662	11,184	5,162	10,291
October–December 2020	10,517	4,549	9,555	16,807	7,081	15,361	11,924	5,075	10,840
January–March 2021	10,462	4,425	9,391	17,046	6,996	15,420	11,924	4,967	10,757
April–June 2021	10,104	4,648	9,232	15,699	7,052	14,349	11,345	5,170	10,363

Source: Periodic Labour Force Survey, Annual Report, 2020–2021, Government of India.

duty in their absence and this is the main reason for not engaging in paid work. Similarly, out of the total females responded that they spend most of their time in domestic duties, 66% reported that they are not willing to work (Sanghi et al., 2015). This may be due to the reason that they have better income and standard of living. Also, across various NSSO surveys, there is no reduction in the females engaged in unpaid domestic duties.

Conclusion

This study analysed the status of informal employment in India with reference to their employment category, employment status and industry classification. The study has also looked into the status of wages paid to the informal workers in India. The main focus of the study was to analyse the gender gap amidst the various indicators of information employment such as LFPR, categories of employment, employment status and average earnings of informal workers. The analysis shows that there is an increase in the LFPR in both the usual status and CWS during all the PLFSs. The gender gap in LFPR is also visible for usual status and CWS in all the PLFSs. The data on the state/union territory wise LFPR show that female work participation rate is much lower compared to their male counterpart in all the states and union territories. The findings show that there is an increase in informal and formal employment during 2004–2005 to 2011–12. Informal sector constitutes the highest share of employment to the total employment in India. Among the informal workforce, self-employed category of employment contributes the highest followed by casual workers and regular wage workers. Half of the workforce in both the rural and urban regions is not eligible for paid leave and other social security benefits. The gender gap in this regard is much lower in both the rural and urban areas. There is a huge difference in the wages paid to regular wage employees in the rural and urban regions. The rural wage is only half of the urban wage. The rural women who engage in domestic duties have increased across the NSSO surveys. Out of the females who have reported that they spend most of their time in domestic duties, 60% of them reported that they do not have anyone else to engage in domestic work in their absence and this is the main reason for their inability to take up paid work. These findings raise a number of policy suggestions. They include the introduction of female friendly and flexible non-farm employment opportunities in both the rural and urban areas, increase in female wage rates, provision of social security measures, skill up-gradation and gender sensitisation programmes to reduce the patriarchal practices. The study also brings out some of the issues for further research. They include the study on the best practices adopted by the states or regions in which the female LFPR is high and to understand sectoral dimensions of job absorption. This study is based on secondary data and could not explore the detailed dimensions of the informal employment and female participation rate in various sectors and sub-sectors. This would also enrich the knowledge about the growing state of informal employment and its various challenges from a development ankle.

References

Abraham, R. (2019). Informal employment and the structure of wages in India: A review of trends. *The Review of Income and Wealth*, *65*, S102–S122. https://doi.org/10.1111/roiw.12435.

Abraham, V. (2009). Employment growth in rural India: Distress-driven? *Economic and Political Weekly*, *xliv*(16), 97–104.

Abraham, V. (2013). Missing labour or consistent de-feminisation. *Economic and Political Weekly*, *xlviii*(31), 99–108.

Chakraborty, S. (2020). Covid-19 and women informal sector workers in India. *Economic and Political Weekly*, *V*(35), 17–21.

CII Discussion Paper. (2018). *Declining female labour force participation in India: Concerns, causes and policy options*. CII.

Deininger, K., Jin, S., & Nagarajan, H. (2013). Wage discrimination in India's informal labor markets: Exploring the impact of caste and gender. *Review of Development Economics*, *17*(1), 130–147. https://doi.org/10.1111/rode.12020

Ferrant, G., Pesando, L. M., & Nowacka, K. (2014). *Unpaid care work: The missing link in the analysis of gender gaps in labour outcomes*. OECD Development Centre.

Government of India, Periodic Labour Force Survey. (2020–2021). *Ministry of statistics and programme implementation*. Government of India.

IWWAGE. (2021). *Initiative for what works to advance women and girls in the economy*. KREA University.

Kapsos, S., Silberman, A., & Baourmpoula, E. (2014). *Why is female labour force participation declining so sharply in India* [Research paper no. 4]. ILO.

Mehrotra, S. (2019). *Informal employment trends in the Indian economy: Persistent informality, but growing positive development* [Working paper no. 254]. ILO.

Mehrotra, S., & Parida, J. K. (2017). Why is the labour force participation of women declining in India. *World Development*, *98*, 360–380.

Neetha, N. (2014). Crisis in female employment analysis across social groups. *Economic and Political Weekly*, *xlix*(47), 50–59.

Rai, S. M., Brown, B. D., & Ruwanpura, K. N. (2019). SDG 8: Decent work and economic growth – A gendered analysis. *World Development*, *113*, 368–380.

Raveendran, G., & Vanek, J. (2020). Informal workers in India: A statistical profile. *Statistical Brief*, *24*, 1–16.

Sanghi, S., Srija, A., & Vijay, S. S. (2015). Decline in rural female force participation in India: A relook into the causes. *The Journal for Decision Makers*, *40*(3), 255–268.

Sankaran, K., & Madhav, R. (2011). Gender equality and social dialogue in India. ILO.

Sheikh, R. A., & Gaurav, S. (2020). Informal work in India: A tale of two definitions. *The European Journal of Development Research*, *32*, 1105–1127.

Singhari, S., & Madheswaran, S. (2017). Wage structure and wage differentials in formal and informal sectors in India: Evidence from NSS data. *The Indian Journal of Labour Economics*, *60*, 389–414.

Sita, L., & Rajarshi, M. (2018). Gender inequality in wage and employment in Indian labour market. *Journal of Academic Research in Economics*, *10*(3), 482–500.

Sorsa, P., Mares, J., Didier, M., Guimaraes, C., Rabate, M., Tang, G., & Tuske, A. (2015). *Determinants of the low female labour force participation in India* [Working paper no. 1207]. OECD, ECO/WKP.

Srija, A., & Shirke, S. (2012). *An analysis of informal labour market in India* (pp. 40–46) [Special feature] Confederation of Indian Industry.

Srivastava, R. (2019). Emerging dynamics of labour market inequality in India: Migration, informality, segmentation and social discrimination. *The Indian Journal of Labour Economics*, *62*, 147–171.

Chapter 19

Challenges of Women Workers in the Solid Waste Management Sector of Kerala: On the Path to Formalization

Fathima Sherin Ottakkam Thodukayil[a], Rahana Salahudeen Raseena[a], Udhayakumar Palaniswamy[a] and Sigamani Panneer[b]

[a]Department of Social Work, Central University of Tamil Nadu, India
[b]Centre for the Study of Law and Governance, Jawaharlal Nehru University, India

Abstract

In line with global initiatives, the state of Kerala in southern India is actively working towards formalizing its informal solid waste management (SWM) sector. Despite this, there is a dearth of studies on formalization processes, particularly focusing on the conditions of workers within this sector. This study addresses the gap by examining the challenges faced by women workers operating within the formalized framework of Kerala's SWM sector. It aimed to investigate challenges faced by grassroots women workers in Kerala's SWM sector during its transition from informal to formal, identifying gaps in the process through their experiences. Using a qualitative methodology, the research gathered data from 10 women workers in the SWM sector in Kozhikode, Kerala, who were part of the *Haritha Karma Sena* (green task force). Thematic analysis of in-depth interviews revealed two major challenges faced by these women. Firstly, there was a negative societal perception towards them, and secondly, there was a lack of appropriate state response to their needs and requirements. These challenges were attributed to gaps and pitfalls in the formalization process, leading to a lowered socio-economic status for the women, increased vulnerability to health hazards, and societal stigma. The findings underscore the need for significant improvements in the formalization process of Kerala's waste management sector. The study advocates for targeted

Informal Economy and Sustainable Development Goals:
Ideas, Interventions and Challenges, 373–397

doi:10.1108/978-1-83753-980-220241020

policy interventions to enhance the working conditions of SWM workers, emphasizing the importance of expediting and streamlining the formalization process. This, in turn, would contribute to the overall effectiveness of the SWM system in the state.

Keywords: Formalization process; informal sector; solid waste management; women workers; social policies

1. Introduction

Originating in the 1970s, the concept of the informal sector encapsulates a diverse and significant realm comprising productive entities and labourers operating beyond the scope of regulated economic activities and safeguarded employment arrangements. The informal sector's significance has amplified not only due to its proliferation across numerous nations but also due to the emergence of novel facets within this expansion, which are increasingly acknowledged as avenues to foster economic development and alleviate poverty (Aguilar & Campuzano, 2009; Aguilar & López Guerrero, 2020). The prevailing prominence of the informal sector has emerged as a pivotal characteristic within India's labour market landscape. Despite accounting for approximately half of the country's gross domestic product, the informal sector's ascendancy in the realm of employment is undeniable, encompassing a staggering proportion of over 93% of the entire workforce engaged in the informal economy or proportion of informal workers in the total participating labour-force (Naik, 2009). The predominant informal sectors in India encompass agriculture, dairy production, waste management, construction, manufacturing, trade and transportation, street vending, domestic labour, and home-based work (Gunsilius et al., 2011). While informal employment constitutes 79% of total urban jobs, this figure rises significantly to 96% in rural India. Despite the substantial presence of informal workers in India's labour market and economy, they encounter challenges that not only confine them to informality but also render them unrecognized. It has been documented that 66% of wage/salaried employees and 93% of casual workers in informal sector lack written employment contracts (Mehrotra, 2023). A substantial portion of these workers lack access to social welfare programmes, and a significant proportion is compelled to work up to 15 hours daily and all 7 days of the week. These workers contend with severe health risks, operating in unsafe conditions with inadequate protections (Oxfam India, 2022).

Gender disparity remains another prominent challenge within India's informal sector (Singh & Gupta, 2011). Women are more frequently engaged in the informal workforce across both rural and urban areas of the country. Notably, sectors like waste management and the construction industry employ a significant number of women workers, including those who are young mothers caring for infant children. Regrettably, these workplaces lack adequate childcare facilities (Oxfam India, 2022). Furthermore, a substantial 85% of rural women in India work within the informal agriculture sector, often facing suboptimal social and economic conditions (Dubey, 2016). Despite their significant presence in agriculture, women experience lower wages and are not recognized as farmers. Similarly, women in the waste management sector are commonly either unpaid or underpaid, confined primarily to door-to-door waste collection and segregation tasks (Dubey, 2016; Singhari & Madheswaran, 2017).

1.1. Formalizing the SWM Sector: Strengthening the Circular Economy and SDGs

The formalization of the informal waste management sector is a pressing concern for governments on both global and regional scales. This concern stems from two key factors. Firstly, when the informal sector is organized and reinforced by public policies and inclusive governance, it has the potential to contribute significantly to the achievement of sustainable development goals (SDGs) (Gutberlet, 2021). Secondly, enhancing the circular economy is imperative, encompassing the holistic evaluation of a product's environmental, social, and economic impact across its entire lifecycle and facilitating the closed-loop recycling of materials (Singh, 2021). Informal recycling workers, operating independently or in groups, gather, categorize, and reintegrate a diverse array of discarded materials into the economy. These grassroots initiatives have accumulated valuable knowledge and offer innovative insights into waste management, driven by their everyday experiences. Waste picker organizations play a pivotal role by providing specialized waste collection services to communities and businesses, contributing to resource recovery and social inclusivity. Such practices form the core of a circular economy (Gutberlet & Carenzo, 2020). Crucially, formalizing the work of waste workers and integrating them into municipal SWM systems can yield multiple benefits. This approach not only enhances their living and working conditions but also renders waste management more cost-efficient. This efficiency stems from reduced waste handling and transportation costs, diminished land use for garbage disposal, and the supply of recovered waste materials, particularly plastics, to manufacturers (Chaddha, 2020).

Waste management stands out as a significant informal sector in India, wielding substantial influence over waste disposal, recycling, and resource retrieval. In the context of developing nations like India, the informal sector plays a pivotal role in waste management, recycling, and the reclamation of resources (Singh, 2021). Informal waste workers are acknowledged as a crucial workforce within the informal economy due to their integral role in enhancing resource utilization efficiency and contributing significantly to environmental conservation. Their efforts are essential for recovering a substantial volume of municipal waste in India (Abdel-Shafy & Mansour, 2018; Gunsilius et al., 2011). Approximately 20% of the country's annual waste output is managed and recycled by informal waste labourers. Preliminary approximations indicate that India is home to around 3 million waste workers, while the World Bank's assessments propose that anywhere from 1% to 2% of the nation's populace could be involved in informal waste recycling (Dias, 2016).

According to the Ministry of Environment, Forest and Climate Change's report, the terms 'waste worker' or 'waste picker' pertain to individuals or groups operating informally to gather and recover reusable and recyclable waste from various locations of waste generation, which include streets, bins, material recovery facilities, processing centres, and waste disposal sites. The primary purpose of this activity is to sell the collected materials directly to recyclers or through intermediaries, thereby generating income to support their livelihoods (Ministry of Environment, Forest and Climate Change, 2016).

1.2. Formalization Process of Informal SWM Sector in India

As part of the global trend in formalization of the informal waste management sector, specifically as part of achieving SDGs, India has been adopting mechanisms for the formalization of informal waste management. This move is crucial as the informal labour force associated with the waste management sector in our country is evidently identified as a vulnerable group in many respects. Despite their crucial role in promoting sustainable recycling practices, informal waste workers in India continually face systemic marginalization both economically and socially (Dubey, 2016). This marginalization is exacerbated by societal attitudes, such as unsorted solid waste disposal at the source, and social taboos. Moreover, disparities in wages and living conditions persist among different segments of informal waste workers (Kumar & Agrawal, 2020). A significant proportion of these workers, particularly street waste pickers, toil and reside in hazardous environments. They often lack access to fundamental amenities such as sanitation and healthcare facilities (Singh et al., 2023). Regrettably, the prevalence of child labour remains notable, contributing to a lower life expectancy among these workers (Singh, 2021). Similar to the broader situation of informal labour in India, waste pickers are excluded from labour regulations, leaving them without the benefits of social security provisions and medical insurance schemes (Singh, 2021). Adding to this, women waste workers are reportedly caught in the dilemma of double marginalization, earning less than their male counterparts (Chaddha, 2020).

As a crucial initial stride towards formalization, several legislations have been enacted in India as components of both national and state-level waste management policies. These include significant regulations such as the National Environment Policy of 2006, the National Action Plan for Climate Change of 2009, the Solid Waste Management Rules of 2016, and the Plastic Waste Management Rules of 2016. In India, SWM is governed by the 'Solid Waste Management Rules, 2016' which were introduced under the Environment (Protection) Act, 1986 (Ministry of Environment, Government of India, 2016). These rules provide a comprehensive framework for the management of solid waste in the country, covering various aspects from waste collection and transportation to disposal and treatment. They emphasize the importance of waste segregation at the source, categorizing waste into biodegradable, non-biodegradable, and hazardous types. The responsibility for waste management, including segregation, collection, transportation, and disposal, lies with local authorities. The rules promote waste processing through methods like composting, recycling, and waste-to-energy technologies, while discouraging open dumping. Additionally, the concept of extended producer responsibility is introduced, making manufacturers and producers responsible for managing post-consumer waste from their products (Ministry of Environment, Government of India, 2016).

All these regulations incorporate clauses that specifically address the informal waste management sector within the country. They underscore the need to acknowledge the pivotal role played by the informal sector, encompassing waste pickers, waste collectors, and the recycling industry, in curtailing waste and provide comprehensive guidelines pertaining to the integration of waste pickers or informal waste collectors into the waste management framework (Bonnet et al., 2023; Da Silva et al., 2019). Besides these national level legislative actions, there were some state legislations too, including the state legislations of Government of Maharashtra, Government of Karnataka, and Government of Kerala. These states were active in the formalization process of informal waste management in the respective states, through adopting either a centralized or decentralized mechanism in waste management. Among these, the plastic waste management in Mumbai, the dry waste collection centres of Bengaluru, and SWM in Pune were all recognized as successful models (Singh, 2021). However, these cases were not executed flawlessly; they still exhibit shortcomings and are not entirely triumphant in achieving full formalization of the sector or complete integration of the informal workforce into the formal sector. Even after 4 years of SWM rule of 2016, only 13% of the urban local bodies (ULBs) in India have initiated and actively implemented the formalization process of SWM sector. Many ULBs in India face challenges such as insufficient funding, a shortage of suitable technology, and a lack of trained personnel, among other issues (Joshi & Ahmed, 2016). The estimated overall municipal revenue in India amounts to INR 1 lakh crore, with a significant portion allocated for staff salaries, pensions, and day-to-day operational costs, leaving very little available for capital investments. This limitation hampers the capacity of ULBs to undertake new projects. Moreover, the absence of adequate financial backing for ULBs results in insufficient infrastructure, which, in turn, results in the unsuccessful execution of policy recommendations (Ahluwalia et al., 2019).

1.3. Formalization of SWM in Kerala

Kerala, the southern-most state of India, shares similarities in informal labour market with that of other Indian states, with a notable concentration of agricultural labourers. However, Kerala distinguishes itself by also hosting distinctive state-specific informal sectors, including noteworthy activities like toddy tapping and engagement in the coir industry (Heller, 1996). Waste management sector is also identified as one of the major informal sectors in Kerala. However, Kerala is attempting to formalize its system for SWM through a decentralized approach, where the process of decentralization refers to the treatment of waste at the source including households or institutions (Ganesan, 2017).

For the formalization process, Kerala government has formalized a state policy on SWM in 2018, in terms of the rules 11 and 15 of the SWM rule of 2016 (Government of Kerala, 2018). As per this, different Government departments have to work collaboratively to achieve the formalization process, with the local self-governments having the regulatory and service delivery responsibilities. SWM in Kerala now involves multiple stakeholders working closely together, sharing expertise and resources to establish decentralized waste management and circular economy solutions (Government of Kerala, 2020). The key participants include local governments, Clean Kerala Company Limited for non-biodegradable waste removal and resource conversion, which is also responsible for the establishment of material collection facilities (MCF), and technical support agencies like *Haritha Keralam Mission* (Green Kerala Mission) and *Suchitwa Mission* (Hygiene Mission), offering guidance and promoting behavioural changes. Monitoring, financial backing, and coordination are facilitated by the Directorate of Panchayats and the Directorate of Urban Affairs (Ambat & Jayanti, 2022). Most importantly, *Kudumbashree mission*, a poverty eradication and women empowerment programme established by Government of Kerala, is entrusted with the responsibility of providing the human resource for the door-to-door waste collection and segregation process, meaning that this will be driven completely by the women where women will be the grass root level workers of the formalized waste management sector in the state. With a strong community network extending over the entire state, *Kudumbashree* has enough human resource and leadership networks to contribute the workers for the waste management activities at the grass root level (Kudumbashree, 2023).

The existing systems in the state have gaps not in the services per se but in terms of inter linkages across various service providers from response.

The groups, thus, formed through Kudumbashree units in each ward are referred to as the *Haritha Karma Sena*, meaning the 'green task force', the micro enterprise units created within local self-government institutions, featuring two women workers in every ward. Designated as a skilled team of women who receive comprehensive training for waste management procedures, the members of the green task force hold a pivotal role as stakeholders in the formalized management of non-biodegradable solid waste. The incorporation of an exclusively female group at the grassroots level of the formalized waste management structure stemmed from a notion embedded in Kerala's SWM policy. This concept aimed to introduce expanded employment and income-generation opportunities, along with heightened involvement of women in the waste management process. The formalized waste management initiative aspires to ensure equitable prospects and advantages for women staff and workers, promoting enhanced employment conditions and work environments (Government of Kerala, 2020). With a predominant focus on inorganic waste, green task force operates through a network of 1,018 units spanning the state. Of these, 926 units are active in rural regions, while 92 units operate within urban areas. A force of 23,546 women contributes to the initiative in rural settings, with an additional 4,678 women participating in urban areas (Kudumbashree, 2023).

Kerala has yet to attain the status of a fully formalized SWM system, and the current systems in the state exhibit shortcomings not in the services themselves but rather in the connections and collaborations among different service providers, as acknowledged by the state itself (Government of Kerala, 2020).

Starting from the Kerala state waste management policy of 2018, the formalization process of Kerala's informal waste management system is still under process and is not in its full swing. In fact, there are very few studies on the process of formalization of the SWM of the state and even less on the status of the workers of this formalizing sector. In this specific context, the present study has two major objectives: (i) To explore the diverse challenges encountered by grassroots-level women workers of the green task force as they transition from the informal to the formal sector. (ii) To understand the gaps in the formalization process of the waste management sector by examining the challenges faced by the members of the green task force, as identified in this study.

These objectives were explored by posing the following research questions:

1. What are the specific challenges and barriers faced by grassroots-level women workers during their transition to a formalized waste management sector?
2. How does the society perceive the green task force workers and what is the attitude of society towards them?
3. What are the specific regulatory and bureaucratic hurdles encountered by the women workers during this formalization process?
4. How do the societal perceptions and state interventions affect the working condition of the women workers in the SWM sector?

This chapter is organized to provide a comprehensive understanding of the study. The introduction section elucidates the study's context, along with the research questions and objectives. Subsequently, the adopted research methods are outlined, followed by the presentation of the study's findings. In the findings section, an in-depth exploration of the major themes and sub-themes derived from the study is provided. These results are then discussed in detail in relation to similar studies. The chapter concludes by discussing the policy implications arising from the study's findings.

2. Methods

The present study employed a qualitative methodology to explore the gaps in the formalization process of informal waste management sector in India through the challenges encountered by the grass root level women work force of the waste management sector of the state. The study collected data from women labourers who are part of the green task force in Kozhikode district of Kerala. The study specifically selected samples from Kozhikode, as the Kozhikode Municipal Corporation is reported to be implementing more strict and organized measures for the effective formalization process of the waste management under its jurisdiction. The sample included 10 women who are part of the green task force, selected based on their willingness to participate. The sample was selected based on purposive sampling technique, as the study needed participants with specific characteristics – those who are in the task force at least for the last six months and those who were able to provide rich data on the focus of the study.

The data were collected through in-depth interviews with the respondents, where the researchers did telephonic interview with the participants. The researchers used a self-prepared interview guide as the tool, which consisted of semi-structured questions. Ethical concerns were strictly followed throughout the data collection process, where the participants were informed in advance about the purpose of the study and their consent was sought before participation in the interview. Participants were allowed to withdraw from the interview at any point if they wished so. The telephonic interviews were recorded with the prior consent of the participants. These recorded interviews were later transcribed and did thematic analysis to reach at the findings. During the analysis process, the transcripts were coded and categorized under major themes and sub-themes. The coding and analysis were done manually by the researchers.

The current research included only the SWM workers from the green task force who have been working for a minimum of one year and are residents of the Kozhikode district in Kerala. It is subject to certain limitations. The study's small sample size drawn exclusively from the Kozhikode district may restrict the generalizability of findings to a broader population and this study omits insights from other stakeholders such as local authorities, community members, and waste management experts.

3. Results

Based on the in-depth qualitative analysis of the data, this study identified that the women labourers who are part of the green task force in Kerala face multi-faceted challenges in their occupation, stemming mainly from bad societal perception and inadequate state responses towards their needs. This, in turn, pointed out to the existing gaps in the implementation of formalized waste management system in Kerala. The major findings of the study emerged from the analysis are presented below (Table 19.1) under different themes.

3.1. Societal Perception Towards the Labourers

One significant finding of this study showed that the general attitude of society towards the women workers within the green task force is unfavourable, with stigmatization and a lack of cooperation. The prevalent societal mind set entails lack of cooperation and societal apathy, where the people were unwilling to pay user fees, showed irresponsibility in waste segregation, were teasing the labourer's children, and were resorting to derogatory labels when referring to these labourers. However, the findings also pointed to a noticeable shift in societal perception when uniforms were introduced. People began to regard the service with more respect and dignity as the women engaged in their tasks more professionally while wearing uniforms.

The results clearly showed that the women labourers of Kerala's green task force have been confronted with a disheartening challenge – the lack of cooperation and apathy from certain segments of society.

Table 19.1. Themes and Selected Quotes from Interviews.

Themes	Sub-themes	Selected Quotes
Societal perception towards the labourers	Lack of cooperation and societal apathy Refusal to pay user fee	'We often encounter a frustrating resistance when it comes to user fees. Some households display a lack of enthusiasm or outright refusal to pay the modest fees for our services. This reluctance appears to stem from a perception that our contributions should come free of charge. Despite our explanations regarding the necessity of these fees to sustain our work, we face a recurring challenge in convincing certain individuals to partake in this essential financial aspect of waste management.' (Respondent 1, Interview dated 26 July 2023)
	Irresponsibility in waste segregation	'People think that it's our duty to segregate the waste. Because they give us user fee. So, their mind-set is it is our duty and they are not responsible. People ask that, why they should be responsible for waste segregation when they are already paying money.' (Respondent 2, Interview dated 26 July 2023)
State response to the task force	Showing unfriendly response	'As we navigate the streets, collecting waste and working diligently to maintain a healthier environment, we often encounter households that deliberately choose not to cooperate. Some residents refuse to hand over their waste, viewing our presence as an inconvenience. It's disheartening to witness the lack of recognition for our efforts, as we strive to create a cleaner and greener Kerala for everyone. We face not only closed doors but also closed hearts.' (Respondent 4, Interview dated 27 July 2023)
	Using derogatory labels to address the workers	'I joined Haritha Karma Sena to make a positive impact on the environment and provide for my family. Little did I know that I would have to face sneers and whispers every day. They called us "waste warriors", but it was never meant as a compliment.' (Respondent 3, Interview dated 30 July 2023) 'My children are unfortunately facing teasing from their peers, who mockingly say things like, "Oh, your mother is like a waste picker, she walks around collecting waste," and use insulting terms.' (Respondent 4, Interview dated 27 July 2023)

(Continued)

Table 19.1. (Continued)

Themes	Sub-themes	Selected Quotes
	Teasing workers' children	'Trust is a cornerstone of any positive interaction. People start to trust us. The uniform and ID card serve as visual cues that reassure residents of our authenticity and purpose. People are more inclined to listen to our recommendations on waste segregation and disposal, recognizing us as official representatives of the Haritha Karma Sena initiative.' (Respondent 7, Interview dated 29 July 2023)
	Positive changes in societal perception with professional outlook	'The nature of our work does not provide continuous employment; there are certain months we have just ten days or even fewer days of work. This irregular pattern poses significant challenges for us to maintain a stable livelihood.' (Respondent 3, Interview dated 27 August 2023)
	Low and unstable wages	'Each day, as we step out to manage waste, we are confronted by the absence of equipment. The government's failure to provide gloves, shoes, and other essential equipment leaves us vulnerable to potential hazards.' (Respondent 5, Interview dated 28 July 2023
	Lack of work equipment	'The lack of gloves, shoes, and medical supplies compromises our health and safety as we navigate waste collection and management.' (Respondent 2, Interview dated 2 August 2023)
	Lack of health concerns	'Although we have noted down the concerns raised by each household and the obstacles faced by us, the government has unfortunately not been responsive to these issues. If the government were to initiate a follow-up process, even a modest effort could potentially bring about positive changes.' (Respondent 5, Interview dated 28 July 2023)
	Resource constraints and gaps in implementation	

Source: Author.

3.1.1. Refusal to Pay User Fee

People's unwillingness to pay user fee is one of the most observed forms of social apathy towards the activities of the green task force members. The data showed that this unwillingness comes mainly from people's misunderstanding and lack of awareness of the nature of the user fee.

> We often encounter a frustrating resistance when it comes to user fees. Some households display a lack of enthusiasm or outright refusal to pay the modest fees for our services. This reluctance appears to stem from a perception that our contributions should come free of charge. Despite our explanations regarding the necessity of these fees to sustain our work, we face a recurring challenge in convincing certain individuals to partake in this essential financial aspect of waste management. (Respondent 1, Interview dated 26 July 2023)

This verbatim clearly shows that people are unaware of the details regarding the user fee for the waste management, resulting in a conflict between the task force member and the user. In fact, this wrong societal perception was evident in many other interviews, where the respondents shared their difficulties in correcting people's misunderstanding about the user fee.

> People think that, the collection of user funds benefits us directly, implying that substantial profits can be generated from each household contributing Rs 50. This is a misunderstanding among the people. Some individuals hold the perception that the government's prior disbursements suffice, leading to questions about the necessity of contributing extra funds. They argue that providing financial assistance is the government's role. In various regions, governments provide money to citizens for waste disposal. Some of them think that by entrusting the waste to 'Akri' (colloquial term for informal garbage collection person), we can get money and no need to give a user fee to take our waste. (Respondent 6, Interview dated 28 July 2023)

The analysis clearly showed that the people are mostly unwilling to pay user fee because of the novelty of the concept and the resulting confusion and suspiciousness. This clearly seems affecting the smooth functioning of the task force.

3.1.2. Irresponsibility in Waste Segregation

Another apathetic act from the people towards the task force members is when it comes to waste segregation. Many of the people are not ready to properly segregate the waste at the source, making the task members' work more challenging.

> We often find bins filled with mixed waste, where items like soiled diapers, napkins, and even used condoms are messily thrown

> together. It's disheartening to see unsorted waste piled up, knowing the potential harm it brings. We believe that waste segregation isn't just a duty; it's a commitment to our environment and future. (Respondent 4, Interview dated 27 July 2023)

> People think that it's our duty to segregate the waste. Because they give us user fee. So, their mind-set is it is our duty and they are not responsible. People ask that, why they should be responsible for waste segregation when they are already paying money. (Respondent 2, Interview dated 26 July 2023)

It is apparent from the narratives that people often mess with different kinds of waste materials, making it extremely difficult for the workers to handle them. Provision of user fee is considered by the people as a means to skip from the segregation duties too, which often stems from the lack of awareness about responsible handling of waste. However, it is worthy to note down here that the labourers are often having a much clearer and responsible perception about their duties while the people were not.

3.1.3. Showing Unfriendly Responses

Expressing unfriendly or harsh behavioural responses to waste collectors is another major feature of societal perception towards them. Such behaviours include refusing to hand over the waste or closing the doors when the workers come to collect the waste materials.

> As we navigate the streets, collecting waste and working diligently to maintain a healthier environment, we often encounter households that deliberately choose not to cooperate. Some residents refuse to hand over their waste, viewing our presence as an inconvenience. It's disheartening to witness the lack of recognition for our efforts, as we strive to create a cleaner and greener Kerala for everyone. We face not only closed doors but also closed hearts. (Respondent 4, Interview dated 27 July 2023)

This conscious non-cooperation not only becomes a barrier in disposing their duty but also a disheartening experience to many. This may point out the lack of dignity of their work.

> When we knock on doors to collect waste and contribute to a healthier environment, we frequently encounter residents who shut their doors without a hint of empathy. Few of them are very cooperative and treat us as a human being. Occasionally, misinformation spread through social media platforms, leading to a misconception that individuals are opposed to contributing user fees, and that the government assumes financial responsibility for workers.

This can result in a breakdown of trust, as people begin to express doubts and uncertainties about our intentions and action. (Respondent 1, Interview dated 26 July 2023)

The narrative above points out to the interference of social media as a threatening factor that spreads misinformation regarding the activities of the green task force, including user fee. This will further worsen the already confused relationship between the task force members and the general public.

3.1.4. Using Derogatory Labels to Address the Workers

The findings showed that the women labourers of green task force, despite their noble efforts, have been vulnerable to the deeply ingrained stereotypes and prejudices prevalent in society. Their profession, it seems, has led to the emergence of derogatory names used to describe them. One of the respondents of this study narrates her experience:

> I remember walking down the street in our green uniforms, collecting waste and contributing to a cleaner environment. People would pass by and mutter words like *perukki, chavaruperkki* (meaning 'waste picker', here in an offensive tone). At first, it hurt deeply. We were doing something important, something that benefited everyone, yet we were reduced to these hurtful labels. (Respondent 9, Interview dated 30 July 2023)

Another respondent had a similar view to share:

> I joined Haritha Karma Sena to make a positive impact on the environment and provide for my family. Little did I know that I would have to face sneers and whispers every day. They called us 'waste warriors', but it was never meant as a compliment. (Respondent 3, Interview dated 30 July 2023)

These narratives clearly illustrate that the general public still are having a stigmatized and prejudiced view of the workers of the waste management sector, and the formalization process has little impact on this attitude.

3.1.5. Teasing Workers' Children

The study results pointed out another disturbing observation, where it was found that even the children of the task force members are sometimes getting teased by their peers on the name of their parents' profession.

> My children are unfortunately facing teasing from their peers, who mockingly say things like, 'Oh, your mother is like a waste picker, she walks around collecting waste', and use insulting terms. (Respondent 4, Interview dated 27 July 2023)

This negative attitude that comes even from children can be viewed as a reflection of the prejudice of the general public towards these workers.

3.1.6. Positive Changes in Societal Perception with Professional Outlook

Indeed, a noticeable shift is emerging in societal attitudes towards waste management and those who are involved in waste collection. The study showed that uniform and ID card have played a significant role in fostering trust and credibility between the labourers and the community.

> Trust is a cornerstone of any positive interaction. People start to trust us. The uniform and ID card serve as visual cues that reassure residents of our authenticity and purpose. People are more inclined to listen to our recommendations on waste segregation and disposal, recognizing us as official representatives of the Haritha Karma Sena initiative. (Respondent 7, Interview dated 29 July 2023)

The above narrative evidently shows how the societal perceptions towards the waste management workers changed with proper implementation of uniforms and identity cards for them. This, in fact, gave them a professional outlook, leading people to change their attitude and recognize them as knowledgeable resource persons who can be sought out to clear their doubts regarding waste segregation and management.

> Now there's a subtle change in the attitude of people. They call us by names and recognize us as the Haritha karma sena workers instead of calling us ill names and making fun of our work. Now some folks actually appreciate what we do. They see the importance of clean surroundings and how it impacts their lives. It is encouraging to know that our efforts are making a difference. (Respondent 10, Interview dated 30 July 2023)

> I remember when we first started, it wasn't easy. People would tease our children, saying hurtful things about us. But today, I see a difference. As societal attitudes shift, we feel a sense of empowerment that transcends our daily tasks. People now approach us with questions, seeking advice on waste segregation and disposal. (Respondent 10, Interview dated 30 July 2023)

The analysis pointed out that professionalization can make noticeable change in societal perception towards the workers, which is one of the essential factors in effective formalization of the waste management sector.

3.2. State Response to the Task Force

The state's response to the women labourers is a pivotal aspect that reflects the commitment of the government towards sustainable waste management and its formalization process. The present study identified the general nature of the state's response to the needs of the green task force workers, which were often inadequate. This includes a delay in provision of necessary equipment such as gloves, shoes, and medical supplies to safeguard their health and safety of the workers, their low and unstable salary, resource constraints, and gaps in implementation.

3.2.1. Low and Unstable Wages

The results of the study revealed that the women workers of the green task force are having lower and unstable wage for their work. The economic challenges posed by the low wages have a tangible impact on the livelihoods and well-being of these workers. Financial stress and limited resources add an additional layer of complexity to their efforts.

> Our work as Haritha Karma Sena labourers is essential, but the reality of low salaries introduces hardships that extend beyond our professional roles. As we contribute to waste management, we also navigate the challenges of meeting our families' needs and ensuring their well-being. The struggle to strike a balance between our commitments to the environment and our financial responsibilities weighs heavily on us. We aspire to contribute meaningfully while also providing for our families, without the need for titles like 'warriors'. We're not seeking titles; we're seeking the well-being of our environment and our families. We want our efforts to make a difference, cleanliness of Kerala, also in the quality of life for our loved. It's also important. For all the challenges we face – the mocking, closed doors, and the demanding work of waste management – the compensation we receive is very less. (Respondent 9, Interview dated 30 July 2023)

> The nature of our work does not provide continuous employment; there are certain months we have just ten days or even fewer days of work. This irregular pattern poses significant challenges for us to maintain a stable livelihood. (Respondent 3, Interview dated 27 July 2023)

Even though the waste management process is being formalized and the workers are recognized not just as regular labourers but as professionally trained task force members, their wages are relatively low and unstable, that can be fluctuated greatly where they will get very less amounts sometimes. It seems that the government does not take initiatives to regularize a minimum wage for these workers, which is one of the most necessary steps to recognize them as formal employees.

Here, another respondent narrates her experience related to this issue:

> We are at the forefront of waste management. However, the issue of low wages casts a shadow over our efforts. It's disheartening to realize that our vital contributions are undervalued in

terms of compensation. We receive an insufficient wage, in this
we should cover all our needs and other expenses such as transportation, uniform, and mobile data recharge. Nowadays, having internet connectivity on our phones is crucial, especially
since many financial transactions are done through platforms
like Google Pay. People pay the user fee, the fifty rupees, through
Google pay. Additionally, transportation costs, including bus and
auto fares, continue to rise, while our salaries remain stagnant.
(Respondent 8, Interview dated 29 July 2023)

This narrative raises another important but unaddressed concern of the workers about the financial burden that arises from their work. Since they are not
provided with travel allowance or additional financial support than the wage,
they are forced to meet the additional requirements with the already lower wages.
The analysis clearly revealed that the green task force members are confronted
with inadequate state responses related to the financial aspects of their work even
though it is a pressing concern.

3.2.2. Lack of Work Equipment

Another important observation raised from the analysis of the data is the lack of
equipment for the work of the task force members. In fact, to ensure the effectiveness of their work and safety, there is an urgent need to equip them adequately.
They are not given essential equipment such as shoes, gloves, and medicine. These
equipment are not only for the primary health concerns of the workers but are
also essential to enhance their work efficiency.

The following narrative of one of the respondents of the study echoes their
concerns on this:

One of the most glaring obstacles we encounter is the lack of substantial support from the government. It's hard to manage waste
when we lack even the simplest tools like gloves, boots, and proper
medical supplies. The government provides one set of gloves, but
that is not enough for us. They also provide one set of uniforms.
But after that, we buy uniforms for ourselves. It's all included in
this salary. We're putting our health on the line, and having access
to the right equipment and safety gear is not a luxury – it's a
necessity. (Respondent 10, Interview dated 30 July 2023)

Similar concerns were raised by almost all respondents of this study. Two more
narratives are presented here regarding this:

The government's neglect in providing necessary equipment
has repercussions beyond our individual experiences. Our efficiency is compromised, leading to longer hours and increased
physical strain. With proper tools, we could enhance our waste

management efforts and contribute more significantly to the communities we serve. (Respondent 7, Interview dated 29 July 2023)

Each day, as we step out to manage waste, we are confronted by the absence of equipment. The government's failure to provide gloves, shoes, and other essential equipment leaves us vulnerable to potential hazards. (Respondent 5, Interview dated 28 July 2023)

The analysis showed that the workers recognize this issue themselves, where they are aware that this lack of necessary equipment for work affects their efficiency and also put them into more dangerous and vulnerable situations. They also identify this as an irresponsibility from government, where they are not provided with sufficient resources.

3.2.3. Lack of Health Concerns

As an addition to the government's inattention in providing the task force members with proper equipment, their health concerns are also found to be at risk since government does not recognize their immediate needs or respond properly. The following narratives from three of the respondents of the present study shed light to this pressing concern:

The lack of gloves, shoes, and medical supplies compromises our health and safety as we navigate waste collection and management. (Respondent 2, Interview dated 2 August 2023)

The government's lack of concern about our health becomes increasingly evident. We handle waste daily, often without the necessary protective gear. It's disappointing to realize that our well-being is not a priority for the very institutions we contribute to through our efforts. (Respondent 6, Interview dated 28 July 2023)

Our health is on the line each day as we handle waste without proper protection. The government's disregard for our well-being erodes our morale and leaves us feeling undervalued. It's a stark reminder that our dedication comes at a personal cost. (Respondent 2, Interview dated 26 July 2023)

The respondents clearly recognize that with not much protective gears or health equipment, they are vulnerable to health threats, which is not properly addressed by the state. They identify it not only as a personal issue, but as government's lack of concern for the whole process of waste management.

3.2.4. Resource Constraints and Gaps in Implementation

The analysis led to another significant finding of this study, where it disclosed that the formalization of waste management in the state is still at its infancy,

where there are many existing gaps that potentially impact the smooth functioning of the process, which was evident from the difficulties and uncertainties
encountered by the task force members. It showed that the formalization process
of waste management presents its own set of challenges for the government. As
it seeks to establish structured and sustainable waste disposal practices, various
hurdles emerge that demand careful consideration and strategic planning, which
is currently lacking in the state. Here, one of the respondents points out the gaps
in implementation of the programme, which eventually affect the quality and
consistency of their work.

> Government itself have the scarcity of Material Collection Facili-
> ties (MCF). We didn't work for two months because of this. This
> raise a range of issues. Notably, residents in the locality of waste
> disposal sites have voiced their worries due to a worsening situ-
> ation. The onset of the rainy season make worsen the problem,
> causing waste to emit unpleasant Smells and flow towards residen-
> tial areas. The current Material Collection Facility (MCF) covers
> a compact area, and don't have any proper restroom and toilet
> facilities within it. (Respondent 4, Interview dated 27 July 2023)

It is of at most concern to note down here that the government does not have
enough MCF that not only affect the works of the task force members but also
result in creation of a negative attitude of general public towards the workers and
to the whole process of waste management.

Some other respondents voiced out their concerns about the lack of proper
response from the government:

> Although we have noted down the concerns raised by each house-
> hold and the obstacles faced by us, the government has unfor-
> tunately not been responsive to these issues. If the government
> were to initiate a follow-up process, even a modest effort could
> potentially bring about positive changes. (Respondent 5, Interview
> dated 28 July 2023)

> When we seek assistance or make inquiries, the responses are often
> unclear reflecting a complex issues due to the involvement of multi-
> ple departments in the process. Upon seeking clarification, we often
> encounter the response that the matter falls beyond the scope of
> their department. (Respondent 8, Interview dated 29 July 2023)

Absence of adequate resource allocation, lack of follow up system, absence of
adequate waste disposal facilities, and issues in allocation of job are all becoming of pivotal concern. Additionally, the coordination and collaboration required
between different governments departments and agencies involved in waste management often seems lacking, which results in complexities that require efficient
communication and synergistic efforts.

4. Discussion

In Kerala, the formalization of the waste management sector through a decentralized approach represents a positive step towards improving waste management practices and environmental sustainability. However, the findings of this research highlight a stark reality where the trained women work force in the SWM sector who are part of the green task force are confronted with numerous hurdles that indicate issues and gaps affecting the formalization process.

One of the foremost challenges faced by the green task force workers as found in this study is the negative social perception surrounding their occupation. In fact, this is a frequently observed issue in the waste management sector, both in the Indian (Kumar & Anand, 2017; Singh, 2021) and global contexts (Fadhullah et al., 2022; Muiruri et al., 2020; Nuzrath & Ruzaik, 2017). This negative perception is generally expressed as societal apathy towards the workers, and such apathetic societal behaviours similar to the ones identified in this study were mirrored in many other studies (Eneji et al., 2016; Kumar & Agrawal, 2020; Sapkota et al., 2020; Singh, 2021). This apathetic behaviours include harassment both from the general public and from the officials such as police, especially towards the women workers in the sector (Routh, 2014), or calling ill-names and making comments about them (Lissah et al., 2020) which is similar to the findings of this study that people still use derogatory names to address the workers. Irresponsibility in waste segregation and irregular payment of user fees (Eneji et al., 2016) were other forms of negative societal perception towards the workers of the waste management sector. In fact, the narratives of the respondents of this study clearly showed that the general public still does not accept the workers as formal employees, or does not treat them as equal. The harsh and unfriendly responses of the people to the workers as observed in this study align with the observations in other studies that waste workers persistently encounter systemic marginalization, stigma, and discrimination in the social fronts (Sapkota et al., 2020; Singh, 2021), which become doubled when it comes to women workers in the sector. Several studies pointed out that the mental strain resulting from this societal apathy leads to mood fluctuations, sleep disturbances, and heightened anxiety in them (Kappan, 2021; Muiruri et al., 2020). It is important to note down here that all the challenges encountered by the green task force members as identified in this study is generally reported to be experienced by the workers of informal waste management sector. This clearly indicates that the women workers of the formal waste management sector of Kerala still are in the social status of informal waste management workers.

Another major finding of the study revealed that there was a positive change in the societal perception towards the task force members when they started to wear uniforms regularly. This finding resonates with the observations of Rao (2023), where unfavourable perception of waste pickers were connected to their physical appearance, which hindered their integration and recognition within society. In case of the green task force members, they were unable to wear the uniforms properly since they were given only one uniform each from the authorities, making it impossible for them to wear it regularly. This points out to two important concerns.

Firstly, it shows that positive societal perception towards the workers can be cultivated through professionalization of the task force, which is actually an essential component of the formalization process. Secondly, it points out to an important gap in the formalization of informal waste management sector in Kerala, where the workers' primary needs are not properly addressed by the state. Positive societal perception is also needed to cultivate through extensive and effective awareness campaigns.

Coming to the third major finding of the present study, the results disclosed that there is an insufficient state response to the needs and concerns of the green task force members, characterized by inadequate remuneration, scarce provision of resources and equipment, and a lack of attention to health concerns, which, in turn, results as a hindrance to the effective formalization of the waste management sector in the state. Based on the narratives provided by the respondents, it was evident that there is a prevailing lack of adequate equipment, including gloves, footwear, and other necessary kit, to effectively handle waste. This can subsequently contribute to health issues among them. Waste pickers may be exposed to a wide range of occupational hazards (Cruvinel et al., 2019; Gutberlet & Uddin, 2017). The occurrence of respiratory symptoms, such as breathing difficulties (dyspnoea) and persistent coughing, was notably higher among waste pickers because of that a significant proportion of waste pickers were not utilizing any protective attire like gloves, masks, or gumboots, thereby amplifying their susceptibilities to health hazards (Chokhandre et al., n.d.). One of the studies found that workers in the waste industry could encounter elevated levels of psychological stress, a result of the heightened vigilance in ensuring environmental safety and handling hazardous materials (Kageyama et al., 2022). Considering the fact that the government is not responding adequately even to the health concerns of the women workers of waste management sector of the state, this needs attention.

Another barrier faced by the workers due to the absence of proper state response, as identified by this study, is the low salary that can't even meet the basic needs of the workers. The process of formalization often involves the introduction of predetermined salaries funded through waste fees collected from residents. Yet, the reluctance to financially support waste services can detrimentally impact the financial security of formalized waste workers. This unwillingness becomes a significant obstacle for initiatives aiming to formalize waste management (Aparcana, 2017). To address the issue of income insecurity, some regional governments have established collecting and storage facilities with the goal of raising sales volumes and improving negotiating power in the face of shifting prices (Medellin and Bogotá, Colombia; Pune, India; Londrina and Diadema, Brazil). This metric can also be paired with a mixed income structure based on fixed trash fees (for collection and other cleaning services) and variable revenues from the sale of recycled materials, as seen in Londrina and Diadema (Brazil), Iloilo City (Philippines), and Pune (India) (Lohri et al., 2014). Such kind of interventions are essential from the part of government to ensure effective financial back up of workers in a formalized system of waste management.

The research highlighted another obstacle faced by the women workers in the formalization process as the lack of coordination between the stakeholders within the system that hindered their smooth functioning. The scarcity of information from stakeholders has been identified as another contributing factor. It is striking that deficient management among formalized waste-workers and a dearth of administrative capabilities within public management may constitute the root causes of the most enduring institutional obstacles (Guerrero et al., 2013; Velis et al., 2012). Challenges arise from insufficient transparency within institutional and organizational formalization processes, coupled with unclear policy and legal structures surrounding formalization. Ambiguity in explaining roles and obligations between the formal sector and formalized waste-workers is also identified as potential pitfalls in formalization process of the waste management system (Wang & Geng, 2012), which were also identified as one of the major gaps in formalization of waste management sector in Kerala. Conflicting interests and competitive dynamics among stakeholders result in an erosion of trust, fostering an environment conducive to corruption and illicit practices within the waste services sector (Aparcana, 2017).

The present study results revealed that the government itself has resource constraints and gaps in implementation of a proper formalized system of waste management in the state. The lack of adequate MCF coupled with the improper disposal of waste poses a multi-faceted challenge that demands immediate attention. India generally has such constraints, where the allocated budgets to the responsible authorities for the SWM often fall short of meeting the necessary expenses for establishing comprehensive waste collection, appropriate storage, efficient treatment, and proper disposal systems. The absence of well-defined strategic plans for municipal SWM, inadequate measures for waste collection and segregation, and a lack of regulatory framework concerning government finances collectively act as significant obstacles in the path towards achieving efficient waste management in India (Kumar et al., 2017). Looking into the successful models of formalized waste management in developed countries, there is a revolution in waste management, which includes transition from landfills to resource reutilization, elevated environmental criteria for waste facilities, altered public perception of waste, and revolutionized corporate accountability. These multi-faceted changes collectively define a pivotal juncture in waste management strategies, where sustainability, responsibility, and resource optimization converge (Hossain, 2022).

5. Conclusion

The formalization process of SWM sector in Kerala is still under process and is not fully achieved the status of a fully functioning formalized sector. This transitional phase, often characterized with ambiguities even in the state machinery, is reflected in the challenges faced by the women members green task force, the trained group of women for grass root level activities in the waste management process. The state, as the responsible figure in the formalization process, must recognize its role in addressing these challenges, thereby catalysing effective formalization process. It is imperative for policymakers to implement measures that ensure fair wages, eradicate societal stigma, and provide adequate resources for the women workers at the grass root level of waste management process.

The transformation from informality to formality demands a comprehensive approach that goes beyond mere policy changes. A holistic strategy should encompass not only legal and regulatory reforms but also targeted initiatives to address the socio-economic empowerment of the workers. Education and skill development programmes can help enhance their capacities, thereby elevating their status and opening doors to improved opportunities. Collaborative efforts between governments, non-governmental organizations, and local communities are crucial in creating an inclusive environment where waste workers are valued and respected in the society. The Kerala's SWM policy clause is not really achieved regarding women's participation in the whole system. Currently, women primarily engage as waste pickers at the grassroots level, without the representations in higher strata and upper-level structures. Recognizing this disparity, it is imperative for the government to acknowledge and undertake measures for substantial improvements in this aspect.

It is strongly advised that future studies in this area should expand the sample size to include a more diverse and representative group of waste management workers, which would enhance the external validity of the findings. Conducting comparative studies across different regions could provide insights into regional variations and challenges. Additionally, incorporating the perspectives of various stakeholders, including policymakers, community members, and experts, would provide a more comprehensive understanding of the waste management ecosystem and facilitate the formulation of holistic and effective interventions. The longitudinal studies that track changes over time could offer insights into the dynamics of waste management practices and the impact of policy changes.

References

Abdel-Shafy, H. I., & Mansour, M. S. M. (2018). Solid waste issue: Sources, composition, disposal, recycling, and valorization. *Egyptian Journal of Petroleum, 27*(4), 1275–1290. https://doi.org/10.1016/j.ejpe.2018.07.003

Aguilar, A. G., & Campuzano, E. P. (2009). Informal sector. In R. Kitchin & N. Thrift (Eds.), *International encyclopedia of human geography* (pp. 446–453). Elsevier. https://doi.org/10.1016/B978-008044910-4.00102-4

Aguilar, A. G., & López Guerrero, F. M. (2020). Informal sector. *International Encyclopedia of Human Geography, Second Edition, 1*, 279–288. https://doi.org/10.1016/B978-0-08-102295-5.10272-0

Ahluwalia, I. J., Mohanty, P. K., Mathur, O., & Roy, D. (2019). *State of municipal finances in India* (No. 19-r-03). Indian Council for Research on International Economic Relations (ICRIER). https://ideas.repec.org/p/bdc/report/19-r-03.html.

Ambat, B., & Jayanthi, T. A. (2022). *Review of solid waste management – Approach and strategy for India with special focus to state of Kerala.* In Proceedings of 12th Hanseatic India colloquium, Germany solid waste management: An Indo-German dialogue. https://www.nswai.org/docs/Review%20on%20Solid%20Waste%20Management%20Practice%20in%20India%20-%20A%20State%20of%20Art.pdf

Aparcana, S. (2017). Approaches to formalization of the informal waste sector into municipal solid waste management systems in low- and middle-income countries: Review of barriers and success factors. *Waste Management, 61*, 593–607. https://doi.org/10.1016/j.wasman.2016.12.028

Rao, B. G. (2023). *Shifting perceptions on India's invaluable waste pickers | FairPlanet.* Retrieved August 22, 2023, from https://www.fairplanet.org/editors-pick/shifting-perceptions-on-indias-invaluable-waste-pickers/

Bonnet, F., Lahboubi, N., Habchi, S., & El Bari, H. (2023). Waste management institutional and legislation aspects in developing countries. In H. El Bari & C. Trois (Eds.), *Waste management in developing countries: Waste as a resource.* Springer. https://doi.org/10.1007/978-3-031-28001-6_6

Chaddha, K. (2020). *Informal waste workers: The issue of formalization.* Social and Political Research Foundation. https://sprf.in/wp-content/uploads/2021/02/24.07.2020_Informal-Waste-Workers_-The-Issue-of-Formalisation.pdf.

Chokhandre, P., Singh, S., & Kashyap, G. C. (n.d.). *Prevalence, predictors and economic burden of morbidities among waste-pickers of Mumbai, India: A cross-sectional study.* https://doi.org/10.1186/s12995-017-0176-3

Cruvinel, V. R. N., Marques, C. P., Cardoso, V., Novaes, M. R. C. G., Araújo, W. N., Angulo-Tuesta, A., Escalda, P. M. F., Galato, D., Brito, P., & Da Silva, E. N. (2019). Health conditions and occupational risks in a novel group: Waste pickers in the largest open garbage dump in Latin America. *BMC Public Health, 19*(1), 1–15. https://doi.org/10.1186/s12889-019-6879-x

Da Silva, C. L., Weins, N., & Potinkara, M. (2019). Formalizing the informal? A perspective on informal waste management in the BRICS through the lens of institutional economics. *Waste Management, 99,* 79–89. https://doi.org/10.1016/j.wasman.2019.08.023

Dias, S. M. (2016). Waste pickers and cities. *Environment and Urbanization, 28*(2), 375–390. https://journals.sagepub.com/doi/abs/10.1177/0956247816657302

Dubey, S. Y. (2016). Women at the bottom in India: Women workers in the informal economy. *Contemporary Voice of Dalit, 8*(1), 30–40. https://www.researchgate.net/publication/301914117_Women_at_the_Bottom_in_India_Women_Workers_in_the_Informal_Economy; https://doi.org/10.1177/2455328X16628776

Eneji, C. V. O., Eneji, J. E. O., & Ngoka, V. N. (2016). Attitude towards waste management and disposal methods and the health status of Cross River State, Nigeria. *SCIREA Journal of Agriculture, 1*(2), 231–247. https://www.researchgate.net/publication/312369217

Fadhullah, W., Imran, N. I. N., Ismail, S. N. S., Jaafar, M. H., & Abdullah, H. (2022). Household solid waste management practices and perceptions among residents in the East Coast of Malaysia. *BMC Public Health, 22*(1), 1–20. https://doi.org/10.1186/s12889-021-12274-7

Ganesan, P. (2017). Landfill sites, solid waste management and people's resistance: A study of two municipal corporations in Kerala. *International Journal of Environmental Studies, 74*(6), 958–978. https://doi.org/10.1080/00207233.2017.1374076

Government of Kerala. (2018). *Kerala local self-government.* https://lsgkerala.gov.in/system/files/202107/haritha%20karmasena%20guidelines%20%281%29.pdf

Government of Kerala. (2020). *Kerala solid waste management project.* https://documents1.worldbank.org/curated/en/273131589796044061/pdf/Social-Management-Framework.pdf

Gunsilius, E., Chaturvedi, B., & Scheinberg, A. (2011). *The economics of the informal sector in solid waste management: Based on information from: Scheinberg, A., Simpson, M., Gupt, Y. et al. (2010).* CWG. https://swachcoop.com/pdf/theeconomicsoftheinformalsector.pdf

Gutberlet, J. (2021). Grassroots waste picker organizations addressing the UN sustainable development goals. *World Development, 138,* 105195. https://www.sciencedirect.com/science/article/abs/pii/S0305750X20303223

Gutberlet, J., & Carenzo, S. (2020). *Waste pickers at the heart of the circular economy: A perspective of inclusive recycling from the Global South.* https://worldwidewastejournal.com/articles/10.5334/wwwj.50

Gutberlet, J., & Uddin, S. M. N. (2017). Household waste and health risks affecting waste pickers and the environment in low- and middle-income countries. *International Journal of Occupational and Environmental Health, 23*(4), 299–310. https://doi.org/10.1080%2F10773525.2018.1484996

Guerrero, L. A., Maas, G., & Hogland, W. (2013). Solid waste management challenges for cities in developing countries. *Waste Management, 33*(1), 220–232. https://doi.org/10.1016/J.WASMAN.2012.09.008

Heller, P. (1996). Social capital as a product of class mobilization and state intervention: Industrial workers in Kerala, India. *World Development, 24*(6), 1055–1071.

Hossain, M. (2022). Solid waste management in developing and developed countries. *A Review, 9*(4), 698–714. https://ideas.repec.org/a/eee/wdevel/v24y1996i6p1055-1071.html

Joshi, R., & Ahmed, S. (2016). Status and challenges of municipal solid waste management in India: A review. *Cogent Environmental Science, 2*(1), 1139434. https://doi.org/10.1080/23311843.2016.1139434.

Kageyama, I., Hashiguchi, N., Cao, J., Niwa, M., Lim, Y., Tsutsumi, M., Yu, J., Sengoku, S., Okamoto, S., Hashimoto, S., & Kodama, K. (2022). Determination of waste management workers' physical and psychological load: A cross-sectional study using biometric data. *International Journal of Environmental Research and Public Health, 19*(23), 15964. https://doi.org/10.3390/ijerph192315964

Kappan, R. (2021). *No empathy for informal waste pickers, seen as dirty: Study by BBC media action.* Retrieved August 21, 2023, from https://www.deccanherald.com/india/karnataka/bengaluru/no-empathy-for-informal-waste-pickers-seen-as-dirty-study-by-bbc-media-action-974707.html

Kudumbashree. (2023). *About Haritha Kama Sena.* https://www.kudumbashree.org/pages/677.

Kumar, A., & Agrawal, A. (2020). Recent trends in solid waste management status, challenges, and potential for the future Indian cities – A review. *Current Research in Environmental Sustainability, 2*, 100011. https://www.kudumbashree.org/pages/677

Kumar, A., & Anand, S. (2017). Community perception towards solid waste management in NCT of Delhi, India. *International Journal of Research & Review* (Www.Gkpublication.In), *4*(July), 47. https://www.ijrrjournal.com/IJRR_Vol.4_Issue.7_July2017/IJRR008.pdf

Kumar, S., Smith, S. R., Fowler, G., Velis, C., Kumar, S. J., Arya, S., Rena, Kumar, R., & Cheeseman, C. (2017). Challenges and opportunities associated with waste management in India. *Royal Society Open Science, 4*(3), 160764. https://doi.org/10.1098/RSOS.160764

Lissah, S. Y., Ayanore, M. A., Krugu, J., & Ruiter, R. A. (2020). Psychosocial risk, work-related stress, and job satisfaction among domestic waste collectors in the Ho municipality of Ghana: A phenomenological study. *International Journal of Environmental Research and Public Health, 17*(8), 2903. https://doi.org/10.3390/ijerph17082903

Lohri, C. R., Camenzind, E. J., & Zurbrügg, C. (2014). Financial sustainability in municipal solid waste management – Costs and revenues in Bahir Dar, Ethiopia. *Waste Management, 34*(2), 542–552. https://doi.org/10.1016/j.wasman.2013.10.014

Mehrotra, S. (2023). *How – Kerala solid waste management project – (KSWMP).* Retrieved August 18, 2023, from https://kswmp.org/how/

Ministry of Environment, Forest and Climate Change. (2016). *Solid waste management rules 2016. Ministry of Environment, Forest and Climate Change, Government of India.* http://bbmp.gov.in/documents/10180/1920333/SWM-Rules-2016.pdf/27c6b5e4-5265-4aee-bff6-451f28202cc8.

Muiruri, J. M., Wahome, R., Karatu, K., Muiruri, J. M., Wahome, R., & Karatu, K. (2020). Study of residents' attitude and knowledge on management of solid waste in Eastleigh, Nairobi, Kenya. *Journal of Environmental Protection, 11*(10), 779–792. https://doi.org/10.4236/JEP.2020.1110048

Naik, A. K. (2009, September). *Informal sector and informal workers in India.* In Special IARIW-SAIM conference on 'Measuring the informal economy in developing countries' (pp. 23–26). https://catalog.ihsn.org/citations/28178.

Nuzrath, A., & Ruzaik, F. (2017). Public perceptions of the effectiveness of solid waste management in the Colombo municipality area. *Sri Lanka Journal of Population Studies,* *17*(November), 31–38. https://www.researchgate.net/publication/321330758_Public_ Perceptions_on_Effectiveness_of_Solid_Waste_Management_in_Colombo_ Municipality_Area

Oxfam India. (2022, March 1). *A glance at the informal sector in India.* https://www.oxfam-india.org/knowledgehub/factsheets/glance-informal-sector-india.

Singh, R. (2021). *Integration of informal sector in solid waste management: Strategies and approaches.* Centre for science and environment, New Delhi. https://cdn.cseindia.org/attachments/0.89670700_1626944339_integration-of-the-informal-sector-richa.pdf

Routh, S. (2014). *Enhancing capabilities through labour law: Informal workers in India.* Routledge. https://www.routledge.com/Enhancing-Capabilities-through-Labour-Law-Informal-Workers-in-India/Routh/p/book/9781138670372

Sapkota, S., Lee, A., Karki, J., Makai, P., Adhikari, S., Chaudhuri, N., & Fossier-Heckmann, A. (2020). Risks and risk mitigation in waste-work: A qualitative study of informal waste workers in Nepal. *Public Health in Practice, 1,* 100028. https://eprints.whiterose.ac.uk/163685/

Singh, K., Singla, N., Sharma, M., & Singh, J. (2023). Urban informal economy and vulnerabilities of domestic waste-pickers: A case of Chandigarh, India. *Waste Management & Research,* 0734242X231154141. https://doi.org/10.1177/0734242X231154141

Singh, T., & Gupta, A. (2011). Women working in the informal sector in India: A saga of lopsided utilization of human capital. *International Proceedings of Economics Development and Research, 4,* 534–538. https://www.researchgate.net/publication/266806200_Women_Working_in_Informal_Sector_in_India_A_saga_ of_Lopsided_Utilization_of_Human_Capital

Singhari, S., & Madheswaran, S. (2017). Wage structure and wage differentials in formal and informal sectors in India: Evidence from NSS data. *The Indian Journal of Labour Economics, 60,* 389–414. https://ideas.repec.org/a/spr/ijlaec/v60y2017i3d10.1007_ s41027-018-0110-y.html

Velis, C. A., Wilson, D. C., Rocca, O., Smith, S. R., Mavropoulos, A., & Cheeseman, C. R. (2012). An analytical framework and tool ('InteRa') for integrating the informal recycling sector in waste and resource management systems in developing countries. *Waste Management and Research, 30*(9 Suppl. 1), 43–66. https://doi.org/10.1177/ 0734242X12454934.

Wang, X., & Geng, Y. (2012). Municipal solid waste management in Dalian: Practices and challenges. *Frontiers of Environmental Science and Engineering in China, 6*(4), 540–548. https://doi.org/10.1007/s11783-011-0361-z

Index

414   Index

Workforce participation (WPR), 337
and gender, 337–340
Working population ratio (WPR), 242
World Bank Institute, 218
World Commission on Environment
and Development (WCED),
214

World Food Programme (WFP),
162
World Health Organization (WHO),
156, 214

Youth unemployment, 300

Printed and bound by CPI Group (UK) Ltd, Croydon, CR0 4YY

18/12/2024

14614797-0005